A COMMENTARY ON
HOMER'S ODYSSEY

A COMMENTARY ON
HOMER'S ODYSSEY

VOLUME I
INTRODUCTION AND BOOKS I–VIII

ALFRED HEUBECK
STEPHANIE WEST
J. B. HAINSWORTH

CLARENDON PRESS · OXFORD
1988

Oxford University Press, Walton Street, Oxford OX2 6DP

Oxford New York Toronto
Delhi Bombay Calcutta Madras Karachi
Petaling Jaya Singapore Hong Kong Tokyo
Nairobi Dar es Salaam Cape Town
Melbourne Auckland

and associated companies in
Berlin Ibadan

Oxford is a trade mark of Oxford University Press

Published in the United States
by Oxford University Press, New York

Originally published in Italian under the title Omero: Odissea
© Fondazione Lorenzo Valla

English edition © Oxford University Press 1988

British Library Cataloguing in Publication Data

A Commentary on Homer's Odyssey.
Vol. 1: Introduction and books I–VIII
1. Homer, Odyssey
I. Heubeck, Alfred   II. West, Stephanie
III. Hainsworth, J. B.   IV. Homer, Odyssey
V. Omero, Odissea. English
883'.01   PA4167
ISBN 0–19–814037–1

Library of Congress Cataloging in Publication Data

Heubeck, Alfred, 1914–1987
A commentary on Homer's Odyssey.
Revised English version of: Omero: Odissea.
Bibliography: p.
Includes index.
Contents: v. 1. Introduction and Books I–VIII.
1. Homer. Odyssey.   2. Odysseus (Greek mythology)
in literature.   I. West, Stephanie.   II. Hainsworth,
J. B. (John Bryan)   III. Homer. Odyssey.   IV. Title.
PA4167.H48   1988   883'.01   87–18509
ISBN 0–19–814037–1 (v. 1)

Set by H Charlesworth & Co Ltd, Huddersfield
Printed in Great Britain
at the University Printing House, Oxford
by David Stanford
Printer to the University

PREFACE

THIS volume is the first of three that aim to provide an introduction and commentary to the *Odyssey*. It is a revised version, without text and translation, of the first two parts of the six-volume edition commissioned by the Fondazione Lorenzo Valla and published by Mondadori. In keeping with the *Odyssey*'s wide geographical range this undertaking has involved Homerists of five nationalities, from both sides of the Atlantic Ocean, and it is hardly surprising if we have approached our task in different ways. Inevitably there is diversity of opinion and variation in emphasis; we do not think that, in principle, this lack of uniformity calls for apology, and, though we realize that at first it may seem disconcerting, we believe that a multifarious approach will in the end prove more stimulating than confusing.

There has been no complete commentary in English on the *Odyssey* since W. B. Stanford's compendious edition, first published forty years ago; a fuller treatment seems intrinsically desirable, and the intervening years have, in any case, seen major developments in Homeric scholarship on many fronts. The Valla commentary was accompanied by the luxury of our own text, but economy and the convenience of the user, we decided, would be better served if the reader were to have the text of the *Odyssey* before him in a separate volume; the lemmata of the commentary have accordingly been taken from T. W. Allen's Oxford Classical Text (second edition, 1917), but this should not present any difficulty for anyone using a different edition.

For the spelling of Greek proper names we have generally adopted the most familiar form.

αἱ δεύτεραί πως φροντίδες σοφώτεραι. In revising our manuscript we have been able to take advantage of the comments of reviewers and friends, and we welcome this opportunity to thank them; we are especially indebted to Professor J. Bremmer, Dr I. de Jong, Professor G. S. Kirk, Professor H. van Thiel, and Professor M. M. Willcock.

Our thanks are also due to the Delegates of the Press for accepting a work which, owing to its unconventional genesis, might be expected to cause peculiar problems. We should like to record our admiration for the unfailing courtesy and efficiency with which the staff of the Press have met all difficulties. It is a particular pleasure to thank John Cordy and John Waś, whose patient guidance has piloted our *Odyssey* from Rome to Oxford, and Daphne Nash, the Press's vigilant and forbearing copy-editor.

We deeply regret that Alfred Heubeck, the leader of our θίασος, did not live to see the publication of this volume.

Oxford   J.B.H.
August 1987   S.R.W.

CONTENTS

BIBLIOGRAPHICAL ABBREVIATIONS

The abbreviations used for ancient authors correspond to those employed in the ninth edition of Liddell and Scott, *Greek–English Lexicon* (LSJ) and in the *Oxford Latin Dictionary*, for periodicals to those of *L'Année philologique*.

Editions of the *Odyssey* referred to in the Commentary:

Allen	T. W. Allen, *Homeri Opera*, iii², iv² (Oxford Classical Text), Oxford, 1917, 1919.
Ameis–Hentze–Cauer	*Homers Odyssee* f. den Schulgebrauch erklärt von K. F. Ameis u. C. Hentze, bearbeitet von P. Cauer, i 1¹⁴, 2¹³, ii 1⁹, 2¹⁰, Leipzig, 1920, 1940, 1928, 1925.
Heubeck*	*Omero, Odissea, libri ix–xii; xxiii–xxiv: Introduzione, testo e commento* a cura di Alfred Heubeck, Fondazione Lorenzo Valla, Rome, 1983, 1987.
Hoekstra*	*Omero, Odissea, libri xiii–xvi: Introduzione, testo e commento* a cura di Arie Hoekstra, Fondazione Lorenzo Valla, Rome, 1984.
Merry–Riddell	W. W. Merry and J. Riddell, *Homer's Odyssey: Books i–xii*, Oxford, 1886.
Russo*	*Omero, Odissea, libri xvii–xx: Introduzione, testo e commento* a cura di Joseph Russo, Fondazione Lorenzo Valla, Rome, 1985.
Stanford	W. B. Stanford, *The Odyssey of Homer²*, Macmillan, London, 1959.
von der Mühll	P. von der Mühll, *Homeri Odyssea³*, Basel, 1961 (Stuttgart, 1984).

Works mentioned by abbreviated title:

Apthorp, *Evidence*	M. J. Apthorp, *The Manuscript Evidence for Interpolation in Homer*, Heidelberg, 1980.
Archaeologia	*Archaeologia Homerica: Die Denkmäler u. das frühgriechische Epos*, ed. F. Matz and H. G. Buchholz, Göttingen, 1967.
Arend, *Scenen*	W. Arend, *Die typischen Scenen bei Homer*, Berlin, 1933.

* The present volume is the first of three in the English edition (introductions and commentary only); the second (Books ix–xvi) and third (Books xvii–xxiv) volumes are forthcoming (also from OUP).

Austin, *Archery* — N. Austin, *Archery at the Dark of the Moon: Poetic Problems in Homer's* Odyssey, Berkeley–Los Angeles, 1975.

Bechtel, *Lexilogus* — F. Bechtel, *Lexilogus zu Homer*, Halle, 1914.

Besslich, *Schweigen* — S. Besslich, *Schweigen–Verschweigen–Übergehen: Die Darstellung des Unausgesprochenen in der Odyssee*, Heidelberg, 1966.

Bethe, *Homer* — E. Bethe, *Homer: Dichtung und Sage*, i–iii, Leipzig–Berlin, 1914, 1922, 1929².

—— *Odyssee* — vol. ii of the above.

Bolling, *Evidence* — G. M. Bolling, *The External Evidence for Interpolation in Homer*, Oxford, 1925.

Burkert, *Religion* — W. Burkert, *Greek Religion: Archaic and Classical*, trans. John Raffan, Oxford, 1985.

Chantraine, *Dictionnaire* — P. Chantraine, *Dictionnaire étymologique de la langue grecque*, Paris, 1968–80.

—— *Grammaire* — —— *Grammaire homérique*, i³, ii², Paris, 1958, 1963.

Clay, *Wrath* — J. S. Clay, *The Wrath of Athena: Gods and Men in the* Odyssey, Princeton, 1983.

Companion — A. J. B. Wace and F. H. Stubbings (eds.), *A Companion to Homer*, London, 1962.

Delebecque, *Télémaque* — E. Delebecque, *Télémaque et la structure de l'Odyssée*, Annales de la Faculté des Lettres d'Aix-en-Provence, NS xxi, 1958.

Denniston, *Particles* — J. D. Denniston, *The Greek Particles²*, Oxford, 1954.

Dindorf, *Scholia* — G. Dindorf, *Scholia Graeca in Homeri Odysseam*, Oxford, 1855.

Ebeling, *Lexicon* — H. Ebeling, *Lexicon Homericum*, Leipzig, 1880–5.

Eisenberger, *Studien* — H. Eisenberger, *Studien zur Odyssee*, Wiesbaden, 1973.

Erbse, *Beiträge* — H. Erbse, *Beiträge zum Verständnis der Odyssee*, Berlin–New York, 1972.

Fehling, *Wiederholungsfiguren* — D. Fehling, *Die Wiederholungsfiguren u. ihr Gebrauch bei den Griechen vor Gorgias*, Berlin, 1969.

Fenik, Studies — B. Fenik, *Studies in the* Odyssey, *Hermes* Einzelschriften, xxx, Wiesbaden, 1974.

Finley, *World* — M. I. Finley, *The World of Odysseus* (second revised edn.), Harmondsworth, 1979.

Finsler, *Homer* — G. Finsler, *Homer* i. 1–2, ii, Leipzig, ²1918, ³1924.

Focke, *Odyssee* — F. Focke, *Die Odyssee*, Stuttgart–Berlin, 1943.

Fränkel, *Gleichnisse* — H. Fränkel, *Die homerischen Gleichnisse*, Göttingen, 1921.

Frisk, *GEW* — H. Frisk, *Griechisches etymologisches Wörterbuch*, Heidelberg, 1954–73.

Germain, *Genèse* — G. Germain, *Genèse de l'Odyssée*, Paris, 1954.

Griffin, *Homer on Life and Death* — J. Griffin, *Homer on Life and Death*, Oxford, 1980.

Hainsworth, *Flexibility* — J. B. Hainsworth, *The Flexibility of the Homeric Formula*, Oxford, 1968.

Heubeck, *Dichter* — A. Heubeck, *Der Odyssee-Dichter und die Ilias*, Erlangen, 1954.

Hoekstra, *Modifications* — A. Hoekstra, *Homeric Modifications of Formulaic Prototypes*, Amsterdam, 1965.

Hölscher, *Untersuchungen* — U. Hölscher, *Untersuchungen zur Form der Odyssee*, Leipzig, 1939.

Kirchhoff, *Odyssee* — A. Kirchhoff, *Die Homerische Odyssee und ihre Entstehung*, Berlin, 1879.

Kirk, *Commentary* — G. S. Kirk, *The* Iliad: *A Commentary*, i. *Books 1–4*, *Cambridge, 1985*.

—— *Songs* — —— *The Songs of Homer*, Cambridge, 1962.

Kühner–Gerth — R. Kühner, *Ausführliche Grammatik der griechischen Sprache*, ii. *Satzlehre*[3], besorgt v. B. Gerth, Hanover etc., 1898–1904.

Kurt, *Fachausdrücke* — C. Kurt, *Seemännische Fachausdrücke bei Homer*, Göttingen, 1979.

Leaf, *Iliad* — W. Leaf, *The* Iliad[2], London, 1900–2.

Lesky, *Homeros* — A. Lesky, *Homeros, RE*, Supplementband xi, Stuttgart, 1967.

Leumann, *Wörter* — M. Leumann, *Homerische Wörter*, Basel, 1950.

LfgrE — *Lexicon des frühgriechischen Epos*, ed. B. Snell and H. Erbse, Göttingen, 1955– .

Lord, *Singer* — A. B. Lord, *The Singer of Tales*, Cambridge, Mass.–London, 1960.

Lorimer, *Monuments* — H. L. Lorimer, *Homer and the Monuments*, London, 1950.

Ludwich, *AHT* — A. Ludwich, *Aristarchs Homerische Textkritik*, i, ii, Leipzig, 1884–5.

Marzullo, *Problema* — E. Marzullo, *Il problema omerico*[2], Milan–Naples, 1970.

Mattes, *Odysseus* — W. Mattes, *Odysseus bei den Phäaken*, Würzburg, 1958.

Meister, *Kunstsprache* — K. Meister, *Die homerische Kunstsprache*, Leipzig, 1921, repr. Darmstadt, 1966.

Merkelbach, *Untersuchungen* — R. Merkelbach, *Untersuchungen zur Odyssee*[2], Zetemata, ii, Munich, 1969.

Monro, *Homeric Dialect* — D. B. Monro, *A Grammar of the Homeric Dialect*[2], Oxford, 1891.

Moulton, *Similes* — C. Moulton, *Similes in the Homeric Poems*, Hypomnemata, xlix, Göttingen, 1977.

Nickau, *Untersuchungen* — K. Nickau, *Untersuchungen zur textkritischen Methode des Zenodotos von Ephesos*, Berlin, 1977.

Nilsson, *Geschichte* — M. P. Nilsson, *Geschichte der griechischen Religion*[3], i, Munich, 1967.

Onians, *Origins* — R. B. Onians, *The Origins of European Thought*, Cambridge, 1951.

Pack[2] — R. A. Pack, *The Greek and Latin Literary Texts from Greco-Roman Egypt*[2], Ann Arbor, 1965.

Page, *Odyssey* — D. L. Page, *The Homeric* Odyssey, Oxford, 1955.

Palmer, *Interpretation* — L. R. Palmer, *The Interpretation of Mycenaean Greek Texts*, Oxford, 1963, 1969[2].

Parry, *Blameless Aegisthus* — Anne Amory Parry, *Blameless Aegisthus*, Leiden, 1973.

—— *Homeric Verse* — Adam M. Parry (ed.), *The Making of Homeric Verse: The Collected Papers of Milman Parry*, Oxford, 1971.

RE — *Paulys Realencyclopädie der classischen Altertumswissenschaft*, ed. G. Wissowa, W. Kroll, K. Mittelhaus, and K. Ziegler, Stuttgart, 1893– .

Risch, *Wortbildung* — E. Risch, *Wortbildung der homerischen Sprache*[2], Berlin, 1973.

Roscher, *Lexikon* — W. H. Roscher–K. Ziegler, *Ausführliches Lexikon der griechischen u. römischen Mythologie*, Leipzig, 1884–1937.

Rüter, *Odysseeinterpretationen* — K. Rüter, *Odysseeinterpretationen: Untersuchungen zum ersten Buch u. zur Phaiakis*, Hypomnemata, xix, Göttingen, 1969.

Ruijgh, *τε épique* — C. J. Ruijgh, *Autour de 'τε épique': Études sur la syntaxe grecque*, Amsterdam, 1971.

—— *Élément* — —— *L'Élément achéen dans la langue épique*, Assen, 1957.

Schadewaldt, *Welt* — W. Schadewaldt, *Von Homers Welt und Werk*[4], Stuttgart, 1965.

Schulze, *Quaestiones* — W. Schulze, *Quaestiones epicae*, Gütersloh, 1892.

Schwartz, *Odyssee* — E. Schwartz, *Die Odyssee*, Munich, 1924.

Schwyzer, *Grammatik* — E. Schwyzer, *Griechische Grammatik*, i–iii, Munich, 1939–53.

Severyns, *Homère* — A. Severyns, *Homère*, i[2], ii[2], iii, Brussels, 1944, 1946, 1948.

Shipp, *Studies* — G. P. Shipp, *Studies in the Language of Homer*[2], Cambridge, 1972.

Thompson, *Motif Index* — Stith Thompson, *Motif Index of Folk Literature*, Copenhagen, 1955–8.

Thornton, *People* — A. Thornton, *People and Themes in Homer's Odyssey*, London, 1970.

Touchefeu-Meynier, *Thèmes* O. Touchefeu-Meynier, *Thèmes odysséens dans l'art antique*, Paris, 1968.

van der Valk, *Textual Criticism* M. van der Valk, *Textual Criticism of the Odyssey*, Leiden, 1949.

van Leeuwen, *Enchiridium* J. van Leeuwen, *Enchiridium dictionis epicae*, Leiden, 1918.

Ventris–Chadwick, *Documents* M. Ventris–J. Chadwick, *Documents in Mycenaean Greek*², Cambridge, 1973.

von der Mühll, 'Odyssee' P. von der Mühll, 'Odyssee', *RE*, Supplementband vii. 696–768, Stuttgart, 1940.

von Kamptz, *Personennamen* H. von Kamptz, *Homerische Personennamen*, Göttingen, 1982.

Wackernagel, *Untersuchungen* J. Wackernagel, *Sprachliche Untersuchungen zu Homer*, Göttingen, 1916.

Wathelet, *Traits* P. Wathelet, *Les Traits éoliens dans la langue de l'épopée grecque*, Rome, 1970.

Webster, *Mycenae* T. B. L. Webster, *From Mycenae to Homer*, London, 1958.

Werner, *H. u. ει vor Vokal* R. Werner. *H u. ει vor Vokal bei Homer*, Fribourg, 1948.

Wilamowitz, *Heimkehr* U. von Wilamowitz-Moellendorff, *Die Heimkehr des Odysseus*, Berlin, 1927.

—— *Untersuchungen* —— *Homerische Untersuchungen*, Berlin, 1884.

Woodhouse, *Composition* W. J. Woodhouse, *The Composition of Homer's Odyssey*, Oxford, 1930, repr. Oxford, 1969.

Wyatt, *Lengthening* W. F. Wyatt, jun., *Metrical Lengthening in Homer*, Rome, 1969.

INTRODUCTION TO
HOMER'S ODYSSEY

Alfred Heubeck's Introduction *was translated for this volume by Yana Spence.*

GENERAL INTRODUCTION

Alfred Heubeck

The two epic poems, the *Iliad* and the *Odyssey*, which the ancient Greeks ascribed to a man named Homer, are the earliest examples of Greek poetry and thought we possess. They have shaped and influenced the whole development of Greek cultural life in all its varied aspects to an extent almost impossible to grasp today. The Greeks themselves were aware of this, adopting and honouring Homer as their instructor in every conceivable sphere of life; and later historians of Greek culture have been able to do no more than illustrate and confirm the fact. That the Homeric epic has also rightly held a position of unsurpassed esteem and influence in the history of Western thought can only be noted here in passing, as the primary object of this short introduction is to prepare the way for an understanding of the *Odyssey*, and little can be said about wider considerations.

Any attempt to understand a literary phenomenon of the distant past, that is, to discern behind the façade of the written word the individuality of the author, to grasp his intentions, and to identify his place in his own world, has unavoidable limitations. They are inherent in the conditions to which every interpreter of such a work is subject, namely his own position in space and time, and his own personality. Any statement about the nature and value, the subject-matter, and the importance of the Homeric epic is influenced by the point of view of the interpreter, which is in turn conditioned by his nationality and his cultural environment.

In view of all this it is not surprising that in the course of well over two thousand years of wrestling with the problem of Homer—debate has been continuous since at the latest the sixth century BC and is particularly lively today—opinions should have differed to a frightening extent. All a commentator can hope to achieve is to touch the periphery of the problem; he cannot reach its centre.

These considerations form the basis of our attempt here to elucidate Homer, and in particular the *Odyssey*. Some widely differing views will have to be mentioned, but the knowledge that no statement made about something which is ultimately impenetrable can avoid subjectivity gives one the right, even lays the duty upon one, to state the case openly for one's own position and not conceal it beneath the variety of other opinions. I shall therefore not merely report other views but will also put forward my own without shirking controversy where it is unavoidable.

It is obviously impossible to discuss everything that has been said in recent times about the *Odyssey*, considering the vast amount of material published by scholars on the central linguistic problems, not to mention the contributions to the better understanding of the poem made by linguistic and comparative studies, or by religious, mythological, mycenological, and historical research. There is another factor, too, which compels us to be brief and selective: the close relationship between the *Iliad* and the *Odyssey*. Because the problems raised by the two poems are similar, in fact to some extent the same, we have to keep the Trojan epic constantly in mind and not limit ourselves to the *Odyssey* alone.

In all the efforts of modern scholars to reach a proper understanding of the Homeric epics, the *Odyssey* has stood constantly in the shadow of the *Iliad*. This applies especially to a line of scholarship—somewhat arbitrarily summed up under the term 'Homeric analysis'—that has increasingly shaken the belief that both poems were the work of one poet, a belief which had endured almost unquestioned for some two thousand years. Homeric analysis began with a famous paper dealing exclusively with the *Iliad* by the Abbé François Hédelin d'Aubignac, published anonymously in 1715, long after the author's death in 1676.[1] Another work, also concerned solely with the *Iliad* and to some extent taking up the observations and conjectures of the Abbé, was the *Prolegomena ad Homerum* of F. A. Wolf, published in 1795. Its persuasive force was such that it started a movement the effects of which are still felt today. It is unnecessary to set out all the arguments by which Wolf and those who followed more or less faithfully in his footsteps tried to demonstrate that belief in the unity of the Homeric poems was ill-founded, or to list all the scholars involved or summarize their often widely differing conclusions. A rapid survey is available in books by G. Finsler[2] and J. Myres.[3]

Wolf had not worked on the *Odyssey* and it was only much later that it became the focal point of research, in the first instance by the great scholar G. Hermann[4] who believed that he recognized in it a combination of originally independent poems. In several articles

---

[1] *Conjectures académiques ou dissertation sur l'Iliade* (Paris, 1715).
[2] *Homer* i. 1³, 71–225 ('Die Homerkritik').
[3] *Homer and His Critics*, ed. D. H. F. Gray (London, 1958).
[4] *De interpolationibus Homeri* (Leipzig, 1832).

published at about the same time as Hermann's book[5] K. L. Kayser expressed his conviction that in the poem as we have it a series of 'layers' can be isolated, and that these layers must be attributed to several successive poets. In his work we also find for the first time the notion of a 'redactor' who eventually combined these hypothetical thematically related poems into a single unit, the *Odyssey* as we know it.

In the chequered history of research on the *Iliad* the most diverse analytical solutions have been proposed, amongst which the so-called 'redactor hypothesis' is only one of many. In contrast, where the *Odyssey* is concerned, the concept of a final editor has predominated. Most scholars who were convinced by Kayser's pioneering work that the *Odyssey* must be explained analytically have argued in favour of this concept, whatever their differences in reconstructing the older poems and their sequence, and have thus understood the *Odyssey* as a consciously assembled unit. Where there are differences of opinion they occur mainly in the evaluation of this editor's poetic talent and extend over the whole range of possibilities: at one end of the scale he is seen as an incapable, uncritical bungler, at the other as a sensitive master of his art with a great poetic gift.

The redactor hypothesis also plays an important part in the ideas of A. Kirchhoff, who was the first scholar to treat the *Odyssey* comprehensively, making critical use of previous opinions and adding acute observations of his own.[6] His work is a landmark in the study of the *Odyssey*, and later research has found little to add to the critical observations on the text which served as the starting point for his analytical reasoning. It is only in the conclusions they have drawn from these observations that other scholars have differed from him.

U. von Wilamowitz-Moellendorff[7] and E. Schwartz[8] in their seminal works on the *Odyssey* also accept the idea of a final redaction, although in very different ways, and modern analysis of the poem is indebted to them for the most important observations and suggestions since Kirchhoff.[9] Modern analysis in the true sense, however, begins with P. von der Mühll's valuable article 'Odyssee'[10] and continues with F. Focke,[11] E. Howald,[12]

---

[5] Collected and published under the title *Homerische Abhandlungen* by L. Usener (Leipzig, 1881).

[6] *Odyssee* (Berlin, 1859); 2nd edn. 1879, with important additions. For the basic ideas and the importance of this work see Finsler, *Homer*, 145–7; A. Heubeck, *Die homerische Frage* (Darmstadt 1974), 8–9.

[7] *Untersuchungen; Heimkehr.*

[8] *Odyssee.*

[9] Reviewed by A. Heubeck, op. cit. 10–13.

[10] *RE*, Suppl. vii (1940), 696–768.

[11] *Odyssee.*

[12] *Der Dichter der Ilias* (Zürich, 1946), 166–81.

W. Schadewaldt,[13] W. Theiler,[14] R. Merkelbach,[15] and D. L. Page,[16] to name only the most important and influential. What characterizes most of these interpretations is the attempt to simplify the complex picture of the development of the *Odyssey* drawn in many earlier works. Von der Mühll and Focke, for instance, postulate only three poets. For von der Mühll the process began with poet 'A' as the creator of the 'Ur-Odyssey'; poet 'T' wrote a related shorter poem on the fortunes of Telemachus; and finally redactor 'B' fused epics 'A' and 'T' together. Focke believes that there was originally an ancient 'wanderings-saga', which poet 'O' set into the context of an extensive 'Homecoming of Odysseus', while poet 'T' enlarged this version by adding the deeds of Telemachus and a concluding piece, and made it into the *Odyssey* we know. Schadewaldt takes a further step towards simplification. He assumes a poet 'A', corresponding somewhat to von der Mühll's 'A' and perhaps identical with the author of the *Iliad*, and an editor 'B', who enlarged the older poem by adding the Telemachy (which was thus entirely his own work) and made all the consequent adjustments.

This wealth of analytical literature for a long time eclipsed the efforts of the 'unitarians' to achieve an understanding of the *Odyssey* as the creation of one single poet—works such as those of C. Rothe (of which the title, *Die Odyssee als Dichtung* (Paderborn, 1914), proclaims its intention), and W. J. Woodhouse,[17] a book which deserves attention even today, in spite of certain idiosyncrasies. But in recent decades the voice of the unitarians has at last become too strong to be ignored. This phase began in earnest with U. Hölscher's *Untersuchungen zur Form der Odyssee* (Berlin, 1939). Many contributions, substantial or brief, have followed since then, of which only those by G. Germain,[18] Lydia Allione,[19] G. Bona,[20] S. Besslich,[21] K. Rüter,[22] Agathe Thornton,[23] H. Erbse,[24] and H. Eisenberger[25] can be mentioned here. The findings of these and other unitarian works will

---

[13] *Die Heimkehr des Odysseus* (Berlin, 1946), now in *Welt*, 375–412; and several more recent articles, for which see the bibliography in A. Heubeck, op. cit. 289–90, and D. W. Packard and T. Meyers, *A Bibliography of Homeric Scholarship* (Malibu, 1974), 120–1.

[14] In several articles, now collected in *Untersuchungen zur antiken Literatur* (W. Berlin, 1970).

[15] *Untersuchungen zur Odyssee* (Munich, 1951; 2nd edn., Munich, 1969).

[16] *Odyssey.*   [17] *Composition.*   [18] *Genèse.*

[19] *Telemaco e Penelope nell'Odissea* (Turin, 1963).

[20] *Studi sull'Odissea* (Turin, 1966).   [21] *Schweigen.*

[22] *Odysseeinterpretationen.*   [23] *People.*   [24] *Beiträge.*

[25] *Studien.*

frequently be cited below (though not always with full references), the more so since I am myself fully committed to this school of thought.[26]

The line of enquiry pursued by the analysts has had the effect of putting the question of Homer himself (unhesitatingly accepted until modern times as the author of both poems) on to a different plane or pushing it into the background as in the end irrelevant or insoluble. But for modern unitarians too the question appears in a new form: if one believes that the *Iliad* and the *Odyssey* were each created by a single poet, one must also ask—in view not only of the contrast in subject matter between the two epics, but also of the conspicuous differences in form and content, in linguistic and stylistic structure, and in human behaviour and intention—whether the poet of the *Iliad* (whom we follow the ancient tradition in calling Homer) can also have written the, undoubtedly later, *Odyssey*. This question was of course already being asked in antiquity. At that time the few scholars who denied a single authorship, and were therefore called 'chorizontes' ('separatists'),[27] failed to carry the day against their 'unitarian' colleagues. The anonymous author of the treatise *On the Sublime* (Περὶ ὕψους 9. 13) probably expressed the opinion of many of his contemporaries when he attempted to solve the problem by suggesting that Homer wrote the *Iliad* as a young man and the *Odyssey* in old age.

Modern unitarians for the most part adopt the more radical position and postulate two different authors. When they want to differentiate they use the name Homer only for the poet of the *Iliad*; the second poet—as there is no traditional name for him—has to be described as 'the Poet of the *Odyssey*', or, occasionally, 'Deutero-Homer'.[28] The view expressed in this introduction, and supported by observations of language, style, composition, and design, is that each of the Homeric epics is a poetic whole; and this view leads by necessity to the position of the 'chorizontes'—as F. Jacoby[29] first pointed out in an article which is still worth reading today. Since then other scholars have begun to see this with increasing clarity,[30] and it is in fact my own position.

---

[26] *Dichter.*

[27] See J. W. Kohl, *De chorizontibus*, Diss. Giessen (Darmstadt, 1917).

[28] G. Nebel, *Homer* (Stuttgart, 1959), *passim.*

[29] 'Die geistige Physiognomie der Odyssee', *Die Antike* ix (1933), 159–94 = *Kleine philol. Schriften*, i (Berlin, 1961), 107–38.

[30] Especially Rüter, *Odyseeinterpretationen*, 13–25, and R. Friedrich, *Stilwandel im homerischen Epos: Studien zur Poetik und Theorie der epischen Gattung* (Heidelberg, 1975).

But in commenting like this on recent research on the *Odyssey* we have hurried on too fast, since we have not yet dealt with an explanation of the nature of Homeric poetry which has been gaining ground steadily since the thirties, particularly (though not exclusively) in Anglo-American circles, where it now almost entirely holds the field. This is the so-called 'oral poetry' theory originated by Milman Parry and developed by his disciples.

It must suffice here to mention briefly the essential points of this approach. Parry based his first two works[31] on an observation which almost forces itself on any impartial reader: namely that the language of ancient Greek epic poetry is highly formulaic. Similar circumstances and events are, wherever possible, related in the same words; the same objects and persons have the same epithets, even when the context leads one to expect otherwise. It is clear that the formulaic combinations of name and adjective and their variants—to which Parry first turned his attention—follow certain fixed rules imposed by the metrical requirements of heroic verse. When the poet of the *Odyssey* speaks of his hero in the nominative he calls him δῖος Ὀ., διογενὴς Ὀ., ἐσθλὸς Ὀ., πολύμητις Ὀ., πτολίπορθος Ὀ., πολύτλας δῖος Ὀ., while in the genitive he is Ὀδυσσῆος θείοιο, Λαερτιάδεω Ὀδυσῆος, Ὀδυσσῆος ταλασίφρονος, Ὀδυσσῆος ἀμύμονος, and so on, as may be required by the form and length of what he wishes to say within the framework of the hexameter.

Considerations of this kind led Parry to distinguish between 'individual' and 'traditional' poetry and to classify the Homeric epics as 'early Greek traditional poetry', in which the freedom of the individual poet to formulate his own verses, though by no means removed, is closely circumscribed by the existence of a well-developed system of fixed modes of expression ('formulaic patterns'), serving at the same time to help and to constrain.

Observations of Yugoslav heroic poetry, the practice of which was still just alive before the Second World War, induced Parry to redraw the dividing line and to shift the emphasis slightly. The distinction he now made was between written poetry, which had its legitimate place in a literate world, and oral poetry, which was the mode of expression of totally or largely illiterate peoples or cultures; and he had no hesitation in classifying the Homeric epics as purely oral traditional heroic poetry. That this gave a new dimension to what we call the 'Homeric question' is beyond dispute. It does not matter that the

---

[31] *L'Épithète traditionnelle dans Homère: Essai sur un problème de style homérique* (Paris, 1928); *Les Formules et la métrique d'Homère* (Paris, 1928). Both works in English translation, together with all Parry's articles, now also in *Homeric Verse*.

literary, comparative, stylistic, and linguistic argume͏͏͏
Parry were not all new; that, in fact, their essential ele͏͏
founded on conjectures and discoveries of earlier researc͏͏͏
important point is that he drew together considerations
kinds from different fields of study and combined the͏͏
impressive overall picture, the inner cohesion and balanc͏͏͏ ͏͏͏͏͏
could not fail to make an impact, particularly at a time when
research had apparently come to a halt in well-worn and by now
largely unrewarding paths.

In many important respects Parry's views were undoubtedly
correct, and the description he and his successors, above all his pupil
A. B. Lord,[33] and G. S. Kirk,[34] have drawn of oral poetry and its
transmission seems to be valid. Modern research has shown how
heroic poetry, orally composed, recited and handed on, has flour-
ished among many illiterate cultures in different areas of the world at
various periods, and how in form and content it displays striking
similarities across the bounds of time and space.[35] Often the tradition
is carried on by members of a guild who cultivate the art of poetry as
a craft and hand it on from generation to generation by teaching,
example, and practice. Guild members learn to use, in addition to
their everyday speech, a special language which is appropriate in
vocabulary and structure to the themes from myth and heroic tale
the singer is called upon to unfold. It conforms to rules governing
rhythm and metre and follows certain principles of economy, produc-
ing a ready supply of formulae or formulaic patterns to describe
persons and objects, events and situations, of the kind which in epic
poetry necessarily recur many times in the same or a similar form; the
correct placing, varying, and combining of these formulae is impor-
tant. A master of the art is able to extemporize fluently in this
artificial language on any theme from heroic tale or myth, just as any
man in the street is capable of recounting an actual event in the
language of daily life.

The picture of the oral poet's art thus derived from a wide range of
studies seems to fit the world of early Greek epic very well. When the
poet of the *Odyssey* brings singers (ἀοιδοί) on to the scene at the
princely courts of Ithaca and Scheria to delight their hearers with

[32] See e.g. the works of M. Murko for the study of Yugoslav heroic poetry; and on
questions of language and metre the basic studies of C. Witte (1909–14), now collected
in K. Witte, *Zur homerischen Sprache* (Darmstadt, 1972).

[33] *Singer*; 'Homer and Other Epic Poetry' in *Companion*, 179–214. Further works
listed in D. W. Packard and T. Meyers, op. cit., 81; A. Heubeck, *Hom.Fr.* 274–5.

[34] *Songs*, 55–101.   [35] C. M. Bowra, *Heroic Poetry* (Oxford, 1951).

songs of gods and heroes, he is blending into the heroic world of which his story tells pictures of his own day: he has himself seen and heard singers like Phemius and Demodocus who can turn any given theme immediately into song, even if that theme has not previously been in the repertoire of the bards (a good example at viii. 487 ff.). For is he not himself a product of the training which shaped the oral singers of the eighth century BC? Does not the way in which he—like the poet of the *Iliad*—manages to give a formal shape to his tale clearly support this view? Both poets use an idiom which was certainly not spoken anywhere or at any time in any Greek house or market-place, in which a profusion of elements from different sources lies concealed behind a seemingly homogeneous façade. Embedded in a language with the basic structure of the Ionic dialect as it was perhaps spoken at the time of the poet we find words and forms which are either borrowed from the northern Aeolic dialect,[36] or preserve old Ionic forms, or are the result of a deliberate attempt to sound archaic. Others are more or less bold improvisations and neologisms.[37]

As we have shown above, a large part of this epic diction consists of phrases, figures of speech, and whole verses that not only operate as formulae but are obviously intended to do so. Both the extraordinary range of application of these formulaic elements and their linguistic character suggest that, like the mixed dialect, they were, at least in part, not the creation of the poets who used them, but traditional features of their craft. The artificial language of the epic[38] is the result of a continuous development over hundreds of years among a circle of bards who in post-Mycenaean times preserved and handed on the heritage of myths and legends in the form of oral poetry.[39] That the poets of the *Iliad* and the *Odyssey* were both deeply rooted in this craft tradition and that their creativeness can only be understood against the background of an epic poetry which had been flourishing for a long time can hardly be doubted.

But does one do justice to the character and individuality of these

---

[36] The most recent full treatment of Aeolisms is Wathelet, *Traits*.

[37] Leumann, *Wörter*.

[38] In addition to the works already mentioned by K. Witte and M. Leumann, see also Meister, *Kunstsprache*, and Chantraine, *Grammaire*, i³, ii².

[39] The case for the post-Mycenaean origin of hexameter epic poetry is convincingly argued by C. Gallavotti, 'Tradizione micenea e poesia greca arcaica', *Atti e Memorie del 1° Congresso Internaz. di Micenologia, Roma 27 Sept.–3 Oct. 1967* (Rome, 1968), ii 831–61. For the contrary–and perhaps more frequently expressed–view that the tradition of epic poetry goes back to Mycenaean or even earlier times, cf. most recently M. Durante, *Sulla preistoria della tradizione poetica greca*, i (Rome, 1971), ii (Rome, 1974).

poets by regarding them, and trying to understand them, as typical representatives of an ancient craft, even if far superior in quality to their predecessors and colleagues? Do the exponents of the oral poetry theory really get to the heart of the matter, and are they correct in classifying the Homeric epics as pure oral poetry? At this point opinions divide, and since clear proof of the rightness of one theory or another is now, and perhaps always will be, unattainable, it remains for the individual to stand by his own opinion, however reached. My own views ought not to be concealed, but as a detailed discussion would be impossible here, I shall just briefly state the main points of my position.[40]

The conclusion that the poets of the *Iliad* and the *Odyssey* took substantial elements of their work from the oral tradition of the bards seems to me no longer open to doubt, and I believe that the acceptance of this helps us to grasp an important, though not the decisive, aspect of their intentions and achievements. The fact that they dealt with material already exploited in oral poetry, and that they continued to shape this material by methods very like those of their predecessors and colleagues, seems to me of less relevance than other observations which force themselves on the interpreter. Even if our lack of precise knowledge of the pre-Homeric epic means that we cannot prove any particular claim, we can yet sense how enormous an advance Homer made on his predecessors.

All that we know suggests that the art of the oral poet consisted in his ability to turn any subject suggested by his audience into epic poetry on the spot. We are surely justified in assuming that the greatest applause was given to the singer who could do this in an especially original and exciting way, in a manner which was particularly well-suited to his listeners and their expectations; in short, a singer able to improvise with particular skill and effectiveness. But even a superficial glance at the Homeric epics shows that in their creation free improvisation has played only the smallest part, and the more one examines them the clearer this becomes. Their most important characteristic is the structure of form and content, the ordering of the material, which is planned precisely and in detail from the very beginning. Heroic events are not simply added one

---

[40] Of the scholars to whose work I am indebted the following shall be particularly mentioned: A. Parry, 'Have we Homer's *Iliad*?', *YClS* xx (1966), 177–216; Lesky, *Homeros*, 698–709; H. Patzer, *Dichterische Kunst und poetisches Handwerk im homerischen Epos*, Sitz.-Ber. d. Wiss. Ges. an d. J. W. Goethe-Universität, Frankfurt/Main, x.1 (Frankfurt, 1971); also A. Heubeck, *Gnomon* xlvi (1974), 529–34. The state of research is well summarized by Fenik, *Studies*, 133–42.

after the other; they are interrelated in many different ways and are given certain functions within the framework of the whole. A network of references to future or past events, extensive preparatory sections, expectations aroused and fulfilled, parallelisms, climaxes, and reversals: all these bind each of the poems together into a harmonious and balanced structure, in which each episode and scene has its proper place, in which nothing can change places and nothing can be added or left out. The strength of the Homeric poets lies in skilful composition, that of the oral poets in improvisation. The creations of oral singers are always new, as chance and the immediate situation dictate; their songs are for the moment and ephemeral. But there is nothing ephemeral about the Homeric epics: they are meant to be permanent and permanently valid, they are not creations of the moment, but reveal planning and careful arrangement. We can recognize how much mental effort and detailed polishing lie behind them, and how many preliminary attempts and drafts must have preceded the finished works.

I believe we can even take the argument a step further. Not only were the *Iliad* and the *Odyssey* products of long and careful planning and polishing; they could not have been created at all without the aid of writing. The new concept of epic poetry, destined to create out of traditional methods and possibilities something that would both continue the tradition and yet surpass it, could only be realized by using the art of writing,[41] which the Greeks had learnt at the beginning of of the eighth century BC from their Phoenician trading partners in the Near East and adapted to their own needs. In short, the poet of the *Iliad*, I believe, took the decisive step from oral poetry to written composition, a step of epoch-making importance whose effects cannot be overestimated.

This account takes us a lot further towards an understanding of the *Odyssey*, our main concern here. If we rightly see Homer as the one who broke out of the old oral tradition and became the creator of a new kind of heroic epic, and if the *Odyssey* (as we can hardly doubt) was composed somewhat later by a second poet who already knew the *Iliad*, then the implications of this poet's situation need to be pointed out. Undoubtedly he, too, was part of the old tradition and took from it important elements of his poetry, but side by side with

[41] This opinion has also lately been expressed by A. Lesky, 'Mündlichkeit und Schriftlichkeit im homerischen Epos', in *Festschrift f. D. Kralik* (Horn, 1954), 1–9 (also in *Gesamm. Schriften* (Berne–Munich, 1966), 63–71); *Homeros*, 698–709; F. Dirlmeier, 'Das serbo-kroatische Heldenlied und Homer', Sitz.-Ber. Heidelberg 1971, 1; Erbse, *Beiträge*, 177–88; Eisenberger, *Studien*, 327.

this tradition there was now a work which superseded it, the *Iliad*; and it would be absurd to suppose that this did not have at least as much influence on him. Indeed, it can be shown that in many ways the *Iliad* provided the inspiration for the *Odyssey*, whose poet to a great extent took his bearings from the earlier work and modelled his writing on it. F. Jacoby[42] aptly described this process as 'conscious rivalry' and 'creative mimesis'. The terms underline both the affinity between the two poems and their differences: while the *Iliad* set the standards against which the poet of the *Odyssey* felt obliged to measure himself, yet the latter's own creative ability lifted him far above the status of a mere imitator. In quality, importance, and intrinsic value his creation fully matches up to its exemplar.

There is no doubt that by comparing the two epics—in structure, language and style, and in the way the two poets conceived of the world, men, and gods—and by thinking of the younger poet as a creative imitator and rival of Homer, we open up important new approaches to an understanding of the later epic. Here it must suffice to mention only a few points.

The poet of the *Iliad* put a pre-eminent hero at the centre of his work. The deeds and sufferings of Achilles inform and direct all the events of the epic; everything in the tale refers to him, and he is present to a remarkable degree even when he remains in the background. By his passivity when absent and inactive he shapes events no less effectively than when he is active. In this respect, one assumes, Homer keeps within the framework of oral tradition, which no doubt frequently made the lives and deeds of outstanding warriors the subject of its songs. What is new is the limitation the poet has imposed upon himself by selecting a relatively short episode from the life of his hero—the wrath of Achilles and its consequences—and making it the kernel of his epic. We can only guess at the considerations which led to this bold and original scheme, but whatever they were they made it possible for him to present the total situation lying behind the selection of events he describes far more completely and vividly than he could have done in a chronologically ordered epic with a series of events covering a long period of time, of the kind we believe typical of the oral period of heroic poets. By this device he turns the Achilleis into the *Iliad*, into an impressive portrayal of the whole memorable war which kept the Greeks for ten years before their enemy's stronghold.

The influence of this new concept on the poet of the *Odyssey* can

---

[42] See above, n. 29.

easily be seen. He, likewise, makes no attempt at a blow-by-blow account of his hero's adventures through the ten long years between his departure from Troy and his final home-coming, but merely projects the events of a short span of time; on a careful reckoning of the days barely six weeks elapse between the intervention of the gods with which the story starts and the slaying of the suitors. By limiting the time element, he, too, succeeds in bringing to life a picture of a whole mythical epoch, which could well be given the overall title 'The Victors' Return from Troy'—represented for us by a single outstanding example, Odysseus, the Lord of Ithaca.

Yet by much the same methods as in the *Iliad* the many events which occurred in the years before those last six weeks are included in the tale, mostly by indirect report. The participants recount what they themselves have seen and experienced or heard from others. From Odysseus' kin and from the suitors we hear of events in Ithaca since the end of the Trojan War—naturally from very different points of view. The accounts given by Nestor and Menelaus to Telemachus (iii–iv) and by the spirit of Agamemnon to Odysseus (xi) give a rounded picture of the fortunes of the other great warriors who set out for home with Odysseus. Lastly there is above all the long and detailed tale of his own wanderings that Odysseus tells to the spell-bound Phaeacians, from his adventures in the land of the Cicones to his lucky rescue on the shore of Scheria. In this way the poet has created a clever network of retrospective information, particularly in the first part of the epic. The way in which this information is co-ordinated and added to—even after long digressions—to give a full picture of everything we need to know reveals careful planning on the part of the poet.

It is the use made here of the restricted time-span—though the device can hardly have derived from anywhere but the *Iliad*—that particularly highlights the creative freedom and independence of the imitation. The episode picked out by the poet of the *Iliad* to represent the entire campaign before Troy is only one of many, belongs to the middle of the action, and for the outcome of the war is almost irrelevant. The only effect it can have on the course of events is a short and ineffectual delay. But with the *Odyssey* the situation is quite otherwise: here the poet has selected the very last and decisive phase as the standpoint of his epic. The difference in subject-matter may have influenced his choice and may even have forced him to it. But the manner in which he has used the possibilities provided by this choice to unfold events of unparalleled drama deserves our utmost admiration.

The poet starts with the moment when Zeus puts the fate of Odysseus, who has clearly been away from home for all too long, before the gods for counsel and decision. At this point, hitherto separate strands of events begin to converge towards the now unavoidable crisis, in a way that is poetically acceptable though hardly comprehensible by reason.[43] This is not only the day when Odysseus frees himself from the fatal numbness which has overcome him in the house of Calypso; simultaneously events begin to move in Ithaca, where his son, resigned and powerless up to now, comes to himself and begins to act independently, responsibly, and courageously to put an end to an intolerable situation. This is also the moment, the poet ordains, when Penelope can no longer resist the pressure from the suitors. In despair and yet not without hope, of her own free will and yet following some inner compulsion, she sets the contest of the bow, which is to decide not only her own and her family's fate, but also that of the throne and the whole country.

The poem thus begins at a moment of great crisis, the *kairos*, when all the different strands come together and everything is at stake: Penelope very nearly has to honour her dreaded promise to the suitors, Telemachus' initiative very nearly finds a sudden and cruel end in the suitors' ambush, and Odysseus very nearly returns either not at all or a day too late. But the gods—and the poet—have arranged everything in the best possible manner: what very nearly happened does not, and when the crisis comes there is a relaxing of the tension, which might have become intolerable for the listener, had he not been able from the very beginning to hope that the gods would let justice triumph and bring everything to a satisfactory conclusion. In the end order rules again.

In this connection another remarkable feature should be mentioned. The poet's bold idea of compressing his narrative into a short time-span and his desire to give in the course of it a full and vivid picture of the hero's homeward journey compel him to explain at some point why Odysseus has not returned home earlier to take up his old privileges. By letting Odysseus himself relate his earlier adventures he turns poetic necessity into an opportunity to tell a tale which could hardly have found a place in the model 'Homeric' epic. The characters of the *Iliad* play their parts in a milieu which is familiar to the hearers from their own experience, a world that in every respect, good and bad, is a human one. Odysseus, however, passes beyond the limits of reality after the storm off Cape Malea and

[43] O. Seel, 'Variante und Konvergenz in der Odyssee', in *Studi in onoro di U. E. Paoli* (Florence, 1955), 643–57.

finds himself in a sphere where heroic and human standards fail utterly. Beyond this frontier, which is fortunately impassable for most mortals, there are still seas, lands, and islands, and the points of the compass still apply, but in this different world there exist beings and forms that cannot be comprehended by the human mind. It is a fantastic and imaginary world, irrational and unreal, a realm of magic and sorcery which bears no relation to human experience, a world (we should particularly note) that was shunned by the early Greek epic and more recently by the poet of the *Iliad* himself, so that only faint traces of it are visible. Within the set framework of the epic, the poet could not in his own person relate the occult and fabulous events of the world of magic and fairy-tale, but if they were recounted by a character in the poem who had himself experienced them, then these fabulous events were in a sense brought back into the known world and could be incorporated into the epic. It is significant that Odysseus is made to tell his adventures in front of the Phaeacians who by their nature and origin represent the slender bridge between the realm of fairy-tale and the world of man. In helping Odysseus the Phaeacians fulfil for the last time their task of mediating between the two worlds.[44]

We have already mentioned how skilfully the poet creates a homogeneous whole from a colourful variety of mythical events which extend over a whole decade, occur in very varied localities, and involve a large number of characters. As we have seen, one of the devices he uses to achieve this is the restriction of direct narrative to an account of the brief period of the crisis. There is another device, however, that goes hand in hand with this and also involves a deliberate restriction: concentration on the main character. In everything that the poet says in his own person or lets the characters in his epic say, Odysseus is always the focus, even when he is not actually mentioned; there is nothing which does not in a wider or narrower sense refer to the hero.

The experiences of the other warriors exhaust almost all possible variations on the theme of 'home-coming'; yet they are all merely a foil for the return of the one who surpasses them in suffering but achieves the most glorious fulfilment in the end. In particular, throughout the *Odyssey* the fate of Agamemnon is kept vividly in front of the listener with its darker parallels and contrasts: on one side there

---

[44] For Odysseus' wanderings (ix–xii) cf. Germain, *Genèse*; K. Reinhardt, 'Die Abenteuer des Odysseus', in *Von Werken und Formen* (Godesberg, 1948), 52–162 (also in C. Becker (ed.), *Tradition und Geist*, (Göttingen, 1960), 47–124); W. Suerbaum, 'Die Ich-Erzählungen des Odysseus', *Poetica* ii (1968), 150–277.

are Agamemnon–Clytaemestra–Aegisthus–Orestes, on the o...
Odysseus–Penelope–the suitors–Telemachus. The similarity in the
situations and the roles of the participants is remarkable, yet the final
solution presents the greatest contrast. Agamemnon was one of the
first, and Odysseus the last, to reach home. But against the back-
ground of Agamemnon's shameful end at the hands of a faithless wife
and wicked rival Odysseus' happy fate stands out in full relief. The
faithful waiting of Penelope in a situation which appears hopeless, her
resistance to the suitors, and her good sense have spared him
Agamemnon's doom, and at last brought fulfilment of his yearn-
ings.[45]

A part of the epic which analytical criticism has frequently
condemned as an interpolation in the 'pure', 'original' *Odyssey* and
attributed to a later expansion is the so-called Telemachy, in which
the actions and experiences of the hero's son are narrated. But this,
too, is closely interwoven with the fate and character of Odysseus.
Unlike the analysts,[46] I believe that the inclusion of the Telemachy in
the epic is a master-stroke on the part of the poet,[47] since it allows
him to start events in different places at the same time, and so to
create from the beginning two strands of narrative which run parallel
until he brings them together at the conclusion. The gods—and the
poet—have carefully arranged that at almost the same moment as
the father on a distant island embarks on the craft he has built
himself, the son leaves his home to find news of his father in the world
outside. We thus have here two opposite courses of action which are
destined to come together and to culminate in common endeavour
and achievement; in other words, they are two aspects of the same
process: that of bringing Odysseus home.

This device was surely the poet's own invention, and he must have
been delighted by it, all the more perhaps because he could have
found no example of such virtuosity in construction either in the *Iliad*
or the earlier oral epics. For epic before the *Odyssey*, we suppose, was
characterized by its linear development, keeping strictly to a chrono-
logical sequence of events. This is even true to a large extent of the

[45] For the function of the 'Atreidae-Paradigm' cf. E. F. D'Arms and K. K. Hulley,
'The Oresteia Story in the *Odyssey*', *TAPhA* lxxvii (1946), 207–13; H. Hommel,
'Aigisthos und die Freier', *SG* viii (1958), 237–45; U. Hölscher, 'Die Atridensage in
der Odyssee', in *Festschrift f. R. Alewyn* (Cologne–Graz, 1967), 1–16.

[46] Above, p. 6.

[47] See esp. F. Klingner, *Über die ersten vier Bucher der Odyssee*, Sitz.-Ber. Leipzig xci.1
(Leipzig, 1944), (also in *Studien zur griech. und röm. Literatur* (Zürich–Stuttgart, 1964),
39–79); K. Reinhardt, 'Homer und die Telemachie', in *Von Werken und Formen*, 37–51
(also in *Tradition und Geist*, 37–46).

Iliad, although it occasionally allows glimpses of events occurring at the same time in different places.

The poet of the *Odyssey* still accepts the rules of epic narrative which forbid him to break out of the chronological sequence, to stop at a certain point and return to a moment his narrative has already passed. But he has a sure eye for seeing how to use the principles of presentation displayed in the *Iliad* for his own purpose and how to describe simultaneous events without breaking with formal tradition. In epic the sequence in which events occurring in different places are narrated represents an actual chronological sequence, and it is obvious that the poet keeps strictly to this rule. Yet we can also see how he manages to convey the simultaneity of two separate strands of events: through the assembly of the gods at the beginning of the *Odyssey* we are prepared for imminent action in Ogygia, and this expectation remains while we hear of the events in Ithaca and accompany Telemachus on his journey to Pylos and Sparta. Nor are we disappointed, for at the moment when the son is persuaded by the allure of royal splendour and hospitality to stay on there in idleness the gods take action again and put their plan into operation. Odysseus departs, and we follow him on his journey (which turns out to be longer than expected) till he finally spends his first night back in Ithaca. Now the time has come for the son's conscience to awaken and we are prepared for this, we have long expected it. During the days Odysseus spends with Eumaeus—it is unnecessary to enquire what he does during that time—Telemachus tears himself away from Sparta and reaches Ithaca after an uneventful journey. At last father and son meet at Eumaeus' farm; their journeys and their search are over. From now on the separate strands of the narrative are united, and father and son act together.[48]

So much for the poet's technique. I hope that we have not been too far off the mark in stressing its continuity with epic tradition and in trying to understand and interpret the *Odyssey* against the background of earlier oral poetry and in particular the *Iliad*. Tradition and progress, conservation and innovation, constraint and freedom—it is between such poles, whatever we may call them, that the richness and individual quality of the poet's epic technique unfolds.

What has been said about the epic technique also applies *mutatis*

---

[48] For these structural problems cf. G. M. Calhoun, 'Télémaque et le plan de l'Odyssée', *REG* xlvii (1934), 133–63; Heubeck, *Dichter*, 40–63; Delebecque, *Télémaque*; H. W. Clarke, 'Telemachus and the Telemacheia', *AJP* lxxiv (1963), 129–45; L. Allione, *Telemaco e Penelope nell'Odissea* (cit. n. 19), 7–59; G. Bona, *Studi sull'Odissea* (cit. n. 20), 189–226; Lesky, *Homeros*, 810–12.

mutandis to all other aspects of the work. What the poet tells us and how he arranges it, the way in which he makes his gods and heroes speak and act, the manner in which he re-creates in his poem the world in which Odysseus' fate was worked out—all this shows an individual cast of mind, with its own brand of sympathetic under-standing of the world. It is not easy to put this 'mental physiognomy' (F. Jacoby) into words, but one can give examples to show how the old has been joined to the new and how tradition has been blended into the poet's own invention to construct a new, consistent whole from opposing elements.

There is, for instance, the hero at the centre of the epic, Odysseus himself. What kind of man is he, this man who, like his surviving comrades and peers, sets off for home with his contingent after the conquest of Troy, but then is separated from the others, suffers more adventures, is kept longest away from his loved ones, and can in the end only reclaim his own by the exertion of all his physical and mental powers? How did the poet want us to see him?

There are many answers to this question and we need not discuss them all individually. Most interpretations try to explain Odysseus from his origins, and this is certainly an important starting point.[49] There are many indications that Odysseus is a very ancient figure in Greek myth. Not only is there his name, which, like that of Achilles, cannot be explained from Greek and points back to older strata. There are also many adventures and situations which seem to be closely connected with our hero from the very beginning of literate tradition: encounters with witches and giants, monsters and canni-bals, his journey to the underworld, his contacts with daemonic beings. All this suggests that Odysseus' roots lie in the world of fairy-tale, perhaps even in the realm of magic and shamanism.[50] No doubt there is some truth in this, but we should be cautious about going beyond what we know for certain or can deduce with a high degree of probability.

What is certain is that the figure of Odysseus as it appears in the *Odyssey* is shaped by what the poet found in the *Iliad* and took from there. In that epic he is one of the kings who take part in the

[49] F. Focke, 'Odysseus: Wandlungen eines Heldenideals', *Antike, alte Sprachen und deutsche Bildung*, ii (1944), 41–52; Paula Philippson, 'Die vorhomerische und die homerische Gestalt des Odysseus', *MH* iv (1947), 8–22; E. Wüst, 'Odysseus', *RE* xvii (1957), 1905–96.

[50] K. Meuli, 'Scythica', *Hermes* lxx (1935), 121–276, esp. 164 ff. = *Gesammelte Schriften* ii 817 ff. (Basle–Stuttgart, 1975); R. Carpenter, *Fiction, Folktale and Saga in the Homeric Epics* (Berkeley–Los Angeles, ¹1946; ²1956), *passim*; Merkelbach, *Untersuchung-en* (¹1951), 224.

retaliatory expedition of the Atreidae. He, too, rules over a sizeable kingdom, from which he brings twelve ships to join the Achaean host. In the circle of leaders he has few peers. Apart from Achilles and Ajax, few are his equal in valour and strength; in political astuteness and military judgement he is superior to most. In short, he is an ideal warrior in whom all the virtues of an aristocratic hero are harmoniously blended. We may even go a step further and suggest that this picture of Odysseus in all essential features already existed in pre-Homeric poetry. There are some indications which show that his place in the Trojan epic is of long standing. In particular, the epithet given him in the *Iliad*, 'Sacker of Cities', only makes sense if in pre-Homeric epic too it was Odysseus who used the ruse of the Trojan horse and made the conquest of Troy possible.

This makes one wonder how it is that this warrior-king with his firm place among the heroes in both the pre-Homeric and Homeric epic becomes involved, for much of the *Odyssey*, in a world separated by a deep gulf from that of the heroes, and shows features which connect him rather with Sinbad the Sailor than with his noble peers and fellow warriors before Troy. Did the poet here follow an independent tradition running parallel to the epic, which preserved a more ancient picture? A different explanation, however, is perhaps more likely. It is possible that it was the poet of the *Odyssey* himself who sent the hero of the Trojan epic on his journey into fairyland, ascribing to him adventures which were originally connected with others, characters now nameless, perhaps from folk-tales, old seafarers' yarns, or even pre-Homeric poetry. Research has shown with great probability that some of the events and characters now connected with Odysseus originally belonged to the saga of the Argonauts.[51]

If it was indeed our poet who enriched the traditional picture of Odysseus with new elements which initially belonged somewhere else we can perhaps guess what led him to take this bold step. The plan of the poem required that Odysseus should return home very late, or almost too late, but a decade of wandering on a journey from Troy to Ithaca—which, though not without peril, is not an extraordinary undertaking—is only plausible if Odysseus strays into far-off lands, from which he cannot return to the world of men unless the gods give him their help.

On this journey, not only are the dimensions of space and time extended. Odysseus is faced with dangers nobody has faced before; all that he possesses and everything dear to him is taken from him bit by

[51] See especially K. Meuli, 'Odyssee und Argonautika' (Basle, 1921, = *Gesammelte Schriften*, ii 593 ff.).

bit in the long wandering from the battle with the Cicones, where he is still the man the *Iliad* describes, to the point of deepest humiliation, when the last vestige of glory has gone, his friends and comrades have all perished, and of his fleet only the keel of his own ship is left.

But the loss of power and glory and possessions is perhaps not the bitterest experience. A remorseless fate has thrown him into an environment where the virtues of an aristocratic warrior reveal their fragility and lose their value, where heroic aims turn into empty posing and become ridiculous gestures, while the world into which he was born is unattainably distant and exists only in the longing of his memory.

I believe that we can detect in this the spirit of a young poet who has himself become conscious of the questionable and limited validity of those aristocratic values which for earlier heroic poetry had been the props of an idealized view of the world and the pillars of a healthy society. It is the spirit of a man who has a different answer to the questions of life and human existence from that of his predecessors. While they set an ideal picture of a fictitious world where life, battle, and death were worth while against the reality of a bitter, toilsome, and grievous existence, and took their audience into a realm of glory, our poet unmasks this ideal in its one-sided narrowness and relativity. He, too, takes his listeners into a mythical world of dreams, but it is a mirror-image of the real world, where there is want and grief, terror and suffering, and where man is helpless. Yet for the poet this grim perception is not the end of the matter: life in the real world must still be lived and mastered, its challenges must be accepted in the proper spirit.

In this changed view of man and his existence the aristocratic virtues of courage, valour, and honour, of wisdom and prudence do not lose their validity completely, but something has to be added: wisdom alone can achieve very little without subtle and calculating shrewdness. There are threats and dangers in life which cannot be overcome by courage and valour alone, there are situations in which clinging to rigid aristocratic ideals is senseless, and sometimes one must simply endure fate patiently or give up. Odysseus is the 'hero' who has learnt—perhaps in spite of himself—to adopt this outlook and to master whatever suffering and anguish life holds in store. He is equipped for this by virtues which are rooted in the old ideals of aristocratic life and conduct but transcend them in a new ability to plan and calculate shrewdly, to hide and dissemble, but also to endure with incredible patience. The common notion of Odysseus as the archetypal bold seafarer and restless adventurer, as an explorer whose world has become too small for him and who craves the new and unknown, misses the essential point, and has little place in what we believe to be the true picture of the hero.

Yet it is not by chance that, along with this disillusioned and pessimistic view of man and his situation, which later found its full expression in early Greek lyric poetry, there is also reconciliation and solace. In our epic all the toil and suffering comes to a happy end; Odysseus, reaching the Phaeacians at the nadir of his fortunes, recovers his strength; in Ithaca the destroyers of a time-honoured order get their deserts, while those who are loyal and god-fearing are rewarded. 'Eunomia', the condition under which everyone has his appointed place and follows his daily life in peace and security, spreads bright happiness over the land.

This prospect of harmony at the end, which puts the disastrous and terrifying events of the epic in a new light, is founded, I believe, in the poet's faith. Although he sees man's plight in a harsh existence with more clarity and fewer illusions than others, he is able to incorporate this awareness in a deeper and more comprehensive view of the world, which is both rooted in traditional ideas and yet shaped by an independent and strong-willed spirit.

The poet of the *Iliad* had shown the events of the Trojan War taking place as it were on a two-tiered stage. The fierce struggle for the city involves men and gods alike, earthly situations and events are mirrored in the realm of the Olympian gods, and often the two strands running side by side become inextricably interwoven, when the gods descend to earth and actively intervene in human affairs, protecting and helping, restraining, encouraging, joining in battle. At such times they are possessed by the same violent feelings and emotions, and entangled in the same situations, as the mortals they love or hate, help or harm. And over mortals and gods alike stands inscrutable and inescapable fate which sets strict terms for all who live under it: it limits the life of men, but it also limits the power of the immortals when they seek to help their mortal descendants, for the gods, too, are powerless to alter the frontiers of death.

The extent to which the poet of the later epic was influenced by this concept should not be overlooked and some divergences from it in the *Odyssey* may simply be due to the different subject-matter. For here it is not the destiny of peoples, but the fate of a single man that is at stake, and it suffices that a single divine enemy, Poseidon, should pile up obstacles to his return,[52] while a single divine helper, Athena,

---

[52] J. Irmscher, *Götterzorn bei Homer* (Leipzig, 1950), esp. 52–77.

should counsel and assist him on his way.[53] It is more significant that in the younger epic the gods intervene less frequently. Whereas in the *Iliad* the activities of gods and men are continuously entwined,[54] here single gods are content with single actions, though with more enduring consequences. Furthermore, their actions are at bottom no more than intervention on behalf of and under the guidance of the one highest god who knows how to ordain everything aright. Zeus himself has changed in the poet's vision. His actions are no longer directed by irrational impulses and emotions, and he no longer has any need to boast of his superior power. He is further removed from the world inhabited by men and controlled by the gods, and not only in the spatial sense. With perceptiveness and wisdom Zeus now directs the fate of the world according to moral principles, which alone create and preserve order. The father of the gods has only a little way to go to become the just ruler of the world.

Consistent with the ethical transformation of the gods is the poet's own conviction, put into the mouth of Zeus, that man can by his own conduct change the fate laid upon him. This human freedom is for now explicitly referred to only in negative terms: the wrongdoer must expect punishment and a shameful end 'before his time' (i 34–5.).[55] That there is a positive side, however, is expressed by the whole work: the man who holds to justice and order and honours the gods may expect the appropriate reward for his efforts. It seems to me that in this respect the *Odyssey* is farther removed from the *Iliad* than it is from Solon and Aeschylus.[56]

We have traversed a very wide field in different ways and from different points of view, and we are aware that we have seen only parts of it, never the whole, and those from a subjective point of view, but any study of poetry is subject to such constraints and limitations; nobody can escape them. Any statement about poetry, however intelligent and knowledgeable, can only be an aid to understanding; at best it can point a way to the poetry itself, and it is that alone which matters.

[53] Marion Müller, *Athene als göttliche Helferin in der Odyssee* (Heidelberg, 1966).

[54] Cf. A. Lesky, *Göttliche und menschliche Motivation im Homerischen Epos*, Sitz.-Ber. Heidelberg 1961: 4.

[55] For this much-discussed passage see esp. W. Jaeger, *Solons Eunomie*, Sitz.-Ber. Berlin 1926: 11, 69–85; also *Scripta Minora*, i (Rome, 1960) 315–37; Focke, *Odyssee*, 25–31; Rüter, *Odysseeinterpretationen*, 64–82.

[56] For the theology of the *Odyssey* as a whole see, among others, A. Lesky, Sitz.-Ber. Heidelberg 1961: 4, 35 ff.; W. Burkert, 'Das Lied von Ares und Aphrodite', *RhM* (1960), 130–44.

THE EPIC DIALECT

J. B. Hainsworth

The Homeric language is artificial, a *Kunstsprache*, but not in the way that the language of Apollonius or Nonnus is artificial. Theirs is a conscious artificiality: the poet of the *Odyssey* used as his natural idiom the language of ἀοιδή in its contemporary form. From our standpoint we may describe this as a special form of the Ionic dialect of the day. It was special in that it combined with the Ionic in simultaneous use a certain number of words and formations taken from other dialects, retained from earlier periods, or generated within the *Kunstsprache* itself. The principle that governed the creation of this special dialect was given definitive form by Witte, 1908–12;[1] it was to produce, for a given sense, the maximum metrical diversity from the least infusion of 'foreign' material. Thus the Aeolic forms of the first person plural pronoun ἄμμες, ἄμμε, and ἄμμι(ν) are admitted beside the metrically different Ionic ἡμεῖς, ἡμέας, and ἡμῖν, but never ἀμμέων beside the metrically identical ἡμέων:[2] likewise an archaic genitive singular -οιο beside -ου, but not an archaic accusative -ονς beside -ους.

Because it was a form of spoken Ionic, the *Kunstsprache* was not fixed from one generation of poets to another, but shared in the linguistic development of the vernacular. It could not do so, however, totally and at once, if the changes affected the metrics of words: otherwise the systems of formulae upon which the ἀοιδοί relied would have been disrupted.[3] Consequently, at any point in time, the *Kunstsprache* contained both archaisms and neologisms in respect of the same feature: the digamma, to quote a notorious example, is

[1] K. Witte, 'Zur homerischen Sprache', *Glotta* i (1909), 132–45; ii (1910), 8–22; iii (1912), 104–56: also 'Homerische Sprach- und Versgedichte', *Glotta* iv (1913), 1–21, and 'Ueber die Kasusausgänge -οιο und -ου, -οισι und -οις, -ησι und -ης im griechischen Epos', *Glotta* v (1914), 8–47. The results are summarised in *RE* viii, coll. 2213 ff. s.v. Homeros: 'Sprache', and brought to completion in Meister, *Kunstsprache*.

[2] The most comprehensive discussion of Aeolic forms in Homer is that of Wathelet, *Traits*. It is, or ought to be, debatable how 'foreign' forms entered the *Kunstsprache*. The conventional view that Aeolic forms reflect an antecedent Aeolic ἀοιδή (see e.g. M. Durante, 'La fase eolica della poesia omerica', in *Studia Classica et Orientalia A. Pagliaro oblata*, ii (Rome, 1969), 85–130) is contested by W. F. Wyatt, 'Homer's Linguistic Ancestors', Ἐπιστημονικὴ Ἐπετηρὶς Θεσσαλονίκης xiv (1975), 133–47, who proposes the Aeolisms as a late importation.

[3] M. Parry, *HSPh* xliii (1932), 9–12 (= *Homeric Verse*, 331–3).

sometimes 'observed' (i.e. is notionally present in order to provide correct metre) and sometimes neglected. On the other hand, if metre were not affected, there was no reason why *Kunstsprache* and vernacular should not evolve *pari passu*: the Ionic $\eta < a$ is (discounting forms classed as Atticisms) universal in words and forms that occurred, as we may judge, in contemporary Ionic. In a vernacular dialect, however, sound changes are typically rapid and complete, but in poetical speech the feeling of ἀοιδοί for the sound of their language, a factor now scarcely ponderable, might render sound laws less than absolute, or lead to a preference for dialect or archaism: Homer has the Aeolic -ά in θεά but the Ionic -ῇ- in θεῇσι, Hesiod a formula λαμπράν τε Σελήνην (for λαμπρήν).[4]

As the idiom of the ἀοιδοί the *Kunstsprache* had, like any other form of language, its own internal dynamism: but whereas anomalous innovations tend to be rejected by the vernaculars, in a tradition that evoked the heroic world by its exotic language anomalies were protected by their very oddity. The peculiar -δ- perfect ἐληλάδατο vii 86 < ἐλαύνω rests on forms such as ἐρηρέδατο vii 95 < ἐρείδω (itself a modification of *ἐρηρίδατο). Philology is not a warrant for the correction of either.

The evolution of the *Kunstsprache* was progressive throughout its existence as a living idiom. If the composition of the *Odyssey* is put at some point between the late eighth and mid-seventh centuries, then it had by that time been evolving for several centuries and was to continue its natural development for at least another century, for as long as ἀοιδή survived. Even after the *Kunstsprache* became a 'dead' language, enshrined in written texts, evolution did not entirely cease (see notes on ἐπιβήομεν—or -βείομεν—vi 262).[5] An editor's raw material is the final stage of this process, as contained in the papyri and the medieval MSS. Since Bentley's discovery of the digamma, many have preferred linguistically antecedent forms to those in the paradosis: κεδνὰ (ἔργα, λυγρὰ, πάντα) ἰδυῖα for κέδν' εἰδυῖα etc. Likewise the effects of contraction and metathesis, which are certain at some points, can be undone at others. One such restored form, ἦος for ἕως (or εἴως) is sanctioned by LSJ[9] (but see iii 126 n.), and it is

---

[4] Such abnormal phonology is rare, but it must not be supposed that ἀοιδοί were uncritical users of their language: there are striking anomalies in *Scutum* and *h.Merc.*, on which see Janko 1982 (n. 8), which betray a taste for archaism and interrupt the otherwise insensible assimilation of the *Kunstsprache* to the vernacular.

[5] For the broad direction of the development see Janko 1982 (n. 8), and for particular formulae A. Hoekstra, *The Sub-epic Stage of the Formulaic Tradition* (Amsterdam, 1969).

easy to see that certain formulae, or certain habitual placings of words, are likely to have been established at a time when the older forms were in use, e.g. *ἠόα δῖαν for ἠῶ δῖαν, *'Ωαρίωνος for 'Ωρίωνος, *ἀγανόο for ἀγανοῦ (see v 1, v 274, vii 288 nn.) Linguistic development here resulted at most in an inelegance. The ἀοιδοί, who could offer θυγατέρα ἦν (Il. v 371 etc.) as –∪∪––, may have taken it in their stride. The paradosis offers no evidence that they did not. But it is conceivable that the older forms, with varying success, resisted replacement: ἀγήραος (v 136 etc.) is well attested in mid-verse, while the contracted ἀγήρως (v 218) coexisted at the verse-end. Editors print the older forms if there is evidence for them besides that of linguistic science, but the persistence of such forms, whether they survived Homer or predeceased him, cannot usually even be conjectured.[6]

In the simplest terms our texts of Homer bear witness simultaneously to two stages in the evolution of the *Kunstsprache*: first, the stage reached when the text was first stabilized; second, the stage endorsed in the late classical and Hellenistic periods. To the second we owe the fact that the orthography of the paradosis is uniform: no manuscript or papyrus writes digamma, all show aspiration, if it is indicated, diectasis, the same odd flexion of σπέος (datives σπῆι and σπέσσι —see i 15 n.) and some other s-stems (see viii 73 n.), and η > ει in certain circumstances before vowels. Some accidents at this stage were actually attributed by Alexandrian scholars to a μεταχαρακτηρισμός from the Old Attic to the Ionic alphabet (see n. on καιροσέων, vii 107). In an age when many children were taught epic poetry from a written text by schoolmasters (cf. the school scene on the red figure cup by Douris; J. D. Beazley, *Attic Red Figure Vase Painting*[2] (Oxford, 1963), 431, 48), it is understandable that spelling pronunciations of obscure words became established and were reflected in subsequent forms of the text. For the most part, however, the orthography and even the accentuation of the transmitted text represents the tradition of the Homeric rhapsodes.[7] But how many features are actually due to the evolution of the language within that tradition? Aspiration almost certainly, since words which should be aspirated on etymological grounds but were absent from the Attic

---

[6] For the prehistory of some aspects of the *Kunstsprache* see the two monographs of Hoekstra, *Modifications*, and *Epic Verse before Homer* (Amsterdam, 1981).

[7] Orthography: J. La Roche, *Die homerische Textkritik im Altertum* (Leipzig, 1866), has an invaluable account of the paradosis. Accentuation: Chantraine, *Grammaire*, i, 189–92—observe the 'archaisme remarquable' by which paroxytone words of trochaic shape receive an oxytone accent on the final syllable when followed by an enclitic: type ἔνθά τε (Allen's OCT prints the normal accents, however.) For other special accents see also Schwyzer, *Grammatik*, 384–5.

vernacular (e.g. ἦμαρ, ἤμβροτε) retain *spiritus lenis*: some *lectiones faciliores* (e.g. τηλεθοῶσα for τηλεθάουσα v 63, and some repairs to apparently bad metre (see v 34 n.). But we can detect, or suspect, these only when the tradition fluctuates. For contraction, diectasis, and similar phenomena belong generally to the first stage, the first stabilization of the text: only radical and unacceptable rewriting can eliminate them.

The form of the *Kunstsprache* found in the *Odyssey* may be defined first in relation to certain linguistic developments which are guaranteed by metre, then in relation to other early hexameter poetry. An attempt is often made to describe the language in quantitative terms, e.g. the rate of neglect of initial digamma is 17.2% in *Il.*, 17.9% in *Od.*, 33.7% in Hes. *Th.*, 37.9% in *Op.*, 27.7% in *Sc.*, 53.6% in *h.Merc.*, and 15.9% in *h.Ven.*[8] As a chronological argument a single criterion is deceptive: a poet may archaize—the author of *Scutum* diligently observed digamma, that of *h.Merc.* had a penchant for the -οιο genitive. More importantly, if the poet embarked on a topic where the tradition provided little formulaic diction, he naturally drew (for there was no other source) on his vernacular: similes in Homer are notoriously replete with neologism.[9] Thus the quantity of secondary linguistic features in a given block of verse chiefly reflects a fact of subject matter (see viii 266 ff. n.), the proportion of traditional to non-traditional material.[10] Where the material is very extensive, on the other hand, or where subject matter is comparable, R. Janko (1982, see n. 8) has shown that effective arguments can rest on quantitative premises. It is useful, however, for the present purpose, to consider how deeply a given neologism has penetrated the *Kunstsprache*, rather than its absolute frequency. A linguistic development of the vernacular quickly penetrated the fluid and non-formular part of the *Kunstsprache* (where it differed least), or took effect at the junctions between formulae: next the development would appear in modified formulae, 'formulae by analogy', and other

---

[8] Figures taken from R. Janko, *Homer, Hesiod and the Hymns: Diachronic Development in Epic Diction* (Cambridge, 1982). He comments (p. 46), 'The important observation to be made is that *Od.* is slightly more advanced than *Il.*, but less than Hesiod and most Hymns, and that *Op.* is more advanced than *Th.*'. The pattern is recurrent. Janko's other criteria are: the gen. sgs. of *a*- and *o*-stems, the gen. pl. of *a*-stems, the dat. pl. of *a*- and *o*-stems, the acc. pl. of *a*- and *o*-stems, the declension of Ζεύς, and the movable -ν.

[9] Details in Shipp, *Studies*, 7–200. To similes may be added comments, anecdotes, and such like material standing to one side of the narrative proper.

[10] Janko (op. cit.) cites figures for individual books. Of interest also is K. A. Garbrah, 'A Linguistic Analysis of Selected Portions of the Homeric Odyssey' *Glotta* xlvii (1969), 144 ff., on the distinctive character of the Telemachy.

derivatives of primary formulae: last of all would the development be found attested among regular formulae. Thus (ϝ)οἶνος + epithet is a common turn of phrase in the *Odyssey* (41 times). Digamma is observed in 35 instances, mostly examples of frequent formulae. Three instances are ambiguous, οἶνος standing at the beginning of the verse. Two instances of neglect occur among derivative expressions, ἡδέος οἴνου and μελιηδέος οἴνου, by declension from the accusative or dative cases, and there is one unique expression ἀθέσφατος οἶνος. No regular noun–epithet formulae show neglect (but cf. δαμασσάμενος or βεβαρηότα με φρένας οἴνῳ, where the plural φρένας is supported by xxi 297 ἐπεὶ φρένας ἄασεν οἴνῳ). The loss of digamma, at this point, had hardly begun to affect the formulaic diction.

In addition to the loss of digamma Hoekstra (*Modifications*) has closely examined two other features from this point of view, the quantitative metathesis and the movable -ν; he has also animadverted on vowel contraction, loss of the dual, -σαν plural, and -θη- aorist. The general conclusion is the same in each case: the secondary features are established in the text (in the fluid part of the diction), but not in the formular system. The linguistic developments in the vernacular of Ionia probably antedate the end of the eighth century, though not by any long period of time.

The works of Hesiod and the Homeric *Hymns* give an impression of the epic dialect more deeply penetrated by secondary linguistic features. Much of this impression is due to the increased frequency of secondary features in the non-formular diction, for the features themselves usually have occasional parallels in Homer. Yet some of the increased frequency is found in areas which are very conservative in Homer: Hes. *Op.* neglects the digamma of οἶνος 3 times out of 7, *Od.* 8 times out of 88; *h.Merc.* that of ἔργον 3 times out of 13, *h.Cer.* 4 times out of 7, against only 5 times in *Od.* out of 129 examples.[11] Some new formulae appear, made possible by the evolving vernacular, e.g. Κρονίδεω διὰ βουλάς Hes. *Op.* 71, *Th.* 572; and in *h.Merc.* a complete system exploiting the contraction of Ἑρμῆς < Ἑρμείας:

κύδιμος			Κυλλήνιος	
	} Ἑρμῆς			} Ἑρμῆς.
ἀγλαός			ἐριούνιος	

---

[11] The issue is complicated by the nature of the vernacular from which the poet was seeking to distinguish the *Kunstsprache*. 'He [Hesiod] neglected the digamma, therefore, in conscious imitation of the traditional poetic language; while the Ionian rhapsode did the opposite for the same reason.' (M. L. West, *Theogony* (Oxford, 1966), 91.) The Boeotian retained initial ϝ until a remarkably late date: East Ionic lost it before the earliest documentation

For an editor of Homer these facts have two important implications. First, he is strongly counselled not to correct the transmitted text in the face of a unanimous tradition. No doubt ἀοιδοί sometimes accepted a faulty but traditional rhythm for later generations to correct, but poets as much as rhapsodes must be granted a feeling for metre and the ability to use all the resources of *Kunstsprache* and vernacular to 'correct' it. Second, the text—the ultimate ancestor of our text—was stabilized at a very early date, earlier than the date of composition of *Hymns* and other early hexameter poetry.

In a strictly oral culture the ἀοιδός never completes his poem in the sense that he makes the last corrections to the final draft and lets it pass from his control. For him a poem is not a text, but a sequence of themes and incidents. These he endeavours to recreate as well as his talents permit and his audience deserve on the occasion of each performance. We should not expect in these circumstances that any version of a long poem would be precisely identical to any other version, or consistently of the highest standard. Modern comparative studies confirm this expectation. The divergences are not always substantial. On the lips of the same performer, working in similar circumstances, a poem may acquire a remarkable degree of stability. But such stability is unlikely, in an oral milieu, to survive the poet. For it is when the poem passes from one performer to another that the greatest deformation takes effect. The new poet adopts the story, the sequence of themes and incidents, but recreates those themes according to his own habits.[12]

It is important to realize that the transmutation of the poem at this stage is likely to be considerable. Even within one of the Homeric poems, where certain frequent themes, the so-called 'typical scenes' of arming, sacrificing, etc., tend towards a certain form and diction, uniformity is never actually achieved. In the closest instance the scenes of sacrifice at *Il.* i 458–68 and ii 421–31 share nine lines, but not the two for the roasting of the entrails. At the other extreme it is instructive to compare *h.Merc.* 1–9 and *h.* xviii 1–9.

h.Merc.   Ἑρμῆν ὕμνει Μοῦσα Διὸς καὶ Μαιάδος υἱόν,
Κυλλήνης μεδέοντα καὶ Ἀρκαδίης πολυμήλου,
ἄγγελον ἀθανάτων ἐριούνιον, ὃν τέκε Μαῖα

[12] The doctrine is that of Lord, *Singer*, 68–98 (esp. 78 and 95–8): some of the material on which his generalizations are based may be read in *La Poesia Epica e la sua Formazione*, (Problemi Attuali di Scienza e di Cultura, cxxxix, Rome, 1970), 13–28 (esp. 16–18). For stability of an oral text see *Singer* 94–5 and G. S. Kirk, *CQ* x (1960), 271–81 (= *Language and Background of Homer* (Cambridge, 1964), 79–89 = *Homer and the Oral Tradition* (Cambridge, 1976), 113–28).

νύμφη ἐϋπλόκαμος Διὸς ἐν φιλότητι μιγεῖσα,
αἰδοίη· μακάρων δὲ θεῶν ἠλεύαθ᾽ ὅμιλον
ἄντρον ἔσω ναίουσα παλίσκιον, ἔνθα Κρονίων
νύμφῃ ἐϋπλοκάμῳ μισγέσκετο νυκτὸς ἀμολγῷ,
ὄφρα κατὰ γλυκὺς ὕπνος ἔχοι λευκώλενον Ἥρην,
λήθων ἀθανάτους τε θεοὺς θνητούς τ᾽ ἀνθρώπους.

h. xviii   Ἑρμῆν ἀείδω Κυλλήνιον Ἀργεϊφόντην,
Κυλλήνης μεδέοντα καὶ Ἀρκαδίης πολυμήλου
ἄγγελον ἀθανάτων ἐριούνιον, ὃν τέκε Μαῖα
Ἄτλαντος θυγάτηρ Διὸς ἐν φιλότητι μιγεῖσα
αἰδοίη· μακάρων δὲ θεῶν ἀλέεινεν ὅμιλον
ἄντρῳ ναιετάουσα παλισκίῳ, ἔνθα Κρονίων
νύμφῃ ἐϋπλοκάμῳ μισγέσκετο νυκτὸς ἀμολγῷ
εὖτε κατὰ γλυκὺς ὕπνος ἔχοι λευκώλενον Ἥρην.
λάνθανε δ᾽ ἀθανάτους τε θεοὺς θνητούς τ᾽ ἀνθρώπους.

Both passages seem to recreate the same praise of Hermes, yet only three lines are shared, exactly, between them. Ἀοιδή, it is clear, could not conserve the special character of the text of Homer, if these two passages are in any way typical of different performances of the 'same' material.

Yet something important may have happened to the art of narrative poetry in the early seventh century and reduced the instability of the poems. It is clear that ἀοιδή was literally singing, and required the accompaniment of the lyre. Modern analogies suggest that the poet could not have performed without it.[13] Yet Hesiod's account of his 'call' (*Th.* 29 ff.) tells how the poet was given not a φόρμιγξ but a σκῆπτρον. In the epic the σκῆπτρον is the insignia of the orator; we meet it later as the staff of the unaccompanied reciter of verse, the ῥαψῳδός. Hesiod, accordingly was dubbed the first rhapsode (Nicocles, *FGrH* 376 F 8). It is permissible, when the lyre is discarded, to infer a change in the mode of performance of hexameter poetry, and therefore, in a tradition where composition and performance had been identical, in the mode of its recreation. The skills of the actor, in short, supplanted those of the bard; a version of the text was memorized, and so fixed.[14] Naturally it did not happen all at once, nor were the new skills invariably trustworthy. The celebrated François vase (J. D. Beazley, *Attic Black Figure Vase Painting* (Oxford, 1956), 76, 1) depicts the funeral games of Patroclus with a personnel quite different from that of *Il.* xxiii.

[13] Lord, *Singer*, 126–7.
[14] For an attempt to evaluate the scanty evidence for these crucial developments see R. Sealey, 'From Phemius to Ion', *REG* lxx (1957), 312–55.

The alternative would be to postulate a written text from a very early period. The expense and labour of such an enterprise, and the lack of materials, are grave obstacles to such a view. A graver obstacle is the lack of motivation. The earliest literacy did not confront the oral culture with the realization of its full potential: the reverse was true. In its perfection the oral culture was both subtle and satisfying, for audiences and for performers, and the written word offered no advantages. The motivation of a written text, therefore, had to be external to the tradition of ἀοιδή, something felt by those whose interest in epic poetry went beyond that attributed to Alcinous and his court in *Od.* viii. It is natural at this point to think of the bodies who called themselves 'Homeridae' and 'Creophyleioi', but what role they performed, if any, in the creation of a written text is entirely uncertain.[15] Evidence appears only with those who organized the recitations of Homer at the Panathenaea in the sixth century. Their action reflects and culminates that shift in attitude towards the epic which established Homer as the 'educator of the Greeks'. What distinguished the Athenians was their dissatisfaction with the material immediately available to them and their determination to make use of the complete poems.

As to the process by which the first written texts of Homer were produced, whatever their date and provenance, no information, obviously, exists. Modern investigators have distinguished (1) the actual performance (electronically recorded, and irrelevant to the present enquiry), (2) the autograph text, created by a poet who has acquired literacy, and (3) the dictated text.[16] The last has been thought the most probable origin of the first written texts, yet no study in depth exists of the effect of dictation on the text dictated. For the poets the situation, obviously, is novel. For most of them novelty is merely irksome: the pace is too slow, the 'audience' unresponsive and probably critical. But should a poet successfully adapt himself,

[15] Homeridae: P. *N.* ii 1–3 with schol.; Pl. *Ion* 530 d, *Phdr.*, 252 d, *R.* 599 e; Isoc., *Helena* 65 with Harpocration, *Lex.*, s.v. Ὁμηρίδαι from which it appears they were a γένος in Chios who performed (or were supposed to have performed) Homer's poems, and were the custodians of arcane information and even of ἀνέκδοτα. There are notes on modern controversies in H. T. Wade-Gery, *The Poet of the Iliad* (Cambridge, 1952), 19–21. Creophyleioi: Arist., fr. 611 Rose, Neanth. *FGrH* 84 F 29, Plu. *Lyc.* 4, Iamb. *VP* 11: discussion in W. Burkert, 'Die Leistung eines Kreophylos', *MH* xxix (1972), 74–85.

[16] C. M. (Sir Maurice) Bowra, *Homer and his Forerunners* (Edinburgh, 1955), 8–13, favoured the literate poet: cf. his *Heroic Poetry* (London, 1952), 240; A. A. Lord, 'Homer's Originality: Oral Dictated Texts', *TAPhA* lxxxiv (1953), 124–34, the dictated text. For the subsequent controversy (not much of which rested on firsthand knowledge of oral literature) see Lesky, *Homeros*, coll. 17–23, and A. Heubeck, *Archaeologia* X, 126–84.

the result is often *a more elaborate treatment both of the story and of the themes within it*. For the scribe the task bears some relation to that of an editor. At the least he adjusts language and diction to what he believes to be the norm; he corrects metre; he emends what he conceives to be mistakes, and ensures the match of repeated passages; if he botches his transcription, he must reconstruct the passage as best he can.[17] If the scribe is also a collector, his awareness of alternative versions may tempt him into a truly editorial role, the preparation, by conflation, of a 'consolidated' text. What seem to be echoes of this phase in the story of the text are found in the scholia to *Iliad* x, and might also have been heard, if the scholia were fuller, in the conclusion to the *Odyssey*. Its effects may also be suspected at the beginning of *Odyssey* v, and of course in innumerable other places where the hand of the *Bearbeiter* was detected during an older phase of Homeric criticism.

[17] Lord, *Singer*, 124–8. Some of the consequences of dictation as the method of recording are outlined by M. Skafte Jensen, *The Homeric Question and the Oral-Formulaic Theory* (Copenhagen, 1980), 81–95.

THE TRANSMISSION OF THE TEXT

Stephanie West

The history of the Homeric text in antiquity is at many points obscure and controversial, but discussion of the two epics is hardly possible without some understanding of the way in which they were handed down from the time when they were first recorded in writing until the text was set on a relatively secure footing in the Hellenistic age. The following brief sketch, offered simply as background to the commentary, is intended to alert the reader to the critical phases and the major hazards in the *Odyssey*'s transmission.[1]

Our starting-point is a manuscript of the *Odyssey* produced by (or at least with the co-operation of) its author. The study of contemporary oral epic traditions in many cultures over the last century does not encourage us to suppose that without a written text long and complex poems like the *Iliad* and *Odyssey* could be reproduced beyond the lifetime of their composers in what, by the standards of a literate society, would seem even an approximately accurate form; fluidity and constant reconstitution of its materials are characteristic of oral heroic poetry, and the extraordinary powers of memorization demonstrated by those who have mastered its traditional techniques are accompanied by a facility in improvisation fatal to the accurate transmission of a work of any length or elaboration. Nor does either of the Homeric poems seem quite as well suited to the normal conditions of oral epic performance as a cycle of short, self-contained lays would have been; the composition of a long, carefully structured, poetic narrative might in itself be thought to suggest a seminal appreciation of the advantages of script.

The composer of the *Iliad* appears to have heard of the revived greatness of Egyptian Thebes under the pious Nubian kings of Dyn. XXV (715–663); the reopening of Egypt to the Greeks at this period seems to be reflected in the *Odyssey*'s penchant for Egyptian adven-

---

[1] An excellent introduction to the subject is given by Lesky, *Homeros*, 145 ff.; see also G. Pasquali, *Storia della tradizione e critica del testo*[2] (Florence, 1952), 201 ff., J. A. Davison in *Companion*, 215 ff.; still useful, though somewhat eccentric at times, is the section on transmission in T. W. Allen, *Homer: The Origins and the Transmission* (Oxford, 1924), 202 ff.; on the early stages see also R. Sealey, 'From Phemios to Ion', *REG* lxx (1957), 312 ff.

tures.[2] These are the most definite indications which the two epics offer of a *terminus post quem*, while the general ancient belief that they came at, or near, the beginning of Greek literary history discourages hypotheses which would put the date of their composition later than the seventh century. The first surviving examples of Greek alphabetic writing belong to the second half of the eighth century. Some controversy surrounds the date of its invention (i.e. of the adaptation of Phoenician script to Greek),[3] but certainly even rudimentary literacy must have been extremely restricted in Greek lands before 700, and it seems most unlikely that anyone would have attempted to record a long poetic text in writing before the seventh century. The resumption of regular contacts with Egypt in the reign of Psammetichus I (663–610) brought the advantage of direct access to supplies of papyrus, destined to be the most popular material for Greek books throughout antiquity. Increased contact with their Near Eastern neighbours perhaps stimulated awareness of the advantages of recording poetry in writing.[4] At all events, by the last third of the seventh century the practice was well established; Archilochus, Hesiod, and Tyrtaeus are all to be dated before then, and their precisely worded compositions could not long have survived their authors without a written record.

We should not underestimate the difference between setting down a poem of fifty (or even five hundred) lines and committing to writing a long heroic epic; perhaps the poet of the *Iliad* was not the first to attempt adapting the traditional techniques of formulaic composition to the slow pace of the pen, but had himself benefited by observing the less successful experiments of earlier pioneers. At all events the feasibility of this application of script had been satisfactorily demonstrated by the time that the poet of the *Odyssey* conceived the idea of a monumental epic on Odysseus in emulation of his great predecessor. How long elapsed between the composition of the *Iliad* and the *Odyssey* we cannot hope to say; scholarly convention favours a generation.

[2] *Il.* ix 381–4; see further W. Burkert, 'Das hunderttorige Theben u. die Datierung der Ilias', *WSt* NF x (1976), 5 ff., A. Heubeck, *Gymnasium* lxxxix (1982), 442–3. On the *Odyssey*'s fascination with Egypt see below p. 192.

[3] See further L. H. Jeffery, *The Local Scripts of Archaic Greece* (Oxford, 1961), *CAH* iii[2] i 819 ff., A. Heubeck, *Archaeologia* X, A. Johnston, 'The Extent and Use of Literacy: The Archaeological Evidence', in R. Hägg (ed.), *The Greek Renaissance of the Eighth Century BC: Tradition and Innovation* (Stockholm, 1983), 63–8.

[4] See further W. Burkert, *Die orientalisierende Epoche in der griechischen Religion u. Literatur*, SHAW 1984, 1, esp. 29 ff., 85 ff.

Some time before 600, then, we may with reasonable confidence assume that a poem recognizable as our *Odyssey* was set down in writing. The existence of a written text did not, however, by itself offer much protection against deliberate alteration. We know that the text of tragedy has suffered extensively from actors' interpolations;[5] rhapsodes,[6] on whom for some generations the transmission of the Homeric poems depended, had equally powerful motives for 'improving' the text. The poet of the *Odyssey* himself thought novelty important in song (i 351–2), and no doubt very many of those who recited his work agreed. While oral poetry was still a living art it must have been common for rhapsodes to elaborate and embroider the text, to glorify a patron's heroic ancestors, and to add extra episodes; the study of contemporary oral poetry in Yugoslavia has shown the liberties which a poet may take with a written (even a printed) text.[7] Such individual enterprise would normally be ephemeral in its effects, but the prestige and initiative of an influential rhapsode might secure a longer life for his additions.[8] The looseness of Homeric

[5] See D. L. Page, *Actors' Interpolations in Greek Tragedy* (Oxford, 1934), M. D. Reeve, 'Interpolations in Greek Tragedy', *GRBS* xiii (1972), 247 ff., 451 ff.; xiv (1973), 145 ff.; A. Dihle, *Der Prolog der 'Bacchen'*, SHAW 1981, 2. The arguments are strong for regarding most interpolations in tragedy as histrionic in origin, rather than as products of the period of purely literary transmission. That the ancients were well aware of the danger is shown by the decree of Lycurgus in 330 regarding the three tragedians ([Plut.] *Vit. X Orat.* 841 f.): τὰς τραγῳδίας αὐτῶν ἐν κοινῷ γραψαμένους φυλάττειν καὶ τὸν τῆς πόλεως γραμματέα παραναγινώσκειν τοῖς ὑποκρινομένοις· οὐκ ἐξεῖναι δὲ ἄλλως ὑποκρίνεσθαι. But considerable damage had already been done.

[6] The term *rhapsodos* came to denote mere reciters like Plato's Ion, but even in the fourth century the verb *rhapsodein* could be used of original composition: cf. Pl. *R.* 600 d (of Homer and Hesiod). The tendency to restrict these terms to those who declaimed the works of others must have come with the decline of oral technique; contrast Hes. fr. 357, 1–2 ἐν Δήλῳ τότε πρῶτον ἐγὼ καὶ Ὅμηρος ἀοιδοὶ | μέλπομεν, ἐν νεαροῖς ὕμνοις ῥάψαντες ἀοιδήν, Pi. *N.* ii 1–2, Ὁμηρίδαι ῥαπτῶν ἐπέων ... ἀοιδοί.

[7] Well illustrated by Avdo Međedović's version of 'The Wedding of Smailagić Meho', in M. Parry, A. B. Lord, D. Bynum (eds.), *Serbo-Croatian Heroic Songs*, iii (Cambridge, Mass., 1974). This song was dictated by the singer Ahmed Isakov Šemić in 1885 and published the following year by Friedrich Krauss; reproduced in various popular editions it became widespread among singers. The version dictated by Međedović in 1935 was considerably expanded and seems artistically more effective; though Međedović was himself illiterate, he learned the song from hearing it read.

[8] Compare what we are told about the rhapsode Cynaethus of Chios (schol. Pi. *N.* ii 1 c): Ὁμηρίδας ἔλεγον τὸ μὲν ἀρχαῖον τοὺς ἀπὸ τοῦ Ὁμήρου γένους, οἳ καὶ τὴν ποίησιν αὐτοῦ ἐκ διαδοχῆς ᾖδον· μετὰ δὲ ταῦτα καὶ οἱ ῥαψῳδοὶ οὐκέτι τὸ γένος εἰς Ὅμηρον ἀνάγοντες. ἐπιφανεῖς δὲ ἐγένοντο οἱ περὶ Κύναιθον, οὓς φασι πολλὰ τῶν ἐπῶν ποιήσαντας ἐμβαλεῖν εἰς τὴν Ὁμήρου ποίησιν. ἦν δὲ ὁ Κύναιθος τὸ γένος Χῖος, ὃς καὶ τῶν ἐπιγραφομένων Ὁμήρου ποιημάτων τὸν εἰς Ἀπόλλωνα γεγραφὼς ὕμνον ἀνατέθεικεν αὐτῷ. οὗτος οὖν ὁ Κύναιθος πρῶτος ἐν Συρακούσαις ἐραψῴδησε τὰ Ὁμήρου ἔπη κατὰ τὴν ξθ' Ὀλυμπιάδα, ὡς Ἱππόστρατός φησιν (*FGrH* 568 F 5).

narrative and the traditional formulaic style made minor alteration simple even for bards with no pretensions to creativity.

In these circumstances the epics might have been expected to develop along diverging paths in different parts of the Greek world. Yet when, in the third and second centuries BC, copies from as far apart as Marseilles and Sinope were collated at Alexandria,[9] the text, despite a vast range of trivial variants, was substantially the same.[10] This essential uniformity is the more remarkable inasmuch as each of the two epics has absorbed a substantial body of material regarded in antiquity as alien to the original conception (*Od.* xxiii 297–xxiv, *Il.* x), and yet, so to speak, canonical.[11] Many great popular heroic epics impose on their editors a choice between different recensions;[12] but the history of the Homeric text, as far back as it can be traced, shows only a very slight degree of redactional freedom.

This strongly suggests that something was done to standardize the text and inhibit the proliferation of variants, and it is reasonable to connect this standardization with the tradition of what has come to be known, rather grandiosely, as the Pisistratean recension.[13] In the Hellenistic age it was widely believed that Pisistratus or Solon had tampered with the text of Homer, permanently imposing a version in accordance with Athenian interests; legend subsequently magnified yet further Pisistratus' role in the redaction of the poems. It was long

[9] On the so-called 'city editions' see below pp. 44–5.

[10] At an earlier date Herodotus' manner of referring to Homer implies that he, at least, was unaware of significant regional differences.

[11] Schol. *Od.* xxiii 296: Ἀριστοφάνης δὲ καὶ Ἀρίσταρχος πέρας τῆς Ὀδυσσείας τοῦτο ποιοῦνται. M, V, Vind. τοῦτο τέλος τῆς Ὀδυσσείας φησὶν Ἀρίσταρχος καὶ Ἀριστοφάνης. H, M, Q. Cf. Eust. ad loc. (This note is sometimes taken as an aesthetic comment, to the effect that the *Odyssey*'s story has now reached its consummation, but it seems to me much more likely to represent textual criticism; I hope to deal with this question at greater length elsewhere. For more detailed discussion (and a rather different view) see Heubeck on xxiii 297 ff., introduction to xxiv, xxiv 205 ff.) Schol. *Il.* x 1: φασὶ τὴν ῥαψῳδίαν ὑφ᾽ Ὁμήρου ἰδίᾳ τετάχθαι καὶ μὴ εἶναι μέρος τῆς Ἰλιάδος, ὑπὸ δὲ Πεισιστράτου τετάχθαι εἰς τὴν ποίησιν. (See further Lesky, *Homeros*, 105–6.)

[12] There is an obvious danger of over-simplification in attempting comparisons, but it is clear that editors of the *Nibelungenlied*, the *Chanson de Roland*, the medieval Greek epic of Digenis Akritas, and, outstandingly, the *Mahabharata* face a far more complex task than the editor of Homer. See further H. Brackert, *Beiträge zur Handschriftenkritik des Nibelungenliedes* (Berlin, 1963), 169 ff., J. Bédier, *La Chanson de Roland commentée* (Paris, 1927), 65 ff., S. Impellizieri, *Il Digenis Akritas* (Florence, 1940), 87 ff., M. Winternitz, *Geschichte der indischen Literatur* (Leipzig, 1908), i 397 ff., V. S. Sukthankar, *The Mahabharata for the First Time Critically Edited* (Poona, 1933), i Introduction.

[13] The Pisistratean recension has been restored to scholarly respectability as a result of R. Merkelbach's careful study of the ancient testimony (*RhM* lxxxv (1952), 23 ff. (= *Untersuchungen*, 239 ff.). See also M. Skafte Jensen, *The Homeric Question and the Oral Formulaic Theory* (Copenhagen, 1980), 128 ff.

fashionable to dismiss this as a Hellenistic invention, but already in fourth-century sources there is some evidence pointing in this direction, though Pisistratus is not actually named. The most important testimony is [Pl.] *Hipparch.* 228 b: Ἱππάρχῳ ... ὃς ἄλλα τε πολλὰ καὶ καλὰ ἔργα σοφίας ἀπεδείξατο, καὶ τὰ Ὁμήρου ἔπη πρῶτος ἐκόμισεν εἰς τὴν γῆν ταυτηνί, καὶ ἠνάγκασε τοὺς ῥαψῳδοὺς Παναθηναίοις ἐξ ὑπολήψεως ἐφεξῆς αὐτὰ διιέναι, ὥσπερ νῦν ἔτι οἵδε ποιοῦσιν. The specific attribution of these measures to the relatively unromantic figure of Hipparchus inspires confidence. We should not infer that the author of this dialogue supposed the Homeric poems to have been unknown at Athens before Hipparchus; more probably he believed that, though the epics themselves were familiar from recitation, no text was available in Attica until Hipparchus acquired one and established it as the version to be followed at the Panathenaea. This Panathenaic regulation is also mentioned by Lycurgus (*in Leocr.* 102): οὕτω γὰρ ὑπέλαβον ὑμῶν οἱ πατέρες σπουδαῖον εἶναι ποιητὴν [sc. Ὅμηρον], ὥστε νόμον ἔθεντο καθ' ἑκάστην πεντετηρίδα τῶν Παναθηναίων μόνου τῶν ἄλλων ποιητῶν ῥαψῳδεῖσθαι τὰ ἔπη.[14] The vagueness of Lycurgus' ascription of this measure to ὑμῶν οἱ πατέρες may be due to genuine uncertainty, but more probably reflects reluctance to mention one of the Pisistratids in a context which would set him in a favourable light.

The introduction of Homeric recitation to the programme of the Pisistratean Panathenaea would have quickly revealed the need for an agreed form of the text if the competition was to run smoothly. While no one was likely to be troubled by slight verbal discrepancies between one rhapsode's version and another's, administrative difficulties would have been inevitable if there were disagreement about the inclusion or omission of interesting episodes (such as the Doloneia). If the Athenian authorities decided to insist on a particular text (as they surely must have done), we should expect them to have chosen one deemed to be of respectable provenance, but we should not imagine that anyone in the sixth century would have undertaken a systematic comparison of the various versions available, or that the copy selected must have been what we should judge the best, much less that it had preserved the original composition with complete

---

[14] Cf. Isoc. *Paneg.* 159 (even vaguer). To this fourth-century testimony we should perhaps add that of the Megarian historian Dieuchidas, cited by DL (i 57): τά τε Ὁμήρου ἐξ ὑποβολῆς γέγραφε [sc. Solon] ῥαψῳδεῖσθαι, οἷον ὅπου ὁ πρῶτος ἔληξεν, ἐκεῖθεν ἄρχεσθαι τὸν ἐχόμενον. μᾶλλον οὖν Σόλων Ὅμηρον ἐφώτισεν ἢ Πεισίστρατος· ⟨ἐκεῖνος γὰρ ἦν ὁ τὰ ἔπη εἰς τὸν κατάλογον ἐμποιήσας καὶ οὐ Πεισίστρατος, suppl. Leaf⟩ ὥς φησι Διευχίδας ἐν πέμπτῳ Μεγαρικῶν (*FGrH* 485 F 6). ἦν δὲ μάλιστα τὰ ἔπη ταυτί· 'οἳ δ' ἄρ' Ἀθήνας εἶχον' καὶ τὰ ἑξῆς (*Il.* ii 546 ff.). But Dieuchidas' date is not entirely certain: see further J. A. Davison, *CQ* liii (1969), 216 ff.

fidelity. Once an official Athenian version had been prescribed, rhapsodes who intended to perform in Attica would have wanted copies for themselves; outside this fairly restricted professional group there can hardly have been much demand for some time. Rhapsodic acceptance, hastened, no doubt, by the increasing importance of Athens at this period, would have ensured the success of the Attic text over potential rivals.

It may be thought unlikely that an Athenian version could have won such acceptance if it had been extensively reworked and revised. But a few obviously Athenocentric passages must certainly belong to this phase. References to Athens are not of course in themselves suspect, but in some instances the desire to appeal to an Athenian audience seems blatant: the most striking is the Attic entry in the Catalogue of Ships (*Il.* ii 546–56).[15] No doubt it was common for local colour to be added in recitation; but such insertions would not normally have been long lasting or widespread in their effects, and the perpetuation of this Attic material is not adequately explained by Athenian domination of the nascent book trade in the fifth and fourth centuries. We are not, however, entitled to assume that the only additions which a Pisistratean editor would have thought proper will betray themselves by their obvious patriotic intent. More drastic interference is certainly implied by the tradition which ascribes the insertion of the Doloneia to Pisistratus.[16]

[15] The equation of Attica with Athens, ignoring the other Attic towns, is in itself suspicious; the details of cult-practice have no parallel in the Catalogue, and the fulsome praise lavished on the obscure Menestheus justifiably excited the suspicions of Zenodotus. In the *Odyssey* it is tempting to connect the reference to Orestes' sojourn at Athens (iii 307) with the Pisistratean recension; but in Zenodotus' text Orestes' exile was spent in Phocis, and it would be rash to dismiss his reading as a conjecture: see n. ad loc. However, the description of Athena's visit to Athens (vii 80–1) is of little interest to anyone except an Athenian, and was suspected in antiquity: see schol. ad loc. The third-century historian Hereas of Megara (*FGrH* 486 F 1) believed that Pisistratus had inserted xi 631 Θησέα Πειρίθοόν τε, θεῶν ἀριδείκετα τέκνα; he was surely right in thinking that the selection of these two heroes for special mention points to Athens. It has also been suggested that the part played by Nestor and his family has been expanded, by way of compliment to Pisistratus, who claimed descent from them: see further below, iii 36 n. The orthography has undoubtedly assumed an Attic appearance, but this could adequately be explained by the prominence of Athens in the early development of the book trade and the tendency of scribes to replace unfamiliar forms with Attic ones. Irreducible Atticisms are very few, and there is in any case no reason why metrically convenient Atticisms (like ἐπέκειντο for ἐπεκείατο *Od.* vi 19) should not have entered the epic language before Pisistratus.

[16] If (as I believe) the end of the *Odyssey* was added at this period (see above, n. 11), there must also have been alterations earlier in the poem to prepare for the concluding episodes.

This sixth-century Athenian recension must be regarded as the archetype of all our Homeric MSS and of the indirect tradition represented by ancient quotations and allusions; we can only speculate about what preceded it.[17] It would of course have lacked such aids to the reader as word-division, accentuation, punctuation, and the distinction between capital and small letters; these sophistications, which would have resolved many of the perplexities which beset Homeric scholarship, were not to be introduced to Greek book production for many centuries. We should also expect a scribe working in Attica in the sixth century to use the Attic alphabet, which differed from the Ionic (officially adopted at Athens in 404/3) in making no distinction between the three e-sounds (ϵ, $\epsilon\iota$, η) or between the three o-sounds (o, ov, ω) and in failing to use double letters; no doubt to Attic scribes these refinements seemed merely a nuisance. Cut off as we are from the living tradition of Homeric recitation, we must regret the fact that the Attic alphabet denied to the orthography of unfamiliar words a protection which Ionic script would have afforded. But in the archaic and classical periods these disadvantages would have seemed unimportant; people knew the Homeric poems primarily from hearing them, and anyone with a sufficiently serious interest to acquire (or even consult) a text must generally have had a clear enough idea of how it was supposed to sound.[18]

The familiar twenty-four-fold division of the two epics very

---

[17] The point was well stressed by Erich Bethe (*Homer* i, 52–3): 'Für die Überlieferung der Ilias kommt also nur eine einzige attische Handschrift aus der Zeit des Peisistratos in Betracht. Ebenso für die Odyssee … Das kann nicht oft, nicht scharf genug betont werden. Denn nach keiner Richtung hin ist diese unbestreitbare Tatsache hinlänglich beachtet oder ausgenutzt worden, weder für die Analyse noch für die Textkritik. Ihr Ziel kann kein anderes sein als die Rekonstruktion dieser attischen Mutterhandschrift des sechsten Jahrhunderts für Ilias wie Odyssee … Dieser attische Homertext des sechsten Jahrhunderts ist das einzige Objekt aller Homerforschung. Er ist und muss für uns Homer schlechthin sein, denn es gibt keinen andern als diesen einen'.

[18] We sometimes find it suggested in the scholia that mistakes have arisen in the course of transliteration from the old Attic alphabet: e.g. schol. *Od.* i 52 Ἄτλαντος θυγάτηρ ὀλοόφρονος: ἢ ἐγέγραπτο κατὰ τὴν ἀρχαίαν γραφὴν ⟨ολοοφρον⟩, εἶτά τις μὴ νοήσας προσέθηκε τὸ ος, schol. i 275 μητέρα δ᾽ εἴ οἱ θυμὸς ἐφορμᾶται γαμέεσθαι, ἂψ ἴτω: τῇ ἀρχαίᾳ συνηθείᾳ ἐγέγραπτο μετερ ἀντὶ τοῦ μητηρ. τοῦτο ἀγνοήσας τις προσέθηκε τὸ α; see also schol. *Il.* vii 238, xi 104, xiv 241, xxi 363. This theory is in accordance with Aristarchus' belief that Homer was an Athenian (see schol. *Il.* xiii 197), but it unrealistically presupposes a solitary reader deciphering an unfamiliar text, and none of the examples put forward in the scholia is intrinsically convincing (though some good modern conjectures presuppose similar misunderstandings); see further Cauer, *Homerkritik*, 105 ff., Hainsworth vii 107.

probably goes back to this period; at all events it is almost certainly pre-Alexandrian.[19] The use of the term *rhapsodia* for what we call a book indicates that the system was based on rhapsodic practice. Panathenaic regulations must in any case have prescribed the length of a rhapsode's stint.

This sixth-century standardization of the text could not prevent the proliferation of superficial variation. Fourth-century quotations, particularly in Plato and Aristotle, show a high proportion of variants. This evidence is not, by itself, entirely reliable, since we have to allow for inaccurate quotation from memory. But it is confirmed by the earliest surviving fragments of Homeric MSS, papyri of the third and second centuries BC, which contain many trivial variants, often evidently intended to remove difficulties of one sort or another, and numerous additions, flaccid and inorganic lines or groups of lines.[20] It is uncertain whether rhapsodes are to be held entirely responsible for this diversification; it may to some extent be due to the misplaced creativity of copyists. Certainly papyrological discoveries during the last century have made possible a much more accurate view of the work accomplished by the great Homeric scholars of the Hellenistic age.

Homeric scholarship did not of course begin with the foundation of Alexandria. Rhapsodes, sophists, and schoolmasters had long had a professional interest in the interpretation of Homer.[21] The poet

---

[19] The twenty-four-fold scheme, which works reasonably well for the *Iliad*, appears to have been imposed on the *Odyssey* to make it correspond, and results in some very short books, some of which might easily have been combined (e.g. vi + vii = 678 lines, xx + xxi = 828 lines). If the division had been Alexandrian, we should expect something more severely rational; if it were the work of Aristophanes or Aristarchus, xxiii 297–xxiv would surely have been relegated to a separate book (cf. n. 11). It is true that the only ancient writer to discuss the book division ascribes it to the school of Aristarchus: [Plu.] *Vita Hom.* ii 4 (xxv 22–25 Wil.): εἰσὶ δὲ αὐτῷ ποιήσεις δύο, Ἰλίας καὶ Ὀδύσσεια, διῃρημένη ἑκατέρα εἰς τὸν ἀριθμὸν τῶν στοιχείων, οὐχ ὑπ' αὐτοῦ τοῦ ποιητοῦ, ἀλλ' ὑπὸ τῶν γραμματικῶν τῶν περὶ Ἀρίσταρχον. But in view of the ancient tendency to attribute to Aristarchus any innovation connected with the Homeric text (cf. Plu. *de aud. poet.* 26–7, Ath. 180 c), we should view this testimony with some scepticism, though there may be some substance to the writer's belief that the practice of designating the several books by the letters of the Ionic alphabet originated under the influence of Aristarchus.

[20] See further S. West, *The Ptolemaic Papyri of Homer* (Papyrologica Coloniensia, iii, Cologne and Opladen, 1967); subsequent papyrus discoveries have only confirmed the general picture.

[21] Rhapsodes were expected not only to recite but also to explain Homer (Pl. *Ion*, *passim*, Xen. *Smp.* iii 6), and indeed it would hardly have been possible for them to recite it effectively unless they at least believed that they understood it. A famous fragment of Aristophanes' *Daitaleis* (233 *PCG*) suggests that instruction in recondite

Antimachus of Colophon, who was probably born about the middle
of the fifth century, produced a text from which readings are
sometimes cited in the scholia (e.g. on i 85).[22] Aristotle discussed
Homeric problems with some shrewdness, and is even said to have
produced a text of the *Iliad* for his pupil Alexander, though this may
be a myth; certainly it left no trace in subsequent Homeric scholar-
ship.[23]

It is unlikely that anyone realized how much variation existed
among current Homeric manuscripts before the foundation of the
great library at Alexandria brought together vast numbers of texts.[24]
The production of critical editions for the use of the library was an
important aspect of this great Ptolemaic enterprise; it fell to Zenodo-
tus of Ephesus, the first librarian, to attempt to produce order out of
the chaos of contemporary Homeric texts.[25]

Modern scholars have differed widely in their estimate of Zenodo-
tus' work; he has been regarded by some as cautious and conserva-
tive, by others as irresponsible and freakish. This disagreement results
largely from the unsatisfactory nature of our sources. Almost every-
thing we know about Zenodotus' work on Homer comes from the
scholia, marginal notes culled from what were originally elaborate
commentaries composed by the pupils of Aristarchus, and our
information about his text is very incomplete, particularly for the
Odyssey. While he composed monographs on particular problems, he

Homeric vocabulary was a regular part of Athenian education (the speaker is a father,
apparently engaged in an altercation with his son): πρὸς ταῦτα σὺ λέξον Ὁμήρου ἐμοὶ
γλώττας, τί καλοῦσι κόρυμβα; . . . τί καλοῦσ' ἀμενηνὰ κάρηνα; Two stories in Plutarch's
Alcibiades (vii 1) indicate that the quality of teaching was rather variable: in the one
case Alcibiades rebuked a schoolmaster who had no text of Homer, in the other he
expressed his admiration for a colleague who used one 'corrected' by himself. The
interpretation of early poetry played an important part in sophistic education,
illustrated (no doubt a little unfairly) by the exposition of Simonides which Plato puts
in the mouth of Protagoras (*Prt.* 338 e 6 ff.). Protagoras also turned his attention to
Homer; he was dissatisfied with the opening of the *Iliad* (DK 80 A 29, 30). See further
H. I. Marrou, *Histoire de l'éducation dans l'antiquité* (Paris, 1965), 39 ff.

[22] *Antimachi Colophonii reliquiae*, ed. B. Wyss (Berlin, 1936), xxix–xxxi, frr. 129–42; see
also R. Pfeiffer, *History of Classical Scholarship*, i (Oxford, 1968), 93–5.

[23] Plu. *Alex.* viii. Aristotle published six books on Homeric problems (Ἀπορήματα
Ὁμηρικά, frr. 142 ff. Rose); *Poetics* 25 is devoted to such difficulties and their solutions.

[24] On the rise of scholarship at Alexandria see Pfeiffer, op. cit. 88 ff., 105 ff., 171 ff.,
P. M. Fraser, *Ptolemaic Alexandria* (Oxford, 1972), i 320 ff., W. J. Slater, *CQ* xxxii
(1982), 336–49 (a slightly deflationary view).

[25] The old edition of H. Duentzer, *De Zenodoti studiis Homericis* (Göttingen, 1848
(Hildesheim, 1981)) is still useful, though somewhat antiquated; see further *RE* x A
23 ff. s.v. Zenodotos (3) (Nickau), K. Nickau, *Untersuchungen zur textkritischen Methoden
des Zenodotos von Ephesos* (Berlin, 1977).

left no commentary to accompany his text,[26] and though anecdotal tradition may occasionally have transmitted his interpretation of disputed passages, it seems that on the whole later scholars could only guess his reasons for adopting readings which differed from those of Aristarchus. We should try to dissociate ourselves from the Aristarchean bias of our informants. It is clear that Aristarchus and his pupils did not understand the principles on which Zenodotus had worked, and we should not accept the assumption implicit in our sources that where he differed from Aristarchus he necessarily knew the reading which Aristarchus was to prefer. It must be emphasized that we have no idea how many manuscripts Zenodotus consulted, how he evaluated them, or whether he was consistent in his use of them.

The most interesting feature of his work was the use of a marginal sign, the obelos (—), to mark lines which he regarded as suspect. This procedure was called athetesis (rejection); it was an important element in Alexandrian Homeric scholarship, not properly appreciated by modern scholars until Ptolemaic papyri revealed how widespread was the tendency to expand the text, often by borrowings from elsewhere in the poems (sometimes termed 'concordance interpolation'). In many cases, given enough manuscripts, interpolation could be established with reasonable certainty on external evidence alone; an inorganic formulaic line found in only one out of ten manuscripts could safely be disregarded. But an editor had to face the possibility that an interpolation might have spread to all the manuscripts available to him, and might accordingly suspect the authenticity of material attested by all his sources if it seemed to him somehow to deviate from what he regarded as the Homeric norm; athetesis reflects such suspicions. Excision evidently presented a further, though less frequent, threat to the integrity of the text, and it would not have been a safe editorial rule of thumb to ignore any line which did not enjoy unanimous manuscript support, though it must often have been hard to assess the significance of omission in a particular copy (cf. *Od.* i 99–101, 356–9, with nn.). The marginal obelos alerted the user to a doubt about authenticity.

Modern discussions of Zenodotus' work have centred on the question of whether, and, if so, to what extent, he introduced his own conjectures. Some of his readings seem to us blatant conjectures, but it cannot be shown that they originated with him. Stated in general terms the question may seem of slight importance: we can hardly

---

[26] Or, if he wrote one, it was lost by the time of Aristarchus; but this seems unlikely.

argue that an ancient editor was never entitled to include his own emendations in his editions, though undoubtedly the possibility makes it harder for us to gain a clear view of the transmission. We shall do better to consider a particular case.

According to the scholia on *Od.* iii 313 Crete, not Sparta, was mentioned as the terminus of Telemachus' journey in Zenodotus' text at i 93, 285: οὗτος ὁ τόπος ἀνέπεισε Ζηνόδοτον ἐν τοῖς περὶ τῆς ἀποδημίας Τηλεμάχου διόλου τὴν Κρήτην ἔναντι τῆς Σπάρτης ποιεῖν· οἴεται γὰρ ἐκ τούτων τῶν λόγων κατὰ τὸ σιωπώμενον ἀκηκοέναι τὸν Νέστορα παρὰ τοῦ Τηλεμάχου ὅτι καὶ ἀλλαχόσε περὶ τοῦ πατρὸς πευσόμενος παρεσκεύαστο πλεῖν, διὸ καὶ ἐν τῇ α΄ ῥαψῳδίᾳ ἔγραψε "πέμψω δ' ἐς Κρήτην τε καὶ ἐς Πύλον ἠμαθόεντα" (i 93) καὶ ἡ Ἀθηνᾶ ἀλλαχοῦ (284-6) "πρῶτα μὲν ἐς Πύλον ἐλθέ, κεῖθεν δ' ἐς Κρήτην τε [δὲ Κρήτηνδε Buttmann] παρ' Ἰδομενῆα ἄνακτα· | ὃς γὰρ δεύτατος ἦλθεν Ἀχαιῶν χαλκοχιτώνων." Despite the dogmatic tone of this note, what is alleged about Zenodotus' reasoning can be no more than a guess, and the absence of corresponding Cretan variants where Sparta is mentioned as Telemachus' destination in ii (214, 327, 359)[27] implies that Zenodotus was not systematically altering the text in accordance with some private theory.

These readings are generally dismissed as arbitrary and eccentric conjectures; yet they are so glaringly inconsistent with the subsequent narrative that they might be thought to deserve serious consideration as *lectiones difficiliores*. If Zenodotus, having found these readings in a manuscript to which (rightly or wrongly) he attached importance, judged them too odd to be conjectures, we should respect his reasoning. It is tempting to speculate that we might have here an authentic relic of an earlier design for the Telemachy; certainly Odysseus' cover-stories reveal a keen interest in Crete,[28] and it would not be surprising if the poet had contemplated taking Telemachus to visit Idomeneus but changed his mind before he was far advanced. Yet even if the poet himself had failed to notice the anomaly, we should expect it to have been eradicated in the course of transmission. Was Zenodotus perhaps deceived by an alteration designed to gratify a Cretan audience? If these readings are in fact conjectures (whether Zenodotus' or another's), our failure to discern the reasoning behind them is worrying; if they are his own conjectures, they suggest an approach to the text so high-handed as to create a strong prejudice against his peculiar readings elsewhere.[29]

[27] Cf. schol. ii 359 οὐδ' ἐνταῦθα μνήμη τίς ἐστι τῆς Κρήτης.

[28] xiii 256 ff., xiv 199 ff., xix 172 ff.; cf. the (quite unnecessarily) precise topographical detail of iii 291 ff. [29] As e.g. at iii 216 ff., 296, 307, iv 366.

This curious puzzle serves at any rate to illustrate how little we know about the sources of Zenodotus' text and the principles on which he constituted it. Tempting as it is to try to extrapolate general rules for evaluating Zenodotean variants, the hope is almost certainly illusory. Even if we were completely informed as to Zenodotus' text (and even in Aristarchus' day there appears to have been some uncertainty about his readings (see schol. *Il.* xiv 37)), we could not deduce his critical principles without knowing what he found in the manuscripts available to him. As it is, the attempt to evaluate his work is further complicated by the suspicion that he paid insufficient attention to the preparation of a fair copy of his text; certainly it is hard to believe that if he had given the matter any thought he would have sanctioned such modernisms as οὐθέν for οὐδέν (xviii 130), ἐκαθέζετο (*Il.* i 68), ἐκάθευδε (*Il.* i 611), and we should hesitate to infer from the presence of such forms that his sources were all of relatively late date.

Though Zenodotus' systematic work represents a new development in Homeric scholarship, it is unlikely that his text, intended to serve as a work of reference for scholars rather than to meet the needs of the reading public (itself very much a creation of the Hellenistic age), had much influence outside the Library. Homeric reminiscences in Callimachus and Apollonius of Rhodes show certain affinities with Zenodotus' text (e.g. *Od.* iv 1: see n.), but these may well reflect readings widespread in pre-Aristarchean manuscripts.[30]

Before considering the two other great Alexandrian Homeric scholars something should be said about a group of texts occasionally cited in the scholia which may or may not have been among Zenodotus' sources, but which were certainly used by Aristophanes and Aristarchus. These are the so-called 'city-editions' (αἱ ἀπὸ τῶν πόλεων, αἱ κατὰ πόλεις, αἱ πολιτικαί (scil. ἐκδόσεις)). The *Iliad*-scholia mention texts from Argos, Chios, Crete, Cyprus, Marseilles, and Sinope; for the *Odyssey* texts from Argos and Marseilles are cited, and also one designated as Aeolic.[31] It is uncertain whether these titles merely indicate provenance, or whether they imply that these were in some sense official texts, copies which had been carefully checked and were kept for reference in public libraries or city archives. But in general the variants for which they are cited (e.g. at *Od.* i 38, 424) are not of great interest or apparent antiquity. It is significant that these

[30] See H. Erbse, 'Homerscholien u. hellenistische Glossare bei Apollonios Rhodios', *Hermes* lxxxi (1953), 163 ff., Pfeiffer on Call. fr. 12. 6.

[31] For a detailed account of these texts see Allen op. cit. (n . 1) 283 ff.

texts are never called in evidence in connection with alleged Athenian interpolations.

Another third-century edition of some interest was that of the Cretan epic poet Rhianus.[32] We do not know whether he ever visited Alexandria (though in view of his interests we should expect him to have been attracted there), and his relationship to Alexandrian scholarship is uncertain. The Scholia record his readings in forty-five places, thirty-three of these being from the *Odyssey*, a remarkably large number in view of the scantiness of our *Odyssey*-scholia; they suggest good sense and acute observation of Homeric usage.

The second of the great Alexandrian Homeric scholars was Aristophanes of Byzantium, said as a boy to have been the pupil of Zenodotus.[33] As well as producing a text of Homer, he composed many lexicographical works, but he left no commentary. It is not altogether easy to form a clear picture of his achievement, or to distinguish it from that of his pupil Aristarchus. The two were evidently on the whole in harmony, and it is likely that Aristarchus' critical methods very largely derive from his master; for an interesting difference of opinion see *Od.* iii 71–4 (with n.).

The evidence of contemporary papyri suggests that the labours of Zenodotus and Aristophanes had little if any effect on the book trade. But from about 150 BC a change is observable, as 'wild' texts, characterized by a high proportion of variants and additions, die out; later papyri offer a text which differs little from that of the medieval manuscripts. Given the date of this development, it must surely be connected, directly or indirectly, with the activity of Aristarchus.[34] Quite apart from this change, it is clear that his work enjoyed an authority denied to his predecessors, and indeed there was a tendency to ascribe to him innovations relating to the Homeric text for which he cannot have been responsible; for antiquity he came to epitomize the serious, scholarly critic.[35] Undoubtedly he built on foundations laid by his predecessors, and it would be futile to try to demarcate his individual contribution to the detailed knowledge of Homeric usage

---

[32] See C. Mayhoff, *De Rhiani Cretensis studiis Homericis* (Leipzig, 1870), Pfeiffer, op. cit. (n. 22), 122, 148–9.

[33] For the fragments of Aristophanes' work on Homer see *Aristophanis Byzantii Fragmenta*, ed. W. J. Slater (Berlin, 1986); see also Pfeiffer, op. cit. (n. 22), 171 ff.

[34] The fundamental study of Aristarchus is K. Lehrs, *De Aristarchi studiis Homericis*[3] (Leipzig, 1882); see also A. Ludwich, *Aristarchs homerische Textkritik* (Leipzig, 1884), and, for a useful brief account, Pfeiffer, op. cit., 210 ff.

[35] See above, n. 19. Aristarchus' prestige may be illustrated from schol. *Il.* iv 235, where discussion of a point of accentuation is concluded thus: καὶ μᾶλλον πειστέον Ἀριστάρχῳ ἢ τῷ Ἑρμαππίᾳ, εἰ καὶ δοκεῖ ἀληθεύειν.

on which his text was founded. But certainly the subsequent tradition would have looked very different without his work.

We are fairly well informed about his principles and methods, since he composed both commentaries to accompany his text and monographs on particular problems, and his arguments are often recorded in the scholia. It is easy to get the impression that he was preoccupied with what seem to most people rather trivial points of textual criticism, but in fact his main concern was to produce a text which, without omitting genuine material, was free from subsequent accretions. We tend to overlook this much more important aspect of his work because we take for granted the standardization of the text which resulted from it.

Our most serious difficulty in assessing his work is a lack of information about the MSS which he used and the relative importance which he attached to them. The scholia divide them into two classes, χαριέστεραι and κοιναί (κοινότεραι, εἰκαιότεραι, δημώδεις). The first group comprises carefully prepared texts, including the 'city-editions' as well as those associated with individual scholars, and it is very uncertain whether we know the names of all the texts of this group used by Aristarchus. It is generally assumed that when such a text is mentioned it was a text of the whole epic, but this goes beyond the evidence. The second group might be regarded as ordinary commercial copies; we have no idea how large a stock of these Aristarchus used. It is impossible to say whether a modern scholar, given the same range of MSS, would assess their merits in much the same way as Aristarchus did.[36] Hellenistic scholars could not use palaeographical criteria, and the lack of anything like an *apparatus criticus* meant that the distinction between conjecture and variant was not kept clear. The importance attached to the χαριέστεραι might be interpreted as reflecting a preference for texts of known provenance and (approximate) date, though no doubt other factors were involved. But we should certainly reject the theory that an official Athenian copy, never mentioned because everywhere taken for granted, provided the basis for Aristarchus' text; his method of argument would look very different if he had proceeded in this way.

Aristarchus' general principles emerge most clearly from the discussion of athetized lines. Occasionally external evidence is adduced (as e.g. at *Od.* i 97–8, 171 ff., 185–6, iv 285 ff.), but usually the

---

[36] A story told about the philosopher Timon suggests that some in antiquity might not have rated the χαριέστεραι so highly (D.L. ix 113): φασὶ δὲ καὶ Ἄρατον πυθέσθαι αὐτοῦ [Timon] πῶς τὴν Ὁμήρου ποίησιν ἀσφαλῆ κτήσαιτο, τὸν δὲ εἰπεῖν, εἰ τοῖς ἀρχαίοις ἀντιγράφοις ἐντυγχάνοι, καὶ μὴ τοῖς ἤδη διωρθωμένοις.

arguments are subjective. In general his critical assumptions do not seem much different from those of a modern scholar dealing with a great poet whose text may be supposed to have suffered interpolation. To us his arguments sometimes appear strange because they make few, if any, concessions to the difference between traditional, oral poetry and written literature (though Aristarchus himself might well have objected that modern scholars are too easily satisfied with the second-rate). But it should be emphasized that the practice of athetesis was based not only on a belief in the splendour of Homeric epic but also on extrapolation from what might be observed in contemporary manuscripts. Evidence that the text had been exposed to alteration and expansion was everywhere to hand in current copies, and it would have been naïve to suppose that the full extent of the damage could be revealed by industrious collation. Such alteration might be observed commonly to follow certain trends, recognition of which was bound to give rise to corresponding prejudices. Thus, what may at first sight seem a rather arbitrary dislike of repeated passages (see e.g. schol. *Od.* i 185–6, 356 ff., iii 72 ff., 199–200) should be viewed in relation to the widespread practice, revealed by our earliest papyri, of expanding the text with lines taken from elsewhere in Homer; in these circumstances a degree of prejudice against repeated passages not wholly appropriate to their context is a sensible critical reaction.

From about 150 BC a change is observable in Homeric papyri, which henceforth offer a text very little different from the medieval tradition; the contrast to what had preceded is very striking. In the number of their lines these papyri conform very closely to Aristarchus' text, though they offer too wide a range of variants to allow the hypothesis that they might all be copies of a single edition. This purification of ordinary commercial copies is most plausibly ascribed to the book trade.[37] Many readers must by now have been aware that scholars had established a text relatively free from spurious accretions, and a popular demand for copies is readily understandable. But the common reader was unlikely to be interested in the minutiae of textual criticism, particularly since the choice of one reading rather than another would seldom much affect the sense. Booksellers and proprietors of *scriptoria* could thus easily fall in with popular demand by cancelling lines omitted by Aristarchus, without needing to alter the wording of their texts extensively. Copies so corrected would become commercially fashionable, while any alter-

---

[37] See further P. Collart, 'Les Papyrus de l'*Iliade*', *RPh* vii (1933), 52 ff.

native would die out naturally. This process may be seen as part of a general rise in standards of book-production at this period. The Alexandrian scholars did not impose a single specialist's version on the tradition, but effected a general purge of extraneous material and an increase in knowledge which afforded some permanent protection.

Even this second standardization of the text did not altogether stop interpolation by copyists, which continued, on a fairly modest scale, until the first printed editions. Such post-Aristarchean additions are practically limited to borrowings from other parts of Homer (e.g. i 148, 148a, ii 393, 407, 429, iii 19); their absence from papyri of the Roman period has often revealed such lines as later additions even though they are found in all the medieval manuscripts.[38] But the basic text was now firmly established.

The vicissitudes of its transmission are clearly relevant to any serious study of the *Odyssey*. Its original excellent workmanship enabled it to withstand much later tinkering but we should not approach it as if its textual history were as secure as that of the *Aeneid*. Purely mechanical copying errors appear to have affected it very little; the dangers to which it was exposed were more insidious. Many of the inconcinnities which seemed to the analysts to indicate multiple authorship, and are now more commonly defended as the natural licences of oral composers, may in fact result from tampering designed to produce an *ad hoc* effect without regard to its implications for the poem as a whole, and the modern critic ought not to ignore the threats to authenticity of which the ancient scholars were well aware.

---

[38] Much useful work on this subject was done by G. M. Bolling, *The External Evidence for Interpolation in Homer* (Oxford, 1925), 3 ff.; Bolling's tendency to exaggerate the significance of his observations perhaps explains why they seem not to receive as much attention as they deserve; see also M. J. Apthorp, *The Manuscript Evidence for Interpolation in Homer* (Heidelberg, 1980).

BOOKS I–IV

Stephanie West

PREFATORY NOTE

An unexpectedly early death cut short the work of the scholar to whom these four books were originally entrusted. From Douglas Young, ποιητὴς ἅμα καὶ κριτικός, we might with good reason have looked for something quite out of the ordinary in Homeric criticism, the product of his characteristic style of wide-ranging and lively-minded scholarship. I have often found myself wondering what he would have said; but this pointless speculation serves only to heighten regret for the loss of a peculiarly distinctive contribution to our understanding of the *Odyssey*. What I have written will often seem a poor and pedestrian substitute.

In the preparation of this commentary I have incurred many debts which it is a pleasure to acknowledge. I should like to thank Dr S. P. Brock, Professor A. E. Davies, Professor J. Gwyn Griffiths, Mr C. G. Hardie, Dr A. Robson, Dr C. Walters, and Dr P. Wernberg-Møller for the help with various problems. I have frequently derived both pleasure and profit from discussion with Dr Hainsworth. But my greatest debt is to my husband, Martin, whose patience, learning, and lucidity have repeatedly extricated me from difficulty. For the errors which remain the responsibility is mine alone.

S. R. W.

INTRODUCTION

I

The first four books of the *Odyssey* are centred not on Odysseus but on Telemachus. Telemachus shines by reflected light; though an interesting and attractive poem might be composed with him as its hero, his significance derives from his father. His importance for the *Odyssey* as a whole should not be underestimated; he speaks more than anyone else except Odysseus, and his presence does much to unify the poem.[1] That he was not invented by the poet of the *Odyssey* is clear from the *Iliad*, where Odysseus twice refers to himself as $T\eta\lambda\epsilon\mu\acute{a}\chi o\iota o$ $\pi a\tau\acute{\eta}\rho$ (ii 260, iv 354); the name reflects his father's distinction as an archer. The prominent part which he plays in our *Odyssey* leaves Penelope little more than an onlooker, though vestiges remain of an earlier version in which she was Odysseus' accomplice in exacting vengeance from the suitors (the more obvious conception if her loyalty were above suspicion).[2] The development of Telemachus' role was a natural corollary of the prolongation of Odysseus' wanderings. Familiarity makes us take for granted the fantastic *nostos* recounted in the *Odyssey*, but the story clearly evolved, and we may still perhaps discern, in the prologue and in Odysseus' cover-stories, traces of a more realistic and less time-consuming alternative.[3] The poet's decision to extend Odysseus' *nostos* to nearly ten years, to equal the

[1] See further *RE* v A 1, 325 ff. s.v. Telemachos (Herter).

[2] As the ghost of the suitor Amphimedon alleges (xxiv 149 ff.). Penelope's behaviour at xviii 158 ff., Odysseus' reaction to it, and her decision to arrange the competition which will settle her future husband, despite indications that Odysseus will soon be home (xix 555 ff.), all suggest that she not only knows he is back but is acting in concert with him; see further Page, *Odyssey* 122 ff.

[3] On the prologue see below, i 1–10 nn. An itinerary is perhaps deducible in outline from the constant elements in the autobiographies which Odysseus devises on his return to Ithaca, when he is masquerading as a Cretan (xiii 256 ff., xiv 199 ff., xvii 419 ff., xix 172 ff., 270 ff.; see further Woodhouse, *Composition*, 25 ff., 126 ff., S. West, *LCM* vi (1981), 169 ff.). A briefer *nostos* appears to be indicated by the chronology of the suitors' endeavours; if we are to understand that, when the poem opens, Penelope has been under pressure to remarry for nearly four years (ii 89, 106–7 (= xix 151–2, xxiv 141–2), xiii 377), this implies a period of six years during which she was left in peace, though an unexplained delay of a year would be quite long enough to make it unlikely that Odysseus would ever return.

length of the Trojan War, made it necessary for the son whom he had left as a baby to play a prominent part if he were not to be judged a milksop.

The plan of the *Odyssey* is extremely ambitious, and we must not underestimate the problems of organizing the material. The decision to begin the story of Odysseus' adventures near the end complicates the structure of the poem. The theme of Telemachus' efforts to restore his family's fortunes is used as a kind of prelude, to be developed when father and son unite in vengeance. It is not surprising, given this sophisticated plan, that we find certain inconcinnities at the points where Telemachus' story is linked with his father's. Undeniably there is some awkwardness in the division of the divine council, which starts the action, between the beginning of i and the beginning of v, and in the bisection of Telemachus' leave-taking at Sparta, interrupted at iv 621 to be resumed in xv; the reflective reader may well be puzzled, when Athena chides Telemachus for dallying at Sparta (xv 10 ff.), as to whether his absence from Ithaca has lasted less than a week or (as the timetable of Odysseus' homeward journey demands) a month.[4] It has often been suggested that the Telemachy[5] was either an originally independent poem incorporated rather mechanically into the *Odyssey* or simply a late addition. But Telemachus' story is not as easily detachable as the earlier analysts supposed, and it is not surprising that the 'problem' of the Telemachy came to be regarded as crucial for the analysis of the *Odyssey*. The awkwardness observable at the points of junction with Odysseus' story result from the poet attempting something more elaborate than was quite feasible. Without the Telemachy the *Odyssey* would fall into two rather disparate parts, the deep-sea stories and the revenge; as it is, Odysseus' adventures form a centre-piece framed by two Ithacan sections. The Telemachy also serves to link the *Odyssey* with the larger heroic world and to bridge the gap of nearly a

---

[4] See Hoekstra on xv 1 ff., M. J. Apthorp, 'The Obstacles to Telemachus' Return', *CQ* xxx (1980), 1 ff.

[5] The first to use this term appears to have been P. D. C. Hennings, 'Über die Telemachie', *Jahrbücher f. klass. Philologie*, Suppl. iii (1858), 135 ff. It has become convenient to treat it simply as a title for i–iv, but no one could imagine that this section might form an independent poem without some alteration, and the precise demarcation of the Telemachy is the analysts' fundamental problem. For a lucid survey of the controversy see F. Klingner, *Über die vier ersten Bücher der Odyssee*, Ber. sächs. Akad. Leipzig. xcvi. 1 (Leipzig, 1944), Lesky, *Homeros*, 123 ff., where references to earlier discussions may be found; see also K. A. Garbrah, 'A Linguistic Analysis of Selected Portions of the Homeric Odyssey', *Glotta* xlvii (1969), 144 ff., Eisenberger, *Studien*, 1 ff., H. van Thiel, 'Telemachie u. Odyssee', *MH* xxxvi (1979), 65 ff.

decade since the end of the *Iliad*. It must be regarded as integral to our *Odyssey*.)

It was noted in antiquity that Telemachus' journey is ill-timed and inadequately motivated.[6] Penelope is under constant pressure from the suitors, and her son's attempt to assert himself might reasonably be expected to induce them to terminate the current stalemate, hitherto, from their point of view, highly satisfactory. In Telemachus' absence there is an obvious risk that Penelope might be compelled to remarry. Telemachus' mission is not justified by its results; the information which he brings back is, as might have been expected, inconclusive. The imprudence of the project did not escape the poet, as may be seen from Nestor's warning against the dangers of prolonged absence from home (iii 313 ff.).[7] Athena, who knows that Odysseus will soon return independently of any efforts on Telemachus' part, explains that she sent the boy out to give him the chance to win distinction (xiii 422, cf. i 95). This sounds a little thin; the poet was clearly more interested in the venture itself than in its motivation; Odysseus' journey to Hades is similarly both dangerous and inadequately motivated.[8]

It would be otherwise if the poet had laid less stress on the increasing danger from the suitors. Telemachus' natural concern to end the long uncertainty about his father's fate provides sufficient reason, and the mere presence of the suitors does not make his journey ill-advised, so long as they have no reason to suspect a threat to their security. Telemachus' public denunciation of the suitors in ii is an important preliminary if Odysseus' vengeance is to appear fully justified, but it creates a situation in which we should think it essential for him to remain at his mother's side.

It is tempting to suppose that Telemachus' journey was originally conceived as an independent narrative,[9] a framework for the popular theme of the *nostoi*,[10] of central importance in iii and iv. The returns of all the major heroes are dealt with, in a manner suggesting that the poet saw them not simply as a sequence of stories, but as an ordered

---

[6] Schol. i 93, 284. [7] Cf. ii 363 ff., xiii 417, xiv 178 ff.

[8] See Page, *Odyssey*, 27 ff.

[9] This view of iii and iv is much indebted to Bethe, *Odyssee*, 7 ff., esp. 29 ff., and Merkelbach, *Untersuchungen*, 36 ff.

[10] Cf. i 326–7, x 15. The Epic Cycle (the corpus of early epic dealing with the Trojan War, its causes and aftermath) included a poem on the returns of the Greek heroes, in five books, known to us largely from a summary by the fifth-century neoplatonist Proclus; it was evidently a later composition than the *Odyssey*, which it presupposed; see Bethe, *Homer*, ii[2] 2, 184 ff. (= *Der troische Epenkreis* (Darmstadt, 1966), 36 ff.).

whole consisting of comparable, related destinies, the quarrel between Agamemnon and Menelaus after the sack of Troy (iii 141 ff.) being central to the structure. The division of the narrative between Nestor and Menelaus is masterly. It was a happy coincidence for the poet that Nestor, whose tendency to reminiscence is well established in the *Iliad*, was geographically the most accessible of the returned heroes. Nestor's information is incomplete, and it is left to Menelaus to supplement it by relating his own adventures, including Proteus' account of those whose fates would otherwise be mysterious, the lesser Ajax, Agamemnon, and Odysseus. As it now stands, Proteus' account of Odysseus (iv 555–60) is extraordinarily cursory, though the immediately following prophecy of Menelaus' translation to Elysium distracts us sufficiently to avoid an anticlimax (just as Telemachus' unexpected encounter with the seer Theoclymenus (xv 222 ff.) diverts our attention from the inconclusive outcome of his journey). But we might wonder whether a brief account of Odysseus' adventures was once the climax of Proteus' narrative, culminating, since Proteus is a prophet, in a prediction of the hero's imminent return. We find elsewhere in the *Odyssey* this mannerism of postponing an expected denouement; thus we are disappointed in our expectation that Odysseus will make himself known to the Phaeacians after Demodocus' first recital (viii 83 ff.) and to Penelope in xix. It might be regarded as a rather unsophisticated method of heightening suspense, but to some extent its employment is likely to reflect the combination of alternative versions.

Whether the poet incorporated, with modifications, a theme already familiar to him as an independent poem (whether the conception was his own or another's) or first developed this *Rahmenerzählung* in its present position cannot be established with any certainty, but the former seems to me much the more probable. At all events, we should not underestimate what this section contributes to the epic as a whole. Both in space and time it greatly extends the *Odyssey*'s range. Menelaus' adventures neatly complement (and to some extent foreshadow) those of Odysseus, and the narrative of the *nostoi* takes the story back to the end of the Trojan War. We are also offered a unique, and attractive, view of the heroic world at peace; at Pylos and at Sparta we see heroic excellence find its scope in hospitality, and the picture is the more attractive for its contrast with the lawlessness of Ithaca, a contrast which serves to emphasize the sad consequences of Odysseus' long absence. Many critics, from antiquity onwards, have seen the Telemachy as a *Bildungsroman*: wider experience of the heroic world is to make Telemachus a more effective ally to his father.[11] But the real psychological change in Telemachus comes in i (320 ff.), and after his public denunciation of the suitors he could hardly be regarded as too immature to assist his father adequately.

What he learns about his father at Pylos and Sparta is important. No one in Ithaca could tell him about Odysseus' achievements in the Trojan War, and the general respect in which Odysseus is held (cf. iii 126 ff., 218 ff., iv 105 ff., 169 ff., 240 ff., 267 ff., 333 ff.) enhances the picture of the father whom he has yet to meet, while heightening our expectations in preparation for the moment when Odysseus actually appears. Moreover, Telemachus' journey demonstrates to the suitors that he is in earnest (iv 638 ff.) and that his public protest was not merely an adolescent outburst; it thus precipitates counter-measures, while removing him from the immediate consequences of the suitors' increasing hostility.

The poet does not suggest that there is any causal connection between the failure of Telemachus' ultimatum to the suitors in ii and his journey. Athena-Mentes gives him no reason to suppose that his denunciation will have any immediate practical effect (i 272 ff.), nor does Telemachus seem much surprised by its ill success; but his journey does not depend on the outcome of the assembly, and is not to be regarded as a compromise or a second-best solution. His public protest looks forward to the latter part of the poem; if Odysseus' vengeance is to appear justified, the suitors must have fair warning. The poet has taken some pains to link the journey with the assembly; hence, exceeding Mentes' specific instructions, Telemachus publicly asks for a ship (ii 212 ff.), and the lack of any immediate response effectively demonstrates his isolation and want of resources. But the omen which Halitherses interprets as a sign that Odysseus is already at hand (ii 146 ff.) makes nonsense of this request; the poet was evidently at this point more interested in Odysseus' forthcoming revenge than in Telemachus' mission.

The suitors and the question of Penelope's remarriage loom large in the first two books.[12] The situation is somewhat illogical, but the

[11] The idea that Telemachus' journey constitutes a παιδεία was already suggested by Porphyry (schol. i 284); this conception is reflected in the novel of the seventeenth-century Abbé Fénélon, Les Aventures de Télémaque (1699); cf. W. Jaeger, Paideia i (Berlin–Leipzig, 1934), 55 ff. (= English ed. (Oxford, 1939), 27 ff.). Wilamowitz is to be regarded as the most formidable opponent of this still very popular view (Heimkehr, 106, 118).

[12] Particularly helpful on this topic are W. Allen, 'The Theme of the Suitors in the Odyssey', TAPhA lxx (1939), 104–24, F. Wehrli, 'Penelope u. Telemachos', MH xvi (1959), 228–37, N. Matsumoto, 'Die Freier in der Odyssee', Gnomosyne: Festschrift f. W. Marg (Munich, 1981), 135–41.

poet avoids exposing its oddities by simply taking the suitors' presence in Odysseus' palace for granted. We are nowhere given anything like a systematic account of what is going on in Odysseus' home, though it would be quite natural for Nestor or Menelaus to question Telemachus further about his unwelcome guests (e.g. at iii 211 ff., iv 333 ff.), or for Odysseus himself to ask Athena for more details than she gives him (xiii 376 ff.).

Two folk-tale motifs are combined in the story of Odysseus' return and vengeance. The first of these, the tale of the husband's return,[13] has for its theme a husband (or lover) who comes home after long absence, often in disguise or otherwise unrecognizable, just as his wife (or intended bride) has married, or is about to marry, another; the subsequent development of the plot varies considerably. This story, a *Weltmärchen* if ever there was one, is found all over the world, repeatedly gaining new life from actual instances; in the *Odyssey* we find the same theme developed rather differently in the account of Agamemnon's return. In the story of Odysseus' home-coming it is united with another type of folk-tale, that of a contest between suitors with a bride as the prize.[14] Familiarity with the *Odyssey* might lead us to suppose this to be the natural denouement of the first type of story; certainly the two themes combine very easily. It is normally thought that these tales had been connected with Odysseus before our *Odyssey*, and this view is supported by indications that the poet was not altogether happy about the ethical implications of the hero's savage vengeance, but felt unable to modify a traditional element in the story. To forestall the objection that Odysseus' revenge was out of all proportion to the suitors' crimes he constantly emphasizes that they were wicked men who fully deserved their fate, but does not make explicit the charge against them until we are fully persuaded of their guilt.

Odysseus' indictment of the suitors (xxii 35 ff.) centres on their offences against his property; they have treated his house as if it were

---

[13] N 681 in Thompson's *Motif Index*. See further W. Splettstösser, *Der heimkehrende Gatte u. sein Weib in der Weltliteratur* (Berlin, 1898), W. Crooke, 'The Wooing of Penelope', *Folklore* ix (1898), 97 ff., D. B. Monro, *Homer's Odyssey, Books xiii–xxiv* (Oxford, 1901), 301 ff., L. Radermacher, *Die Erzählungen der Odysse*, SAWW clxxviii. 1 (1915), 47 ff.

[14] Thompson, *Motif Index*, H 331. A curious, and surely significant, parallel to the culmination of the *Odyssey* is found in the widespread central Asiatic tale of the hero Alpamysh; here too the returned hero has to compete with suitors and wedding guests in shooting an arrow from a mighty bow which he alone, its owner, can wield; see further V. Zhirmunsky, 'The Epic of "Alpamysh" and the Return of Odysseus', *PBA* 1966, 267 ff. Parallels from Indian epic are studied by Germain, *Genèse*, 11 ff., who plausibly argues that the theme must have originated on the steppes of central Asia.

their own, and their wooing of Penelope is simply one aspect of this abuse. He does not even mention their conspiracy to murder Telemachus (iv 669 ff.), which to a modern reader appears the most obvious argument in defence of this massacre, though he is aware of it (xiii 425 ff.). The poet has prepared the ground so well that we are unlikely to question the justification of Odysseus' revenge. From the outset it is stressed, not by authorial comment but indirectly and through the reactions of the various characters, that the suitors' actions cry out to heaven for vengeance. The point is firmly established in i by Athena-Mentes; particularly remarkable is the calm assumption (i 294 ff.) that justice and honour require the death of the suitors, where the implied analogy with Aegisthus, guilty of murder and adultery, diverts attention from the justification of the death-penalty. Athena's condemnation is echoed by other right-minded people, Halitherses (ii 161 ff., xxiv 454 ff.), Nestor (iii 210 ff.), Menelaus (iv 332 ff.), Eumaeus (xiv 81 ff.), Penelope (xvii 499 ff., xxiii 63 ff.), Philoetius (xx 215), Theoclymenus (xx 367 ff.), and Laertes (xxiv 282 ff.).

The attempt to win Penelope should not be regarded as in itself improper or unconventional. When the *Odyssey* opens, Odysseus' return is no longer a serious possibility, and there is a general assumption that sooner or later Penelope must marry again. We should not ask whether the poet imagined that she might, in principle, have absolutely refused to consider a second marriage; certainly that option is no longer open to her. But the presence of suitors in such numbers calls for some explanation, and it is significant that the poet never offers one, but simply underlines the point that they have been there for three years (ii 89, 106–7 (= xix 151–2, xxiv 141–2), xiii 377), thus inducing us to take their presence for granted. Yet, though they may now be hard to dislodge, it is scarcely possible to imagine that they could have established themselves in the first place without an invitation.

Stories involving a concurrence of suitors are not uncommon in Greek legend. The outstanding example is the wooing of Helen, as related in the Hesiodic *Catalogue of Women* (frr. 196–204); a similar procedure was followed by Cleisthenes, tyrant of Sicyon, c.575, in arranging a match for his daughter Agariste (Hdt. vi 126 ff.).[15] Such

---

[15] Probably to be seen as imitation of heroic practice, rather than as independent evidence for the custom; Cleisthenes had strong views about the contemporary relevance of traditional epic (Hdt. v 67. 1). We may also compare the foot-races organized by Danaus and Antaeus to dispose of their respective daughters' hands (Pi. *P.* ix 105 ff.); according to Spartan legend Penelope's father Icarius had adopted the same selection procedure (Paus. iii 12. 1).

stories require a formal announcement by the bride's κύριος (normally her father) to ensure that the best candidates learn of the opportunity.[16] In the case of a woman whose husband's death was merely presumed, there would be the more need for such a formal declaration. An invitation to prospective suitors would surely imply hospitality; Cleisthenes, who entertained his daughter's suitors for a year, clearly thought so. But the implications of such an invitation are awkward in the *Odyssey*. If the suitors have been encouraged to assemble, they have a right to generous entertainment, and the point at which they go beyond what convention might entitle them to expect is hard to determine. They have, moreover, a legitimate grievance against Penelope for her failure to co-operate with their reasonable aspirations.

Penelope's heroic constancy and unswerving loyalty to her absent husband are qualities better suited to epic than to folk-tale. In the end her stance is triumphantly justified, against all probability, and results are what matter in the success-orientated heroic world. But her attitude conflicts with the reasonable expectations of almost everyone else involved. She herself says (xviii 257 ff.) that Odysseus at his departure told her to take a second husband if he had not returned by the time Telemachus had grown up; though this detail of Odysseus' farewell looks like *ad hoc* invention, it shows that there could be no objection to a bona fide suitor, and we should not attach too much weight to references to gossip (δήμοιο φῆμις xvi 75, xix 527) as a deterrent. Elsewhere she admits that both her son and her parents wish her to decide on a second husband (xix 158 ff., 530 ff.). Her attempt to postpone indefinitely an apparently inevitable decision is bound to cause problems, as the suitors' spokesman, Antinous, points out (ii 87 ff.).

The suitors' behaviour makes it entirely intelligible that Penelope should be reluctant to choose a second husband from among them. Their speeches in ii show them to be not merely unmannerly and extravagant but also brutal and unscrupulous. They make no attempt to commend themselves to Penelope, though her ruse with Laertes' shroud (ii 89 ff., cf. xix 137 ff., xxiv 128 ff.) has made plain her reluctance to marry again. Like the conventional villains of melodrama, they continue to press their claims even after Penelope has revealed that she knows of their plot to murder her son.

---

[16] Compare Cleisthenes' advertisement (Hdt. vi 126. 2): Ὀλυμπίων ὢν ἐόντων καὶ νικῶν ἐν αὐτοῖσι τεθρίππῳ ὁ Κλεισθένης κήρυγμα ἐποιήσατο, ὅστις Ἑλλήνων ἑωυτὸν ἀξιοῖ Κλεισθένεος γαμβρὸν γενέσθαι, ἥκειν ἐς ἑξηκοστὴν ἡμέρην ἢ καὶ πρότερον ἐς Σικυῶνα ὡς κυρώσοντος Κλεισθένεος τὸν γάμον ἐν ἐνιαυτῷ, ἀπὸ τῆς ἑξηκοστῆς ἀρξαμένου ἡμέρης.

From Penelope's point of view there is in fact some advantage in their numbers; a single determined wooer would have been much harder to put off. The principle on which she might select her second husband is variously represented.[17] It is implied that the decision rests wholly with her, even if technically a male κύριος is involved, either her father Icarius or, once he is grown up, Telemachus (cf. xv 20, xvi 391, xviii 270, xix 528–9). Personal preference appears to be, on the whole, irrelevant, though it might seem to be implied by her tactic of surreptitiously encouraging individuals (ii 91–2, xiii 380–1). The usual assumption is that she will marry the suitor who gives most gifts (xv 17–18, xvi 76–7, xix 528–9, xx 335): compare Hesiod's account of the wooing of Helen (frr. 198–204), in which Menelaus wins πλεῖστα πορών (204, 85–7). The contest with the bow, a much more primitive idea, introduces an alternative criterion.

It is usually assumed that, once married to her second husband, Penelope would leave Odysseus' house, allowing Telemachus to enjoy his inheritance undisturbed (xi 177–9, xvi 33–4, xviii 258 ff., xix 528, xx 337 ff., xxi 77 ff., 114 ff.). As a corollary it is sometimes suggested that, before remarrying, she should return to her father's house (i 275–8, ii 195 ff.), and that the suitors should apply to Icarius as the competent authority. All this is in accordance with classical practice. Yet the story of the test with the bow requires that the returned husband should find his rivals in his house, and occasionally, in other contexts, the poet envisages Penelope's second marriage being celebrated in Odysseus' palace (iv 769–71, xxiii 149–51), which must imply that this would remain her home.

Potentially there is also a political aspect to Penelope's remarriage, as Antinous sees when Telemachus first attempts to assert himself (i 386–7).[18] In theory no one disputes Telemachus' right to succeed his father, but in a crisis calling for qualities of leadership Penelope's husband would be in a strong position. Certainly if Telemachus were dead, his mother's husband could confidently hope to enjoy the power which had once been Odysseus',[19] and this, we are told, was Antinous' aim (xxii 50 ff.). But generally the threat to Odysseus'

[17] 'The marital fortunes of Penelope are indeed a constant embarrassment to those who believe in a consistent social pattern in Homer' (A. M. Snodgrass). See further W. K. Lacey, 'Homeric ἔδνα and Penelope's κύριος', *JHS* lxxxvi (1966), 55–68, A. M. Snodgrass, 'An Historical Homeric Society?', *JHS* xciv (1974), 115–25, G. Wickert-Micknat, *Archaeologia* R, 89 ff., M. I. Finley, *Economy and Society in Ancient Greece* (New York, 1981; Harmondsworth, 1983), 233–45, 290–7.

[18] See further S. Deger, *Herrschaftsformen bei Homer* (Vienna, 1970), 132 ff.

[19] Thus Aegisthus gained the throne at Mycenae (iii 304–5), Oedipus at Thebes (xi 273 ff.), and Gyges in Lydia (Hdt. i 11–12).

house represented by the suitors is treated as a purely private problem.

The implied analogy between Aegisthus and the suitors is, as I have said, one of the means by which the poet persuades us that the latter were wicked men who fully deserved their punishment. But this is only one aspect of the recurrent leitmotif of Agamemnon's return and its consequences.[20] The theme is introduced almost at the start of the poem (i 29 ff.), and is particularly prominent in i–iv (cf. i 298 ff., iii 193 ff., 306 ff., iv 512 ff.), though the poet returns to it elsewhere (xi 409 ff., xiii 383 ff., xxiv 193 ff.). It offers both analogy and antithesis. The poet can exploit the parallelism between Aegisthus and the suitors, Orestes and Telemachus, and the contrast between Clytaemestra and Penelope, between the imprudent Agamemnon's speedy but disastrous return and the long-delayed but ultimately happy home-coming of the circumspect Odysseus. Orestes' matricide does not fit the pattern, and is therefore ignored. The development of this theme in relation to Odysseus' story is made possibly by the *Odyssey*'s extended time-scale; the story of Orestes' vengeance requires an interval in which the boy grows up, and the prolongation of Odysseus' absence makes it possible to link the two. Reflection on the circumstances of Agamemnon's death and Orestes' vengeance probably suggested the idea that Menelaus' return must somehow have been greatly delayed (cf. iii 248–9), leading the poet to devise his far-flung travels.

Only Athena's warning, Odysseus says, saved him from a fate like Agamemnon's (xiii 383 ff.); the general principle is sound, though his own innate caution and Penelope's unwavering loyalty would have prevented his falling so easy a victim. The action of the *Odyssey* depends on the special relationship between Odysseus and Athena, whose support extends not only to Telemachus but also to Penelope. Divine favour for an individual hero is a motif familiar from the *Iliad*; for its extension from father to son there is an Iliadic parallel in Athena's relationship with Tydeus and Diomedes (*Il.* v 800 ff.). The bond of sympathy between Athena and Odysseus is, as she herself makes clear, their common intelligence (xiii 296 ff.); a somewhat similar affinity existed between Odysseus' grandfather Autolycus and Hermes (xix 395 ff.). Nestor speaks of the favour shown by Athena to

[20] See further S. Bassett, 'The Second Nekyia', *CJ* xiii (1918), 521–6, E. F. D'Arms and K. K. Hulley, 'The Oresteia Story in the *Odyssey*', *TAPhA* lxxvii (1946), 207–13, H. Hommel, 'Aigisthos u. die Freier', *Studium Generale* viii (1958), 237–45, U. Hölscher, 'Die Atridensage in der Odyssee', *Festschrift f. R. Alewyn* (Cologne–Graz, 1967), 1–16, A. Lesky, 'Die Schuld der Klytaimestra', *WS* lxxx (1967), 5–21.

Odysseus at Troy as unparalleled (iii 218 ff., cf. viii 520, xiii 388), but though this judgement may have been justified by stories to be found in some of the Cyclic epics, such as the ὅπλων κρίσις, it is not borne out by the *Iliad*. There, despite Ajax's petulant complaint of favouritism (xxiii 782–3), Odysseus is only one among several heroes who receive Athena's support, and certainly there is no suggestion of any intellectual bond between them. In the *Iliad* Athena is primarily a warrior-goddess, giving practical help more often than counsel; her reputation for wisdom seems to have developed with her connection with Odysseus.

It is entirely due to Athena that the long deadlock is broken, and Odysseus' home-coming and triumph over his enemies would alike be impossible without her repeated intervention. Her prominence in the opening scene on Olympus prepares us for her supremely important role in the epic as a whole. She controls the complex action almost as if the characters were marionettes and she the puppet-master. We have here a clear contrast with the *Iliad*, where the Olympians are collectively involved in the action. To some extent this difference corresponds to that between a world war and the troubles of a single family. But the Odyssean Zeus is more dignified and remote; though he approves of Odysseus (i 65 ff.), he leaves it to Athena to contrive his home-coming. Though the wrath of Poseidon is repeatedly mentioned, it has little effect; the poet deliberately avoids conflict between Poseidon and Athena over Odysseus (cf. xiii 341 ff.). The goddess's paramountcy in the *Odyssey* must have considerably enhanced the poem's appeal to Athenians; perhaps that partly explains its selection for performance at the Panathenaea.[21]

In the first four books the poet laid the foundations of his monumental narrative; repeated rereading can only strengthen our admiration for the skill with which he solved the problems inherent in his grand design. Here we have the mature work of one who had long reflected on his subject and experimented with its several parts. Analytic critics have often expressed themselves as if the poet was working with fixed, i.e. written, texts of earlier short poems from which he compiled his epic rather mechanically. This picture requires some modification if it is to fit the now generally accepted view of the *Odyssey* as the product of a long tradition of oral poetry.

[21] See further M. W. M. Pope, 'Athena's Development in Homeric Epic', *AJP* lxxxi (1960), 113–35, Marion Müller, *Athene als göttliche Helferin in der Odyssee* (Heidelberg, 1966), M. M. Willcock, 'Some Aspects of the Gods in the *Iliad*', *BICS* xvii (1970), 1–10, M. Skafte Jensen, *The Homeric Question and the Oral-Formulaic Theory* (Copenhagen, 1980), 167 ff.

Whether or not the *Odyssey* itself was composed with the aid of writing, the poet's sources must have been very largely (and indeed most probably entirely) oral, and therefore fluid and mutable. Many of the difficulties to which critics have adverted arise from the poet's tendency to sacrifice overall consistency for short-term effect by combining striking elements from different versions of his story. It is relatively easy to detect and censure such inconsistency, but much that is memorable (including Telemachus' journey) would very likely have been lost for ever if the poet had concentrated on a tidier story-line. This rather hospitable attitude towards incompatible elements is an interesting aspect of the *Odyssey*, and we should admire the skill which allows us at times to benefit from alternative narrative possibilities rather than feel the need to defend or explain away discrepancies which, though they may slightly disconcert the reflective reader, would not be noticed by a listening audience. Only long experience could show how far logically incompatible elements might be combined without confusing the listener, and the poet's practice provides better evidence of what would work than we can ever hope to find elsewhere.

II

Frequent change of scene is characteristic of the first half of the *Odyssey*, and the Telemachy covers a very wide range geographically. From the Western Isles we move to the Peloponnese, and the narratives of Nestor and Menelaus extend our view to include most of the Levant and even Africa. The poet's topographical conceptions are often a source of difficulty to the commentator, and various oddities collectively leave the impression that neither he nor his audience was acquainted with many of the places prominent in the narrative. In an age before maps were familiar even a relatively well-travelled man would find it hard to retain much information of this sort,[22] and the transmission of heroic epic in places far from the scenes described would constantly tend to confuse and obscure topographical detail. While it is often possible to explain away individual difficulties, the accumulation of examples suggests that this may be wasted ingenuity. This topic has received relatively little

[22] Greek tradition credited Anaximander of Miletus (*c*.610–546) with the first map of the inhabited world (DK 12 A 6); Aristophanes (*Nu.* 206 ff.) extracts a joke from Strepsiades' bewilderment when shown a local map. The earliest map we have is in fact Babylonian, a clay tablet map of northern Mesopotamia, dating to the dynasty of Sargon of Akkad (2400–2200).

attention, though its implications should effectively discourage the more popular pastime of locating Odysseus' adventures in ix–xii on the map of the Mediterranean. The following remarks are confined to what is relevant to i–iv.

First, Ithaca. The difficulties presented by the poem's references to its hero's kingdom were already a subject of controversy in antiquity; Strabo opens his discussion thus (454): οὐ γὰρ εὐκρινῶς ἀποδίδωσιν ὁ ποιητὴς οὔτε περὶ τῆς Κεφαλληνίας οὔτε περὶ τῆς Ἰθάκης καὶ τῶν ἄλλων πλησίον τόπων, ὥστε καὶ οἱ ἐξηγούμενοι διαφέρονται καὶ οἱ ἱστοροῦντες. The most important and perplexing passage is ix 21–7, where Odysseus describes his home to Alcinous.[23] Ithaca, he says, is one of a numerous group of islands lying close together, among which are Doulichion, Same, and Zacynthus. It is natural to identify Ithaca and Zacynthus with the islands which still bear those names, but Doulichion and Same are not so easy; the most probable explanation is that they are both parts of Cephallenia.[24] Further details about Ithaca follow: αὐτὴ δὲ χθαμαλὴ πανυπερτάτη εἰν ἁλὶ κεῖται | πρὸς ζόφον, αἱ δέ τ᾽ ἄνευθε πρὸς ἠῶ τ᾽ ἠέλιόν τε. We should naturally take this to mean that Ithaca is low-lying (χθαμαλή) and situated furthest west (or north-west) of the whole group (cf. xxi 347). But Ithaca is in fact mountainous, with steep-to coasts, and lies east of Cephallenia. A radical solution to these difficulties was attempted by Dörpfeld, who suggested that the Homeric Ithaca was the classical Leucas (modern Lefkas), which could reasonably be described as πανυπερτάτη πρὸς ζόφον, if this is understood as 'furthest to the north-west'; following a suggestion of Strabo, he interpreted χθαμαλή as 'close to the main-land', a sense for which it would be hard to find a parallel. But the other islands do not lie 'around' or 'on either side of' Leucas (ἀμφὶ δὲ νῆσοι πολλαί), and the standard epithets of Odysseus' homeland, κραναή, τρηχεῖα, παιπαλόεσσα (cf. iv 605 ff.), are peculiarly appropriate to Ithaca and do not suit Leucas nearly as well; in any case, the transfer of the name has not been convincingly explained. Corfu (Corcyra) and Cephallenia have also been proposed. But Merry was surely right when he wrote[25] 'The most probable view, in our opinion, is that Homer intended to make the home of his hero in the actual island of Ithaca; but in the absence of any personal acquaint-ance with the scene, the poet could only draw upon such vague information as might be accessible, as to the geographical position of the place; the details being only a poet's conception of the natural scenery common to many Greek islands, and probably reproduced

---

[23] See Heubeck's n. on ix 21–7. [24] See i 246–7 n.

[25] Merry–Riddell 561. See further *Companion*, 398 ff. Lorimer, *Monuments*, 494 ff.

with more or less similarity in many places with which he was actually familiar.'[26]

With the end of ii the scene moves southward to Nestor's Pylos. Its identification was disputed in antiquity: see Strabo 339 ff., 349 ff. The name was common, and Nestor's narrative at *Il.* xi 670 ff. implies that his home lay further north than the famous Pylos in Messenia. Strabo believed that Nestor came from an obscure place of the same name in Triphylia, and this theory seemed to be confirmed by Dörpfeld's discovery in 1907 of Mycenaean remains near Kakovatos in Triphylia. However, excavations in 1939 revealed a great Mycenaean palace among the foothills of Mount Aegialon, on the high ridge now called Epano Englianos, about six miles north of Messenian Pylos; it is now generally agreed that this is the historical counterpart of Nestor's home.[27] The data in the *Odyssey* merely indicate the western coast of the Peloponnese. At first sight the speed of Telemachus' journey from Ithaca might seem to suggest a more northerly situation than Messenian Pylos: a single night brings him to his destination, whereas the journey from Ithaca to Navarino Bay, even in ideal conditions such as Telemachus enjoys, would take a small sailing-ship at least twenty-four hours, and more probably thirty. But we should not treat these data as a reliable indication of distance. It was artistically appropriate that the journey should be speedily accomplished and Telemachus arrive in the early morning rather than at suppertime. Realistically regarded, such a voyage, through coastal waters and among islands, would be extremely foolhardy at night.

Telemachus' two-day chariot-journey from Pylos to Sparta (iii 485–97) is even less realistic. The poet was more interested in providing Telemachus with a suitably dignified form of transport. But an extended journey by chariot would be intolerably uncomfortable, even over level ground, and Telemachus would have to traverse some very mountainous country. Two days would scarcely be enough for the distance, whether on foot or mule-back;[28] a traveller from Messenian Pylos to Sparta would need to allow a day for crossing Mount Taygetus and two days for the journey from Pylos to Pherae. Even on Dörpfeld's hypothesis that Nestor's home lay in Triphylia, the distance and the rugged terrain would make it difficult to reach Sparta in two days.[29]

The poet's unfamiliarity with the Peloponnese creates more obvi-

[26] See also Hoekstra on xiii 103–7, 217–18, xiv 335, xv 33.
[27] See further *Companion*, 422 ff. and iii 4 ff. n.
[28] See *Guide Bleu*, ed. 1911, 436–7, 454. [29] See further iii 484 ff. n.

ous difficulties in his account of Agamemnon's home-coming. When Telemachus hears how Agamemnon was killed he asks (iii 249 ff.) ποῦ Μενέλαος ἔην; τίνα δ' αὐτῷ μήσατ' ὄλεθρον | Αἴγισθος δολόμητις; ... ἦ οὐκ Ἄργεος ἦεν Ἀχαϊκοῦ, ἀλλά πη ἄλλη | πλάζετ' ἐπ' ἀνθρώπους; His question implies that the two brothers are envisaged living together, or at any rate close to one another (cf. 256–7, 311). Yet in reality Mycenae, Agamemnon's city (iii 304), is c.80 kilometres, as the crow flies, from Menelaus' city of Sparta (iv 1). The use of Ἄργος to mean both 'the Argolid' and 'the Peloponnese' no doubt fostered misconception.[30] Even odder is the detail that Agamemnon was blown off course on his homeward journey while trying to round Cape Malea, the most southerly point of the Peloponnese (iv 514 ff.), an incomprehensible route if he was making for the Argolid; but this passage presents several strange features, and may well be interpolated.[31]

Menelaus' *nostos* greatly extends our horizons. He thus describes his route (iv 83–5): Κύπρον Φοινίκην τε καὶ Αἰγυπτίους ἐπαληθείς, | Αἰθίοπάς θ' ἱκόμην καὶ Σιδονίους καὶ Ἐρεμβοὺς | καὶ Λιβύην. He was blown southward to Egypt while trying to round Cape Malea (iii 286 ff.), and it would be sensible to return via Phoenicia and Cyprus. But the rest of the list appears to represent travel undertaken for its own sake, and it is hard to suggest a reasonable route; the separation of Σιδονίους from Φοινίκην is rather disconcerting. The poet was concerned to account for Menelaus' seven-year journey, but seems not to have had a definite conception of his itinerary. We should certainly not overestimate the real geographical knowledge involved.

Egypt is prominent in Menelaus' *nostos*.[32] The poet was obviously interested in the land of the Nile, though perhaps not very knowledgeable. He has heard of the town of Thon (iv 228) at the Canopic mouth of the Nile, though the place has become a person. He knows of Egypt's river (iv 477, 581), but appears not to know its name.[33] Thebes (iv 126) was surely no more than a name to him; the rather casual way in which it is mentioned suggests that he had no idea of its distance from the coast. His error over the location of Pharos (iv 355–7) has attracted a good deal of attention, but is not really very significant; the story demands a desert island, and Pharos has been made to fill that role.[34]

By contrast with this catalogue of topographical vagueness and inaccuracy we may note that the poet is strikingly well informed about Crete. He indicates with remarkable precision the point on the coast where most of Menelaus' company made landfall (iii 291–6),

[30] See i 344, iii 251. nn.   [31] See iv 514–20 n.   [32] See further p. 192.
[33] See iv 477 n.   [34] See iv 354–9 n.

irrelevant as it is for the narrative. This is only a detail: his knowledge is displayed more fully when Odysseus, in support of his alias as a Cretan nobleman, describes the island to Penelope (xix 172 ff.)[35]—a splendid example of early Ionian ethnography.

[35] Crete figured even more extensively in Zenodotus' edition: see i 93 (with n.) and introduction p. 43.

BOOK I: COMMENTARY

The beginning of the *Odyssey* posed peculiar difficulties for the poet because of the work's complicated structure; it starts when the hero's wanderings are almost over, and his earlier adventures are not related until a third of the poem has been completed. The poet has first to set in motion two series of events which are designed to coalesce in their final stages, and to achieve this he has to disturb the apparently stable situation on Ithaca and break the deadlock on Calypso's island. The *Iliad* starts with a definite event, Agamemnon's outrageous treatment of Chryses; the *Odyssey* begins in stalemate. The poet rapidly outlines the main features of the background, and then fills in more detail once the action is under way.

We cannot tell how much of the story the poet might assume to be, in its general outlines, familiar to his audience, and how far he was consciously innovating; but there are signs that he knew more than one way of telling the story, and the relative importance of the various people and themes introduced in this book may have differed greatly in different versions. Characters are firmly but economically delineated; we do not feel we need to know more about them than the poet tells us. From their behaviour and conversation we realize the cumulative misery produced by Odysseus' long absence, and though the hero of the poem does not appear till v, he is the centre of interest from the outset. Telemachus' 'awakening' is an important element in this book; though many critics, from antiquity onwards, have seen an educational purpose in his journey, the real change in him occurs in i, and a series of scenes in this book and the next demonstrates that he has come of age. Many details in this book gain an added significance from the subsequent unfolding of the story. Above all, we notice the poet's concern, from the outset, to justify Odysseus; the savage tale of vengeance is to assume a strongly moral slant, so that the massacre of the suitors appears as the will and work of heaven.

1–10. The proems of the *Iliad* and *Odyssey* are strikingly similar, particularly at the beginning. The theme comes first ($\overset{\,}{α}νδρα/μῆνιν$; cf. *Il. parv.* fr. 1 Allen Ἴλιον ἀείδω, *h.Cer.* 1, *hMerc.* 1), next the invocation ($μοι$ ἔννεπε, Μοῦσα/ἄειδε, θεά), then a four-syllable adjective characterizing the theme ($πολύτροπον/οὐλομένην$), expanded by a relative clause ($ὃς$ μάλα πολλὰ πλάγχθη/ἣ μυρί' Ἀχαιοῖς ἄλγε' ἔθηκε), further elaborated by two δέ-clauses ($πολλῶν$ δ', πολλὰ δ'/πολλὰς δ', αὐτοὺς δέ). In both the poet refers to the vast possibilities of the theme ($μάλα$ πολλά, πολλῶν δ', πολλὰ δ'/μυρί') and sorrows to be described ($πάθεν$ ἄλγεα/ἄλγε' ἔθηκε). Both openings presuppose in the listener a general familiarity with the legendary framework; the poet, as Horace puts it (*AP* 148–9), 'in medias res | non secus ac notas auditorem rapit'. The general effect is well summed up by Quintilian

67

(x 1. 48): 'Age vero, non utriusque operis ingressu in paucissimis versibus legem prohoemiorum non dico servavit sed constituit? Nam et benivolum auditorem invocatione dearum quas praesidere vatibus creditum est et intentum proposita rerum magnitudine et docilem summa celeriter comprensa facit.' The resemblance between the two proems may partly reflect a traditional pattern for beginning a long heroic narrative, but the parallelism is so close as to suggest that the poet of the *Odyssey* modelled his opening on that of the *Iliad*. See further S. E. Bassett, 'The Proems of the *Iliad* and the *Odyssey*', *AJPh* xliv (1923), 339 ff., B. A. van Groningen, 'The Proems of the *Iliad* and the *Odyssey*', *Mededeelingen der koninklijke nederlandsche akademie van wetenschappen* NR ix. 8 (1946), 279 ff., Rüter, *Odysseeinterpretationen*, 28 ff., A. Lenz, *Das Proöm des frühen griechischen Epos* (Bonn, 1980), esp. 49 ff., 71 ff.

The proem begins and ends with an invocation of the Muse. Such an appeal was clearly conventional for epic narrative; but what is the significance of the convention? The invocation of the Muses at the beginning of the Catalogue of Ships (*Il.* ii 484 ff.) is of great importance for understanding the poet's view of their role. There the poet is about to embark on a long, circumstantial enumeration of the various contingents fighting at Troy; whether or not this is, in essentials, true, it is of little interest unless it is believed to be. The poet looks to the Muse to supply knowledge of what lies outside his own experience: ὑμεῖς γὰρ θεαί ἐστε, πάρεστέ τε, ἴστέ τε πάντα. A similar view of the Muses' function emerges very clearly from Odysseus' praise of Demodocus (viii 487 ff.). The goddess provides the singer's material and validates his narrative. By thus invoking the Muse the poet gives us to understand that his account of events which, as he and his audience well know, happened long ago, does not depend on his own invention, but is sanctioned by a divinity whose mouthpiece he is; whatever stories we have previously heard about Odysseus, what we are about to hear is what really happened. See further Lenz, op. cit., 27 ff., M. Skafte Jensen, *The Homeric Question and the Oral-Formulaic Theory* (Copenhagen, 1980), 62 ff., Clay, *Wrath*, 9 ff.

Despite the care which has obviously been bestowed on its composition, this is, as has often been pointed out, an odd opening for our *Odyssey*. It covers only a third of the poem (v–xii), not very accurately, and gives disproportionate emphasis to a single incident. The stress laid on the sacrilegious gluttony of Odysseus' comrades no doubt reflects the poet's concern to anticipate the charge that his hero failed to bring home his men (cf. xxiv 426–8), but his censure is not altogether borne out by his narrative in xii (see below, 7–9 n.); in any case, the suitors' sins are of far more importance for the poem as a whole than those of Odysseus' comrades. Moreover, though the prominence afforded to the Phaeacians may prevent us noticing the oddity, Odysseus' wanderings do not take him much among the cities of men (3), but far from human society. None of the *speciosa miracula* which we associate with Odysseus—Polyphemus, Aeolus, Circe, the Sirens, Scylla and Charybdis—is mentioned. We do not expect a comprehensive summary of what is to come; but if the poet's purpose was, as it would be natural to suppose, simply to indicate enough of his theme to catch his audience's attention, his choice of detail is strange. It is a natural conjecture that this opening was composed for a poem devoted to Odysseus' wanderings, related in a less fantastic form, and the outlines of such a *nostos*, bringing him back by way of Crete, Egypt, and Thesprotia, may be discerned behind the cover-stories which Odysseus tells to Eumaeus, Antinous, and Penelope (xiv 199 ff., xvii 419 ff., xix 172 ff., 270 ff.); see further p. 51. It is understandable if the poet was anxious to preserve this splendid and carefully constructed proem, even though he must have realized that it no longer quite fitted a narrative which was to culminate in Odysseus' heroic vengeance, already in prospect in i.

Horace produced two versions of the opening of the *Odyssey*: *AP* 141–2: 'Dic mihi, Musa, virum, captae post tempora Troiae | qui mores hominum multorum vidit et urbes'; *Epp.* i 2. 19 ff.: '[Ulixen] qui domitor Troiae multorum providus urbis | et mores hominum inspexit, latumque per aequor, | dum sibi, dum sociis reditum parat, aspera multa | pertulit, adversis rerum immersabilis undis.'

1. Cf. Livius Andronicus' famous translation (*poet.* 1): 'virum mihi, Camena, insece versutum'. **ἔννεπε:** the archaic verb imparts a certain solemnity to what follows. It is uncertain whether the -νν- is original or due to metrical lengthening: see further Wyatt, *Lengthening*, 94 ff. **Μοῦσα:** the poet invokes the Muse emphatically at the outset (cf. 10), but not thereafter; contrast *Il.* ii 484 ff., xi 218, xiv 508, xvi 112. The Muses are the daughters of Zeus (cf. 10, *Il.* ii 491, Hes. *Th.* 52, etc.) and, according to Hesiod, Memory (*Th.* 54); in Hesiod's catalogue they are nine (*Th.* 76 ff., cf. *Od.* xxiv 60 (with Heubeck's n.)), but probably they were generally regarded as a vague plurality, without individual identities; see further Hainsworth on viii 63, M. L. West on Hes. *Th.* ll. c. **πολύτροπον:** the meaning was disputed in antiquity: 'turning many ways, of many devices, ingenious' or 'much wandering'. The epithet recurs in only one other place in Homer, at x 330, where either sense would be suitable. Later writers evidently understood it as 'ingenious' (e.g. *h.Merc.* 13, 439, Pl. *Hi. Mi.* 364 e, Th. iii 83. 3, cf. πολυτροπίη Hdt. ii 121 ε 3), a synonym for the epithets more commonly applied to Odysseus, πολύμητις, πολύφρων, πολυμήχανος, ποικιλομήτης, etc., and corresponding to the self-characterization of ix 19–20 εἴμ' Ὀδυσεὺς Λαερτιάδης, ὃς πᾶσι δόλοισιν | ἀνθρώποισι μέλω. Thus, from the outset, the poet stresses the importance of intelligence. The alternative explanation, that πολύτροπος is equivalent to πολύπλαγκτος and glossed by the following clause (just as πατροφονεύς is glossed at 299–300), is less attractive. Such exegesis is out of place here, and alien to the rather summary style of the proem; moreover, Odysseus' travels resulted from accident rather than *Wanderlust*, and a reference to something genuinely characteristic of him is more appropriate. The scholia on Ar. *Nu.* 260 indicate a variant πολύκροτον (cf. Eust. on this line); in the Hesiodic *Catalogue* Odysseus is described as υἱὸς Λαέρταο πολύκροτα μήδεα εἰδώς (fr. 198. 3).

2. **πλάγχθη**: in epic language, as in Vedic and Avestan, the syllabic augment is optional. It used to be generally accepted that such optional augmentation, as against the mandatory augmentation of prose texts in Greek and Indo-Iranian languages, represented a characteristic of Indo-European poetic style, reaching back to the period before the separate IE languages came into existence. But the fact that the augment is normally omitted from Mycenaean texts, which in view of their essentially non-poetic nature would have been expected to show augmented verb-forms, seriously undermines this theory, though it is not clear how the facts should be explained. See further L. Bottin, 'Studio dell'aumento in Omero', *SMEA* x (1969), 69–145, Chantraine, *Grammaire*, i 478 ff., §§ 230 ff. **Τροίης ἱερὸν πτολίεθρον**: a unique designation for Troy, but cf. *Τροίης ἱερὰ κρήδεμνα* (*Il.* xvi 100), *Κικόνων ἱερὸν πτολίεθρον* (*Od.* ix 165). ἱερός is a frequent epithet for Troy (normally in the formula Ἴλιος (-ον, -ου) ἱρή (-ήν, -ῆς)); as often in Homer, it is used to convey a sense of something solemnly impressive, without obvious religious connotations. For non-Trojan examples of ἱερός with toponyms cf. iii 278 (Sunium), ix 165 (Ciconian city), xi 323 (Athens), xxi 108 (Pylos), *Il.* i 366 (Thebe), ii 506 (Onchestus), 535 (Euboea), 625 (the Echinades), iv 103 (= 121) (Zeleia). See further P. Wülfing-v. Martitz, ' Ἱερός bei Homer u. in der älteren griechischen Literatur', *Glotta* xxxviii (1959–60), 272–307, C. Gallavotti, 'Il valore di "hieros" in Omero e in Miceneo', *AC* xxxii (1963), 409–28, J. P. Locher, *Untersuchungen zu* ἱερός hauptsächlich bei Homer (Bern, 1963), esp. 36 ff., O. Szemerényi, *SMEA* xx (1979), 207 ff. πτολίεθρον seems to be a poetic coinage; the Ionic equivalent, *πολίεθρον, is not attested. **ἔπερσε**: cf. xxii 230; Odysseus is the real conqueror of Troy because he devised the stratagem of the Wooden Horse.

3–4. **πολλῶν ... πολλά**: anaphora with expressions of number is common in Greek, and there are many Homeric examples with πολύς (e.g. iii 273, iv 230); see further Fehling, *Wiederholungsfiguren*, 199. **ἴδεν ἄστεα**: Bentley's ἴδε would allow the lost initial digamma (ϝ, corresponding to English *w*) of ἄστεα to be metrically effective, but such changes are pointless in view of the many places where this phoneme is neglected. Digamma in initial prevocalic position seems to have disappeared from epic diction at the same time as it was lost in the Ionian vernacular, and cannot have been pronounced even where it was metrically feasible. See further Palmer in *Companion*, 100–1, Chantraine, *Grammaire*, i 116 ff., §§ 50 ff., R. Janko, *Homer, Hesiod and the* Hymns (Cambridge, 1982), esp. 42 ff. **νόον**: 'attitude, outlook, disposition, way of thinking', cf. iv 267, vi 121, ix 176; see further K. v. Fritz, '*NOOΣ* and *NOEIN* in the Homeric poems', *CPh* xxxviii (1943), 79 ff., G. Bona, *Il 'NOOΣ' e i 'NOOΓ nell'Odissea* (Turin, 1959), S. M. Darcus, *Glotta* lviii (1980), 33 ff. Zenodotus read νόμον, which is surely implied by Horace's translation 'mores' (quoted in 1 n.), since 'mentem' would have been the obvious rendering of νόον. This reading has found some distinguished supporters: see Bona, op. cit., 8 n. 20. But νόμος, though common in Hesiod (*Op.* 276, 388, *Th.* 66, 417, frr. 280. 14, 322), does not occur elsewhere in Homer, δίκη and θεσμός being preferred, though εὐνομίη is found once (*Od.* xvii 487); in any case, the sg. is awkward. Zenodotus' text was not provided with accents, and it is conceivable that what he intended was, as Nauck suggested, νομόν, 'their range, dwelling places' (cf., perhaps, *Il.* xx 249), but this seems a strange expression.

4. The antithesis with the preceding line is highly effective, but in fact Odysseus does not spend more than sixty days at sea from the time when he leaves Troy. xiii 90 looks like a conscious reminiscence. ὅ γ': often in Homer where the subject of two successive clauses is the same, it is picked up in the second clause by a pronoun strengthened with γε or δέ.

5. 'Trying to secure his own life and the home-coming of his companions.' Except (significantly) in his encounter with the Cyclops (ix 170 ff.), Odysseus is not represented as seeking his adventures; he is well aware of the obligations of a leader to his followers and of a king to his subjects (cf. ii 230 ff. (= v 8 ff.), xix 107 ff.). The *Wanderlust* of Tennyson's Ulysses derives from Dante (*Inferno* xxvi), not Homer: see further W. B. Stanford, *The Ulysses Theme* (Oxford, 1954), 175 ff. ἑταίρων: companions, especially companions in arms. The term, which often implies a high degree of mutual trust, has nothing to do with kinship; the heroes at Troy are ἑταῖροι to one another regardless of family and nationality: cf. e.g. *Il.* iv 266, xvii 150, xxiii 252. For ἑταῖροι used to describe the whole following of a hero cf. *Il.* xvi 204, xxiii 5, of Achilles' Myrmidons. See further A. Andrewes, *Hermes* lxxxix (1961), 134–7, H. T. Kakridis, *La Notion de l'amitié et de l'hospitalité chez Homère* (Thessaloniki, 1963), 51 ff., M. L. West on Hes. *Op.* 183.

6. οὐδ' ὥς: 'not even so, not for all that'. The accentuation of ὥς is uncertain; ancient grammarians in fact prescribe a circumflex accent in this expression and in καὶ ὥς, μηδ' ὥς and κἂν ὥς. ἱέμενός περ: 'eager though he was'.

7–9. The emphasis given to this episode (on which see Heubeck on xii 260 ff.) is striking. In fact this severe condemnation of Odysseus' companions is not borne out by the narrative. Eleven of his twelve ships are destroyed by the Laestrygonians, through no fault of the victims, and even on board Odysseus' own ship there are several casualties before Thrinacia is reached (ix 288 ff., 311, 344, x 551–2, xii 245 ff.). The men are driven to their sacrilegious act by the gods who punish them for it. Their decision to avoid the dangers of sailing by night by landing on Thrinacia is sensible (xii 279 ff.), but Zeus forces them to stay by sending a contrary wind (313), which blows for a month (325) until their supplies are exhausted (329). When at last they decide to eat the cattle as the only alternative to starvation (341 ff.), they do all they can to mitigate the offence; meanwhile Odysseus, who might have restrained them, has been sent to sleep by the gods (338). The significance of this discrepancy, not as to the facts but in their interpretation, is controversial: see further Fenik, *Studies*, 212 ff. For a historical case of trouble over a sacred herd see Hdt. ix 93.

7. The moral of the whole poem, to be echoed in Eurylochus' justified censure of Odysseus' foolhardiness in Polyphemus' cave (x 437), τούτου γὰρ καὶ κεῖνοι ἀτασθαλίῃσιν ὄλοντο. **αὐτῶν . . . σφετέρῃσιν**: the word-order, genitive *before* possessive adjective, is quite abnormal; presumably this reflects the modification of a formulaic prototype like *Il.* iv 409 κεῖνοι δὲ σφετέρῃσιν ἀτασθαλίῃσιν ὄλοντο: see further J. Wackernagel, 'Indogermanische Dichtersprache', *Philologus* lxxxxv (1943), 12–13 (= *Kl. Schr.* (Göttingen, 1953), i 197–8). **ἀτασθαλίῃσιν**: ἀτασθαλίη is an important word in the *Odyssey* and recurs shortly in Zeus's speech on human perversity as a cause of suffering (34). It is mainly used with reference to the suitors' conduct; it denotes behaviour for which men not only suffer but deserve to suffer, culpable recklessness implying a selfish disregard for the decencies of social life. See Hainsworth on viii 166, *LfgrE* s.v. ἀτασθαλίη, ἀτασθάλλω, ἀτάσθαλος, D. M. Jones, *Ethical themes in the Plot of the* Odyssey (Inaugural lecture, London, 1954).

8. **κατά**: to be taken adverbially with ἤσθιον. **Ὑπερίονος**: for Homer Ὑπερίων is simply a title of the Sun-god; it is usually joined with Ἠέλιος, but can stand alone (i 24, *Il.* xix 398); Ὑπεριονίδης (xii 176) is apparently regarded as equivalent. But in Hesiod Hyperion is a Titan and father of Helios (*Th.* 374). The etymology is uncertain, but it is probably best taken as equivalent to Latin *superior*: see H. Usener, *Götternamen* (Bonn, 1896), 19–20.

9. **αὐτάρ**: the coexistence of Achaean αὐτάρ and Ionic ἀτάρ within the formulaic system should be noted; despite the frequency with which αὐτάρ occurs, its second syllable is never in arsis: the few apparent exceptions can be eliminated by adopting the variant ἀτάρ given in every instance. On αὐτάρ and its place in the formulaic system see further Ruijgh, *Élément*, 29 ff. **νόστιμον ἦμαρ**: ἦμαρ, already an archaism, but metrically far more convenient than ἡμέρη of contemporary Ionic, is often so used in Homer with an adjective (cf. δούλιον, νηλεές, αἴσιμον ἦμαρ) to denote a state or condition, such periphrases being used particularly in connection with what does not in fact happen: see H. Fränkel, 'Die Zeitauffassung in der frühgriech. Literatur', *Wege u. Formen frühgriechischen Denkens*² (Munich, 1960), esp. 5–6, R. A. Santiago, 'Observaciones sobre algunos usos formularios de ἦμαρ en Homero', *Emerita* xxx (1962), 139–50. ἡμέρη is not used in this way in Homer.

10. The poet no doubt took pride in his flashback technique; he did not need to begin at the beginning, but could start at a point relatively near the end, and thus concentrate the action within a period of approximately forty days. He does not specify a particular event as his starting-point, and there is a smooth and natural transition to the description of Odysseus' circumstances. **τῶν ἁμόθεν γε**: 'from some point, from whatever point you will, in this story'; cf. viii 500 ἔνθεν ἑλών. Nowhere else in Homer does

any form of *ἀμός occur. It is disputed whether it is an Atticism (cf. Pl. *Grg.* 492 d etc. ἀμόθεν γέ ποθεν) or an archaism, but if it were a genuine archaism we might expect to find more examples: see Shipp, *Studies*, 314 n. 2. **εἰπὲ καὶ ἡμῖν:** the force of καί is not quite clear: is it 'Tell us too, share your knowledge with us' or 'Tell us as well as others', an appeal to precedent? The former seems more likely; for the general idea cf. *Il.* ii 485 ff., and for the use of καί cf. *Od.* ix 16–17 νῦν δ' ὄνομα πρῶτον μυθήσομαι, ὄφρα καὶ ὑμεῖς | εἴδετ', 'in order that you may know it as well as me' **ἡμῖν:** the poet and his audience.

11–21. A brief sketch of the conflict of divine interests over Odysseus' return to Ithaca.

11. ἔνθ' marks the point in time at which the *Odyssey* opens; we are not given a more precise indication until ii 175, where we learn that it is the twentieth year since Odysseus left home for Troy; see below, ii 174–6 n. **ὅσοι ... ὄλεθρον:** the *nostoi* of the other Greek survivors are related by Nestor and Menelaus in iii and iv. **αἰπὺν ὄλεθρον:** αἰπύς is similarly used metaphorically with φόνος, δόλος, πόνος, and χόλος; though it is not quite clear what metaphor is presupposed, the general sense seems to be 'merciless, hard to overcome': see further Hoekstra on xvi 379, W. J. Verdenius, 'The Metaphorical Use of ΑΙΠΥΣ', *Mnemosyne* Ser. 4, vi (1953), 115, *LfgrE* s.v. αἰπά, H. J. Koch 'αἰπὺς ὄλεθρος and the Etymology of ὄλλυμι', *Glotta* liv (1976) 216 ff.

13. Odysseus' preference for his middle-aged wife over Calypso in her earthly paradise (v 63 ff.) is rightly stressed at the outset.

14. We learn more about Calypso at 51 ff. Her father is Atlas, and she has nothing but her name in common with Hesiod's ἱμερόεσσα Καλυψώ, listed among the daughters of Tethys and Oceanus in the *Theogony* (359); she has no place in myth independent of the *Odyssey*. She has much in common with Circe (as Odysseus himself is aware (ix 29 ff.)), who may well have served as her model. But Calypso represents a much more serious temptation to Odysseus. Though we cannot be certain, it looks as if Calypso was invented at a late stage in the development of the story, when the poet, having decided to extend Odysseus' *nostos* to ten years, had to devise a means of detaining his hero for a long period without implying any weakening in his resolve to get home. Her name underlines her function in the story. See further Hainsworth, introduction to v and v 57 n. Heubeck on x 133 ff., *RE* x 1772 ff. (Lamer), Woodhouse, *Composition*, 46–53, 215–17, F. Dirlmeier, 'Die "schreckliche" Kalypso', *Lebende Antike: Symposion f. Rudolf Sühnel* (Berlin, 1967), 20 ff. **πότνια:** a title of honour, applied to mortal women as well as goddesses, in origin fem. of πόσις; see further Russo on xx 61, Frisk, *GEW*, Chantraine, *Dictionnaire*. **δῖα θεάων:** the partitive gen. might be expected to imply distinction within the group, as it clearly does in δῖα γυναικῶν, almost certainly the model for this formula (cf. Hainsworth on v 159). But the expression is used without regard to pre-eminence in the divine hierarchy, and was evidently regarded as appropriate to any goddess.

COMMENTARY

15. σπέσσι: the declension of σπέος, an archaic word of unknown etymology, presents several problems: see Monro, *Homeric Dialect*, 88 § 105 (5), Chantraine, *Grammaire*, i 7 § 1, Ruijgh, *Elément*, 126–7, Werner, *H u. ει vor Vokal*, 36–40. σπέσσι occurs only in the Odyssean formula ἐν σπέσσι γλαφυροῖσι (7 times, always at the beginning of the line); it may have replaced σπέεσι, which is sometimes given as a variant and would be morphologically more satisfactory (cf. ἔπεσι). An alternative form, σπήεσσιν, occurs four times, but no other part of the pl.

16. ἔτος ... ἐνιαυτῶν: the use of these words in Homer indicates that they were regarded as equivalent, though originally ἐνιαυτός meant 'anniversary, the day on which the year's cycle is completed': see C. J. Emlyn-Jones, 'ἔτος and ἐνιαυτός in Homeric Formulae', *Glotta* xlv (1967), 156–61, R. S. P. Beekes, ibid., xlvii (1969), 138 ff.   **περιπλομένων ἐνιαυτῶν:** cf. Verg. *A.* i 234 'volventibus annis'.

17. ἐπεκλώσαντο: 'spun to, assigned by spinning', i.e. appointed, ordained. κλώθω and its cpds. are regularly used of the spinning of fate (cf. vii 197 ff., with Hainsworth's n.), but here the verb seems to be used rather loosely. The following dialogue between Zeus and Athena does not suggest that anything had previously been determined about the date of Odysseus' return, yet according to common belief a man's destiny, not in precise detail, but as regards the time of his death and the general balance of good and ill, was fixed for him at birth (vii 196 ff., *Il.* x 70–1, xx 127–8, xxiii 79, xxiv 209 ff., Hes. *Th.* 218–19 = 905–6).

18–19. οὐδ' ἔνθα ... φίλοισι: there is some doubt about the interpretation and punctuation. Is this the apodosis to ἀλλ' ὅτε δὴ κτλ; a reference to the difficulties which delayed his return ('not even then was he safe out of danger or among his friends')? Or is it a parenthesis foreshadowing the latter part of the poem ('though even there and among his own people he was not free from trials'), with θεοὶ δ' beginning the apodosis? The second interpretation was evidently adopted by Aristarchus (see schol. *Il.* xvi 46), but this isolated allusion to subsequent events is rather awkward. It is probably better to adopt the first interpretation, though it is somewhat flat. Either way, the passage seems clumsy.

20–1. The cause of Poseidon's anger is explained more fully at 68 ff.; on the importance of divine wrath in the *Odyssey* see J. Irmscher, *Götterzorn bei Homer* (Leipzig, 1950), 52 ff. Poseidon is not of course directly responsible for Odysseus' enforced sojourn with Calypso, but the static condition of Odysseus' affairs is due to his hostility.   **ἀντιθέῳ Ὀδυσῆϊ:** ἀντίθεος refers to physical qualities such as beauty or strength, not to moral superiority; it is even used of the Cyclops (i 70) and of the suitors (xiv 18). We have long realized that Odysseus was meant, but the name adds a certain emphasis to the conclusion of this section.

22–95. The stage being now set, the action opens. Athena takes advantage of Poseidon's absence to raise with Zeus the question of Odysseus' long-delayed home-coming, and, being encouraged by her father's response, outlines her plan for restoring Odysseus' fortunes. The episode is often

74

described, over-formally, as a divine council, but though its function in initiating action is analogous (cf. Hainsworth on v 1 ff.) the tone is rather that of casual conversation, which provides a natural medium for conveying further details of the background to Odysseus' predicament, above all, the grounds for Poseidon's hostility.

22. A visit to the Ethiopians similarly explains the absence from Olympus of Zeus and the other gods at *Il.* i 423 ff., cf. xxiii 205-7. They are normally located in the far east (cf. Mimn. fr. 12. 9 West, [A.] *Pr.* 809), Memnon their king being the son of Eos (Hes. *Th.* 984-5). The identification of the Ethiopians with the people living south of Egypt is not certainly attested before Hecataeus (*FGrH* 1 F 325-8, with Jacoby ad loc.), though *Od.* iv 83 ff., Hes. fr. 150, 17-19 might be taken as evidence of this conception. But for the poet of the *Odyssey* they are clearly a mythical race, and some vagueness about their homeland is not surprising.

Αἰθίοψ is a properly formed Greek cpd., and, despite some uncertainty about its derivation, the interpretation 'with burnt face' is the most probable; there is no reason to regard it as a foreign word distorted by popular etymology; see further Schwyzer, *Grammatik*, i 447, *LfgrE*, Frisk, *GEW*, Chantraine, *Dictionnaire*. As a personal name it has been found on tablets from Pylos, in the form *Ai-ti-jo-qo*, though the significance of this is debatable: see Ventris–Chadwick, *Documents*, 243-4 (PY 115), 248 (PY 121), 250-2 (PY 131, 133). Negroes are depicted in frescoes from Cnossus and Thera; see Sir Arthur Evans, *The Palace of Minos* (London, 1921), ii 755 ff., pl. xiii, iv 886-7, fig. 869, S. Marinatos, 'An African in Thera', *AAA* ii (1969), 374-5, D. L. Page, 'The Miniature Frescoes from Acrotiri, Thera', *PAA* li (1976), 135 ff. So the Mycenaeans must have had a word for 'negro', and there is nothing against supposing this to have been the original meaning of Αἰθίοψ. But we do not know how the poet and his audience understood the word. Neither in Homer nor in Hesiod is there any suggestion that Ethiopians were dark-skinned, though Hesiod refers (*Op.* 527) to κυανέων ἀνδρῶν δῆμόν τε πόλιν τε, and in the *Catalogue* (fr. 150, 17-19) Αἰθίοπες are associated with Μέλανες, Κατουδαῖοι, Πυγμαῖοι, and, probably, Λίβυες (all, incidentally, descended from Poseidon). The concept of this just and pious race, whose righteousness won them the friendship of the gods, retained its attraction throughout antiquity, culminating in Heliodorus' *Aethiopica*; it is against this background that we should set the New Testament story of Philip's encounter with the Ethiopian courtier (Acts 8: 26 ff.). See further E. H. Berger, *Mythische Kosmographie der Griechen* (supplement to Roscher's *Lexikon*, 1904), 22-4, A. Lesky, 'Aithiopika', *Hermes* lxxxvii (1959), 27 ff. (= *Gesammelte Schriften* (Berne–Munich, 1966), 410 ff.), A. Dihle, *Umstrittene Daten* (Cologne, 1965), 65 ff., F. M. Snowden, *Blacks in Antiquity* (Cambridge, Mass., 1970), esp. 101 ff., *Before Color-Prejudice* (Cambridge, Mass., 1983), esp. 46 ff.

23-4. This partition of the Ethiopians is new, western Ethiopians being apparently a product of Ionian speculation. The geographical detail is distracting, as we naturally wonder which group Poseidon is visiting and are not told until v 283, where we infer from the fact that his return journey brings him via Cilicia that he must have been east. Herodotus (vii 69–70) interprets this conception of Ethiopians divided between east and west in terms of Indians and Africans. **Αἰθίοπας:** for epanalepsis used to introduce supplementary information cf. 50–1, *Il.* ii 671–3, 837–8, 849–50, 870–1, vi 153–4, 395–6, xii 95–6, xxi 85–6, 157–8; see further Fehling, *Wiederholungsfiguren*, 184–5. **ἔσχατοι ἀνδρῶν:** 'remote from men', like the Phaeacians (vi 204–5). ἔσχατος is not in origin a superlative (*pace* LSJ), but a local adjective meaning 'situated outside'; see further Leumann, *Wörter*, 158 n. 1. **δυσομένου:** cf. Hes. *Op.* 384 (where δυσομενάων is contrasted with ἐπιτελλομενάων); in both places δυσόμενος is evidently used with present sense. Though it looks like a fut., it should probably be regarded as the participle corresponding to δύσετο, a so-called 'mixed aorist'. These forms were regarded by ancient scholars, and apparently by Homer and Hesiod, as imperfects: see Chantraine, *Grammaire*, i 416–17 § 199, Monro, *Homeric Dialect*, 43 § 41, and below, 330 n. **Ὑπερίονος:** see above, 8 n.

25. ἑκατόμβης: as ancient scholars realized, ἑκατόμβη is derived from ἑκατόν and βοῦς (see Chantraine, *Dictionnaire* s.v. ἑκατόν, Frisk, *GEW*, *LfgrE*), but where the number of beasts is specified it is always much smaller than a hundred, and the victims need not include cattle: cf. *Il.* vi 115 (cf. 93) (twelve oxen), xxiii 147 (fifty sheep).

26. γε τέρπετο: here, as often, our MSS are divided between augmented and unaugmented forms, and there is no obvious reason for preferring one to the other. Aristarchus appears to have avoided the syllabic augment at certain places in the line (cf. e.g. iii 461) but we do not know his reasons: see Chantraine, *Grammaire*, i 481–2 § 231. **δαιτὶ παρήμενος:** for Homer it is normal to sit at table (cf. iii 389, xx 136, *Il.* ix 199 ff., xxiv 472 ff.), and similarly for Phocylides (fr. 13 West). At Athens, at least, the custom of reclining begins *c.*600; Crete still followed the ancient practice in the Hellenistic period (Heraclid. Lemb. fr. 15 Dilts, Pyrgion *FGrH* 467 F 1).

27. ἐνὶ μεγάροισιν: initial λ, μ, ν, ρ, and σ may make a long syllable of a preceding short vowel (normally only in arsis except in the first foot). Our MSS sometimes mark this by doubling the initial consonant, and this orthography was preferred by Aristophanes; the evidence of contemporary papyri indicates that it was normal practice.

29–31. Cf. iv 187–9. This sounds like the opening of an Oresteia; the poet surely intended us to be surprised. Orestes' vengeance is the latest important event, and, in heaven as on earth, naturally forms a topic of conversation: cf. i 298 ff., iii 194 ff. There is nothing artificial or contrived about the way in which the poet introduces the leitmotif of Agamemnon's return and its consequences, a theme important throughout the poem but particularly so in the first four books: see above, pp. 16–7, 60. Here the emphasis on Aegisthus is important; the poet implies a close parallel between his case and that of the suitors, and though this conception will not stand up to logical analysis, it contributes significantly to the presentation of the suitors as wicked men whose crimes provoked the just wrath of heaven.

Aegisthus, son of Thyestes (and therefore Agamemnon's cousin), is not mentioned in the *Iliad*. The etymology of the name is uncertain, but it is more likely to be pre-Greek than a short form of *Αἰγισθένης: see further *LfgrE*.

29. ἀμύμονος: traditionally explained as 'blameless', from privative ἀ- and the stem found in μῶμος, cf. Hsch. μῦμαρ· αἶσχος, φόβος, ψόγος. This derivation is questionable, and the translation 'blameless' is scarcely ever natural in Homer, where the primary meaning seems to be rather 'beautiful, handsome', from which develops the sense 'excellent, expert'; see further Parry, *Blameless Aegisthus*; for an ingenious attempt to defend the conventional interpretation see F. M. Combellack, *AJPh* ciii (1982), 361 ff. (The article in *LfgrE* is unsatisfactory.) At iii 310 Aegisthus is given a different, but metrically equivalent, epithet, ἀνάλκιδος.

30. Ἀγαμεμνονίδης: the honorific force of the patronymic is unmistakable. Homeric epic preserves an extremely ancient usage in its extensive employment of patronymics; on their use see further W. Meyer, *De Homeri patronymicis* (Göttingen, 1907), J. A. Scott, 'Patronymics as a Test of the Relative Age of the Homeric Books', *CPh* vii (1912), 293–301. They are much less common in the *Odyssey* than in the *Iliad*.

32 ff. The theology implied by Zeus' speech has received much attention, and it should be stressed that its main function is to start the action. This would not be a natural point to introduce unfamiliar ideas, and there is in fact nothing new in Zeus' moralizing. The emphasis lies on the particular case of Aegisthus, which suggests the opening generalization (not vice versa); we are all familiar with the conversational mannerism which dignifies items of gossip with prefatory remarks about people who go looking for trouble, and this is not very different. Aegisthus' story, foreshadowing the fate of the suitors, is told in such a way as to sharpen the antithesis between his well-merited punishment and Odysseus' largely undeserved sufferings. The passage seems to have been in Solon's mind when he composed his elegy on *Eunomia* (fr. 4, cf. fr. 11 West): see W. Jaeger, 'Solons Eunomia', *SPAW* 1926, xi 69–85 (= *Scripta Minora*, i (Rome, 1960) 315–37). On the speech as a whole see further Wilamowitz, *Der Glaube der Hellenen*, ii (Berlin, 1932), 116 ff., E. R. Dodds, *The Greeks and the Irrational* (Berkeley–Los Angeles, 1951) 32, 52 n. 21, D. M. Jones, *Ethical Themes in the Plot of the* Odyssey, 15 ff., Rüter, *Odysseeinterpretationen*, 64 ff., Fenik, *Studies*, 208 ff., L. Allione, *Telemaco e Penelope nell'Odissea* (Turin, 1963), 39 ff. Nilsson, *Geschichte*, 363.

32–3. Zeus refers to the practice of attributing to a god (often himself) any misfortune for which there is no obvious cause. This is a standard feature of Homeric conversation, sometimes serious and sincere, sometimes a way of disclaiming responsibility: e.g. i 347–9, vi 188–90, xi 558–60, xii 371–2, *Il.* iii 164–5, xix 86–8. A certain degree of suffering is part of the human condition, since men are exposed to forces outside their control, and for this, in terms of Homeric theology, the gods must be held responsible. Zeus does not attempt to deny this; his point is that men bring further troubles upon themselves by their own folly and perversity. The thought requires us to supply πάντα with κακά; cf. viii 167.

34–5. ἀτασθαλίῃσιν: see above, 7 n. **ὑπὲρ μόρον:** at first sight this looks like a theological paradox, but if the poet had meant that wicked men can frustrate or circumvent destiny, he would surely have explained so abnormal a view in greater detail. Contrast the consolatory commonplace of *Il.* vi 487–8: οὐ γάρ τίς μ' ὑπὲρ αἶσαν ἀνὴρ Ἄϊδι προϊάψει· | μοῖραν δ' οὔ τινα φημὶ πεφυγμένον ἔμμεναι ἀνδρῶν. Though we find several times in the *Iliad* the idea that something nearly happened contrary to destiny, ὑπὲρ μοῖραν, ὑπὲρ μόρον (ii 155, xx 30, 336, xxi 517, cf. ὑπὲρ Διὸς αἶσαν xvii 321), these expressions are to be regarded as a way of increasing tension, emphasizing a critical point in the narrative. Even Zeus himself will not try to override destiny (*Il.* xvi 431 ff., xxii 167 ff.), and what is contrary to fate simply cannot happen. But αἶσα and μοῖρα are both used in a looser sense of what is fitting, right, or reasonably to be expected, and in this sense there is nothing paradoxical in an action ὑπὲρ αἶσαν or οὐ κατὰ μοῖραν: e.g. ii 251 σὺ δ' οὐ κατὰ μοῖραν ἔειπες; viii 397, ix 352, *Il.* iii 59, vi 333 ἐπεί με κατ' αἶσαν ἐνείκεσας οὐδ' ὑπὲρ αἶσαν; xvi 367 οὐδὲ κατὰ μοῖραν πέραον πάλιν, 'they crossed in disorder'; xvi 780 ὑπὲρ αἶσαν Ἀχαιοὶ φέρτεροι ἦσαν, 'the Greeks were victorious beyond their share, beyond what might reasonably have been expected' (cf. Leaf, *Iliad*, ad loc.). ὑπὲρ μόρον here is to be interpreted similarly; the phrase is not used in quite the same way in 34 as in 35, but in both there is the idea of going beyond the normal limit, of getting more than one's due share of something. We may compare the analogous, weakened, use of its adjective μόρσιμος at xvi 392 (= xxi 162) ἥ δέ κ' ἔπειτα | γήμαιθ' ὅς κε πλεῖστα πόροι καὶ μόρσιμος ἔλθοι, where it means little more than 'suitable, well-qualified'. The poet was no doubt not unaware of a certain rhetorical effectiveness in using ὑπὲρ μόρον in this way.

36. μνηστήν: 'wooed', i.e. lawfully wedded.

37 ff. Hermes' mission to Aegisthus is surely an *ad hoc* invention, intended to underline the latter's criminal folly, and perhaps partly suggested by Hermes' forthcoming mission to Calypso (cf. 84 ff.); it is not found in any later treatment of the story; cf. iii 266–71, with nn., and on similar inventions in the *Iliad* see M. M. Willcock, 'Mythological Paradeigma in the *Iliad*', *CQ* xiv (1964), 141 ff. Here too the fate of Aegisthus foreshadows that of the suitors, who similarly ignore divine warnings (cf. ii 146 ff., with nn.), warnings which are not arbitrary prohibitions but simply reminders of what should be obvious to any right-minded person.

In the *Iliad* Iris acts as messenger of the gods, but Hesiod's view of Hermes as θεῶν κῆρυξ (*Op.* 80, cf. *Th.* 939, fr. 170) is unlikely to derive solely from the *Odyssey*,[1] and we should not imagine that the poet was innovating in assigning this role to Hermes.

---

[1] Not only because the *Theogony* and the *Works and Days* are very probably earlier than the *Odyssey* (see M. L. West, *Hesiod, Theogony* (Oxford, 1966), 46–7).

Hermes, the son of Zeus and Maia, was always reckoned among the major Olympians, but in Homer his role is normally subordinate (though at x 275 ff. he appears to act on his own initiative in preparing Odysseus against Circe's magic arts). According to the Hesiodic *Catalogue* (fr. 64) he was the father of Odysseus' maternal grandfather, the sinister Autolycus; this is unlikely to be post-Homeric invention, but though the poet of the *Odyssey* knows of a special relationship between the god and Autolycus, he explains it in terms of the latter's particular devotion to Hermes' cult (xix 395–8). The derivation of Ἑρμείας is uncertain, but there is much to be said for a connection with ἕρμα, in the sense of 'cairn', the ancient means of marking a boundary or path. 'That a monument of this kind could be transformed into an Olympian god is astounding. In effecting this transformation, narrative poetry combined two motifs: the widespread mythical figure of the trickster who is responsible for founding civilization, and the epic role of the messenger of the gods, which was already familiar in Near Eastern epic.' (W. Burkert). See further Nilsson, *Geschichte*, i 501 ff., Frisk, *GEW*, Chantraine, *Dictionnaire*, W. Burkert, *Griechische Religion der archaischen u. klassischen Epoche* (Stuttgart–Cologne–Mainz, 1977), 243 ff. (= *Greek Religion* (Blackwell, Oxford, 1985), 156 ff.), H. Herter, 'Hermes: Ursprung u. Wesen eines griechischen Gottes', *RhM* cxix (1976), 193 ff.   ἀργειφόντην: like many of Hermes' distinctive titles, obscure and evidently very ancient (cf. ἀκάκητα, διάκτορος, ἐριούνιος, σῶκος). It is used as if it were an alternative name (and therefore would be better printed with a capital); it designates Hermes alone, and only rarely occurs, as here, in apposition to the name. Ancient scholars offer various wild guesses about its meaning; the usual interpretation was 'slayer of Argus', recalling Hermes' role in the story of Io, an obviously ancient tale, even though the first surviving references to it come from the pseudo-Hesiodic *Catalogue of Women* and *Aegimius* (Hes. frr. 122 ff., 294 ff.). It seems fair to infer that the poet and his audience understood ἀργειφόντης thus; certainly the second element was already interpreted as 'killer' when the *Iliad* was composed, since it must have provided the model for ἀνδρειφόντης (*Il.* ii 651 etc., cf. Πολυφόντης *Il.* iv 395). This, however, can hardly have been the original meaning; we expect a standing epithet to refer to a permanent or recurrent function or characteristic, not to a single exploit, and the change from *ἀργο- to ἀργει- has not been satisfactorily explained. Some ingenious derivations have been proposed by modern scholars: 'dog-killer' (J. Chittenden, *AJA* lii (1948), 24 ff., see also M. L. West, *Hesiod, Works and Days* (Oxford, 1978), 368–9), 'shining in splendour' (A. Heubeck, *BN* v (1954), 19 ff., cf. H. Koller, *Glotta* liv (1976), 211 ff.), 'shining at Argos' > 'killer at Argos' (W. Burkert). None of these seems immediately convincing, and the difficulty of finding a satisfactory Greek etymology lends force to Chantraine's view that the word is pre-Greek. See further Hainsworth on v 43, Chantraine, *Dictionnaire*, Frisk, *GEW*, *LfgrE*, W. Burkert, *Homo Necans* (Berlin, 1972), 185 n. 18 (= Engl. ed. (Berkeley–Los Angeles, 1983), 165 n. 18).

Another form of 38 was widely current in antiquity: Ἑρμείαν πέμψαντε διάκτορον ἀργειφόντην. This was the reading of Zenodotus and Aristophanes, and the line is quoted in this form in the learned *Iliad*-commentary of *P.Oxy.* 1087 (Pack² 1186), col. i 31–2 (first century BC) and in Epictetus (iii 1. 39). This version is not obviously inferior to that preferred by Aristarchus and given in all the medieval MSS; the use of the dual is easily defended, since the poet here concentrates on Zeus and Athena, and the common tendency of scribes to replace duals with plurals would argue in favour of its priority. But διάκτορον ἀργειφόντην is so much commoner than ἐΰσκοπον ἀργειφόντην that a mechanical error in the second half of the line would have been very easy, entailing the alteration of πέμψαντες to πέμψαντε to restore the scansion. A further ancient variant is recorded from the Massaliot edition (on which see above, introduction p. 44), πέμψαντες Μαίης ἐρικυδέος ἀγλαὸν υἱόν, untraditional in its language and an obvious modernization.

40. The change from indirect to direct speech underlines the importance of this part of Hermes' message, but seems extraordinarily abrupt; *Il.* iv 301 ff., xxiii 855 ff. offer partial parallels. Ἀτρεΐδαο: with τίσις, 'vengeance for Atreus' son', not with Ὀρέσταο; it is abnormal in Homer to use the grandfather's name as a patronymic, except for Achilles.

41. ἱμείρεται: epic aor. subj.

43. ἀπέτισε: the medieval MSS invariably offer this orthography for the aor. of τίνω instead of the philologically correct ἔτεισα given in early inscriptions; similarly we regularly find ἔμιξα, ἔφθισα instead of ἔμειξα, ἔφθεισα. (Papyri sometimes give the correct spelling, but probably only by accident.) See further Chantraine, *Grammaire*, i 13 § 5, 412 § 195, LSJ. (But cf. Hoekstra on xiii 15.)

44. γλαυκῶπις: obviously parallel to βοῶπις, a standing epithet of Hera in the *Iliad*. These epithets have been connected with a (putative) theriomorphic phase in Greek religion, but Athena is never in Homer associated with the owl, as she is with other birds (vulture iii 372, *Il.* vii 59, swallow xxii 240, dove *Il.* v 778), and γλαύξ does not occur in Homer, though σκώψ, the little horned owl, is mentioned (v 66). Presumably the poet connected γλαυκῶπις with γλαυκός (cf. *Il.* xvi 34), and understood it as 'with gleaming, flashing, eyes'. See further *LfgrE*, Kirk, *Commentary* on *Il.* i 551, C. J. Ruijgh, *Mnemosyne* S. iv, xxxvii (1984), 156–7.

47. Athena's imprecation foreshadows the death of the suitors; it is said to have been quoted by Scipio Africanus on the death of Tiberius Gracchus (Plu. *TG* xxi. 4).

48–9. Note the repeated syllables δαΐφρονι δαίεται, δὴ δηθά and alliteration in δ and π. Such effects are not unusual in Homer: see further L. P. Rank, *Etymologiseering en verwante verschijnselen bij Homerus* (Assen, 1951). δαΐφρονι: it is uncertain what meaning the poet attached to this adjective. In the *Iliad* it is a conventional epithet of warriors (including Odysseus (xi 482)); the first element was evidently connected with δάϊς, 'battle'. In the *Odyssey* δαΐφρων is used much more widely, to describe the Phaeacian

craftsman Polybus (viii 373) and Odysseus' mother (xv 356, cf. Hoekstra's
n.) as well as Telemachus (iv 687) and Alcinous (viii 8, 13, 56), neither of
whom is particularly warlike; the poet apparently connected the first
element with δαῆναι, 'to learn', and interpreted it as 'sensible, prudent', a
sense in which it seems to be used already in the *Iliad* occasionally (vi 162;
xi 123, 138). The fact that it is metrically interchangeable with περίφρων
and πολύφρων has probably fostered confusion about its specific meaning;
at i 83 the MSS are divided between δαΐφρονα and πολύφρονα, while the
scholia on xv 356, which refer to δαΐφρων as a frequent epithet of
Penelope, imply its presence in places where our MSS are unanimous in
reading περίφρων. For a detailed discussion see Parry, *Blameless Aegisthus*,
25–6 n. 1, B. Snell, *Glotta* lv (1977), 41–3, *LfgrE*. **δαίεται**: presumably
'is torn, distracted', from δαίομαι, not 'burns', from δαίω; as is observed in
the scholia τὸ καίεται ἐπ' ἐρώσης.

50–1. The punctuation of the OCT with a stop at the end of 50 produces a
very clumsy asyndeton. It is better to punctuate with a comma after
θαλάσσης and take νῆσος δενδρήεσσα as in apposition to ὀμφαλός: the tree-
covered island stands out from the sea like the navel from the body or the
boss from the surface of a shield. For the anaphora cf. 22–3 Αἰθίοπας and n.
Taken strictly ὀμφαλὸς θαλάσσης presupposes a landlocked sea, and hence
a location in the Mediterranean, but the poet stresses that Calypso's island
lies in the far west (cf. iv 498, v 100 ff., 278, xii 447–8), and attempts to
identify it with any Mediterranean island are misguided; on ancient
theories about its situation see Hainsworth on v 55.

52–4. These details are in a sense gratuitous, but they lend substance to the
newly invented Calypso, and by thus linking her with a malign giant in the
depths of the sea the poet effectively evokes a sense of incalculable menace.
But inconsistent cosmological conceptions have been conflated, to the
bewilderment of anyone who tries to visualize what Atlas actually does. In
Hesiod (*Th.* 509, 517–20, 746–8) this stout-hearted (κρατερόφρων) son of
the Titan Iapetus stands in the far west (or in the underworld), supporting
the sky by Zeus' command: Ἄτλας δ' οὐρανὸν εὐρὺν ἔχει κρατερῆς ὑπ'
ἀνάγκης, | πείρασιν ἐν γαίης πρόπαρ' Ἑσπερίδων λιγυφώνων | ἑστηώς,
κεφαλῇ τε καὶ ἀκαμάτῃσι χέρεσσι· | ταύτην γάρ οἱ μοῖραν ἐδάσσατο μητίετα
Ζεύς. In the *Odyssey* this picture is combined with the idea, widespread in
the ancient Near East, of pillars supporting the sky (cf. Ibyc. 55 (336)).
The resulting conception of Atlas as a kind of buttress is partly reflected in
[A.] *Pr.* 348 ff.: (Ἄτλας) πρὸς ἑσπέρους τόπους | ἕστηκε κίον' οὐρανοῦ τε καὶ
χθονὸς | ὤμοιν ἐρείδων, ἄχθος οὐκ εὐάγκαλον; there, however, Atlas has only
one pillar to support,[2] and appears to be based, as in Hesiod, on land.
Lesky threw light on the *Odyssey*'s location of Atlas in the sea by comparing
the partly parallel situation of the giant Upelluri of Hittite/Hurrian myth
('Hethitische Texte u. griech. Mythos', *AAWW* 1950, 148–55 (= *Gesam-
melte Schriften* (Berne, 1966) 363–8); Upelluri, according to the *Song of*

---

[2] κίον' could conceivably be dual, but the sg. is surely much more natural.

Ullikummi, lives in the sea and has heaven and earth built upon him. The poet has evidently combined elements selected from various current views on the difficult questions of what holds up the sky and what supports the earth; our perplexities arise partly because we are prepared to study these lines more minutely than the poet could have envisaged anyone doing. (There would be no problem if ἔχει (53) could be interpreted as 'has charge of', but αὐτός establishes its sense to be physical (like ἔχουσι 54)). We do not know why Atlas is described as ὀλοόφρων, 'malignant, destructive, bent on mischief', an epithet restricted to dangerous animals in the *Iliad* and reserved in the *Odyssey* for a formidable trio, Atlas, Aietes (x 137), and Minos (xi 322), each of whom is introduced apropos of a female relative, daughter or sister. Aietes' dealings with the Argonauts and Minos' with Theseus are recalled by the epithet, but it is not clear why Atlas is so described; the probability that the duties imposed on him would have soured his temperament is insufficient explanation. The epithet was evidently found strange in antiquity: Cleanthes read ὀλοόφρονος, i.e. περὶ τῶν ὅλων φρονοῦντος, and the scholia record a further variant, ὀλοόφρων, which must likewise be a conjecture. ὀλοόφρονος is for us all the more impressive because of this uncertainty, but I doubt if the poet intended mystification. **ὅς τε θαλάσσης πάσης βένθεα οἶδεν**: the same phrase is used of Proteus (iv 385–6), who, however, is highly mobile. On Atlas see further *RE* ii 2119 ff. (Wernicke), M. L. West on Hes. *Th.* ll. c., *LfgrE*.

56–7. Calypso's efforts to beguile Odysseus seem to have had some initial success, to judge by v 153 ἐπεὶ οὐκέτι ἥνδανε νύμφη. **αἱμυλίοισι λόγοισι**: exemplified by v 206 ff. αἱμύλιος is not found elsewhere in Homer, but is applied to λόγοι by Hesiod who associates it with feminine wiles (*Th.* 890, *Op.* 78, 374, 789); its etymology is uncertain: see Frisk *GEW*, Chantraine, *Dictionnaire*, *LfgrE*. λόγος occurs in only one other place in Homer, *Il.* xv 393, where it is used of soothing speech to a wounded man. **θέλγει**: the verb's connotations are well explored by Heubeck on x 213. **ὅπως ... ἐπιλήσεται**: the only Homeric instance of ὅπως with indic. in a purpose clause (at *Il.* i 136 ἄρσαντες κατὰ θυμόν, ὅπως ἀντάξιον ἔσται, ὅπως has rather the meaning 'how'); there are a few examples of ὄφρα used thus with the fut.: see Chantraine, *Grammaire*, ii 273 § 402.

58–9. Odysseus wishes to die because his longing to see Ithaca again seems hopeless; cf. v 151–8 (but the idea at vii 224–5 is rather different). Penelope too feels she would rather die than continue to live in perpetual mourning for Odysseus (xviii 202–5, xx 61 ff.). **καί:** 'were it but'.

59–62. The use of νυ to introduce three successive questions underlines Athena's impatience. **οὐδέ:** connective, 'yet ... not.'

60. **φίλον ἦτορ:** attributive φίλος in Homer is hardly to be distinguished from a reflexive (direct and indirect) possessive, used predominantly of what may be regarded as inalienable property (parts of the body, relatives etc.): see further M. Landfester, *Das griechische Nomen 'philos' u. seine Ableitungen* (Spudasmata xi, Hildesheim, 1966), 3 ff. The usage is imitated by Horace, 'cuncta ... amico quae dederis animo' (*O.* iv 7. 19–20). **Ὀλύμπιε:** the vocatives here and in 62 express strong feeling and make the reproach more forceful.   **τ'**: probably better taken as τε than as τοι; for οὔ νύ τ' cf. 347; see further Ruijgh, τε épique, 842–3.

61. A similar consideration almost induces Zeus to spare Hector (*Il.* xxii 170–1); cf. also *Il.* iv 44 ff.

62. τί νύ οἱ τόσον ὠδύσαο Ζεῦ: the ending of Athena's speech was perhaps suggested by ἐπεὶ μέγας ὠδύσατο Ζεύς (*Il.* xviii 292). For the implied derivation of Odysseus' name from *ὀδύσσομαι ('doomed to odium' Stanford) cf. xix 406 ff. (his grandfather Autolycus named him in remembrance of the hatred he had incurred (by his crimes) on the way to Ithaca), v 340, 423, xix 275, S. fr. 965 (with Pearson's n.); see further E. Risch, 'Namensdeutungen u. Worterklärungen', *Eumusia: Festgabe f. Ernst Howald* (Zurich, 1947), 72 ff. = *Kl. Schr.* (Berlin–New York, 1981), 294 ff., L. P. Rank, *Etymologiseerung en verwante verschijnselen* (Assen, 1951), 51–63, W. B. Stanford, 'The Homeric Etymology of the Name Odysseus', *CPh* xlvii (1952), 209–13. The name is clearly non-Greek, and probably non-Indo-European, and its true etymology is mysterious; though the form Ὀδυσσεύς was canonized by epic, Ὀλυσσεύς (cf. Lat. *Ulixes*) is widely attested and may be older: see further *RE* xvii 2, 1906 ff. (Wüst), Frisk, *GEW*, Chantraine, *Dictionnaire*, von Kamptz, *Personennamen*, 355–60.

63–4. = v 21–2.   **νεφεληγερέτα**: see Hainsworth on v 21.   **ποῖόν σε ἔπος φύγεν ἕρκος ὀδόντων**: the teeth are regarded as a barrier which should have prevented the words from escaping. Constructions like this, with a double acc., 'of the whole and part', are very common in Homer: see Chantraine, *Grammaire*, ii 42 § 51, Monro, *Homeric Dialect*, 134–5 § 141. See also Hainsworth on v 22.

65. Zeus indignantly rejects the imputation of personal hostility.   **ἔπειτ'**: 'after all this', i.e. 'in these circumstances (of which you speak)'.   **θείοιο**: 'godlike'; see further Hainsworth on v 11.

66. The first περί is to be taken with ἐστί, governing βροτῶν, 'he surpasses all men in wisdom'; the second is adverbial, equivalent to περισσῶς, 'beyond all other men'.

68–75. If we compare Odysseus' own account of his dealings with Polyphemus (ix 105–566) we may be surprised by Zeus' dispassionate tone: the Cyclops blatantly defies Zeus (ix 275 ff.) and Odysseus sees himself as the agent of divine vengeance (ix 477–9). Poseidon (like Helios: see 7–9 n.) takes no account of mitigating circumstances, nor does Zeus think them worth mentioning here.

68. γαιήοχος: in Homer this title is Poseidon's alone. Its origin and meaning are controversial, mainly because of uncertainty about -οχος. The poet and his audience, like the tragedians (cf. A. *Supp.* 816, S. *OT*, 160), probably connected it with ἔχω and understood the compound as 'earth-holding, the Earth Sustainer', but Laconian Γαιάροχος (*IG* v 1. 213, 9, etc.) rules out this etymology. The usual assumption that the second element is related to ὀχέω, Lat. *veho* etc., leaves the interpretation of the compound debatable: 'he who rides (as a river) beneath the earth (and thereby shakes it)' Nilsson, 'husband of Gaia' Borgeaud. Meillet's suggestion that the root is *wegh- 'shake', cf. Lat. *vexare*, is attractive. Cf. Hainsworth on viii 322 and see further Frisk *GEW* s.v. γαιάοχος, Chantraine, *Dictionnaire*, s.v. γῆ, *LfgrE*.

69. The poet's failure to mention that Polyphemus had only one eye should be noted (contrast Hes. *Th.* 142 ff.); it is not satisfactorily explained by the assumption that everyone took it for granted that Cyclopes were one-eyed. Here, in this rather summary account, the omission of any explicit reference to Polyphemus' abnormality is understandable; but it is not made good in ix, where it would be natural to alert the audience to this essential precondition for Odysseus' stratagem. On this and some related problems see R. Mondi, *TAPhA* cxiii (1983), 17 ff.

70. ἀντίθεον: a somewhat surprising epithet; though it well serves Zeus' attempt to justify Poseidon's anger, it is probably best explained as imitation of *Il.* i 264, where it is applied to a different Polyphemus; it should not be taken as referring to Polyphemus' divine parentage (see *LfgrE*). ὅου κράτος ἐστὶ μέγιστον: a similar formula applied to Zeus (v 4, *Il.* ii 118, ix 25) refers to supreme authority, but we can hardly envisage Polyphemus as a recognized leader ruling over a community of Cyclopes, and the phrase surely means simply that Polyphemus is the strongest among them (cf. *Il.* xiii 484); see further G. Bona, *Studi sull'Odissea* (Turin, 1966), 72 ff. The variant ἔσκε looks like a conjecture intended to meet the objection that Polyphemus would have had difficulty in maintaining his position after being blinded by Odysseus. ὅου: this form is also found at *Il.* ii 325 (ὅου κλέος). A single MS gives ὅο, probably by accident, though this must have been the original form of the gen. in such phrases. In several places in Homer metre indicates an original gen. in -οο even though this has virtually vanished from the MS-tradition and may indeed never have stood in any written text: see further Chantraine, *Grammaire*, i 45 § 18, 82 § 34, Monro, *Homeric Dialect*, 83 § 98.

71–3. Polyphemus' mother Thoosa seems to be an *ad hoc* invention, her name recalling the swift movement of the waves; cf. the Phaeacian Thoon (viii 113). For Phorcys cf. xiii 96, 345, and see iv 349 n. Polyphemus' parentage was already a source of perplexity in Aristotle's time (fr. 172 Rose); since neither his father nor his mother is a Cyclops, in what sense can he be said to be one? Nothing is said about the lineage of the other Odyssean Cyclopes, and it is left unclear whether they too are regarded as sons of Poseidon (cf. esp. ix 412). The Hesiodic Cyclopes, who forge Zeus' thunderbolts, are children of Uranus and Gaia (*Th.* 139 ff., 501 ff.). ἀτρυγέτοιο: in Homer applied only to the sea, except at *Il.* xvii 425, where it qualifies αἰθήρ. Etymology and meaning are quite uncertain, though the initial ἀ- is generally taken as privative. The scholia offer the (philologically impossible) explanation 'sterile, infertile, unharvested', from τρύγη; Herodian connects it with τρύω and interprets it as 'unwearied, indefatigable'—apt enough for the incessantly moving sea, but not for αἰθήρ; a derivation from τρύξ, 'lees of wine, dregs', has also been suggested, giving the sense 'pure'. See further *LfgrE*.

73. σπέσσι: see above, 15 n.

74. ἐκ τοῦ δή: probably temporal, 'from that time forward', rather than 'for that reason'.

75. οὔ τι κατακτείνει: this may be taken either as a conative present, or as parenthetic, 'though he does not kill him'.

76. ἡμεῖς οἴδε: 'we who are here'. The agreement of the other gods, in the absence of Poseidon, is assumed without discussion.

81-95. Athena outlines her programme, thus providing us with some guidance as to the course which this complicated narrative is to follow. Her first proposal (84 ff.) is almost predictable, but nothing has prepared us for her second suggestion (88 ff.). The first part of her plan is postponed until the second has been carried out; the poet proceeds to what is foremost in his mind, and Hermes is not dispatched until v 28 ff. This inverted order is quite common in Homer when a twofold instruction or proposal is related: see further S. E. Bassett, ' Ὕστερον πρότερον Ὁμηρικῶς', HSPh xxxi (1920), 39 ff. In this instance there is an unusually long stretch of narrative before the poet returns to the first item on the agenda, and Athena is therefore made to reopen the question of Odysseus' return at the beginning of v; this quasi-recapitulation is better suited to the needs of a listening audience than to those of a reflective reader, who may be puzzled by Athena's apparent failure to take account of what has already been decided; see further Hainsworth, introduction to v.

83. ὅνδε δόμονδε: Hoekstra on xiv 424 considers the implications of the fact that the ending -δε is found with possessive ὅς only in this formula.

84. As a genealogical curiosity we may note that Hermes is Calypso's nephew (his mother Maia being like Calypso a daughter of Atlas, though not by the same mother), but the relationship is quite irrelevant here, as is the tradition that he was the father of Odysseus' maternal grandfather, Autolycus (schol. xix 432). **διάκτορον:** another of Hermes' peculiar titles, in the *Iliad* invariably, in the *Odyssey* usually, combined with ἀργειφόντης (on which see 38 n.). Etymology and meaning are mysterious; of the various suggestions offered by ancient scholars the only one worth taking seriously is the derivation from διάγω, with the apparent meaning 'conductor, guide' (of travellers in general and of souls on their way to Hades, as at xxiv 1 ff.), though διάκτορος is not a normally formed agent noun from διάγω. R. Janko (*Glotta* lvi (1978), 192-5) argues for derivation from the rare διάκτωρ known from Bianor (*AP* x 101. 3 = *Garland* Gow–Page 1751), βούταν διάκτορα (διώκτορα cj. Buttmann), and Hesychius' gloss διάκτορσι· ἡγεμόσι, βασιλεῦσι; for earlier theories see Frisk, *GEW*, Chantraine, *Dictionnaire*, *LfgrE*.

85. Ὠγυγίην: cf. vi 172, vii 244, 254, xii 448, xxiii 333. It is not clear whether this is to be regarded as the name of Calypso's island or as an epithet, as it is in Hesiod, who uses it to describe the water of Styx (*Th.* 806), and in later poets. Its derivation and meaning are quite uncertain, but ancient scholars interpreted it as 'very old, primeval'. See further Hainsworth on vi 172, Roscher, *Lexikon*, iii 690-4, Wilamowitz,

Untersuchungen, 16–17, Frisk, *GEW*, Chantraine, *Dictionnaire*. Antimachus (see introduction pp. 40–1) read Ὠγυλίην, evidently identifying Calypso's island with Ogylus, which is located by Stephanus of Byzantium between the Peloponnese and Crete and is probably Anticythera.   ὀτρύνομεν: short vowel aor. subj.

86. ἐϋπλοκάμῳ: see Hainsworth on v 58.   νημερτέα: 'sure', i.e. that will not fail to be put into force.

87. νόστον: in apposition to βουλήν.

88. Ἰθάκην ἐσελεύσομαι: Ἰθάκηνδε ἐλεύσομαι is probably to be preferred here, the other variants being best explained as conjectures intended to eliminate the hiatus, though this is not uncommon at the main caesura; for similar variants cf. xvii 52, *Il.* vi 365.

89. μᾶλλον ἐποτρύνω: Athena will reinforce a mood already present in Telemachus (cf. 115–17).

90. καλέσαντα: with οἵ in 89.   κάρη κομόωντας Ἀχαιούς: Ἀχαιοί is often used when in fact only the people of Ithaca are meant: cf. ii 7, 265, 306; similarly Κεφαλλῆνες: see Heubeck on xxiv 355. The poet was clearly hampered by the metrical intractability of Ἰθακήσιοι (and apparently unfamiliar with the alternative form of the ethnic, Ἴθακος). Homeric gods (cf. *Il.* i 529, xx 39, *h.Ap.* 134) and heroes alike wear their hair long; though nothing is said about non-aristocratic hairstyles, there would be little point in this formula if long hair was supposed to be normal for everyone. It remained the fashion for the wealthy until well into the fifth century; the palaestra finally led to the prevalence of a shorter style. See further Marinatos, *Archaeologia* B, 1 ff., *RE* vii 2110 ff. (Bremer).

91. μνηστήρεσσιν: the suitors are introduced as if they were a familiar part of the story.   ἀπειπέμεν: 'speak out, give notice'.

92. ἀδινά: 'thick-thronging'.   εἰλίποδας: in Homer this epithet is restricted to cattle (while sheep are ταναύποδα (ix 464) and horses ἀερσίποδες (*Il.* iii 327, xviii 532, xxiii 475)). In antiquity the first element was connected with εἴλω, ἐλίσσω; the failure to observe an initial ϝ is against this explanation, but may only mean that the word is a late formation; the word would then mean 'rolling their feet as they walk, shambling'. See further Hainsworth on viii 60, Frisk, *GEW*, Chantraine, *Dictionnaire*, *LfgrE*.   ἕλικας: an epithet likewise restricted to cattle in Homer and very often combined with εἰλίποδας, of uncertain meaning. In antiquity it was generally explained as referring to twisted horns (cf. *h.Merc.* 192–3 βοῦς . . . κεράεσσιν ἑλικτάς), or else to their shambling gait; in either case it must be regarded as an abbreviated cpd. (*ἑλικόκραιρα, *ἑλικόπους); a third explanation, 'black', is surely merely a scholiast's guess. See further Frisk, *GEW*, Chantraine, *Dictionnaire*, *LfgrE*.

93. The inadequate motivation of Telemachus' journey, involving as it does considerable risk without obvious advantage, was criticized in antiquity, as we learn from the scholia here and on 284; the question is discussed above, p. 53.   Σπάρτην: Zenodotus read Κρήτην, and at 285, correspondingly, δ' ἐς Κρήτην τε [δὲ Κρήτηνδε cj. Buttmann] παρ' Ἰδομενῆα ἄνακτα for δὲ Σπάρτηνδε παρὰ ξανθὸν Μενέλαον; these are the strangest and perhaps the most significant of Zenodotean variants, and raise important questions about his methods: see further introduction pp. 43–4. Some MSS give two extra lines after 93, κεῖθεν δ' ἐς Κρήτην τε παρ' Ἰδομενῆα ἄνακτα· | ὃς γὰρ δεύτατος ἦλθεν Ἀχαιῶν χαλκοχιτώνων (cf. 285–6), a rather clumsy attempt to combine both versions.   **Πύλον:** on the location of Nestor's Pylos see below iii 4 n.   **ἠμαθόεντα:** a standing epithet of Pylos, applied to no other place in Homer, and evidently created by analogy with ἠνεμόεις; ἀμαθόεις does not occur, but cf. the Cypriot town Ἀμαθοῦς. ἠμαθόεις and ἠνεμόεις have similar functions, both being used to describe places and appearing in the same position in the line; see further Wyatt, *Lengthening*, 106. Epithets formed with the suffix -ϝεντ- are commonly treated as having two terminations: see K. Witte, *Glotta* iii (1912), 109–10.

95. Telemachus will be praised for his exertions.

96–143. Athena in the guise of the Taphian Mentes is welcomed by Telemachus.

96–101. 96: cf. v 44, xvii 2, *Il.* xxiv 340; 97–8 = v 45–6, *Il.* xxiv 341–2; 99 = *Il.* x 135, xiv 12, xv 482; 100–1 = *Il.* v 746–7, viii 390–1. The characteristic preparations for departure (cf. xv 550–1, xvii 2–4) have been elaborated to suit a god; however, doubts were cast on this elaboration in antiquity. Aristarchus and earlier, unnamed, critics questioned the authenticity of 97–8, as being more appropriate to Hermes; the lines' absence from the Massaliot edition probably reflects similar critical doubts rather than genuine tradition. Aristarchus also athetized 99–101 as borrowed from the *Iliad*. To many modern scholars such objections seem simply to betray a failure to appreciate the techniques of oral composers, who habitually elaborate their work with passages originally devised for other contexts. Yet if we allow that the poet of the *Odyssey* appears to expect us to recognize verbal allusions to the *Iliad*, we should not immediately dismiss this ancient expression of disquiet, engendered by a sense of inappropriate pastiche combined with some knowledge of the practices of scribes (and, no doubt, rhapsodes) who, as our papyri show, were given to expanding the text with lines borrowed from other parts of Homer.

97. ἀμβρόσια χρύσεια: there is a clear semantic connection between the two adjectives; gold, being imperishable, is symbolic of immortality, and the gods' possessions are characteristically of gold or silver, however inconvenient or impractical this might seem.   **ὑγρήν:** this substantival use of the fem. adjective to mean 'the sea' is already established in the *Iliad* (x 27, xiv 308, xxiv 341); Hesiod uses γλαυκή similarly (*Th.* 440).

101. κοτέσσεται: short vowel aor. subj.

102. = xxiv 488, *Il.* ii 167, iv 74, vii 19, xxii 187, xxiv 121. Here Olympus is clearly a mountain (very probably the original meaning of this evidently pre-Greek word), but this earlier conception (cf. Nilsson, *Geschichte*, i 353) is losing ground in the *Odyssey* to the tendency, already observable in the *Iliad* (viii 18 ff.), to equate it with οὐρανός. See further Hainsworth on vi

COMMENTARY

42-7. **Οὐλύμποιο:** as often the metrical lengthening reflects convenience rather than necessity: see further Wyatt, *Lengthening*, 90.

103-4. Athena's arrival is dealt with rather abruptly; we might have expected some description of Odysseus' palace, but the poet evidently wished to introduce the suitors without delay. **'Ιθάκης ἐνὶ δήμῳ:** as often in epic δῆμος is used in a predominantly local sense, of the land belonging to a community. **ἐπὶ προθύροις ... οὐδοῦ ἐπ' αὐλείου:** 'in the outer porch at the entrance to the court'; the only entrance to the house lies through the courtyard. Various more or less plausible reconstructions of Odysseus' home have been proposed, but we cannot hope to establish in detail what the poet had in mind (if indeed he himself had a clear overall conception). He certainly ascribed to the heroic age a more imposing style of building than was feasible in Greek lands in his own day, but the elements in his picture which seem to reflect the realities of Late Helladic palaces, as revealed by excavation at Mycenae, Pylos, and Tiryns, do not justify the inference that he was accurately enough informed about Mycenaean architecture to allow us to supply the deficiencies of his account by reference to the archaeological evidence (or vice versa). The observable ruins of Mycenaean palaces and the traditional stock of formulae and narrative motifs could often have perpetuated the memory of features which had no counterpart in the architecture of the Geometric age, but some distortion would have been inevitable. Contact with the Near East may also have contributed some details (particularly to the splendours of Menelaus' and Alcinous' palaces). See further Hainsworth on vi 303, 304, H. Plommer, 'Shadowy megara', *JHS* xcvii (1977), 75 ff., H. Drerup, *Archaeologia* O. **παλάμη ... ἔγχος:** it is normal for a traveller to carry arms, even when he is going only a short distance (cf. ii 10, Th. i 6. 1), and to lay down his weapons when he is received as a guest (121, cf. xv 282, xvi 40).

105. **ξείνῳ:** here best translated 'stranger, foreigner'; contrast 176, where it is 'guest, guest-friend'. **Ταφίων ἡγήτορι Μέντῃ:** cf. *Il.* xvii 73 Κικόνων ἡγήτορι Μέντῃ (where Mentes merely provides an alias for Apollo). The Taphians are mentioned elsewhere in the *Odyssey*, generally in rather an unfavourable light, as slave-traders and raiders (xiv 452, xv 427, xvi 426, cf. [Hes.] *Sc.* 19 (where they are coupled with the Teleboai)). Mentes' speeches indicate commercial interests and a certain lack of scruple (181 ff., 260 ff.); his reference to the Trojan War as if it were no concern of his (210 ff.) seems to imply that the Taphians are not Greeks. The ancients located Mentes' kingdom on Meganisi, a small island about nine miles from Ithaca, lying immediately east of Leucas, from which it is separated by a strait only half a mile wide; in Strabo's time it was called Taphious (Str. 456). Whether the poet had any definite locality in mind is obviously debatable, but since Mentes is supposed to be quite unknown to Telemachus and the suitors, the poet must have imagined his kingdom to lie some distance away. See further N. G. L. Hammond, *Epirus* (Oxford, 1967), 378-9.

Wilamowitz was probably right in arguing (*Untersuchungen*, 6–7) that Mentes is modelled on Mentor, the elderly Ithacan in whose guise Athena subsequently appears to Telemachus (ii 268 ff. etc.). The resemblance of their names, probably to be understood as 'adviser' (from *men- 'think', as in μέμονα) can hardly be coincidence, and was presumably intended to underline the similarity of their roles (cf. Eurycleia/Eurynome/Eurymedusa, Melanthius/Melantho). But while it may be that Mentor-Athena had a more deep-rooted connection with the story of Odysseus' return (cf. xxii 205 ff., xxiv 502 ff.), Mentes is not to be dismissed as a colourless, insufficiently motivated *Doppelgänger* of Telemachus' other adviser. Mentes' part could be played only by a stranger with a fresh view of the situation. Athena's purpose is to goad Telemachus into action, and one of the chief obstacles to be overcome is the general Ithacan acquiescence in the suitors' outrageous conduct. The shocked reaction of a stranger is far more effective than any words which could be put in the mouth of Mentor who, however reluctantly, has accepted the situation hitherto. Telemachus' exposition of the problem throws light on his own character, and provides a natural vehicle for background information which needs to be conveyed to the audience. In this episode we may also see a foreshadowing of the later part of the poem, when Odysseus himself appears as a stranger in his own home.

In the *Iliad* the gods quite often appear on earth in the guise of mortals, to urge individual heroes to action and to give an unexpected turn to the development of events. But the alias is not normally maintained for a long conversation; Hermes' dealings with Priam (*Il.* xxiv 346 ff.) offer the closest parallel for Athena's procedure here.

106. δ' ἄρα: the particles mark a new and interesting stage in the story. ἔπειτα: apparently otiose; contrast the same formula at 144. We must take it as indicating the next thing which Athena observed, not the next thing to happen.

107. πεσσοῖσι: pebbles used for playing a board-game, counters; the commonly favoured translation 'draughts' is misleading. Such pastimes have no place in the *Iliad*. Sophocles (frr. 429, 479) is the earliest authority for the tradition which associated the invention of board-games with Palamedes; representations of Achilles and Ajax thus occupied were popular with black-figure vase-painters, and presumably reflect an episode in one of the Cyclic epics. In fact the Greeks probably owed their board-games to the Near East (cf. Pl. *Phdr.* 274 d); see further *RE* xiii 1900 (Lamer), H. J. R. Murray, *A History of Board-games other than Chess* (Oxford, 1952), 24 ff.

108. οὓς ἔκτανον αὐτοί: the brief phrase well conveys the wickedness of the suitors, who waste another's substance; like Odysseus' comrades (7–9), they have killed cattle to which they have no right.

109–12. The meal being prepared here is not consumed until 149 ff.; further preliminaries are described at 136 ff. κήρυκες and θεράποντες are free-born subordinates; since the same man may be both κῆρυξ and θεράπων (cf. xviii 424, *Il.* i 321), we should not follow the scholia in interpreting οἱ μέν (110) and οἱ δέ (111) in terms of a demarcation of duties between two distinct groups. Even in the *Iliad* we occasionally find a κῆρυξ employed in the preparations for feasting (*Il.* ix 174, xviii 558), a natural enough extension of the herald's duties in connection with sacrifices (e.g. *Il.* iii 245 ff., 268 ff.); this is very much commoner in the *Odyssey*. The conception of the herald as an official envoy or representative (e.g. xix 135, *Il.* i 334, vii 274 ff.) merges rather uncomfortably with his role as a kind of personal assistant, and we may wonder how far the Homeric picture corresponds to reality at any period. For a survey of the miscellaneous duties of the Homeric κῆρυξ see Ebeling, *Lexicon*. θεράπων is a more general term, 'assistant, attendant, follower, companion'; it denotes a non-kinsman of noble, but dependent, status (Patroclus was Achilles' θεράπων (*Il.* xviii 152)). θεράποντες must be prepared to turn their hands to many tasks which might also be done by slaves, according to the needs of the moment. See further G. Ramming, *Die Dienerschaft in der Odyssee* (Erlangen, 1973), 23 ff., 91 ff., 133 ff., P. A. L. Greenhalgh, 'The Homeric *Therapon* and *Opaon* and their Historical Implications', *BICS* xxix (1982), 81 ff.

110. ἄρ' οἶνον: it is tempting to follow Bentley in deleting ἄρ', and thus allow its proper force to the original initial ϝ of οἶνος: see above, 3 n. Particles have often been wrongly inserted to remedy what were regarded as metrical defects.

111–12. τραπέζας ... πρότιθεν: individual tables were regularly used at Greek banquets; they did not form part of the room's permanent furnishing, but were brought in for the guests and cleared away at the end of the meal. The common Odyssean formula παρὰ δὲ ξεστὴν ἐτάνυσσε τράπεζαν (i 138 etc.) seems to imply some kind of folding table, a type known from Hittite monuments, though no Greek example has been found; see further S. Laser, *Archaeologia* P, 56 ff., G. M. A. Richter, *The Furniture of the Greeks, Etruscans and Romans* (London, 1966), 63 ff. **πρότιθεν, τοὶ δέ**: this was the reading of Aristarchus; the alternative word-division, προτίθεντο ἰδέ, found in all our medieval MSS, surely represents an attempt to eliminate the unique πρότιθεν (impf., = προυτίθεσαν), comparable with μέθιεν (xxi 377) and ξύνιεν (*Il.* i 273): see Monro, *Homeric Dialect*, 5 § 5.

113 ff. There is a typical schema in Homer for scenes describing the reception of a visitor, whether friend or stranger; details may vary according to circumstances, but there emerges very clearly a general picture of what is regarded as the proper conventional treatment to be accorded to a ξεῖνος. A particularly good example is Nestor's description of the welcome accorded to him and Odysseus when they came to the palace of Peleus (*Il.* xi 765 ff.); it corresponds closely to what we find here. (1) The new arrival waits at the entrance until (2) one of the company notices him, (3) gets up from his seat and hastens to the doorway, (4) takes the visitor by the hand, (5) leads him in, (6) offers him a seat, (7) fetches food and invites him to eat; (8) after a meal come questions. There are many examples of such scenes in the *Odyssey*: well worth comparing are the

ξενια

descriptions of Telemachus' reception at Pylos (iii 5 ff.) and at Sparta (iv 20 ff.), and of Odysseus' welcome by Eumaeus (xiv 29 ff.). The emphasis or variation of particular details within the conventional framework serves to convey an impression of the household to which the visitor has come; here we should notice the way in which the poet underlines Telemachus' conscientiousness and his isolation among the crowd of potentially hostile suitors. See further W. Arend, *Scenen*, 34 ff., M. W. Edwards, 'Type-scenes and Homeric hospitality', *TAPhA* cv (1975), 61–7.

Telemachus' welcome marks the start of the first of the *Odyssey*'s many scenes of hospitality, the sphere in which the virtues of the heroic world most distinctively manifest themselves in peacetime (a rare condition). Generosity in feasting kinsmen and friends is natural enough, but hospitality towards strangers involves an element of risk and may be deemed a fair index of morality in general. The ambivalence of *xeinos*, both 'stranger' and 'guest, host, guest-friend', indicates the tensions inherent in such relationships; as Menelaus learnt to his cost, a host might occasionally have grounds to regret admitting even an apparently respectable stranger to his home, even though abuse of hospitality exposed the offender to the wrath of Zeus Xenios. But under normal circumstances such entertainment established a tie of guest-friendship which could be regarded as hereditary (cf. 175 ff.), its implications well illustrated by the behaviour of Glaucus and Diomedes, who consider themselves bound to refrain from fighting one another because their grandfathers had exchanged hospitality, and give each other valuable gifts instead (*Il.* vi 119 ff.). A well-established etiquette guides the dealings of host and guest until the latter has been set on his way to his next destination; its most noteworthy features, from the modern reader's point of view, are the practice of allowing the new arrival to remain incognito until he has eaten (potentially rather hazardous) and the custom of presenting him with a keepsake on departure. Though the material lavishness of Homeric hospitality can hardly correspond to historical reality, the poet's own world is surely reflected in the high value attached to the proper entertainment of strangers and in the system of manners deemed appropriate to such encounters; the experiences of modern travellers have repeatedly demonstrated the prevalence of similar customs in places where the provision of temporary accommodation has not been put on a business footing. See further Finley, *World*, 99 ff., Thornton, *People*, 38 ff., H. J. Kakridis, *La Notion de l'amitié et de l'hospitalité chez Homère* (Salonika, 1963), 86 ff.

113. Telemachus is named here for the first time in the *Odyssey*, but he is twice mentioned by name in the *Iliad* (ii 260, iv 354), and the detail should have been familiar to the poet's first audience. His name reflects his father's characteristic method of fighting; for Odysseus' skill at archery cf. viii 215 ff. (with Hainsworth's n.), xxi 393 ff., xxii 1 ff. The children of many Homeric heroes bear names which recall some aspect of their fathers' lives—Eurysaces (Ajax), Astyanax (Hector), Megapenthes (Menelaus), Iphianassa, Chrysothemis, and Laodice (Agamemnon), Pisistratus

COMMENTARY

(Nestor); the story of how Odysseus was named by his grandfather involves the same principle (xix 407–9; see above, 62 n.). See further von Kamptz, *Personennamen*, 31–2.

115–17. Telemachus' abstraction sets him apart from the suitors, intent on their diversions; he is already in a receptive frame of mind for Athena's plan, but the idea of taking the initiative against his unwanted guests has not occurred to him.

116. Cf. xx 225; ἔκλησιν θέωμεν xxiv 485. **μνηστήρων τῶν μέν:** for the article with μέν following the noun cf. *Il.* vii 461; the expression is strange, but probably results from the adaptation of a formulaic pattern, cf. 151 μνηστῆρες, τοῖσιν μέν

119–20. νεμεσσήθη . . . ἐφεστάμεν: the detail suggests Telemachus' hospitable instincts. We note that the poet does not envisage either a porter or any means for a visitor to announce his arrival.

121. See 104 n.

122. A common, but slightly puzzling, formula, used to introduce 125 speeches of very different content and length, when the character who is to speak has been the subject of the last verses. The metaphor of πτερόεντα more probably derives from archery than from ornithology; the feathers of an arrow help it to fly straight (for πτερόεις, 'well-feathered', applied to arrows cf. *Il.* iv 117, v 171), and the image of utterance as an arrow is common in Greek (e.g. A. *Supp.* 446, *Eu.* 676, Pi. *O.* ix 11–12, E. *Supp.* 456, fr. 499 N., Pl. *Smp.* 219 b, Luc. *Nigr.* 36). Some have held that ἔπεα πτερόεντα are apt, well chosen words, flying straight to the listener's comprehension, but in view of the variety of utterance so described the epithet is probably better understood as expressing an essential characteristic of the thing to which it is applied (cf. λαμπρὸν φάος, νὺξ ἐρεβεννή); the poet who coined the phrase was attempting to answer the question how words pass from speaker to listener, and any word, once uttered, is πτερόεν. See further Hainsworth on viii 346, Hoekstra on xiii 165. Russo on xvii 57, M. Parry, 'About Winged Words', *CPh* xxxii (1937), 59 ff. (= *Homeric Verse*, 414 ff.), M. Durante, ' "Epea pteroenta": La parola come "cammino" in immagini greche e vediche', *RAL* xiii (1958), 3–14 (= R. Schmitt (ed.), *Indogermanische Dichtersprache* (Wege der Forschung, clxv, Darmstadt, 1968), 242–60), J. Latacz, 'ἄπτερος μῦθος—ἄπτερος φάτις: ungeflügelte Worte?', *Glotta* xlvi (1968), 27 ff. **φωνήσας:** intrans., both μιν and ἔπεα being governed by προσηύδα.

123–4. Χαῖρε: cf. iv 60; 'welcome', 'greetings', do less than justice to the meaning; in such contexts the imperat. expresses a wish for the other's general physical and mental well-being. See further J. Latacz, *Zum Wortfeld 'Freude' in der Sprache Homers* (Heidelberg, 1966), 50. **φιλήσεαι:** the emphasis is on the outward expression of φιλία, 'you will be treated kindly'. **αὐτὰρ ἔπειτα κτλ:** similarly Nestor (iii 69–70), Menelaus (iv 60–2), and Eumaeus (xiv 45–7) postpone questions until their guests have eaten. Breaches of this convention may however be observed: Calypso asks Hermes to state his business before she feeds him (v 85 ff.), but does not get

92

an answer until he has finished (95 ff.), and Alcinous is snubbed by Odysseus for questioning him before he has satisfied his hunger (vii 215 ff.).   ὅττεό σε χρή: this construction of χρή (originally a noun) with acc. of the person and gen. of the thing needed is peculiar to the Epic dialect; see further Chantraine, *Grammaire*, ii 40 § 49 (F).

125. Παλλάς: see Hainsworth on vi 328.

128. δουροδόκης: the word occurs nowhere else, nor any later synonym. The ancients supposed that the spear-shafts rested in the flutings of the columns; alternatively, we might envisage a rack or a large jar (like an umbrella-stand) set against the pillar. The detail is added, it seems, for the sake of the reference to the absent master of the house.   ἄλλα: 'as well, besides'.

130. θρόνον: the grandest type of Greek chair, generally provided with a straight back and armrests: cf. Ath. 192 ef (evidently quoting from earlier sources): ὁ γὰρ θρόνος αὐτὸ μόνον ἐλευθέριός ἐστιν καθέδρα . . . ὁ δὲ κλισμὸς περιττοτέρως κεκόσμηται ἀνακλίσει. τούτων δ' εὐτελέστερος ἦν ὁ δίφρος. This type of chair is regularly offered to guests as a mark of honour: cf. iv 51, v 86, 195, vii 162–3, *Il.* xviii 389, xxiv 522, 553. Telemachus himself sits on a κλισμός (132), described by ancient scholars as a light easy chair with a sloping back. But the distinction between the two is not always kept clear and the two terms are sometimes used as if they were synonyms: cf. *Il.* xi 623, 645, xxiv 515, 597. See further G. M. A. Richter, *Furniture of the Greeks, Etruscans and Romans* (London, 1966), 13 ff., S. Laser, *Archaeologia* P, 38 ff.   λῖτα: 'fine cloth' (not necessarily linen, *pace* LSJ); it is uncertain whether this form should be regarded as acc. sg. masc. or n. pl.; cf. *Il.* xviii 352, xxiii 254 ἑανῷ λιτί: see further Heubeck on x 353, Frisk, *GEW*, Chantraine, *Dictionnaire* s.v. λίς.

131. θρῆνυς: it is undoubtedly comfortable to have a rest for the feet when sitting in a high chair; in addition, and perhaps more important, a footstool would keep the feet clear of the general mess, including puddles of wine from libations, inevitable during a Homeric banquet.

132–3. ποικίλον: the epithet suggests wood of contrasting colours, or a contrast of materials, e.g. wood and ivory.   ἔκτοθεν ἄλλων | μνηστήρων: 'apart from the others, the suitors'; ἄλλος, as often, is followed by an epexegetic noun. Telemachus is constantly aware of the problem presented by the suitors.

134. ἀδήσειεν: the MSS are divided between this form and ἀηδήσειεν; the meaning is not affected. If ἀδήσειεν is sound, it must come from the same verb as the rather puzzling pf. ptcp. ἀδηκότες (xii 281 (see Heubeck's n.), *Il.* x 98, 312, 399, 471) and is presumably to be explained by reference to ἄδην as 'become sated, disgusted with'. ἀηδήσειεν seems more natural, though ἀηδέω, the denominative of ἀηδής, is not otherwise attested in Hesychius. Confusion probably arose when the contracted Ionic form ἀδέω replaced ἀηδέω. See further *LfgrE* s.v. ἀηδέω, Wackernagel, *Kl. Schr.*, i 613–4.   ὑπερφιάλοισι: an epithet frequently applied to the suitors, even by their leader, Antinous (xxi 289); it implies violence and insolence. Its

COMMENTARY

derivation is uncertain; it is generally connected with ὑπερφυής, but this is not wholly convincing, and the ancient derivation from ὑπὲρ φιάλην, 'running over the cup', has found some recent supporters: see further Frisk, *GEW*, Chantraine, *Dictionnaire*.

135. ἀποιχομένοιο ἔροιτο: a very unattractive hiatus; Bentley's conjecture ἀποιχομένοι' ἐρέοιτο eliminates this, and avoids neglect of ϝ in ἔρ(ϝ)οιτο: but cf. 405, iii 77.

136 ff. Descriptions of meals are common in the *Odyssey*; the emphasis lies on the details of preparation, and hospitality rather than gastronomy is the keynote; the food itself is not regarded as interesting. Conversation among the company after the meal provides a natural context for many of the stories told in the *Odyssey*, above all Odysseus' account of his adventures (ix–xii); it foreshadows the later popularity of the symposium as a literary genre. See further Arend, *Scenen*, 68 ff., and on practical details G. Bruns, *Archaeologia* Q, 45 ff.

136–40. = iv 52–6, vii 172–6, xv 135–9 (and x 368–72, but the passage must be a late interpolation, being absent from a papyrus and many medieval MSS). This stereotyped description of a meal is normally an element in the welcome extended to a guest; exceptionally, in a different context at xv 135 ff. Here it merges into the description of the feast which was being prepared when Athena-Mentes arrived (109–12).

136. The heroes of the *Iliad* do not wash their hands before meals, but the custom is general in the *Odyssey*, and observed even if the diner has just emerged from the bath (iv 48 ff., xvii 86 ff.); this suggests that it has, at least in part, a religious significance: see further R. Ginouvès, *Balaneutiké* (Paris, 1962), 151–2.

138. παρὰ ... τράπεζαν: see above, 111 n.

139–40. The scholia on iv 55–6 note that Aristarchus regarded these lines as suspect: εἰκότως δὲ νῦν τὰ περὶ τῆς ταμίας παράκειται· οὐ γὰρ ἐν τῷ ξενίζεσθαι παρὰ Τηλεμάχῳ τὴν Ἀθηνᾶν· ἐπεισεληλύθασι γὰρ οὗτοι [Telemachus and Pisistratus] τοῖς περὶ τὸν Μενέλαον, ἐξ ἀρχῆς δὲ παρὰ τῷ Τηλεμάχῳ πάρεστιν ὁ Μέντης. Ath. (193 b) also criticizes the passage: εἰ γὰρ εἴδατα παρέθηκεν ἡ ταμίη, δῆλον ὡς κρεάτων λείψανα τυγχάνοντα, τὸν δαιτρὸν οὐκ ἔδει παρεισφέρειν. 139 is inoffensive, though it duplicates 147, but 140 is pointless, if not positively misleading: it is appropriate where a meal is produced at short notice, but Mentes has arrived just as the feast was about to be served, and it would be absurd to feed the visitor on a combination of left-overs and freshly roasted meat. The couplet has surely been inserted to increase the resemblance to similar passages elsewhere; in the same way 141–2 have been added after iv 56, where they are equally unsuitable (see n.).

141. κρειῶν: this form has perhaps replaced an earlier κρεάων; but see Chantraine, *Grammaire*, i 109–10 § 89. **πίνακας:** 'plates' (of wood or metal), not, as has been suggested, 'slices of meat'.

143. αὐτοῖσιν: Telemachus and Mentes.

144–324. While the suitors are intent on feasting and song, Telemachus and Athena-Mentes talk. The latter identifies himself, gets Telemachus to

94

explain the situation, and advises measures for dealing with the suitors. He then departs; his sudden disappearance leads Telemachus to suspect that his visitor was divine.

144. Cf. xx 160. The suitors enter while Mentes and Telemachus are being served.

145. κατὰ κλισμούς τε θρόνους τε: on this common Odyssean formula see Hoekstra on xv 134; on the difference between θρόνος and κλισμός see 130 n. ἐξείης perhaps implies some order of precedence, so that those of higher rank occupy the θρόνοι.

147. Cf. xvi 51 σῖτον δ' ἐσσυμένως παρενήνεεν [-ον] ἐν κανέοισιν, the only other place where the cpd. παρανηνέω occurs; cf. ἐπενήνεον (*Il.* vii 428); at *Il.* xxiii 139 νήνεον is a weakly attested variant for νήεον. -νήνεον is hard to explain, and has often been altered to -νήεον, νηέω being the Homeric form of νέω; but the unanimity of the MSS suggests that if -νήνεον is a mistake, it is an early one, and may go back to the poet. See further Hoekstra on xvi 51, Frisk, *GEW* s.v. -νέω, Chantraine, *Dictionnaire* s.v. νηέω. **δμῳαί:** women slaves; see further 398 n. **κανέοισι:** normally translated 'baskets', but 'bowls' might be better, as they are sometimes said to be of metal (x 355, *Il.* xi 630).

148. = iii 339, xxi 271, *Il.* i 470, ix 175. A first-century papyrus (P. 106 = Pack² 1024) and a few medieval MSS omit the line; its position varies, some MSS putting it after 146, a few after 149. The external evidence thus strongly suggests post-Aristarchean interpolation. Moreover, the mixing of the wine was described earlier (110), and since Telemachus and his guest have already been served (143), this stage in the preparations should now be over. Some MSS actually add a further line (148a = iii 340, xxi 272, *Il.* i 471, ix 176). The passage thus well illustrates the common tendency to assimilate typical scenes and partially parallel passages by interpolation, which often imports details inappropriate to the particular context; cf. 139-40. For the convention that κοῦροι, boys or young men of noble birth, serve the wine cf. also xv 141, *Il.* xx 234 (with schol.); see further H. Jeanmaire, *Couroi et Courètes* (Lille, 1939), 30-1. **ἐπεστέψαντο:** 'they filled to the brim', cf. ii 431, *Il.* viii 232 κρητῆρας ἐπιστεφέας οἴνοιο; Alcm. 19. 1-2 τραπέσδαι μακωνιᾶν ἄρτων ἐπιστεφοίσαι: cf. schol. on *Il.* i 470 ἐπεστέψαντο· ὑπὲρ τὸ χεῖλος ἐπλήρωσαν, ὡς δοκεῖν ἐστέφθαι τῷ ὑγρῷ; references to other ancient discussions of this expression are collected by Erbse ad loc. Vergil evidently found the phrase suggestive: cf. *G.* ii 528 'cratera coronant', *A.* i 724 'vina coronant', iii 525-6 'magnum cratera corona | induit'; there is no reason to suppose he misunderstood its meaning.

149. οἱ: includes Telemachus and Mentes as well as the suitors.

150. This very common formula marks the conclusion of the first part of the meal; conversation is postponed until hunger and thirst are satisfied and the company relaxes over their wine. **ἐξ:** with ἕντο, 'they had put from them, dismissed, i.e. satisfied.'

152. Cf. xxi 430. **μολπή:** dance or rhythmical movement (including ball games, cf. vi 101) combined with song. Aristarchus denied this musical element to μολπή and μέλπομαι, athetizing *Il.* i 474 where μέλποντες must include singing; but this is arbitrary, and a general survey of the other contexts where μολπή and μέλπομαι occur strongly suggests that singing is involved. Here μολπή would be tautologous with ὀρχηστύς if it did not imply song. See further M. Wegner, *Archaeologia* U, 42–3.   **τά**: attracted to the gender of its predicate.   **ἀναθήματα δαιτός**: a puzzling expression, perhaps 'proper accompaniments of feasting'; similarly the lyre is δαιτὸς συνήορος (viii 99) and δαιτὸς ἑταίρην (xvii 271). See further *LfgrE* s.v. ἀνάθημα.

153–4. The professional bard is an important figure in the *Odyssey*, by contrast with the *Iliad*, where the musicians are gifted amateurs, Apollo and the Muses on Olympus (*Il.* i 603–4), Paris (iii 54) and Achilles (ix 186 ff.) on earth (though the legendary Thamyris (ii 595 ff.) sounds like a professional). The outstanding practitioner is Demodocus in viii, and we cannot fail to observe the respect and sympathy shown to him by Odysseus; hence Alcinous' comparison of Odysseus himself to a skilled bard (xi 368–9) is peculiarly apt. We should also note the curious responsibility which Agamemnon assigns to a minstrel (iii 267 ff.), and the poet's interesting choice of a simile drawn, unusually, from his own craft at perhaps the most critical moment in the story (xxi 406 ff.). It is obviously debatable how far any historical reality is reflected in the Odyssean picture. The place (if any) of professional bards in the Mycenaean world must be a matter for conjecture, but the position of Hesiod, whose poetry was a sideline to his smallholding, was very likely nearer to life as the poet knew it than that of Phemius or Demodocus. See further Hainsworth on viii 62 ff., Schadewaldt, 'Die Gestalt des homerischen Sängers', *Welt*, 54 ff., H. Maehler, *Die Auffassung des Dichterberufs im frühen Griechentum bis zur Zeit Pindars* (Hypomnemata, iii, Göttingen, 1963), 21 ff. Demodocus is blind (viii 62 ff.), as Homer himself was supposed to have been (cf. *h.Ap.* 172–3),[3] but there is no reason to think that Phemius is; 153 does not mean that he could not have found his instrument for himself, but represents a way of conveying an order to sing (rather than a courteous gesture). The poet emphasizes, both here and in xxii (351 ff.), that Phemius is not among the suitors' henchmen.

153. **κίθαριν**: in Homer κίθαρις and φόρμιγξ are treated as synonymous, cf. 155 φορμίζων, *Il.* xviii 569–70. The instrument had a body of wood and a sound-box made of, or shaped like, a tortoise's shell, with ox-hide stretched over the face and two curved horns rising from it, joined by a cross-bar

---

[3] On the interpretation of these lines cf. W. Burkert (*Arktouros: Hellenic Studies Presented to B. M. W. Knox* (Berlin–New York, 1979), 57): 'Most modern interpreters ... seem to acquiesce in the assumption that this is some anonymous Chian poet speaking, accidentally blind, otherwise unknown. This overlooks the implications of verse 173, with the poet "all of whose songs are the very best among posterity". What a strange claim for an obscure, anonymous author! The very best poet of all times, the absolute classic: this is meant to be Homer.'

carrying the pegs, to which strings of gut were attached. Phemius' lyre should be the four-stringed instrument often represented on Geometric vases; the Greeks regarded this as the original form, though seven- and eight-stringed lyres had in fact been in use among the Minoans and Mycenaeans. The traditional date of the change to seven strings, associated with Terpander's victories at the Spartan Carneia some time in the seventh century, receives some support from vase-paintings; but though the poet of the *Odyssey* may thus himself have known the seven-stringed instrument, he could hardly fail to be aware that it was an innovation. The early lyre had a very limited compass, and its music was simply an adjunct to song; significantly Homer has no separate noun for a cithara-player: the musician is the ἀοιδός. Phemius' manner of delivery should probably be imagined as a recitative over a range of four notes (one for each string). See further Wegner, *Archaeologia* U, 1 ff., M. L. West, 'The Singing of Homer', *JHS* ci (1981), 113 ff.

154. **Φημίῳ:** 'the man who spreads report, the rich in tales'; like many Homeric minor characters Phemius bears a name indicating the conception which the poet wished to arouse in the listener's mind. On this important aspect of Homeric style see further H. Mühlestein, *SMEA* ix (1969), 67–94, von Kamptz, *Personennamen*, 25 ff.

155. **ἤ τοι:** better ἤτοι, an emphatic equivalent of preparatory μέν; see further Ruijgh, τε épique, 198–200.   **ἀνεβάλλετο:** for this use with ἀείδειν to mark the beginning of a recitation cf. viii 266, xvii 262. The scholiast on viii 266 glosses it with ἀνεκρούετο, προοιμιάζετο, 'struck up, played some preliminary notes as a prelude'; we should not envisage anything elaborate.

156. Telemachus takes advantage of the fact that the rest of the company are concentrating on Phemius' song, which thus provides some privacy for his conversation.

157. = iv 70, xvii 592. According to the scholia on iv 70 Aristarchus read πευθοίατο ἄλλοι; this produces an unusual hiatus at the end of the fifth foot (see Chantraine, *Grammaire*, i 91–2 § 39), but cf. iv 236 (ἄλλοτε ἄλλῳ) and n. There is nothing unhomeric in this use of the article with ἄλλος: see Chantraine, *Grammaire*, ii 162 § 242, Monro, *Homeric Dialect*, 228 § 260.

158 ff. Telemachus' words reflect his embarrassment at the suitors' behaviour (cf. 119–20, 132–4), and are evidently intended to forestall any reproach at his allowing such disorder in his house. He obviously behaves somewhat unconventionally in speaking so freely to his guest before he knows whom he is entertaining, but some apology is called for, since the suitors behave as if the place belonged to them, and yet ignore the visitor. His reluctance to name his father is noticeable.

163. Some editors punctuate with a strong stop at the end of this line, but it seems simpler and smoother to treat it as a conditional protasis which takes on the force of a wish from its context: see further D. Tabachovitz, *Homerische εἰ-Sätze* (Lund, 1951), 60 ff.

164–5. **ἐλαφρότεροι . . . ἀφνειότεροι:** the only Homeric example of the use of

97

the double comparative where two qualities are contrasted in the same subject: see Kühner–Gerth, ii 312 § 541 (5).

166–8. Telemachus denies what he most wishes: cf. 413–16, iii 241–2; similarly Eumaeus tells of hopes raised only to be disappointed (xiv 122 ff., 372 ff.). **μόρον**: cognate acc., cf. ix 303 ἀπωλόμεθ' αἰπὺν ὄλεθρον. **εἴ περ**: 'even if', a common Epic use; cf. ii 246, xiii 138, 143, *Il.* ii 597, iii 25, x 225, xi 116, xii 223, 245, xxii 389. **φῆσιν**: elsewhere (xi 128 = xxiii 275) φῇ is used; on this and similar forms see Chantraine, *Grammaire*, i 426 § 219. The use of the pure subjunctive with εἰ to express the idea that the contingency envisaged is indefinite, one which may happen repeatedly or not at all, is quite common in Homeric Greek, though it has disappeared from Attic-Ionic: see Chantraine, *Grammaire*, ii 279 § 410, Monro, *Homeric Dialect*, 266 § 292 (b).

169–70. The request to a stranger to introduce himself, generally after a meal, is a typical feature of the *Odyssey*'s many scenes of hospitality: e.g. iii 71 ff., viii 550 ff., xiv 187 ff., xvi 57 ff. The nearest counterpart in the *Iliad* occurs when warriors on the battlefield recount their family history, e.g. vi 121 ff., xxi 150 ff.

169. εἰπὲ καὶ ἀτρεκέως κατάλεξον: formulae consisting of a pair of virtual synonyms are an important feature of Homeric style, well studied by K. O'Nolan, 'Doublets in the *Odyssey*', *CQ* xxviii (1978), 23–7.

170. = x 325, xiv 187, xv 264, xix 105, xxiv 298. **τίς πόθεν εἰς ἀνδρῶν**: often taken as 'Who are you and where do you come from?', though the following question is then superfluous. It is better to take πόθεν closely with ἀνδρῶν, referring to descent: cf. xvii 373 πόθεν γένος εὔχεται εἶναι, xix 162; the meaning then is 'Who are you and who was your father?' See further J. Wackernagel, *Vorlesungen über Syntax*², i (Basel, 1926), 299–300, who notes that precisely this type of question is found in Sanskrit epic and in the oldest parts of the *Avesta* (cf. 30 n.).

171–3. = xiv 188–90, cf. xvi 57–9, 222–4. The lines were absent from some ancient editions and regarded as suspect by Aristarchus who argued that while these were proper questions for Eumaeus to put to the ragged Odysseus, whose appearance would make it surprising that he had found a passage, they were out of place here (see schol. on xiv 188). Aristarchus thus postulated an interpolation of a common type (see 148 n.), and there is much to be said for this view. The point of Eumaeus' interrogation is obscured if we have been led to suppose that these enquiries are normal Ithacan custom, and it would better express Telemachus' preoccupation with his missing father if he proceeded without delay to ask if his visitor had known Odysseus. 185–6, likewise suspected in antiquity, answer the questions put here; the two passages stand or fall together.

171. ὁπποίης: indirect interrogative, as if κατάλεξον had immediately preceded; the direct question is resumed with πῶς.

172. εὐχετόωντο: the range of meanings conventionally ascribed to εὔχομαι and its cognates (see LSJ) is a long-standing source of difficulty, and much ingenuity has been expended in explaining how the same verb can mean both 'boast' and 'pray'. The problem seems to have been solved by L. C. Muellner (*The Meaning of Homeric* εὔχομαι *through its Formulas* (Innsbrücker Beiträge zur Sprachwissenschaft, xiii, Innsbruck, 1976)), who argues that it is 'a functionally marked word for "say" '; in secular contexts (as here) it means 'say (proudly, accurately, contentiously, as the case may be)', in sacral 'speak, say sacredly'.

173. Usually taken as a rather naïve joke, except by proponents of the view that Homer's Ithaca is really Lefkas (see above pp. 63-4) which, according to Strabo (451-2), was a peninsula until *c*.650 when the Corinthians severed the isthmus connecting it to the mainland.

175-7. Not a conventional question.

176. ἴσαν: better taken as impf. of εἶμι than as plupf. of οἶδα; for the construction with acc. and no preposition cf. xviii 194 εὖτ' ἂν ἴῃ ... χόρον. **δῶ:** this word, which clearly functions as a substantive, occurs 23 times in Homer, always at the end of the line with a sg. adj. or gen. and always acc. sg., except at i 392, where it is nom. sg. (cf. Hes. *Th.* 933: acc. pl.). Ancient scholars interpreted it as an abbreviation of δῶμα (like κρῖ for κριθή). It has been argued that it was originally a directional suffix, meaning 'to', as the parallelism between ἡμέτερόνδε and ἡμέτερον δῶ might suggest, but this theory has come to seem less attractive with the discovery of Mycenaean *do-de* evidently meaning 'to the house' in Linear B tablets from Thebes. See further Hoekstra on xiii 4, Heubeck on xxiv 115, Szemerényi, *SMEA* xx (1979), 224-5, Frisk, *GEW*, Chantraine, *Dictionnaire*, *LfgrE*. On Homeric vocabulary for houses see M. O. Knox, ' "House" and "palace" in Homer', *JHS* xc (1970), 117-20.

177. ἐπίστροφος: a puzzling Homeric *hapax*, though it was read by Aristophanes at viii 163 instead of ἐπίσκοπος, and Ἐπίστροφος is a popular name for minor characters in the Catalogue of Ships (*Il.* ii 517, 692, 856). The scholia offer various explanations: concerned, respectful, hospitable; respected and attracting men to him; inclined to go around visiting (ἐπερχόμενος καὶ ἐπιδημῶν); the last seems the most attractive. Aeschylus (*Ag.* 397) evidently understood the word as 'conversant with' (though we cannot be sure that he had this passage in mind), but this rendering, though commonly adopted, is not quite satisfactory here, unless we take it as a litotes.

179 ff. Mentes' cover-story is obviously comparable with the fictions which Odysseus himself devises (xiii 256 ff., xiv 199 ff., xvii 419 ff., xix 172 ff., xxiv 304 ff.); note, in particular, the reference to a meeting with Odysseus himself long ago (cf. xix 185 ff., xxiv 265 ff.).

180. Ἀγχιάλοιο: cf. viii 112, *Il.* v 609; the compound might be thought slightly inept as a personal name, but cf. Ἀμφίαλος, Ὠκύαλος, Εὐρύπυλος, Ὑψιπύλη; see further von Kamptz, *Personennamen*, 10. **δαΐφρονος:** see above, 48-9 n. **εὔχομαι:** see above, 172 n.

181. ἀτάρ: see 9 n. **Ταφίοισι:** see 105 n.

182. ὧδε: 'so, just as you see'.

183-4. Trading is evidently not regarded as dishonourable; a rather different attitude seems to be implied at viii 159–64, though perhaps the objection is to an obsession with profits rather than to trade as such.   πλέων: monosyllable by synizesis; the formula πλέων ἐπὶ οἴνοπα πόντον elsewhere (iv 474, *Il.* vii 88) occupies the second part of the line.   οἴνοπα: a puzzling epithet, frequently applied to the sea and twice to oxen (xiii 32, *Il.* xiii 703, in both places in the dual). The conventional rendering 'wine-dark' follows the interpretation of ancient scholars; though it does not inspire complete confidence, it is more convincing than alternative suggestions. See further Hainsworth on v 132.   ἐπ' ἀλλοθρόους ἀνθρώπους: cf. iii 302, xiv 43, xv 453.

184. Τεμέσην: an ancient variant Τάμασιν (or -σον) is recorded. Mentes' destination was variously identified in antiquity with Tempsa in Bruttium and Tamassos in Cyprus. Strabo (255–6) favours Tempsa, but though it might have been an entrepôt there is no evidence of copper-workings (see *RE* V A 459–60 (Philipp)), while Cyprus was famous for its copper (cf. Lat. *cuprum = aes Cyprium*). It is not a serious difficulty that Tamassos (Politiko) lies in the centre of the island, whereas Mentes' words would more naturally suggest a port; the poet simply named a place which he associated with copper. (K. Hadjioannou (*AA* lxxxi (1966), 205–10) sees a reference to the important Cypriot town of Alasia, and would read ἔς τ' Ἄλασιν but the τε is awkward, and emendation unnecessary).   αἴθωνα: the epithet seems to have been extended to iron from copper; against the conventional interpretation 'flashing' R. J. Brown (*Glotta* lxi (1983), 31 ff.) argues persuasively that αἴθων is properly 'brown', its metaphorical use arising from the association between a sunburnt skin and manly, spirited behaviour; see also Frisk, *GEW*, Chantraine, *Dictionnaire* s.v. αἴθω, *LfgrE* s.v. αἴθοπ-. On Homeric metallurgy see further D. H. F. Gray, 'Metal-working in Homer', *JHS* lxxiv (1954), 1 ff., R. J. Forbes, *Archaeology* K.

185–6. 185 = xxiv 308. The lines were athetized by Aristophanes and Aristarchus, and omitted in some ancient editions; they are evidently intended to answer 171–3. The rest of the poem throws no light on the topography of 186. The harbour Rheithron is not mentioned elsewhere; the Attic ῥεῖθρον, instead of the normal Ionic ῥέεθρον, is noteworthy. Neion may represent a misunderstanding of the obscure epithet ὑπονήϊος applied to Ithaca at iii 81. Odysseus speaks of Mount Neriton as the outstanding feature of his island (ix 22, cf. xiii 351, *Il.* ii 632); the names are oddly alike.

187–8. With Mentes' claim to a longstanding relationship of guest-friendship with Odysseus we may compare the (disguised) Odysseus' own claim to have entertained Odysseus twenty years before (xix 185 ff.), which leads Penelope, once she has tested it, to treat the stranger as a confidant (253 ff.).

188–93. Mentes' detailed knowledge of Laertes' circumstances no doubt implies a long-standing interest in Odysseus' family supporting his claim to be a πατρώϊος ξεῖνος, but the main purpose of this passage (incidentally noteworthy for its extensive use of enjambment) is to reveal that Laertes, familiar as Odysseus' father from the frequent use of the hero's patronymic in the *Iliad*, is still alive. This must surprise us, since already in the *Iliad* Odysseus is one of the senior chieftains (cf. *Il.* xxiii 790–1); we shall presently learn that Odysseus was already ruling in Ithaca before the Trojan War (ii 47). No doubt physical as well as mental vigour is needed for the exercise of power in the heroic world; but a chief who is supported by a loyal and competent son could, like Nestor and Priam, retain his position until an advanced age,[4] and we may be puzzled to account for Laertes' retirement, particularly since he is still active, despite the lapse of a further twenty years and the austerities to which he has subjected himself. Moreover, even a very frail old man might be expected to offer advice and moral support in the face of the problems which beset Penelope and Telemachus; yet Laertes' presence in the neighbourhood is not allowed to affect our sense of their isolation (though the arguments by which Eurycleia dissuades her mistress from seeking her father-in-law's help may strike the reader as hardly cogent (iv 735 ff., 754 ff.)). Conversely, Telemachus does not react to Mentes' words as if he were aware of an implied reproach for neglecting his grandfather; Laertes' misery is not treated as any direct concern of his. The poet has had to strike a delicate balance to account both for Laertes' non-involvement and for his continued survival. This improbable longevity is best explained as a device to avoid the awkward dilemma which his death would have created in the Nekuia: Odysseus could hardly have foregone all converse with his dead father, but such an episode would have greatly weakened the impact of the scenes with Anticleia and Tiresias. The reunion in xxiv (205 ff.) exploits this prolongation of Laertes' life, but should not be regarded as motivating it.

Unlike the fathers of other major Homeric heroes Laertes is an obscure figure; his name is unique, and its etymology mysterious: see further *RE* xii (1) 424 ff. (Lamer). His austere way of life is self-imposed, an expression of his grief for his son; cf. xi 187–96, xvi 138–45.

188. ἐξ ἀρχῆς: 'from of old', cf. ii 254, xi 438, xvii 69.

189. ἥρωα: ἥρως is applied very generally to men of noble birth: cf. 272 ἥρωας Ἀχαιούς.

190. ἐπ' ἀγροῦ: 'in the country'.

192. παρτιθεῖ: = παρατίθησιν, cf. *Il.* xiii 732; the accentuation is disputed: see Chantraine, *Grammaire*, i 298–9 § 138, Monro, *Homeric Dialect*, 18–19 § 18. **κατά:** with λάβῃσιν.

193. γουνόν: an obscure word, possibly to be connected with γόνυ and understood as 'hill, high ground'; see Frisk, *GEW*, Chantraine, *Dictionnaire*,

---

[4] We find parallels in Euripides for the situation implied here. In *Alc.* Admetus rules in Pherae though his father Pheres is still alive; in *Hipp.* Theseus rules in Troezen in the lifetime of his grandfather Pittheus, the former king; similarly in *Ba.* Pentheus has taken over from his grandfather Cadmus at Thebes; at *Andr.* 22–3 it is implied that Neoptolemus might have driven his grandfather Peleus to abdicate at Pharsalus. But we do not know whether Euripides had any grounds, apart from the evidence of the *Odyssey*, for regarding this as common practice in the heroic age.

LfgrE.   **ἀλωῆς:** it is odd that the same word can mean both 'cultivated ground, vineyard, orchard' (as here) and 'threshing floor'. Possibly its original sense was rather more general, so that it could be used of any plot of land unoccupied by buildings; or two different words may be involved. See further Frisk, *GEW*, Chantraine, *Dictionnaire*, *LfgrE*.

194. ἔφαντ': the subject is left vague.

195. βλάπτουσι κελεύθου: 'hinder him from his journey', cf. iv 380 πεδάᾳ καὶ ἔδησε κελεύθου, A. *Ag.* 120 βλαβέντα λοισθίων δρόμων.

196. Odysseus is here named for the first time in this conversation; we have been expecting this for some time, and it surely adds emphasis to Mentes' confident assertion.   **δῖος:** see Hainsworth on v 171.

198–9. An interesting mixture of truth and falsehood.

200 ff. The first of many predictions that Odysseus will soon be home: cf. ii 160 ff., xiv 158 ff., xv 172 ff., xvii 154 ff., xix 303 ff., 535 ff. Telemachus evidently regards it as no more than a confident expression of hope, and is not markedly cheered by it.

201. ἀθάνατοι: the lengthening of the first syllable of this common epic term reflects (as often) metrical convenience rather than necessity; Homeric language has synonyms in αἰὲν ἐόντες and αἰειγενέται. See further Wyatt, *Lengthening*, 79–80.

202. There is a nice irony in this disclaimer. In the *Iliad* μαντική, the gift of Apollo (*Il.* i 87), is restricted to the quasi-rational technique of inductive divination from omens, especially from the behaviour of birds in flight; the *Odyssey* also admits ecstatic prophecy in the symbolic vision of the hereditary Apolline seer Theoclymenus (xx 351 ff.).

204. ἔχῃσι: the subject must be δέσματα, and the lack of an expressed object is awkward; Cobet's cj. ἔ for τε is attractive.

205. The asyndeton adds weight to Mentes' words.

207–9. Telemachus' resemblance to his father is a recurrent theme: cf. iii 122–5, iv 141–6. It appears that he now looks more like Odysseus as the latter's friends remember him than Odysseus himself does, if we may judge by the ease with which Odysseus escapes recognition on his return to Ithaca.   **τόσος:** cf. 296–7.   **αἰνῶς:** 'strangely, uncannily'; cf. Nestor's reaction (iii 123) σέβας μ' ἔχει εἰσορόωντα.   **ἐπεί** introduces the reason why he can observe the likeness; there is a slight, but natural, ellipse. **τοῖον** emphasises θαμά.

213. πεπνυμένος: a standing epithet of Telemachus, restricted to occasions when he is about to speak; it is unlikely that πέπνυμαι is cognate with πνέω, though the two were easily confused; see further Hainsworth on viii 388, Chantraine, *Dictionnaire*.

215–16. Telemachus' reply is slightly surprising, but Mentes has practically answered his own question. For 216 cf. Men. fr. 227 αὐτὸν γὰρ οὐθεὶς οἶδε τοῦ ποτ' ἐγένετο, | ἀλλ' ὑπονοοῦμεν πάντες ἢ πιστεύομεν. The idea must already have been a commonplace, and the tone is surely mildly ironical, though Telemachus might well be somewhat diffident in asserting that the hero whom his visitor knows so much better and so much admires is in fact his father. **γόνον:** for the sense 'parentage, stock' cf. xi 234, xix 166. **ἀνέγνω:** 'gnomic' aor., used in general truths irrespective of time: see Chantraine, *Grammaire*, ii 185 § 273, Monro, *Homeric Dialect*, 67 § 78.

219. Cf. v 105 ff., xx 33.

222–3. 'Yet (sad as your father's fate is, and yours too at present), fame is assured to your race because of your own excellence'. **ὀπίσσω:** 'in the future'. **Πηνελόπεια:** here named for the first time; she is not mentioned in the *Iliad*. Her name is probably derived from πηνέλοψ, a particoloured duck. The theory that she was originally a bird-goddess has found some support, but is extremely speculative. Germain (*Genèse*, 468 ff.) has drawn attention to the monogamous habits of ducks which, whether wild or domesticated, remain inseparably paired with a single partner throughout their lives, so that in Chinese and Russian folklore the duck has become a symbol of marital fidelity; though there is no evidence of this notion in Greek, it is possible that the choice of such a name for an ideally faithful wife reflects the influence of a people whose folklore employed the symbolism of the duck thus. However, women's names were quite commonly derived from birds' names in Greek (see F. Bechtel, *Die historischen Personennamen* (Halle, 1917), 591), and the poet does not encourage us to attach any particular significance to Penelope's name. An alternative etymology was current in antiquity, from πήνη, 'thread'; this is quite unconvincing in itself, but it is possible that the story of Penelope's web (ii 93 ff. etc.) arose from false etymology from πήνη and λέπω or ὀλόπτω 'strip off', though it should be noted that none of these words is used in the account of Penelope's weaving. See further *RE* xxxvii 461 ff. (Wüst), Frisk, *GEW*, Chantraine, *Dictionnaire*, von Kamptz *Personennamen*, 275–6, M.-M. Mactoux, *Pénélope: Légende et mythe* (Paris, 1975), 233 ff.

224 ff. Mentes now raises the questions which Telemachus had earlier tried to forestall (158 ff.). He approaches the subject rather abruptly, as if he had only just noticed what was going on, and Telemachus cannot avoid explaining the situation in much more detail, and thus providing us with a clearer picture of the background. The topic is obviously painful to him, but Athena's purpose is to overcome his resignation and goad him into action, and she cannot achieve her ends without causing him some distress.

225. δαί: so Aristarchus; almost all our MSS read δέ. δαί is a colloquialism, frequent in Ar., but not found in formal prose, adding liveliness to the question: see further Denniston, *Particles*, 262–3; for the parechesis τίς δαίς, τίς δαί cf. 48 δαΐφρονι δαίεται and n. It has, however, been suspected that δαί is merely a conjecture, intended to eliminate the (relatively rare) hiatus δὲ ὅμιλος; whether δαί is properly to be regarded as Homeric is debatable, since in neither of the two other places where it was read by Aristarchus (xxiv 299, *Il.* x 408) does it have unanimous MS-support. See further Heubeck on xxiv 299, Erbse, *Beiträge*, 212–13. **τίπτε δέ σε χρεώ:** cf. *Il.* x 85; the phrase is slightly elliptical: understand e.g. ἱκάνει. It is used somewhat loosely: 'What has this to do with you?' The syntax of χρεώ is confused; its usage has to be compared with that of both χρείω and χρή, which though originally a noun came to be regarded as a verbal form: see further Chantraine, *Grammaire*, ii 40 § 49 (F), Shipp, *Studies*, 31.

226. For the three types of feast cf. xi 415. **εἰλαπίνη ἠέ**: the last vowel of εἰλαπίνη is amalgamated with the initial vowel of ἠέ to make one long syllable. Synecphonesis of this type is otherwise almost confined in Homer to the monosyllables δή, ἦ, μή, with a following long vowel or diphthong, and ἐπεὶ οὐ; other examples comparable to this are xxiv 247 ὄγχνη οὐ, *Il.* ii 651 Ἐνναλίῳ ἀνδρειφόντῃ, xvii 89 ἀσβέστῳ οὐδ', xviii 458 ἐμῷ ὠκυμόρῳ (v. l.); see further Erbse, *Beiträge*, 206–7. The metrical oddity, along with the absence of any opening interrogative particle (cf. iv 140, vi 149), contributes to the staccato effect of the questions. **γάμος**: a wedding-feast: cf. iv 3 ff., xxiii 131 ff., *Il.* xix 299. **ἔρανος**: a dinner to which all contribute (cf. iv 621 ff.), ruled out by the general extravagance and lack of restraint.

227–9. Cf. 133–4. The poet has not actually described the suitors doing anything which could be so regarded; he presents them through the eyes of his characters, and avoids a direct description of drunkenness and gluttony.

Some editors put a comma at the end of 226, and take τε in 227 as connective. But the use of τε, 'and', to co-ordinate clauses with different subjects is relatively rare in Homer, and particularly awkward here since the second clause is quite long. It is impossible to take ὥς τέ μοι κτλ· as a result clause; it does not suit the context, and this construction of ὥστε with a finite verb does not occur in Homer. It seems best to take ὥς τε as introducing a comparison, the participle here functioning like the substantive ὑβρισταί: cf. viii 491, x 295, 322. The sentence elucidates what has just been said, and asyndeton is normal with such an explanation. See Ruijgh, τε épique, 597–8 § 488, Chantraine, *Grammaire*, ii 325 § 473. **αἴσχεα**: 'disgraceful deeds', an unusual use of αἶσχος.

232. μέλλεν: 'was likely to be', i.e. presumably was. **ἀμύμων**: 'fine, beautiful': see above, 29 n.

233. κεῖνος ἀνήρ: Telemachus continues to refer to his father rather obliquely.

234 ff. Cf. xiv 366 ff., where Eumaeus develops the same theme.

234. ἑτέρως ἐβόλοντο: cf. *Il.* xv 51 βούλεται ἄλλη. For ἐβόλοντο cf. xvi 387 (with Hoekstra's n.), *Il.* xi 319; this form is attested also in Arcadian, and must be old. In many MSS the more familiar ἐβούλοντο has replaced it; ἐβάλοντο, recorded as an ancient variant, is also found.

235–6. περὶ πάντων | ἀνθρώπων: 'above all other men', cf. iv 231; the construction is not quite logical with ἄϊστος.

237–40. Cf. v 306 ff., xxiv 30 ff., A. *Ch.* 345–53, E. *Andr.* 1182 ff.

238. = iv 490, xiv 368. The logic of this passage is much improved if we follow Hennings in deleting this line. τῷ, 'in that case', in 239 must refer to 237: if Odysseus had died in Ithaca, the Παναχαιοί, dispersed after their return from Troy, could not have celebrated his funeral. The same illogicality has been imported into Eumaeus' speech in xiv, where this line is in place, but 369-70 (= i 239-40) must be a late interpolation, since they are absent from many MSS. On the tendency to increase the correspondence between similar passages, see above, 139-40 n. **φίλων:** 'those near and dear to him, his family', contrasted with ἑταῖροι, his comrades in arms. **ἐπεὶ πόλεμον τολύπευσε:** 'when he had finished winding the thread of war'. For the metaphor cf. 17. From Ar. *Lys.* 585-6 κἄπειτα ποῆσαι | τολύπην μεγάλην κᾆτ' ἐκ ταύτης τῷ δήμῳ χλαῖναν ὑφῆναι it seems clear that τολύπη is a ball of spun thread, not wool ready for spinning.

239-40. = xxiv 32-3; in the *Odyssey* Παναχαιοί occurs only in this formula. The dead are normally cremated in Homer; a barrow is raised over the pyre to keep alive the dead man's memory for generations to come: cf. iv 584 (a cenotaph), xi 74 ff., xii 13, xxiv 80 ff., *Il.* iv 176 ff., vi 419, vii 86-91 (a very clear exposition of the idea), 336, xvi 457, xxiii 245-8, xxiv 797-801. The idea is not peculiar to heroic poetry: cf. Plato Com. fr. 183 (Kock), (of Themistocles' tomb): ὁ σὸς δὲ τύμβος ἐν καλῷ κεχωσμένος | τοῖς ἐμπόροις πρόσρησις ἔσται πανταχοῦ, | οὓς ἐκπλέοντάς τ' εἰσπλέοντάς τ' ὄψεται | χὠπόταν ἅμιλλ' ᾖ τῶν νέων θεάσεται. The words of the dying Beowulf (*Beowulf* 2802 ff.), curiously close to *Od.* xxiv 80 ff., should remind us that it was not a peculiarly Greek idea. See further M. Andronikos, *Archaeologia* W, 32 ff., 107 ff.

240. ἤρατ': aor. of ἄρνυμαι, an artificial form which seems to have been substituted for ἤρετο by confusion with aor. of ἀείρω: see Chantraine, *Grammaire*, i 387-8 § 185, *LfgrE*.

241. = xiv 371 (see Hoekstra's n). **ἀκλειῶς:** 'without report, so that there is no news of him' (cf. ἀκλέα iv 728); the verbal antithesis with κλέος in 240 can scarcely be reproduced in English. (Shewring's 'ingloriously' is not really satisfactory, since it suggests 'ignominiously' rather than 'obscurely'.) **ἅρπυιαι ἀνηρείψαντο:** cf. xx 66, 77, where ἀνέλοντο θύελλαι and ἅρπυιαι ἀνηρείψαντο describe the same event. ἅρπυιαι are personified storm-winds; their genealogy is given by Hesiod (*Th.* 265 ff.); for further details see *LfgrE*. ἀνηρείψαντο is probably a cpd. of ἐρέπτομαι; though the simple verb is attested only in the sense 'devour', comparison with cognates in other languages suggests an earlier meaning 'snatch, seize'; see further Frisk, *GEW*, Chantraine, *Dictionnaire* s.v. ἐρέπτομαι. Confusion with ἐρείπω appears to have affected its spelling in Homeric MSS; on the MS-evidence for its spelling elsewhere see M. L. West on Hes. *Th.* 990. The obvious similarity between noun and verb in this formula suggests that the verb was intended to indicate the etymology of ἅρπυιαι; for similar glosses on the names of fabulous creatures cf. xii 85-6 (Scylla), 104 (Charybdis), Hes. *Th.* 252-3, 775-6, 901-3. The form ἀρέπυιαι, attested in the *EM* and found on a vase from Aegina (P. Kretschmer, *Griech. Vaseninschriften* (Gütersloh, 1894), 208) increases the resemblance; ἀνηρέ(ι)ψαντ' ἀρέπυιαι, which some would read here, would incidentally improve the metre by removing a rare word-break after the trochee of the fourth foot (violation of Hermann's Bridge).

242. ἄϊστος, ἄπυστος: an impressive asyndeton; for the use of co-ordinated adjectives with negative prefix in asyndeton cf. iv 788 ἄσιτος, ἄπαστος, *Il.* ix 63 ἀφρήτωρ ἀθέμιστος ἀνέστιος ἐστιν ἐκεῖνος, *h.Cer.* 200; see also Shipp, *Studies*, 11–12.

245–51. = xvi 122–8, cf. xix 130–5.

246–7. Cf. ix 21–6 (with Heubeck's n.), *h.Apoll.* 428–9. Same (Samos) is identified by Strabo (453) with Cephallenia, where there is still a town of that name; this well suits the location of the suitors' ambush (iv 671) ἐν πορθμῷ Ἰθάκης τε Σάμοιό τε παιπαλοέσσης. Doulichion is more difficult. Unlike Same, it is not part of the realm assigned to Odysseus in the Catalogue of Ships (*Il.* ii 631 ff.), but is said to be ruled, together with the Echinades, by Meges (625 ff.). Strabo (458) identifies it with Dolicha, one of the Echinades, a small, desolate island; but Doulichion in the *Odyssey* is rich in grass and grain (xvi 396 πολυπύρου ποιήεντος, cf. xiv 335) and sends almost as many suitors as Same, Zacynthus, and Ithaca (xvi 247–53), implying that it was both large and prosperous; the size of Meges' contingent at Troy (forty ships to Odysseus' twelve) supports this inference. These data suit Leucas well, and this identification is indirectly supported by Strabo's testimony (452) that the island had once had a different name and was renamed by Corinthian settlers. The only difficulty with this identification arises from xiv 334–5, where Odysseus speaks of breaking a journey from Thesprotia to Doulichion at Ithaca, which should imply that Doulichion lies south of Ithaca; but given the poet's generally imprecise conception of his hero's homeland (see above, pp. 63–4) this is not serious. The Odyssean data would also fit Cephallenia, but this identification (advocated by Hoekstra on xiv 335) creates difficulties for the *Iliad*; a mainland situation, in Acarnania or Elis, has also been suggested. See further *Companion*, 398 ff., R. Hope Simpson and J. F. Lazenby, *The Catalogue of the Ships in Homer's Iliad* (Oxford, 1970), 101, *LfgrE*. **ὑλήεντι Ζακύνθῳ:** cf. ix 24 ὑλήεσσα Ζάκυνθος; ὑλήεις is often treated as an adjective of two terminations. For the retention of a short final vowel before ζ with a name which could not otherwise be accommodated in the hexameter cf. *Il.* ii 824 δὲ Ζέλειαν, iv 103; see further Wyatt, *Lengthening*, 183 n. 1.

247. Cf. xv 510, xvi 124, xxi 346; see 388 ff. n.

249–50. Cf. xxiv 126. **ἀρνεῖται:** 'decline, refuse'. **στυγερὸν γάμον:** so Penelope herself describes it (xviii 272). **τελευτὴν | ποιῆσαι:** 'make an end', i.e. through marriage to one of the suitors.

251. Telemachus' exposition of the situation is now complete; his prediction sounds alarmist, but prepares us for the suitors' plot to murder him (iv 669 ff.). **οἶκον:** i.e. substance; cf. iv 318 ἐσθίεταί μοι οἶκος. **τάχα:** 'soon'; the meaning 'perhaps' is not Homeric.

252–305. This speech forms the centre-piece of i and sets in motion the subsequent train of events; it is the means by which Athena achieves her purpose in coming to Ithaca. Telemachus has to be convinced that he must, and can, act to restore order in his household, and he needs some guidance towards the ultimate solution of the problem presented by the suitors. The first part of the speech (253–69) is intended to make Telemachus more receptive to the instructions which follow; the poet was surely conscious of the oddity of Telemachus taking seriously such drastic advice from a complete stranger. Mentes does not spare the boy's feelings; sympathetic though his visitor is, Telemachus is left in no doubt that he is not half the man his father was, and that the advice he receives is based on a realistic assessment of his capabilities. In the second part (269 ff.) the plan which Athena outlined earlier (90 ff.) is further elaborated.

252. ἐπαλαστήσασα: presumably 'in indignation, deeply moved'; the sound effect ἐπαλαστησασα ... Παλλάς no doubt partly influenced the poet's use of this rare verb (not found again until A.R. (iii 369, 557)).

254. δεύῃ: 'you stand in need of'; the ancient variant δεύει, given by a few MSS, is to be understood as an impersonal 3rd pers. sg., equivalent to δεῖ.

255 ff. Athena's wish echoes Telemachus' own thoughts (115–17). The incomplete protasis is taken up again at 265.

256. δύο δοῦρε: the Homeric warrior is commonly, though not invariably, equipped with a pair of throwing spears.

257 ff. The first of a series of reminiscences preparing Telemachus for the father he is to meet in xvi; like Nestor (iii 120 ff.) and Helen (iv 240 ff.), Mentes emphasizes Odysseus' resourcefulness and the devotion which he inspired in his friends. It is not clear whether this disquieting story of Odysseus' quest for arrow-poison, so much at odds with the normal Odyssean conception of the god-fearing hero, is meant to be taken as a real episode in Odysseus' biography or as Athena's *ad hoc* invention. Odysseus does not use a bow for fighting in the *Iliad*, where it is evidently regarded as no proper weapon for a major hero; nor does he even compete in the archery contest at Patroclus' funeral games (*Il.* xxiii 850–83), though Telemachus' name presupposes that Odysseus took pride in this skill (see 113 n.). In the *Odyssey* his normal weapons are spear and sword, and he is presented as an archer in only two other places, among the Phaeacians, to whom he boasts of, but does not demonstrate, his prowess (viii 214–33: see Hainsworth on 215–18), and when he exacts his revenge from the suitors (xxi, xxii). Nowhere else in Homer is arrow-poison explicitly mentioned, even in connection with hunting, though its use may be implied at *Il.* iv 218, where Machaon sucks out Menelaus' arrow-wound, the result of a gross violation of the solemnly agreed truce, and thus peculiarly likely to raise suspicions of a tactic normally deemed illicit. Heracles uses arrows poisoned with the blood of the Hydra against Geryon (Stesich. *SLG* S 15 (*LGS* 56 E) ii 1 ff.) and against the centaurs (Apollod. ii 85–6, 152), but these are monsters, not men. Mentes indicates that this early application of chemical warfare might be thought unethical (264), and the detail calls to mind the unscrupulous Odysseus of Attic tragedy. In the scholia it is suggested that the poet was here preparing the ground for Odysseus' slaughter of the suitors, since the use of arrow-poison would make it much easier for every shot to prove fatal; this may well be right. In the event the poet preferred a more heroic conception, and Odysseus achieves his victory by nerve and superb marksmanship. See further F. Dirlmeier, 'Die Giftpfeile des Odysseus', *SHAW* 1966, 2, Clay, *Wrath*, 71–2.

Only relatively few plants are suitable sources for arrow-poison, which must not only be lethal in small quantities but also rapid in its effect on the heart or nervous system. Though several plants grow in Greece which a modern toxicologist, even with relatively primitive apparatus, could use for this purpose, their poisonous properties were in general not appreciated in antiquity, and the only possibility seems to be black hellebore (*Helleborus orientalis*). See further O. Schmiedeberg, *Über die Pharmaka in der Ilias u. Odyssee* (Strasburg, 1918), 14–25, where details of the manufacturing procedure may be found.

Ephyra is also mentioned as a source of poison at ii 328–9. It was a fairly common place-name (cf. Str. 338), but only two towns need to be considered here, both in western Greece: Thesprotian Ephyra, later called Κίχυρος (cf. Th. i 46. 4), and a town in Elis. If the Taphians' home is indeed Corcyra (see above, 105 n.), it seems more likely that Thesprotian Ephyra is meant; though Corcyra is not on the direct homeward route from Thesprotian Ephyra to Ithaca, both places lie well north of Ithaca, whereas Odysseus' route would be rather circuitous if he came from Elis.

259. Ἴλου: a nonentity, not mentioned elsewhere; his father Mermerus, son of Jason and Medea, has connections with both Elis and Ephyra.

260. θοῆς: the commonest Homeric epithet for ships; see further C. Kurt, *Seemännische Fachausdrücke bei Homer* (Göttingen, 1979), 47 ff.

261–2. ὄφρα . . . χαλκήρεας: 'in order that he might have it for anointing his bronze-tipped arrows', cf. ix 248–9, ὄφρα οἱ εἴη | πίνειν.

263. Ilus' conscientious scruples may seem strange, since it might be thought equally as impious to possess poison as to let someone else have it, but there could be no objection to the use of arrow-poison in hunting (cf. Verg. *A.* ix 772–3, [Arist.] *Mir.* 837 a 13). νεμεσίζετο: 'stood in awe of, had regard to the wrath of'; only here is this verb used with an acc., and the sense is rather strained; we might have expected ὀπίζετο.

264. In view of the Taphians' reputation as pirates (see above, 105 n.), it is perhaps not surprising that Anchialus did not share Ilus' scruples. But the important point is Anchialus' overriding affection for Odysseus.

265–6. = iv 345–6, xvii 136–7. τοῖος picks up 257.

267. Cf. i 400, xvi 129, *Il.* xvii 514, xx 435. It is not quite clear what image is involved, but it is tempting to connect this expression with the notion of the gods spinning what is to be (cf. i 17 and n.); spinning is generally a sedentary task, and the thread as it is being spun passes over or lies on the spinner's knees. See further Hainsworth on vii 197 ff., Onians, *Origins*, 303 ff., B. C. Dietrich, *Death, Fate and the Gods* (London, 1965), esp. 289 ff.

268. ἀποτίσεται: see above, 43 n.

269 ff. Mentes' instructions fall into three main parts (271 ff., 279 ff., 293 ff.), the first two of which are of crucial importance for motivating Telemachus' subsequent actions. Since Kirchhoff's fundamental discussion

(238 ff.) various oddities have exposed this section, the vital link between Telemachus' adventures and the rest of the narrative, to the assaults of analytical critics, who have seen in its alleged incoherence and in certain other inconcinnities the hand of a redactor welding a separately conceived Telemachy onto an essentially complete poem about Odysseus' return: see further Page, *Odyssey*, 52 ff., 73 ff. (though his own interpretation of the data is idiosyncratic). But there has undoubtedly been a tendency to exaggerate difficulties and to discount alternative explanations, without due allowance being made for the effect on Athena's counsels of background information which Mentes cannot be permitted to reveal. She knows, as does the audience, that the gods have determined on Odysseus' return in the near future, and her plan of action for Telemachus makes sense only in the light of this knowledge. The audience could reasonably be expected to find nothing strange in all this, and it would be captious to complain that Telemachus ought to have been more alert to inadequacies in the advice offered by this authoritative stranger. From the last part of Mentes' speech we realize that Athena's plan includes vengeance on the suitors; the poem's scope is thus shown to be more extensive than has previously been indicated. See further F. M. Combellack, *Gnomon* xxviii (1956), 413 ff. (review of Page, *Odyssey*), Rüter, *Odysseeinterpretationen*, 148 ff., Eisenberger, *Studien*, 37 ff., E. Siegmann, 'Die Athene-Rede im ersten Buch der Odyssee', *WJA* NF ii (1976), 21 ff.

269. φράζεσθαι: 'consider'.

271. This line may seem fussy so soon after 269 (cf. 279), but Mentes needs to appear tactful and aware that the position of a stranger offering gratuitous advice is delicate.   **εἰ δ' ἄγε:** 'come now'; on this interjectional use of εἰ see Chantraine, *Grammaire*, ii 274 § 404, Monro, *Homeric Dialect*, 291-2 § 320.

272-4. Cf. 90-1.

272. Cf. *Il.* xix 34 ἀλλὰ σύ γ' εἰς ἀγορὴν καλέσας ἥρωας Ἀχαιούς. The poet seems slightly at a loss for the right words for an Ithacan assembly; see above, 90 n.

273-4. This public denunciation of the suitors before gods and men is Athena's object in arranging the assembly: see introduction to ii. No time is wasted over the possibility that the suitors might actually accede to Telemachus' request, and Mentes' subsequent instructions (295-6) presuppose that they will take no notice of it. Some critics have seen a difficulty in this, but Telemachus can reasonably be expected to share the assumption that nothing will come of it; indeed, the suitors would seem less formidable if it appeared worth considering the possibility that they would peaceably depart if formally requested to do so.   **πέφραδε:** redupl. aor. imper. of φράζω.   **ἐπὶ μάρτυροι:** or ἐπιμάρτυροι? It is hard to decide; cf. *Il.* vii 76 Ζεὺς δ' ἄμμ' ἐπιμάρτυρος [v.l. ἐπὶ μάρτυρος] ἔστω. For the cpd. form cf. e.g. ἐπίουρος, ἐπιβουκόλος, ἐπιβώτωρ. Zenodotus appears to have consistently read (ἐπι)μάρτυρες, the form in more general use, where Aristarchus preferred (ἐπι)μάρτυροι: cf. schol. *Il.* ii 302.

275-8. Cf. ii 195-7 (part of the speech by the suitor Eurymachus). This is the

least satisfactory part of Mentes' speech, being both irrelevant and
confusing. Telemachus has already said that Penelope does not want to
marry again (249–50); this is not a casual detail, but an essential part of his
dilemma, and it is hard to see why Mentes should be made to overlook it.
Mentes offers Penelope no advice applicable to her actual situation,
though he might, without any loss of verisimilitude, at least have
counselled qualified optimism, or prayer; the absence of any alternative
suggestion makes it seem as if he supposes that Penelope really does wish to
remarry. Moreover, it would be ridiculous for her father to start negotiat-
ing a second marriage before Telemachus returns from the journey which
Mentes is about to propose, and thus to set in hand arrangements which
might have to be cancelled a few weeks later, with considerable loss of face,
if Telemachus heard that Odysseus was still alive; 277–8 are simply a
distraction and create confusion in relation to 292. Furthermore, the
presence of these lines here diminishes their effectiveness in the mouth of
Eurymachus; in particular, what would otherwise strike us as a rather
mercenary detail (277 = ii 196) is reduced to a commonplace. This
directive for Penelope thus creates several difficulties without any compen-
sating advantages, and there is much to be said for Hermann's view that it
is a later interpolation, modelled on the corresponding passage in ii and
presumably inserted for the sake of a meretricious comprehensiveness.

It would be hard to find a Homeric parallel for the abrupt change of
construction in 275–6 (μητέρα . . . ἂψ ἴτω), corresponding to the straight-
forward μητέρ' ἐὴν ἐς πατρὸς ἀνωγέτω ἀπονέεσθαι of Eurymachus' speech,
but this anomaly is irrelevant to the question of authenticity; it could easily
have been avoided with μήτηρ for μητέρα or ἴμεν (Bentley's cj.) for ἴτω.

Although the question of Penelope's remarriage is frequently raised, it is
left unclear what roles are to be played by Telemachus, her father Icarius,
and Penelope herself in arranging it. Telemachus' words at ii 52 ff. suggest
that he regards Icarius as responsible, while Antinous (ii 113–14) seems to
contemplate an arrangement involving all three; yet later (iv 769 ff., xxiii
135 ff.) it is assumed that Penelope's marriage would be celebrated in
Odysseus' palace, and it is hard to see how Icarius could then be involved.
The marriage-settlement of 277–8 raises related, but more complex,
problems. Since οἱ δέ (277) can only be Penelope's kinsmen, ἔεδνα (ἕδνα)
must be understood (as also at ii 196) as gifts from the bride's family, a
dowry; cf. ii 53, where ἐεδνώσαιτο θύγατρα is most naturally interpreted as
referring to the provision of a dowry. However, in the twelve other places
in Homer where the term is used, it denotes presents from a suitor to the
bride's kin, as it invariably does in the Hesiodic *Catalogue of Women*; the
word is rare outside early epic, and must already have been obsolete in
normal usage when the *Odyssey* was composed. Terminologically, then, this
passage is anomalous, though there are other Homeric references to what
sounds like a dowry (the clearest being ii 132, iv 736, xx 341–2, xxiii 227–8,
Il. xxii 51) to set against the many references to valuable gifts from a suitor
to the bride or her kin (e.g. viii 318, xi 282, xv 16 ff. (Penelope), 367, xvi

391–2 (P.), xix 529 (P.), xxi 161–2 (P.), *Il.* xi 243 ff., xiii 365 ff. (where the suitor undertakes military service instead), xvi 178, 190, xxii 472), and the implications of such heroic names as Ἠερίβοια (*Il.* v 389) and Περίβοια (*Od.* vii 57) (cf. παρθένοι ἀλφεσίβοιαι *Il.* xviii 593, *h.Ven.* 119). There have been many ingenious attempts to construct a consistent system from what appears to be evidence of two quite different types of marriage-settlement; much, but not everything, might be harmonized by positing the not uncommon practice of indirect dowry, whereby the bridegroom pays over property which will be used to endow the newly established household. But it is most probable that Homeric marriage-customs represent an amalgam of practices from different historical periods and different places, further complicated, perhaps, by misconception: see further A. M. Snodgrass, 'An Historical Homeric Society?', *JHS* xciv (1974), 114 ff. (where references to earlier discussions may be found) and above, p. 59 f.   **δυναμένοιο:** on the rather surprising lengthening of the first syllable (cf. xi 414) see Wyatt, *Lengthening*, 120–1.

278. φίλης ἐπὶ παιδὸς ἕπεσθαι: the force of ἐπί is not quite clear: possibly indicating purpose, 'towards,', i.e. in order to get; see Chantraine, *Grammaire* ii 107 § 152; or perhaps it should be taken more closely with the verb and φίλης παιδός interpreted as a gen. of price. The phrase is a little odd applied to a middle-aged widow.

279–92. Cf. 93–5. This second suggestion does not depend on the result of the first; however the suitors react, Telemachus ought to be concerned to find out what has happened to his father. Significantly, when he goes to bed at the end of the day it is this journey which occupies his thoughts (444), not the more immediate prospect of the assembly.

280. Mentes assumes that Telemachus will have no problem about getting hold of a ship; in fact, without divine assistance it would have been difficult (cf. ii 265–6, 319–20). The relatively carefree manner in which this voyage is proposed and undertaken is inconsistent with the indications later in the poem that it is winter (xiv 457, 529 ff., xvii 25, 191, xix 319).   **ἄρσας:** aor. participle of ἀραρίσκω, 'equipping, fitting out'.   **ἐρέτῃσιν ἐείκοσιν:** a modest size; the Phaeacian ship which brings Odysseus home has a crew of 52 (viii 35) and this was probably the size of the normal 'capital' ship of this period: see J. S. Morrison and R. T. Williams, *Greek Oared Ships* (Cambridge, 1968), 46–7.

282–3. ὄσσαν . . . ἐκ Διός: a rumour of which the origin cannot be traced: cf. S. *OT* 43 εἴτε του θεῶν | φήμην ἀκούσας εἴτ' ἀπ' ἀνδρὸς οἶσθά που.   **κλέος:** 'report, news', cf. ἀκλειῶς in 241.

285. On Zenodotus' reading κεῖθεν δ' ἐς Κρήτην τε [δὲ Κρήτηνδε Buttmann] παρ' Ἰδομενῆα ἄνακτα (cf. 93) see above, introduction pp. 43–4.

286. ὅς: demonstrative.   **δεύτατος:** 'last', an illogical but natural meaning for the superlative in view of the use of δεύτερος to mean 'later' (e.g. *Il.* x 368, xxii 207).   **Ἀχαιῶν χαλκοχιτώνων:** a very common formula in the *Iliad*. The poet and his audience probably understood the epithet as 'armed with bronze', but most likely it originally referred to the use of a metal-plated tunic; see further Lorimer, *Monuments*, 208 ff., D. L. Page, *History and the Homeric* Iliad (Berkeley–Los Angeles, 1959), 245 ff., 284 ff.

287–92. Mentes reviews alternative possibilities, the first happy (and relevant), the second unhappy (and irrelevant). This apparent uncertainty adds verisimilitude, but the instructions given in 293 ff. in fact ignore the second alternative. This section is parenthetical; ταῦτα in 293 must refer to Telemachus' journey. Mentes' advice is not as comprehensive as it looks; it does not cover the most likely contingency, that Telemachus might fail to get any definite information about his father's fate.

288. The sense is 'you could endure even for as long as a year'; τρυχόμενος refers to the troubles Telemachus would suffer from the suitors. It is not suggested that he should stay away for a year (as some interpreters have supposed).

289. τεθνηῶτος: this was the form adopted by Aristarchus, and is certainly to be preferred to τεθνειῶτος, given by most of the medieval MSS. In this and similar cases -ηώς, -ηότ-, -ηῶτ- are original, while -ειώς, -ειότ-, -ειῶτ- could have been produced under the influence of the quantitative metathesis which produced -εώς, -εῶτος: see further Werner, *H u. ει vor Vokal*, 51–6.

291 ff. χεῦαι, κτερεΐξαι, δοῦναι, φράζεσθαι: infinitives used with imperatival force: see Chantraine, *Grammaire*, ii 316–17 § 460, Monro, *Homeric Dialect*, 206–7 § 241.

291. σῆμα: a monument, cenotaph; cf. iv 584.   κτέρεα κτερεΐξαι: 'honour the dead by performing the proper funeral rites'; whatever the original meaning of these terms they are used in Homer very generally of gifts and honours offered to the dead: see M. Andronikos, *Archaeologia* W, 27, R. Arena, 'Osservazioni su alcune parole greche risalenti ad una comune radice "κτερ" ', *RIL* lxxxxviii (1964), 3 ff. This kind of *schema etymologicum* is quite common in Homer, e.g. iii 140 μῦθον μυθείσθην, ix 108 φυτεύουσιν . . . φυτόν, x 518 χοὴν χεῖσθαι.

If Odysseus is dead, Penelope must resign herself to remarriage; Telemachus' own position would thus become highly precarious (cf. ii 332–6, xvi 371 ff., xx 241 ff.), but Mentes wastes no time on this depressing contingency, which we know will not arise.

293 ff. Mentes' instructions now go beyond the programme outlined at 90 ff., and look forward to the second half of the poem. Telemachus' greatest task is still to come when he returns from his journey (293). This section is slightly confusing at first sight because Mentes takes Odysseus' survival for granted and discounts the possibility of his death mentioned in the immediately preceding lines, together with its corollary, Penelope's remarriage; obviously the suitors would leave Telemachus' halls if Penelope had made her choice among them. A listening audience, sharing Athena's knowledge of the true state of affairs, would hardly have been troubled by Mentes' curious confidence on a point which he should still regard as uncertain, but this apparent oddity has led to some raising of eyebrows among analytical critics.

Mentes also takes it for granted that Telemachus will want revenge on the suitors, and that no peaceful settlement will satisfy him; only the means to this end require further deliberation. This assumption might shock us if we were not so familiar with the story, but the fact that the goddess of wisdom herself is the first to advocate this massacre stifles at the outset our qualms about its justification. The appeal to Orestes' example (298 ff.) is significant; the force of this paradigm lies largely in the implication that the suitors are as guilty as Aegisthus. The obvious objection that Telemachus faces more serious opposition than Orestes did stimulates our curiosity about the method to be adopted.

293. ἐπήν: the contraction of ἐπεὶ ἄν is thought by many scholars to be post-Homeric; nearly all instances of ἐπήν can easily be replaced by ἐπεί or ἐπεί κ(εν): see further Chantraine, *Grammaire*, ii 259 § 381, Monro, *Homeric Dialect*, 329 § 362. **ταῦτα:** the journey to Pylos and Sparta. **ἔρξῃς:** ancient grammarians recommend a rough breathing for ἔρδω, ἔρξα, though perhaps this is based merely on the convenience of distinguishing the aor. of ἔρδω from that of ἐέργω.

295–6. Cf. xi 119–20.

297. νηπιάας ὀχέειν: 'to continue, keep on with, childish ways' surely suits the context better than 'to put up with folly'. The idea that Telemachus has just reached manhood and now for the first time realizes that he must think and act independently is reflected in Penelope's repeated surprise at his behaviour (i 360–1, xviii 217 ff., xxi 354–5); compare his own comments at ii 313, xviii 229, xx 310, xxi 132. **νηπιάας:** cf. νηπιέη (*Il.* ix 491), νηπιέῃσι (xxiv 469, *Il.* xv 363, xx 411). What we should expect as the abstract noun corresponding to νήπιος is *νηπιίη or *νηπίη; the forms given in our MSS probably represent an artificial re-expansion (diectasis) of *νηπίη, and have the advantage of avoiding confusion with νήπιος. See further Chantraine, *Grammaire*, i 83 § 34, Wackernagel, *Untersuchungen*, 67–9, Risch, *Wortbildung*, 33.

298 ff. Cf. 29–31, and n.

299. πάντας ἐπ' ἀνθρώπους: for ἐπί meaning 'throughout, among' cf. xxiii 124–5 σὴν γὰρ ἀρίστην | μῆτιν ἐπ' ἀνθρώπους φάσ' ἔμμεναι, xix 334, xxiv 94, *Il.* x 213. **πατροφονῆα:** 'murderer of his father' (not 'parricide'); 300 provides a much needed explanation. This passage was probably in Aeschylus' mind when he made Orestes address Clytaemestra as πατρο-κτονοῦσα (*Ch.* 909, cf. 974, 1015, 1028); cf. also S. *Tr.* 1125, E. *Or.* 193.

300–2. = iii 198–200. **ὅ ... ἔκτα:** for this kind of gloss cf. ii 65–6 περικτίονας ... οἳ περιναιετάουσι, iii 383 ἀδμήτην, ἣν οὔ πω ὑπὸ ζυγὸν ἤγαγεν ἀνήρ, xviii 1–2 πτωχὸς πανδήμιος, ὃς κατὰ ἄστυ | πτωχεύεσκ' Ἰθάκης, xx 56–7, *Il.* ii 212–13, v 63, ix 124. ὅ, the reading of Aristarchus, is certainly to be preferred to ὅς of our MSS, since ὅς results in neglect of the digamma of οἱ, which is normally respected in early epic: for details see M. L. West on Hes. *Op.* 526. Aristarchus must have had other reasons for adopting this reading, since no ancient scholar was aware of the relevance of the digamma to Homeric language. It is hardly possible to say whether ὅ should be regarded as the neut. of the relative pronoun, used, as often, with the sense of a conjunction, 'because', or as the definite article functioning as a relative pronoun; see Chantraine, *Grammaire*, ii 284 § 417. **ἔκτα:** the last syllable is short, cf. xi 410, *Il.* xv 432; on this athematic aor. of κτείνω see Chantraine, *Grammaire*, i 380–1 § 181.   **ἔσσ':** ἔσσο, imper. of εἰμί.

304. Telemachus offers a similar excuse at iv 598.   **με:** with μένοντες, not with ἀσχαλόωσι.

305. ἐμῶν ἐμπάζεο μύθων: an emphatic echo of 271.

307–8. ἦ τοι μέν (better ἤτοι, see 155 n.) mark an emphatic asseveration: see Denniston, *Particles*, 389.   **ὥς τε πατὴρ ᾧ παιδί:** the simile reminds us of the close relationship between Athena and Odysseus; later Telemachus uses it ironically in conversation with Antinous (xvii 397).

309. ἐπειγόμενός περ ὁδοῖο: 'though eager to be on your way'; the gen. is often so used with verbs expressing the idea of aiming at something: see Chantraine, *Grammaire*, ii 53–4 § 64, Monro, *Homeric Dialect*, 144–5 § 151 (c).

310. λοεσσάμενος: bath-water normally has to be heated specially, and often some time elapses before a visitor is offered a bath: cf. iii 464 ff., viii 426 ff. It is no doubt an indication of Menelaus' very high standard of living that his guests can be provided with baths on arrival (iv 48 ff.).   **τεταρπόμενος:** reduplicated aor.; see Chantraine, *Grammaire*, i 395 ff. § 189, Monro, *Homeric Dialect*, 39–40 § 36.

311–13. There are many references in Homer to presents given by hosts to their guests: cf. iv 125 ff., 589–619, viii 389 ff., xiii 135 ff., xv 83 ff., xxi 13 ff., xxiv 273 ff., *Il.* vi 218 ff., x 269. This is not represented only as Greek practice: Egyptians, Phoenicians, Lycians, and Phaeacians likewise make lavish gifts to their visitors, and even the Cyclops is aware of the custom (ix 356–65) (though Calypso and Circe appear not to be, unless their generous provision of stores for the next stage of their guests' journeys is supposed to meet this conventional obligation). Such gifts are not of merely sentimental value; precious metal and metalwork are favoured for this purpose, as are elaborately woven textiles; livestock might also be given, at least in theory (iv 589 ff., xv 85). Apart from their intrinsic worth, such presents serve as a material indication of the esteem in which a guest is held and as a reminder of the link with a former host, though (oddly to our minds) there appears to be no objection to giving them away again (iv 617–19). There seems nothing against supposing that the custom existed in the poet's own day among the relatively few Greeks who had the resources to travel: see further J. N. Coldstream, 'Gift Exchange in the Eighth Century BC', in R. Hägg (ed.), *The Greek Renaissance of the Eighth Century BC: Tradition and Innovation* (Stockholm, 1983), 201 ff. On the general importance of gifts in the Homeric world see Finley, *World*, 73 ff. (Pelican ed. 61 ff.) and for a wider sociological perspective M. Mauss, *The Gift* (London, 1954; English translation of *Essai sur le don* (1925)).   **κειμήλιον:** something to be stored up.   **οἷα:** generalizing pl. in apposition to a sg.; a common

Homeric usage.   **φίλοι: φίλος** in Homer is rarely active in sense, and attributive φίλος is normally a reflexive possessive (see above, 60 n.). The epithet seems altogether better suited to the recipient than to the donor, and there is much to recommend Düntzer's φίλοις (*Jahrbücher f. class. Philol.* viii (1862), 754).   **ξεῖνοι ξείνοισι:** polyptoton expressing reciprocity; cf. iii 272, v 97, vii 120–1, ix 47, x 82, xvii 217, *Il.* ii 363, xiii 130–1, xvi 111, Hes. *Op.* 23 ff. See further Fehling, *Wiederholungsfiguren*, 222 ff.

315 ff. Athena has no more to say to Telemachus for the moment, and any further conversation might lessen the impact of what has preceded.

315. περ: intensive.

317. αὖτις ἀνερχομένῳ: i.e. on the way back from Temesa (184). Similarly, Nestor does not give Telemachus a present when he leaves Pylos because it is taken for granted that he will stay there again on his return from Sparta.

318. σοὶ δ' ἄξιον ἔσται ἀμοιβῆς: apparently 'it will be worth a return to you, it will bring you its full value in the shape of a return', sc. if Telemachus visits Mentes. The act of giving is normally the first half of a reciprocal action; the donor expects a counter-gift in due course, though with parting-gifts of this sort there is clearly an element of risk: cf. xxiv 283 ff. The scholia are surely wrong in interpreting the phrase to mean that Mentes, when he revisits Telemachus, will bring him a present. It is generally made quite clear that it is only the host who makes a gift at leave-taking; at *Il.* vi 218–20, where an exchange of presents is described, it is reasonable to suppose that two separate occasions are involved. Telemachus might be expected to assume, without anything being said on the subject, that, if their positions were reversed, he would receive an adequate counter-gift; Mentes' words are meant for reassurance rather than information. In societies where gift-giving plays as important a part as it does in Homer, the refusal of a gift is an awkward breach of convention, liable to cause grave offence: 'One does not have the right to refuse a gift . . . To do so would show fear of having to repay and of being abased in default . . . Failure to give or receive, like failure to make return gifts, means a loss of dignity' (Mauss, *The Gift*, 39–40). Mentes thus emphasizes that he is not refusing Telemachus' gift, merely postponing it.

320. ὄρνις δ' ὡς ἀνοπαῖα διέπτατο: the scholia show that the meaning and accentuation of ἀνοπαια were disputed in antiquity (see also *LfgrE*). Aristarchus thought ἀνόπαια was the name of a species of bird; this is clearly a guess, as is the suggestion that ἀνοπαῖα is an adverb meaning 'unseen' or 'upwards'. Crates and others saw a reference to the hole in the roof-tiles (τὴν τετρημένην κεραμίδα) commonly called καπνοδόκη, 'smoke-vent'. This interpretation, which calls for ἀν' ὀπαῖα, receives some support from the Attic use of ὀπαῖον for a structure on the roof of a temple, probably a kind of lantern (*IG* i³ 476, 112–22 (408/7); cf. Plu. *Per.* xiii 7). The rarity of the term may leave us wondering whether it was a familiar part of the local builder's vocabulary; it is conceivable that a Homeric word (or what was taken to be one) was adopted to dignify an architectural innovation intended for rather grand buildings. But even on the latter hypothesis we should be entitled to infer that Crates' view of the passage was already current in the fifth century, and it is surely the most probable interpretation; various explanations might be offered for its failure to gain general acceptance in antiquity. The poet appears to have deliberately chosen (or perhaps coined) a term less specific than the self-explanatory καπνοδόκη (which surely already existed in his day) and we are perhaps guilty of over-translating in rendering ἀν' ὀπαῖα 'by the smoke-vent'; but it is difficult to suggest an alternative which would not be at least equally misleading. Any such feature of course precludes an upper storey to the megaron.

On this interpretation it is difficult to avoid the inference that Athena is supposed to be transformed into a bird, not merely, as some have thought, compared to one. Though διέπτατο might be used of swift movement other than literal flying (cf. *Il.* xv 83, 172), it is absurd to imagine Mentes suddenly levitating towards the roof and squeezing out through a chink in the tiles; we are surely meant to suppose that he suddenly vanished and Telemachus saw instead a bird flying overhead, like the sparrow whose flight through a nobleman's banqueting-hall seemed to an Anglo-Saxon audience an apt analogue for human existence (Bede, *Hist. eccl.* ii 13). Athena similarly takes her departure from Pylos in the guise of a lammergeyer (iii 371–2: see n.).

320–1. τῷ . . . θάρσος: this was Athena's purpose, cf. 89; the effect of her visit is illustrated in the confrontations which follow.

323. Even the suitors find it a natural supposition that a stranger may be a god (xvii 483 ff.).

325–66. Telemachus asserts himself against his mother.

325–7. Phemius began at 156, and has apparently been singing all the time that Telemachus has been talking with Mentes; his song forms the connecting link with the next episode. In view of the suitors' general rowdiness (cf. 133, 365), their continued silence is to be construed as a remarkable tribute to the power of song and the fascination of Phemius' theme. The *nostoi* of the other Greek heroes form the background to Odysseus' story; their various fates must raise questions about Odysseus and, for Telemachus, Phemius' song reinforces the effect of Athena's visit. The sophisticated way in which the poet treats the various home-comings (iii 130–98, 254–312, iv 351–586) implies that the *nostoi* were a familiar theme; Penelope testifies to its popularity (341–2, cf. x 15). The *Odyssey* is reticent as to the reason for Athena's wrath, though the way in which Nestor and Menelaus allude to it (iii 132 ff., iv 502) shows that the poet knew the story, related in the Cyclic *Iliou Persis* and used by Alcaeus as a political parable (*SLG* S 262 (*LGS* 138)), of the lesser (Locrian) Ajax's attempt to rape Cassandra in Athena's own temple at Troy; the Greek army as a whole incurred the goddess's anger for failing to punish this sacrilege adequately. There is obvious dramatic irony in the fascinated attention with which the suitors listen to the tale of Athena's vengeance, oblivious to the goddess's actual presence; as we recall the disapprobation with which she viewed their conduct, we realize that their apparent security is terribly precarious. Such irony is very characteristic of the poet's treatment of the suitors; see further A. F. Dekker, *Ironie in de Odyssee* (Leiden, 1965), 64 ff.

326. ἦατ': a 'correction' of εἶατ', the form consistently given by our MSS for the simple verb (though they are divided over καθείατο/-ήατο). But these 'incorrect' forms are likely to be old, and it may be wrong to alter them; see further Werner, *H u. ει vor Vokal*, 58 ff., Wyatt, *Lengthening*, 147–8.

328 ff. Penelope's appearance before the suitors, the first of four such scenes (cf. xvi 409 ff., xviii 206 ff., xxi 63 ff.), has been judged insufficiently motivated (cf. Wilamowitz, *Heimkehr*, 123–4); but it is hypercritical to ask why, given her aversion to the suitors, she could not retire to a room where she would not hear Phemius' song. It seems to be normal heroic convention for the mistress of the house to join the men as they drink in the *megaron* after supper (thus Helen (iv 121 ff.), Arete (vi 304–5, vii 140 ff.)); Penelope's appearance at this late stage draws attention to her previous absence and reminds us how uncongenial she finds the company. But, more important, her protest (337 ff.) provokes unexpected opposition from Telemachus, a rapid demonstration of the newly won self-confidence resulting from Athena-Mentes' visit.

328. ὑπερωϊόθεν: 'from upstairs', where Penelope spends most of her time, being forced to withdraw from the *megaron* by the suitors' outrageous behaviour (cf. xv 515–17, xvii 569–72, xxiii 302). The poet imagines sound travelling very easily in Odysseus' palace; thus Penelope from her room gains a clear idea of the indignities suffered by Odysseus at the hands of the suitors (xvii 492 ff.) and Odysseus in the *megaron* hears her weeping in her room (xx 92). **θέσπιν:** shortened form of θεσπέσιος, used only in this formula.

329. Lines of this pattern, consisting of name, father's name, and an epithet qualifying one or the other, are common: e.g. vi 17 Ναυσικάα, θυγάτηρ μεγαλήτορος Ἀλκινόοιο, xv 554 etc. Τηλέμαχος, φίλος υἱὸς Ὀδυσσῆος θείοιο. They are particularly effective used, as here, when a character is first introduced. **περίφρων:** a standing epithet of Penelope, applied only to women in early epic.

330. κλίμακα: 'staircase' (not 'ladder'); the case is to be understood as a kind of internal acc. expressing the space traversed; cf. iii 71 πλεῖθ' ὑγρὰ κέλευθα. **κατεβήσετο:** the forms ἐβήσετο, ἐδύσετο, so-called 'mixed aorists', are found in several places in some MSS, and were preferred by Aristarchus to the *lectio facilior* given by the majority, ἐβήσατο, ἐδύσατο. They were regarded by ancient grammarians as imperfects (see schol. on *Il.* i 496) and it seems best to interpret them as past tenses of the desideratives βήσομαι and δύσομαι which served as futures: see further Chantraine, *Grammaire*, i 416–17 § 199, Monro, *Homeric Dialect*, 43 § 41, C. P. Roth, 'More Homeric "Mixed Aorists" ', *Glotta* lii (1974), 1 ff.

331–5. = xviii 207–11; 332–5 = xxi 63–6; 332–4 = xvi 414–16. Noblewomen are usually attended by maids when they go where they might meet men: cf. iv 123 ff. (Helen), vi 84 (Nausicaa), *Il.* iii 143 (Helen), xxii 450 (Andromache); Penelope herself says (xviii 184) οἴη δ' οὐκ εἴσειμι μετ' ἀνέρας· αἰδέομαι γάρ. The masc. counterpart of this formula provides dogs instead (ii 11).

332. δῖα γυναίκων: cf. 14 δῖα θεάων and n.

333. The formula is used only of women (viii 458 (Nausicaa), xvi 415, xviii 209, xxi 64 (Penelope), cf. *h.Cer.* 186 (Metaneira) ἧστο παρὰ σταθμὸν κτλ.). σταθμός, as a feature of Homeric houses, usually denotes a door-post (though at xvii 96 it must refer to a bearing-pillar of the megaron) and it is tempting to picture Penelope, who never associates with the suitors more than she must, staying as near the doorway as possible; a similar stance would suit the modest Nausicaa in the presence of her father's guests. But this interpretation requires us to take τέγος loosely as 'building', not in its usual meaning 'roof', and does not suit *h.Cer.* 186, since Metaneira would not have chosen to sit at the doorway with her baby. We should probably therefore imagine Penelope standing beside one of the central pillars in her vain attempt to impose her will on the banqueters. See also Hainsworth on viii 458, Hoekstra on xvi 415.

334. λιπαρὰ κρήδεμνα: the κρήδεμνον is a veil, mantilla, or shawl worn over the head and shoulders: see *Companion*, 501–2, S. Marinatos, *Archaeologia* A, 13, 46, Hoekstra on xiii 388. It is not clear why the pl. is used, since the sg. would scan equally well and is used of the κρήδεμνον which Ino gives to Odysseus (v 346 etc.). λιπαρά implies treatment with oil: cf. vii 107 (with Hainsworth's n.). That Penelope goes veiled in the presence of the suitors even in her own home is probably to be interpreted as a gesture advertising her aversion to any familiarity and discouraging any notion that they are her guests. See also Russo on xviii 209–10.

335. On the connotations of κεδνός see Hoekstra on xiv 170.

336. δακρύσασα: Penelope's tears are a visible reminder of her constancy.

337. γάρ: anticipatory; this clause gives the reason for what follows, a common arrangement in Homeric speeches. **βροτῶν θελκτήρια:** cf. xi 334, xii 40, 44, xvii 521. **οἶδας:** found only here in Homer for οἶσθα, which it started to replace in Ionic fairly early: e.g. Hippon. fr. 177 West, Hdt. iii 72. 1, cf. *h.Merc.* 456, 467; see further F. Solmsen, 'Zur griechischen Verbalflexion', *ZVS* xxxix (NF xix) (1906), 207. Presumably the poet chose this form so that the ending of this line would echo those of 336 and 338; cf. 48–9 and n. Zenodotus read something else, variously reported as ἤδεις or εἴδεις, on which the scholia add that Aristarchus had no objection to this reading (καὶ Ἀρίσταρχος οὐ δυσχεραίνει τῇ γραφῇ). If Aristarchus took Zenodotus' reading to be the plpf. of οἶδα, this is a surprising comment; the normal Homeric forms are ἤδησθα (xix 93) and ἠείδης (*Il.* xxii 280), and the sense is relatively feeble. It is worth considering Schwartz's suggestion that what Zenodotus in fact read was θελκτήρι' ἀείδεις, which is unobjectionable.

343. τοίην ... κεφαλήν: the head is in a sense the person; this form of expression in Homer is generally associated with the dead: cf. x 521, 536, xi 29, 49, 549, 557, *Il.* xi 55, xviii 114, xxi 336, xxii 348, xxiii 94, xxiv 276, 579.

344. καθ' Ἑλλάδα καὶ μέσον Ἄργος: cf. iv 726, 816, xv 80 (cf. Hoekstra's n.); the meaning is evidently 'throughout the whole of Greece'. In the *Iliad* Ἑλλάς is the name of the city and kingdom of Peleus, and corresponds to southern Thessaly; in this Odyssean formula it is used in a wider sense, of northern Greece in general. Thucydides (i 3. 3) remarks on Homer's restricted use of Ἑλλάς and Ἕλλην; but Hesiod (*Op.* 653) uses Ἑλλάς to mean 'Greece'. See further *LfgrE*. Ἄργος, as often, denotes the Peloponnese: contrast iii 251, and see n. μέσον is not entirely logical, but reinforces the idea that Odysseus was known in every part of Greece. Aristarchus rejected the line, because he held that the meanings given to Ἑλλάς and Ἄργος were unhomeric: see schol. on *Il.* iv 171, ix 395.

346 ff. Telemachus' reply embodies the earliest literary criticism in Greek literature; he is surely the poet's spokesman in his plea for artistic freedom and his emphasis on the importance of novelty.

346. ἐρίηρον: the epithet is restricted to bards and ἑταῖροι; its exact meaning is uncertain, though its derivation from ἦρα is generally accepted: see Frisk, *GEW*, Chantraine, *Dictionnaire* s.v. ἐρίηρες, R. Gusmani, *SMEA* 6 (1968), 17 ff. We may translate 'loyal' or 'ready to render service'.

347–9. Cf. 32–3 and n.   τ': probably emphatic τε, not τοι.

349. ἀλφηστῇσιν: ἀλφηστής is alien to the *Iliad*, though Hesiod uses it. It seems to be modelled on ὠμηστής, 'eating raw flesh', and its first element is almost certainly ἀλφι-; the etymology 'eater of grain' appears to be indicated in Hes. fr. 211. 12–13, cf. S. *Ph.* 709. 'Grain-eating' men are thus distinguished from gods and savages; cf. *Od.* ix 191, where the Cyclops is contrasted with ἀνδρί γε σιτοφάγῳ. See further Chantraine, *Dictionnaire*. In antiquity some evidently connected the first element with ἀλφαίνω and understood the cpd. as 'enterprising': see Hsch. ἀλφησταί· ἄνθρωποι, βασιλεῖς, ἔντιμοι; ἀλφηστῇσι· τοῖς εὑρετικοῖς καὶ συνετοῖς; cf. A. *Th.* 770.

350. οὐ νέμεσις: 'it is no reason for anger that', cf. xx 330, *Il.* iii 156, xiv 80.   **Δαναῶν:** Δαναοί is not simply a synonym for Ἀχαιοί and Ἀργεῖοι; it has no corresponding toponym, is used only in the pl., and seems to have military connotations. See further *LfgrE*.

351–2. Cf. Pi. *O.* ix 48–9 αἴνει δὲ παλαιὸν μὲν οἶνον, ἄνθεα δ' ὕμνων | νεωτέρων. Since much modern writing on oral epic emphasizes the importance of the familiar and traditional, it is interesting to find the poet stressing the value of novelty. Plato (*R.* 424 b) cites the passage thus: ὅταν τις λέγῃ ὡς τὴν ἀοιδὴν μᾶλλον ἐπιφρονέουσ' ἄνθρωποι, ἥτις ἀειδόντεσσι νεωτάτη ἀμφιπέληται; since it may safely be assumed that he was quoting from memory, we should not attach much importance to the apparent variants ἐπιφρονέουσ' and ἀειδόντεσσι. On Plato's quotations from Homer see G. Lohse, *Helikon* iv (1964), 3–28, v (1965), 248–95, vii (1967), 223–31.

353–5. Penelope cannot reasonably hope to avoid ever hearing of the Trojan war; it was an event of international importance, not merely a personal misfortune.

356–9. Cf. xxi 350–3, *Il.* vi 490–3; for 358–9 cf. also xi 352–3. The lines were absent from some ancient editions and athetized by Aristarchus as being less suitable here than in the other two places where they occur. Modern scholars have often argued that this criticism betrays an inadequate understanding of the function of stock passages in an essentially oral narrative style. Yet the lines raise some awkward questions which are seldom squarely faced. Recalling as they do one of the most memorable scenes of the *Iliad*, Hector's farewell to Andromache, they have for us the effect of a quotation, and their callousness in this context is enhanced by the contrast with their earlier occurrence: there it is war which is said to be the concern of men, a view which no Homeric woman could question, and Hector is attempting to calm Andromache's fears, not telling her to mind her own business. If these lines are authentic here, are we to infer that the poet intended us to recognize an allusion to the *Iliad*, or are we misled by the scantiness of the epic material available to us? Did his original audience see in these lines simply a stock heroic response to women who pester their menfolk?

Certainly the favourable impression created by Telemachus' earlier observations is quite destroyed by this adolescent rudeness, culminating in the outrageous claim that speech ($\mu\hat{v}\theta os$) is not women's business, quite contrary to Homeric custom as we see it at the courts of Menelaus and Alcinous, where Helen (iv 121 ff.) and Arete (vii 141 ff.) play a full part in the conversation after dinner. Some have praised the psychological realism by which Telemachus is made to go too far in his first attempt to assert his authority; I find this an unconvincing defence, and am inclined to follow Aristarchus in suspecting interpolation intended, perhaps, partly to provide a more explicit reason for Penelope's withdrawal and partly to stress Telemachus' newly acquired self-confidence.

356–8. Spinning and weaving, the domestic arts *par excellence*, are the normal occupation of Homeric women without regard to rank: cf. ii 94, xvii 97 (Penelope), iv 130 ff. (Helen), v 62 (Calypso), vi 306 (Arete), x 222–3 (Circe), *Il.* iii 125 ff. (Helen), xxii 440 ff. (Andromache). Skill in textile production is the gift of Athena, and the results represent an important part of a family's wealth. Apart from provision for utilitarian, day-to-day purposes, a rich household would be expected to have a store of more elaborate fabrics for special occasions (including funerals: cf. ii 94 ff., *Il.* xxiv 580 ff., 795) and for formal presentation to gods (cf. *Il.* vi 89–93 etc.) as well as to men (cf. xv 123 ff., *Il.* xxiv 228 ff.). See further G. Wickert-Micknat, *Archaeologia* R, 13, 38 ff., 43. Some see an allusion to Penelope's unsuccessful ruse with Laertes' shroud (ii 93 ff. = xix 138 ff. = xxiv 128 ff.)   **οἶκον:** here used of Penelope's quarters only, not of the whole house; cf. 360, iv 717. The ancient variants attested here ($\dot{a}\lambda\lambda\dot{a}$ σύ γ' $\dot{\epsilon}i\sigma\epsilon\lambda\theta o\hat{v}\sigma a$) and at 360 ($\theta\dot{a}\lambda a\mu o\nu$ δὲ $\beta\epsilon\beta\dot{\eta}\kappa\epsilon\iota$) show that this use of οἶκος was found difficult in antiquity.   **τοῦ:** demonstrative.

360–4. = xxi 354–8; 362–4 = xix 602–4; cf. xvi 449–51.

360. Penelope's reaction underlines the change in Telemachus brought about by Athena's visit.

361. μῦθον πεπνυμένον: perhaps best understood as referring to Telemachus' assertion of authority.

365–6. The suitors are excited by a rare glimpse of Penelope, and aggrieved that she has disappeared so soon, without deigning to offer them a word; 366 is an oblique, but highly effective, way of indicating her beauty (cf. *Il.* iii 154 ff.).   σκιόεντα: a fixed epithet of μέγαρα, regularly applied also to clouds and mountains; it is probably better taken as 'shady, cool' than as 'shadowy, gloomy, badly lit'. For a detailed discussion of the formula see G. S. Korres, 'Μέγαρα σκιόεντα', *Athena* lxxvii (1971), 202–30, 394–5.

366. = xviii 213.   ἠρήσαντο: 'prayed aloud to, expressed a wish to'. παραί: with κλιθῆναι.

367–420. Telemachus warns the suitors of his intention to make a public protest against their intrusion; Antinous and Eurymachus fail to dissuade him.

370–1. Cf. ix 3–4.

373. Cf. *Il.* ix 309 χρὴ μὲν δὴ τὸν μῦθον ἀπηλεγέως ἀποειπεῖν, the opening of Achilles' great speech and the only other place in Homer where ἀπηλεγέως occurs.

374–80. Cf. ii 139–45 (identical apart from its opening, ἔξιτέ μοι). Athena did not tell Telemachus to give the suitors notice of his intention to make a public protest, but he has nothing to gain by letting it take them by surprise, and it is sensible both to offer them a chance of avoiding a formal denunciation and to forestall the excuse that they had no reason to believe their presence unwelcome to him. The formulation of this passage is to some extent influenced by the way in which the poet plans to handle the narrative in ii, but this does not give rise to any serious difficulties (despite Page, *Odyssey*, 74–5, whose criticisms are well dealt with by Rüter, *Odysseeinterpretationen*, 184 ff., and Besslich, *Schweigen*, 11 ff.).

377. Cf. 160.   νήποινον: 'without compensation'.

378. ἐπιβώσομαι: contracted from ἐπιβοήσομαι, cf. *Il.* x 463 (v.l.), xii 337, βωστρεῖν (*Od.* xii 124); this contraction of -οη- is Ionic, not Attic: see Chantraine, *Grammaire*, i 35 § 15.

379. αἴ κέ ποθι Ζεὺς δῷσι: 'in case Zeus may grant...'; for this type of condition see Chantraine, *Grammaire*, ii 282–3 § 414.

381–2. = xviii 410–11, xx 268–9.   ἐν should be taken closely with φύντες, 'biting their lips hard' (in suppressed anger); on ὀδάξ see Frisk, *GEW*, Chantraine, *Dictionnaire*.   ὅ: 'because', like Lat. *quod*; see Chantraine, *Grammaire*, ii 285 § 417, Monro, *Homeric Dialect*, 242 § 269.

383 ff. Antinous and Eurymachus are the two most prominent suitors (ἀρχοὶ μνηστήρων iv 629); the poet tells us nothing about their background here, but confines himself to projecting their personalities: contrast the way in which Eurycleia is introduced (429 ff.). As often, Antinous speaks first. He is consistently presented as the ringleader, and, correspondingly, is the first to fall to Odysseus' arrows (xxii 8 ff.); after his death Eurymachus attempts to cast all the blame on him (xxii 48 ff.).   Ἀντίνοος is best interpreted as 'Contrary-minded, Hostile', and thus belongs to a large group of

Homeric personal names which indicate a character's personality without regard to the considerations by which in real life parents were guided in naming their children; cf. 154 n. (Phemius) and see further von Kamptz, *Personennamen*, 25 ff., 56. Modern novelists follow a similar convention when they give ridiculous names to characters who are not to be taken seriously. (Ἀντίνοος is attested as a historical name, but presumably those who chose it either gave no thought to its derivation or took it to be vaguely complimentary, like Ἀντίκλεια). Antinous is a fluent and effective speaker; his father's name, which surely means 'Persuasive' rather than 'Compliant', looks like an *ad hoc* invention intended to characterize the son (cf. xxii 330–1 Φήμιος Τερπιάδης). Odysseus himself compliments him on his appearance (xvii 415–16, cf. xxi 277 θεοειδέα). He alone of the suitors is not positively proved inferior to Odysseus in the test with the bow, since he sees good reason to postpone his attempt (xxi 256 ff.). The glory of Odysseus' ultimate triumph is enhanced by the quality of his chief adversary; the suitors are not merely a flock of arrogant weaklings.

Antinous replies to the tone rather than the content of Telemachus' speech; here and in ii he consistently tries to undermine Telemachus' attempts to assert his authority by refusing to take him seriously.

384–5. In this condescending comment on Telemachus' sudden display of independence we note the irony characteristic of the poet's treatment of the suitors (cf. 325–7 n.). Antinous describes Telemachus as ὑψαγόρης elsewhere (ii 85, 303, xvii 406); the word does not otherwise occur in Homer.

386–7. Antinous is alert to political implications in Telemachus' attempt to assert himself.   βασιλῆα: 'lord' or 'prince', rather than 'king'. In early Greek epic βασιλεύς covers a range of meanings from 'monarch' to 'nobleman, prominent person', and in translating we should avoid too specific a term. It becomes clear from Telemachus' reply that what Antinous purports to regard as πατρώϊον for Telemachus is some kind of supremacy among the Ithacan nobility, analogous to Alcinous' position in relation to the twelve Phaeacian βασιλῆες (viii 390–1, cf. vii 49, with Hainsworth's n.) and symbolized in the omen which greets Telemachus' return to Ithaca (xv 525 ff.), as Theoclymenus realizes (533 ff.): ὑμετέρου δ' οὐκ ἔστι γένεος βασιλεύτερον ἄλλο | ἐν δήμῳ Ἰθάκης, ἀλλ' ὑμεῖς καρτεροὶ αἰεί. But the position calls for qualities of leadership which the immature Telemachus cannot claim; even though in a struggle for power his status as Odysseus' son might be exploited with advantage, it could not compensate for his lack of experience and confidence against a rival like Antinous. So long as there is neither a crisis calling for strong unified leadership nor any obviously outstanding candidate among the Ithacan nobility, the power vacuum created by Odysseus' continued absence could remain unfilled for a long time without causing practical problems; but Telemachus' determination to upset the status quo suggests to Antinous that a struggle for supremacy may be imminent.

The meaning of βασιλεύς in Homer has been much discussed. A very full bibliography is given by M. Schmidt in his excellent article in *LfgrE*; see also Hainsworth, introduction to viii (pp. 342-3).

The poet's conception of the governance of Ithaca seems imprecise; traditions about the heroic age and the political conditions presupposed by his formulaic stock may at times have been contaminated by contemporary realities. But Odysseus' οἶκος is the focus of his story, and the political implications of the hero's return are hardly regarded.

387. ποιήσειεν: punctuation at this point in the line, after the second trochee, is unusual; see further H. Fränkel, 'Der homerische u. der kallimachische Hexameter', *Wege und Formen frühgriechischen Denkens*[2] (Munich, 1960), 107.

390. τοῦτ': βασιλεύειν. Διός γε διδόντος: on the gen. absol. in Homer see Chantraine, *Grammaire*, ii 324 § 472, Monro, *Homeric Dialect*, 213-14 § 246. The breach of Hermann's Bridge (caesura after the trochee of the fourth foot) is slightly mitigated by the word-break between Διός and γε; see Monro, *Homeric Dialect*, 340 § 368.

391. φῇς: 'think', rather than 'say'.

392-3. Cf. *Il.* ix 155, xii 310 ff. οἵ: βασιλῆϊ, implied in βασιλευέμεν. δῶ: see 176 n.

394-5. βασιλῆες: nobles; cf. 247. At ii 292-3 we find a similar formula used of ships.

396. τῶν κέν τις τόδ' ἔχῃσιν: 'one of them may surely have this, let one of them have this'; the subjunctive expresses Telemachus' emphatic assent; he is not merely stating what is likely to happen: see Chantraine, *Grammaire*, ii 211 § 311, Monro, *Homeric Dialect*, 252 § 275 (b). The vagueness of τόδε is surely deliberate; it is better that we should not enquire too closely what political rights Telemachus would be prepared to resign. ἐπεὶ θάνε δῖος Ὀδυσσεύς: this ready concurrence with the suitors' assumptions may be thought disingenuous, since Telemachus has just been encouraged to hope that his father may still be alive (196 ff., 267-8, 287-8), but it is understandable that he should not wish to expose himself to the charge of wishful thinking (cf. 413).

397. ἐγών: a few MSS read ἐγώ, which respects the initial digamma of οἴκοιο.

398. Raiding and piracy are regarded as perfectly honourable, at least if the victims are foreigners: cf. iii 71 ff. (= ix 252 ff.), xiv 246 ff., xxiii 356-7. The possibility of buying slaves is ignored here, though Eurycleia (i 430) and Eumaeus (xv 452-3, 483) were thus acquired. δμώων: on the connotations of δμώς see G. Ramming, *Die Dienerschaft in der Odyssee* (Erlangen, 1973), 3 ff., 67 ff., 124 ff., 131 ff.

399. Eurymachus similarly speaks after Antinous at ii 177 ff., xxi 320 ff.; the reserve in Telemachus' answer (412 ff.) indicates that his reassurances are to be regarded as insincere (as, even more blatantly, at xvi 435 ff.). Though its elements are perspicuous enough, Εὐρύμαχος seems meaningless as a personal name.

400. See above, 267 n.

402. σοῖσιν: most MSS read οἷσιν, which should probably be preferred as a rare archaism. ὅς (σϝός) seems originally to have served as a reflexive possessive for all three persons, but Aristarchus refused to recognize as Homeric its use for the first and second persons, and there was evidently a tendency for other readings to be substituted. See further M. L. West on Hes. *Op.* 381, Chantraine, *Grammaire*, i 273–4 § 128, Leaf, *Iliad*, i 559–65.

404. ἀπορραίσει': Bentley's emendation of ἀπορραίσει assimilates the mood to that of ἔλθοι. The verb is presumably a cpd. of ῥαίω, literally 'strike down from (possession of)'; for the construction with a double acc., regular with ἀφαιρεῖσθαι and many verbs of similar meaning, cf. xvi 428, Emp. DK 31 B 128. 10; on the form see further M. L. West on Hes. *Th.* 393, Frisk, *GEW*, Chantraine, *Dictionnaire* s.v. ῥαίω.   **Ἰθάκης ἔτι ναιεταούσης:** 'so long as Ithaca is still inhabited'; for this sense of ναιετάω cf. iv 177, ix 23, *Il.* iv 45; on its development see Leumann, *Wörter*, 191–4, G. P. Shipp, *Essays in Mycenaean and Homeric Greek* (Melbourne, 1961), 42 ff. Allen's app. crit. does not mention that all MSS read ναιεταώσης, which is contrary to Homeric usage for verbs in -άω; where this fem. ptcp. occurs in the *Iliad* (ii 648, iii 387, vi 415) the MSS are regularly divided between ναιετάωσα, ναιετάουσα (uncontracted), and ναιετόωσα (with artificial 'distraction' of the contracted vowel (*diectasis*)); Aristarchus preferred the last: see schol. *Il.* vi 415. On this rather puzzling variation see further Chantraine, *Grammaire*, i 79 § 32, Cauer, *Homerkritik*, 108, Shipp, *Studies*, 34–5.

405. ξείνοιο ἐρέσθαι: see above, 135 n. The infin. ἐρέσθαι is otherwise found in Homer only in the Odyssean formula μεταλλῆσαι καὶ ἐρέσθαι (iii 69, 243 etc.); it must be an aor., and therefore accented paroxytone, though our MSS agree with Herodian (on *Il.* xvi 47) in accenting it proparoxytone, as if it were a pres.; see further Chantraine, *Grammaire*, i 394 § 188.

406. ὁππόθεν, ποίης: as at 170–2, direct and indirect interrogatives are combined.   **εὔχεται:** see above, 172 n.

407. πατρὶς ἄρουρα: perhaps more specific than the preceding γαίης, 'his ancestral fields' rather than 'his fatherland'.

408. The sudden change in Telemachus' manner suggests this explanation.   **ἀγγελίην πατρὸς ... ἐρχομένοιο:** 'a message from your returning father' (cf. *Il.* xv 174) or 'news of your father's return'? Cf. ii 30.

409. ἑὸν αὐτοῦ χρεῖος: 'his own business', cf. ii 45. χρεῖος was the orthography preferred by Aristophanes and is given in almost all MSS; but χρῆος would be more correct; see Chantraine, *Grammaire*, i 70 § 28. χρεῖος in Homer commonly has the sense of 'debt' (e.g. iii 367, xxi 17), but if we take it here, the specific ἑὸν αὐτοῦ becomes practically meaningless; moreover, the arrival of a creditor would not naturally suggest itself as an explanation for Telemachus' newly acquired confidence. For ἔλδομαι with acc. cf. xxiii 6, *Il.* v 481.   **τόδ' ἱκάνει:** 'comes this way', a common phrase, cf. x 75, xvii 444, 524.

410. οἷον ... οἴχεται: cf. 320.

411. γνώμεναι: 'for one to know him, for us to know him'; for the omission of the subject of the infin. cf. iv 196, xi 158–9.   **οὐ μὲν γὰρ κτλ:** there is a slight ellipse of a type not uncommon with explanatory γάρ (see Denniston, *Particles*, 61); this clause supplies the reason for Eurymachus' question: the visitor looked distinguished, and his activities are likely to be of interest (as those of a peasant would not be).

413. Cf. 396.

414. Eumaeus speaks of earlier, misleading, reports about Odysseus (xiv 122 ff., cf. 374 ff.). **πείθομαι:** for the sense 'believe, trust in' cf. *Il.* xii 238; cf. *Od.* xvi 192 οὐ γάρ πω ἐπείθετο ὃν πατέρ᾽ εἶναι; its normal Homeric meaning is 'obey'. **ἔλθοι:** sc. ἀγγελίη.

415–16. Cf. ii 201, *Il.* xvi 50 f. Eurymachus did not mention prophecy; this gratuitous denial underlines Telemachus' (disingenuous) claim that he will not believe any such report, whatever its origins.

417. οὗτος is the subject, ξεῖνος ἐμὸς πατρώϊος ἐκ Τάφου predicate.

418–19. Cf. 180–1.

420. Cf. 323; the contrast between Telemachus' words and thoughts implies that he is learning wiliness. **ἀθανάτην:** cpd. adjs. in Homer are often of three terminations; but the fem. is illogical here, since if Telemachus had not identified his divine visitant as Athena, there would be no reason for him to think specifically of a female divinity.

421–3. = xviii 304–6. The suitors have not taken very seriously Telemachus' statement that they are unwelcome. **τρεψάμενοι τέρποντο:** the assonance is surely intentional; see above, 48–9 n.

424–44. The suitors go home; Telemachus, attended by the old nurse Eurycleia, goes to bed.

424. Cf. iii 396, vii 229, xiii 17, *Il.* i 606. **κακκείοντες:** i.e. κατακείοντες; on κατακείω, an alternative form, perhaps desiderative, of κατάκειμαι, see Chantraine, *Grammaire*, i 453 § 215. The scholia quote an alternative version of the line, read by Aristophanes (though hardly, as is alleged, his own invention), and add that both were given in the Argive edition (on which see above, introduction pp. 44–5): ἔνιοι δὴ τότε κοιμήσαντο καὶ ὕπνου δῶρον ἕλοντο' [= xix 427], μεταποιηθῆναι δέ φασιν ὑπὸ Ἀριστοφάνους τὸν στίχον· ἐν δὲ τῇ Ἀργολικῇ προστέθειται. This variant was evidently intended to avoid a problem about sleeping-arrangements for those suitors who were not within easy reach of home: cf. schol. ii 397.

425. ὅθι οἱ θάλαμος ... αὐλῆς: 'where his bedroom was built in the fine courtyard'; it is probably better to take αὐλῆς as a local genitive than as partitive after ὅθι. Compare the extra bedrooms built for Priam's children (*Il.* vi 243 ff.).

426. Cf. xiv 6 (of Eumaeus' hut). **ὑψηλός:** 'lofty', its usual architectural meaning, not 'on high'; there is no suggestion that this is an upstairs room. **περισκέπτῳ:** interpreted by ancient scholars as 'conspicuous' or 'commanding a view all round', from σκέπτομαι; of these two suggestions the first is probably preferable, and certainly we should not infer from the epithet that Telemachus' room is supposed to be free-standing, an unnecessarily extravagant form of construction. But the formula περισκέπτῳ ἐνὶ χώρῳ is also used of Circe's palace (x 211), in the depths of a wood, where this interpretation is inappropriate; hence we should perhaps follow Döderlein's suggestion that περίσκεπτος is connected with σκέπας, and means 'protected on all sides'; even if this is not the correct etymology, the poet may well have understood the epithet in this sense. See further Hoekstra on xiv 6, Frisk, *GEW* s.v. σκέπας, Chantraine, *Dictionnaire* s.v. σκέπτομαι.

427. μερμηρίζων: the connotations of μερμηρίζω are well explored by C. Voigt, *Überlegung u. Entscheidung* (Meisenheim am Glan, 1972), 11 ff.

428 ff. This detailed description of Telemachus going to bed reminds us that, in the eyes of those around him, he is still a child; but its main purpose is to introduce Eurycleia, formerly Odysseus' nurse (xix 354–5), and destined to play an important role later. She is closely involved in the action from the start; she helps Telemachus to prepare secretly for his journey (ii 345 ff.) and consoles Penelope when she hears of his departure (iv 742 ff.). Eurycleia and the swineherd Eumaeus receive far more attention than any slave in the *Iliad*, but, significantly, both are of noble origins (429, xv 403 ff.).

428. δαΐδας: on the various types of torch used in antiquity see *RE* vi 1945 ff. (Mau). The fact that Telemachus is lighted to his bedroom does not mean that he had to go out into the courtyard to get to it; a corridor would need illumination. **κεδνὰ ἰδυῖα:** so Bentley, whom most editors follow; our MSS read κέδν' εἰδυῖα. ἰδυῖα, the old type of fem. ptcp. showing the zero-grade ϝιδ and with digamma effective, is certainly the original form in this and similar formulae, but our MSS of Homer and Hesiod regularly give the e-grade form εἰδυῖα; in only one place (*Il.* ix 270) is there a variant, ἔργα ἰδυίας, while εἰδυῖα is guaranteed by metre at *Il.* xvii 5 (cf. Hes. *Th.* 887). ἰδυῖα may thus already have given way to εἰδυῖα when the *Odyssey* was composed. See further Hoekstra on xiii 417, M. L. West on Hes. *Th.* 264, *Op.* p. 62. οἶδα is used here, as often, of what we should regard as moral rather than intellectual qualities; on this usage see further H. Fränkel, *Dichtung u. Philosophie des frühen Griechentums*[2] (Munich, 1962), 91 (= *Early Greek Poetry and Philosophy* (Oxford, 1975), 82).

429. Eurycleia's father and grandfather are named to show that she is of good family; the poet of the *Odyssey* is sparing with patronymics (see above, 30 n.), and the archaistic hybrid Πεισηνορίδαο is markedly honorific. We are presumably meant to suppose that like Eumaeus (xv 403 ff.) and Eumaeus' Sidonian nursemaid (xv 427 ff.) Eurycleia was kidnapped by pirates. Her father's name is not otherwise attested, and its derivation is mysterious; this is most unusual in the case of a character of no importance whom we should suppose to be the poet's own invention; see further H. Mühlestein, *SMEA* ix (1969), 80–1.

430. Cf. xv 483 (of Eumaeus).

431. ἐεικοσάβοια: evidently a high price: at *Il.* xxiii 705 a skilled woman slave is valued at 4 oxen. For comparison, a set of golden armour and a male prisoner are each worth 100 oxen (*Il.* vi 236, xxi 79), a tripod 12 oxen (*Il.* xxiii 703), a set of bronze armour 9 oxen (*Il.* vi 236), and a cauldron one ox (*Il.* xxiii 885); at xxii 57 Eurymachus suggests that the suitors should each pay Odysseus by way of compensation τιμήν ... ἐεικοσάβοιον. The same use of cattle as a standard of value is reflected in names like Ἀλφεσίβοια, Ἐρίβοια, Πολύβοια, though these envisage marriage-prospects (cf. 275–8 n.) rather than trade.

433. Contrast the behaviour of Amyntor (*Il.* ix 449 ff.) and Agamemnon's callous threat (*Il.* i 31).

434. The virtual repetition of 428 marks the end of the digression and the return to the main narrative (cf. 265), a common feature of Homeric style and of archaic Greek literature in general. For a detailed study of the phenomenon see W. A. A. van Otterlo, *Untersuchungen über Begriff, Anwendung u. Entstehung der griechischen Ringkomposition* (Mededeelingen der Nederlandsche Akad. van wetenschappen, NR vii, 1944). **οἱ, ἑ:** Telemachus, who is the subject also of ὤϊξεν in 436.

437. χιτῶνα: clearly rather short if Telemachus could take it off while sitting on his bed (cf. *Il.* ii 42); contrast the long male chiton implied at *Il.* v 733 ff., viii 384 ff. See further S. Marinatos, *Archaeologia* A, 7–9, 38–41.

439. ἀσκήσασα: a strange use of ἀσκέω, which in Homer is normally used of skilful craftsmanship exercised in making or ornamenting something; here the meaning is more like 'treat with care, look after'; compare the use of κομίζω with a cloak as object, *Il.* ii 183. See further *LfgrE*.

440. τρητοῖσι: 'pierced', cf. xxiii 198; a plausible explanation of the epithet is suggested in the *Etymologicum Magnum*: τρητὸν λέχος· παρὰ τὸ τετρῆσθαι κατὰ τὰ ἐνήλατα, εἰς ἃ ἐμβάλλεται ἡ σπάρτος, i.e. the bedframe is pierced so that a network of cords can be fastened to it, on which the mattress is supported. See further S. Laser, *Archaeologia* P, 30 ff.

442. ἐπὶ ... ἱμάντι: 'she drew the bolt home by its strap'. κληΐς in Homer is more commonly 'bolt' than 'key'. The bolt is on the inside of the door; the strap, which makes it possible to fasten or unfasten the door from outside, passes through a hole in the door (cf. iv 802).

443. οἰὸς ἀώτῳ: the etymology of ἄωτος is uncertain, and discussion of its meaning in Homer has often been confused (as in LSJ) by Pindar's frequent use of ἄωτος to denote 'the best, the quintessence' of its kind. In Homeric contexts ἄωτος is used without qualitative overtones, of wool, whether on the sheep (ix 434) or made up (as at *Il.* xiii 599, 716), and of linen used for bedding (*Il.* ix 661); it is probably to be understood as 'flock, fibres': so *LfgrE*, but see also R. A. Ramin, *Glotta* liii (1975), 195 ff. We should not expect Telemachus to use an untreated fleece as bedding, and οἰὸς ἀώτῳ presumably means a blanket (generally χλαῖνα in Homer).

BOOK II: COMMENTARY

Athena's plan for Telemachus was outlined in i (88 ff., 271 ff.); in ii we see its implementation. More than half the book is occupied with the assembly summoned by Telemachus to witness his formal denunciation of the suitors; in order that Odysseus' massive vengeance may appear justified, his victims must be given due warning. Attempts to relate the function and procedure of this assembly to some historical reality are unsatisfactory; the poet's primary model was surely provided by the assemblies of *Iliad* i and ii, which likewise serve to clarify the moral issues, to give substance to the main characters, and to set the action in a wider context. The proceedings reveal a public aspect to what has hitherto been presented as a domestic misfortune, though this public aspect is rather ambivalently presented. Going beyond Athena's instructions Telemachus seeks to stir up public feeling against the suitors, not, as we might expect, by reminding the Ithacans of the loyalty due to the house of their former prince (though Mentor is well aware of this obligation (229 ff.)), but by presenting the suitors' conduct as a scandal reflecting on the whole community and provoking the wrath of heaven against those who knowingly suffer such wickedness to continue in their midst. The lack of any immediate response to Telemachus' initiative underlines his isolation; as the meeting continues we gain an impression of a community cowed by a small group of arrogant and unscrupulous young noblemen. There is a crescendo of violence in the suitors' speeches; Antinous presents their actions as a justified response to Penelope's delaying tactics, but Eurymachus and Leocritus make no attempt to disguise the reality. With their outright rejection of Telemachus' request the suitors' doom is sealed, their moral blindness being strikingly exemplified by their nonchalant dismissal of the omen which confirms Telemachus' imprecation (146 ff.). We are left to wonder how far the coming vengeance will extend among the community which has connived at the suitors' misdeeds. After this confrontation the preparations for Telemachus' journey may seem an anticlimax; but it is brought home to us that it is the execution of this project, not his public protest, which convinces the suitors that Telemachus' opposition represents a serious threat to their security. Athena's frequent intervention in the latter part of the book demonstrates that, for all his immaturity, she regards him as worth helping.

1–81. The Ithacan assembly is convened; Aegyptius asks why the meeting has been called, and Telemachus appeals for support against the suitors.

1. The beginning of the book, the start of a new phase in the action, coincides with the dawn of a new day: cf. iii, v, viii, xvii, *Il.* viii, xi, xix. This verse, the most famous of all the Homeric formulae for daybreak, is common in the *Odyssey* (iii 404, 491, iv 306, 431, 576, v 228, viii 1, ix 152,

170, 307, 437, 560, x 187, xii 8, 316, xiii 18, xv 189, xvii 1, xix 428), but occurs only twice in the *Iliad* (i 477, xxiv 788). **ῥοδοδάκτυλος**: the rose familiar to the Greeks was red or pink, but the specific visual sense of the epithet seems not have been very precisely felt: Sappho applies it to the moon (96. 8); cf. ῥοδόπηχυς, used as a general ornamental epithet of goddesses and women (Hes. *Th.* 246, 251, fr. 64. 13, Sapph. 53, 58. 19). It is usually taken as referring to a pattern of rays like a spread hand, but, as M. L. West points out on Hes. *Op.* 610, it might also describe a single sliver of red light at the horizon (cf. Alc. 346. 1 δάκτυλος ἀμέρα).

3–5. = iv 308–10, cf. xx 125–6. **ἄντην**: 'to look at, in presence'; see further *LfgrE*.

6–8. Cf. *Il.* ii 50–2, 442–4. The scholia, reflecting the views of Aristarchus, observe that the lines are inoffensive here, but more appropriate in the *Iliad* (οὐδὲν μὲν ἀντιπράττουσιν οἱ στίχοι πρὸς τὴν παροῦσαν ὑπόθεσιν, οἰκειότεροι δὲ μᾶλλον εἰσιν ἐν Ἰλιάδι). The poet was not particularly interested in the details of summoning the assembly; he was content to use a ready-made description, perhaps indeed regarding this kind of cross-reference to the *Iliad* as desirable, and ignored the practical difficulties of convening such a meeting at short notice. **ἀγορήνδε**: the assembly is evidently supposed to be held in a regular place, with special seats for the elders (14).

9. On formulae consisting of a pair of virtually synonymous expressions see above, i 169 n.

10. παλάμη ... ἔγχος: cf. i 104 and n.

11–13. Cf. xvii 62–4. **κύνες πόδας ἀργοί**: here, and at xvii 63, there is a well-supported variant δύω κύνες ἀργοί; it is hard to choose between them. ἀργός has two meanings, 'fast' and 'white, shining'; the former seems more appropriate here, the animal's speed being more important than its colour; see further *LfgrE*. Dogs are used in Homer for hunting (e.g. xvii 291 ff., *Il.* xi 325), for herding and for guarding property (e.g. xvii 200, *Il.* xviii 578); wealthy men may keep them as pets (xvii 309–10, *Il.* xxii 69, xxiii 173). Cf. Verg. *A.* viii 461 'necnon et gemini custodes limine ab alto | praecedunt gressumque canes comitantur erilem'.

12. Athena similarly enhances Odysseus' appearance when it is particularly important that he should make a good impression: cf. vi 229 ff., viii 18 ff., xvi 172 ff., xxiii 156 ff. So too in the *Iliad* she endows Diomedes (v 4–5) and Achilles (xviii 206) with a fiery splendour before a significant appearance. This divine intervention alerts us to the critical nature of what is immediately to follow. **θεσπεσίην**: θεσπέσιος is generally understood as representing *θεσ-σπετος, 'spoken by a god, divinely uttered', cf. θέσφατος; but in Homer its precise significance has faded, and it merely means 'divine'. See further Frisk, *GEW*, Chantraine, *Dictionnaire*. **κατέχευεν**: for the metaphorical use of this verb cf. xiv 38, *Il.* ii 670.

13. θηεῦντο: 'gazed in wonder at'; on the connotations of θηέομαι and related verbs see H. J. Mette, '"Schauen" u. "Staunen"', *Glotta* xxxix (1961), 49 ff.

COMMENTARY

14. For the elders' special seats cf. *Il.* xviii 503 f. οἱ δὲ γέροντες | ἥατ᾽ ἐπὶ ξεστοῖσι λίθοις ἱερῷ ἐνὶ κύκλῳ, *Od.* viii 6. Evidently the elders are not necessarily old, since no objection is made to Telemachus sitting among them in his father's place.

15 ff. The procedure is clearly rather informal; there is no president or chairman. We might have expected that it would fall to the man responsible for summoning the meeting to make the opening speech. Aegyptius does not reappear.

15. Αἰγύπτιος: this is found as a personal name in Mycenaean (see Ventris–Chadwick, *Documents*, 136), but it is more likely that the choice of this name for a minor figure reflects the novelty of reopened communications with Egypt (on which see below, p. 192) than a memory of the Mycenaean age. (It is curious that Odysseus' herald, Eurybates, is described in terms suggesting a negroid appearance (xix 244 ff.): did the poet wish to suggest ancient links between Ithaca and North Africa?)

16. μυρία ἤδη: experience, rather than wide general knowledge.

17. καὶ γάρ: the following parenthesis should probably be taken as giving the reason why he was the first to speak, not as an explanation of 16.

18. Ἴλιον εἰς εὔπωλον: the epithet εὔπωλος is applied to Troy alone in Homer. The *Iliad* contains many references to the excellence of Trojan horses: cf. v 221 ff., 265 ff., 640 ff., xx 221 ff., xxiii 377 ff., cf. *Od.* xviii 261 ff. The military implications of the epithet should be borne in mind; the horse has no agricultural use in Homer.

19–20. According to the scholia these lines were athetized, presumably by Aristarchus; we do not know why, but these details are a slight distraction and we need to remind ourselves that we are being told more than Aegyptius himself or anyone else in Ithaca knew. The Cyclops has already been mentioned (i 69–70), though nothing is said there about his cannibalism (ix 288 ff., 311–12, 344 ff.). **Ἄντιφος:** short form of Ἀντίφονος. **σπῆϊ:** σπέεϊ would be more correct, but the incorrect contraction may well be early, and σπῆϊ should probably be retained. The declension of this archaic word presents several problems: see above, i 15 n. **πύματον δ᾽ ὁπλίσσατο δόρπον:** 'and prepared him last (of the Ithacans who were eaten) for his supper'; the clause might be taken to mean that Antiphus was Polyphemus' last meal, but there is no reason to think the Cyclops stopped eating altogether after he was blinded.

22. Eurynomus reappears briefly at xxii 242. **δύο ... ἔργα:** 'two all the time looked after the family farm-lands'; for this sense of ἔχω cf. iv 737; ἔργα, without further qualification, usually means 'agricultural work'; the transition to the sense of 'farm, tilled land' is easy.

23. τοῦ: i.e. Antiphus.

24. τοῦ: 'for him', cf. ὀδύρεσθαι with gen. iv 104, 819. **δάκρυ χέων:** MSS and scholia take this as one word, but the compound form is unsatisfactory.

25. Halitherses and Mentor, the other two aged Ithacans who speak in this assembly, begin in the same way (161, 229); the others address the man who has last spoken. **δὴ νῦν:** suggesting a certain urgency: see further Denniston, *Particles*, 218. **μευ:** one MS gives μοι; on this variation see below, 262 n.

26-7. The fact that no assembly has been held for nearly twenty years indicates that the poet regarded the institution as peripheral to the political organization of Ithaca. **θόωκος:** 'sitting, session', cf. v 3, xv 468, Hdt. vi 63. 2 ἐν θώκῳ κατημένῳ μετὰ τῶν ἐφόρων; Acgyptius may be supposed to refer to meetings of some more select body, which would normally prepare business to be set before the assembly. θόωκος is an extended form of θῶκος, contracted from *θό(ϝ)ακος. **Ὀδυσσεὺς δῖος:** an untraditional variation of the very common δῖος Ὀδυσσεύς.

28. τίνα χρειὼ τόσον ἵκει: cf. v 189, *Il.* x 142. χρειώ, normally fem., seems occasionally to be neut., though no instance is entirely conclusive: see LSJ s.v. χρεώ. Here it seems more natural to take τόσον as an adjective than adverbially.

30. Two obvious explanations are suggested in order that their subsequent rejection (42 ff.) may emphasize the abnormal character of what is happening. This method of highlighting an unusual situation by negating the typical is very characteristic: cf. xi 171-9, 181-203, xvi 30 ff., 36 ff., 95 ff., 114 ff., *Il.* vi 376 ff., xvi 36 ff., 50 ff. See further Arend, *Scenen*, 16, J. T. Kakridis, *Homeric Researches* (Lund, 1949), 111 ff. **ἀγγελίην στρατοῦ ... ἐρχομένοιο:** either 'news of an invading army' or 'news of the army's return (from Troy), a message from the returning army'; the former, which would call for prompt and well-organized communal action, is surely the more probable interpretation. **ἔκλυεν:** Zenodotus read ἦιον in 42, where our MSS give ἔκλυον: did he read ἦιεν here?

33. ὀνήμενος: aor. med. ptcp. of ὀνίνημι, used of those to (or of) whom one says ὄναιο, ὄναιτο, 'blessed' (with the implication that such a one is a blessing to others), cf. οὐλόμενος, applied to those to whom one says ὄλοιο, ὄλοιτο.

35. φήμη: a casual utterance regarded as an omen, cf. xx 100, 105 ff., also called κληδών (xviii 117, xx 120); cf. Ar. *Av.* 719-20: ὄρνιν τε νομίζετε πάνθ' ὅσαπερ περὶ μαντείας διακρίνει· | φήμη γ' ὑμῖν ὄρνις ἐστί. This idea is not found in the *Iliad*.

36-8. This detailed account of the moments before Telemachus starts to speak forms an interesting contrast to the rather cursory narrative of 6-8; it emphasizes the importance of what is to follow.

36. ἔτι δήν: the lengthening of iota of ἔτι reflects the earlier *δϝήν.

37. σκῆπτρον ... χειρί: the staff is a symbol of authority; for its use to give official sanction to the speaker in an assembly cf. *Il.* i 234 ff., ii 279, iii 218-19, x 321, 328, xxiii 566 ff. In such contexts it may be seen as representing the authority of the community, as also when carried by heralds as a badge of office (*Il.* vii 277). The king's σκῆπτρον, in Homer as throughout the ancient Near East, is a token of divine sanction for the ruler who wields it: cf. *Il.* ii 46, 101 ff., vi 159, ix 37-8, 98-9; kings alone are described as σκηπτοῦχοι, though the king may temporarily hand over

COMMENTARY

his σκῆπτρον to another, as a sign of delegated authority (*Il.* ii 185–6). Priests and seers also carry staffs (*Il.* i 15, 28, *Od.* xi 91), and Hesiod, who relates how the Muses gave him a staff (not a lyre) as a sign of his vocation, evidently regarded it as a normal attribute of a bard (*Th.* 30), a tradition continued in the rhapsode's staff. See further *RE* xi 2128–9 (Pfister), *Encyclopaedia of Religion and Ethics*, ed. J. Hastings (Edinburgh, 1911), xi 811 ff., F. J. M. de Waele, *The Magic Staff or Rod* (Nijmegen, 1927), L. Deubner, *Archiv f. Religionswissenschaft* xxx (1933), 83 ff., A. Alföldi, *AJA* lxiii (1959), 15 ff., M. L. West on Hes. *Th.* 30, J. V. Andreev, *Klio* lxi (1979), 367, Griffin, *Homer on Life and Death*, 9 ff.

38. Peisenor is not mentioned again.   πεπνυμένα ... εἰδώς: a formula regularly used of heralds: cf. iv 696, 711, xxii 361, xxiv 442, *Il.* vii 278.

40 ff. It may at first surprise us that Telemachus' expected ultimatum is not delivered until his second speech (138 ff.), but his denunciation of the suitors requires some preliminary account of their offence; Telemachus allows this to develop into a reproachful indictment of the community as a whole, and is overcome by tears before delivering his ultimatum. Heraclides Ponticus (fr. 174, ap. schol. ii 63) criticized this speech as ἀνοικονόμητον, and it is surely meant to reflect Telemachus' youth and inexperience. He wavers between a desire to be bold and a feeling of helplessness, and though he desperately needs the support of the people of Ithaca, his words are not likely to win them over; his high-flown outburst exposes him to Antinous' deflationary tactics. But the speech has a function beyond its immediate context, since it establishes the community's collective responsibility for the suitors' offences (cf. xxiv 455).

40. οὗτος ἀνήρ: 'this man (about whom you ask)' referring back to 28, not a periphrasis for ἐγώ; only with ἤγειρα does Telemachus reveal that this man is himself.

41. ὃς λαὸν ἤγειρα: lengthening at this point in the line is rather unusual when it does not coincide with punctuation: see van Leeuwen, *Enchiridium*, 91 § 19. This anomaly could be eliminated with Bentley's λαούς for λαόν or Cobet's τὸν λαὸν ἄγειρα, but neither conjecture is quite convincing.

42–4. Cf. 30–2.

42. ἔκλυον: Zenodotus read ἤιον, which deserves serious consideration as the *lectio difficilior*, though elsewhere the Homeric form of the impf. is ἄιον (ā at *Il.* x 532, xxi 388, ă at *Il.* xi 463, xviii 222).

43. εἴπω: the subjunctive replaces the opt. of 31 (εἴποι); grammatically this is anomalous (see Monro, *Homeric Dialect*, 258 § 282), but εἴποιμι would not scan without further alterations to the line.

44. Telemachus' claim that his troubles are not a matter of public concern well illustrates the *Odyssey*'s tendency to minimize the political implications of the situation; see further pp. 59 f. and i 386–7 n.

45. χρεῖος: see above, i 409 n.   ὅ: equivalent to ὅτι, 'in that, inasmuch as'.   κακόν: Aristophanes' reading κακά looks like a conjecture intended to avoid the need to take δοιά (46) rather awkwardly in a semi-adverbial sense, 'in two ways'.

46-9. These lines read like an afterthought (whether the original poet's or another's), intended to underline the pathos of Telemachus' predicament and partially modelled on his earlier account of his troubles (i 231 ff.). They rather unfortunately give the impression that Telemachus regards the destruction of his property as a more important matter than the loss of his father; the scholia (on 48) offer an attempt to meet this criticism: οὐχ ὡς προκρίνων τοῦ πατρὸς τὴν οὐσίαν, ἀλλὰ τὴν κατηγορίαν αὔξων τῶν νέων· ἄλλως τε τοῦτο μὲν ἀμφίβολον, ἐκεῖνο δὲ πρόδηλον.

47. τοίσδεσσιν: for this double dat. form cf. 165, xiii 258, *Il.* x 462; τοίσδεσι x 268, xxi 93; see further Chantraine, *Grammaire*, i 276 § 129.   **πατήρ ... ἦεν:** cf. 234, v 12 (with Hainsworth's n.), xv 152. Such kindly concern for his people is not to be taken for granted in a Homeric ruler; cf. iv 690 ff.; for Odysseus' own conception of a good king see xix 109 ff.

48-9. μεῖζον: sc. κακὸν ἔμπεσεν. The repetition ἅπαντα, πάγχυ, πάμπαν stresses the idea of total destruction.

50. μητέρι μοι μνηστῆρες: striking alliteration underlines the asyndeton. It is hard to say whether the dative μοι should be classified as possessive, ethical or of disadvantage.   **ἐπέχραον:** 'assailed, forced themselves upon'; the cpd. is found in only one other passage in Homer, *Il.* xvi 352, 356 (of physical attack).

51. Telemachus implies that the suitors' fathers ought to have called them to order. The scholia show that it was an old problem (discussed already by Aristotle's pupil, Heraclides Ponticus (fr. 173)) why Telemachus complained only of the Ithacan suitors; we have already been told that not all the suitors are of local origin (i 245 ff.) and later (xvi 247 ff.) Telemachus gives a full list in which only twelve out of one hundred and eight come from Ithaca. The two extra lines of Aristophanes' text (cf. i 245-6) represent an attempt to avoid this problem, which is not, however, very serious: the ringleaders come from Ithaca, and the poem very seldom mentions any except Ithacan suitors.

52 ff. Cf. xiv 90 ff. On the arrangements for Penelope's remarriage see above, i 275-8 and nn.   **πατρὸς ... ἐς οἶκον:** the phrase, as pointed out in the scholia, tends to suggest that Icarius lived in Ithaca; otherwise we might expect ποτὶ ἄστυ or πρὸς γαῖαν; at xv 16 it seems to be similarly implied that he lived nearby. But the detail should not be pressed. Later tradition located Icarius in Acarnania or Sparta.

53. ἐεδνώσαιτο: the verb occurs only here in Homer; its interpretation depends on the meaning of ἔεδνα presupposed here. ἔεδνα is used in Homer both of presents offered by suitors and, much less commonly, of gifts from the bride's kin (see above, i 275-8n.); since ἔεδνα must have the latter sense at 196 and a dowry also seems to be implied at 132-3, it is more natural to take ἐεδνώσαιτο θύγατρα as 'provide his daughter with a dowry' than as 'receive gifts from his daughter's suitors'. However, since the form of marriage-settlement envisaged does not affect Telemachus' argument, we may translate non-committally with 'betroth'. The optative is used here and in 54 instead of the subjunctive after a primary verb because the main clause is negative in sense: see Chantraine, *Grammaire*, ii 249 § 366, Monro, *Homeric Dialect*, 279–80 § 306.

54. οἱ ... ἔλθοι: understand ὅς as the subject; it is quite common in Homer where two relative clauses come together to omit the relative in the second clause. Here the choice is presented as that of Icarius; at 113–14 it is a joint decision and at 128 Penelope's alone.

55–9. = xvii 534–8.

55. εἰς ἡμέτερον: sc. δῶμα. Most MSS give εἰς ἡμετέρου (cf. vii 301, xvii 534), the reading of Aristarchus; the expression is apparently due to false analogy with such phrases as ἐς πατρός (e.g. ii 195), εἰς Αἰγύπτοιο (iv 581); cf. ἐν ἡμετέρου Archil. fr. 196a 4, Hdt. i 35. 4, vii 8 δ 1.

58. τὰ δὲ πολλά: τά should be taken as demonstrative, not with πολλά: 'and these things are largely wasted'. **ἔπ':** i.e. ἔπεστι.

63 ff. Telemachus' tone becomes markedly more impassioned as he appeals to the Ithacans for help against the suitors (inconsistently with his earlier claim (44) that he was not going to raise a matter of public interest); such wickedness, he argues, affects the whole community. The question of the relative guilt of the Ithacans corporately is well discussed by W. Krehmer, 'Volk ohne "Schuld"?', *ZAnt* xxvi (1976), 11 ff.

63–4. ἀνσχετά: i.e. ἀνασχετά, 'tolerable'. **οὐδ' ἔτι καλῶς ... διόλωλε:** 'and the ruin of my house has become a disgrace'. καλῶς occurs nowhere else in Homer; Heyne suggested καλά, but in the *Iliad* and *Odyssey* the middle of the line is the normal place for καλά used adverbially.

64–6. Telemachus appeals to the forces which inhibit wickedness. αἰδώς, shame, which works from within in response to social situations and the judgement of others, and νέμεσις, disapproval, a sense of indignation at another's wrongdoing which may lead one to intervene in the affairs of others, are often coupled: cf. *Il.* xiii 121–2 ἀλλ' ἐν φρεσὶ θέσθε ἕκαστος | αἰδῶ καὶ νέμεσιν, xi 649 αἰδοῖος νεμεσητός, *Cypr.* fr. 7. 5–6 ἐτείρετο γὰρ φρένας αἰδοῖ | καὶ νεμέσει, Hes. *Op.* 199–200 ἀθανάτων μετὰ φῦλον ἴτον προλίποντ' ἀνθρώπους | Αἰδὼς καὶ Νέμεσις, fr. 204. 82 νέμεσίν τ' ἀποθεῖτο καὶ αἰδῶ. Aristotle discusses them together (*EN* 1108 a 32 ff.). On αἰδώς in Homer see *LfgrE*, W. J. Verdenius, 'ΑΙΔΩΣ bei Homer', *Mnemosyne* NS 3, xii (1945), 147–60, J. M. Redfield, *Nature and Culture in the Iliad: The Tragedy of Hector* (Chicago–London, 1975), 113 ff. Athena-Mentes had already observed that a sensible man would feel νέμεσις at the suitors' behaviour (i 228). Arguments involving an appeal to honour and shame are a commonplace of ancient oratory: cf. K. J. Dover, *Greek Popular Morality in the Time of Plato and Aristotle* (Oxford, 1974), 226 ff. For the combined sanctions of fear of the gods and human nemesis cf. xxii 39–40; that the gods are held to guarantee some moral relationships is an important idea in the *Odyssey*, reflected in an epithet unknown to the *Iliad* θεουδής, 'god-fearing', i.e. just (vi 121, viii 576, etc.). **περικτίονας ... οἳ περιναιετάουσι:** cf. i 299–300 πατροφονῆα ... ὅ οἱ πατέρα κλυτὸν ἔκτα, and n.

67. μεταστρέψωσιν ἀγασσάμενοι κακὰ ἔργα: it is not clear whether μεταστρέψωσιν is trans., governing κακὰ ἔργα, in which case the sense is 'turn their

wickedness back upon them in anger'; otherwise, we must take κακὰ ἔργα
with ἀγασσάμενοι (for ἄγαμαι with acc., cf. iv 181, xxiii 64) and translate
'should change their attitude (sc. from passive indifference) in anger at
wickedness'. On the connotations of ἄγαμαι see Heubeck on x 249, *LfgrE*.
Just as the Trojans suffered collectively for Paris' sins and the Greek army
for Ajax's sacrilege (see above, i 325-7, and n.), so the people of Ithaca
may be punished for acquiescence in the suitors' misdeeds.

68. λίσσομαι ... Ζηνός: the asyndeton emphasizes Telemachus' prayer. πρός
is normally used in such adjurations; for the simple gen. cf. *Il.* xxii 345 μή
με ... γούνων γουνάζεο μηδὲ τοκήων. **Θέμιστος:** for the close association
of Zeus and Themis, a common idea later, cf. Hes. *Th.* 901, where she is
said to have been his second wife. Themis stands for the traditional order
of things, whether it depends merely on human convention (as, for
instance, the proper treatment of strangers, cf. xiv 56) or on nature (cf. xiv
130, ἢ θέμις ἐστὶ γυναικός); for the association of Themis with the conduct
of assemblies cf. *Il.* xx 4-5. See further Hoekstra on xiv 56, K. Latte, 'Der
Rechtsgedanke im archaischen Griechentum', *A&A* ii (1946), 63ff., *RE* v
A ii 1626 ff., H. Vos, *Themis* (Diss. Utrecht, 1956), W. Pötscher, 'Moira,
Themis u. τιμή im homerischen Denken', *WS* lxxiii (1960), 31 ff.

69. καθίζει: trans.

70 ff. Instead of appealing for help against the suitors, Telemachus asks the
Ithacans to stop encouraging them; his equation of apathy or acquiescence
with positive complicity is surely to be seen as an emotional distortion
betraying his youth and inexperience. **σχέσθε ... ἐάσατε:** cf. *Il.* xxii
416; σχέσθε: 'forbear, let be'; Aristophanes, who read μή instead of καί,
must have interpreted σχέσθε differently, perhaps 'support me' or 'resist',
though neither is very satisfactory. μή is surely a conjecture, producing a
more straightforward plea for assistance.

71. εἰ μή πού τι: rather heavy-handed irony. **πατὴρ ἐμὸς ἐσθλὸς Ὀδυσ-
σεύς:** cf. iii 98, iv 328. ἐσθλός is better taken with πατήρ than with
Ὀδυσσεύς: cf. 46 and Penelope's πόσιν ἐσθλόν iv 724, 814. Odysseus is
ἐσθλός as Telemachus' father; the collocation ἐσθλὸς Ὀδυσσεύς does not
occur otherwise. See further O. C. Cramer, 'Ulysses the Good?' *TAPhA* civ
(1974), 77 ff.

73. τῶν μ' ἀποτινύμενοι: 'exacting a return from me for this, making me pay
for this'; τῶν refers to the hypothetical wrongs committed by Odysseus.

74 ff. Telemachus contrasts the native Ithacans, against whom he would
have some redress, with the suitors, of whom the majority come from
elsewhere; this is, of course, inconsistent with the earlier part of his speech
(51 ff.), where he concentrated on the Ithacan suitors and ignored the rest.
It is not clear how Telemachus imagines he would enforce restitution of
property consumed without his consent; importunity alone would surely
not suffice. Commentators compare xiii 14, xxii 55, xxiii 357, but in none
of these contexts is the situation really analogous.

77. ποτιπτυσσοίμεθα: for the sense 'entreat' cf. iv 647.

78. ἕως: the only place in Homer where it is an iambus; see further notes on

135

148 and iii 126. The construction with κεν and opt., instead of pure opt., is also unique: cf. Chantraine, *Grammaire*, ii 261 § 386, Monro, *Homeric Dialect*, 282 § 307.

79. νῦν δέ: logical rather than temporal.

80. Cf. *Il.* i 245. **χωόμενος**: the verb has connotations of frustration and disappointment, as well as anger: cf. *Il.* xxii 291, xxiii 385. **ποτί**: to be taken closely with γαίῃ.

81. δάκρυ᾽ ἀναπρήσας: cf. *Il.* ix 433, the only other place in Homer where ἀναπρήθω occurs. Homeric heroes weep easily: e.g. viii 83 ff., 521 ff. (Odysseus), *Il.* i 349 (Achilles), xvi 3 (Patroclus); cf. schol. bT *Il.* i 349 ἕτοιμον τὸ ἡρωϊκὸν πρὸς δάκρυα. καὶ Ὀδυσσεὺς "ὡς δὲ γυνὴ κλαίῃσι" [*Od.* viii 523] καὶ ἡ παροιμία "ἀεὶ δ᾽ ἀριδάκρυες ἀνέρες ἐσθλοί", see also Hoekstra on xvi 191. **οἶκτος ... ἅπαντα**: Telemachus has not succeeded in inspiring any feeling of outrage at the suitors' behaviour, much less any general desire to help him.

82–128. Encouraged by the assembly's lack of response to Telemachus' appeal, Antinous lays the blame on Penelope; Telemachus should send her back to her father's house, so that her marriage may be arranged without delay.

82. ἀκήν: apparently an adverbial acc., but see further *LfgrE*, Frisk, *GEW* s.v. ἀκέων, Chantraine, *Dictionnaire* s.v. ἀκή.

84 ff. Antinous has already been introduced (i 383 ff.); his speech is cool, sophisticated, and uncompromising. His attempt to defend the suitors' consumption of Telemachus' substance as a justified reaction to Penelope's delaying tactics establishes beyond all doubt her extreme reluctance to remarry and the brutality of those who intend to force her to a second marriage whatever her feelings; it also shows Penelope to be not only loyal, but, like her husband, resourceful.

85. Cf. 303, xvii 406 (Antinous is the speaker); on ὑψαγόρη see above, i 385 n.

86. μῶμον: the noun occurs only here in Homer, though the related verbs μωμεύω and μωμάομαι are found (vi 274, *Il.* iii 412). μῶμος normally refers to comparatively trivial fault-finding, niggling criticism, malicious gossip; Antinous thus minimizes the gravity of Telemachus' charge: see further Parry, *Blameless Aegisthus*, 29 ff.

88. περί: 'outstandingly, beyond all others'.

89. This is the first indication of the period during which the suitors have been pestering Penelope; the apparent discrepancy with 106 (cf. xiii 377–8 οἳ δή τοι τρίετες μέγαρον κάτα κοιρανέουσι, | μνώμενοι ἀντιθέην ἄλοχον) may be explained by carelessness in equating ordinal and cardinal numbers: cf. *Il.* ii 134 ἐννέα δὴ βεβάασι Διὸς μεγάλου ἐνιαυτοί and 295–6 ἡμῖν δ᾽ εἴνατός ἐστι περιτροπέων ἐνιαυτὸς | ἐνθάδε μιμνόντεσσι, both referring to the same period of time.

At 175 we learn that Odysseus has been missing for nearly ten years: did the poet intend us to infer that Penelope was left in peace for six years after the fall of Troy? It would surely have been reasonable to assume long before then that Odysseus had failed to survive the journey home, and we might have expected the suitors' interest in Penelope to begin at a correspondingly earlier date. The extension of Odysseus' *nostos* to nearly a decade, which was almost certainly a relatively late development, has left a period unaccounted for; see further pp. 51 ff.

90. ἀτέμβει: 'cheat, frustrate', a strong and unusual verb.

91–2. = xiii 380–1, 'divide et impera'. **μὲν ἔλπει:** most MSS read μέν ῥ' ἔλπει, a clumsy attempt to repair a line which appeared metrically defective to readers unaware of the lost initial ϝ of ἔλπει; cf. Hoekstra on xiii 380.

93–110. The story of Penelope's web is repeated twice, by Penelope herself to Odysseus (xix 138 ff.) and by the ghost of the suitor Amphimedon to Agamemnon (xxiv 128 ff.). The relationship between the three passages has produced keen, but inconclusive, debate. Slight differences between them can largely be explained by the narrators' different viewpoints; but there is a more serious discrepancy over the timing of the ruse. While here we get the impression that the work was finished some time ago, and Penelope herself describes it as her first stratagem (xix 138), in Amphimedon's account the shroud has only just been completed when Odysseus arrives to save Penelope from a decision which can no longer be postponed (xxiv 149 ff.); the latter version, which produces a tauter narrative, is likely to be more faithful to the original conception. But this tale had surely long been a familiar part of Penelope's legend, and we should not suppose that the poet of the *Odyssey* was the first to relate it in verse; in the light of a better understanding of the techniques of oral poetry the question of relative priority among the three Odyssean versions has come to look unimportant. See further Russo on xix 138 ff., Heubeck on xxiv 128 ff., 147 ff., Woodhouse, *Composition*, 66 ff., W. Büchner, 'Die Penelopeszenen in der Odyssee', *Hermes* lxxv (1940), 129–36, Page, *Odyssey*, 120–1, 132–3, F. Wehrli, 'Penelope u. Telemachos', *MH* xvi (1959), 228 ff. = *Theoria u. Humanitas* (Zürich–Munich, 1972), 39 ff., F. M. Combellack, 'Three Odyssean Problems', *CSCA* vi (1973), 17 ff.

The main importance of the story lies in its portrayal of character. It represents a folk-tale of a common type, in which an importunate lover is put off by a trick; for other examples see Thompson, *Motif Index*, K. 1227. It has been suggested that it reflects a derivation of Penelope's name from πήνη 'thread, woof' and λέπω 'strip off'; but neither word occurs in the *Odyssey*, and the poet seems unaware of any such etymology: see above, i 222–3 n.

Penelope's project is slightly surprising. Though the sacrifice of precious fabrics in the course of the funeral ceremony did honour to the dead and was creditable to his family (cf. *Il.* xxii 510 ff.), Greek custom did not, so far as we know, require a special garment for burial; even if it had, and the obligation to make it had fallen on the daughter-in-law, there was nothing to stop Penelope working on it after remarriage, while the suitors might have found it strange that she had not already provided it, in view of Laertes' advanced age. It has been plausibly suggested that in the original

version of the story Penelope was weaving herself a wedding-garment. This
motif is found in the legend of St Agatha who, being pressed by her mother
to marry a rich man despite her wish to remain a virgin, agreed to marry
when she had finished weaving a wedding-veil, and postponed her
wedding-day by the same stratagem as Penelope (*Acta Sanctorum* 1 Febr.,
p. 604 E): see further W. Crooke, 'The wooing of Penelope', *Folklore* ix
(1898), 97 ff., R. Eisler, *Weltenmantel u. Himmelszelt* (Munich, 1910), 131 ff.
Possibly this was replaced by Laertes' shroud in order to strengthen
Laertes' rather insecure position in the plot (on which see above, i
188–93 n.).

93. δόλον τόνδ' ἄλλον: 'this further scheme' (besides leading the suitors on
with false promises).

94. στησαμένη μέγαν ἱστόν: the Greek loom was vertical and the weaver had
to stand. We should expect the loom itself to be a fixture, and the story
presupposes that Penelope cannot take the loom with her to her new home;
the phrase more probably means 'setting up the warp (vertical threads)'
than literally 'erecting the loom'.   **ἐνὶ μεγάροισιν:** 'in the palace':
according to xv 517 Penelope worked in an upper room, and we should in
any case expect her to keep out of the way of the suitors.

95. λεπτόν: the finer the thread, the longer the work would take.   **περί-
μετρον:** used in Homer only of Penelope's web.

96. ff. Penelope's speech consists of a single, unusually complex, periodic
sentence.

96. ἐπεὶ θάνε δῖος Ὀδυσσεύς: Penelope pretends to fall in with the suitors'
assumption, in order to win their confidence, as Telemachus does at i 396.

97. ἐπειγόμενοι τὸν ἐμὸν γάμον: 'though eager for this marriage with me'.

98. μεταμώνια: predicative.

100. τανηλεγέος: the epithet is found only in this formula, always at this
place in the line; it is one of a series of compounds in -ηλεγής, cf. δυσηλεγής,
ἀπηλεγέως, ἀνηλεγής, from ἀλέγω. τανηλεγής is most plausibly explained as
developing from, and equivalent to, ἀνηλεγής, 'pitiless, remorseless', the
initial τ originating from wrong word-division. See Russo on xix 145,
Frisk, *GEW*, Chantraine, *Dictionnaire*.

102. σπείρου: quite a general term, like 'sheet'.   **κεῖται:** subj.; on the form
see Chantraine, *Grammaire*, i 457 § 217, Monro, *Homeric Dialect*, 70 § 81.

105. ἀλλύεσκεν: iterat. impf. of ἀναλύω.   **ἐπεί:** so Allen, following Bekker,
but almost all MSS read ἐπήν; this contracted form has been condemned
by many scholars as post-Homeric, but though in very many places ἐπεί or
ἐπεί κ' could easily be substituted, some instances are less easily eradicated:
see above, i 293 n. Its use with the opt. here, contrary to Attic usage, is
surprising, but cf. iv 222; for further examples see Chantraine, *Grammaire*, ii
260–1 § 384.

106–7. τρίετες ... τέτρατον: some ancient editions had δίετες and δὴ τρίτον,
obvious conjectures to remove the apparent inconsistency with 89.

108. καὶ τότε: καί is emphatic, marking the beginning of the apodosis.

110. τό: this either refers back to φᾶρος (97) or is used rather vaguely.

111. The transition is rather abrupt. ὑποκρίνονται, ἵν' εἰδῇς: Bentley's conjecture ὑποκρίνονθ' ἵνα εἰδῇς not only respects the initial digamma of εἰδῇς (in itself a doubtful gain: see Hoekstra on xvi 236) but also removes a unique instance of punctuation after the trochee of the fifth foot (see Maas, *Greek Metre*, 60–1 § 88).

113–14. On the arrangements for Penelope's remarriage see above, i 275–8 n. τῷ ὅτεῳ ... αὐτῇ: for the omission of the relative pronoun in the second relative clause cf. 54 and n.

115–22. The construction changes, and no apodosis follows the conditional clause of 115; after a long parenthesis (116–22) the sentence is recast.

116. τὰ φρονέουσ' ... Ἀθήνη: 'setting her wits to work in things where Athene has favoured her so richly' (Shewring).

117. Cf. vii 111. ἔργα ... περικαλλέα: spinning and weaving are women's ἔργα *par excellence*; cf. i 357–8 and see further G. Wickert-Micknat, *Archaeologia* R, 38 ff. For the co-ordination of infin. and substantive cf. *Il.* i 258, vii 203, xv 642.

120. Tyro, daughter of Salmoneus, king of Elis, was the mother of Pelias and Neleus by Poseidon (and thus grandmother of Nestor), and also bore three sons to her husband Cretheus, Aeson, Pheres, and Amythaon (xi 235 ff., Hes. frr. 30–2). Alcmene, wife of Amphitryon, bore Heracles to Zeus (xi 266 ff., Hes. frr. 193. 19–20, 195 (= *Sc.* 1 ff.), 248). Mycene, eponymous heroine of Mycenae, daughter of Inachus and mother of Argos, was mentioned by Hesiod (fr. 246), but is only a name to us. Antinous selects three great names from the past, but there is no reason to regard any of these heroines as particularly clever; the antiquarian note is slightly strange, but the comparison undeniably flattering.

121. Cf. Penelope's own self-evaluation xix 325–6. ὁμοῖα ... Πηνελοπείῃ: i.e. ὁμοῖα νοήμασι Πηνελοπείης; for the compendious comparison cf. iv 279 φωνὴν ἴσκουσ' ἀλόχοισιν, xiii 89 ἄνδρα ... θεοῖς ἐναλίγκια μήδε' ἔχοντα, *Il.* xvii 51 κόμαι Χαρίτεσσιν ὁμοῖαι.

122. τοῦτο: understand νόημα from νοήματα in 121. ἐναίσιμον: 'fitting'.

123. ἔδονται: the lack of an expressed subject is awkward; μνηστῆρες must be understood from 111. Aristophanes, who read βίοτός τε τεός, must have taken ἔδονται as pass., thus avoiding the difficulty.

124–5. Antinous finds it hard to describe or comprehend Penelope's attitude; he simply ignores her abhorrence of the group which he represents.

125. τιθεῖσι: on the accentuation see Chantraine, *Grammaire*, i 298 § 138.

126. ποιεῖτ': i.e. ποιεῖται.

127–8. Cf. xviii 288–9. ἔργα: cf. 22 and n. Ἀχαιῶν: the gen. depends on the relative ᾧ.

129–45. Telemachus rejects Antinous' proposal; calling on the suitors to leave his house he prays that if they disregard his request they may die there unavenged.

130. οὔ πως ἔστι: the expression is used both of moral and of physical impossibility. ἀέκουσαν ἀπῶσαι: Antinous' speech has made it absolutely clear that Penelope will not leave willingly.

131–7. The argumentation is curiously weak and presents several oddities. Düntzer suggested that 132–3 were interpolated to elucidate ἐκ γὰρ τοῦ πατρὸς κακὰ πείσομαι (134), but even if these lines are cut out the passage is not free from difficulties; if there was indeed rhapsodic remodelling at this point, it was probably more extensive.

131. ἄλλοθι γαίης: 'in another land, far away'.

132–3. ζώει ὅ γ' ἢ τέθνηκε: cf. iv 110, 837, xi 464; elsewhere the formula is clearly an indirect question, but here the construction is rather loose. Odysseus' survival is not apparently in itself an obstacle to Penelope's remarriage, provided it is safe to assume that he will not return.   **κακὸν ... Ἰκαρίῳ:** it is disputed whether this refers to payment of compensation for an implied slight to Penelope, or to the restitution of her dowry (on which see above, i 275–8 n.). Either way, these financial considerations do Telemachus little credit, and are the more incongruous in view of the suitors' depredations, since any sum which Icarius might reasonably demand might be expected to strain Telemachus' resources less than the continued presence of the suitors.

134. τοῦ πατρός: presumably Penelope's father; though in Telemachus' mouth we might suppose Odysseus to be meant, the whole question of Penelope's remarriage presupposes that Odysseus will not return, and a reference to him here would considerably complicate the picture.   **δαίμων:** Telemachus is thinking of supernatural sanctions in general, not of any particular god.

135. The Erinyes were created as a result of the first act of violence perpetrated by a son against his father, the castration of Uranus by Cronus (Hes. *Th.* 185), and one of their principal functions is to punish crimes within the family; for their support of mother against son cf. xi 280, *Il.* ix 568 ff., xxi 412–13. They are closely associated with curses; cf. *Il.* xxi 412, A. *Eu.* 417.

137. It is not clear why Aristarchus athetized this line; the only reason given in the scholia is that it is superfluous, but this does not in itself seem a sufficient objection. There was, however, clearly a tendency to add lines summing up what has just been said, cf. iv 511, *Il.* v 527, xi 705.   **ἐνίψω:** to be understood as fut. of ἐνέπω, cf. xi 148, *Il.* vii 447; there has evidently been some confusion with ἐνίπτω, 'blame', cf. Chantraine, *Grammaire*, i 442–3 § 209. On the connotations of ἐνέπω see i 1 n.

138. αὐτῶν: strengthens ὑμέτερος, cf. i 7.

139–45. = i 374–80: see n.

146–76. Two eagles fly over the market-place; their strange behaviour impresses the crowd. The aged Halitherses prophesies Odysseus' imminent return and urges his fellow-citizens to restrain the suitors.

146 ff. Zeus similarly sends an eagle, the bird he loves best, τελειότατον πετεηνῶν, in answer to prayer at *Il.* viii 247, xxiv 315; we are thus assured that Telemachus' prayer will be fulfilled. This divine confirmation will seem the more impressive if we bear in mind how seldom Zeus intervenes directly in the events of the *Odyssey* (cf. xx 102 ff., xxi 413, xxiv 539); the omen underlines the seriousness of this moment. Further bird-omens relating to Odysseus' return occur at xv 160 ff., 525 ff., xx 242–3, cf. xix 535 ff.; this is the commonest type of omen in Homer, and the interpretation is invariably easy. There is a useful brief account of Odyssean omens in Thornton, *People*, 52–7; for a more detailed study see H. Stockinger, *Die Vorzeichen im homerischen Epos* (Munich, 1959), esp. 52 ff., 124 ff., 147 ff.

146. εὐρύοπα: in Homer this epithet is applied only to Zeus; originally acc. from *εὐρύοψ it came to be used as a nom. by analogy with μητίετα Ζεύς etc. Its meaning is probably 'with far-reaching voice', cf. Chantraine, *Grammaire*, i 200 § 83, Frisk, *GEW*, Chantraine, *Dictionnaire*.

148. τὼ δ᾽ ἧος: Allen unnecessarily adopts Platt's conjecture for τὼ ἕως μέν; for monosyllabic ἕως cf. v 123 (with Hainsworth's n.), *Il.* xvii 727; see further Chantraine, *Grammaire*, i 12 § 3. For the meaning 'for a time' (= τέως) cf. *Il.* xii 141, xiii 143, xv 277, xvii 727, 730.

150. πολύφημον: cf. Hdt. v 79. 1, where the Pythia's instruction ἐς πολύφημον ἐξενεῖκαι is interpreted to mean 'bring it before the assembly'.

151. ἐπιδινηθέντε ... πυκνά: 'wheeling over it, they beat their wings rapidly'. The scholia interpret the line in terms of a collision resulting in loss of plumage (ἐκεῖσε δὲ ἐνταῦθα συστραφέντες ἐν τῷ καταράσσειν τὰ συνεχῆ αὐτῶν πτερά). But the two birds, which arrive and depart together, are surely supposed to be acting in harmony, and simple clumsiness is out of place in an omen. The contrast between their smooth, powerful flight and this violent flapping as they hover above the assembly is highly effective. There is perhaps a reminiscence of this passage in Sapph. 1. 11–12 (of Aphrodite's στροῦθοι) πύκνα δίννεντες πτέρ᾽ ἀπ᾽ ὠράνω αἴθε|ρος διὰ μέσσω.

152–4. Obscure and strangely expressed; serious corruption has been suspected in 152 and 154. ἱκέτην: ἰδέτην is the better attested reading, given sinister overtones by the second half of the line. ὄσσοντο δ᾽ ὄλεθρον: 'doom was in their eyes, their look threatened doom', cf. *Il.* i 105, xxiv 172.[1] δρυψαμένω: often interpreted as reciprocal, but this outburst of mutual aggressiveness would be hard to explain, since the two birds must represent Odysseus and Telemachus; it is better taken as reflexive, and interpreted as a gesture of mourning (cf. *Il.* ii 700, xi 393), a natural reaction to the situation in Ithaca, though it is hard to envisage a bird on the wing in an attitude which could be so described; on either interpretation παρειάς seems a little strange. It is worth considering a view mentioned but rejected by Eustathius, that the necks and cheeks belong to the assembled Ithacans (πάντων, cf. αὐτῶν 154); this produces a vivid picture, corresponding closely to the tactics of Odysseus' vengeance, an unexpected attack by a determined pair on an unarmed crowd. But if this was what the poet intended, he would surely have used the active,

---

[1] Rhianus had another reading, reported in the scholia as ἔσσατο and explained as ὄσσαν καὶ κληδόνα ἐποίουν. ἔσσατο must be corrupt; I prefer Porson's ὄσσαντο (from an otherwise unattested *ὄσσαμαι, probably Rhianus' own invention) to Ludwich's ὀσσῶντο, as the corruption of the unusual form is easier to account for. See further C. Mayhoff, *De Rhiani Cretensis studiis homericis* (Leipzig, 1870), 59–60.

δρύψαντες.   ἀμφί: probably adverbial, 'all round'.   δεξιώ: right is
east in Greek divination, cf. *Il.* xii 239; see further A. Bouché-Leclercq,
Histoire de la divination dans l'antiquité (Paris, 1879), 137–8.   αὐτῶν: of the
Ithacans; αὐτῶν has been suspected, but the whole passage is clumsily
composed. The accumulation of difficulties in these three lines is disturb-
ing: could they be a later addition intended to make the omen more
sensational, and thus heighten the perversity of the suitors who insist on
ignoring it?

157–9. Halitherses is mentioned among Telemachus' πατρώιοι ἑταῖροι at xvii
69; he plays a more important part at xxiv 451 ff., but his warning again
goes unheeded. His name seems to mean 'Sea-bold'; Mastor, his father,
'Seeker', has apparently been invented, like Antinous' father Eupeithes (i
383), to characterize his son.   ὄρνιθας γνῶναι: not all birds are significant
(cf. 181–2, xv 531–2), and the augur must recognize those that are.

161 ff. Halitherses' speech, a final, vain, appeal to the suitors, should be
compared with other speeches of augural interpretation, xv 172 ff., 531 ff.,
xx 245–6, *Il.* ii 323 ff., xii 211 ff.; *Od.* xix 546 ff. is analogous. In all the
other long speeches there is a careful comparison of sign and reality;
Halitherses merely presents his conclusions, and his speech offers no help
with the difficulties of the preceding description. The numerical element,
where there is one, is important in omens; yet Halitherses speaks as if only
a single eagle had appeared. The poet cannot allow him to be too specific;
a solemn warning against the vulnerable Telemachus would create
difficulties in the development of the story at this point. In the latter part of
the speech (170 ff.) Halitherses' argumentation is circular; he infers from
his interpretation of the present omen that his prophecy twenty years
before was correct, and hence that his interpretation of what has just
happened is trustworthy. But the validity of his warning is not affected by
this illogicality; the omen simply confirms the moral judgment of right-
minded men.

As it stands, Halitherses' speech contains a falsehood in his claim (165)
that Odysseus is near at hand, plotting the suitors' death, a detail which
Telemachus quite ignores (212 ff.); Odysseus is still as far from Ithaca as
he has ever been, and though Tiresias had forewarned him (xi 115 ff.), he
does not address his thoughts to the problem presented by the suitors until
he gets home (xiii 375 ff.). Analytic critics have seen here a reflection of a
different version of the story, in which Odysseus was already back in
Ithaca at the time of this assembly. But the discrepancy might also be due
to the knowledge of subsequent developments which the poet shared with
his audience: Odysseus' return is now certain, despite the distance. See
further Page, *Odyssey*, 170–1.

161. See 25 n.

162. εἴρω: see Hoekstra on xiii 7.

163. πῆμα κυλίνδεται: cf. *Il.* xi 347, xvii 688; the metaphor seems to be that
of a wave.

164–5. ἤδη ἐγγύς: balancing and controverting δὴν ἀπάνευθε.   τοίσδεσσι:

see 47 n.   **κῆρα:** on the connotations of Homeric κήρ see Hainsworth on v 387.

166. κακόν: probably predicative, Odysseus being understood as the subject, cf. iii 306.

167. εὐδείελον: an epithet of places, not found in the *Iliad*, and applied in the *Odyssey* almost exclusively to Ithaca (more generally at xiii 234). Its occurrence in an inscription from Phocis (to be published in *IG* ix 1² 4) indicates that it was not an artificial, poetic coinage, but throws no light on its meaning. Ancient scholars were uncertain whether it should be connected with δῆλος or with δείλη; the former seems more likely. See further Frisk, *GEW*, Chantraine, *Dictionnaire* s.v. δείελος, δῆλος, G. Klaffenbach, *Glotta* xlviii (1970), 204–5.

168. καταπαύσομεν: sc. μνηστῆρας, subject of πανέσθων.

170. ἀπείρητος: 'inexperienced', cf. *h.Ven.* 133.

174–6. Cf. ix 533–4, xi 113–15; a synopsis of the *Odyssey* and the first clear indication of the length of time which has elapsed since Odysseus' departure. The way in which this date is introduced strongly suggests conscious imitation of the *Iliad*, where the information that the action takes place in the tenth year of the war is similarly first given (ii 134) at a public meeting in an account of a portent at the beginning of the campaign.

177–207. Eurymachus mocks Halitherses and repeats the demand that Penelope should return to her father's house so that her wedding may be arranged.

Eurymachus was introduced at i 399. His speech, marked by a specious realism, exemplifies the suitors' disregard for divine warnings (cf. xx 360 ff.), an important motif in the poem (cf. i 37 and n.). It is interesting to compare Agamemnon's reaction to an unpalatable demand by a seer (*Il.* i 106 ff.): angry as the king is, he obeys unquestioningly. Eurymachus' rebuke to Halitherses is combined with advice to Telemachus, in which he covers much the same ground as Antinous; but unlike Antinous he is rude and abusive.

178. εἰ δ' ἄγε: see above, i 271 n.

180. ταῦτα: with μαντεύεσθαι.

181–2. The pious Hector dismisses the whole art of augury in much stronger terms, *Il.* xii 237 ff. But there is an important difference: Hector relies on a divine promise, and though he is wrong, he is not impious.

183. τῆλ': contradicting ἐγγύς in 165.

185. ἀνιείης: from ἀνίημι, 'excite, urge on'.

186. The charge of corruption is often brought against seers by those who find their message unwelcome: cf. S. *OT.* 387 ff., *Ant.* 1055, E. *IA* 520.

188. παλαιά ... εἰδώς: 'with so much long experience'.

190. ἀνιηρέστερον: this comparative, as if from an adj. in -ήρης, was no doubt coined for metrical convenience, since it avoids a succession of 3 short syllables: cf. Chantraine, *Grammaire*, i 95 § 41, 258 § 121.

191. The line is absent from many MSS and ignored by the scholia and Eustathius; it is clearly a late interpolation modelled on *Il.* i 562.

192-3. Eurymachus' threat is puzzling; it has an air of legalism, but what is the implied offence? **ἐπιθήσομεν:** presumably the subject is to be understood as the community as a whole, not just the suitors. **ἦν:** this should be taken with τίνων, ἐνὶ θυμῷ going with ἀσχάλλῃς.

195-7. Cf. i 275-8: see n. ad loc.; but in the earlier passage, where this forms part of Athena-Mentes' advice to Telemachus, Penelope's own desire to marry again (εἴ οἱ θυμὸς ἐφορμᾶται γαμέεσθαι) is an essential condition. **ἐς πατρός:** understand οἶκον. **ἀπονέεσθαι:** for the lengthening of ἀπο- in ἀπονέεσθαι (and some other parts of this verb) cf. ἀποπέσῃσιν xxiv 7, ἀποδίωμαι Il. v 763. Metrical necessity does not satisfactorily explain this puzzling form, since the poet could easily have used the simple verb νέεσθαι; see further Wyatt, *Lengthening*, 84-7, Hoekstra, *Mnemosyne* xxxi (1978), 18-20.

199. ἔμπης: 'all the same, nevertheless'.

200. μάλα περ πολύμυθον ἐόντα: 'for all his long speeches'.

202. μυθέαι: we should expect μυθέεαι, and some editors emend to μυθέε'; but πωλέαι at iv 811 cannot be corrected in this way and thus provides some confirmation: cf. Chantraine, *Grammaire*, i 73 § 30, Monro, *Homeric Dialect*, 352 § 378.

203-4. βεβρώσεται: used as pass. **οὐδέ ποτ' ἶσα | ἔσσεται:** 'will never be equal (to what they were before)': so Eustathius, Ebeling. But the initial digamma of ἶσος is normally observed and the phrase has often been suspected, though no convincing emendation has been suggested: see further G. M. Bolling, *CPh* xxvi (1931), 313.

205-7. The ending of Eurymachus' speech was suspected by Aristophanes, who particularly objected to the use of ἀρετή in 206; according to the scholia ὁ Ἀρίσταρχος λείπειν φησὶ τὸ ἄρθρον, ἵν' ἦ εἵνεκα τῆς ταύτης ἀρετῆς ... Ἀριστοφάνης δὲ ὑπώπτευε τὸν στίχον, νεωτερικὸν λέγων τὸ ὄνομα τὸ τῆς ἀρετῆς. πιθανὸν δὲ συναθετεῖν αὐτῷ καὶ τὸν πρὸ αὐτοῦ καὶ τὸν μετ' αὐτόν. Though Aristophanes' specific criticism of εἵνεκα τῆς ἀρετῆς can be met quite easily, the expression is certainly odd; also noteworthy is the awkward ὃν γάμον of 205, producing an unparalleled construction with a double acc. for διατρίβω ('delays the Greeks with regard to her marriage'). 204 would provide an energetic and satisfactory conclusion to Eurymachus' speech; Aristophanes may well have been right to suspect interpolation.

206. τῆς ἀρετῆς: Aristarchus' interpretation, 'this woman's excellence', has won considerable support among modern commentators; cf. τῆς εὐνῆς (sc. Βρισηίδος) Il. ix 133, 275, xix 176; the alternative, 'this, i.e. such, excellence' is rather flat. Brugmann's conjecture ἧς for τῆς (cf. xxiv 197) would remove this uncertainty. Aristarchus' view is supported by references to Penelope's ἀρετή at xviii 251 (= xix 124), xxiv 193, 197; in the first passage the word includes, or perhaps refers primarily to, her beauty. It is not clear why Aristophanes thought the use of the word here unhomeric; perhaps he took it in the sense 'distinction, success, the reward of excellence' (LSJ s.v. ἀρετή iii).

208–23. Telemachus' third speech. He does not refer to the omen, nor to the two speeches which followed it, but asks for a ship so that he may seek news of Odysseus in Pylos and Sparta.

The assembly has fulfilled its purpose in Athena's plan, and Telemachus now moves on to the second stage of her project for him. Though nothing immediately comes of his request for help (212–13), his speech shows that, despite the suitors' rejection of his appeal, he has not succumbed to resignation and will not try to persuade his mother to remarry until Odysseus' fate is certain.

212–23. Cf. i 279–92, and n. But Athena did not tell Telemachus to ask for a ship in the assembly; at i 280 it is simply assumed that transport will present no problems.

213. ἔνθα καὶ ἔνθα: 'there and back'.

222. χεύω: κτερεῖξω shows that χεύω must be understood as fut., though it does not look like a fut. form. χεύσω, given by many MSS, corresponds to the late ἔχευσα, and must be post-Homeric. Aristarchus' reading is uncertain, perhaps χείω (Porson's conjecture for χρείω/χρειώ of schol.). The adaptation of Athena's commands to statements of intention has produced an anomalous form; see further Shipp, *Studies*, 319.

224–41. Emphasizing the community's collective responsibility for the suitors' depredations, Mentor reproaches the Ithacans for their indifference and seeks to rouse them against the suitors.

This is the only place where Mentor appears *in propria persona*; elsewhere 'Mentor' is Athena who has assumed his appearance. The poet thus prepares us for the role which Mentor is to play as Athena's alias; at the same time this expression of support for Telemachus provides an opening for Leocritus, the most brutal of the suitors.

225. Cf. Odysseus' appeal (xxii 208–9): Μέντορ, ἄμυνον ἀρήν, μνῆσαι δ' ἑτάροιο φίλοιο, | ὅς σ' ἀγαθὰ ῥέζεσκον· ὁμηλικίη δέ μοί ἐσσι. ἀμύμονος: see above, i 29 n.

226–7. A puzzling detail, though we may compare Agamemnon's action in entrusting Clytaemestra to his ἀοιδός (iii 267). But there is no suggestion elsewhere that Mentor has some sort of responsibility, however vaguely defined, towards Odysseus' dependants, nor does Telemachus think of turning to him for advice or moral support. 227 elaborates 226 unnecessarily and awkwardly, but its omission in one MS is surely just an accident.

227. γέροντι: presumably Mentor himself, not, as some commentators take it, Laertes, who is not elsewhere regarded as taking an active interest in Odysseus' household; οἶκον must then be understood as subject of πείθεσθαι and Mentor as subject of φυλάσσειν.

229. Cf. 25.

230–4. Repeated by Athena herself at v 8–12. For the paradox-wish of 230–2 cf. Hes. *Op.* 270 ff. νῦν δὴ ἐγὼ μήτ' αὐτὸς ἐν ἀνθρώποισι δίκαιος | εἴην, μήτ' ἐμὸς υἱός, ἐπεὶ κακὸν ἄνδρα δίκαιον | ἔμμεναι, Thgn. 129–30 μήτ' ἀρετὴν εὔχου Πολυπαΐδη ἔξοχος εἶναι | μήτ' ἄφενος· μοῦνον δ' ἀνδρὶ γένοιτο τύχη.

230. πρόφρων: best translated by an adverb, 'wholeheartedly, willingly'.

COMMENTARY

καὶ ἤπιος: hiatus at the end of the fourth foot is unusual: see van Leeuwen, *Enchiridium*, 83–4 § 14. Here two examples occur very closely: cf. 232 καὶ αἴσυλα; Bentley's conjectures ἀγανός ⟨τε⟩ and ἀήσυλα would remove both very simply.

231. αἴσιμα εἰδώς: a good example of the use of οἶδα to express moral rather than intellectual qualities; cf. i 428 and n.

232. αἴσυλα: in Homer this adjective is found only in n. pl., with ῥέζω and μυθέομαι; its meaning is evidently 'wicked, criminal', but its etymology is quite uncertain.

234. πατὴρ δ' ὣς ἤπιος ἦεν: cf. ii 47 and n.

236. κακορραφίῃσι: cf. κακὰ ῥάπτειν iii 118, xvi 423. The pl. is very often used with abstract nouns in Homer where the sg. might seem to us more natural, perhaps partly for metrical convenience: cf. 346 πολυϊδρείῃσιν, xix 523 ἀφραδίας, *Il.* i 205 ὑπεροπλίῃσι, v 521 βίας, xvi 776 ἱπποσυνάων.

237. παρθέμενοι: 'hazarding, staking', cf. iii 74, ix 255 (of pirates).

238. νέεσθαι: used, as often, with fut. sense.

239. οἷον: 'seeing how'.

240. ἄνεῳ: it was disputed in antiquity whether this should be taken as nom. pl. of an Attic declension adjective *ἄνεως (so Allen) or as an adverb. But the former interpretation is impossible at xxiii 93, and the poet of the *Odyssey* surely understood the word as an adverb; see further *LfgrE*.

242–59. Leocritus replies to Mentor with a threatening speech, bidding the people return home.

The suitors' unscrupulous insolence now appears undisguised; Leocritus makes no attempt to justify their behaviour, but simply assumes that might is right.

242. Ληόκριτος: this is the spelling which we should expect, from ληός = λεώς, but our MSS consistently give Λειώκριτος wherever the name occurs (cf. xxii 294, *Il.* xvii 344); see further Werner, *H u. ει vor Vokal*, 71–2.

243. ἀταρτηρέ: ἀταρτηρός occurs in only two other places in early Greek epic (*Il.* i 223, Hes. *Th.* 610), being applied to men or their utterance, and apparently meaning 'harmful, mischievous', though its etymology is uncertain; subsequently it falls out of use until revived by Hellenistic poets. See further Kirk on *Il.* i 223, Frisk, *GEW*, Chantraine, *Dictionnaire*, *LfgrE*.

244–5. ἀργαλέον .. δαιτί: this can be taken in two ways: (1) It is hard (i.e. oppressive) even for men with an advantage in numbers to fight for the sake of a feast; (2) It is hard to fight against men who actually have an advantage in numbers for the sake of a feast. (2), taking πλεόνεσσι closely with μαχήσασθαι, seems preferable: cf. 251 εἰ πλεόνεσσι μάχοιτο, xvi 88–9 πρῆξαι δ' ἀργαλέον τι μετὰ πλεόνεσσιν ἐόντα | ἄνδρα καὶ ἴφθιμον. This should probably be interpreted as a threat to Mentor: an old man like him cannot hope to achieve anything against the suitors; even Odysseus would find the odds against him too great. It is also true that the people of Ithaca outnumber the suitors, but this is less relevant; Leocritus is surely more concerned to stress that Mentor is in a minority than to consider the possible consequences of collective action.

The ancient variant παύροισι is presumably a conjecture intended to remove any uncertainty, as is εἰ πλέονές οἱ ἕποιντο in 251.

246. εἴ περ: 'even if'; see i 167 n.

249. Cf. *Il.* xiv 503–4 οὐδὲ γὰρ ἡ Προμάχοιο δάμαρ Ἀλεγηνορίδαο | ἀνδρὶ φίλῳ ἐλθόντι γανύσσεται.

250. ἀεικέα: 'humiliating', bringing discredit to the victim.

253. ὀτρυνέει: 'shall urge on, speed', cf. vii 151. Leocritus is of course sarcastic: the only help which Telemachus may expect is from two ineffective old men.

256. τελέει ... ταύτην: not a threat, but an aspersion on Telemachus' competence.

257. αἰψηρήν: proleptic, 'quick to disperse'.

258. Telemachus' lack of popular support is indicated by the Ithacans' ready acquiescence in Leocritus' high-handed dismissal.

260–98. Telemachus goes to the sea-shore and prays to the divinity who visited him on the previous day. Athena, in the guise of Mentor, encourages him, and promises to see to ship and comrades.

260. Similarly Chryses goes to the sea-shore to pray to Apollo (*Il.* i 34 ff.); cf. *Il.* i 348 ff., Pi. *O.* i 71 ff.

261. For the ritual washing of hands cf. iii 440 ff., iv 750 ff., xii 336–7, *Il.* ix 171, xvi 230, xxiv 302 ff., Hes. *Op.* 724–5, 737 ff., etc. **πολιῆς ἁλός:** the genitive is best classified as partitive; verbs expressing the idea of bathing or washing may be constructed with either gen. or dat.: see Chantraine, *Grammaire*, ii 52 § 62. **Ἀθήνη:** Telemachus realized immediately after Mentes' departure that he had been visited by a god (i 323), but does not yet know who it was; for Nestor, who knows that Odysseus was a favourite of Athena's, it is an easy inference that it must have been her (iii 377 ff.).

262. κλῦθι: normally the function of κλῦθι and κλῦτε is to attract the god's attention to the request which follows, but here κλῦθι itself constitutes the appeal; Telemachus' prayer, like that of Achilles to Thetis (*Il.* i 352 ff.), does not contain any specific petition. It is probably wrong to regard κλῦθι and κλῦτε as poetic creations: see further Hainsworth on vi 239, Wyatt, *Lengthening*, 210–11. **μοι:** the dat., given by most MSS, is to be preferred as the *lectio difficilior* to μευ, the reading of Aristarchus; the enclitics μοι, σοι, οἱ often function as genitives in Homer: see Chantraine, *Grammaire*, ii 70 § 88. **χθιζός:** used adverbially. **δῶ:** see above, i 176 n.

264. Cf. i 281.

265–6. τὰ δέ: his voyage. **διατρίβουσιν:** 'thwart, hinder, delay'; Leocritus had ridiculed Telemachus' request.

267. The first hemistich is a very common formula, its usual sequel being τοῦ δ' ἔκλυε – ∪ ∪ – ×. **σχεδόθεν:** 'from nearby'.

268. = 401, xxii 206, xxiv 503, 548; the formula is well discussed by J. S. Clay, *Hermes* cii (1974), 129 ff.

270–80. Mentor's opening is somewhat rambling, and some have suspected interpolation. But its slight incoherence is appropriate for an old man, and Athena's alias must look convincing.

270. ὄπιθεν: 'hereafter, in future'; Mentor combines a compliment on Telemachus' performance in the assembly with encouragement for the future.

An alternative punctuation is possible, with a stop at the end of 270 and a comma at the end of 272; the conditional clause of 271–2 then goes with 273, not with 270.

271. A rather striking way of expressing the idea of heredity; the compound ἐνστάζω occurs only here in Homer.

272. οἷος κεῖνος ἔην: the construction is not quite clear, but it should probably be taken as a kind of indirect exclamation, 'seeing what a man he was'. Alternatively, there might be an ellipse, leaving ὥστε σε εἶναι τοιοῦτον οἷος to be understood, but this seems rather unnatural. **τελέσαι ἔργον τε ἔπος τε:** for the idea of all-round competence compare the aim of the heroic education as described by Phoenix (*Il.* ix 443) μύθων τε ῥητῆρ' ἔμεναι πρηκτῆρά τε ἔργων.

273. ἀλίη: 'in vain'; the epithet is restricted to ὁδός in the *Odyssey*; in the *Iliad* its application is much wider.

274–5. In view of the repeated emphasis on Telemachus' resemblance to his father (cf. i 207–9, and n.), this is clearly meant to seem absurd, a rather laborious joke; it is merely a parenthesis, and γάρ in 276 refers back to 271–2. **οὐ κείνου:** for οὐ as neg. in conditions, especially in antithesis, cf. xii 382, *Il.* iii 289, iv 55, 160, etc. **ἔπειτα:** logical, 'in that case'.

276–7. The general idea of progressive degeneration is a commonplace, expressed on the grandest scale in Hesiod's myth of the ages (*Op.* 106 ff.). This particular passage seems to be reflected in E. *Heracl.* 325 ff.: ἐξ ἐσθλῶν δὲ φὺς | οὐδὲν κακίων τυγχάνεις γεγὼς πατρός, | παύρων μετ' ἄλλων· ἕνα γὰρ ἐν πολλοῖς ἴσως | εὕροις ἂν ὅστις ἐστὶ μὴ χείρων πατρός. Unfavourable comparison with the previous generation is common in paraenesis: cf. *Il.* iv 372 ff., v 800–1. The alliteration in π is very marked; on alliteration in Greek proverbial phrases see M. S. Silk, *Interaction in Poetic Imagery* (Cambridge, 1974), 224 ff. **κακίους, ἀρείους:** these contracted comparatives, normal in Attic, are rare in Homer: see Chantraine, *Grammaire*, i 255 § 118.

278. The obvious echo of 270 marks the end of the digression.

279. οὐδέ ... πάγχυ: probably 'not at all' rather than 'not altogether'.

281. βουλήν τε νόον τε: ideas, attitude, way of looking at things; cf. iv 267, xi 177.

284. ὅς: i.e. θάνατος. **ἐπ' ἤματι:** 'in one day, in a day's space', cf. *Il.* x 48, xix 229.

285 ff. Athena takes over the organization of Telemachus' voyage. On her connection with seamanship see M. Detienne and J. P. Vernant, *Cunning Intelligence in Greek Culture and Society* (Hassocks, Sussex, 1978), 216 ff. (= *Les Ruses de l'intelligence: La Mètis des grecs* (Paris, 1974), 201 ff.). Athena's role in escorting Telemachus to Pylos has much in common with Hermes' guidance of Priam in *Il*. xxiv.

286–7. For τοῖος ... ὅς, 'such ... that', cf. *Il*. vii 231, xxiv 182–3.

289. ἤϊα: normally, as here, 'provisions for a journey'; but at v 368 it must mean 'chaff'. It occurs only once in the *Iliad* (xiii 103), meaning 'food'. It has three scansions, − − ∪ (here, 410, *Il*. xiii 103), − ∪∪ (iv 363, xii 329), and, at the end of the line, − ∪ (v 266, ix 212, cf. v 368). Its etymology is quite uncertain: see Frisk, *GEW*, Chantraine, *Dictionnaire*.

290. ἀμφιφορεῦσι: it is interesting that both this and the later, haplographic, form ἀμφορεύς are attested in the Linear B tablets; see further Heubeck on ix 163–5, Hoekstra on xiii 105, *LfgrE*. ἄλφιτα: 'groats', i.e. either whole grains with the hulls removed or the relatively large particles which result from a rough crushing of such grains; the restriction of the term to barley-groats is almost certainly post-homeric. From ἄλφιτα could be made μάζαι, 'kneaded cakes', which were eaten uncooked. See further L. A. Moritz, '*ΑΛΦΙΤΑ*: A Note', *CQ* xliii (1949), 113–17, *Grain-mills and Flour in Classical Antiquity* (Oxford, 1958), 149 ff. The emphasis on cereals more accurately reflects reality than the abundant roast meat conventional in Homeric meals.

292. ἐθελοντῆρας: the word occurs only here.

294. ἐπιόψομαι: 'I will choose', cf. *Il*. ix 167; whether this should be taken as fut. of ἐφοράω or of a quite different verb (cf. LSJ s.v. ἐπιόψομαι) is uncertain.

295. νῆα may easily be supplied as object of ἐφοπλίσσαντες and ἐνήσομεν from the preceding clause.

296. ἔτι δήν: on the lengthening of a short syllable before δήν see above, 36 n.

298. φίλον τετιημένος ἦτορ: Telemachus is depressed at the prospect of facing the suitors again before his departure.

299–336. Telemachus is welcomed back with mockery by Antinous; his calm determination to proceed with his projected journey provokes taunts from all sides.

300. ἀνιεμένους: 'flaying, skinning', cf. E. *El*. 826 ἀνεῖτο λαγόνας, Hsch. ἀνιέναι· δέρειν; the skin is undone, loosened, so that the flesh below is laid bare.

301 ff. Antinous behaves as if Telemachus' public protest was merely an adolescent outburst; cf. i 383 ff. and n.

301. ἰθύς: with Τηλεμάχοιο; for the separation of ἰθύς from its gen., cf. iii 17, xxiv 241, *Il*. xvi 602, xxiv 471.

302. A common formula. ἔν ... οἱ φῦ χειρί: ἐν should be taken closely with φῦ (cf. i 381); the verb, literally 'was rooted in', comes to mean 'clung closely'. It is not clear whether χειρί is locative, 'he clung closely to Telemachus' hand, grasped Telemachus' hand tightly', or instrumental, 'he took hold of him with his hand'; but in view of 321 the former is more likely. ἔκ τ' ὀνόμαζε: here this might mean 'addressed him by name, called him by name', but in some contexts this is impossible (e.g. v 181, x 319, *Il*. xiv 218) and the verb evidently means merely 'spoke aloud', with ἔπος understood as its object. See also Hoekstra on xiv 52, and for a detailed discussion R. d'Avino, 'La funzionalità di ὀνομάζω e la formula ἔπος τ' ἔφατ' ἔκ τ' ὀνόμαζε', *Studia classica et orientalia Antonino Pagliaro oblata*, ii (Rome, 1969), 7–33.

303. Cf. 85.

305. μοι: ethic dat., cf. Chantraine, *Grammaire*, ii 72 § 93; this element of personal appeal, almost 'to please me', is more interesting than μάλ', though the latter has more MS-support.

306. This rather vague assurance is, as Telemachus sees (319–20), worth nothing.   ταῦτα: explained by the next line.

308. ἠγαθέην: 'sacred', applied only to places (Lemnos, Lesbos, Nysa, Pylos, Pytho); the form is puzzling: see further Wyatt, *Lengthening*, 107.

311. ἀκέοντα: 'quietly', i.e. without expressing his grievance, με being understood; cf. xiv 195. ἀκέων, here apparently a participle, is sometimes treated as adverbial and indeclinable (xxi 89, *h.Ap*. 404, cf. *Il*. iv 22, viii 459); it is uncertain whether this adverbial usage has evolved from its use as a ptcp., or vice versa: see Frisk, *GEW*, Chantraine, *Dictionnaire* s.v. ἀκή, *LfgrE*, Leumann, *Wörter*, 166 ff.

312. ἦ οὐχ ἅλις: cf. *Il*. v 349, xvii 450, xxiii 670.

313. ἐγὼ δ' ἔτι νήπιος ἦα: a good example of Homeric parataxis.

314. ἄλλων: Telemachus means Mentes, despite the generalizing pl.

315. καὶ δή: used like the later καὶ δὴ καί to mark something similar in kind to what has preceded but stronger in degree.   θυμός: in translating we must, unfortunately, choose between 'spirit, courage' and 'anger'; the former is probably preferable.

316–17. According to the scholia on 325 these lines were athetized by Aristarchus, but we do not know exactly what his arguments against them were; the scholia merely say that 325 ff. confirm his objection, since the suitors should not be in any doubt about Telemachus' destination if they had heard 317. This is not in itself very cogent, but certainly it is imprudent of Telemachus to threaten the suitors like this, a pointless and risky gesture of defiance.   κακὰς ἐπὶ κῆρας ἰήλω: not formulaic, though the idea is common enough in Homer.

318. Cf. *Il*. xxiv 92, 224.   οὐδ' ἁλίη ... ἀγορεύω restates εἶμι; it does not mean that Telemachus is confident about the outcome of his journey.   μέν: emphasizes the assertion, though it also has adversative implications—'I *will* go, notwithstanding difficulties'.

319–20. ἔμπορος: 'as a passenger', cf. xxiv 300; the sense 'merchant' is a later development. Its position gives considerable emphasis, and the circumlocutory ἐπήβολος ... γίγνομαι adds further weight to Telemachus' words; ἐπήβολος occurs only here in Homer.

320. ὥς ... εἶναι: Telemachus has seen through Antinous' insincere reassurance at 306, cf. 253 ff.

321. ἦ: impf. of ἠμί.

322. Cf. xxii 199. The line was athetized as superfluous (περιττός) by Aristophanes and Aristarchus; it anticipates and spoils the antithesis in οἱ δ' ἐπελώβευον.   ῥεῖα: 'nonchalantly, without more ado'.

323. ἐπελώβευον: *hapax.*

325 ff. This is simply mockery; iv 663–4 show that the suitors have not taken Telemachus' plan seriously. But, as often in the *Odyssey*, what is said in jest turns out to be truer than the speaker supposes: see above, i 384–5 n.

328. Ἐφύρην: cf. i 259 above, and n.

332 ff. To some extent this speech foreshadows the suitors' plot to ambush Telemachus (iv 670 ff.).

334. Rather heavy-handed mockery.

335–6. Cf. xvi 384–6. Telemachus is the last of his line, and there is no difficulty in supposing that in the event of his death his mother and stepfather would inherit the property which would otherwise have been his; but how the suitors collectively could have any lawful claim on his estate is hard to imagine. This simply illustrates the suitors' general propensity to treat Telemachus' property as if it were their own.

337–81. Telemachus arranges with Eurycleia for necessary provisions.

337. θάλαμον κατεβήσετο: the preposition in κατεβήσετο does not necessarily imply that the store-room was underground, but basement store-rooms were certainly normal in Mycenaean palaces, and would provide a cool location for keeping provisions. On the 'mixed aorist' form -εβήσετο see above, i 330 n.

338–9. Treasure is important in the heroic world not only for its intrinsic value but also as a status symbol. **νητός:** *hapax.*

340. πίθοι: we think of the large storage-jars, sometimes reaching seven feet in height, familiar from excavations of Mycenaean sites.

341. ἕστασαν: plpf.

342. ποτὶ τοῖχον ἀρηρότες: 'fitting close together along the wall'; πίθοι have flat bases, unlike amphorae which are sharp at the bottom, and do not need actually to lean against the wall. **εἴ ποτ':** 'in case'.

344. The doors of a θάλαμος appear to be regarded as a particularly important feature; they are specifically mentioned in connection with almost a quarter of the places where the word occurs.

345. ταμίη: a senior female house-servant, with authority to give out provisions; Eurynome is also a ταμίη (xvii 495, xviii 169, xix 96, xxiii 154). The common translation 'housekeeper' is misleading, since a housekeeper fulfils a unique managerial role in a household. **νύκτας τε καὶ ἦμαρ:** it is disputed whether the use of ἦμαρ as a pl. in this formula is an archaism (so Hoekstra on xv 476, Ruijgh, *Élément*, 121) or has developed from its pl. sense in cpds. like ἐξῆμαρ and ἐννῆμαρ (so Leumann, *Wörter*, 100).

346. ἔσχ': i.e. ἔσκε. The poet does not mean that Eurycleia spent all her time in the store-room, but that she was frequently there; we have already seen (i 428 ff.) that she has other duties.

349. μαῖ': Eurycleia is regularly so addressed not only by Telemachus but also by Odysseus (e.g. xix 482) and by Penelope (e.g. xxiii 11); for this friendly form of address to old women cf. xvii 499, *h.Cer.* 147; it is a hypocoristic formed by adding the suffix -ya to the root μα-, cf. γραῖα: see further Frisk, *GEW*, Chantraine, *Dictionnaire*.

350. λαρώτατος: ω of the superlative strongly suggests that the preceding syllable was once short, and that ᾱ results from contraction, from *λα(ϝ)αρός or *λα(ϝ)ερός; in Homer the first syllable never occurs in the arsis of the foot, and could thus always be resolved into two short syllables; but cf. ὀϊζυρός which despite its long penultimate syllable forms its comparative and superlative in ω (v 105, *Il.* xvii 446).

351. κεῖνον ... τὸν κάμμορον: for the use of the article with the demonstrative cf. xviii 114, xix 372.   **κάμμορον:** i.e. *κατάμορον 'subject to destiny'; for the assimilation cf. καμμονίη (*Il.* xxii 257), and see Chantraine, *Grammaire*, i 87–8 § 37. This epithet is applied only to Odysseus; the allusive and unusual periphrasis has much more point if we follow Blass in excising the next line (= v 387). The insertion of proper names to clarify a descriptive phrase or circumlocution is common: see M. L. West, *Textual Criticism and Editorial Technique* (Stuttgart, 1973), 23.

354. ἄλφιτα: see above, 290 n.

355. μυληφάτου: apparently 'bruised in a mill'; cf. vii 104, xx 105–8. Until Roman times grain was laboriously ground by hand in a small saddle-quern: see Moritz, *Grain-mills and Flour in Classical Antiquity*, Pl. 1 and 2. It makes little difference whether the epithet is taken with ἀλφίτου or with ἀκτῆς.   **ἀλφίτου:** the sg. is used only because the gen. pl. does not fit the hexameter.   **ἀκτῆς:** the once popular derivation of this word from the same root as ἄγνυμι is very dubious, and its etymology must be regarded as quite uncertain.

362. ἔπεα πτερόεντα: see above, i 122 n.

363. φίλε τέκνον: cf. xv 125; *constructio ad sensum*, a metrically convenient alternative to the grammatically correct φίλον τέκνον (xxiii 26).

364. πῇ: almost 'why'; Eurycleia is not asking about his route, but about his motives.

365. μοῦνος ἐὼν ἀγαπητός: Eurycleia could scarcely suppose that Telemachus intended to travel alone, particularly in view of the quantity of provisions he has ordered, and μοῦνος should be taken closely with ἀγαπητός, 'a beloved only son': compare the emphasis on the single heir in each generation at xvi 117 ff.

366. ἀλλογνώτῳ: *hapax*.

367–8. Again, a foreshadowing of the suitors' plot to kill Telemachus, cf. 332 ff.   **αὐτίκ' ἰόντι:** 'as soon as you go'.   **φθίῃς:** intrans., probably aor. subj. with long ῑ *metri gratia*; see also Chantraine, *Grammaire*, i 458 § 218.

370. πόντον ἐπ' ἀτρύγετον: the construction fits ἀλάλησθαι, which is evidently regarded as the important verb in the line, not πάσχειν; on ἀτρύγετος see above, i 72 n.

372. οὔ τοι ἄνευ θεοῦ: cf. xv 531

373 ff. The administration of a solemn oath has many parallels in Homer: cf. iv 253–4, v 178 ff., x 343 ff., xii 298 ff., xv 435 ff., xviii 55 ff., *Il.* iii 268 ff., x 321 ff., xiv 271 ff., xix 108 ff.; see further Arend, *Scenen* 122–3. Here it underlines the importance of Telemachus' journey. It may seem at first sight unreasonable that he should suppose that his absence could be concealed from his mother for so long, but the suitors assume that he is simply somewhere else on the estate (iv 640) until Noemon lets out the truth, and Telemachus might hope that his mother's mind would work in the same way. The poet was evidently concerned not to delay Telemachus' departure with a prolonged and emotional leave-taking, which incidentally could hardly fail to attract the notice of the suitors.

374. Cf. iv 588.   **ἐνδεκάτη τε δυωδεκάτη τε:** the copulative τε has disjunctive force; we must translate it with 'or'; cf. *Il.* i 128 τριπλῇ τετραπλῇ τε, ix 379. The precise number of days is unimportant; a round number is intended; see further Focke's sensible discussion, *Odyssee*, 3 ff.

376. κατά ... ἰάπτῃ: κατά should be taken with ἰάπτῃ, not with χρόα καλόν. ἰάπτω, which normally means 'throw, hurl', must here mean 'hurt, harm, spoil'. LSJ distinguish two different verbs, but this is probably wrong: see Frisk, *GEW*, Chantraine, *Dictionnaire*.

377. θεῶν ... ἀπόμνυ: 'swore that she would not with a mighty oath by the gods'. θεῶν μέγας ὅρκος surely meant originally 'the great oath sworn by the gods, that by which the gods swear', cf. v 185–6, x 299, *Il.* xv 37–8, *h.Cer.* 259, Hes. *Th.* 400, 784, Alc. 304. 4 (LP) (= Sapph. 44A. 4 Voigt); for the sense 'an oath by the gods' cf. Xen. *An.* ii 5. 7 οἱ θεῶν ὅρκοι. See further Leumann, *Wörter*, 81 ff.

378. = x 346, *Il.* xiv 280, cf. *Od.* xii 304, xv 438. τόν might be taken as demonstrative.

382–404. Athena sees to ship and crew, and then calls Telemachus down to the harbour at evening.

382 ff. Preparations for a journey, whether by land or sea, are a stock feature of Homeric narrative. This is the first such scene in the *Odyssey*, and Telemachus' journey is of unusual importance, so that it is natural that these preparations should be related in some detail. It is worth comparing some similar scenes: the departure of the Phaeacians from Scheria (viii 48 ff., xiii 18 ff.), Odysseus' account of the journey from Circe's island (xi 1 ff.), Telemachus' homeward voyage (xv 205 ff., 282 ff.), the suitors' preparations for their ambush (iv 778 ff.), the return journey from Chryse (*Il.* i 478 ff.). A typical pattern may be discerned, though no single scene conforms to it exactly; here we find all the standard elements, with some expansion: (1) a crew is selected (383 ff.); (2) those who are to sail make their way to the ship (391–2); here, unusually, this happens after (3) the ship is drawn down to the sea (389); (4) the ship is made ready for the voyage (389–90) and (5) moored in the harbour (391); (6) equipment and provisions are put on board (410–15); (7) passengers and crew go on board (416–19); (8) the mooring ropes are loosed (418); (9) with a favourable wind the voyage begins (420 ff.). See further Arend, *Scenen*, 81 ff.

Shipbuilding techniques are conservative, and the Homeric data fit equally well Mycenaean and Geometric ships, so far as our evidence goes; the formulaic system for ναῦς is more elaborate than any other except for personal names. See further D. H. F. Gray, *Archaeologia* G, esp. 92 ff., J. S.

Morrison and R. T. Williams, *Greek Oared Ships* (Cambridge, 1968), 43 ff., L. Casson, *Ships and Seamanship in the Ancient World* (Princeton, 1971), esp. 43 ff., 220 ff., Kurt, *Fachausdrücke*.

382. = iv 795, vi 112, xviii 187, cf. xxiii 242, 344; after this formula or transition we regularly find either asyndeton, as here, or ῥα as the connective. It would be natural to suppose that Athena was making these arrangements, as she undertook to do (291), while Telemachus was occupied with the suitors and Eurycleia, but it is normal Homeric convention to narrate simultaneous events as if they happened successively: for a brief introduction to this topic (Zieliński's law) see Page, *Odyssey*, 64 ff. (to the bibliography there given should be added Delebecque, *Télémaque*, T. Krischer, *Formale Konventionen der homerischen Epik* (Zetemata lvi, Munich, 1951), 91 ff.).

384. ἑκάστῳ: i.e. each of the men she had selected; presumably the poet envisaged a crew of twenty, cf. 212.

385. ἀγέρεσθαι: the accentuation is disputed, depending on whether this form is regarded as present (proparoxytone) or aor. (paroxytone); similarly ἀγέροντο (xx 277, *Il.* ii 94, xviii 37, 245) may be either impf. or aor. The MSS agree in accenting it as a pres., and it was certainly so interpreted by Hellenistic poets, cf. A.R. iii 895 ἀγέρονται, Theoc. xvii 94 ἀμφαγέρονται.

386. Φρονίοιο Νοήμονα: obviously significant names, intended to mark father and son as sensible men, by contrast with the suitors. Noemon is not such an uncommon name (cf. *Il.* v 678, xxiii 612; D.L. v 73; Ath. 20 a), but there seems to be no certain instance of Phronius.

387. ὑπέδεκτο: 'undertook, promised' sc. δώσειν. Virtually the same formula is used at xx 372, xxiii 314, but the meaning of ὑπέδεκτο is rather different.

388. = iii 497, xi 12, xv 185, 296, 471. **δύσετο:** see i 24 n. (δυσομένου), 330 (κατεβήσετο). Sailing at night was normally regarded as foolhardy (cf. xii 284 ff.), but cf. iv 786, 842 ff., xiii 35 ff., xv 471.

389. νῆα ... ἅλαδ' εἴρυσε: when a ship was not in constant use, it was hauled up on the beach and steadied with blocks at each side of the keel: cf. *Il.* i 485–6. Normally it takes several men to drag it down to the sea, but Athena manages single-handed.

390. ὅπλ': 'gear, tackle'. **ἐΰσσελμοι:** 'well-constructed' probably conveys the sense better than 'well-benched'.

391. στῆσε: 'moored'; when the ship is loaded and in order, it is pushed out into deeper water where it is held only by the stern-hawsers (πρυμνήσια).

393. = 382. Repetition at so short an interval is unattractive and the line is surely a medieval interpolation, being omitted by at least two medieval MSS and by P. 1 (*P.Oxy.* 773, Pack² 1031; the omission was not noted in the *ed. pr.*, but see the complete transcript published by W. Lameere, *Aperçus de la paléographie homérique* (Brussels, 1960), 113 ff., where the papyrus is redated to the fourth century).

395. ἐπὶ ... ὕπνον ἔχευε: 'made them sleepy' (not, as at xviii 188, 'sent them to sleep'). Athena similarly bewilders the suitors at xx 345–6; so too Hermes, escorting Priam to Achilles, removes a potential danger by sending the Greek guards to sleep (*Il.* xxiv 445–6).

397. ἔτι δήν: see 36 n.

398. ἦατ': see i 326 n.

402. ἐϋκνήμιδες ἑταῖροι: cf. ix 60, 550, x 203, xxiii 319. The epithet seems purely conventional; there is never any suggestion that Telemachus' crew have armour or weapons.

403. ἦατ' ἐπήρετμοι: Athena exaggerates, to make Telemachus hurry; contrast 408. Elsewhere in the *Odyssey* ἐπήρετμος is an epithet of ships, 'equipped with oars'. **τὴν σὴν ... ὁρμήν:** cf. *Il.* x 123; τὴν σήν is very emphatic, 'the impulse, initiative, which must come from you'.

404. It is hard to guess what led Zenodotus to athetize the line; possibly he found suspicious the rather strange expression διατρίβωμεν ὁδοῖο. διατρίβωμεν is best taken as intrans., 'let us not lose time from our voyage, let us not delay our voyage'; for the gen. cf. i 195 βλάπτουσι κελεύθου, iv 380 ἔδησε κελεύθου. The alternative explanation, that ἑταίρους is to be understood as the object, is awkward.

405–34. When all the preparations have been made, Telemachus and Mentor go on board; the wind is favourable, and all night the ship sails on.

407. = iv 428, viii 50, xii 391, xiii 70, cf. iv 573, xi 1; it is surely a late interpolation, being absent from several medieval MSS and from two papyri, P. 1 (iv AD) and P. 138 (107 b, *P.Merton* 52, Pack² 1053; i BC).

409. ἱερὴ ἲς Τηλεμάχοιο: cf. xvi 476, xviii 60, 405, xxi 101, 130, xxii 354; the formula is generally used to introduce a speech by Telemachus or his reaction to someone else's speech. There is a similar formula for Alcinous, ἱερὸν μένος Ἀλκινόοιο (vii 167, viii 2, 4, 385, 421, xiii 20, 24), sometimes reduced to μένος Ἀλκινόοιο (vii 178, viii 423, etc.); on this is modelled ἱερὸν μένος Ἀντινόοιο (xviii 34). The epithet ἱερός is never applied directly to persons in Homer. These formulae are not found in contexts where strength or holiness is particularly relevant, though it may well be that such expressions were originally devised to convey the idea of a charismatic, numinous force associated with royalty; however, the application of such a formula to Antinous shows that any such associations had faded. The grand phrase seems hardly appropriate to the youthful Telemachus, and very likely he has taken over a formula originally devised for another hero with a name of similar metrical pattern. See further Hainsworth on viii 2, Russo on xviii 34, 60, P. Wülfing-v. Martitz, *Glotta* xxxviii (1959/60), 272 ff., esp. 301 ff., J. P. Locher, *Untersuchungen zu ἱερός hauptsächlich bei Homer* (Bern, 1963), 54 ff. Such periphrases are characteristic of epic style: cf. xi 601 βίην Ἡρακληείην, Hes. *Th.* 951 ἲς Ἡρακλῆος, fr. 198. 2 Ὀδυσσῆος ἱερὴ ἴς; similar, but not quite analogous is *Il.* xxiii 720 κρατερὴ δ' ἔχεν ἲς Ὀδυσῆος.

410. δεῦτε: the frequent use of δεῦρο as an interjection led to the creation of a pl. δεῦτε, formed as if it were a 2nd pers. pl. imper. **ἤϊα:** see 289 n.

412. οὐδ' ἄλλαι δμῳαί: 'nor the women-servants either'.

413–17. The repetition of ἄρα in this passage should be noted; its effect is to suggest a lively feeling of interest: see further Denniston, *Particles*, 33.

416. ἄν ... νηὸς βαῖν': it is probably better to take ἄν (i.e. ἀνά) with βαῖνε, rather than with νηός; a similar problem arises at ix 177, xv 284. ἀνά with gen. is otherwise found only in an inscription (see LSJ s.v. ἀνά A.), and νηός may be taken as a locative gen. The construction was surely affected by formulae with ἐπιβαίνω and ἐκβαίνω, e.g. iii 12, xv 547.

417–26. Cf. xv 285–92. Athena seats herself in the place reserved for the pilot.

419. κληῖσι: 'thole-pins', hook-shaped fittings to which the oars were attached for rowing by leather loops, cf. viii 37, 53; on the origins of the erroneous conventional translation 'thwarts, rowing benches' see Leumann, *Wörter*, 33, 209.

420. Cf. *Il.* i 479; here (by contrast with the rather similar scene in xv) Athena sends a favourable wind before preparations for sailing have been made: cf. Pi. *P.* i 33–5 ναυσιφορήτοις δ' ἀνδράσι πρῶτα χάρις | ἐς πλόον ἀρχομένοις πομπαῖον ἐλθεῖν οὖρον· ἐοικότα γὰρ | κὰν τελευτᾷ φερτέρου νόστου τυχεῖν. We find Athena exercising a general control of the winds at v 382 ff.: contrast x 20 ff.   **ἴκμενον οὖρον:** the adj. occurs only in this phrase; its etymology is uncertain, though the ancient theory that it derives from ἴκω, ἱκέσθαι, may well be right: see further Frisk, *GEW*, Chantraine, *Dictionnaire*, C. P. Roth, *HSPh* lxxvii (1973), 186.

421. ἀκραῆ: the original meaning was probably 'blowing on the heights, from the heights', but it seems to be understood simply as 'blowing strongly, fresh'. It is disputed whether the long a in this and similar cpds. (ἁλιαής, δυσαής, εὐαής, etc.) is an archaic feature due to compositional lengthening or should be explained as metrical lengthening: see further Hoekstra on xiv 253, Chantraine, *Grammaire*, i 100 § 44, *Dictionnaire* s.v. ἄημι, ἄκρος, Frisk, *GEW*, *LfgrE*. But the unusual contraction of -εα in the last syllable (cf. Chantraine, *Grammaire*, i 56 § 23) would be avoided with ἀκραέα, keeping the original short a; cf., perhaps, Hes. *Op.* 594 ἀντίον ἀκραέος Ζεφύρου; see further Shipp, *Studies*, 59–60.   **οἴνοπα:** see above, i 183 n.

423. ὅπλων: 'ropes'.

424. μεσόδμης: apparently a box amidships in which the mast was stepped; apart from xv 289 the word is not elsewhere used in connection with ships and appears to have been borrowed from architecture; see further Kurt, *Fachausdrücke*, 116 ff.

425. ἀείραντες: 'raising it'; when not in use the mast lay horizontal, resting in the ἱστοδόκη.   **προτόνοισιν:** shrouds leading from the top of the mast to the gunwale on either side of the ship; helped by the ἐπίτονος (xii 423) they kept the mast in position.

426. ἱστία: though the word for 'sails' in Homer is almost always pl., except in the phrase μέσον ἱστίον (ii 427, *Il.* i 481: ἱστίῳ at *Il.* xv 627 is exceptional), vase-paintings and other pictorial evidence from the archaic period show that there cannot have been more than one sail on a ship. The pl. very probably reflects the use of many pieces of cloth to make one sail; μέσον ἱστίον may then literally be the middle piece.　λευκά: this implies sails made of linen.　βοεῦσιν: for ropes made of leather cf. *h.Ap.* 407; see further Hoekstra on xv 291, Kurt, *Fachausdrücke*, 165 ff.

427-9. Cf. *Il.* i 481-3.

428. στείρη: apparently the cutwater; see further Kurt, *Fachausdrücke*, 89-90.　**πορφύρεον**: a common epithet of the sea in Homer, sometimes, as here, evidently connected with πορφύρω 'surge, heave', but in other contexts better associated with πορφύρα; occasionally (e.g. *Il.* xvii 361) either sense would be equally satisfactory.

429. The line is omitted in several MSS and is surely a late interpolation.

430. The wind being both steady and favourable, they simply need to set the sail at the proper angle and make it fast.　**μέλαιναν**: the most frequent epithet for ships in Homer after θοή, referring to the coating of pitch (or pitch and wax) used on the vessel.

431. Cf. *Il.* viii 232; see above, i 148 n.

432. The libation at the first free moment underlines Telemachus' piety, a sharp contrast to the irreligious suitors. He has not yet identified as Athena the divine visitant of the previous day, and there is a pleasing irony in his particular devotion to the divinity who has made his journey possible and now accompanies him.　**αἰειγενέτῃσιν**: 'everlasting'; see further Hoekstra on xiv 446.

434. As often, the end of a day coincides with the end of a book; but μέν looks forward to δέ in iii 1, and the connection is close. Schol. T *Il.* xxiv 8 implies that the line was suspected in antiquity, but we have no idea why.　**ἠῶ**: 'during the dawn', acc. of length of time.

BOOK III: COMMENTARY

We move from the lawlessness and near-anarchy of Ithaca to the pious, well-ordered life of Nestor's Pylos. Nestor, who περὶ οἶδε δίκας ἠδὲ φρόνιν ἄλλων, knows his obligations and rejoices in fulfilling them; the suitors' outrageous disregard for the laws of hospitality and religion is emphasized by contrast. In his dealings with this patriarchal family, whose activities unfold against a background of religious observance, Telemachus experiences a spontaneous friendliness lacking not only in his own home but also among the somewhat melancholy splendours of Menelaus' palace at Sparta.

Despite his threat to seek help from Pylos against the suitors (ii 316–17) Telemachus does not ask Nestor for assistance, or even for advice, nor does Nestor offer either. Telemachus' purpose is to get news of his father, and his visit to Nestor thus appropriately forms the framework within which is developed the theme of the *nostoi* of the Greek heroes from Troy. Nestor's hospitable ways make it natural that he should be well informed about the vicissitudes of his former comrades, since visitors may be expected to retail news of the outside world. His tendency to lengthy reminiscence, familiar from the *Iliad*, is here turned to good account. His narrative is complemented by that of Menelaus in iv; the ingenuity with which this material is organized and divided between the two books should not be underestimated.

Vergil followed this book very closely in *Aeneid* viii, in his account of Aeneas' visit to Evander; see further G. N. Knauer, *Die Aeneis u. Homer* (Hypomnemata vii, Göttingen, 1964), 249 ff.

1–66. Telemachus and Athena-Mentor are welcomed by Nestor and his people, who have gathered on the shore to sacrifice to Poseidon.

1. The beginning of a new day which, as often, is the beginning of a fresh episode, is here described with unusual elaboration. For λίμνη used of the sea, cf. *Il.* xiii 21, 32, xxiv 79; it is very common in later poetry. Here the all-encircling stream of Ocean is meant.

2. πολύχαλκος is similarly applied to the sky at *Il.* v 504. Elsewhere in Homer it means 'rich in bronze', and it is sometimes so understood here, the home of the gods being no doubt well provided with bronze as with every other convenience and luxury. However, though to many modern readers the epithet rather suggests a vault of bright, burnished metal, ancient commentators preferred the interpretation 'solid, firm'; cf. χάλκεος οὐρανός (*Il.* xvii 425, imitated by Pindar, *P.* x 27, *N.* vi 3), Διὸς χαλκοβατὲς δῶ (*Il.* i 426, xiv 173, etc.), σιδήρεος οὐρανός (*Od.* xv 329); the last unambiguously implies solidity rather than brightness, but does not establish that this was originally the point of these metallic epithets.

3. ζείδωρον: 'grain-giving', an epithet applied in Homer only to ἄρουρα. ζειά (cf. iv 41, 604) is emmer, the ancient Mediterranean cereal. Empedocles

(DK 31 B 151) uses the epithet to mean 'life-giving'; this misinterpretation may well go back much earlier. See further Hainsworth on v 463.

4 ff. The action opens with a typical scene, the reception of a visitor; on the general characteristics of such scenes see i 113 ff. n. Here, unusually, the new arrivals find their host not in his house but on the beach.

The location of Nestor's Pylos was disputed in antiquity: see Str. 339 ff., especially 349 ff. Besides the famous Messenian Pylos, scene of the Athenian landing in 425, there was a town of the same name in Elis, too far inland to be seriously considered except by zealous local historians, and a third Pylos in Triphylia, an obscure place known to us mainly from Strabo, who describes it as somewhat over thirty stades inland from the coast (350). If we take the evidence of the *Odyssey* by itself, there is nothing against supposing the poet to have located Nestor's home in Messenia, a view evidently held by Pindar, for whom Nestor is Μεσσάνιος γέρων (*P.* vi 35), and widespread in antiquity. (No weight should be attached to the objection that the journey from Ithaca to Messenian Pylos is too much for a single night; Telemachus enjoys exceptionally favourable sailing conditions (ii 420 ff., cf. xv 292 ff.), and the constraints of a realistic timetable are quite irrelevant.) But problems arise when we consider the *Iliad*. The topographical indications of the raid which Nestor describes at xi 670 ff. imply that his home was further north, much nearer the Alpheus than the classical Pylos was. Strabo, following earlier scholars, argues that Nestor's home was the obscure Triphylian Pylos; but his attempt to show that this better suits the description of Telemachus' return journey is not at all cogent. However, the topographical data of Nestor's narrative are not altogether satisfactory and strongly suggest that though the author knew the names of some places in that part of the western Peloponnese, he was uncertain about their general relationship: see further Leaf ad loc.

Archaeological discoveries gave the question a fresh interest. In 1907 Dörpfeld found the remains of a Mycenaean palace at Kakovatos in Triphylia, two kilometres from the sea. The view that this was Nestor's capital gained ground until 1939, when Kourouniotis and Blegen found another Mycenaean palace, seventeen kilometres north of the classical Pylos, at Epano Englianos. That this was the original Pylos is made virtually certain by the frequent occurrence of the name 'Pu-ro' in the Linear B tablets discovered there, in contexts suggesting that it was a place of supreme importance; unfortunately, no king has been definitely identified in the tablets.

The palace of Epano Englianos was destroyed by fire *c.*1200 BC, and what we learn of Nestor's home bears little relationship to it. The poet clearly imagined Nestor to live near the shore, since it takes only a short time for a messenger to summon Telemachus' companions from the ship to Nestor's palace (423-32); but the palace at Epano Englianos lies a good morning's walk from the beach. Moreover, the poet presents Nestor's home as relatively modest compared with Menelaus' (cf. iv 44 ff., 71 ff.);

yet Epano Englianos will stand comparison with any Mycenaean site so far discovered.

See further E. Meyer, *RE* xxiii 2, 2113 ff. (a powerful statement of the case for Kakovatos as the Homeric Pylos), C. W. Blegen *et al.*, *The Palace of Nestor at Pylos in Western Messenia* (Princeton, 1966–73), F. Kiechle, 'Pylos u. der pylische Raum in der antiken Tradition', *Historia* ix (1960), 1–67, esp. 13 ff., R. Hope Simpson and J. F. Lazenby, *The Catalogue of the Ships in Homer's* Iliad (Oxford, 1970), 82 ff., Ventris–Chadwick, *Documents*, 141–2, Hoekstra on xv 209–14.   ἐϋκτίμενον: 'well-built'; see further Hoekstra on xv 129.

5 ff. It is surely significant that Telemachus finds Nestor engaged in sacrifice; Nestor's piety, an aspect of his character not particularly noticeable in the *Iliad*, is thus established from the outset. Sacrifice is much emphasized in this book (cf. 338 ff., 390 ff., 418 ff.), and the detailed description of the ritual at 445 ff. is of outstanding importance for our knowledge of Greek sacrificial practice. The absence of any priest should be noted; contrast the great sacrifice at *Il.* i 446 ff. See further E. Vermeule, *Archaeologia* V, 95 ff., and on the interpretation of the ritual K. Meuli, 'Griechische Opferbräuche', *Phyllobolia f. P. v. d. Mühll* (Basel, 1946), 185 ff., esp. 211 ff., (= *Gesammelte Schriften* (Basel, 1975), 907–1021, esp. 935 ff.), W. Burkert, *Homo Necans* (Berlin, 1972), 10 ff. (= English edn. (Berkeley–Los Angeles, 1983), 3 ff.), J. L. Durand, in M. Detienne and J. P. Vernant (eds.), *La Cuisine du sacrifice en pays grec* (Paris, 1979), 133–81 (with very helpful illustrations), G. S. Kirk, *Entretiens Hardt* xxvii (Vandoeuvres–Geneva, 1981), 61 ff.; on typical elements in the narrative see Arend, *Scenen*, 64 ff., Tafel 4, Schema 8.

5. τοὶ δ': the people of Pylos.

6. Black victims were normally offered to chthonic powers (cf. xi 33, *Il.* iii 103), but Poseidon shares certain characteristics with Hades (see Richardson on *h.Cer.* 18). The Neleids claimed to be descended from Poseidon (cf. *Od.* xi 235 ff.). In the Linear B tablets from Epano Englianos Poseidon is the most important divinity: see further M. Gérard-Rousseau, *Les Mentions religieuses dans les tablettes mycéniennes* (Rome, 1968), 181–5. The Peloponnese was very rich in peculiar cults and myths associated with Poseidon, and it seems highly probable that his cult originated there: see further Nilsson, *Geschichte*, i 444 ff.   ἐνοσίχθονι: despite his fixed epithets ἐνοσίχθων and ἐννοσίγαιος, Poseidon causes an earthquake only once in Homer (*Il.* xx 57 ff.), and is regarded as primarily Lord of the Sea.   κυανοχαίτῃ: κύανος, a loan-word from Hittite, denotes in Homer a darkblue substance. Blue hair might be appropriate to a sea-god, but Zeus and Hera have eyebrows of the same shade (*Il.* i 528, xv 102) and the epithet is best understood as 'dark-haired'.

7–8. ἐννέα δ' ἕδραι ἔσαν: 'there were nine sitting-places, they sat in nine groups'. The scene is not altogether clear: should we imagine nine groups in a line, facing the sea, or arranged in a semicircle, of which the sea formed the diameter? In the Catalogue of Ships (*Il.* ii 591 ff.) we learn that

Nestor ruled nine cities and had a force of ninety ships; if each ship held fifty men (cf. *Il.* ii 719, xvi 170), his contingent at Troy was the same size as the assembly here. ἐπίφορός ἐστι πρὸς τὸν ἐννέα ἀριθμόν, observes the scholiast on *Il.* vi 174 (cf. on xii 25); on the use of nine as a typical number in Homer see Erbse, *Beiträge*, 195 ff., J. W. S. Blom, *De typische getallen bij Homeros en Herodotos* (Nijmegen, 1936), 255 ff.   ἧατο: see above, i 326 n.   προὔχοντο: 'they held before themselves', a strange expression.

9. σπλάγχνα: 'spleen, kidneys, liver', probably also heart and lungs; like ἔγκατα, *plurale tantum* in Homer, understandably, since the entrails form a mass within which it may be hard to distinguish the individual items.   μηρία: the original purpose of thus presenting the thigh-bones to the god was apparently to assist in the regeneration of the victim, and thus secure the continuity of animal life, though Hesiod's attempt to explain the origins of this practice (*Th.* 535 ff.) shows that it was no longer understood.

10–12. The landing is dealt with very briefly: contrast the much more detailed descriptions at xiii 93 ff., xv 495 ff., xvi 324 ff., 351 ff., *Il.* i 432 ff., cf. 485 ff.; see further Arend, *Scenen*, 79 ff.

10. οἱ δ': 'the others' (Telemachus and his crew).   ἐΐσης: 'well-balanced'; see further Kurt, *Fachausdrücke*, 42. It has been plausibly suggested that the prothetic vowel of this epic form of ἴσος arose from false division of ἀσπίδα πάντοσε ϝίσην as ἀσπίδα πάντοσ' ἐ(ϝ)ίσην; see also Hainsworth on viii 98.

11. στεῖλαν ἀείραντες: 'they furled the sail by brailing it up'; it could thus be shaken out at short notice. Contrast the more elaborate arrangements at *Il.* i 433 ff., where the sails are taken down and the mast lowered.

14. αἰδοῦς: 'shyness, embarrassment'; for the construction of χρή with acc. and gen. cf. i 124.

17. ἱπποδάμοιο: not an epithet of Nestor elsewhere in Homer, but cf. the formulaic ἱππότα Νέστωρ, and 68 n.

18. εἴδομεν: subjunctive, expressing intention.

19–20. = 327–8. But 19 is omitted by many MSS, and should be rejected here as a medieval interpolation.   ψεῦδος: 'a lie'; normal Homeric usage of ψεῦδος and its cognates shows that deliberate falsehood is meant, not merely misinformation.   πεπνυμένος: for Homer intelligence and sound moral principles largely overlap; cf. 52 and 266.

21 ff. Telemachus had evidently expected his older companion to take the initiative. Some critics have been troubled by his nervousness here after his bold confrontation of the suitors in the Ithacan assembly. But he is no longer the host, whose duty it is to question his guests, and his diffidence indicates a sense of decorum as well as due respect for the venerable Nestor.

23. οὐδὲ ... πεπείρημαι: 'I have not practised myself, am not experienced, in.'

24. αἰδὼς ... ἐξερέεσθαι: 'It is embarrassing for a young man to question someone older.'

27–8. The repeated negative is probably due to slight inadvertence in combining formulae.

33. κρέα τ': the MSS are divided between κρέατ' and κρέα τ'. The nom. and

acc. pl. of κρέας are slightly puzzling. Most often we find κρέα with short α
followed by a consonant (i 112 etc.); short final α is likewise implied by the
elision κρέ(α) at iii 65 etc. But κρέά ἔδμεναι (*Il.* iv 345, xxii 347) points to
either κρέᾱ (contracted from *κρέασα) with α shortened in hiatus, or κρέα'
from κρέαα with elision. The *Odyssey* also has several places where, as here,
most or all MSS give another form of pl., κρέατ', which may well be
ancient (cf. ix 162, 557, x 184, 468, 477, xii 30, xiv 109, mostly in the
formula ἤμεθα δαινύμενοι κρέα τ' ἄσπετα καὶ μέθυ ἡδύ). See further Ebeling,
Lexicon s.v. κρέας, Chantraine, *Grammaire*, i 209–10 § 89.

34 ff. The whole company welcomes the new arrivals: contrast Mentes'
reception at Odysseus' palace (i 113 ff.). The scene is depicted on a late
red-figure vase from Apulia: see Touchefeu-Meynier, *Thèmes*, 216–17.

36. Pisistratus is evidently Nestor's youngest son, and the only one still
unmarried (401). As the most junior among those providing hospitality he
goes to welcome the newcomers; similarly at *Il.* xi 765 ff. when Nestor and
Odysseus come to visit Peleus, they are greeted by Achilles. Like Telema-
chus himself, he bears a name recalling some aspect of his father's life: see i
113 n. He is not mentioned in the *Iliad* and, more significantly, is
apparently omitted in the list of Nestor's sons given in the Hesiodic
Catalogue of Women (fr. 35. 10 ff.), which, though lacunose, seems to have
no room for him. His prominence in the Telemachy raises an interesting
question. Herodotus tells us (v 65. 3–4) that the tyrant Pisistratus, whose
family claimed descent from the Neleids of Pylos, was named after Nestor's
son; but some have thought that the relationship was the reverse, and that
Pisistratus was invented and introduced into the *Odyssey* at the time of the
Pisistratean recension (see introduction, pp. 36 ff.). Pisistratus' role is
essential to the Telemachy, and such a theory might seem to entail dating
the *Odyssey* as a whole to the mid-sixth century. But it might have been
possible without radical or extensive reworking to reassign and enhance a
part originally played by another son of Nestor, as a mark of appreciation
to a generous patron.

39. πατέρι ᾧ: the lengthening of a short vowel in arsis before possessive ὅς (cf.
e.g. xxiii 150 πόσιος οὗ), as before ἕ, οὗ, etc. (e.g. *Il.* v 343 ἀπὸ ἕο), perhaps
reflects the initial s lost before ϝ at the beginning of these words.

40 ff. This book contains two further drink-offering scenes, at 332 ff. and
390 ff.; there is, however, considerable variation in the way they are
related, and monotony is avoided.

As well as wine for a libation Pisistratus offers the newcomers σπλάγχνα
for themselves, a particular honour; the hungry priest Hierocles in Ar. *Pax*
(1103 ff.) hopes for a similar reception.

41. δειδισκόμενος: an obsolete form, cognate with δέχομαι. The spelling
δηδισκ- would probably be more accurate, but there seems to have been
some confusion with δείκνυμι (cf. iv 59 δεικνύμενος), and the traditional
orthography is more likely to reflect the poet's view. See further Hoekstra
on xv 150, Russo on xviii 121, Frisk, *GEW* s.v. δηδέχεται, Chantraine,
Dictionnaire s.v. δηδέχεται, *LfgrE* s.v. δειδέχαται.

42. αἰγιόχοιο: the epithet αἰγίοχος belongs exclusively to Zeus; its original sense is disputed, but in Homer it must mean 'aegis-bearing' or 'aegis-shaking' (cf. Bacchylides' coinage πελέμαιγις (xvii 7, of Athena). From the *Iliad* we learn that the aegis is a goat-skin shield, sometimes lent by Zeus to Athena (v 738 ff., xviii 204, xxi 400) and even to Apollo (xv 308, xxiv 20). It is something more than a defensive weapon, even a magical one, and is clearly related to, perhaps a symbol of, Zeus' control of the weather (cf. *Il.* xvii 593 ff.). See further Nilsson, *Geschichte*, i 436–7, *LfgrE*, Chantraine, *Dictionnaire* s.v. αἰγίς, M. L. West, *Hesiod, Works and Days* (Oxford, 1978), 366 ff.

45. ἥ: the relative is assimilated in gender to its predicate. **θέμις:** see ii 68 n.

46. μελιηδέος οἴνου: cf. *Il.* xviii 545; clearly a secondary development from the older formula μελιηδέα οἶνον (xiv 78 etc.), which respects the initial ϝ of οἶνος. Hoekstra, *Modifications*, 48, discusses how the idea embodied in this formula might have been expressed in the gen. sg. under the same metrical conditions before ϝ was dropped.

49. ὁμηλικίη: while this might here be taken as a true abstract, it is used elsewhere in the *Odyssey* as if it were equivalent to ὁμῆλιξ (364, vi 23, xxii 209), and this seems more natural; see also 364 n.

50. ἄλεισον: a rare synonym for δέπας, often regarded as a Mediterranean loan-word: see *LfgrE*, Frisk, *GEW*, Chantraine, *Dictionnaire*. At 63 the cup is further described as δέπας ἀμφικύπελλον.

51. τίθει: impf.

52. δικαίῳ: as often in Homer, δίκαιος here implies observance of custom and social convention rather than honesty or fair-mindedness. Pisistratus, as we might expect, resembles his father in character (cf. 20, 244).

54. πολλά here surely expresses intensity rather than quantity, not 'much', but 'earnestly'.

57–8. ὄπαζε, δίδου: the present tense is used of long-lasting benefits; contrast the aorist δός (60) with reference to a specific action.

61. οὕνεκα: is to be taken closely with πρήξαντα, i.e. τοῦτο πρήξαντα οὗ ἔνεκα.

62. ἔπειτα: is used resumptively, in restating an act already described: cf. *Il.* v 432–6 Αἰνείᾳ δ' ἐπόρουσε ... τρὶς μὲν ἔπειτ' ἐπόρουσε. ἔνθα is used very similarly at *Od.* vii 1 ὡς ὁ μὲν ἔνθ' ἠρᾶτο.

63. ἀμφικύπελλον: Aristotle (*HA* 624 a 7 ff.) takes it for granted that this means a 'double cup', i.e. two cups joined at the base, like an open-ended hour-glass; he uses the term to illustrate the arrangement of bees' cells. But Aristarchus interpreted it as 'two-handled', while others took it as 'circular, round'. See further Hainsworth on viii 89, *LfgrE*, G. Bruns *Archaeologia* Q, 42–4.

65. κρέ' ὑπέρτερα: the flesh on the carcase, as opposed to the σπλάγχνα.
ἐρύσαντο: 'had drawn it off (the spits)'. This concludes the process begun at 33. Roasting meat, unlike other kinds of cookery, is regarded as a suitable task for the men of the heroic age. As usual, the preparations for a meal receive more attention than the meal itself.

66. δασσάμενοι δαίνυντ' ... δαῖτα: the world-play should be noted. **δασσάμενοι:** aor. ptcp. of δατέομαι.

67–101. In response to Nestor's questions Telemachus explains who he is, and why he has come to Pylos; he begs Nestor to give him whatever information he has about Odysseus.

68. Γερήνιος ἱππότα Νέστωρ: a common formula in both epics. The meaning of Γερήνιος was disputed in antiquity. Some connected it with the town of Gerena (-ia, -os) in Messenia (cf. Hes. frr. 34, 35; see further *RE* vii 1264–5 s.v. Gerenia); but no other Homeric hero has a formulaic epithet derived from a place, and this would be a strange exception, since Gerena was neither Nestor's birthplace nor associated with any exploit of his known to us. An alternative explanation was 'old, venerable'; the use of the formula γέρων ἱππηλάτα Νέστωρ (436, 444) as if it were equivalent suggests that the poet may himself have understood the epithet in this sense (cf. schol. BT *Il.* xvi 196, where γερήνιος ἱππότα Φοῖνιξ is recorded as a variant for γέρων ἱππηλάτα Φ.) but this cannot have been its original meaning. The form suggests a possessive adjective, like Τελαμώνιος, Ποιάντιος, Νηλήιος, in function a patronymic (so Leumann ap. Meyer, *RE* xxiii 2159 s.v. Nestor); but if we accept this interpretation we immediately face the problem raised by the suppression of Nestor's original father in favour of Neleus, and we can hardly suppose that the poet and his audience understood the epithet as 'son of Gerenos'.   **ἱππότα:** like other masc. nouns with nom. sg. in ᾰ (μητίετα, κυανοχαῖτα, εὐρύοπα, etc.) this seems in origin to be a voc. which remained unchanged when the name to which it was attached came to be used in the nom.; such forms are much commoner in the *Iliad* than in the *Odyssey*: cf. Monro, *Homeric Dialect*, 81 § 96, Chantraine, *Grammaire*, i 199 ff. § 83. Delebecque, *Le Cheval dans l'Iliade* (Paris, 1951), 38, 164–5, notes that in Homer ἱππότα and ἱππηλάτα are restricted to characters who have already won their claim to fame before the action of the *Iliad*: either they are, like Nestor, already old men, or they are mentioned as fathers, grandfathers, or more remote ancestors of those involved in the fighting at Troy. Nestor appears as an expert on chariot-tactics at *Il.* iv 301 ff., cf. ii 555, and offers some rather unethical advice on chariot-racing at xxiii 306 ff. There is an interesting discussion of Nestor's formulae by F. Bader in R. Bloch (ed.), *Recherches sur les religions de l'antiquité* (Geneva–Paris, 1980), 11 ff., 53 ff.

69. As usual, the host waits to discover the identity of his guest until they have eaten; cf. i 123–4 n.   **ἐρέσθαι:** on the accentuation see above, i 405 n.

71–4. = ix 252–5, *h.Ap.* 452–5. Aristarchus argued, against Aristophanes, that 72–4 are less appropriate here than in ix, where Polyphemus similarly interrogates Odysseus and his men when he finds them trespassing in his cave; he evidently suspected that they were a secondary addition here, authentic in ix. 72 in itself is unobjectionable, but the diffident Telemachus and the aged Mentor with their small ship would not immediately suggest a raiding party, and if the question is treated as a routine enquiry it loses much of its force in ix, where Polyphemus has to deal with a party of intruders lurking in his home. But without 73–4 Nestor's questions would look disproportionately brief after the rather formal introduction.

Thucydides surely had this passage in mind when he wrote (i 5. 1–3) οἱ γὰρ Ἕλληνες τὸ πάλαι καὶ τῶν βαρβάρων οἵ τε ἐν τῇ ἠπείρῳ παραθαλάσσιοι καὶ ὅσοι νήσους εἶχον, ἐπειδὴ ἤρξαντο μᾶλλον περαιοῦσθαι ναυσὶν ἐπ' ἀλλήλους, ἐτράποντο πρὸς λῃστείαν ... οὐκ ἔχοντός πω αἰσχύνην τούτου τοῦ ἔργου, φέροντος δέ τι καὶ δόξης μᾶλλον· δηλοῦσι δὲ ... οἱ παλαιοὶ τῶν ποιητῶν τὰς πύστεις τῶν καταπλεόντων πανταχοῦ ὁμοίως ἐρωτῶντες εἰ λῃσταί εἰσιν, ὡς οὔτε ὧν πυνθάνονται ἀπαξιούντων τὸ ἔργον, οἷς τε ἐπιμελὲς εἴη εἰδέναι οὐκ ὀνειδιζόντων. It is not, however, wholly true that raiding and cattle-rustling are regarded as perfectly respectable in the heroic world; Eumaeus is quite explicit in his condemnation of marauders (xiv 85 ff.). But there is a double standard, and in general it seems to be assumed that the element of danger is in itself sufficient justification, at any rate when the victims are foreigners; cf. Odysseus' account of his own adventures (true and fictitious), ix 40 ff., xiv 247 ff., xvii 425 ff.

71. ὑγρὰ κέλευθα: see Hoekstra on xv 474.

72. μαψιδίως: 'recklessly'. **κατὰ πρῆξιν:** 'on business, on a trading venture', like Mentes (i 182 ff.); cf. πρηκτῆρες viii 162.

76–7. Cf. i 320–1.

77. ἀποιχομένοιο ἔροιτο: see above, i 135 n.

78. = i 95; it is clearly interpolated here, being absent from two papyri and from most medieval MSS; it also introduces an unhomeric repetition of ἵνα.

79. Νηληϊάδη: Nestor's patronymic has an alternative form, Νηλείδης; cf. Πηλείδης and Πηληϊάδης; see further Chantraine, *Grammaire*, i 105–6 § 46. **κῦδος Ἀχαιῶν:** used also of Odysseus, xii 184, *Il.* ix 673, x 544.

81. ὑπονηΐου: the epithet occurs only here, and the traditional interpretation 'lying under Mount Neion' does not inspire complete confidence. There is only one other reference to Neion, which some have suspected to result from misinterpretation of this epithet: see i 186 n. The scholia compare Θήβη Ὑποπλακίη (*Il.* vi 397), but this is not really analogous, as the topographical epithet serves to distinguish the town near Troy from its more important Boeotian homonym, whereas there was no danger of Odysseus' homeland being confused with some other Ithaca. **εἰλήλουθμεν:** for the form cf. *Il.* ix 49; see further Monro, *Homeric Dialect*, 28 § 25, Chantraine, *Grammaire*, i 425 § 202.

83. Telemachus fails to tell Nestor his name: some may see in this a nicely calculated omission, indicating a sense of his own unimportance or preoccupation with his purpose, but I doubt if it is significant. **κλέος εὐρύ:** 'far-reaching news, news which has spread from far away'; κλέος should not be translated by 'fame' here.

87. πευθόμεθ': 'we have heard'; the pres. is similarly used with ἀκούω where it is more natural to translate with a past tense as at ii 118, iii 193, iv 94, 688, xv 403.

88. κείνου ... Κρονίων: 'even his death (let alone his other troubles) Zeus has made obscure'. As often, Telemachus sounds as if he accepted Odysseus' death as a fact; here he is evidently concerned to show that he has faced the worst possible case, so that Nestor may not be tempted to conceal what he knows in order to spare his feelings. **ἀπευθέα:** at 184, the only other place where ἀπευθής occurs in Homer, its sense is active.

90. ἐπ' ἠπείρου: 'on land', cf. v 56, x 56, etc.

91. In Homer Amphitrite simply represents the sea (cf. v 422, xii 60, 97); Hesiod mentions her among the Nereids and as Poseidon's consort (*Th.* 243, 930). The name is unexplained, though a connection with Triton, and perhaps with Tritogeneia, looks obvious; see further *LfgrE*.

92–101. = iv 322–31; but this duplication may partly result from interpolation intended to assimilate to one another Telemachus' appeals to Nestor and to Menelaus: see below on 98 ff.

92. τὰ σὰ γούναθ' ἱκάνομαι: suppliants sometimes literally clasp the knees of the person entreated (cf. vi 142, 148, xiv 279), but Telemachus merely means 'I beseech you'. Various explanations have been proposed for the value set upon the knees in this gesture peculiarly characteristic of the ritual of suppliancy; for two plausible, but very different, theories see Onians, *Origins*, 174 ff., W. Burkert, *Structure and History in Greek Mythology and Ritual* (Berkeley–Los Angeles–London, 1979), 44–5, and on the conventions of suppliancy in general J. P. Gould, 'Hiketeia', *JHS* xciii (1973), 74–103.

95. πλαζομένου, as the following γάρ shows, refers to Odysseus, and is not to be taken with ἄλλου: 'if you heard from someone else the story of his wanderings'. The line is clumsy and fussy; Bekker's view that it should be regarded as an interpolation is attractive.

96. μ' is the object of both participles. **μειλίσσεο:** 'soften, sweeten, your words', i.e. gloss over the truth.

97. Cf. xvii 44. **ὅπως ... ὀπωπῆς** apparently means 'how you got sight of him', an odd phrase to use here. It is sometimes suggested that it can be given an intellectual interpretation, 'what view you have formed', but this is artificial. The ancient variant ἀκουῆς surely represents an attempt to avoid this difficulty.

98–101. It was suggested by Bérard and Schwartz that these lines, which are peculiarly appropriate in Telemachus' appeal to Menelaus (iv 328 ff.), are interpolated here. 97 forms a perfectly satisfactory conclusion to Telemachus' speech; 98–9 are not particularly appropriate to the relationship between Nestor and Odysseus at Troy, but are exactly right addressed to Menelaus, for whose sake Odysseus had gone to Troy.

99. ἔπος ... ἔργον: see ii 272 n.

101. ἐνίσπες: strong aor. imper. of ἐνέπω (cf. δός, θές, σχές): most MSS have ἐνίσπε. See further Chantraine, *Grammaire*, i 467 § 222.

102–200. Nestor describes the sufferings of the Greeks before Troy and relates the events which led to their separation on the return journey; he lists the heroes whose subsequent histories are known to him, but has no news of Odysseus.

103. There is no apodosis to the clause which begins here with ἐπεί; cf. iv 204, vi 187, viii 236.

106. Cf. Achilles' claims at *Il.* i 163 ff., ix 328 ff.

109 ff. Cf. xi 467 ff., xxiv 15 ff.; for Ajax's suicide cf. xi 543 ff. The poet assumes the stories of these heroes' deaths (but not necessarily any particular poetic treatment of them) to be familiar to his audience.

111–12. The heroic end of Antilochus, slain by the Ethiopian prince Memnon while rescuing his father, is memorably related by Pindar, *P.* vi 28 ff.; Achilles subsequently avenged his friend by killing Memnon. The story, an obvious counterpart to that of Patroclus, was told in the *Aethiopis*, and has given rise to much debate about the relationship between that poem and the *Iliad*: see further Heubeck on xxiv 16–18, M. M. Willcock, *BICS* xx (1973), 5 ff., 'Antilochos in the *Iliad*', *Mélanges Ed. Delebecque* (Aix-en-Provence, 1983), 477 ff., W. Kullmann, 'Zur Methode der Neoanalyse in der Homerforschung', *WSt* xv (1981), 5 ff. (where references to earlier discussions may be found). The admirable restraint of this brief tribute by the usually garrulous Nestor is peculiarly effective in evoking pathos, suggesting as it does the courage of an old man who has steeled himself to speak of his beloved son without breaking down: contrast Pisistratus' adolescent sentimentality (iv 186 ff.). Menelaus praises Antilochus for the qualities which Nestor singles out (*Il.* xv 569 ff.).

115. Homer uses both ἑξέτης and ἑξαέτης. The analogy of forms like ἑπταέτης and εἰναέτης, from numerals ending in -ά probably accounts for the anomalous α in πενταέτης and ἑξαέτης.

117. ἀνιηθείς: almost 'bored'.

118. ῥάπτομεν: the metaphorical use of this verb, 'contrive, plot', is commoner in Homer than the literal; cf. ii 236 n.   ἀμφιέποντες: probably 'carefully, intently', rather than 'pressing them hard'.

119. παντοίοισι δόλοισι: ruses naturally suggest the subject of Odysseus. μόγις: i.e. only after much pain and grief.   ἐτέλεσσε: 'brought to an end'.

120–5. The passage has often been suspected; it offers a rather unconvincing variation on the theme of Telemachus' resemblance to his father, and contains some oddities of expression. Elsewhere (i 208 ff., iv 140 ff.) it is his physical likeness to Odysseus which excites comment, and this is what σέβας μ' ἔχει εἰσορόωντα leads us to expect here. But in fact the resemblance on which Nestor remarks lies in their way of speaking, though the idea is rather confusingly expressed (and wholly unconvincing in the case of a young man who has not seen his father since he was an infant).

122. παντοίοισι δόλοισι: the repetition at so short an interval is clumsy. εἰ ἐτεόν γε: what follows shows that this phrase does not indicate any real doubt.

123. σέβας ... εἰσορόωντα: similarly Helen (iv 142).

124–5. Nestor rather confusingly combines two ideas: first, that Telemachus' way of speaking is strikingly like that of Odysseus, and, second, that it is like what it should be, i.e. remarkably sensible for a young man. ἐοικότες in 124 must refer to resemblance (cf. iv 141–3, xix 380–1), while ἐοικότα in 125 must mean 'fitting, suitable' (cf. iv 239 καὶ μύθοις τέρπεσθε· ἐοικότα γὰρ καταλέξω). The fact that speech resembling that of Odysseus would also be suitable and appropriate makes the confusion easier.

126. ἦος: εἵως, the reading of all our MSS,[1] should not be altered to ἦος, nowhere attested but to be inferred as the early Ionic form: see further on iv 90. There is no parallel for the sense 'all that time', and possibly an anacolouthon is intended, as at the beginning of Nestor's speech (104).

127. The workings of ἀγορή and βουλή in the Greek camp are well illustrated at *Il.* ii 53 ff.

129. φραζόμεθ': impf.

130 ff. The home-comings of the Greek heroes from Troy form a recurrent theme in the Telemachy: cf. i 325–7 n. and pp. 53–4.

130–1. = xiii 316–17; but 131, which anticipates the actual departure in 157 and produces a very awkward connection with 132, is almost certainly interpolated. **αἰπήν:** an artificial but metrically convenient substitute for αἰπεῖαν.

133. ἐπεὶ ... δίκαιοι: cf. ii 282 (of the suitors).

136. As a result of this quarrel, Agamemnon arrives home without Menelaus, so that Aegisthus can dispose of him without trouble: see further on 248–51.

138. ἐς ἠέλιον καταδύντα: normally this formula means 'until sunset', but here it must be 'towards, near, sunset'. Morning was the usual time for assemblies, though we find them held in the evening on occasion (*Il.* viii 489 ff., ix 10 ff., xviii 245 ff.); but the parenthetical 139 explains why it was imprudent to hold this important meeting so late in the day. Such folly might in itself be regarded as evidence of Athena's anger.

142. νόστου: to be taken closely with ἐπ' εὐρέα νῶτα θαλάσσης, cf. v 344–5 νόστου | γαίης Φαιήκων.

143. οὐδ' ... πάμπαν: 'not at all'. **ἐήνδανε:** *ἐάνδανε would be more correct; ἐήνδανε reflects Attic ἥνδανε (cf. 150 ἥνδανε); cf. Monro, *Homeric Dialect*, 61 § 67 (2), Chantraine, *Grammaire*, i 480 § 230.

146. ὅ = ὅτι.

151. ἀέσαμεν: this verb, unknown to the *Iliad*, occurs only in the aor. and in combination with νύκτα(ς). Its derivation is obscure, and it is not clear whether it means 'sleep' or 'spend, pass (the night)'; it is also uncertain whether the variation in the quantity of the initial α is due to metrical lengthening, compensatory lengthening after the loss of ϝ, or contraction; see further Hoekstra on xvi 367, Frisk, *GEW* s.v. ἄεσα, *LfgrE* s.v. ἄεσα, Chantraine, *Dictionnaire* s.v. ἀέσκω. The ancient variant εἰάσαμεν is an obvious conjecture, replacing an obscure word with a more familiar one. **ὁρμαίνοντες:** the connotations of ὁρμαίνω are well explored by C. Voigt, *Überlegung u. Entscheidung* (Meisenheim am Glan, 1972), 13 ff.

152. πῆμα κακοῖο: cf. δύης πῆμα (xiv 338).

153. οἱ μέν: 'some of us'.

---

[1] This important fact is not stated in Allen's apparatus, though cf. his *Praefatio* vi.

154. βαθυζώνους: in Homer this epithet, like βαθύκολπος and ἑλκεσίπεπλος, is not applied to Greek women; the restriction is not observed in later poetry. βαθύκολπος presumably expresses the effect of being βαθύζωνος. Some have interpreted it in terms of a girdle drawn rather tight, accentuating the natural curves of the figure; 'svelte' is Bérard's translation; similarly *LfgrE*. But it is more likely, as Aristarchus held, that βαθύκολπος suggests a style which left a fold of material hanging over the girdle. Cf. Herodotus' description of Alcmaeon's preparations when he wanted to stow about himself as much gold as he could (vi 125): ἐνδὺς κιθῶνα μέγαν καὶ κόλπον βαθὺν καταλιπόμενος τοῦ κιθῶνος κτλ. This produced a convenient and capacious pocket, which the Phoenician girl who kidnapped Eumaeus put to similar use when she secreted three goblets ὑπὸ κόλπῳ (xv 469). The Homeric restriction of these epithets points to an obvious and significant distinction between Greek and Anatolian (or, more generally, Near Eastern) dress styles at the time when they entered the epic tradition; they must belong to a period when Greek women wore something other than the classical peplos with a girdle, a style to which they are remarkably appropriate. Mycenaean women dressed rather differently: Mycenaean art depicts two styles: the more striking, a stiff, full skirt and a bolero, was probably for ceremonial occasions, everyday wear being a long, close-fitting robe, a fuller version of the men's tunic; in both styles the hem is clear of the ground, and a Mycenaean lady could not properly be described as ἑλκεσίπεπλος.

The subject of women's dress in Homer is difficult and unsatisfactory, but plainly the poems do not, in general, present women wearing the distinctive styles of the Mycenaean age. See further Lorimer, *Monuments*, 337 ff., S. Marinatos, *Archaeologia* A, M. Bieber, *Entwicklungsgeschichte der griechischen Tracht*[2] (Berlin, 1967), 23 ff.

156. ποιμένι λαῶν: the metaphor of the king as shepherd of his people is common in both epics.

157. νέας is to be understood as object of ἐλαύνομεν and antecedent of αἱ.

158. ἐστόρεσεν: 'levelled, made calm'. **μεγακήτεα:** explained in the scholia as a possessive cpd., 'containing great sea-monsters'; Theocritus' πολυκήτεα Νεῖλον (xvii 98) looks like a reminiscence of this passage. The epithet was evidently understood rather differently by the poet of the *Iliad*, where it is applied to a dolphin (xxi 22) and to a ship (viii 222, xi 5, 600); some have argued that, like κητώεσσα, it should be connected with an alleged *κῆτος, 'hollow, cleft' (cf. iv 1 n.).

159. ἐς Τένεδον: the first day's journey from Troy is very short.

160. οἴκαδε ἱέμενοι gives the reason for their sacrifice.

161. σχέτλιος: emphatically placed at the beginning of the line, as almost invariably in Homer. **ἔπι:** with ὦρσε.

162-4. Odysseus' own narrative (ix 39 ff.) throws no light on this return to Troy, presumably prompted by belated qualms about setting off without making further efforts to propitiate Athena (cf. 143 ff.).

162. ἀμφιελίσσας: of the three explanations commonly advanced, 'wheeling either way, handy', 'curved at both ends', 'curved at both sides', the last seems much the most probable; the epithet is very commonly used of ships drawn up on a beach, where their form and method of construction would be clearly visible. See further Kurt, *Fachausdrücke*, 39 ff.

164. ἐπ' ... **ἦρα φέροντες:** cf. xvi 375, xviii 56, *Il.* i 572, 578; at *Il.* xiv 132 ἦρα φέρειν is used without ἐπί. ἦρα is evidently equivalent to χάριν; no other part of the noun occurs, and it is uncertain whether it is masc. sg. or neut. pl. We learn from schol. *Il.* i 572 that Aristarchus took it as a neut. pl. adj., ἐπίηρα, and the use of ἐπίηρος in later poetry shows that this was not an isolated view, though Herodian rightly rejected it. See Chantraine, *Dictionnaire*, and Frisk, *GEW* s.v. ἦρα, R. Gusmani, *SMEA* vi (1968), 17 ff.

165. ἀολλέσιν: Nestor's contingent fled as a united group: contrast 155–6, 162–3.

166. γίγνωσκον: impf., implying a gradual realization.

167. Τυδέος υἱός: Diomedes.

168. νῶϊ: the iota is hard to explain; νῶε should perhaps be restored: cf. Wackernagel, *Untersuchungen*, 151 anm. 2.

169. The second day's sail was from Tenedos to Lesbos, not more than 50 km. The δολιχὸς πλόος is the open-sea route across the Aegean (cf. 174–5 πέλαγος μέσον εἰς Εὔβοιαν | τέμνειν); this would take them north of Chios (καθύπερθε Χίοιο) and of Psyra to Geraestus, the most southerly point of Euboea, a distance of about 200 kilometres from Lesbos. This is the shorter route overall, but entails a longer run without any accessible port than the safer route running inside Chios, past the headland of Mimas on the Asiatic coast, then south of Chios (ὑπένερθε Χίοιο), and westwards through the Cyclades.

Sappho (fr. 17) refers to the sojourn of the Greek fleet at Lesbos on the way home from Troy, but implies a rather different story: see further D. L. Page, *Sappho and Alcaeus* (Oxford, 1955), 58 ff.

170. παιπαλοέσσης: 'rugged'; see further Frisk, *GEW* s.v. παιπάλη, Leumann, *Wörter*, 236 ff., G. P. Shipp, *Essays in Mycenaean and Homeric Greek* (Melbourne, 1961), 48 ff.

173. In Homer it is rare to ask for an omen, though cf. xx 97 ff., *Il.* xxiv 314 ff. Rather surprisingly, the poet does not tell us what form it took.

175. τέμνειν: an atticism, the usual epic form being τάμνειν. **ὑπέκ:** with φύγοιμεν.

Nestor and his party choose the more dangerous route, but with the gods' help come quickly and safely home. The moral, *nisi Dominus frustra*, is not over-stressed, but is clear enough, and should be remembered when we come to the death of the impious Ajax, who chose the safer course through the Cyclades and yet was shipwrecked (iv 499 ff.).

179. ἐπί is to be taken closely with ἔθεμεν, 'we laid on his altars'. **πέλαγος μετρεῖν:** cf. Verg. *G.* iv 389–90 'aequor ... metitur'.

180. The fourth day's voyage since their departure from Troy covers about 200 km. **εἴσας:** see 10 n.

182. ἔστασαν: this is the reading of Aristarchus (cf. schol. *Il.* xii 56) and must be regarded as a shortened form of ἔστησαν; the MSS are divided between this form and the plpf. ἔστασαν, which, since it is intrans., is clearly impossible; one MS has the impf. ἵστασαν, presumably a medieval conjecture but adopted by many editors. Similar problems arise at viii 435, xviii 307, *Il.* ii 525, xii 56, xviii 346.[2] **Πύλονδ' ἔχον:** 'I held on for Pylos'; νῆας may be understood as the object of ἔχον (cf. *Il.* xvi 378, xxiii 422). Nestor was fortunate with weather conditions; the difficulty of rounding Cape Malea, the most southerly point of the Peloponnese, is repeatedly stressed (iii 287 ff., iv 514 ff., ix 80 ff., xix 186 ff.).

184. ἀπευθής: 'in ignorance, without getting news', active here: contrast 88.

185. κείνων: i.e. Greeks who had remained at Troy (155) and those who had turned back with Odysseus (162).

187. On ἢ θέμις ἐστί see 45 n. For κεύθω with acc. of the person from whom something is concealed, a usage not found in the *Iliad*, cf. xxiii 273.

188. The Myrmidons are Achilles' men in the *Iliad*; after his death the leadership naturally devolves on his son, Neoptolemus. Further details of their journey were related in the *Nostoi*, as we learn from Proclus' summary: Νεοπτόλεμος δὲ Θέτιδος ὑποθεμένης πεζῇ ποιεῖται τὴν πορείαν. καὶ παραγενόμενος εἰς Θρᾴκην Ὀδυσσέα καταλαμβάνει ἐν τῇ Μαρωνείᾳ, καὶ τὸ λοιπὸν ἀνύει τῆς ὁδοῦ, καὶ τελευτήσαντα Φοίνικα θάπτει· αὐτὸς δὲ εἰς Μολοσσοὺς ἀφικόμενος ἀναγνωρίζεται Πηλεῖ.

ἐγχεσιμώρους: the second element in this word was found puzzling in antiquity; cf. ἰόμωρος, ὑλακόμωρος, and the later prose word σινάμωρος. Frisk (*GEW*) persuasively interprets the word as 'speerberühmt', citing Celtic, Germanic, and Slavic parallels for the second element; his discussion of ἰόμωρος, ὑλακόμωρος, and σινάμωρος (s.v. σίνομαι) should be compared; cf. Leumann, *Wörter*, 37, 272 Anm. 18. It looks as if some of these compounds were formed after the meaning of the second element had been obscured. Beck (*LfgrE*) suggests that the second element was connected with μωρός by popular etymology and the cpd. understood as something like 'berserk'.

190. The prominence here given to Philoctetes (cf. viii 219) no doubt reflects his importance in the events related in the *Little Iliad*; as the Greeks learned from the Trojan seer Helenus, Troy could not fall without Philoctetes' bow, which he had inherited from Heracles and with which he killed Paris. **Ποιάντιον:** the use of possessive adjectives in -ιος as patronymics (cf. Τελαμώνιος, Νηλήιος, Καπανήιος, etc.) is very ancient (cf. Lat. *Tullius*, *Marcius*, etc.), and not to be regarded, as it has sometimes been, as a specifically Aeolic feature; see further, K. Strunk, *Die sogenannten Äolismen der homerischen Sprache* (Cologne, 1957), 79 ff.

192. ἀπηύρα: that this defective verb would have seemed rather abstruse to the poet's audience is indicated by the fact that Hesiod evidently confused it with ἐπαυρίσκω (*Op.* 240); see further K. Strunk, *Glotta* xxxvii (1958), 118–27, *LfgrE* s.v. ἀπηύρων.

---

[2] By analogy we find ἔστασε, *AP* ix 708. 6 (Philip), ἔστασας 714. 2 (Anon.).

193. Again, the theme of Agamemnon's death and Orestes' vengeance; see above, i 29–31 n. **ἀκούετε**: pf. in sense, cf. πεύθομαι 87, 187.

195–7. The punctuation of the OCT (comma at end of 195) is unsatisfactory; it is better to begin a new sentence at 196: 'How good a thing it is...!' **κεῖνος** in 195 means Aegisthus, in 197 Orestes. **ἐπισμυγερῶς**: the form is confined to Epic; Frisk (*GEW* s.v. σμυγερός) well explains it as 'expressive Kontamination', from μογερός and στυγερός with ἐπι- by analogy with ἐπίπονος, or something of the sort.

198–200. = i 300 ff. 199–200 were athetized by Aristophanes and Aristarchus. The fact that 198 escaped athetesis indicates that they had other grounds for suspicion besides repetition, and certainly the lines are awkward here; the compliment of 199 is clumsy in this context, and it is hard to avoid seeing in Nestor's advice a reference to the suitors, and thus an inept anticipation of 211 ff.

Orestes' vengeance forms the climax of Nestor's speech; the theme will be resumed later (248 ff.). We might have expected that the list of safe arrivals would culminate in a formal, negative, statement about Odysseus, highlighting his unusual situation by contrast with the others. But Nestor has already said all he can in answer to Telemachus' question (163, 184), and the direction of his interest has shifted. If 199–200 are removed, there seems to me nothing wrong with the end of this speech; for a different view see Page, *Odyssey*, 174–5, Merkelbach, *Untersuchungen*, 37–8.

201–52. Nestor and Mentor attempt in vain to overcome Telemachus' despair of a solution to the problem presented by the suitors. Telemachus asks for further details of the homecomings of Agamemnon and Menelaus.

203. οἵ: ethic dat.

204. Cf. *Il.* vi 357–8.

205. τοσσήνδε: τόσοσδε has a stronger demonstrative sense than τοσοῦτος; Telemachus means 'so great *now* and to *me*', ⟨ὅσην Ὀρέστης εἶχε⟩ being understood; τίσασθαι κτλ. (206)is epexegetic of δύναμιν. **περιθεῖεν**: most MSS read παραθεῖεν, 'concede, place at my disposal'; this is unobjectionable, but editors generally prefer περιθεῖεν, 'clothe, invest me with'; for the metaphor cf. e.g. ἐπιειμένος ἀλκήν (ix 214, *Il.* vii 164), μένος ἀμφιβαλόντες (*Il.* xvii 742).

206. There is a certain oddity in Telemachus referring to suitors without saying whose, but such things are to be expected in oral narrative. For the construction of τίσασθαι cf. *Il.* iii 366.

208. μοι: amplified and corrected in the next line, somewhat clumsily, by πατρί τ' ἐμῷ καὶ ἐμοί, cf. 380–1. (The alternative explanation of μοι as an ethic dat., 'I would have you know', is surely unnatural.)

209. Condemned as superfluous in the scholia, probably reflecting Aristarchus' view.

211. Cf. 103.

214–15. = xvi 95–6. Telemachus does not answer these questions, though his general attitude implies a negative to the first. **ἑκὼν ὑποδάμνασαι**: 'allow yourself to be oppressed'. **θεοῦ ὀμφῇ**: 'the prompting of a god', to be understood by reference to the common assumption that the gods are at work when men do or say something odd without any discoverable cause, cf. i 384. It would be discourteous to suggest that the people of Ithaca might have reasonable grounds for withholding support from Telemachus; so, if he is unpopular with them, the cause must be supernatural. We may compare ὄσσαν ... ἐκ Διός (i 282–3), of a rumour of untraced origin. (In the scholia the phrase is interpreted as a reference to an oracle demanding the deposition of the king; but oracular sanction is rare in Homer, and this rather unusual contingency seems too specific to provide a satisfactory antithesis to ἑκὼν ὑποδάμνασαι).

216–17. We meet here the first of several connected problems presented by this discussion. All our MSS, with Aristarchus, read ἀποτίσεται in 216 and ὅ γε in 217, so that the lines refer to Odysseus. The abrupt change of subject is rather clumsy; before and afterwards Nestor is concerned with Telemachus' desire for vengeance, and this speculation about Odysseus seems inconsequential, though admittedly the subject of his return is of such overriding interest that the association of ideas is natural. Coherence is produced with Zenodotus' text, reading ἀποτίσεαι in 216 and σύ γε in 217; ἐλθών then refers to Telemachus' return from his travels. Nestor's speech is thus concerned with a single topic, Telemachus' wish (205 ff.) that he might himself take vengeance on the suitors. But with Zenodotus' readings here a problem arises later, since Mentor speaks (232 ff.) as if Nestor and Telemachus had been discussing the possibility of Odysseus' return. It is better to accept some incoherence here, natural enough in a rather garrulous old man and fostered by the poet's liking for dramatic irony, since it affords Telemachus an opportunity to deny what we know will in fact happen. The variants of Zenodotus' text were no doubt intended to impose order on Nestor's train of thought. See further Page, *Odyssey*, 175–6 (defending Zenodotus' text), Nickau, *Untersuchungen*, 213 ff. (against). σφι: 'on them', i.e. the suitors.

222. Cf. Ajax's comment (*Il.* xxiii 782–3) θεά ... ἣ τὸ πάρος περ | μήτηρ ὣς Ὀδυσῆϊ παρίσταται ἠδ' ἐπαρήγει. But Nestor's view of a unique relationship between Athena and Odysseus is not entirely borne out by the *Iliad*, where Odysseus is certainly no more favoured than Diomedes, and the poet probably had in mind later events, such as the Judgment of Arms; see further M. W. M. Pope, 'Athena's development in Homeric epic', *AJPh* lxxxi (1960), 113–35.

223. The wish expressed at 218 ff. is resumed, but now takes on more clearly conditional force.

224. τις: meiosis, 'many a one'; cf. *Il.* xiii 638.   ἐκλελάθοιτο: 'forget', sc. in death, cf. xxii 444.

226. ff. Telemachus' reply picks up Nestor's reference to the possibility of Odysseus' return (not his concluding words). He now believes his father to be dead (cf. 240–2) and in οὐδ' εἰ θεοὶ ὣς ἐθέλοιεν we should see the melancholy commonplace that even the gods cannot help their favourites in the face of death (as Athena-Mentor confirms (236–8)). The paler and more conventional εἰ μὴ θεοὶ ὣς ἐθέλοιεν of Zenodotus' text corresponds to his variants in 216–17.

226. πω: 'at all'; though it has been doubted whether πω is used in this sense in Homer, a temporal meaning would clearly be out of place here; cf. e.g. *Il.* iii 306, xii 270.

227–8. Telemachus reacts similarly to his father's suggestion that they might be able to deal with the suitors without further support (xvi 243–4): ἀλλὰ λίην μέγα εἶπες· ἄγη μ' ἔχει· οὐδέ κεν εἴη | ἄνδρε δύω πολλοῖσι καὶ ἰφθίμοισι μάχεσθαι. **οὐκ ἂν ἐμοί γε | ἐλπομένῳ τὰ γένοιτ':** 'I cannot expect that to happen'; cf. xxi 115 οὔ κέ μοι ἀχνυμένῳ, *Il.* xiv 108 ἐμοὶ δέ κεν ἀσμένῳ.

230. Τηλέμαχε: on the lengthening of a short syllable in arsis, see van Leeuwen, *Enchiridium*, 91–2 § 19; it is mitigated by the slight pause natural after a voc. This metrical irregularity could easily have been avoided by using the nom. for the voc., as often in Homer (cf. Monro, *Homeric Dialect*, 155–6 § 164, Chantraine, *Grammaire*, ii 36 § 45); Τηλέμαχος, given by a few MSS, may be the right reading. **ποῖόν ... ὀδόντων:** see i 64 n.

Zenodotus read Τηλέμαχ' ὑψαγόρη, μέγα νήπιε, ποῖον ἔειπες, a rather surprising variant in view of his reading in 226. Possibly this alternative was introduced to remove the metrical irregularity, though it seems unnecessarily drastic; or perhaps we are not fully informed about Zenodotus' text in the preceding passage. ὑψαγόρης is otherwise restricted to contexts where Antinous chaffs Telemachus (i 385, ii 85, 303, xvii 406), and its use here seems strangely insensitive.

231. Om. Zenodotus. The line has a proverbial look, and admits two interpretations: (1) a god, if he will, can easily bring a man home even from a distant land; (2) a god, if he will, can even at a distance save a man. It may be wrong to ask which the poet really meant. The following lines might support (1), as otherwise there is no logical connection between 231 and 232, though on this interpretation 231 is quite irrelevant to what Telemachus has just said. Aristarchus evidently preferred (2), since he athetized 232–8 on the grounds that 232–5 did not follow on logically from what had been said and that 236–8 were inconsistent with 231. **σαώσαι:** aor. opt. expressing the admission of a possibility, a use rarely found without ἄν or κεν; see Monro, *Homeric Dialect*, 272 § 299 (f), Chantraine, *Grammaire*, ii 216 ff. § 321.

233. = v 220, viii 466.

234. ἐφέστιος: 'at home', used a little loosely, since Agamemnon is said to have been killed in Aegisthus' house (iv 524 ff., xi 409 ff.).

236. ὁμοίϊον: epic adj., applied to γῆρας, θάνατος, νεῖκος, and πόλεμος; of the two explanations current in antiquity, 'common to all, impartial' (cf. ὅμοιος) and 'evil, hateful', the former is to be preferred: see further Russo on xviii 264, Frisk, *GEW*, Chantraine, *Dictionnaire*, Wyatt, *Lengthening*, 174–8, A. N. Athanassakis, *RhM* NF cxix (1976), 4 ff.

238. See ii 100 n.

240–2. Telemachus does not dwell on his disappointment at the lack of definite news; it would be unmannerly for him to burden his host with his troubles.

241-2. Athetized by Aristarchus, an almost inevitable corollary of his athetesis of 232 ff. **ἐτήτυμος**: rather striking applied to νόστος.

244-6. Athetized by Aristarchus as superfluous. The lines lead us to expect that Telemachus is going to ask for advice, or otherwise profit by Nestor's long experience, and it is slightly disconcerting when he merely enquires about a fairly recent event.

244. περὶ οἶδε ... ἄλλων: 'he knows better than others'.

245. This very strangely expressed line is obviously suggested by the description of Nestor, when ten years younger, at *Il.* i 250-2: τῷ δ' ἤδη δύο μὲν γενεαὶ μερόπων ἀνθρώπων | ἐφθίαθ', οἳ οἱ πρόσθεν ἅμα τράφεν ἠδ' ἐγένοντο | ἐν Πύλῳ ἠγαθέῃ, μετὰ δὲ τριτάτοισιν ἄνασσεν. As often, the distinction between ordinal and cardinal numbers seems to be confused (cf. ii 89 n.). Some commentators take γένεα as an acc. of duration, but we should then expect τρία not τρίς, and it is better understood as object of ἀνάξασθαι; for trans. ἀνάσσω cf. iv 177. The med. of ἀνάσσω is not otherwise attested.

246. Telemachus does not of course mean that Nestor looks extremely old, but that his appearance is noble; expressions like ἀντίθεος, θεοείκελος, θεοῖς ἐναλίγκιος ἄντην, etc. regularly refer to physical beauty; see further Parry, *Blameless Aegisthus*, 218 ff.

247. ἐνίσπες: see 101 n.

248. Nestor's reply shows that he takes Telemachus to mean 'How did it come about that Agamemnon was killed?', not 'By what method...?'

249. Telemachus is puzzled because Nestor's narrative at 168 ff. would suggest that Menelaus would have reached home before Agamemnon. His question implies that the brothers are thought of as living together, or at any rate nearby (cf. 256-7, 311), though even as the crow flies Mycenae is about eighty kilometres from Sparta. But clearly neither the poet nor his audience was very familiar with the geography of the Peloponnese: see above, pp. 64-5.

251. Ἄργεος ... Ἀχαϊκοῦ: a local gen., giving a less definite localization than the dat. Ἄργος cannot here mean 'the city of Argos', since that is Diomedes' capital (cf. 180-1), and is evidently used in a wider sense, to denote Agamemnon's kingdom (cf. 263), as described in *Il.* ii 569-75. The various senses of Ἄργος, which may also be used to refer to the whole Peloponnese (cf. i 344), surely contributed to the poet's topographical confusion.

252. ἐπ': 'through, among', cf. xiv 43, with Hoekstra's n.   **ὁ δέ**: Aegisthus; the following clause, expressing the result, 'so that A. had the confidence to kill him', well exemplifies Homeric parataxis.

253-328. Nestor tells of the seduction of Clytaemestra and of Menelaus' wanderings; he deals briefly with Agamemnon's murder, and at greater length with Orestes' revenge, and advises Telemachus to visit Menelaus.

255. τόδε: subject of ἐτύχθη.   **καὐτός**: crasis is rather rare in Homer; see Monro, *Homeric Dialect*, 350 ff. § 377.   **ὀίεαι**: 'you imagine, guess', an inference from 249 ff.

258 ff. Nestor's hypothesis is a measure of the enormity of Aegisthus' offence; but Orestes' regard for his mother evidently entailed a proper funeral for her paramour as well (309–10). On the role of dogs in such contexts see M. Faust, 'Die künstlerische Verwendung von κύων "Hund" in den homerischen Epen', *Glotta* xlviii (1970), 8–31; the connotations of this motif (which incidentally implies that the Homeric hero was supposed to be untroubled by any notion of the vengeful dead) are well explored by C. Segal, *The Theme of the Mutilation of the Corpse in the* Iliad (Leiden, 1971).

260. ἄστεος: the MSS are divided between this and Ἄργεος. But Ἄργος could not here mean 'the city of Argos', and a more extended sense does not suit the context. Intrusive proper names are a common type of corruption: see further M. L. West, *Textual Criticism and Editorial Technique* (Stuttgart, 1973), 23.

261. μέγα ἔργον: for the use of this formula to refer to a wicked deed cf. xi 272, xii 373, xix 92.

262. The answer to Telemachus' question begins here.   **κεῖθι:** at Troy.

266. δῖα refers to position or birth rather than character.   **Κλυται-μνήστρη:** better Κλυταιμήστρη, established as the correct spelling from the evidence of inscriptions and Latin, and supported by the ancient derivation παρὰ τὸ κλυτὸν καὶ τὸ μήδω, to which there is perhaps an allusion in the latter half of the line (cf. i 298 ff. and n.); Κλυται- is probably to be regarded as a metrical adaptation of Κλυτα- or Κλυτο-. The spelling with ν, given by nearly all the medieval MSS here,[3] results from late etymologizing fantasy, which derived the name from μνάομαι; but the correct spelling is found in two papyri at *Il.* i 113 (P. 30, *P.Oxy.* 748, 3rd cent. AD; *P.Köln* 70, Augustan), and in a fragment of the Hesiodic *Catalogue* (23 (a) 27). See further *RE* xi 890–1, Fraenkel on A. *Ag.* 84, v. Kamptz, *Personennamen*, 79–80.   **φρεσὶ ... ἀγαθῇσι:** the phrase implies proper moral feeling rather than high intelligence, but the distinction between the two is often blurred; cf. ii 231 n. This detail of Clytaemestra's initial resistance is not found elsewhere (cf. i 37 ff. with n.).

267. The minstrel as the queen's guardian is another curiosity of which there is no trace in any other authority. The ancient commentators were clearly puzzled, but inclined to the view that the minstrel was supposed to recount stories of womanly excellence, and thus inspire Clytaemestra to emulation while diverting her mind from improper thoughts; cf. Athen. 14 b. This implies a more Hesiodic style of poetry; the minstrels of the *Odyssey* do not offer advice or exhortation. But εἴρυσθαι (268) rather suggests physical protection, though a bard sufficiently able-bodied to be an effective guardian might himself be tempted to rape or seduction. It is worth considering an alternative explanation, rejected in the scholia but perhaps reflected (or corroborated?) in Hesychius' *Lexicon*, where ἀοιδός is glossed with ὁ εὐνοῦχος, σπάδων. Certainly castration in boyhood would account

---

[3] Allen (*PBSR* v (1910), 26) records the spelling without ν from four late MSS (M¹, P⁴, U³, U⁴), but this can hardly be more than a happy accident.

for this odd combination of duties; but though the castration of animals was evidently familiar (cf. *Il.* xxiii 147 ἔνορχα μῆλα), Greek literature does not refer to the castration of men before the fifth century, when it was evidently regarded as a barbarous Oriental practice (A. *Eu.* 187 ff., Hdt. iii 48. 2, viii 105–6). Still, there are few literary references to the *castrati* who played an important part in opera from the seventeenth to the late nineteenth century, and the argument from silence may not be a conclusive objection in this case.

For a stimulating discussion of this passage (with a rather different approach) see D. L. Page, 'The Mystery of the Minstrel at the Court of Agamemnon', *Studi classici in onore di Quintino Cataudella*, i (Università di Catania, 1972), 127 ff.

269. μιν: the minstrel, Aegisthus, or Clytaemestra? Most probably C., since ἀλλ' ὅτε δή evidently balances τὸ πρὶν μέν (265). For δαμάζω used of yielding to lust or passion cf. *Il.* xiv 316, 353. **ἐπέδησε:** probably from πεδάω; there is no certain instance of ἐπιδέω in Homer.

272. ἐθέλων ἐθέλουσαν: cf. v 155 παρ' οὐκ ἐθέλων ἐθελούσῃ, *Il.* vii 197 ἑκὼν ἀέκοντα; for polyptoton expressing reciprocity see above, i 311 ff. n.

273–4. πολλὰ ... πολλά: on the anaphora see above, i 3–4 n. **ἀγάλματ':** 'pleasing gifts', valuable things which bring pride to their owner, whether god or man; for the sense cf. iii 438, viii 509. **ἀνῆψεν:** 'fastened up', i.e. dedicated. **ὑφάσματα:** cf. *Il.* vi 302 ff.

278. Σούνιον: the SE tip of Attica, the next landmark after C. Geraestus. **ἱρόν:** the splendid columns of the temple of Poseidon are a familiar tourist attraction; the remains of the temple of Athena Sounias are less spectacular. **Ἀθηνέων:** as in the Catalogue of Ships (*Il.* ii 546 ff.), Athens and Attica are treated as virtually synonymous.

279–80. Sudden death without any obvious cause is regularly explained by the visitation of Apollo, or, when the victims are women, of Artemis: cf. e.g. vii 64, xi 173, xv 411 (with Hoekstra's n.).

282–3. Φρόντιν Ὀνητορίδην: Phrontis seems not to have been current as a personal name in real life, but Onetor, 'beneficial', is attested in Attic inscriptions. **ὃς ... ἄελλαι:** the relevance of this tribute becomes apparent shortly (289–90). For an interesting examination of Phrontis' role see M. Detienne and J.-P. Vernant, *Cunning Intelligence in Greek Culture and Society* (Hassocks, Sussex, 1978), 241 ff. (= *Les Ruses d'intelligence: La Mètis des grecs* (Paris, 1974), 233–4).

285–6. On the importance of proper funeral rites see i 239, 291 nn. No details are given, but we may compare the ceremonies performed for Elpenor (xii 9 ff.); his corpse is cremated with his armour, and the remains then covered by a mound with a pillar and Elpenor's oar on top.

286. καὶ κεῖνος: Menelaus, like Nestor, sailed south down the east coast of the Peloponnese.

287. γλαφυρῇσι: γλαφυρή is one of the three commonest Homeric epithets for νηῦς, reflecting, it seems, the earliest method of ship-construction, by hollowing out a tree-trunk: see further Kurt, *Fachausdrücke*, 33 ff. **Μα-**

COMMENTARY

λειάων ὄρος αἰπύ: C. Malea, the SE point of the Peloponnese, rises to a height of 793 m.; contrary winds were a constant source of difficulty to vessels trying to round in either direction, and provided the Corcyraeans with a plausible excuse for their absence from Salamis in 480 (Hdt. vii 168). Strabo quotes a proverb (378), Μαλέας δὲ κάμψας ἐπιλάθου τῶν οἴκαδε. Agamemnon (iv 514) and Odysseus (ix 80, cf. xix 187) are similarly blown off course.

288. θέων: a little awkward after ἰών, and ἷξε θέων seems better suited to ship than sailor. M. S. Haywood, discussing word-play between θέω/θεός and θοός in Homer (*Papers of the Liverpool Latin Seminar* iv (1983), 215 ff.), suggests that its appearance here, in proximity to Ζεύς, was influenced by a standard word-play on θέω and θεός.

290. τροφόεντα: otherwise found only at *Il.* xv 621; cf. τρόφις (*Il.* xi 307, Hdt. iv 9. 4); it is evidently connected with τρέφω, cf. κῦμα ... ἀνεμοτρεφές (*Il.* xv 624–5); see further Frisk, *GEW* s.v. τρέφω, Chantraine, *Dictionnaire* s.v. τρέφω.

291–9. It may surprise us that so much attention is devoted to the ships which lost touch with Menelaus; admittedly, they form the greater part of his contingent (he brought sixty ships to Troy (*Il.* ii 587)), but their vicissitudes are quite irrelevant to Nestor's narrative. However, the poet was clearly interested in Crete for its own sake (cf. Odysseus' choice of Cretan origins for his cover-story (xiii 256 ff., xiv 199 ff., xix 172 ff.)). The apparent precision with which the site of the shipwreck is described might suggest first-hand knowledge, but there are several difficulties, and it is doubtful whether any site satisfies all the conditions implied by the narrative. On the navigational hazards of this coast see *The Mediterranean Pilot* iv⁷ (London, 1941), 30–1.

292. Strabo, commenting on the account of Crete given at xix 172 ff., says (475) that the Cydonians occupied the western part of the island. Their city, Cydonia, was on the north coast, near the modern Chania, not far from the river Iardanos, now the Platanias. Since the ships are said to have been wrecked on the south coast, the Iardanos is presumably mentioned because it is associated with the Cydonians, not for the sake of topographical precision; otherwise we should have to assume that the ships put into land near its mouth, and then sailed round to the south of the island. The poet apparently means that the group approached Crete at its western end, and then was driven along the south coast. ἔναιον: the impf. is used, as often, of what was, and still is, true. 'Ιαρδάνου: the name is sometimes said to be Semitic, representing Jordan; but the same formula is used at *Il.* vii 135 of an unidentifiable river in Elis.

293. ἔστι δέ τις: a rather stately phrase, generally used, as here, to introduce set-piece descriptions; cf. iv 844, *Il.* ii 811, xi 711, 722. This usage, found also in Sanskrit and Latin, is clearly very ancient; for a full discussion see E. Fraenkel, *De media et nova comoedia quaestiones selectae* (diss. Göttingen, 1912), 46–7, E. Kieckers, *Die Stellung des Verbs im griechischen u. in den verwandten Sprachen*, i (Strassburg, 1911), 50 ff., G. W. Williams, *Tradition* *and Originality in Roman Poetry* (Oxford, 1968), 640 ff.   λισσὴ … πέτρη: often taken to refer to C. Lithinos, the promontory SW of Phaistos and the most southerly point of Crete, 'a bold and well-defined headland, distinguished by a high, wedge-shaped cliff, the cape forming the acute angle of the wedge' (*The Mediterranean Pilot* iv⁷ (London, 1941)); in antiquity this was known as Λισσῆς or Λισσήν (cf. Str. 479, St.Byz. s.v. Φαιστός), and Crates read Λισσήν here, though this is stylistically impossible.

294. ἐσχατιῇ Γόρτυνος: 'on the outskirts of the territory of Gortyn'; on ἐσχατία see further L. Robert, *Opera Minora Selecta* (Amsterdam, 1969), 820–22.

295. σκαιὸν ῥίον: 'a headland on the left, to the west'.

296. Sir Arthur Evans, whose knowledge of the terrain was unrivalled, argued that the topographical indications point to the vicinity of the port of Komo: 'About a mile to the North [of Matala, the port of Phaistos] there juts out, beyond a dry torrent-bed, a headland of white rock, which is the natural boundary between it [Gortynian territory] and that of Phaestos and may indeed be the actual point that the poet had in view in his λισσὴ πέτρη. This headland at the same time offers the first real shelter available for small craft escaping, like those of Menelaos, the sea-beaten rocks of Cape Lithinos itself in a southerly gale' (*The Palace of Minos*, ii (London, 1928), 86). On this interpretation λισσὴ πέτρη, σκαιὸν ῥίον and μικρὸς λίθος are one, the σκαιὸν ῥίον itself being a relatively inconspicuous feature compared with the great western headland of C. Lithinos a few miles further south.   **μικρός:** Zenodotus read Μαλέου, for which the Suda provides the following explanation (s.v. Μάλεος): Μάλεος γάρ τις τελέσας τὸν λίθον τοῦτον ἀνιέρωσε τῷ Ποσειδῶνι, πρὸς τὸ μὴ τὰ κύματα προσπελάζειν τῷ Φαιστῷ; the scholia similarly describe it as a kind of breakwater to the port of Phaistos. The information retailed by these ancient scholars may not ultimately be based on anything more solid than speculation about this line; but, if so, Μαλέου must surely once have been current in other texts besides that of Zenodotus. It is attractive; an unfamiliar Μαλέου might well have been changed to the immediately comprehensible μικρός, but the reverse process is unlikely.

299. τὰς πέντε νέας: those separated from the others as described in 291.   **κυανοπρῳρείους:** the epithet occurs only here; νέας κυανοπρῳρείους has evidently been modelled on νεὸς κυανοπρώροιο, κυανόπρωρος being probably just a grander synonym for μέλαινα, referring to the pitch with which the vessel was coated; see further Kurt, *Fachausdrücke*, 57 ff.

300. Αἰγύπτῳ: see below, p. 192.

301. Cf. iv 90–1 and the description of some of the gifts collected by Menelaus and Helen at iv 125 ff., 614 ff.; similarly Menelaus, in proposing a trip round Greece to Telemachus, emphasizes that no one would send them away empty-handed (xv 80 ff.). The theme of treasure-collecting is also prominent in Odysseus' cover-stories (xiv 323 ff., xix 283 ff.); cf. also xi 356 ff. On the custom of presenting a visitor with a parting gift see i 311 ff. n.; but it is slightly strange to regard this practice as a potential source of immense wealth, since the traveller who collects presents from his hosts incurs corresponding obligations. The poet's view of heroic convention has here perhaps been influenced by the conditions of his own time, when mercenary soldiers might make lucrative careers for themselves in the service of foreign rulers, and trading ventures in unfamiliar lands and unexploited markets could bring vast profits (cf. Hdt. iv 152).

303. ταῦτ' ... ἐμήσατο ... λυγρά echoes μέγα μήσατο ἔργον (261).

304–5. Two late MSS and schol. S. *El.* 267 give 304 after 305; some editors prefer this order, since it makes the reference of ταῦτ' in 303 clearer.

ἑπτάετες: similar periods of seven years at vii 259–61, xiv 285–7; cf. seven day periods at x 80–1, xii 397–9, xiv 249–52, xv 476–7. The only comparable case from the *Iliad* is ἔβδομος μείς (xix 117). On seven as a significant or typical number see further W. H. Roscher, *Die Sieben- u. Neunzahl im Kultus u. Mythus der Griechen*, ASAW, liii (1906), J. W. S. Blom, *De typische getallen bij Homeros en Herodotos* (Nijmegen, 1936), 202–3, D. Fehling, *Die Quellenangaben bei Herodot* (Berlin, 1971), 154–67. **ἤνασσε:** on the form see Chantraine, *Grammaire*, i 480 § 230. **πολυχρύσοιο Μυκήνης:** cf. *Il.* vii 180, xi 46. We naturally think of the treasures excavated from the sixteenth- and fifteenth-century shaft graves; the tombs of later Mycenaean princes, which would probably be more relevant to the genesis of this formula, have been robbed of their riches. We do not know whether the Mycenaeans got their gold by trade or by warfare, but certainly there was no source close at hand.

306. τῷ δέ οἱ ὀγδοάτῳ: ἔτει is to be supplied from ἑπτάετες. **κακόν:** nom., to be taken predicatively, 'as a disaster'; cf. xii 118, xvi 103 (and probably ii 166), *Il.* v 63.

307. ἀπ' Ἀθηνάων: some MSS read ἀπ' Ἀθηναίων.[4] In Attic tragedy, as in Pindar (*P.* xi 34 ff.), Orestes' exile is set in Phocis, and this offhand reference to an Athenian sojourn left ancient scholars at a loss; modern scholars have generally been content to associate it with the Pisistratean recension (see above, introduction pp. 36 ff.), but this does not explain very much. If the tragedians knew ἀπ' Ἀθηνάων here, it is amazing that they ignored it, and though Zenodotus' ἀπὸ Φωκήων has often been dismissed as a conjecture (whether his own or another's) designed to remove an anomaly, I suspect that it represents the form of the text familiar in fifth-century Athens.[5] (What Aristarchus meant by ἀπ' Ἀθηναίης is uncertain, but it is probably best taken as 'from Athens'; cf. vii 80, where the sg. Ἀθήνη is used for the city (so schol.)).

308. = i 300, iii 198; it is omitted by a few MSS and should probably be excised as a medieval interpolation.

309–10. Cf. iv 547; for funeral feasts cf. *Il.* xxiii 29 ff., xxiv 802–3. There is no doubt something disconcerting in the notion of a banquet given by a murderer in honour of his victims, but the feast was an essential part of

---

[4] Allen's apparatus omits this variant.

[5] It is an odd coincidence that Ἀθηναίων is recorded as an ancient variant for Φωκήων at *Il.* xv 516.

the funeral ritual; see further M. Andronikos, *Archaeologia* W, 15 ff., W. Burkert, *Homo Necans* (Berlin, 1972), 61 ff. (= Engl. ed. (Berkeley–Los Angeles–London, 1983), 50 ff.). Orestes is not associated with the death of Clytaemestra elsewhere in Homer, but though this reference would be consistent with suicide occasioned by the death of her paramour, it would be far-fetched to suppose that Orestes' matricide is a post-Homeric development; normally the poet concentrates on Aegisthus and those aspects of Orestes' vengeance which won unqualified approval (see above, pp. 16–7, 60 and i 29–31 n.). But it is not surprising that these lines were absent from some ancient editions; they raise awkward questions and might well be suspected of being a post-Homeric addition.[6]   **δαίνυ τάφον**: cf. δαινύναι γάμον iv 3, *Il.* xix 299.   **ἀνάλκιδος Αἰγίσθοιο**: contrast ἀμύμονος Αἰγίσθοιο (i 29), an interesting exception to normal principles of formulaic economy.

311. βοὴν ἀγαθός: a formula regularly applied to Menelaus and Diomedes, and occasionally to others (Ajax, Hector, Polites); it was found puzzling in antiquity, but of the various interpretations which have been offered the only one worth serious consideration is 'good at shouting, strong-voiced'; a powerful voice is an obvious asset to a commander in the field and also an indication of the strength and vitality essential for heroic distinction; on shouting in heroic battles see Griffin, *Homer on Life and Death*, 37 ff.

312. ἄχθος: 'as freight', i.e. all that his ships could carry.

313. καὶ σύ: the theme of Menelaus' travels and their conclusion brings Nestor back to the subject of Telemachus' journey.

314–16. = xv 11–13 (where Athena in effect rebukes Telemachus for ignoring Nestor's warning).   **κτήματα δασσάμενοι**: as the suitors themselves suggest (ii 332 ff.).   **τηϋσίην**: the adj. occurs only in poetry, and its etymology is obscure; see Frisk, *GEW*, Chantraine, *Dictionnaire*.

317 ff. There is no inconsistency between this and the preceding instruction not to wander a long time away from home: a few days spent at Sparta, in which Telemachus may achieve the purpose with which he set out, cannot be so described. We know already that Telemachus intends to fulfil Athena's instruction to go to Sparta (i 93, 285, ii 214, 359), but he has not told Nestor this, and there is no discrepancy in the latter suggesting it to him now.   **ἐς Μενέλαον**: ἐς is unusual with a person.

318. νέον: in fact, nearly three years before.   **ἄλλοθεν**: 'from abroad', cf. xvi 26.

319. ἐκ τῶν ἀνθρώπων further defines ἄλλοθεν.   **ἔλποιτο**: the subject is left indefinite; it is the antecedent of ὅν τινα. The optative here expresses the admission of a possibility, a use rare without ἄν or κεν; Nauck's conjecture κε for γε produces a more regular construction, cf. Monro, *Homeric Dialect*, 272–3, § 299 (f).

320. ὅν τινα πρῶτον ἀποσφήλωσιν: 'if once they have driven him off his course'; for this use of πρῶτος cf. x 328, xiii 127, LSJ s.v. πρῶτος iii 3 e.

---

[6] Schol. T *Il.* xxiii 29 cite 309 and 311 without 310, but I doubt whether this is significant.

321–2. τοῖον: emphasizing μέγα, cf. i 209.   **ὅθεν ... οἰχνεῦσιν:** the birds which migrate south to Egypt in autumn, among them perhaps most conspicuously the cranes (cf. *Il.* iii 3 ff., Hes. *Op.* 448 ff.), do not return until the following year; Nestor's manner of expression implies that it is too far for them to undertake the journey more than once a year. The distance is more prosaically expressed at xiv 257, where the voyage from Crete to Egypt is said to take five days; the return journey, in the teeth of the prevailing winds, would of course take much longer.   **τε δεινόν:** δεινός (< δϝεινός) normally lengthens a preceding short vowel.

324. ἐθέλεις: sc. ἰέναι, to be understood from ἴθι (323). πομπή, facilitating the next stage in a guest's journey, is a regular, and important, part of a host's duty. It may take many forms according to circumstances; we see it at its most magnificent when the Phaeacians convey Odysseus home to Ithaca.

326. The line reads like a rather fussy afterthought and has been suspected by some modern scholars; it spoils the connection of thought between 325 and 327—'my sons can escort you, but you yourself must ask'.   **δῖαν:** on the connotations of δῖος applied to places see Hainsworth on v 20.

327–8. = 19–20.

329–408. Nestor invites the strangers to stay the night with him. Mentor accepts for Telemachus but will himself return to his ship. As the goddess departs in bird form Nestor recognizes her and vows a sacrifice. They go indoors and after a last drink together retire.

329. Sunset marks the end of Poseidon's festival.

330 ff. It is no doubt an indication of the authority emanating from Athena even in disguise that no one appears to find it strange that a visitor should take the initiative in urging the conclusion of the rites.

332. ἄγε with pl., as at ii 252 etc.; it is treated as an interjection.   **τάμνετε ... γλώσσας:** cf. Ar. *Av.* 1705, *Pax* 1060, ἡ γλῶττα χωρὶς τέμνεται. The tongues are those of the oxen sacrificed at the beginning of the day; these had evidently been reserved to be burnt as a final offering. We do not hear of this rite elsewhere in Homer; it is discussed by Meuli op. cit. (on 5 ff.), 222–3.

334. For libation before going to bed cf. vii 137–8, xviii 419, *Il.* ix 712.

337. ἦ: 3rd pers. sg. impf. of ἠμί.

339. See i 148 n.

340. The procedure here is made somewhat clearer by comparison with xviii 418 ff. There the instruction is given οἰνοχόος μὲν ἐπαρξάσθω δεπάεσσιν | ὄφρα σπείσαντες κατακείομεν and its fulfilment is thus described (425–6) νώμησεν δ' ἄρα πᾶσιν ἐπισταδόν· οἱ δὲ θεοῖσι | λείψαντες μακάρεσσι πίον μελιηδέα οἶνον. The cpd. ἐπάρχομαι is restricted to this ritual sense of pouring into each cup a few drops which each man poured out in libation, with the server standing by, before he was given a drink for himself.

341. ἐπέλειβον: the prefix should probably be understood to mean 'over' rather than 'in addition' or 'afterwards'; cf. 459–60 (= *Il.* i 462–3) καῖε δ' ἐπὶ σχίζης ὁ γέρων, ἐπὶ δ' αἴθοπα οἶνον | λεῖβε, xii 362. The impf. is used because the action is repeated; each participant in turn stands up, goes to the altar, and pours his offering over the burning tongues.

346 ff. Nestor regards the proper fulfilment of the duties of hospitality as a matter of honour, and expects his guests to assume this attitude in him; he treats Mentor's move to depart as based on a misconception of both his resources and his moral standards.

346. τό γ': explained by 347.

348. i.e. ὥς τε παρά τευ πάμπαν ἢ ἀνείμονος ἠὲ πενιχροῦ. ἀνείμων is not found elsewhere before Hellenistic poetry; we expect it to mean 'without clothing', but the sense is rather 'short of clothing, without spare clothing'.

349. χλαῖναι: often used as blankets, cf. iv 299, xi 189. χλαῖνα and φᾶρος are evidently synonymous, but φᾶρος is the more archaic and solemn term; see further Hoekstra on xiii 67, xiv 132. **ῥήγεα:** ῥῆγος is not found outside epic.

352. τοῦδ' ἀνδρός: a strange use of ὅδε, which predominantly marks what is present and can be pointed out, perhaps to be explained by the prominent position which Odysseus holds in Nestor's thoughts (though he has not actually been mentioned since 242); the anomaly rather suggests that the poet has been a little careless in employing a form of words devised for a different context.

353. Cf. xiii 74-5. The conventional translation of ἴκρια as 'deck' suggests a more elaborate structure than Homer can have envisaged (even Odysseus' σχεδίη has ἴκρια (v 163, 252)). A kind of rough platform seems to be meant; see further Hainsworth on v 163, Kurt, *Fachausdrücke*, 128 ff.

355. ὅς τις: this distributive use of ὅς τις and ὅς κε(ν) after a pl. noun is fairly common in Homer (cf. e.g. xii 40, xvi 228, xx 295).

357-8. Τηλέμαχον is the subject, σοί the object of πείθεσθαι. **οὕτως:** i.e. 'as you suggest'.

364. ὁμηλικίη: see 49 n. The links of friendship stemming from membership of the same age-group are often mentioned in Homer; cf. xv 196-7, xxii 208-9, *Il.* iii 174-5, v 325-6.

366. Καύκωνας: Strabo (321 ff., 342, 345-6) assembles what information he can about the Kaukones, whom he regards as a pre-Greek stock, like the Pelasgians; they no longer existed in his day, but their territory had lain in the western Peloponnese, in Triphylia and Elis. Herodotus mentions them briefly (i 147. 1, iv 148. 4); see further *RE* x 2, 64 ff. (s.v. Kaukones).

367. χρεῖος: used especially of the obligation to restore or offer recompense for stolen cattle or other plunder, cf. xxi 17, *Il.* xi 686, 688, 698; on the orthography see i 409 n.

371-2. Mentor vanishes, and the spectators see instead a vulture flying off; Nestor is quick to interpret this manifestation correctly (375 ff.). **εἰδομένη** must mean that the goddess assumes the form of a bird (cf. i 105, ii 268, 401, vi 22, viii 8, xxii 206, xxiv 503, 548, *Il.* ii 280, iii 122, v 462, xiii 69); similarly, she watches the fight with the suitors in the shape of a swallow (xxii 239-40); cf. *Il.* vii 58 ff., xiv 286 ff. To some scholars the notion that the Olympians might thus manifest themselves in the guise of birds, of extreme interest to the historian of Greek religion, has seemed to imply unacceptably theriomorphic conceptions of divinity, and the attempt has been made to interpret all such passages as similes, most recently by F. Dirlmeier, *Die Vogelgestalt homerischer Götter* (SHAW, 1967), 2; his arguments are, however, satisfactorily met by H. Bannert, *WSt* NS xii (1978), 29–42 and H. Erbse, *Hermes* cviii (1980), 259–74. **φήνη**: the bearded vulture or lammergeyer; see D'Arcy Thompson, *A Glossary of Greek Birds* (St Andrews, 1936), 303.

374. See ii 302 n.

375. Nestor sees that what has just happened disproves what Telemachus had said at 208–9, 227 ff.

378. τριτογένεια: various explanations of this title, exclusively Athena's, were offered in antiquity, none very convincing; for details see LSJ. P. Kretschmer ('Mythische Namen 6', *Glotta* x (1919), 38 ff.) argued persuasively for the interpretation 'true-born, legitimate daughter', comparing Τριτοπάτορες, 'the fathers of the race, the true ancestors'; the adjective marks Athena's motherless, indisputably legitimate, birth from the head of Zeus. See further Frisk, *GEW* s.v. Τρίτων, Chantraine, *Dictionnaire*.

380. ἴληθι: probably a reduplicated pres. (from *σι-σλη-θι), not a pf.; see Chantraine, *Grammaire*, i 13 § 5, 299 § 138. **δίδωθι:** the imperat. ending in -θι in non-thematic tenses is commoner in Homer than in Attic; but δίδου is also found (cf. iii 58).

382–4. = *Il.* x 292–4. **ἦνιν:** in Homer the epithet is used only in acc. (sg. and pl.), and restricted to cows destined for sacrifice. In antiquity it was explained as 'sleek' or 'one year old, yearling'; the latter is very probably right, the root being ἔνος, an old word for 'year' from which the first element of ἐνιαυτός comes; see further Frisk, *GEW*, Chantraine, *Dictionnaire*. Ancient scholars disagreed over the accentuation. ἦνιν, given by almost all MSS and advocated by Herodian, produces a trochaic fourth foot, a metrical licence for which there is no certain Homeric parallel. It is surely better to regard it as a rare suffix in -ῑ, and therefore paroxytone, ἤνιν; cf. Chantraine, *Grammaire*, i 207–8 § 88. **ἀδμήτην:** glossed by ἦν ... ἀνήρ; cf. i 300–2 n. **περιχεύας:** the gilding, described at 432 ff., is done by a metal-worker, not by Nestor personally.

389. Cf. i 130, 145 nn.

390. ἀνά with κέρασσεν. The scholia and Eustathius explain ἀνά as 'a second time' or 'twice', but more probably it is intended to indicate thorough mixing, as in English 'mixed *up*': cf. iv 41, ix 209, x 235; see also Hoekstra on xiii 50.

391. ἐνδεκάτῳ: the scholia imply a reading ἐν δεκάτῳ.

392. κρήδεμνον: the word is not used elsewhere in connection with wine-jars, and it is unclear whether the cover itself is meant, or a string to keep it in place; cf. the metaphorical use of κρήδεμνον at *Il.* xvi 100. Note the paronomasia κρήδεμνον ... κρητῆρα; cf. i 48 n.

393. τοῦ: sc. οἴνου.

396. οἱ μέν: 'the others'; Nestor's married sons evidently have θάλαμοι in the palace. **κακκείοντες:** see i 424 n.

398. On this formula see Russo on xvii 3.

399. τρητοῖς ἐν λεχέεσσιν: see i 440 n. **αἰθούσῃ:** visitors are normally bedded down under the αἴθουσα or in the πρόδομος: cf. iv 296 ff., vii 335 ff., *Il.* xxiv 643 ff. The αἴθουσα is evidently envisaged as a structure outside the μέγαρον, either adjacent to or in the πρόδομος; for a detailed discussion see S. Hiller, *WSt* NF i (1970), 14–27 and cf. i 103–4 n. on Odyssean house-plans in general. The traveller, who might be a complete stranger, is thus sheltered without being given access to every part of the house.

400–1. Zenodotus athetized these two lines; we do not know why, but it is certainly not normal Homeric convention to give a visitor a companion for the night—Odysseus in vii and Priam in *Il.* xxiv sleep alone—and he may have suspected that the couplet had been added to introduce homosexual overtones. But it serves to make the point that Pisistratus is the only one among Nestor's sons still unmarried, so that in due course, without the question ever being discussed, it will appear natural that he should be chosen to accompany Telemachus to Sparta. See further Nickau, *Untersuchungen*, 227–8. **ἐϋμμελίην:** this Iliadic epithet occurs only here in the *Odyssey*. **ὄρχαμον ἀνδρῶν:** cf. 454, 482. ὄρχαμος is found only in poetry, and in Homer is restricted to this formula and ὄρχαμε λαῶν; it was plainly highly archaic, and its etymology is obscure. Ancient scholars explained it as 'leader', which fits the *Iliad* perfectly, but is less satisfactory in the *Odyssey*, where we find the swineherd Eumaeus and the goatherd Philoetius so designated (xiv 121, xv 351, 389, etc., xx 185, 254). The poet probably thought the word vaguely honorific, without attaching a precise meaning to it.

402. μυχῷ δόμου ὑψηλοῖο: not architecturally precise; the same formula is used when Menelaus and Helen retire for the night (iv 304), but next morning Menelaus emerges ἐκ θαλάμοιο (310).

403. λέχος πόρσυνε: an expression reserved in Homer for the wife who shares her husband's bed; no difference is discernible between λέχος and εὐνή. We are not told the name of Nestor's wife until 452.

404–72. Next morning Nestor makes the sacrifice promised to Athena. Telemachus bathes and takes part in the following feast.

404. See ii 1 n.

407. The seats are not precisely localized; θύραι could mean the doors of the μέγαρον (cf. xxii 76) or the gates of the courtyard (cf. vii 112).

408. ἀποστίλβοντες ἀλείφατος: the judgement seat has been anointed as a mark of its sanctity. Stones at crossroads were similarly anointed (cf. Thphr. *Char.* 16. 5, Lucian, *Alex.* 30, Apul. *Flor.* 1), and at Delphi the stone which Cronus swallowed by mistake for Zeus was anointed daily (Paus. x 24. 6). See further Onians, *Origins*, 279–80, *Encyclopaedia of Religion and Ethics* ed. J. Hastings (Edinburgh, 1908), i 553–4.

411. οὖρος Ἀχαιῶν: the formula is exclusively Nestor's.

412. σκῆπτρον: see ii 37 n.

413 ff. For the list of Nestor's sons cf. Hes. fr. 35. 10–11: [τοῦ δ' ἦν Ἀντίλοχός τε κα]ὶ αἰχμητὴς Θρασυμήδης | [Περσεύς τε Στρατίος τε καὶ Ἄρητος κα]ὶ

Ἐχέφρων. Each plays his part in the ensuing scene of sacrifice, the longest and most detailed in Homer, in accordance with Athena's peculiar importance in the poem.

415–16. Pisistratus enjoys the distinction of a line to himself; the immediately following mention of Telemachus reinforces the idea suggested at 400–1, that the question which of Nestor's sons should accompany Telemachus to Sparta needs no discussion.

420. ἐναργής: used especially of the gods appearing in corporeal form, cf. vii 201, xvi 161, *Il.* xx 131.   **θάλειαν:** this epithet occurs only in fem., and in Homer is reserved for banquets.

421. ἐπὶ βοῦν: 'for a cow, to fetch a cow', cf. ἐπὶ τεύχεα ἐσσεύοντο xxiv 466, *Il.* ii 808; μετά is generally used in this sense.

422. βοῶν ἐπιβουκόλος: for the pleonasm cf. αἰπόλος αἰγῶν (xvii 247), προδόμῳ δόμου (iv 302), ἀμφασίη ἐπέων (iv 704), συῶν συβόσια, αἰπόλια αἰγῶν (xiv 101), ποδάνιπτρα ποδῶν (xix 343). ἐπιβουκόλος: = βουκόλος; he is *over* the cows, not an over-herdsman; cf. ἐπιβώτορι (xiii 222), ὑποδμώς (iv 386); see further Leumann, *Wörter*, 92.

425. χρυσοχόον: he is later called χαλκεύς (432) and is evidently supposed to work in other metals beside gold. The way in which Nestor summons him suggests that his status is similar to the cowherd's, i.e. that he is a slave and not, as we might expect, an independent worker like the δημιοεργοί listed at xvii 383 ff. But it would be unsafe to use this detail as the basis for any inference about the status of smiths in the poet's own day.   **Λαέρκεα:** a rather grand name, 'defender of the people', perhaps borrowed from the *Iliad* (xvi 197, xvii 467); it is not historically attested.

428. δαῖτα πένεσθαι: explained by 429 as the preparations for cooking, not the cooking itself, which is an integral part of the sacrificial meal and done by Nestor and his sons (455 ff.).

429. ἀμφί: strange; βωμόν, or some similar term, is to be understood. Various conjectures have been made: αὖα Nauck, ἄμμι van Herwerden; Schwartz suggested that the whole line should be excised as being a later addition intended to remove the suspicion of a slight inconsistency created by δαῖτα πένεσθαι.   **οἰσέμεν:** epic aor., an artificial creation combining the sigma of the sigmatic aor. with a thematic conjugation; see further Chantraine, *Grammaire*, i 417–18 § 199, C. L. Prince, *Glotta* xlviii (1970), 155–63.

430 ff. The anaphora of ἦλθε (430, 431, 432, 435) marks a kind of procession; cf. viii 322 ff.

432–3. χαλκεύς, χαλκήϊα: the terms are used, as elsewhere, to cover metal-working in general; cf. ix 391 ff., where the χαλκεύς works with iron. Here the tools which the smith brings (434) are more appropriate to iron-working, which alone requires the heavy hammering of red-hot metal; gold is hammered cold, with a light hammer. The poet was evidently impressed by the spectacular and mysterious processes of the blacksmith's forge, and imported the equipment into a context where it has no place. The only way in which the horns of a living ox could be gilded is by affixing gold foil; περιχεύειν (384, 426, 437) should be translated 'cover, spread over'. See further D. H. Gray, 'Metal Working in Homer', *JHS* lxxiv (1954), 1 ff., esp. 4, 12–13, F. Eckstein, *Archaeologia* L, 5, 21. **πείρατα τέχνης**: 'the means of accomplishing his art'; for this sense of πεῖραρ cf. *Il.* xxiii 350.

435–6. Athena is present in person, but invisible. **ἱρῶν ἀντιόωσα**: 'to meet the offering'; the poet clearly wished to avoid suggesting that the goddess in any sense fed on the sacrifice; contrast *Il.* ix 535. **ἱππηλάτα**: see 68 n.

438. **ἀσκήσας**: perhaps best translated by an advb., 'skilfully'.

439. **κεράων**: 'by the horns'; for the gen. cf. *Il.* xi 258 ἕλκε ποδός, xxiv 515.

440–2. Aretus, Thrasymedes, and Perseus apparently act on their own initiative, being familiar with the ritual; Nestor gave no instructions on these points.

440. **ἀνθεμόεντι**: 'adorned with flowers, with a floral pattern', cf. xxiv 275, *Il.* xxiii 885.

444. **ἀμνίον**: the word occurs only here in Homer, and the senses in which it is used by later authors do not suit this context. It must refer to the bowl in which the victim's blood was collected before being sprinkled on the altar-stone (σφαγεῖον), a piece of equipment clearly required here since the animal is too big to be raised over the altar. This part of the ritual is then indicated only indirectly.

445 ff. The preparations are now complete, and the sacrifice itself begins: see above, 5 ff. n. The element of repetition characteristic of typical scenes in Homer is very conspicuous in descriptions of such sacrificial banquets, where the nature of the ritual allows less deviation than is natural in other recurrent activities. The other sacrifices narrated at length are at xii 353 ff., xiv 413 ff., *Il.* i 447 ff., ii 402 ff., vii 314 ff., xxiv 621 ff. They fall into well-marked sections: (1) preliminary offering and prayer, (2) killing of victim and preparations for cooking, (3) cooking, (4) meal, (5) conversation. Here (5) is very brief, but (1) and (2) are treated with unusual elaboration; see further Arend, *Scenen*, 64 ff. The passage is an extremely valuable source of evidence for Greek sacrificial ritual; it is interesting to compare Euripides' account of a similar scene, *El.* 790 ff.

445. **χέρνιβα ... οὐλοχύτας**: 'began the rite with the lustral water and the barley meal for sprinkling'; cf. *Il.* i 449 χερνίψαντο δ' ἔπειτα καὶ οὐλοχύτας ἀνέλοντο, 458, ii 410, 421. Before prayer or sacrifice the hands must be washed; for the principle cf. *Il.* vi 266 ff., Hes. *Op.* 725, E. *El.* 791 ff. (with Denniston's n.), for the practice ii 261, iv 750, 759, xii 336, *Il.* xvi 230, xxiv 303 ff. See further R. Ginouvès, *Balaneutiké: Recherches sur le bain dans l'antiquité grecque* (Paris, 1962), 299–318. **οὐλοχύτας**: unground coarse barley meal, the most ancient of agricultural products, the οὐλαί of 441; hidden beneath the barley meal is a knife, which is now uncovered. The participants throw the barley 'forward' at the victim and the altar, a primitive gesture of aggression transformed into something harmless. In the absence of barley Odysseus' men use leaves at xii 357–8.

446. The cutting of a few hairs from the head, while it does no damage, means that the victim is no longer physically inviolate. For this feature of the ritual cf. xiv 422, *Il.* iii 273, xix 254, E. *El.* 811–12; similarly at E. *Alc.* 73 ff. the human victim is dedicated to the gods below when Thanatos has cut off a lock of her hair. ἀπαρχόμενος so soon after κατάρχετο emphasizes the importance of these preliminaries.

448–9. Cf. *Il.* xvii 520 ff.

450. The victim is stunned (cf. xiv 425–6). It may surprise us that the ritual cry (ὀλολυγή), the contribution of the women participants, comes now, before any blood has been shed; cf. iv 767, *Il.* vi 301, A. *Th.* 269 Ἑλληνικὸν νόμισμα θυστάδος βοῆς, *Ag.* 595, 1118, Hdt. iv 189. 3. See further L. Deubner, *Ololyge u. Verwandtes* (APAW, 1941), 1.

452. Εὐρυδίκη: Nestor's wife is a nonentity, named only here in Homer, and variously called Mnesioche and Anaxibia by other writers. πρέσβα: only here used of a mortal; the meaning must surely be 'eldest', not 'august, honoured'.

453. οἱ μέν: the other sons of Nestor, by contrast with Pisistratus. For this part of the ritual cf. *Il.* i 459 αὐέρυσαν μὲν πρῶτα καὶ ἔσφαξαν καὶ ἔδειραν, E. *El.* 813–14 κἄσφαξ' ἐπ' ὤμων μόσχον ὡς ἦραν χεροῖν | δμῶες. The forequarters are raised off the ground and the beast's head drawn back; the throat is thus exposed to the knife and the victim's head turned upward towards the gods in whose honour it is being slain. All this demands considerable physical strength; hence Nestor delegates it to his sons. It remained the task of the ephebes in later times: see further F. Graf, *MH* xxxvi (1979), 14–15. εὐρυοδείης: in Homer only in the formula χθονὸς εὐρυοδείης; a lengthened form of *εὐρύοδος created by analogy with feminines in -εια. Schulze's suggestion (*Quaestiones*, 487–8) that it should be corrected to εὐρυεδείης (cf. Simon. 542. 24 εὐρυεδοῦς ... χθονός) is unnecessary. See further Frisk, *GEW*, Chantraine, *Dictionnaire*.

454. Once again, a prominent role for Pisistratus.

455. For the ascription of a θυμός to animals cf. *Il.* xiii 704 (oxen), xvi 468, xvii 451 (horses), xii 150, xvii 22 (boars), xxii 263 (wolves and sheep), xvii 678 (hares), xxiii 880 (birds).

456. διέχευαν: 'they dismembered it, cut it up into joints', the regular meaning of this cpd. in Homer (cf. xiv 427, xix 421, *Il.* vii 316). ἐκ μηρία τάμνον: 'they cut out the thigh-bones'. On the significance of this and the following parts of the ritual see 9 n.

457. κνίση: fat is widely regarded as the stuff of life (at *Il.* xxii 501 mutton fat is singled out as a delicacy particularly suitable for an infant prince): see further Onians, *Origins*, 279 ff.

458–62. = *Il.* i 461–5.

458. δίπτυχα: it seems more natural to interpret this as an advb. rather than as a metaplastic acc. sg. formed as if from δίπτυξ and agreeing with κνίσην understood. For the double layer of fat cf. *Il.* xxiii 243. ἐπ' αὐτῶν δ' ὠμοθέτησαν: 'they set little pieces from every part of the carcass on top of them (sc. the fat-encased thigh-bones)'; cf. the slightly fuller description at xiv 427–8 ὁ δ' ὠμοθετεῖτο συβώτης, | πάντων ἀρχόμενος μελέων, ἐς πίονα δῆμον. Hesiod perhaps refers to this practice (*Th.* 541); an Attic *lex sacra*, perhaps of the third century BC (*Hesperia* xxxix (1970), 48 ll. 16–17) shows that a similar rite was occasionally performed in later centuries: see R. Parker, *LCM* ix, 9 (1984), 138. Like the offering of the thigh-bones, it seems originally to have been intended to assist the animal's regeneration.

461. When the σπλάγχνα have been eaten, preparations for the main meal begin. Roasting meat, unlike other sorts of cooking, is regarded as men's work because of its close connection with religion; here it is apparently done out of doors. Characteristically, more attention is paid to the preparations than to the meal itself.

464 ff. While the meat is cooking Telemachus bathes. Baths in Homer are normally treated as part of the preparations for feasting; people may of course eat without having bathed, but they do not normally bathe unless they intend to eat; cf. iv 48 ff., vi 96 ff., 210 ff., viii 426 ff., x 358 ff., 449 ff., xvii 87 ff., xix 320 ff., xxiv 365 ff., *Il.* x 576 ff. The only cases in Homer where a meal does not follow a bath are *Od.* v 264 and xxiii 153 ff. Bathing in preparation for feasting was of course normal in the classical period (e.g. Pl. *Smp.* 174 a, Ar. *Av.* 131–2). The offer of a bath is not regarded as normal in the reception of a visitor; Odysseus gets the opportunity only on his second evening among the Phaeacians (viii 450 ff.); Telemachus does not suggest it to Athena-Mentes in i until 310, and has not himself previously bathed during his stay in Nestor's household. The emphasis in such descriptions lies on the effect produced by the bath (cf. 468), not on the details of the actual ablutions. See further Arend, *Scenen*, 124 ff., R. Ginouvès, *Balaneutiké* (Paris, 1962), 156 ff.

It is not clear where the poet imagined this activity taking place, whether in a side-room or in the megaron itself. A lack of concern for privacy is indicated by the fact that normally in Homer a woman helps with the bath, sometimes a slave (iv 49, viii 454, xvii 88, xix 317 ff., xxiii 154, xxiv 366), sometimes the mistress of the house (iv 252 (Helen), v 264 (Calypso), x 361, 450 (Circe)), occasionally, as here, her daughter (cf. *Il.* v 905 (Hebe); Ath. (10 e) refers to the daughters of Cocalus bathing Minos). It is quite clear from x 361 that assistance during the bath is meant, and λοῦσεν (464) should not be translated by 'got a bath ready for' or 'caused to bathe'. Odysseus displays an unexpected delicacy about accepting such help from Nausicaa's maids (vi 217 ff.: see Hainsworth's n.). In the classical period men managed on their own: see Fraenkel on A. *Ag.* 1109.

According to the Hesiodic *Catalogue of Women* (fr. 221) Polycaste bore a son, Persepolis, to Telemachus; I imagine that the poet of the *Odyssey* devised this episode to foreshadow a union already familiar in legend.

465. ὁπλοτάτη: a positive of this Epic comparative and superlative is not attested. Ancient scholars derived ὁπλότερος from ὅπλον, 'more capable of bearing arms', characterizing the young by contrast with the old; but it should perhaps rather be connected with an IE *oplo, 'strength' (cf. Lat. op-, opulens); see O. Szemerényi, *Gnomon* xlix (1977), 6. As there was no home-leave during the Trojan War Polycaste should be either under ten or over twenty; but such arithmetic is out of place.

466. λίπ': found in Homer only in this elided form, with verbs meaning 'anoint', and to be regarded as an advb. in -α, like σάφα; see Hainsworth on vi 96, Russo on xix 505, Frisk, *GEW*, Chantraine, *Dictionnaire* Leumann, *Wörter*, 309–10.

467. *Hysteron proteron*, since the tunic must be put on before the cloak; cf. iv 50, v 264. Though metrical reasons partly account for this common feature of Homeric style, the inverted order often reflects relative importance; here the cloak, being the outer garment, makes the more striking impression.

468. ἀσαμίνθου: the ending -νθος indicates that the Greeks took over ἀσάμινθος from the pre-Greek population, but its etymology is obscure; it has been found on a Linear B sealing from Knossos, KN Ws 8497. No details are given of the form or the normal material of the heroic bath-tub (Menelaus' silver bath-tubs (iv 128) clearly represent exceptional luxury). The Mycenaean examples so far discovered are of earthenware, which is compatible with the Homeric epithet εὔξεστος (iv 48, xvii 87, *Il.* x 576). The Homeric practice of anointing oneself and dressing before leaving the bath seems to imply a hole to let the water out. See further *LfgrE* Hainsworth on viii 450.

471. ἐπὶ ... ὄροντο: ὄρομαι occurs otherwise only at xiv 104, where the context requires a meaning like 'watched over', which suits the present passage. It is evidently from the same root as ὁράω and apparently represents a more archaic form; see Frisk, *GEW*, Chantraine, *Dictionnaire*, *Grammaire*, i 311 § 144.

472. οἰνοχοεῦντες: the variant ἐνοινοχοεῦντες surely represents an attempt to remedy what was regarded as a trochaic first foot when the initial ϝ was forgotten.

473–97. Accompanied by Pisistratus Telemachus leaves for Sparta; they spend the night with Diocles at Pherae.

473. = i 150. Usually Homeric banquets only cease when the company goes to bed, but this began early in the day and further activity follows.

475. ἄγε: used with a pl., as at ii 252 etc.

476. ἄρματ': only one chariot is in fact meant, but ἄρματα is regularly so used in Homer as equivalent to ἄρμα. On this use of the pl. for objects which it is more logical to think of in the sg., see Monro, *Homeric Dialect*, 160 § 171, Chantraine, *Grammaire*, ii 31 § 39 (but see also Hoekstra on xv 145). **πρήσσησιν ὁδοῖο:** this use of the gen. with verbs of motion, expressing the area within which the movement takes place, is basically partitive; see Monro, *Homeric Dialect*, 143 § 149, Chantraine, *Grammaire*, ii 58 § 72. πρήσσω in this sense of 'pass over, traverse' is used only in the present.

480. Schwartz proposed deleting this rather feeble line; the first half, which is not formulaic, is metrically clumsy, with hiatus both before and after οἷα.

481. Telemachus is expected to return to Nestor's palace on his homeward journey, and so there are no formal farewells; contrast the elaborate scene of leave-taking at Sparta (xv 59 ff.). **βήσετο:** see i 24 n.

482. It is now treated as self-evident that Pisistratus should accompany Telemachus; contrast 325, 369, and see 400–1, 415–16 nn.

484 ff. Telemachus' journey from Pylos to Sparta should not be regarded as reflecting the traffic conditions of any historical period. The chariot, in which driver and passenger normally stood upright in a restricted space, was not a vehicle for long-distance travel, certainly not for a journey taking two days; here it imparts an impression of grandeur which would not be achieved by mounting the travellers on mules. A journey from Pylos to Sparta would entail crossing Mt. Taygetus; but there was no road capable of taking wheeled traffic over any of the passes in antiquity. See further Lorimer, *Monuments*, 503–4, *RE* xxiii 2, 2144 s.v. Pylos (5) (Meyer), iii A 1345 s.v. Sparta (Bölte); on chariots see J. Wiesner, *Archaeologia* F, 25, J. H. Crouwel, *Chariots and Other Means of Land Transport in Bronze Age Greece* (Amsterdam, 1981).

The return journey is related at xv 182 ff.

486. σεῖον ... ἔχοντες: both σεῖον and ἀμφὶς ἔχοντες ('supporting at either end') govern ζυγόν; a strange expression. Aristophanes read θεῖον, an evident conjecture; various attempts, none convincing, have been made to emend ἀμφὶς ἔχοντες.

487. = ii 388 etc.; it is omitted by the first-century AD P. 3 (Pack² 1039, *P.Lit.Lond.* 30) and should very probably be rejected as a late interpolation.

488. The classical Pherae is the town now called Kalamata, lying roughly midway between Pylos and Sparta; comparison with xxi 15–19 confirms this identification here, and this was certainly a settlement of some importance in Mycenaean times. Diocles' descent from the river Alpheus (cf. *Il.* v 543 ff.) might suggest a location further north, somewhere near Megalopolis, but this detail is clearly connected with the general vagueness about the location of Pylos, on which see 4 n.

Stretches of an ancient, quite probably Mycenaean, high road from Pylos to Kalamata have been discovered: cf. W. A. MacDonald, 'Overland Communications in Greece during LH III', *Mycenaean Studies* (Madison, 1964), 217 ff.

489. 'Ορτιλόχοιο: Wackernagel, *Untersuchungen*, 236–7 A. 1, argues cogently that 'Ορτίλοχος is to be preferred to 'Ορσίλοχος as being the older, authentic, form of the name; see also Hoekstra on xiii 260.

490. ἄεσαν: see 151 n.

491. See ii 1 n.

493. = xv 146, 191; it is omitted by most MSS including P. 3 and *P.Köln* 40 (III/IV AD), and should not be admitted to the text; probably it was inserted to produce a closer correspondence with the description of Telemachus' return journey.

495. πυρηφόρον: πυροφόρος is more usual (cf. *Il.* xii 314, xiv 123, xxi 602).

496. ἦνον: the impf. has conative force, 'sought to finish their journey'. τοῖον: used like οὕτως; it seems more natural to take it with ὑπέκφερον than with ὠκέες.

BOOK IV: COMMENTARY

Telemachus' visit to Sparta, the counterpart of his visit to Pylos, occupies three-quarters of the book. Menelaus' narrative of his adventures complements Nestor's account, and by the end we have learnt the details of the *nostoi* of all the major figures on the Greek side, including Helen, except for Odysseus. With a certain sense of anticlimax we return in the last part of the book to Ithaca and the reactions of the suitors and Penelope to the news of Telemachus' journey.

The luxurious splendour of Menelaus' palace forms an obvious contrast to the unostentatious comfort of Nestor's Pylos; the poet develops the antithesis between the two households in other details (cf. 20 ff., 49, 209, and nn). But the sense of purposive activity manifested in the pious festivities at Pylos lacks a counterpart; the wedding celebrations with which the book opens rapidly fade from view, and can scarcely be reconciled with the subsequent development of this episode.

Menelaus' account of his adventures forms the climax of the Telemachy, and is carefully constructed in relation not only to Nestor's narrative but also to that of Odysseus. Menelaus and Odysseus between them box the compass, and many details of Menelaus' experiences on Pharos may be paralleled from Odysseus' Deep Sea Stories. The general tenor of Proteus' exposition suggests that it will culminate in an account of Odysseus' fortunes since leaving Troy; but this would obviously not have suited the poet's grand design, and, as often in the *Odyssey*, the expected result is postponed.

The Egyptian emphasis in Menelaus' adventures is noteworthy (cf. 125 ff., 228 ff., 351 ff., and nn.); it is paralleled in Odysseus' cover-stories (xiv 245 ff., xvii 425 ff.). This interest in Egypt has important implications for the date of composition. Regular contacts between Greece and Egypt ceased with the end of the Mycenaean age, and were not resumed until the mid-seventh century, under Psammetichus I, though occasional Greek adventurers certainly visited the country during the preceding half-century. Odysseus' imaginary Egyptian experiences have much in common with those of the Greek mercenaries whose intervention proved decisive for the fortunes of Psammetichus and thus led to the resumption of relations between Greece and Egypt (cf. Hdt. ii 152 ff.). The *Odyssey*'s interest in Egypt surely mirrors contemporary developments, the excitement of renewed contacts with this extraordinary country, and not, as has often been supposed, a dim tradition preserved from the Mycenaean age. See further Chr. Froidefond, *Le Mirage égyptien dans la littérature grecque, d'Homère à Aristote* (Aix, 1971), 15 ff., T. F. R. G. Braun, 'The Greeks in Egypt', *CAH*² iii 3, 32 ff. (where further bibliography may be found).

1–67. When Telemachus and Pisistratus reach Sparta they find a double wedding being celebrated in Menelaus' palace. After a slight delay they are hospitably entertained.

1. κοίλην ... κητώεσσαν: cf. *Il.* ii 581. **κοίλην:** 'lying in a hollow, hemmed in by mountains'; Sparta lies in the Eurotas valley, between the ranges of Taygetus and Parnon. Λακεδαίμων is best understood as the name of a district of which the chief city was Sparta, not as the name of a town; it is nowhere necessary to take it in the latter sense, while at *Od.* xxi 13 it must mean the district, and the epithets favour that interpretation. **κητώεσσαν:** a highly archaic epithet, occurring in Homer only in this formula, of very uncertain meaning. According to Strabo (367) it was interpreted as either 'great' or 'infested with huge fishes, sea-monsters'; Hesychius adds a further explanation, 'damp, well-watered'. The reading preferred by Zenodotus, καιτάεσσαν or καιετάεσσαν was said to mean either 'full of mint' or 'full of hollows, ravines'; the fissures produced by earthquakes were called καιετοί (Str. 367), and the subterranean cavern at Sparta into which state prisoners or their corpses were thrown was known as ὁ καιέτας (or καιάδας (cf. Th. i 134. 1, Paus. iv 18. 4)). This last explanation is attractive, and may equally be valid for κητώεσσαν which, if it is correct here, may be connected with an alleged *κῆτος, 'hollow, cleft'; cf. iii 158 n. (μεγακήτεα). See further Frisk, *GEW*, Chantraine, *Dictionnaire*, S. P. Morris, *HSPh* lxxxviii (1984), 1–11.

Callimachus' ἵππους καιετάεντος ἀπ᾽ Εὐρώταο κομίσσαι (fr. 639, from the *Hecale*) reflects the text adopted by Zenodotus here; on the relationship between Callimachus and Zenodotus see Pfeiffer on fr. 12. 6.

3 ff. As at Pylos, Telemachus arrives in the middle of festivities. Here a double wedding is being celebrated, surely a very unusual event. The background is sketched with some care; yet once Telemachus and Pisistratus are inside the palace, the celebrations are forgotten, and Menelaus and Helen appear to have no other concern than entertaining the two young men. The poet seems to have found it hard to integrate the wedding festivities with the rest of the narrative. (According to Athenaeus (180 e) Diodorus the Aristophanean 'rejected the wedding as spurious' (ὅλον τὸν γάμον περιέγραψε). It is difficult to take this as serious textual criticism; the excision of 3–19 would produce a very clumsy connection between 2 and 20, and in any case some background to Telemachus' visit is needed.)

3. δαινύντα γάμον: cf. iii 309 δαίνυ τάφον. **ἔτησιν:** ἔται is found only as a pl. in Homer, and is used as a kinship term, denoting a group wider than κασίγνητοι (cf. xv 273, *Il.* vi 239, xvi 456 (= 674)), less immediate relatives as well as close kin; see further Hoekstra on xv 273, Frisk, *GEW*, Chantraine, *Dictionnaire*, A. Andrewes, *Hermes* lxxxix (1961), 134–7.

4. ἀμύμονος: 'lovely' (cf. 14); see i 29 n. But Hermione, born before Helen went to Troy (263), would be a rather elderly bride.

5. ῥηξήνορος: exclusively Achilles' epithet in Homer. The poet expects us to recognize Neoptolemus without difficulty; we may note that, as this splendid marriage shows, Achilles' son is not thought to suffer any social disadvantage from his father's failure to marry his mother.

6. The *Odyssey* ignores, or does not know, the story of Hermione's betrothal to Orestes, familiar from Euripides' *Andromache* and *Orestes* (and also used in Sophocles' lost *Hermione*); cf. Pherecyd. *FGrH* 3 F 63, 64.

9. Μυρμιδόνων ... περικλυτόν: a convenient phrase, but we may doubt whether the poet had a particular place in mind. For Achilles the Spercheus valley, not any town, evidently represents the heart of his father's kingdom (cf. *Il.* xvi 173–6, xxiii 142 ff.). **ἄνασσεν:** sc. Neoptolemus.

10. Alector, according to the scholia and Eustathius, was of distinguished ancestry, being the son of Pelops and Hegesandra daughter of Amyclas. The poet will have understood his name as 'defender' (not 'cock'); see further *LfgrE*. **Σπάρτηθεν:** *Σπάρτη* is the town of Sparta, *Λακεδαίμων* the whole district of Laconia. **ἤγετο:** the middle is similarly used of bringing home a bride for someone else at xv 238, xxi 214, Hdt. i 34. 3, etc.

11. τηλύγετος: the precise meaning of this epithet was disputed in antiquity, and its etymology is uncertain. In Homer it is always used of a dearly loved, special, or favourite child, once (*Il.* xiii 470) with an evidently pejorative sense, 'spoilt darling'. The ancient explanation 'late born, born to aged parents' does not suit very well either this passage or *Il.* iii 175, where Helen so describes Hermione. See further Frisk, *GEW*, Chantraine, *Dictionnaire*, M. G. Ciani, 'La parola omerica *τηλύγετος*', *AIV* cxxiii (1964–5), 157–66. **Μεγαπένθης:** the name is evidently chosen to express Menelaus' grief at Helen's desertion, reflecting his character as a wronged husband, the most important thing about him in epic; see further i 113 n.

12. δούλης: *δοῦλος* is not attested in early epic, *δμώς* being used instead, but *δούλη* occurs also at *Il.* iii 409 (likewise in a context suggesting concubinage); cf. the derivatives *δούλιος* (xiv 340, xvii 323, *Il.* vi 463) and *δουλοσύνη* (xxii 423). Some ancient scholars, rejecting the Iliadic instance on other grounds, held that *δούλη* must be a name here διὰ τὸ μηδέποτε λέγειν οὕτω τὸν ποιητὴν τὴν θεράπαιναν: a distressingly circular argument. The cyclic *Nostoi*, elaborating on this passage (see p. 53 n. 10), rescued Megapenthes' mother from anonymity. **Ἑλένη ... ἔφαινον:** Menelaus' lack of a legitimate son gives a particular poignancy to his conversation with Pisistratus (206 ff.); the point is made at the outset because it is important for a just appreciation of Menelaus' situation. The Hesiodic *Catalogue* (fr. 175. 2) gives Menelaus and Helen another child, Nicostratus, whose name indicates that he was born after the war. **ἔφαινον:** 'granted'; cf. xv 26.

13. ἐπεὶ δή: for this line beginning cf. viii 452, xxi 25, xxiv 482, *Il.* xxii 379, xxiii 2. Leaf (on *Il.* xxii 379) suggested that the licence was encouraged by the π/ππ alternation in ὅπως/ὅππως (similarly Wyatt, *Lengthening*, 219–20); but though this explanation is attractive it is perhaps surprising, if the analogy was widely accepted, that the spelling *ἔππεί is nowhere found in our MSS. On so-called acephalous lines (i.e. lines which apparently open with a short syllable) see Wyatt, *Lengthening*, 201–22.

14. ἥ ... Ἀφροδίτης: the same formula is used of Helen herself in [Hesiod] (fr. 196. 5). **χρυσέης:** χρύσεος is not applied to any other god in Homer; some have seen a reference to golden hair-ornaments, but more likely it is simply metaphorical.

17–19. Cf. *Il.* xviii 604–6. **ἐμέλπετο, μολπῆς:** see above, i 152 n.

20 ff. On the reception of guests as a typical scene see i 113 ff. n. There is an obvious contrast here with the spontaneous welcome extended to Telemachus at Pylos. Eteoneus' uncertainty about admitting the strangers, despite their obvious respectability, no doubt is meant to reflect the peculiar circumstance of the wedding celebrations rather than a failure to recognize the normal obligations of hospitality or a caution engendered by the disastrous results of extending a welcome to a young man of princely appearance a quarter of a century or so earlier; but no explanation of this unusual and discourteous delay is offered. Odysseus himself is subjected to similar embarrassment at the Phaeacian court (vii 153 ff.), though unlike Telemachus he has not waited to be invited inside, and his host's hesitation is understandable given the unorthodox manner of his arrival.

22. Eteoneus reappears at xv 95, where we learn that he lived nearby; κρείων implies fairly high status, as does his patronymic Βοηθοΐδης (31).

27. γενεῇ Διός: implies royalty, kings being διογενεῖς; cf. 63–4. **ἔϊκτον:** 3rd pers. dual of ἔοικα.

28. καταλύσομεν: deliberative subj.

29. ἄλλον: to be taken with ἱκανέμεν. **φιλήσῃ:** 'entertain'; a common sense of φιλέω in Homer.

30 ff. Menelaus' reaction shows clearly that he, like Nestor (iii 346 ff.), regards proper fulfilment of the duties of hospitality as a matter of honour.

30. = 332, *Il.* xvii 18.

33–5. The stress in this sentence falls on the participial phrase—'we enjoyed the hospitality of many on our travels (and so should extend it to others)'. **αἴ κέ ... ὀϊζύος:** 'in the hope that Zeus may rid us of sorrows in days to come'; the note of uncertainty may be taken as reflecting Menelaus' vivid recollection of past dangers.

36. θοινηθῆναι: θοινᾶσθαι and θοινή do not occur elsewhere in Homer; the use of this verb rather than δαίνυσθαι implies that this feast is something out of the ordinary.

39–43. Cf. *Il.* viii 433–5 for a similar scene on Olympus.

41. ζειάς: a kind of emmer; see further W. Richter, *Archaeologia* H, 111–12. **κρῖ:** = κριθή, confined to Homer, and used only in nom. and acc., always qualified by λευκόν; see further Frisk, *GEW*, Chantraine, *Dictionnaire* s.v. κριθή.

42. πρὸς ἐνώπια παμφανόωντα: cf. xxii 121, *Il.* viii 435, xiii 261; probably the faces of crude brick walls covered with plaster are meant; cf. Lorimer, *Monuments*, 428 n. 1.

43–6. Cf. 71–5; Telemachus' admiration for the splendours of Menelaus' residence foreshadows his father's reaction to Alcinous' palace (vii 81–102,

133–4).   **θεῖον:** not elsewhere applied to δόμος in Homer; a tribute to extraordinary magnificence. 45–6: cf. vii 84–5.

47. τάρπησαν ὁρώμενοι: 'gazed to their hearts' content, gazed enough'.   **ὀφθαλμοῖσι:** this kind of redundancy, natural enough in an oral style, is common in Homer: cf. e.g. xvii 27 ποσὶ προβιβάς, *Il.* iii 161 ἐκαλέσσατο φωνῇ, xii 442 οὔασι πάντες ἄκουον.

48–50. = xvii 87–9; see iii 464 ff. and 468 nn.

51. παρ' Ἀτρεΐδην Μενέλαον: in the place of honour.

52–8. = i 136–42: see nn. Hand-washing is treated as an indispensable preliminary to the meal, even though Telemachus and Pisistratus have just bathed. 57–8 are absent from many of the medieval MSS, and are surely a late interpolation, as Athenaeus evidently thought (193 b).

59. The wedding celebrations are now forgotten; Menelaus devotes his attention to the two young strangers, and there is no suggestion that he has other, invited, guests as well.   **δεικνύμενος:** a formal gesture of welcome is evidently meant; on the form see iii 41 n.

60. χαίρετον: see i 123 n.

61. δείπνου πασσαμένω: cf. i 124. δεῖπνον seems to be used carelessly for what is clearly an evening meal (cf. iii 497); it denotes the main Homeric meal, dinner, normally taken at midday, while δόρπον is supper. Bentley's conjecture δόρπου deserves serious consideration, being supported by 194, 213. The MSS are often divided between the two words (vii 166, 215, ix 311, 344, x 116, *Il.* xi 86), and the substitution of a familiar word for a less common one is a widespread form of corruption.   **εἰρησόμεθ':** the typical questions about a stranger's name and origins are in fact replaced by a carefully prepared scene of *anagnorisis* foreshadowing Odysseus' self-revelation to Alcinous.

62–4. Athetized by Zenodotus, Aristophanes, and Aristarchus, though the scholia do not properly explain their objections. Certainly 62 is strangely expressed.

63. γένος: probably acc. of respect.

65. νῶτα: the chine was regarded as the portion of honour; cf. viii 474 ff., xiv 437–8, *Il.* vii 321–2, ix 207. It was still the perquisite of the Spartan kings in the fifth century (Hdt. vi 56).

67–8. = i 149–50; see i 150 n.

68–112. Telemachus' amazement at the palace's magnificence leads Menelaus to relate how he collected his treasures during seven years' wanderings. He recalls the friends for whom he must mourn, above all Odysseus.

69 ff. As at Pylos (iii 22 ff.), Telemachus is rather reluctant to address his host.

70. = i 157; see n.

71. τῷ ... θυμῷ: cf. *Il.* v 243, 826, x 234, xi 608, Verg. *A.* xii 142 *animo gratissima nostro.*

72. κάδ is Barnes' conjecture; all our MSS read καί, but a preposition is clearly required and the phrase is quoted with κατά in schol. T *Il.* xxiv 323; the corruption is easier to explain if κάδ was originally written (cf. xviii 355 κὰκ κεφαλῆς).

73. ἠλέκτρου: ἤλεκτρον can denote both amber and an alloy of gold and silver produced naturally in Lydia (cf. Paus. v 12. 7, with Frazer's n.); it is often hard to decide which is meant. It must be amber in the two other places where it occurs in Homer, *Od.* xv 460 χρύσεον ὅρμον ἔχων, μετὰ δ' ἠλέκτροισιν ἔερτο and xviii 295–6 ὅρμον ... χρύσεον, ἠλέκτροισιν ἐερμένον, ἠέλιον ὥς; the use of the pl. obviously suits pieces of amber but would be very peculiar if the metal was meant, while the attractive contrast between gold and amber would be lacking in a necklace made from two sorts of precious metal. Some have thought that its association with στεροπή here suggested a metal, but amber may certainly be said to shine or glitter, and there seems no need to give ἤλεκτρον a different sense here from that of its other two Odyssean occurrences. Amber, which comes mainly from the coasts of the Baltic, first appears in Greek lands in the shaft graves of Mycenae; very little has been found from the period between the end of the Mycenaean age and the eighth century, but in the late eighth and seventh centuries it was evidently very popular. See further D. E. Strong, *Catalogue of the Carved Amber in the Department of Greek and Roman Antiquities* (London, British Museum, 1966), 1–36, C. W. Beck, 'Amber in Archaeology', *Archaeology* xxiii (1970), 7–11, L. Deroy and R. Halleux, *Glotta* lii (1974), 36 ff., A. Harding and H. Hughes-Brock, *ABSA* lxix (1974), 145–70. **ἐλέφαντος:** in Homer ἐλέφας always means ivory, not the animal which produces it. Ivory was highly valued and skilfully worked in the Mycenaean period; as with other luxury articles, the demand evidently fell during the Dark Ages, but revived from the ninth century onwards. The chief exploiters of the ivory trade were the Phoenicians, and the main source was originally Syria, though as the Syrian herds became extinct supplies were acquired from India and Africa. See further Hainsworth on viii 404, Russo on xviii 296, R. D. Barnett, 'Early Greek and Oriental Ivories', *JHS* lxviii (1948), 1 ff., C. Singer, E. J. Holmstead and A. R. Hall (eds.), *A History of Technology* (Oxford, 1954), 663 ff., M. Treu, 'Homer u. das Elfenbein', *Philologus* xcix (1955), 149 ff., H. H. Scullard, *The Elephant in the Greek and Roman World* (London, 1974), 260 ff.

74. αὐλή: here used, exceptionally for Homer, of the dwelling as a whole; Seleucus' reading τοιαῦτα δόμοις ἐν κτήματα κεῖται avoids this anomaly. There is perhaps a reminiscence at [A.] *Pr.* 122 τὴν Διὸς αὐλήν.

75. ὅσσα: i.e. ὅτι τόσα.   **ἄσπετα:** 'countless'.

78. Menelaus forestalls the risk of divine φθόνος with an immediate disclaimer.

80. ἐρίσσεται: subj. 'may rival'.   **ἢ κέν τις ... ἠὲ καὶ οὐκί:** 'few or none'; cf. Hdt. iii 140. 2 ἀναβέβηκε δ' ἤ τις ἢ οὐδείς κω παρ' ἡμέας αὐτῶν.

81 ff. Menelaus' emphasis on his own sufferings is well calculated to reduce Telemachus' awe at his surroundings.

82. ἠγαγόμην: sc. κτήματα.

83. Nestor has already told us (iii 300) that Menelaus was blown south to Egypt on the way back from Troy. We should suppose that he visited Phoenicia (cf. 617 ff.) and Cyprus on the way home.   **Αἰγυπτίους:** to be scanned as a trisyllable, cf. 127, 229, xiv 263, 286, xvii 432, *Il.* ix 382; but at ii 15, iv 385 Αἰγύπτιος scans as four syllables. For this synizesis with metrically intractable proper names cf. *Il.* ii 537 Ἱστίαια, Tyrt. fr. 23. 6 Μεσσηνίων, Hes. fr. 58. 5 Ἀσκληπιοῦ.

84. The poet was evidently conscious that, even allowing for three weeks' delay in Egypt caused by contrary winds (360 ff.), the distance was insufficient to explain Menelaus' absence for seven years, the interval required by the rest of his narrative. Consequently Menelaus is sent on further wanderings, collecting treasure. His route was much discussed in antiquity: cf. Str. 37–43; some held that he must be supposed to have circumnavigated Africa, a view recently revived by W. von Soden, 'Die Eremboi der Odyssee u. die Irrfahrt des Menelaos', *WSt* lxxii (1959), 26 ff. The poet's intention was evidently to increase Menelaus' mileage, but I doubt whether he had a definite conception of the itinerary.   **Αἰθίοπας:** see i 22 n.   **Σιδονίους:** cf. 618. The apparent separation of Sidonians from Phoenicians is strange. Strabo says that some thought Phoenician colonies were meant, but if the poet had really intended this, we should expect him to have made it clearer.   **Ἐρεμβούς:** completely mysterious; all later references to them derive from this passage, and we cannot even tell in which continent they should be sought. Strabo thought they might be Arabs; other ancient scholars proposed far-fetched emendations (Ἐρεμνούς Crates, Ἀραμβούς Posidonius, Ἀραβάς τε Zeno).

85 ff. This digression on pastoral life in North Africa surely reflects an interest in the colonization of Cyrenaica; cf. Λιβύην ... μηλοτρόφον in the oracles recorded by Hdt. (iv 155. 3; 157. 2); see further J. Boardman, *The Greeks Overseas*² (London, 1980), 153 ff. We find echoes of the colonial movement elsewhere in the poem, e.g. in the detailed description of the Isle of Goats (ix 116 ff.), an obviously promising site for settlement, and in the account of the foundation of Scheria (vi 4 ff.).   **ἵνα ... τελέθουσι:** 'where lambs are immediately horned', i.e. mature quickly. The horns are the most obvious sign that the animal is adult; the poet surely did not mean that in Africa sheep acquire horns at an earlier stage in relation to their general development than they do elsewhere.

86. **τρίς:** no ewe could lamb three times in a year, since the gestation period is about five months. Sheep normally breed only once annually, but may produce two lots of lambs in ideal conditions. Three lambing seasons might be arranged by mating the animals at three different times, but can hardly be what the poet had in mind; the emphasis is not on careful stock-farming but on astounding fertility. The ancient variant δίς must be a conjecture intended to bring Menelaus' wild claims into line with reality.

Since 86 provides an explanation for the constant supply of milk described in 87–9, Bekker transposed it to follow 89.

88. Milk as an article of diet, both in Homer and in archaic Greek literature in general, is sheep's or goat's milk, not cow's. The constant supply of milk is simply the effect of better diet than Greek livestock were used to.

89. **ἐπηετανόν:** confined to poetry, in Homer only in the *Odyssey*. The original sense seems to have been 'lasting the whole year': cf. Frisk, *GEW*, Chantraine, *Dictionnaire*. **θῆσθαι**: Hesychius quotes the phrase *ἐπ-ηετανὸν γάλα νᾶσαι*, without any indication of author (s.v. *νᾶσαι*); some have taken this as evidence for an ancient variant *νᾶσαι*, but the quotation more probably comes from a Hellenistic poet remodelling a Homeric expression; the aor. of *νάω* is not otherwise attested.

90–1. ἦος, τῆος: our MSS read *ἕως* or *εἵως* (see iii 126 n.) and *τείως*. Where, as here, metre requires a trochee, *ἕως* points to an earlier **ἦος*, nowhere attested but to be inferred as the early Ionic form from comparison of Doric *ᾶς* and Ionic *ἕως*. Most editors restore either *ἦος* or, following Hermann, the compromise *εἶος*, for which, in a few passages, there is very slight MS-support. But the virtual unanimity of the MSS (including papyri) and the apparently unquestioning acceptance by ancient scholars of *ἕως* with trochaic scansion suggests that long-standing rhapsodic tradition lies behind *ἕως/εἵως*, and it seems likely that this was the form normally to be heard when the text was recited in the classical period. It should be noted that in most cases this phenomenon occurs at the beginning of the line (particularly in the formula *ἕως ὁ ταῦθ' ὥρμαινε κατὰ φρένα καὶ κατὰ θυμόν*) where there was an unusual degree of metrical freedom, especially with words which were bound to stand at the beginning of their clauses (cf. 13 *ἐπεὶ δή* and n.), though often this is disguised by artificial lengthening. The problem is among the most awkward to be faced by a modern editor, and its failure to engage the attention of Aristarchus is surprising. See further Hainsworth on v 123, 365, Hoekstra on xiii 315, Russo on xix 530, Ebeling s.v. *ἕως*, *τέως* Chantraine, *Grammaire*, i 11 § 3, Werner, *H u. ει vor Vokal* 25–6, M. L. West, *Glotta* xliv (1967), 135 ff. **κεῖνα**: 'those parts'. **βίοτον**: 'means of living, substance'. **ἄλλος**: Menelaus cannot bring himself to name Aegisthus.

94–6. We may find it hard to sympathize with this lament for bygone prosperity in view of the preceding emphasis on Menelaus' riches. The speech would in fact be more coherent without these lines; the antecedent of *ὧν* in 97 must be *τοῖσδε κτεάτεσσιν* (93), and Bekker was perhaps right to excise what might be regarded as an infelicitous attempt to enhance the pathos of Menelaus' situation. **τάδε**: prospective, referring to his pre-war wealth. **μέλλετ' ἀκουέμεν**: 'you are likely to have heard', cf. iii 87 n. **ἀπώλεσα**: 'I lost', cf. i 354, ii 46, iv 724, 814, etc. **εὖ μάλα ναιετάοντα**: 'well-established'; see i 404 n.

99. Ἄργος: here the Peloponnese; cf. iii 251 n.

100–3. Menelaus' speech becomes somewhat flaccid and incoherent; the poet (characteristically) postpones the expected reference to Odysseus.

102. γόῳ φρένα τέρπομαι: 'I satisfy my heart with weeping'. Homeric heroes do not take positive pleasure in lamentation, but they may satisfy a desire to weep (cf. 103). For this use of *τέρπομαι* in connection with lamentation cf. xi 212, xix 213, 251, 513, xxi 57, *Il.* xxiii 10, 98, xxiv 513; see further J. Latacz, *Zum Wortfeld 'Freude' in der Sprache Homers* (Heidelberg, 1966), 187 ff.

104-5. Cf. *Il.* xxii 424-5. **ἀπεχθαίρει**: 'makes hateful', a most unusual sense.

107. With an irony very characteristic of the *Odyssey*, Menelaus speaks spontaneously of what most concerns Telemachus (cf. e.g. viii 73 ff., xiv 37 ff.). See further A. F. Dekker, *Ironie in de Odyssee* (Leiden, 1965). **ἤρατο**: probably best taken as aor. med. of ἀείρω, 'undertook, took upon himself'; cf. Chantraine, *Grammaire*, i 387 § 185 n. 1. But at i 240 the same form must be aor. of ἄρνυμαι; see n. **τῷ**: better interpreted as a demonstrative, strengthened by αὐτῷ, than as 'therefore'.

112. νέον: adverbial, with γεγαῶτα.

113-82. Mention of Odysseus moves Telemachus to tears, and Menelaus is led to suspect that the boy must be Odysseus' son. His guess is put into words by Helen, who comes with her spinning to join the men. Pisistratus confirms their inference, and explains why Telemachus has come. Menelaus weeps for Odysseus.

   This episode, which in some ways foreshadows the process by which Odysseus makes himself known to the Phaeacians in viii, is well discussed by N. J. Richardson, 'Recognition Scenes in the *Odyssey*', *Papers of the Liverpool Latin Seminar* iv (1983), 219 ff., esp. 223 ff.

114. βάλε: 'let fall'.

115. Odysseus similarly draws his cloak over his face to hide his tears from the Phaeacians (viii 83 ff.); cf. A. *Ch.* 81, E. *Hipp.* 243-6, *Supp.* 111, 286, *Or.* 280, *IA* 1122 ff., Pl. *Phd.* 117 c. **ἄντ'**: i.e. ἄντα.

116 ff. Deliberation between two possibilities is a recurrent situation in Homer, typically marking heightened tension, a critical point in the development of events; cf. e.g. vi 141 ff., xx 10 ff.; see further Arend, *Scenen*, 108 ff., C. Voigt, *Überlegung u. Entscheidung*, 18 ff., esp. 74 ff.

120 ff. We have been waiting for Helen to appear since the beginning of the book, and her entry, given a rather ceremonial quality by its detailed description, brings the recognition scene to a climax. Again we are conscious of the contrast with Pylos: Nestor's wife is a virtuous nonentity, Helen dominates the following scene, taking charge in a way which might be judged unsuitable for a wife when her husband is present (though whether she may fairly be charged with flirting with Telemachus depends on one's view of what constitutes flirting). Commentators, perhaps unduly impressed by her spinning, have often been inclined to supply Helen and Menelaus with an atmosphere of domestic contentment not really to be found in the text. Helen's presence does little to lighten the prevailing mood of melancholy reminiscence. Menelaus' comments on Nestor's happiness in his sons (206 ff.) remind us of Helen's failure to give him a son (11 ff.), a misfortune not unconnected with their long separation, and the story which he tells to illustrate Odysseus' characteristic shrewdness and self-control presents his wife in a very poor light (271 ff.). It was not, we may infer, the poet's purpose to present Menelaus and Helen as fairy-tale characters who, once home, lived happy ever after.

   Though Helen's origins as a goddess are indisputable, in Greek epic she has been thoroughly humanized, and her former divine status is virtually irrelevant to our appreciation of her role in Homer.

See further J. T. Kakridis, 'Problems of the Homeric Helen', *Homer Revisited* (Lund, 1971), 25 ff., M. L. West, *Immortal Helen* (Bedford College, London, 1975), L. L. Clader, *Helen: The Evolution from Divine to Heroic in Greek Epic Tradition* (*Mnemosyne* Suppl. xlii, 1976), C. Calame, *Les Choeurs de jeunes filles en Grèce archaïque*, i (Rome, 1977), 333 ff.

120. ἦος: see 90 n.

121. The detail of Helen emerging from the privacy of an inner room is a further indication that the wedding party with which the book opened has been forgotten. ἐκ Ἑλένη: the MSS read ἐκ δ' Ἑλένη; Bentley's excision of δ' allows for the initial digamma of Ἑλένη (cf. 130), formerly disputed but now established by epigraphic evidence, probably to be dated to the sixth century, from Helen's sanctuary at Therapne: see H. W. Catling and H. Cavanagh, 'Two Inscribed Bronzes from Sparta', *Kadmos* xv (1976), 145–57 (= *SEG* xxvi 458), C. de Simone, *Glotta* lvi (1978), 40 ff. Few traces of this lost digamma are discernible in Homer; we may instance the lengthening of the last syllable of Ἀλέξανδρος in the formula Ἀλέξανδρος Ἑλένης πόσις ἠϋκόμοιο (*Il.* iii 329 etc.), though lengthening before the caesura is too common for this to have much weight; see also Hoekstra on xiv 68. Whether we should follow Bentley here is debatable; there is a danger of 'correcting' the poet himself. Certainly apodotic δέ after a temporal protasis is very common in Homer: see Denniston, *Particles*, 177 ff., Kirk on *Il.* i 194.

122. Nausicaa (vi 102 ff., 151–2) and Penelope (xvii 37, xix 54) are similarly compared to Artemis. χρυσηλακάτῳ: in Homer exclusively an epithet of Artemis (cf. *Il.* xvi 183, xx 70). The distaff is not readily associated with Artemis, and some ancient scholars argued that ἠλακάτη could be used for 'arrow', and interpreted χρυσηλάκατος correspondingly (cf. ἰοχέαιρα). But the almost immediately following reference to Helen's χρυσέη ἠλακάτη (131) surely implies that the poet of the *Odyssey* (whatever may be true of the *Iliad*) gave the epithet what seems its obvious sense, 'with golden distaff'; it seems to have been similarly interpreted by Pindar, who applies it to Amphitrite, the Nereids and Leto, (*O.* vi 104, *N* v 36; vi 36). See further Frisk, *GEW*, Chantraine, *Dictionnaire* s.v. ἠλακάτη.

123. κλισίην: to be identified with the κλισμός of 136, on which see i 132 n.

124. τάπητα: to cover the κλισίη.

125 ff. Like Arete (vi 305 ff.), Helen does not intend to sit idle when she joins her husband to entertain his guests. Spinning, with a little practice, can, like plain knitting, be done whenever the hands are not otherwise occupied, needing little light or attention. Even at Troy Helen busied herself with wool-working (*Il.* iii 125 ff.), and her industry should not be regarded as marking a return to domestic propriety. On spinning and weaving as the ἔργα γυναικῶν *par excellence* see i 356–8 n.

125–7. Cf. *Il.* ix 381–4: οὐδ' ὅσ' ἐς Ὀρχομενὸν ποτινίσεται, οὐδ' ὅσα Θήβας | Αἰγυπτίας, ὅθι πλεῖστα δόμοις ἐν κτήματα κεῖται, | αἵ θ' ἑκατόμπυλοί εἰσι, διηκόσιοι δ' ἀν' ἑκάστας | ἀνέρες ἐξοιχνεῦσι σὺν ἵπποισιν καὶ ὄχεσφιν.[1] The pre-eminence which Egypt's southern capital enjoyed under Dyn. XVIII, above all in the reign of Amenophis III (c.1417–1379), ended when Akhenaten (c.1379–1362) moved the royal residence northwards to Tell-el-Amarna, but was briefly revived under the pious Nubian kings of Dyn. XXV (715–663), until the city was sacked by Assurbanipal. Do the Homeric allusions to its extraordinary wealth reflect Mycenaean conditions or recent history? Cogent reasons for the latter view have been advanced by W. Burkert ('Das hunderttorige Theben u. die Datierung der Ilias', WSt NF x (1976), 5 ff.) who, among other arguments, explores the implications of the city's Greek name. An architectural resemblance to Boeotian Thebes can hardly have been discernible at any period, and none of the regular Egyptian designations can have sounded like Θῆβαι (for details see Lloyd on Hdt. ii 3. 1). Presumably some adventurous Greek traveller mistook the name of a prominent temple or a district, or a descriptive phrase, for the name of the city; the range of possible misconception is vast—we may recall the story of the foreign visitor who concluded that the most popular British drink was 'same again'.[2] But it seems inconceivable that this nomenclature could go back to the Mycenaean age; once Greek contacts with Egypt were broken off the situation of the city which the Greeks had called by this name would have been forgotten, and seventh-century Greek travellers would have got no help in identifying it from native Egyptians, since the name would have meant nothing to them. Yet there was never any doubt or controversy about the identification of Thebes (as there was, for instance, about Pylos and Doulichion), never any suggestion that the much more accessible, and normally more important, Memphis might be meant. The name surely belongs to the period when Greek contacts with Egypt began again in the late eighth and seventh centuries.

The *Iliad*'s reference to the city's hundred gates must derive from reports of the famous pylons (ceremonial gateways), but we do not know whether news of its revived splendours penetrated to Greek lands before the city was sacked by the Assyrians. However, the long trail of caravans carrying home to Nineveh the booty of which Assurbanipal boasted (see J. B. Pritchard (ed.), *Ancient Near Eastern Texts Relating to the Old Testament*[3] (Princeton, 1969), 295, 297) advertised throughout the Near East the wealth which had failed to save the ancient and pious city from Assyrian aggression.

Menelaus' Theban hosts have Greek names and habits of hospitality. It is curious that the poet does not assign any official status either to them or to Menelaus' other Egyptian friends, Thon and Polydamna (228); contrast 617–18.   ἔναι': in an unusual position; normally ἔναιεν, ἔναιον stand before the main caesura or at the end of the line.   Αἰγυπτίης: on the trisyllabic scansion see 83 n.

---

[1] It has been suggested that 382 was borrowed from the *Od.*; but it is essential to the structure of Achilles' speech.

[2] I am indebted for help on this point to Dr Mark Smith.

128 ff. None of the gifts mentioned in this catalogue is characteristically Egyptian.

129. δέκα ... τάλαντα: the weight of the Homeric talent (mentioned only in connection with gold) is unknown; the order of the prizes at *Il.* xxiii 262–70 suggests that it was not great.

130. αὖ Ἑλένῃ: nearly all MSS read αὖθ' Ἑλένη, neglecting the original initial digamma of Ἑλένη; see 121 n.

131–2. A golden distaff would be unconveniently heavy. The closest Homeric parallels for Helen's wheeled work-basket are the wheeled tripods of *Il.* xviii 375–6. Fragments of a wheeled tripod have been found in a cave at Polis Bay in Ithaca: see S. Benton, *ABSA* xxxv (1938), 88–9, Lorimer, *Monuments*, 73. The technique of mounting things on castors belongs to Phoenicia rather than Egypt; cf. the bronze lavers on wheels which Hiram of Tyre provided for Solomon's temple, 1 Kgs. 7: 30. Helen's work-basket combines unusual design and precious material, ordinary ones being of wickerwork. **χρυσῷ ... κεκράαντο:** 'the rims were finished off with gold' (κεκράαντο plpf. pass. of κραίνω). The same formula is used of the Phoenician bowl which Menelaus gives Telemachus (616); for the juxtaposition of the two precious metals cf. also x 355, 357, *Il.* xi 31.

133. We return to the point we left at 125.

134. νήματος ἀσκητοῖο: 'yarn already spun'.

135. ἰοδνεφές: Polyphemus' sheep are naturally that colour (ix 426), and we should not infer that the wool was dyed before it was spun.

138 ff. Similarly at xv 169 ff. Helen intervenes while Menelaus is still making up his mind. **ἴδμεν:** polite use of the 1st pers. pl. where the 2nd pers. would be more logical: cf. 632.

139. δῶ: see i 176 n.

140. = *Il.* x 534. In both places the interpretation of ψεύσομαι has caused difficulty, since there can be no question of the speaker seriously contemplating a deliberate lie, and ψεύδομαι is not normally used in Homer of unintentionally saying what is not true (though *Il.* v 635 could perhaps be so taken); thus the phrase cannot be understood as 'Shall I be wrong or right in what I say?'. Cf. iii 20 n. (ψεῦδος). But the real question for Helen is whether to say nothing or to speak out; the emphasis falls on ἔτυμον ἐρέω, and ψεύσομαι enhances its force by contrast. The formula was perhaps originally devised for a soliloquy.

141 ff. Athenaeus comments on this episode (190 e): πάνυ γὰρ αἱ γυναῖκες διὰ τὸ παρατηρεῖσθαι τὴν ἀλλήλων σωφροσύνην δειναὶ τὰς ὁμοιότητας τῶν παίδων πρὸς τοὺς γονέας ἐλέγξαι. Catullus alludes to it at lxi 214 ff. On the theme of Telemachus' resemblance to his father see nn. on i 207–9, iii 120–5. It would be more natural for Helen to comment on Telemachus' likeness to his father rather than to (her mental picture of) Odysseus' son, and her immediate inference that he must be, specifically, Telemachus is too glib; though it might be common knowledge that Odysseus had only one legitimate son, the unknown youth might be a νόθος like Megapenthes.

145. κυνώπιδος: cf. Helen's self-reproaches in the *Iliad*, iii 180, 404, vi 344,

356, xxiv 764. 'The dog's affection can be bought with pleasure; he fawns on the master who brings him sweetmeats (*Od.* x 216). Thus the adulterous woman is a dog—Helen preeminently, even in her own description of herself..., but also Clytemnestra (*Od.* xi 424, 427), Aphrodite (*Od.* viii 319), and Penelope's faithless serving maids (*Od.* xix 154)' (J. M. Redfield). On the literal and figurative uses of κύων in Homer see M. Faust, 'Die kunstlerische Verwendung von κύων "Hund" in den homerischen Epen', *Glotta* xlviii (1970), 8–31.

146. ὑπὸ Τροίην: ὑπό conveys the idea of coming close up to something lofty.

149–50. Cf. Verg. *A.* iii 490 'sic oculos, sic ille manus, sic ora ferebat'.

151. νῦν: 'just now': contrast νῦν in 148.

153. εἶβε: the etymology of εἴβω is obscure. It functions as a doublet of λείβω, though it is more restricted in its position and use, and has been plausibly explained as an artificial development of λείβω, created by its decapitation *metri gratia*: see further Hainsworth on viii 531, M. W. Haslam, 'Homeric Words and Homeric Metre: Two Doublets Examined (λείβω/εἴβω, γαῖα/αἶα)', *Glotta* liv (1976), 201 ff.

157. μέν τοι: affirmative in tone.

158–60. These lines were absent from Rhianus' edition and athetized by Aristarchus. They are untraditional in expression and may reasonably be viewed with some suspicion: were they added because a need was felt to explain why Pisistratus was acting as spokesman? See further Wilamowitz, *Heimkehr*, 114, Bolling, *Evidence*, 230 ff., Merkelbach, *Untersuchungen*, 42. **νεμεσσᾶται:** 'he thinks it wrong, unseemly'. **ἐπεσβολίας:** the noun occurs only here in Homer, though cf. ἐπεσβόλον *Il.* ii 275; it was used by later poets to mean 'scurrility, violent abuse', but here the sense seems rather to be 'uninvited speech'. Zenodotus is credited with the reading ἐπιστομίας, otherwise unattested and of uncertain meaning.

161. Γερήνιος ἱππότα Νέστωρ: see iii 68 n.

163–7. These lines were suspected by some ancient critics, surely with good reason. Menelaus ignores them; he does not refer to Telemachus' difficulties and alleged need for advice, but simply expresses delight at this visit by the son of his old friend. Moreover, Telemachus has come to seek news of his father, not counsel. In any case, it is Homeric custom for a visitor to wait until he is asked before explaining why he has come; Menelaus courteously postpones enquiries until the next morning (312 ff.), when the explanation given here by Pisistratus is completely ignored. See further Merkelbach, *Untersuchungen*, 42–3, Page, *Odyssey*, 177, Eisenberger, *Studien*, 74 n. 5. **ὑποθήσεαι:** ὄφρα with fut. indic. is unusual, hence v. Leeuwen's cj. ὑποθήεαι; but cf. xvii 6–7, *Il.* viii 110–11, xvi 242–3. **ἔπος ... ἔργον:** see ii 272 n. **οἱ:** enclitic.

171. καί μιν continues the relatival construction of ὃς εἵνεκ' ... ἀέθλους. **ἔφην:** 'I thought' rather than 'I said'. **ἐλθόντα:** 'when he returned'. **φιλησέμεν:** 'treat him well'.

174–7. Menelaus' proposal for wholesale resettlement is reminiscent of Agamemnon's offer of seven εὖ ναιόμενα πτολίεθρα to Achilles at *Il.* ix

149 ff. But it should not be taken as a reflection of political reality, either in the Mycenaean age or subsequently. There is no danger of the absent Odysseus accepting this offer, which would in any case put him and his people to considerable inconvenience, but it serves as a vivid expression of Menelaus' high regard for him. See further J. V. Andreev, *Klio* lxi (1979), 365 ff. **νάσσα:** trans., 'I would have given him for his home'. **ἐξαλαπάξας:** 'emptying, clearing', an abnormal sense for this verb, which elsewhere implies destruction (cf. iii 85, viii 495, etc.), perhaps due to misunderstanding of *Il.* ix 328 δώδεκα ... πόλεις ἀλάπαξ' ἀνθρώπων.

179. φιλέοντε: reciprocal in sense, 'entertaining each other'.

181. μέλλεν: 'must have'. **ἀγάσσεσθαι:** 'feel jealous at, begrudge'. The idea that the gods resent human happiness and success is found elsewhere in the *Odyssey*: cf. viii 565–6 = xiii 173–4, xxiii 210 ff. (all in speeches); the spirit of Calypso's protest at v 118 ff. is similar. The poet of the *Iliad* evidently attached little importance to it, but this view is widespread in the literature of the archaic and early classical periods. See further E. R. Dodds, *The Greeks and the Irrational* (Berkeley–Los Angeles, 1951), 28 ff.

183–218. Menelaus' grief proves infectious. Even Pisistratus is moved to weep for Antilochus, the brother whom he never knew, but he takes the lead in bringing the company to a more cheerful frame of mind.

This passage displays in an extreme form the sentimentality characteristic of the *Odyssey*, and is further marred by a contradiction with the earlier narrative, since Menelaus' proposal to resume the meal (213) is inconsistent with 68, where we are told that Telemachus and Pisistratus had finished eating. To modern taste, at least, Pisistratus asserts himself more than might be thought proper in a guest so much junior to his hosts, and his observations on the tribute due to the dead, though fitting in themselves, seem a little out of place on the lips of the one who, of all the company, has least real cause for grief; Menelaus' commendation may surprise us. Was the passage perhaps added to enhance Pisistratus' role (cf. Schwartz, *Odyssee*, 308–9)? In defence, see Eisenberger, *Studien*, 75–6.

183. On Homeric susceptibility to tears see ii 81 n.

187–9. Cf. i 29–31. **Ἠοῦς υἱός:** Memnon; see iii 111–12 n.

190. περί: with βροτῶν, expressing superiority, 'above, beyond'.

192. Athetized by Aristarchus. **οἷσιν** is used to mean ἡμετέροις, a sense unique in Homer; to defend it, as some commentators do, by taking it closely with Νέστωρ φάσχ' ὁ γέρων, produces an unnaturally involved sentence-structure.

193. εἴ τί που ἔστι: 'if it is at all possible'. **πίθοιο:** opt. used as a courteous imperative. Pisistratus does not actually say what he proposes, though it may be easily inferred.

194. μεταδόρπιος: only here in Homer; elsewhere it means 'after supper', but 'during supper' is indicated by Menelaus' subsequent proposal to resume their meal, though a listener might well misinterpret the word at first hearing. **ἀλλὰ καὶ Ἠώς ... ἠριγένεια**: Pisistratus surely does not mean 'It will soon be morning'; the company is in no hurry to retire after this. The sense is rather 'Morning will be time enough for that'; he goes on to explain that he has no objection to lamentation at the right time.

195. νεμεσσῶμαι: 'regard as unseemly'. **γε μέν**: adversative; see Denniston, *Particles*, 387.

197–8. Parenthetic. τινά must be understood as the subject of κείρασθαι; for the custom cf. xxiv 46, *Il.* xxiii 46, 135.

202. Cf. iii 112; as at 107, the name is kept back till the end.

204. There is no proper apodosis to the protasis which begins here; cf. iii 103 ff. Menelaus returns Pisistratus' compliment (190).

205. καὶ ῥέξειε is strictly superfluous, but the familiar combination of word and deed expresses the comprehensive, all-round, nature of Pisistratus' intelligence.

206. τοίου refers back to πεπνυμένος; **ὅ**: 'because', i.e. 'as I infer because'; cf. xviii 392; see Monro, *Homeric Dialect*, 242 § 269, Chantraine, *Grammaire*, ii 284 § 417.

208. γαμέοντί τε γεινομένῳ τε: 'at marriage and at birth', prothysteron, cf. iii 467 n.; for the combination of events cf. *Il.* iii 40. **γεινομένῳ**: i.e. γενομένῳ with metrical lengthening of the first syllable (perhaps by analogy with οὐλόμενος); see Wyatt, *Lengthening*, 119–20.

210. λιπαρῶς γηρασκέμεν: cf. λιπαρὸν γῆρας xi 136, xix 368, xxiii 283; imitated by Pi. *N.* vii 99.

211. αὖ: answers μέν (210); see Denniston, *Particles*, 376.

212. ὃς πρὶν ἐτύχθη: i.e. before Pisistratus spoke; the phrase is rather feeble, and van Herwerden's cj. ὧν πρίν is attractive.

213–14. Hand-washing is regularly mentioned as a preliminary to eating: see i 136 n.; the detail is interesting here, where the meal has merely been temporarily interrupted. But it is debatable whether we should take it as a genuine reflection of current convention or whether the poet has simply inserted a detail which he associates with feasting without thinking whether it is quite appropriate in this particular context. **χευάντων**: 3rd pers. pl. aor. imper.; as often, the subject is left vague: cf. xix 599 θέντων. **ἠῶθεν** picks up Pisistratus' ἀλλὰ καὶ Ἠώς | ἔσσεται ἠριγένεια (194–5); presumably we should understand the words as intended not to exclude Pisistratus but to encourage the shy Telemachus, who has hitherto left all the talking to his friend. For the infin. after ἔσονται cf. *Il.* xiii 312 ἀμύνειν εἰσὶ καὶ ἄλλοι, 129 οὔατ' ἀκουέμεν ἐστί.

219–305. After Helen has soothed their spirits with a drug added to the wine, she and Menelaus tell stories of Odysseus' resourcefulness and determination.

220 ff. It has often been suggested that the description of Helen's wonder-drug is based on opium, which is not mentioned in Greek literature before the fourth century and cannot have been widely known in Greek lands when the *Odyssey* was composed; henbane (*Hyoscyanus niger*) has also been proposed. But there is no reason to think that it was customary in antiquity, either in Egypt or anywhere else, to add either drug to wine;[3] nor indeed is it quite certain that opium was known in Egypt at this period. See further M. D. Merlin, *On the Trail of the Ancient Opium Poppy* (London–Toronto, 1984), esp. 179 ff. It was, however, Egyptian practice to mix with wine an elaborately concocted incense called *kyphi*; Plutarch (*de Iside* 80), probably drawing on the Egyptian priest Manetho, lists sixteen ingredients, of which the most important appear to be resin and myrrh, and claims for it the power to dissolves sorrow and tension without drunkenness; it cannot, of course, have been as potent as opium. See further *RE* xxiii 52 ff. (κῦφι). Greek experience of Egyptian hospitality may thus lie behind this passage, but like the *soma*-pills of Aldous Huxley's *Brave New World* Helen's drug represents an extrapolation from pharmacological actuality; we may also see a tribute to the elaborate Egyptian pharmacopoeia. The realistic limitation of ἐφημέριος (223) marks the difference from such fantasies as the amnesiac lotus (ix 94 ff.) and Circe's enchantments (x 235 ff.). We should note that knowledge of *materia medica* seems here regarded as of particular interest to women (though cf. ἰητροὶ πολυφάρμακοι (*Il.* xvi 28)); it is a natural part of a general concern with household provisions. See further G. Wickert-Micknat *Archaeologia* R, 35–7.

Plutarch (*Mor.* 614 b) and Macrobius (vii 1, 18) offer an allegorical explanation: the φάρμακον represents Helen's bewitching eloquence.

221. Unusual vocabulary; νηπενθής and ἐπίληθος are otherwise found only in what are clearly reminiscences of this passage; ἄχολος is used, uniquely, in an active sense, 'banishing anger'.

222. ἐπεί: most MSS read ἐπήν; see ii 105 n.

226. δηϊόῳεν: the subject is left vague.

227. μητιόεντα: elsewhere in early poetry μητιόεις is exclusively an epithet of Zeus, evidently equivalent to μητίετα (e.g. *h.Ap.* 344, Hes. *Op.* 51, 769).

228. Πολύδαμνα: peculiarly appropriate to an expert in φάρμακα, neither this name nor its masc. counterpart, *Πολύδαμνος, is historically attested. Θῶνος: Thon is the only character in Menelaus' Egyptian adventures who bears what looks like a genuine Egyptian name, but it is primarily a place-name, once widespread and still surviving in Coptic. Thon seems to have been invented by the Greeks as the eponymous founder of the town where they put into land; see further A. Fick and F. Bechtel, *Die gr. Personennamen* (Göttingen, 1894), 366, J. Yoyotte, 'Notes de toponymie égyptienne', *MDAI* (*Kairo*) xvi (1958), 423–30. Thon and Polydamna may thus be regarded as located in the Delta, representing Lower Egypt as Polybos and Alkandre (126) represent Upper. (Herodotus, whose elaborate account of Helen's sojourn in Egypt (ii 113 ff.) skilfully combines Homer, Stesichorus, and rationalizing speculation, makes Thon warden of the Canopic mouth of the Nile.)

---

[3] It should also be noted that initiation to opium is normally found unpleasant (addicts have usually started by taking it medicinally, often as a specific for dysentery), so that Telemachus and Pisistratus, at least, would have been unlikely to enjoy the evening; but some poetic licence might be conceded on this point.

229. Αἰγυπτίη: on the trisyllabic scansion see 83 n.   **τῇ**: sc. ἐν Αἰγύπτῳ.

230. μεμιγμένα: it is not quite clear whether the poet means that the wholesome and the poisonous grow together (cf. xix 175 ἄλλη δ' ἄλλων γλῶσσα μεμιγμένη) or whether μεμιγμένα simply picks up ἐπεὶ κρητῆρι μιγείη (222).

231–2. ἰητρὸς ... ἀνθρώπων: 'everyone is a physician skilled above all (other) men'; cf. Hdt. ii 84 (in Egypt) πάντα δ' ἰήτρων ἐστι πλέα. Paieon appears in the *Iliad* (v 401, 899) as the physician of the gods; cf. Hes. fr. 307 (M–W). Later he was identified with Apollo, but in Homer Apollo has no healing function. On the origins of Paieon see Nilsson, *Geschichte*, i 159; the name seems to be Mycenaean: see Ventris–Chadwick, *Documents*, 126.

The scholia mention an alternative version of 231–2, ἰητρὸς δὲ ἕκαστος, ἐπεί σφισι δῶκεν Ἀπόλλων | ἰᾶσθαι; this slightly more logical reading is ascribed to Aristarchus, but rejected because of the identification of Paieon and Apollo. However, the information in this note has probably been distorted, and it is more likely that the argument against this version represents Aristarchus' view; see further Ludwich, *AHT* i, 541–2. A further ancient variant, φαρμακέων for ἀνθρώπων, likewise results from an attempt to improve the logic; but φαρμακεύς is unhomeric.

234. ἐξαῦτις: referring back to 138 ff.

236–7. ἀτὰρ ... ἅπαντα: Helen's point and the exact force of ἀτάρ are not clear. Some commentators see a contrast with ἐσθλῶν ('Sons of good men, *but* success and failure are in the hands of Zeus'), some regard it as looking forward to δαίνυσθε, expressing in advance the antithesis which might be expected to follow the main clause. But though this type of anticipation is quite common with causal clauses (e.g. i 337, v 29), it is hard to find a parallel for an anticipatory adversative clause, and the former interpretation, though slightly elliptical, thus seems preferable.   **ἄλλοτε ... ἄλλῳ**: for the hiatus cf. *h.Herm.* 558, Hes. *Op.* 713, Sol. 13. 76 West, Thgn. 157, 992, Phoc. 5. 1 West, Xenoph. DK 21 B 26. 2.   **διδοῖ**: cf. xvii 350, *Il.* ix 519, as if from a contracted verb in -όω; see Monro, *Homeric Dialect*, 19 § 18, Chantraine, *Grammaire*, i 299 § 138.

239. ἐοικότα: 'suited to the occasion'.

240. Cf. xi 328, 517.   **μυθήσομαι**: subj., like ὀνομήνω.

242 ff. The story which Helen tells to illustrate Odysseus' exceptional resourcefulness and courage will be balanced by Menelaus' reminiscence (267 ff.). Both relate to the period after the end of the *Iliad* and draw on the body of saga which was to form the subject-matter of Cyclic epics by Lesches and Arctinus; in both Helen herself plays a prominent part. In her own tale she herself dominates the action: she held Odysseus at her mercy, but did not betray him because she had come to see the folly of her desertion and longed for a Greek victory. Menelaus replaces Helen's favourable self-portrait with something much less pleasant which, because it comes second, is likely to leave a lasting impression. He tells how Helen later had all the Greek leaders in her power, when the Horse was brought into Troy, and by her folly nearly destroyed them. The juxtaposition of these two complementary tales suggests the lability of Helen's character, and a rather coquettish pride in dangerous secrets. Though we must beware of reading into this episode psychological subtleties alien to the poet's purpose, it might be thought to reveal the tensions inherent in Helen's apparently placid relationship with Menelaus; she would have done better to resist the temptation to reminisce about her days at Troy, and her initiative goads her husband to reveal to the young men whom she seeks to impress an incident bound to embarrass her. See further Bethe, *Odyssee*, 253-4, 259-60, A. Severyns, *Le Cycle épique dans l'école d'Aristarque* (Liège, 1928), 334 ff., 347 ff., J. T. Kakridis, 'Helena u. Odysseus', *Homer Revisited* (Lund, 1971), 40 ff., R. Schmiel, 'Telemachus in Sparta', *TAPhA* ciii (1972), 463-72, Ø. Andersen, 'Odysseus and the Wooden Horse', *SO* lii (1977), 5-18.

The poet appears to assume in his audience some familiarity with the circumstances of Odysseus' reconnaissance at Troy. In Proclus' summary of Lesches' *Little Iliad* it occurs after the construction of the Wooden Horse, as a preliminary to the theft of the Palladium. But the prominence of Helen in this adventure is surely an *ad hoc* invention; it is hard to imagine that earlier poetry offered ready-made an episode so exactly suited to the purpose of directly involving Helen in the conversation and illustrating Odysseus' characteristic qualities in a light so favourable to her. It is suggested in the scholia that the tale was intended to prepare the way for Odysseus' appearance as a beggar on his return to Ithaca; for a similar theory see n. on i 259. There too his disguise is penetrated when he is being washed by a woman who knows him well (xix 386 ff.). How far such foreshadowing results from conscious planning is hard to say; but Helen's role in her story might well have been suggested by Eurycleia's.

Herodotus (iii 154 ff.) has a somewhat similar story about the Persian Zopyrus, who pretended to be a deserter from the Persians and so enabled Darius to take Babylon; for further examples of such ruses see Thompson, *Motif Index*, K 2357.

245. οἰκῆϊ: οἰκεύς in the *Iliad* means 'an inmate of one's household'; in the *Odyssey* it becomes a euphemism for 'menial, slave'; cf. xiv 4 (with Hoekstra's n.), 63.

246-9. It was persuasively argued by L. Friedländer ('Doppelte Recensionen in Iliade u. Odyssee', *Philologus* iv (1849), 580 ff.) that εὐρυάγυιαν (246) ... Τρώων πόλιν (249) represent an alternative to the preceding three lines (αὐτὸν (244) ... πόλιν (246)). 248 raises particular problems. If we follow Aristarchus in taking δέκτῃ as an otherwise unattested noun, 'beggar', it is inconsistent with οἰκῆϊ (245). But if we take it as a personal name, as we are told it was in the *Little Iliad* (fr. xi Allen), the following relative clause is clumsy and perplexing: does it mean '(Odysseus) who was in no respect such (as the otherwise unknown Dectes)' or '(Dectes) who was not there at all in the Greek camp'? It is assumed in the scholia that the composer of the *Little Iliad* derived Dectes from this passage, but the converse may be nearer the truth: was the passage intended to enliven the story further with a detail drawn from the *Little Iliad*? There has perhaps been similar tampering with Menelaus' tale (see 285–9 n.).

249. ἀβάκησαν: the word occurs only here; meaning and etymology are uncertain. Sappho (120, 2) has ἀβάκης, apparently meaning 'calm, gentle, peaceful'. The scholia interpret as ἠγνόησαν: a reasonable guess.

250. ἐγὼ ... ἀνέγνων: we have already seen that Helen is good at faces (141 ff.). **τοῖον ἐόντα:** ambiguous: 'as the man he was' or 'though thus disguised'? It makes little difference.

251. Odysseus' skill in evading questions is very noticeable in his dealings with the Phaeacians and Penelope.

252. Helen presents herself to Telemachus as his father's hostess, performing from friendship the duties of hospitality which she might have delegated to a slave; cf. iii 464 n. In this rather summary account we are not immediately struck by the implausibility of the wife of a Trojan prince bathing an unkempt, runaway slave.

254. It does not of course follow that Helen revealed what had happened to the Trojans after Odysseus had reached the Greek camp; once he was out of danger the information compromised her. **μὴ μέν:** negative form of ἦ μέν, appropriate to oaths and solemn asseverations; cf. *Il.* xxiii 585.

256. νόον: 'plan, intentions', including the stratagem of the Wooden Horse, since it is clear from Menelaus' story that Helen understood its function.

258. φρόνιν ἤγαγε: 'brought back information'. A strange expression: ἤγαγε suggests that it is conceived as a kind of booty or spoil, and the scholia note that φρόνις was in fact used in that sense by later writers: οἱ δὲ νεώτεροι φρόνιν τὴν λείαν ἀπεδέξαντο; they perhaps saw a veiled allusion to the theft of the Palladium, which Homer never mentions: cf. Severyns, op. cit. (242 ff. n.), 350–1.

259. ἔνθ' ... ἐκώκυον: the murders reveal the penetration of Trojan defences by a spy, and the Trojan women are alert to the implications.

260. Cf. 145, and n.; for Helen's remorse cf. also *Il.* iii 139 ff., 173 ff., 399 ff.

261. ἄτην: mental aberration supernaturally imposed, folly, infatuation; cf. xxiii 223–4. Helen is not disclaiming responsibility for her actions; she means that she acted under the influence of overwhelming passion, not rationally or from calculation. For a lucid discussion of ἄτη in Homer, see E. R. Dodds, *The Greeks and the Irrational*, 2–8.

263. παῖδα: Hermione, cf. 4 ff. **νοσφισσαμένην:** 'abandoning'.

266 ff. In Idomeneus' view men's ἀρετή is most clearly manifested when they lie in ambush (*Il.* xiii 277 ff.), and Menelaus' account of Odysseus in the Wooden Horse well illustrates that quality of the hero's character which led Pope to describe him as 'upon all emergencies master of his passions'; his self-control and strength of purpose save the Greek leaders from the unexpected hazard created by Helen's recklessness. The poet assumes that in its general outline the story of the Wooden Horse is well known to his audience (cf. viii 492 ff. (with Hainsworth's n.), xi 523 ff.), but again we may suspect that he himself invented the curious part here assigned to Helen. Her behaviour does not suggest deliberate treachery; if she had changed her mind since her encounter with Odysseus she could have destroyed the Greeks in the Horse easily enough without visiting it. But she could bring only danger to the Greek leaders by this irresponsible demonstration of complicity, which was also a reminder that, at this critical juncture, their lives depended on her goodwill and silence, and not surprisingly Menelaus finds her folly unaccountable. We are left with the impression of a spoilt, bored woman craving excitement and a sense of power.

266. To be understood as approval for Helen's whole speech, not just as an acknowledgment of the neat concluding compliment.

268. For the way in which Menelaus develops his sentence cf. xi 416 ff., xxiv 87 ff., *Il.* ii 798-9, iii 184 ff., x 548 ff.

269. τοιοῦτον: probably masc., as Ὀδυσσῆος ... κῆρ is only a periphrasis for Ὀδυσσεύς.

270-1. Cf. 241-2. Ὀδυσσῆος ... κῆρ: cf. the Iliadic periphrases with λάσιον κῆρ + gen., ii 851, xvi 554.

272. ξεστῷ: cf. E. *Tr.* 534 ξεστὸν λόχον Ἀργείων.

273. = viii 513, *Il.* ii 352; it is omitted by a few MSS and is very likely a later addition.

274-5. Menelaus' inference reflects the same assumptions as Helen's reference to Aphrodite (261); he resorts to a theological explanation because her behaviour seems quite irrational. κελευσέμεναι ... ἔμελλε: 'some god must have bidden you'; κελευσέμεναι: aor. inf., cf. οἰσέμεναι xviii 291, ἀξέμεναι *Il.* xxiii 50.

276. Athetized by Aristarchus and some earlier scholars; they argued that it had been interpolated to introduce a reference to Helen's leviratical marriage to Deiphobus after the death of Paris (as related in the *Little Iliad*), a development of the legend which they held to be post-Homeric, suggested by the reference to Deiphobus at viii 517. But the line is surely indispensable; if Helen had not been observed by a Trojan there would have been no danger to the Greeks and Odysseus' precaution would have been unnecessary. θεοείκελος: i.e. handsome.

278. ἐκ δ' ὀνομακλήδην: the undivided form ἐξονομακλήδην at xii 250, *Il.* xxii 415; for the tmesis cf. διὰ δ' ἀμπερές (*Il.* xi 377).

279. It is not actually recorded that Aristarchus athetized this line, but the scholia emphasize its absurdity in terms which imply that he must have done: πόθεν γὰρ ὅλας ᾔδει, ἵνα καὶ τὰς φωνὰς αὐτῶν μιμήσηται; πάνυ δὲ γελοῖος ἡ τῶν φωνῶν μίμησις καὶ ἀδύνατος. πῶς δ' ἂν ἐπίστευον ὅτι πάρεισιν αὐτῶν αἱ γυναῖκες; (Cf. Ludwich, *AHT* i, 543, Severyns, op. cit. (on 242 ff.), 336). The line is awkward in expression and implausible in content. Commentators compare *h.Ap.* 162 ff., where we are told that the chorus of Delian girls πάντων δ' ἀνθρώπων φωνὰς καὶ κρεμβαλιαστὺν | μιμεῖσθ' ἴσασιν· φαίη δέ κεν αὐτὸς ἕκαστος | φθέγγεσθ'· οὕτω σφιν καλὴ συνάρηρεν ἀοιδή. But the ability to sing in dialect is rather different from successful mimicry of individuals, and the Delian girls' virtuosity throws little light on this strange trick. If the line is indeed a later addition, the interpolation perhaps reflects a craving for sensationalism; but there may be more to this curious detail than meets the eye. **πάντων Ἀργείων**: to be understood as restricted to those in the Wooden Horse. **ἀλόχοισιν**: i.e. ἀλόχων φωναῖς, compendious comparison; cf. ii 121 n.

283. ὑπακοῦσαι: 'to answer'; cf. x 83.

285–9. The passage was absent from many ancient editions and athetized by Aristarchus; the only ancient argument recorded against it, that Anticlus is not mentioned in the *Iliad* but comes from the Epic Cycle, is more substantial than it looks at first sight, since he is mentioned as if he were a familiar figure. 285–8 were surely composed as an alternative to 280–4 (cf. 246–9, and n.); 285–6 are inconsistent with 282–3. The incident might well have been suggested by (and intended to foreshadow) Odysseus' rather violent handling of Eurycleia (xix 479 ff.), the obscure Anticlus being introduced because it would not have been fitting for Odysseus to lay hands on some more distinguished hero. The case against 289 is less clear. It makes a more impressive end to the story than 284, nicely balancing Helen's concluding reference to Aphrodite (261), and though Homeric characters are not usually so specific about the identity of the god responsible when they infer divine intervention, Menelaus might reasonably conclude that Athena had been at work on the strength of the special relationship between her and Odysseus (cf. iii 222).

286. Ἄντικλος: short form of Ἀντικλέης, of uncertain meaning.

287. ἐπί: with πίεζε.

290. Telemachus, for whom these stories must have somewhat the effect of an obituary, now enters the conversation for the first time.

292. ἄλγιον: 'all the sadder'; cf. xvi 147.

293. There is a slight ellipse: 'nor (would it have saved him) even if his heart had been of iron'. The metaphor (for which cf. v 191 ff., xii 280, xxiii 172, *Il.* xx 372, xxii 357, xxiv 205) reflects the Iron Age in which the poet lived; Homeric weapons are of bronze.

294. τράπεθ': aor. imper. of τρέπω, 'send us off'; Telemachus does not mean that the whole company should retire, merely that he and Pisistratus would like to do so; cf. *Il.* xxiv 635.

296–305. This scene has much in common with vii 335–47, *Il.* ix 658–62, xxiv 643–8; see further Arend, *Scenen*, 100. **αἰθούσῃ**: see iii 399 n.; the poet does not envisage regular guest-rooms even in Menelaus' splendid palace. **τάπητες, χλαῖναι**, and **ῥήγεα** all seem to be rugs or blankets; cf. iii 349 n. Pillows as such are not mentioned, but a rolled-up rug might be used.

302. προδόμῳ δόμου: for the pleonasm cf. iii 422 and n.

303. = 21. The line is omitted by P. 140 (2nd cent. AD) and two medieval MSS; it is clearly unnecessary and almost certainly a later addition.

305. This is the last we shall see of Helen until xv 100. **τανύπεπλος**: cf. Hoekstra on xv 171. **δῖα γυναικῶν**: cf. δῖα θεάων, i 14 n.

306–50. Next morning Menelaus informs himself more exactly about the reason for Telemachus' journey.

306–10. Cf. ii 1–5, with nn. This is the sixth day of Telemachus' journey.

312. χρειώ: see ii 28 n.

314. ἐνίσπες: see iii 101 n.

316 ff. Some critics complain that Telemachus' speech is incoherent, that there is no connection between his desire for news (317) and his account of the suitors' depredations (cf. Merkelbach, *Untersuchungen*, 43). But this is hypercritical: Telemachus has been moved to go in search of news by the progressively worsening situation at home.

318. πίονα ἔργα: 'rich farms'.

322–31. = iii 92–101 (but see iii 98–101 n.); Telemachus has no reason to change the form of words with which he achieved good results at Pylos.

329. ἔπος ... ἔργον: see ii 272 n.

333–50. Retailed *verbatim* by Telemachus to Penelope (xvii 124–41).

335–40. This is the first developed simile in the *Odyssey*; the rarity of such similes in the Telemachy is noteworthy, however it is to be explained. Much has been written about Homeric similes; the following works provide a good introduction: Fränkel, *Gleichnisse*, C. M. Bowra, *Heroic Poetry* (London, 1952), 268 ff., Shipp, *Studies*, 208 ff., Moulton, *Similes*.

Lions appear very frequently in Homeric similes. See further Annie Schnapp–Gourbeillon, *Lions, héros, masques: les représentations de l'animal chez Homère* (Paris, 1981), C. Wolff, 'A note on lions and Sophocles, *Philoctetes* 1436', *Arktouros: Hellenic Studies presented to Bernard M. W. Knox* (Berlin–New York, 1979), 144–50, R. Friedrich, 'On the compositional use of similes in the *Odyssey*', *AJPh* 102 (1981), 120–37. Their geographical distribution was far more widespread in antiquity than it is now—there were lions in remote and mountainous areas of northern Greece at least as late as the fourth century BC (see Arist. *HA* 579 b 6 ff., 606 b 14 ff., Paus. vi 5. 4–5, cf. Hdt. vii 125–6)—but the poet's information about their habits was probably a matter of hearsay rather than direct observation. The lion symbolizes superior strength and courage, just as the deer exemplifies the lack of these qualities; cf. *Il.* xi 113 ff., where a lion falls upon some fawns in their lair. Odysseus is compared to a lion again at vi 130 ff. and after his slaughter of the suitors at xxii 402 ff. (xxiii 48 is probably an interpolation).

This simile undoubtedly brings out the weakness of the suitors against Odysseus and the inevitability of their destruction. But its general development is bizarre and many critics have commented on its absurdity. The situation is in itself incredible, since lions have a strong and distinctive odour, while deer are nervous creatures with an extremely keen sense of smell and an instinctive fear of lions.[4] There is a pathos in the innocent fawns' predicament which is out of place, as is the implication that not the suitors, Odysseus' prospective victims, but their parents are to blame; the emphatic ἀμφοτέροισι (339), which suggests that the careless doe herself escaped, is also awkward. We may suspect that the simile was taken over ready-made and not originally devised for this context.

---

[4] *The Times* (1 Aug. 1984) reports the use by a Scottish landowner (acting on Israeli advice) of lion droppings from Edinburgh Zoo to keep red deer off his winter barley.

Cf. Anacr. 408: ἀγανῶς οἷά τε νεβρὸν νεοθηλέα | γαλαθηνὸν ὅς τ' ἐν ὕλῃ κεροέσσης | ἀπολειφθεὶς ἀπὸ μητρὸς ἐπτοήθη.

335. ξυλόχῳ: apparently 'lair', cf. εὐνήν (338); elsewhere in Homer its meaning is 'copse, thicket'.

337. ἐξερέῃσι: ἐξερέω, not found in the *Iliad*, is used elsewhere in the *Odyssey* to mean 'enquire, question', but here its sense is evidently 'search, investigate'.

338. εἰσήλυθεν: the change from subj. to indic. is common in similes; cf. e.g. v 368 ff., *Il.* iv 141 ff.

339. ἀμφοτέροισι: 'on both fawns'; deer do not normally bear more than two young at a time. It is quite artificial to take ἀμφοτέροισι as 'the two parts of the family', doe and fawns, as some commentators suggest. Aristophanes interpreted it as 'doe and fawn', which implies that in 336 he read νεβρὸν ... νεηγενέα γαλαθηνόν.

340. Menelaus' confidence is irrational, reflecting the knowledge which the poet shares with the audience; Proteus had revealed (558–60) that Odysseus' prospects of return were poor.

341–6. Cf. i 255–66.

342–44. The scholia quote the account of Philomeleides given by Hellanicus of Lesbos (*FGrH* 4 F 150): οὗτος βασιλεὺς ὢν Λέσβου τοὺς παρίοντας εἰς πάλην ἐκάλει· καὶ τοὺς Ἕλληνας δὲ προσορμισθέντας. ὃν Ὀδυσσεὺς καὶ Διομήδης δολοφονήσαντες τὸν τάφον αὐτοῦ καταγώγιον ξένων ἐποίησαν, ὡς Ἑλλάνικός φησιν. Wherever Hellanicus got this additional information, the poet almost certainly did not expect his listeners to know more about Philomeleides than he relates here; we are perhaps meant to link this episode with the *Iliad*'s allusions to a Greek raid on Lesbos (ix 129, 664). **ἐϋκτιμένῃ ἐνὶ Λέσβῳ:** cf. Anacr. 358. 5–6 εὐκτίτου Λέσβου. **ἐϋκτιμένῃ:** see iii 4 n. **ἐνὶ Λέσβῳ:** some manuscripts read ἐν Ἀρίσβῃ. The more precise localization is attractive; the common tendency to replace terms judged obscure with more familiar words would easily explain why it was ousted by ἐνὶ Λέσβῳ. **Φιλομηλεΐδη:** the name was found puzzling in antiquity; it looks like a patronymic, but it would be strange to introduce an unfamiliar character by his patronymic alone, and such obscurantism is quite unhomeric. The suffix should probably be regarded as meaningless, a simple expansion of Φιλομηλεύς (though this is not attested as a personal name) or Φιλόμηλος; with the possible exception of Naubolides (viii 116) there is no Homeric parallel to this type of name, but from the classical period we may compare, e.g., Aristides, Euripides. The scholia record a variant, corrupted to Φιλομήδη; we can only conjecture what this conceals. See further v. Gersau, *RE* xix 2519–20.

345–6. = i 265–6. Menelaus' outburst of indignation may seem somewhat inadequate; Telemachus might be thought entitled to an offer of assistance (such as the suitors envisage (ii 325 ff.)), since his troubles result from Odysseus' willingness to help Menelaus. But the story of Odysseus' vengeance has no place for intervention by outsiders.

349. τά: the article when used as a relative normally follows the noun or

pronoun to which it refers, though cf. *Il.* i 125 ἀλλὰ τὰ μὲν πολίων
ἐξεπράθομεν, τὰ δέδασται. Monro, *Homeric Dialect*, 231 § 262 suggests reading
ἀλλά θ' ἅ μέν; see also G. M. Bolling, *CPh* xli (1946), 233. **γέρων ἅλιος**
νημερτής: the Old Man of the Sea is properly anonymous (cf. xxiv 58, *Il.* i
358, 538, 556, xviii 141, xx 107, xxiv 562), but is known under various
names; cf. Paus. iii 21. 9 ὅν δὲ ὀνομάζουσι Γυθεᾶται Γέροντα, οἰκεῖν ἐν θαλάσσῃ
φάμενοι, Νηρέα ὄντα εὑρίσκον; see further U. v. Wilamowitz-Moellendorff,
Der Glaube der Hellenen (Berlin, 1932), i 214-19, Nilsson, *Geschichte*, i 240-4,
Burkert, *Religion*, 172. **νημερτής** is partially explained by 385-6
(θαλάσσης | πάσης βένθεα οἶδε), though Proteus' knowledge extends be-
yond marine affairs; cf. Hesiod's account of Nereus, likewise νημερτής (*Th.*
233-6). On prophetic water-spirits see Thompson, *Motif Index*, F 420, 4. 10.

351-586. Menelaus' *nostos*.

351-424. He was detained on the island of Pharos, where Eidothea,
daughter of Proteus, took pity on him; she showed him how to induce her
father to reveal what he must do to get home.

352. Menelaus learns why he is delayed from Proteus (472 ff., cf. iii
144-5.) **ἐπεὶ οὐ:** synizesis. **τελήεσσας:** the epithet is used in Homer
only of hecatombs; it is not clear whether it refers to the quality of the
victims or to the efficacy of the sacrifice; but the two are, in any case,
closely linked.

353. Athetized by Zenodotus,[5] and probably also by Aristarchus, on the
grounds of obscurity: ποῖαι γάρ, φησίν, ἐγένοντο ἐντολαί; the objection is
cogent. We do not hear elsewhere of any general divine ordinance that
men should offer sacrifice before important undertakings, though clearly it
was regarded as a matter of common prudence to do so; but if we are
supposed to imagine that a specific command had been given to Menelaus
on this particular occasion, we must be perplexed by Proteus' failure to
allude to it; see further Nickau, *Untersuchungen*, 256-7. The line is in any
case clumsily expressed; we should expect βούλονται, and the lack of an
expressed subject to μεμνῆσθαι is awkward. Ἀ γνώμη of some later
rhapsodist' (Merry).

354-9. On the use of a topographical introduction to mark a new phase in
the narrative see Hoekstra on xiii 96. Pharos, the site of the great
lighthouse of Alexandria (Ras-el-Tin), in fact lies less than a mile from the
coast; the discrepancy (even worse at 483) was most commonly explained
in antiquity by the (geologically quite unacceptable) hypothesis that the
coastline had advanced as a result of alluvium brought down by the river:
cf. Str. 30, 37, Plin. *HN* ii 201, Sen. *Quaest.Nat.* vi 26; see further
A. Calderini, *Dizionario dei nomi geografici e topografici dell'Egitto Greco-Romano*
(Cairo, 1935), i 156 ff., *RE* xix 1857 ff. (Kees). It has also been suggested
that the poet gave the distance not from the nearest point on the coast but
from Naucratis (cf. Arist. fr. 169 R.), or from the Bolbitinic mouth of the
Nile, where the Milesians had their trading post before the foundation of

---

[5] Allen's apparatus wrongly says that Zenodotus omitted it.

Naucratis; but this approach is artificial and unconvincing. The poet appears to have borrowed an Egyptian toponym for the desert island which his story required without regard to geographical reality. Pharos looks like a Greek rendering of an authentic Egyptian place-name; it could be taken to represent *Pr-Ḥr*, 'House of Horus', a common Egyptian toponym (cf. H. Gauthier, *Dict. des noms géographiques* ii (Cairo, 1925), 112–16); the cult of Horus was prominent in the Western Delta. Another, but less likely, possibility is *Pr-Rᶜ*, 'House of Re' (cf. Gauthier ii 100–1).[6]

354. ἔπειτα: logical, not temporal; cf. ix 116.

357. ἤνυσεν: 'gnomic' aor., used of something generally or customarily true, irrespective of time; see further Monro, *Homeric Dialect*, 67 § 78 (2), Chantraine, *Grammaire*, ii 185 § 273.

358–9. εὔορμος: 'a good place to put in to land', cf. ix 136; the epithet should not be rendered 'with a good anchoring-place', as the ships are not moored, but drawn up on the beach(426 ff.).   ἀπὸ ... βάλλουσιν: 'they launch, push off'; an unusual use of βάλλω; the subject is left unexpressed.   μέλαν ὕδωρ: water from deep places where the light cannot reach.

361. ἁλιαέες: 'blowing seawards'.

363. ἠΐα: see ii 289 n.

365–6. On Proteus see 385 n. The daughter who acts against her father is a common *Märchen*-motif: see Thompson, *Motif Index*, G 530. 2. We know nothing about Eidothea apart from what we are told here, and she may well be the poet's invention. The meaning of her name, not otherwise attested, is not clear, but Risch's suggestion that it is to be understood as a reversal of θεοειδής seems more plausible than other explanations which take it to reflect a characteristic of her father's (cf. i 113 n.), either 'the knowing goddess' (> εἰδυῖα) or 'the goddess of many forms' (> εἶδος); see further *LfgrE*. Aeschylus in his *Proteus* (fr. 5 Mette) called her Eido (cf. E. *Hel.* 11). In Zenodotus' text she was Eurynome; cf. *Il.* xviii 398, Hes. *Th.* 358 (with M. L. West's n.). Her role is somewhat similar to that of Leukothea (v 334 ff.); particularly noteworthy is the absence of any apparent motive for the assistance which the two goddesses provide.

367. μ': i.e. μοι; for the elision of the diphthong cf. xxiii 21, *Il.* vi 165, x 544, xiii 481, xvii 100.   ἔρροντι: ἔρρω in Homer always has connotations of misery.

368. Similarly at xii 331–2. Odysseus' men are reduced to fishing when their supplies run out. Fish is absent from the normal heroic diet, as Plato observed (*R.* 404 bc): οἶσθα γὰρ ὅτι ἐπὶ στρατιᾶς ἐν ταῖς τῶν ἡρώων ἑστιάσεσιν οὔτε ἰχθύσιν αὐτοὺς ἑστιᾷ [sc. Ὅμηρος], καὶ ταῦτα ἐπὶ θαλάττῃ ἐν Ἑλλησπόντῳ ὄντας, οὔτε ἐφθοῖς κρέασιν ἀλλὰ μόνον ὀπτοῖς. But Odysseus includes fish in his list of the blessings resulting from the rule of a just king (xix 108 ff.), and fishing is mentioned in many similes (v 432 ff., x 124, xii 251 ff., xxii 383 ff., *Il.* v 487, xxiv 80 ff.). As often, the similes reflect the poet's own world and ignore the conventions normal in describing the heroic way of life, where the regular consumption of great quantities of

---

[6] I am indebted to Professor J. Gwyn Griffiths for this information.

roast meat represents what the poet and his audience regarded as an ideal diet, not a genuine recollection of the Mycenaean age; in fact archaeological evidence (the remains of fish and fishing tackle) establishes that fish was an important element in Mycenaean diet; see further H.-G. Buchholz–G. Jöhrens–I. Maull, *Archaeologia* J, 131–80.

370. ἔπος φάτο φώνησέν τε: not a regular Homeric formula, but cf. *h.Cer.* 53; we might have expected προσηύδα δῖα θεάων (cf. x 400, 455). Zenodotus read ἥ δέ μοι ἀντομένη (presumably ἔπεα πτερόεντα προσηύδα or πτερόεντ' ἀγόρευεν).

371. Saving advice, as often, is preceded by insulting sarcasm; cf. xx 33 ff., *Il.* v 800 ff., xv 244 ff. νήπιος and χαλίφρων are similarly combined at xix 530.

372. μεθιεῖς: a pres. is clearly intended, but orthography and accentuation are uncertain; see Monro, *Homeric Dialect*, 18 ff. § 18, Chantraine, *Grammaire*, i 298–9 § 138.

373–4. Cf. 466–7.

376. It is not explained how Menelaus recognizes Eidothea as a goddess (or how he knows her name), but her authoritative tone and her presence in circumstances where no mortal girl was to be expected make this a reasonable inference. It tends to be characteristic of Homeric style to account for every detail, but this lack of explanation is undeniably effective here.   περ: emphasizes the universality of the relative.

377–8. μέλλω ... ἀλιτέσθαι: 'I must have offended the gods', cf. 94 μέλλετ' ἀκονέμεν.

379–81. = 468–70. Homer's gods are omniscient in a rather limited sense: if they turn their minds to a question they know the answer to it. Thus Poseidon knows that Odysseus will be safe once he has reached Scheria (v 288–9) and can predict with confidence that twins will be born to Tyro (xi 248 ff.). But they can still be deceived or eluded when they are off guard: Menelaus is able to trick Proteus (452 ff.); the other Olympians can come to Odysseus' aid in Poseidon's absence (i 19 ff., v 286–7); the Sun does not immediately realize, but has to be told, that Odysseus' companions have eaten his cattle (xii 374 ff.). Similarly, in the *Iliad*, Hera distracts the attention of Zeus so that Poseidon can help the Greeks (xiv 153 ff.) and sends Iris with a message to Achilles κρύβδα Διὸς ἄλλων τε θεῶν (xviii 166 ff.).

380. μ' ... ἔδησε κελεύθου: for the metaphor cf. v 383, x 20, xiv 61; for the construction cf. i 195 τόν γε ... βλάπτουσι κελεύθου.

381. νόστον: direct obj. of εἰπέ (379).

384 ff. The Old Man of the Sea is known under various names in different places. This is Proteus' first appearance in Greek literature. His name has been connected with his gift of prophecy, *fatidicus*, cf. πρωτόν, πέπρωται (see further Schulze, *Quaestiones*, 22 n. 3), though the poet's audience would probably have derived it from πρῶτος. νημερτής is partially explained by 385–6, though Proteus' knowledge extends beyond marine affairs; cf. Hesiod's account of Nereus, likewise νημερτής (*Th.* 233–6), and on prophetic water-spirits in general see Thompson, *Motif Index*, F 420, 4.

10. But Proteus will not give up his knowledge without a struggle, and has

the advantage of a capacity for self-transformation for which, though Greek legend knew of other shape-shifters, he was to become proverbial.

His Egyptian connection may well have been an innovation by the poet of the *Odyssey*. In later legend we also find him linked with Chalcidice (so Lyc. 115 ff., Call. *Victoria Berenices* (*Suppl. Hell.* 254), 5–6 εἰς Ἑλένη[ς νησῖδ]α καὶ εἰς Παλληνέα μά[ντιν,] ποιμένα [φωκάων], Verg. *G.* iv 390–1, schol. A.R. i 598, Apollod. ii 5. 9), and the persistence of this tradition, despite the *Odyssey*'s authority, strongly suggests that Proteus was originally associated with the north Aegean and relocated to serve the poet's interest in Egypt. Of course, a sea-god may be deemed to be equally at home on any coast, but Αἰγύπτιος suggests that the poet wanted to stress a particularly close link with Egypt. In Hdt. (ii 112–16) Proteus is no longer a god but a Memphite pharaoh, and it has been argued that this euhemerization was suggested by the resemblance to an Egyptian royal title *prouti*; possibly this similarity had already influenced the poet of the *Odyssey*.

The episode has much in common with Odysseus' consultation of Tiresias in xi; see further Heubeck on x 539–40, P. Plass, 'Menelaus and Proteus', *CJ* lxv (1969), 104 ff. We notice that both heroes are not only told how to get home but also how their lives will end. In fact, despite such phrases as ὁδὸν καὶ μέτρα κελεύθου (iv 389 = x 539), νόστον θ', ὡς ἐπὶ πόντον ἐλεύσεαι ἰχθυόεντα (iv 390, 424 = x 540, cf. 470), Menelaus does not want advice on his route, but favourable winds. Perhaps this betrays the use of Odysseus' consultation of Tiresias as the model for this episode; but it may have been a commoner theme. What principally interested the poet was clearly the opportunity to recount various *nostoi*.

This episode has slight similarities to the Egyptian *Story of the Shipwrecked Sailor* (see M. Lichtheim, *Ancient Egyptian Literature*, i (Berkeley–Los Angeles–London, 1973), 211 ff.), in which the hero, marooned on an uninhabited island, is greatly helped by a prophetic serpent; there too the incident formed part of a *Rahmenerzählung*. But I doubt if these resemblances are as significant as has sometimes been supposed.

See further Herter, *RE* xxiii 940 ff. (s.v. Proteus), K. O'Nolan, 'The Proteus legend', *Hermes* lxxxviii (1960), 1–19.

Vergil's use of this episode (*G.* iv 387 ff.) well illustrates some of the characteristic features of his approach to Homeric material.

385–6. ἀθάνατος: not otiose; Proteus is a lesser supernatural being, whose immortality might not be immediately assumed; cf. xii 302 ἀθανάτη ... Κίρκη. **ὅς τε ... οἶδε:** cf. i 52–3 (of Atlas). **ὑποδμώς:** hapax in Homer; 'servant', not 'under-servant'; cf. ὑποδρηστήρ (xv 330), ὑφηνίοχος (*Il.* vi 19), ἐπιβουκόλος (iii 422). δμώς is properly 'slave', but we should not press too hard the implications for Proteus' juridical status.

387. Eidothea's caution is the more understandable in view of Proteus' capacity for self-transformation, but is probably not intended to imply more than the uncertainty of paternity in general; cf. i 215–16.

388–9. The construction is not quite clear: either εἴ πως introduces a wish and ὅς κεν a purpose clause or εἴ πως is a conditional protasis and ὅς, which introduces the apodosis, has demonstrative force. **λελαβέσθαι:** reduplicated aor., by analogy with λελαθέσθαι, 'un hapax qui semble expressif au lieu de λαβέσθαι' (Chantraine); cf. Chantraine, *Grammaire*, i 395–6 § 189, Monro, *Homeric Dialect*, 39 § 36, Risch, *Wortbildung*, 243.

389–90. = x 539–40. **μέτρα κελεύθου:** the meaning is not quite clear: 'the length of the way' (in days, presumably) or 'the length of the various stages', implying details of stopping-places?

393. ὁδόν: cognate acc. after οἰχομένοιο; cf. ὁδὸν ἐλθεῖν (iii 316, *Il.* i 151), ἰέναι ὁδόν (xvii 426).

395. φράζευ: 'explain, suggest'.

399. Omitted by P. 5 (*P.Oxy.* 775, Pack² 1050; 3rd cent. AD) and by a few of the medieval MSS; surely a late interpolation. Elsewhere after the formula τοιγάρ ... ἀγορεύσω no connecting particle is used.

400. Cf. *Il.* viii 68. **δ':** used, as often, to mark the answer to a second question (cf. e.g. *Il.* iii 229). **ἀμφιβεβήκῃ:** the subj. is given by one MS while the rest have ἀμφιβεβήκει. The plpf. indic. is appropriate where the line occurs in the *Iliad*, but not here, and most editors read ἀμφιβεβήκῃ; but ἦμος is not used elsewhere in Homer with the subj. and the absence of ἄν is awkward. It is perhaps simplest to suppose that the poet adopted a striking formula for 'midday' without sufficient regard to the tense; possibly he thought of ἀμφιβεβήκει as a pres. from a new form in -ω: cf. κεκλήγοντες (*Il.* xii 125 etc.), implying κεκλήγω, γεγωνέμεν (*Il.* viii 223), ἐγέγωνεν (*Il.* xiv 469), implying γεγώνω.

402. Cf. *Il.* vii 63–4 οἵη δὲ Ζεφύροιο ἐχεύατο πόντον ἔπι φρὶξ | ὀρνυμένοιο νέον, μελάνει δέ τε πόντος ὑπ' αὐτῆς.

403. σπέσσι: on the declension of σπέος see i 15 n.

404. φῶκαι: only one species of seal occurs in Mediterranean waters, the Mediterranean monk seal, *Stenorhynchus albiventer*, now an endangered species, found as far south as C. Blanc in West Africa. The poet's emphasis on their smell (406, 441 ff.) suggests he found them less attractive than we do; cf. also xv 480. **νέποδες:** variously interpreted in antiquity (cf. LSJ); the most plausible explanation, associated with Aristophanes, is 'descendants, children', cf. Latin *nepotes*; see further Wackernagel, *Vorlesungen zur Syntax*, ii 252, Frisk, *GEW*, Chantraine, *Dictionnaire*. **ἁλοσύδνης:** at *Il.* xx 207 an epithet of Thetis, but here used substantivally as a designation of another sea-goddess; its meaning and etymology were very likely as obscure to the poet as they are to us, but he no doubt associated it with ἅλς, ἅλιος; see further Frisk, *GEW*, Chantraine, *Dictionnaire*, *LfgrE*. J. U. Powell (*CQ* xv (1929), 125), comparing Aeschylus' description of fishes as ἀναύδων ... παίδων τᾶς ἀμιάντου (*Pers.* 577–8) suggested that the curious phrase marked the fact that seals are salt-water creatures in a different sense from fishes.

406. For the seal's strong smell cf. Ar. *V.* 1035. **πικρόν:** may be taken either as an adj. of two terminations agreeing with ὀδμήν (cf. ὀλοώτατος ὀδμή 442) or as an adv. with ἀποπνείουσαι.

408. κρίνασθαι: infin. for imperat., as often. Eidothea does not explain her plan very clearly.

410. ὀλοφώϊα: cf. x 289 ὀλοφώϊα δήνεα Κίρκης; its derivation is uncertain: later poets associated it with ὄλλυμι and used it to mean 'destructive', but in Homer it seems to be 'deceptive, tricky'.

411. ἔπεισιν: 'will go over them, go his rounds among them', cf. 451 ἐπῴχετο.

412. πεμπάσσεται: aor. subj.

413. λέξεται: from λέχομαι.

417. πειρήσεται: understand ἀλύξαι. The theme of successive transformations is found elsewhere in early Greek epic: cf. *Cypr.* fr. vii Allen (Nemesis), Hes. fr. 33 (Periclymenus), fr. 43 (Mestra). This capacity is particularly appropriate to a water-spirit; we may compare the stories of Nereus and Achelous wrestling with Heracles. See further M. Detienne and J. P. Vernant, *Les Ruses d'intelligence: La Mètis des grecs* (Paris, 1974), 28–9, 109 ff. (= *Cunning Intelligence in Greek Culture and Society* (Hassocks, Sussex, 1978), 20–1, 112 ff.), Thompson, *Motif Index*, D 610 ff.

418. ἑρπετά: 'moving things'; the specific sense 'reptiles' is a later development.

420. αὐτός: either 'in his own shape', explained by 421, or 'of his own accord'.

422. καί introduces the apodosis. **σχέσθαι ... βίης:** 'cease your violence'.

425–80. Menelaus and his men seize Proteus and induce him to speak; he advises Menelaus to return to Egypt and there atone for his failure to sacrifice before his homeward voyage.

425–31. Cf. 570–6.

429. ἀμβροσίη: the epithet is often applied to night, but its exact significance is not clear. It is usually supposed that night is called divine because it is a divine gift, bringing sleep and an end to the day's labours. But a more precise meaning is suggested by P. Thieme (*Ambrosia*, Ber. Akad. Leipzig, 98. 5 (Berlin, 1952), 15 ff. (= R. Schmitt (ed.), *Indogermanische Dichtersprache* (Darmstadt, 1968), 113 ff.), who interprets ἀμβρόσιος as 'Lebenskraft enthaltend', 'containing life-force, vital power'; night may thus be so described because it brings sleep which restores and refreshes.

430. ἐπὶ ῥηγμῖνι: 'at the sea's edge'.

431. See ii 1 n.

432. Omitted by many MSS; surely a late interpolation.

434. Odysseus similarly emphasizes the reliability of those who were to assist him in his assault on Polyphemus (ix 334–5) **ἰθύν:** no other case of this archaic noun, found only in epic, is attested; see further Frisk, *GEW*, Chantraine, *Dictionnaire*.

435. ὑποδῦσα: 'having plunged into', taking up ὑπὸ πόντον ἐδύσετο (425); but we expect the ptcp. to refer to an action more closely linked with the main vb., and Düntzer's conjecture ἀναδῦσα, 'emerging from', is very attractive (cf. *Il.* i 496). **εὐρέα:** this acc. sg. occurs in six places in Homer, always in connection with the sea (cf. xxiv 118, *Il.* vi 291, ix 72, xviii 140, xxi 125). The common formula εὐρέϊ πόντῳ evidently produced εὐρέα πόντον by analogy, perhaps encouraged by εὐρέα νῶτα θαλάσσης; see further Chantraine, *Grammaire*, i 97 § 42, Hoekstra, *Modifications*, 112.

436–7. Eidothea's trick resembles Odysseus' ruse for escape from the Cyclops' cave (cf. ix 424 ff.); for the motif of disguise as an animal see Thompson, *Motif Index*, K 1823.

441–2. Cf. 406 n. The stench of a newly flayed sealskin under a hot sun would be quite appalling; smells are seldom mentioned in heroic epic, and this unusual touch of realism makes the whole fantastic scene more vivid and credible. **ἁλιοτρεφέων:** the only example of a cpd. with ἁλιο- for ἁλι-; see further Risch, *Wortbildung*, 195. **ὀλοώτατος:** for the two-termination superlative cf. x 279 (v.l.), xii 11 (v.l.), *h.Cer.* 157, Hes. *Th.* 408, Pi. fr. 152 Snell = 139 Bowra; the few instances of two-termination comparatives and superlatives in prose are confined to words where the positive is a cpd. and has only two terminations. Its use here is probably to be explained by a tendency to avoid shortening η and ω at the end of the fifth foot; see further A. Platt, *CR* xxxv (1921), 142. On the general use of masc. forms of adjectives with fem. nouns see K. Witte, *Glotta* iii (1912), 106 ff., Shipp, *Studies*, 72 ff.

443. This type of question-comment is very unusual in Homer. **εἰναλίῳ:** see Hainsworth on v 67.

444. As often, the more important point is put first, though later in time; see iii 467 n.

445. **ἀμβροσίην:** cf. 429 n.; the fem. adj. is used substantivally. Ambrosia, which corresponds etymologically to the *amr̥ta* drunk by the gods of Indian mythology, is the food of the gods (cf. v 93 (with Hainsworth's n.), Hes. *Th.* 640; fodder for their horses, *Il.* v 777), who occasionally allow men to eat it (e.g. v 199, *Il.* xix 347 ff.); it is also used as soap at *Il.* xiv 170 and as an unguent at *Il.* xvi 670 ff., xix 38–9, xxiii 186–7, *h.Cer.* 237. In general it seems to be regarded as a divine, age-retarding, counterpart of olive-oil or animal grease; its deodorant properties are due to the fragrance characteristic of the gods and their possessions (e.g. *h.Cer.* 275 ff., Thgn. 8 ff., [A.] *Pr.* 115 ff.). See further *LfgrE*, Onians, *Origins*, 292 ff., E. Lohmeyer, *Vom göttlichen Wohlgeruch*, SHAW 1919, 9, 12 ff., Clay, *Wrath*, 145 ff.

447. **ἠοίην:** like ἀμβροσίη a fem adj. used substantivally. **τετληότι θυμῷ:** a common Odyssean formula, not found in the *Iliad*.

451. **λέκτο:** aor. med. of λέγω 'count, reckon', cf. 452; in 453 from λέχομαι, 'lie down'. The word-play is clearly deliberate: cf. i 62 n.

454. **δὲ ἰάχοντες:** there are 17 examples in Homer of a short final vowel lengthened before ἰάχω, reflecting earlier *ϝιϝάχω: see further Chantraine, *Grammaire*, i 139–40 § 54.

456. **ἠϋγένειος:** applied in Homer only to lions; apparently modelled on ἠΰκομος, the only other Homeric compound in ἠϋ- and presumably expressing a similar idea, 'with a splendid mane' (rather than 'well-bearded', which would be more logical in view of its apparent connection with γένειον); the alternative explanation, that it is a lengthened form of εὐγενής, seems much less likely.

457. πάρδαλις: an Oriental loan-word of unknown origin: cf. Frisk, *GEW*, Chantraine, *Dictionnaire*. The Greeks and Romans confused leopards and panthers, and the various words for them are treated as synonyms; we cannot tell which is meant here. They appear in the similes of the *Iliad* (xiii 103, xvii 20, xxi 573) and in Semonides (fr. 14 West); they were still to be found in Caria in Cicero's time (*ad fam.* ii 11. 2; viii 4. 5, 9. 3). πάρδαλις was the spelling preferred by Aristarchus; the grammarian Apion distinguished between πόρδαλις, the male, and πάρδαλις, the female, but this is surely groundless pedantry; πόρδαλις may well be an Atticism: cf. Shipp, *Studies*, 18.

458. This line has attracted some suspicion, primarily because the sense seems to require an aor. rather than the impf. γίγνετο; in any case, Proteus' metamorphosis into a tree, instead of the fire which Eidothea had predicted (418), appears a tactical error, a mere display of transformational virtuosity presenting no problem to his captors. I suspect that the poet took it over ready-made as a stock element in the description of a shape-shifter; such imprecision is a common enough feature of oral style. (For a defence on rather different lines see W. Ludwig, *Hermes* lxxxix (1961), 189–90).

459. Cf. 419.

460. Proteus has now exhausted his range of transformations.   **ἀνίαζ':** intrans., 'grew tired', cf. 598.   **ὀλοφώϊα:** see 410 n.

462. θεῶν: to be taken with τίς, not with βουλάς. Proteus, who does not need to be told who Menelaus is, presumably knows the answer.

466–7. Cf. 373–4.

468–70. Cf. 379–81.

472. Cf. 352. ἀλλὰ μάλ' perhaps expresses a certain impatience; Proteus does not waste time answering the question which Menelaus actually asked, but deals immediately with what would have been his next question.

473. The emphasis falls on ῥέξας, on which ὄφρα κτλ. depend.

477. Αἰγύπτοιο: in the *Odyssey* the name of both land and river, here evidently the latter (cf. 581, xiv 258 = xvii 427, cf. *h.Bacch.* 9); we may see in the use of the same term for both a reflection of Egypt's dependence on the Nile for its existence. Νεῖλος, which heads Hesiod's list of the world's great rivers (*Th.* 338), does not occur in Homer;[7] this was regarded in antiquity as evidence that Hesiod was later than Homer, but the argument is scarcely watertight.   **διιπετέος:** found only in this formula in Homer (cf. vii 284, *Il.* xvi 174, xvii 263, xxi 268, 326), and evidently an archaism. The most popular of the various explanations canvassed in antiquity, 'fallen from Zeus', i.e. 'rain-fed', is generally preferred by modern scholars, though the ablatival-genitive use of the first part of the cpd. is surprising and the first non-formulaic instance, *h.Ven.* 4 οἰωνούς τε διιπετέας, seems to link the second element with πέτομαι, not with πίπτω. It is doubtful

---

[7] The name was long mysterious, but has recently been convincingly explained as an attempt to render an Egyptian term for the branches of the river traversing the Delta: see further H. Goedicke, *AJPh* c (1979), 69–72, H. S. Smith, in J. Ruffle, G. A. Gaballa, and K. A. Kitchin (eds.), *Glimpses of Ancient Egypt: Studies in Honour of H. W. Fairman* (Warminster, 1979), 163–4.

whether διαιπετής, which Alcman uses to mean 'falling through' or 'flying through' (3. 67), should be regarded as another form of the same adj., as some scholars have argued; but its concurrence may well have contributed to a shift in the meaning of διιπετής. A certain Zenodorus is said to have read διειπετέος, though his reasons are unknown; he may merely have intended to mark the metrical lengthening of the second syllable. See further Hainsworth on vii 284, *LfgrE*.

481–586. Menelaus asks how the other Greeks fared after leaving Troy. Proteus tells him what has happened to Ajax, Agamemnon, and Odysseus, and prophesies Menelaus' eventual translation to Elysium. Menelaus follows Proteus' instructions and gets safely home.

481. Menelaus' distress seems disproportionate.

486. Menelaus now acts on his own initiative.

489. ἀδευκέϊ: this Odyssean epithet occurs in only two other places, being applied also to φῆμις (vi 273) and πότμος (x 245); ancient scholars explained it as 'cruel', or 'unexpected', or 'concealed, mysterious', but these interpretations seem to be merely guesses; see further Hainsworth on vi 273, *LfgrE*.

490. = i 238, xiv 368. The question seems to be framed with Agamemnon's fate in mind, and though it is obviously unrealistic that Menelaus should think murder at the hands of one's kin almost as likely as shipwreck, it would not be uncharacteristic for the poet thus to anticipate subsequent developments; for a trenchant attack on its authenticity see Kirchhoff, *Odyssee*, 189.

494. ἄκλαυτος: 'free from tears'; pass. in sense at xi 54, 72, *Il.* xxii 386. ἀπευθής (iii 88, 184) and ἀπήμων (487, *Il.* xiv 164) are similarly used in both act. and pass. senses.

495 ff. Proteus now continues and supplements Nestor's narrative of the *nostoi* (iii 132 ff., 254 ff.).

496. χαλκοχιτώνων: see i 286 n.

498. Cf. 552. The line was omitted by Zenodotus, though, as is pointed out in the scholia, it is presupposed by Menelaus' question at 551; its omission must have been accidental, unless there were further differences in Zenodotus' text either here or at 551 ff.

499. The poet takes it for granted that we shall realize that this is the lesser Ajax, son of Oileus and leader of the Locrians, whose sacrilegious attempt to rape Cassandra brought upon the Greeks the wrath of Athena (cf. i 325–7 n.). **μέν:** answered by δέ in 512.

500–1. Γυρῆσιν ... πέτρησιν: located by ancient scholars near Myconos, which claimed one of the reputed graves of Ajax (schol., Eust., Hsch. s.v. Γυρῆσι πέτρησιν). On the south side of Tenos, the island a little north of Delos, was a cliff or mountain called Γύρας (Hsch. s.v. Γύρας); probably a rock or reef in the channel between the two islands was believed to have broken off from it and was identified as Ajax's rock; see further F. H. Sandbach, *CR* lvi (1942), 63 ff. Ajax thus took a different route from Nestor and Menelaus, the longer but more sheltered course through the

Cyclades; cf. iii 169 n. Later tradition placed his death off C. Caphereus, the south-east point of Euboea, where Nauplius engineered his shipwreck in revenge for his son Palamedes' death (E. *Tr.* 88 ff., Verg. *A.* xi 259–60); see further Bethe, *Odyssee*, 278 ff.

503. ἀάσθη: acted under the influence of ἄτη; see 261 n. Excessive self-confidence is similarly punished at viii 224 ff., *Il.* ii 594 ff., xxiv 605 ff.; the fate of the suitors points the same moral.

505. μεγάλ' ... αὐδήσαντος: 'his loud boast'.

509. τῷ: with ἐφεζόμενος.

510. κατὰ πόντον: 'over the sea'; some distance seems to be implied.

511. The line was evidently not well attested in antiquity. According to the scholia ἐν οὐδεμιᾷ ἐφέρετο: this presumably represents a précis of a note which listed editions from which 511 was absent, and should not be taken too literally (cf. the summary use of πᾶσαι in the scholia on e.g. *Il.* i 585, 598, where fuller versions of the same note give a list of names; see further Ludwich, *AHT* i, 118 ff.). The scholiast continues καὶ λίαν γάρ ἐστιν εὐτελής· θαυμάσαιμεν δ' ἂν πῶς παρέλαθε τὸν Ἀρίσταρχον ὀβελίσαι αὐτόν, but clearly it must be regarded as doubtful whether Aristarchus knew the line at all. Lines which round off an episode by an explicit statement of death are a fairly common type of interpolation; cf. *Il.* v 42, viii 315, xv 578, all of which are omitted by some manuscripts and were almost certainly added after Aristarchus. However, such lines are normally borrowed from elsewhere in Homer, while 511 appears to have been composed specially; for the first half cf. i 166, xiv 137, xix 85, for the second cf. xi 98.

514–20. After 513 we do not expect Agamemnon to face further perils by sea, and the route here described is quite extraordinary; though some oddities might be explained by the vagueness about Peloponnesian topography observable elsewhere in the poem, considerable difficulties remain, and critics have with good reason suspected interpolation and/or accidental dislocation. If Agamemnon was making for the Argolid, we should not expect him to be near C. Malea, the southernmost tip of the Peloponnese (cf. iii 287 n.); there is no suggestion that this is an unplanned change of route forced on him by the storm which wrecked Ajax. Moreover, elsewhere in the *Odyssey* ships driven off course at C. Malea are blown south or south-west (iii 287 ff., ix 80 ff., xix 187 ff.), and this would be natural here, since Agamemnon would have needed a north or north-east wind to get there from Troy. But if Aegisthus' estate is in the Argolid, as the rest of the narrative implies, Agamemnon would need to be blown northwards. One ancient scholar, Andron (*FGrH* 10 F 11), put Aegisthus' home on Cythera, presumably on the strength of this passage; but τότ' ἔναιε is awkward if the poet in fact imagined him to be far away at Mycenae. Bothe, by transposing 517–18 to follow 520, avoided this difficulty, but καὶ κεῖθεν (519) seems to require a more specific localization than πόντον ἐπ' ἰχθυόεντα. That Agamemnon was almost delivered into Aegisthus' hands once, but then got safely away, introduces a further element of suspense into the saga of his homecoming, but surely needs further development to be properly effective, and it mars the antithesis between the many sufferings experienced by Odysseus on his protracted homeward journey and Agamemnon's swift and uneventful voyage (cf. iii 232–5). I believe the passage must be an interpolation, based on a version of Agamemnon's homecoming otherwise unknown to us; the reference to C. Malea may imply that its composer envisaged Agamemnon ruling jointly with Menelaus at Sparta, anticipating the double kingship of historical times, but may merely be the result of carelessness, C. Malea being the regular place for ships to be blown off course. See further K. Kunst, 'Die Schuld der Klytaimnestra', *WSt* xliv (1924/5), 18 ff., v. d. Mühll, *Odyssee*, 708, Merkelbach, *Untersuchungen*, 47 ff., Eisenberger, *Studien*, 82 n. 18.

517. ἀγροῦ ἐπ' ἐσχατίην: land beyond the limit of agriculture; for an interesting discussion of this formula see J. M. Redfield, *Nature and Culture in the* Iliad (Chicago–London, 1975), 189 ff.

522. Cf. v 463, xiii 354.

525. ὑπό: with ἔσχετο, 'promised'.

526. χρυσοῦ δοιὰ τάλαντα: see 129 n. **εἰς ἐνιαυτόν:** Calchas had prophesied that Troy would fall in the tenth year of the expedition (*Il.* ii 329), and the poet may have imagined Aegisthus appointing his watchman at the beginning of that year. The detail is picked up by Aeschylus, *Ag.* 2 φρουρᾶς ἐτείας μῆκος. **ἐνιαυτόν:** see i 16 n.

527. The subject of both verbs is Agamemnon. The second hemistich recalls the common Iliadic formula μνήσασθε δὲ θούριδος ἀλκῆς (*Il.* vi 112, viii 174, etc.); it reflects the notion that attack is the best method of defence.

529 ff. In Proteus' account of Agamemnon's murder there is no mention of Clytaemestra, though Agamemnon's ghost recalls her as Aegisthus' callous accomplice (xi 409 ff., xxiv 97) and this is Menelaus' view (iv 92).

531. ἑτέρωθι: sc. of the palace; the incident takes place ἐν μεγάροισιν (537).

532. καλέων: to invite him to the feast.

534. ἀνήγαγε: 'brought him up from the shore'.

535. = xi 411. **τε:** to be taken closely with ὥς; the particle has a generalizing force, expressing the customary nature of the action involved; see further Denniston, *Particles*, 533, Ruijgh, τε épique, 571–2, 617–18. **κατέκτανε:** gnomic aor.; see 357 n.

537. We infer from the first hemistich that Agamemnon's comrades put up a determined resistance, which is inconsistent with xi 412–13, where Agamemnon's ghost says that they were butchered like swine; the much greater complicity of Clytaemestra in xi suggests some fluidity in the poet's conception of the story. Here the implication that no human witness survived (except Aegisthus himself) enhances the value of Proteus' information. (N. E. Crosby's conjecture, δώματ' ἐς for οὐδέ τις (*CPh* xviii (1923), 72–3) has often been cited with approval, but presupposes a type of mechanical copying error unlikely to have had much effect on the transmission of Homer).

538–41. Cf. x 496–9. We may compare Plato's animadversions on the Homeric heroes' lack of self-control (*R.* 388 a).

544. οὐκ ... δήομεν: 'we shall achieve nothing by it'; cf. x 202. For the use of the 1st pers. pl. where the 2nd pers. would be more logical cf. 138; commentators generally interpret it as expressing sympathy, but here the tone is surely ironic and slightly condescending.

546–7. ἤ κεν Ὀρέστης | κτεῖνεν: 'or Orestes must, will, have killed him'; κεν and the aor. indic. are used almost like a fut. pf., to express an act which will probably have taken place: a strange use; cf. Monro, *Homeric Dialect*, 294–5 § 324, Chantraine, *Grammaire*, ii 227, § 334. Bekker conjectured καί for κεν, but the aor. alone would be clumsy.   **σὺ ... ἀντιβολήσαις:** it might seem an unlikely coincidence that Menelaus should arrive home on the day of the funeral, but this is in fact what happened (iii 309).

548–9. Menelaus is cheered by the prospect of vengeance; Aegisthus will not escape scot-free.

552. Cf. 498.

553. According to the scholia ἐν ἁπάσαις ἠθετεῖτο. Proteus made it quite clear at 498 that the third leader was not dead but marooned. The line appears to result from a craving for antithesis, whether the poet's or another's.

555 ff. The whole construction of this episode seems designed to lead up to an account of Odysseus' adventures as the climax of Proteus' exposition, but we have to make do with this brief survey of the hero's present situation, because the poet chose to let Odysseus tell his own story; as often, the anticipated effect is postponed. We also expect Proteus, since he is a prophet, to predict Odysseus' imminent return, and it is highly probable that this formed part of the episode as originally conceived; such a prediction would justify Menelaus' confident forecast of the suitors' destruction (340) and the apparently unreasonable optimism which Telemachus displays at xv 156 ff.; see further Bethe, *Odyssee*, 33 ff., Merkelbach, *Untersuchungen*, 51–2.

556. τὸν ἴδον: Bentley's deletion of δ', to allow its force to the original initial digamma of ἴδον, is supported by our earliest witness, a papyrus of the late first or early second century (*PSI* inv. CNR 66–7; see M. Manfredi, *Papiri dell'Odissea* (Florence, 1979), 19 ff., no. 5).

557–60. = v 14–17, xvii 143–6. Proteus' account of Odysseus' predicament exactly corresponds to the latter's situation when first we meet him.

557. μεγάροισι: μέγαρον used of a cave (cf. i 15, v 57 ff.) should be noted; the connotations of the term were evidently not very precise. On Calypso see i 14 n.

559–60. Cf. v 141–2.   **ἐπήρετμοι:** see ii 403 n.

561 ff. Proteus now volunteers some information unasked; similarly Tiresias, who knows without being told that Odysseus has come to consult him about his voyage home, tells him much about subsequent developments (xi 100 ff.). The transition is very abrupt.

562. Ἄργει: not 'the city of Argos', but the surrounding region, perhaps to be understood as the Peloponnese as a whole; see i 344 n.

563 ff. Menelaus will not die, but will be translated to Elysium. His good fortune, the more striking by contrast with his brother's horrible death, does not depend on any merits of his own, but on his status, unique for a mortal, as Zeus' son-in-law; Helen will of course accompany him (cf. Isoc. *Helen* 62, Apollod. *Epit.* vi 30). Elysium is in many ways like Olympus: cf. vi 43 ff.; we may also compare the description of Alcinous' garden (vii 117 ff.) and of the island where Eumaeus was born (xv 403 ff.). The name itself does not reappear until Apollonius Rhodius (iv 811), but the same conception of a paradise reserved for a privileged few appears in Hesiod's account of the νῆσοι μακάρων (*Op.* 167 ff.): τοῖς δὲ δίχ' ἀνθρώπων βίοτον καὶ ἤθε' ὀπάσσας | Ζεὺς Κρονίδης κατένασσε πατὴρ εἰς πείρατα γαίης. | καὶ τοὶ μὲν ναίουσιν ἀκηδέα θυμὸν ἔχοντες | ἐν μακάρων νήσοισι παρ' Ὠκεανὸν βαθυδίνην, | ὄλβιοι ἥρωες, τοῖσιν μελιηδέα καρπὸν | τρὶς ἔτεος θάλλοντα φέρει ζείδωρος ἄρουρα. Originally νῆσοι μακάρων must have meant 'Isles of the gods', in accordance with the normal sense of μάκαρες in early epic, and we should compare the myth of the gods' garden in the far west, where Zeus lay with Hera at their marriage and to which Heracles went to get the golden apples of the Hesperides (see further Barrett on E. *Hipp.* 742-51). Later descriptions of the Isles of the Blessed (e.g. Pi. *O.* ii 68 ff.) combine the material offered by Homer and Hesiod with later ideas; the qualifications for admission become increasingly ethical, and cannot be used as independent evidence for the original conception. Menelaus' prospects are clearly exceptional; we may wonder who else, besides Rhadamanthys, the poet imagined in Elysium. The great heroes of the Trojan War, Agamemnon, Ajax, and Achilles (despite his goddess mother) are in Hades (xi 387 ff., xxiv 15 ff.), and when Zeus deplores the fate that dooms his beloved son Sarpedon to die at Troy (*Il.* xvi 433 ff., 490 ff.), there is no consoling suggestion of a happier afterlife. Hesiod's paradise is less exclusive, and subsequent writers relaxed the qualifications for inclusion still further. The Cretan provenance of this conception, so much at odds with the normal Greek belief in a shadow-like afterlife in Hades, is indicated by the brief reference ὅτι ξανθὸς Ῥαδάμανθυς; the association of Rhadamanthys with Elysium was evidently familiar. Rhadamanthys, adopted into Greek legend as the son of Zeus and Europe (*Il.* xiv 321-2), bears a pre-Greek name (-νθ-) and is closely associated with Crete. This view of the afterlife accords with what little may be inferred about Minoan beliefs from their funerary monuments; the Minoans themselves perhaps owed the conception to Egypt. See further M. P. Nilsson, *Geschichte*, i 324 ff., *The Minoan-Mycenaean Religion*² (Lund, 1950), 621 ff. The name Ἠλύσιον has been convincingly explained by W. Burkert, 'Elysion', *Glotta* xxxix (1960/1), 208 ff., cf. Chantraine, *Dictionnaire*, from the adj. ἐνηλύσιος, 'struck by lightning'. In Greek belief lightning consecrates; a place struck by lightning was ἄβατος, not to be trodden by men, and death by lightning, as in the case of Semele and Asclepius, was a form of apotheosis. Ἠλύσιον must have arisen from misinterpretation of ἐνηλυσίῳ as ἐν Ἠλυσίῳ; for other Homeric examples of new words created from the second part of a cpd. see Leumann, *Wörter*, 109-10, 122 ff.

565. ῥηΐστη βιοτή: normally characteristic of the gods; cf. θεοὶ ῥεῖα ζώοντες 805 etc. In Hesiod's νῆσοι μακάρων there are three crops a year (*Op.* 172–3). βιοτή occurs only here in Homer; βίοτος is common.

566. Cf. the tricolon of similar content at vi 43–4.

567. A spring-like west wind similarly prevails in Alcinous' orchard (vii 119); cf. Hes. *Op.* 592–4; Pindar reproduces this detail (*O.* ii 71 ff.), ἔνθα μακάρων νᾶσον ὠκεανίδες αὖραι περιπνέοισιν. Aristotle (*Pr.* 943 b 23) quotes this line in the form ἀλλ' αἰεὶ Ζεφύροιο διαπνείουσιν ἀῆται, implying the absence of 568; but the exact wording does not affect his point, and he was almost certainly quoting from memory.

568. The river Oceanus separates the living from the dead, cf. x 508 ff., xi 157 ff., xxiv 11 ff. Elysium is in the far west, but on this side of Oceanus.

569. σφιν: 'in their eyes', ethic dat., referring back to ἀθάνατοι (564), though after the intervening description of Elysium this is barely intelligible. According to the schol. the line was absent from some copies διὰ τὸ ἀκύρως ἔχειν τὴν ἀντωνυμίαν (because the pronoun is used improperly); the explanation alleged is presumably mere speculation, and its defective attestation may indicate that the line is a late addition, making explicit what might easily be inferred. **ἔχεις:** 'have to wife'; cf. vi 281, vii 313.

570–6. Cf. 425–31.

577. On putting out to sea as a typical scene see ii 382 ff.

579. The change from 1st pers. pl. to 3rd is slightly clumsy, reflecting a certain difficulty in adapting the 3rd pers. formula to the 1st; cf. ix 53–4.

581–2. Cf. 477–8. The elliptical construction εἰς ... ποταμοῖο (sc. ὕδωρ) arises from the repetition of the phrase used in Proteus' instructions with minimal change, so that the command and its execution correspond as closely as possible; grammatically it may be explained by comparison with the apparent ellipse of οἶκον or δῶμα in such phrases as ἐς πατρός (ii 195), εἰς Ἀΐδαο (xi 164, 277, etc.); see Chantraine, *Grammaire*, ii 105 § 149. **στῆσα νέας:** 'I stopped my ships, brought my ships to anchor'; cf. xiv 258 (= xvii 427); for στῆσα ἐς there is a partial parallel in such phrases as ἐς θρόνους ἕζεσθαι (iv 51), cf. LSJ s.v. εἰς i 2.

584. Normally cenotaphs are erected in a dead man's homeland if his bones cannot be recovered or if he has been buried in a foreign country (cf. i 289 ff.). But Menelaus has no reason to suppose that Agamemnon had not been properly buried, nor does he say that he performed funeral rites (contrast i 291 ἐπὶ κτέρεα κτερεΐξαι). We may compare the *tumulus honorarius* erected by his soldiers in memory of Drusus (Suet. *Cl.* i 3). For the idea that a barrow may preserve a hero's memory even in a foreign land cf. xi 75 ff., xxiv 80 ff., *Il.* ii 813–14, iv 176 ff., vii 87 ff. Here however the association between funerary monument and κλέος ἄσβεστον seems more conventional than realistic, since it would have been unreasonable to hope that Menelaus' cenotaph would secure for Agamemnon a place in the legends of a land with which the hero himself had no association. The notion, if we take it seriously, reflects the assumptions of a literate society; the use of writing to mark gravestones is among its earliest applications.

585–6. = xvii 148–9. Menelaus deals very briskly with this part of his homeward journey, though it must have included his visits to Phoenicia and Cyprus (83, 617 ff.). **νεόμην:** *νέομαι* has no aor., and the impf. is here used with aoristic meaning.

587–623. Menelaus urges Telemachus to stay with him for some time, and offers him a chariot and horses as a present; but Telemachus wants to get home, and requests a gift better suited to conditions in Ithaca. Menelaus promises him a silver mixing-bowl. Guests gather at the palace for the common meal.

588. Cf. ii 374.

589. On the regular presentation of a substantial gift to a guest see i 311 n.

590. τρεῖς ἵππους: a pair of horses to draw the chariot and a third as a spare. In two episodes in the *Iliad* (viii 86 ff., xvi 152 ff., 462 ff.) we find references to the use of a third horse, an outrunner, described as παρήορος, not harnassed to the yoke but attached more loosely; the poet may have had in mind this Iliadic practice. (There would have been considerable problems in using a tracehorse on a battlefield, and it has been suggested that the conception derives from a misunderstanding of the adjective παρήορος, which is also used in a quite different sense, 'sprawling'; see further E. Delebecque, *Le Cheval dans l'*Iliade (Paris, 1951), 98 ff., J. Wiesner, *Archaeologia* F, 20 ff.)

592. Cf. viii 431. **ἐμέθεν:** see Chantraine, *Grammaire*, i 243 § 110.

594 ff. Telemachus' reply to Menelaus' invitation falls short of outright refusal, and though it has usually been supposed that he declines, the scene shifts back to Ithaca before any definite arrangements are made which would remove all doubt as to his meaning. This ambiguity should be understood as deliberate obfuscation on the poet's part. Before Telemachus' story is resumed in xv there intervene ten books recounting Odysseus' adventures, and if we follow the reckoning of time implied there, Telemachus must remain a month at Sparta; yet when the poet returns to Telemachus, the action is resumed at this point, and it is strongly suggested that the events of xv 1 ff. belong to the night immediately following this conversation. The creation of a slight uncertainty as to Telemachus' immediate intentions is an important part of the poet's strategy for preventing the inconsistent chronologies implied by the two strands of his narrative from bewildering the audience. See further above pp. 17–8, 51 ff., Hoekstra on xv 1 ff., Page, *Odyssey*, 78 ff., Eisenberger, *Studien*, 84 ff., M. J. Apthorp, *CQ* xxx (1980), 1–22. Telemachus has of course more serious reasons for declining Menelaus' invitation than concern for his comrades left at Pylos; the longer he is away, the greater the danger from the suitors (cf. xv 10 ff.). But a reference to his troubles at home would remind us rather uncomfortably that Menelaus has offered him neither advice nor help.

594. ἔρυκε: cf. *ἐρύκεις* (599); Telemachus implies that his freedom to depart depends on Menelaus' decision.

595–8. The fascination of story-telling is a recurrent theme in the *Odyssey*: cf. 239 ff., x 14 ff., xi 333 ff., xiii 2 ff., xvii 513 ff.

596. τοκήων: the pl. is evidently used rather loosely.

598. For the excuse cf. i 304.

600. δοίης: we should expect the subj., and δώῃς (cj. Nauck) is a simple change. But the opt. may be used for politeness' sake, to avoid seeming to assume too much; cf. Monro, *Homeric Dialect*, 279 § 305 (d), Chantraine, *Grammaire*, ii 248–9 § 366. **κειμήλιον:** 'something to treasure up', i.e. not livestock; cf. ii 75 where Odysseus' wealth is said to consist of κειμήλιά τε πρόβασίν τε.

602. ἄγαλμα: predicative, 'as a glory, delight'.

603. λωτός: a word of uncertain origin, used for various plants providing fodder or fruit; cf. Frisk, *GEW*, Chantraine, *Dictionnaire*. Here some kind of trefoil or clover is evidently meant.

604. ζειαί, κρῖ: see 41 n. **εὐρυφυὲς κρῖ λευκόν:** spondaic ending with a diaeresis after the fifth foot is very rare: cf. xii 64, *Il.* x 574, xi 639; κρῖ λευκόν also ends the line at *h.Cer.* 452. Most other apparent examples involve resolvable contractions; see Meister, *Kunstsprache*, 7 ff.

605 ff. We may compare Athena's description at xiii 242 ff., where there is more stress on Ithaca's advantages. Odysseus, like Ajax, whose kingdom is mountainous Salamis, has no chariot at Troy. Cf. Hor. *Ep.* i 7, 40 ff.: Haud male Telemachus, proles patientis Ulixei, | 'non est aptus equis Ithace locus, ut neque planis | porrectus spatiis nec multae prodigus herbae: | Atride, magis apta tibi tua dona relinquam'. There is surely also a recollection in Simonides fr. 591: ὁ Σιμωνίδης τὴν ἱπποτροφίαν φησὶν οὐ Ζακύνθῳ ὀπαδεῖν ἀλλ' ἀρούραισι πυροφόροις.

606. The line is awkward in its present position; the asyndeton and change of subject are harsh, and instead of καί we should expect an adversative conjunction. Bergk (*Philologus* xvi (1860), 577–8) suggested that its proper place was after 608, where it forms an effective culmination to the speech. If there has been some dislocation, it must be ancient; Aristarchus' readings, αἰγίβοτον and ἱππόβοτον (sc. πέδιον), evidently conjectures intended to mitigate the abrupt change of subject, imply that he knew of no other order of lines.

608. αἵ ... κεκλίαται: 'lie sloping towards, near'; cf. xiii 234–5. ἀκτὴ ... ἁλὶ κεκλιμένη. The fact that Ithaca is said to be the least suited of all the islands for driving horses is a serious objection to Dörpfeld's once fashionable view that the Ithaca of the *Odyssey* is in fact Leucas (see above, pp. 63–4); there is virtually no level ground on Thiaki, while Leucas has quite extensive plains round Nidri and at its northern end.

610. κατέρεξεν: 'caressed'; the verb occurs several times in this formula, but the only other part found in Homer is καρρέζουσα (*Il.* v 424).

611. Telemachus shows himself a true son of Odysseus by the adroitness with which he declines gifts which, though splendid, are useless to him. **οἵ:** i.e. ὅτι τοιαῦτα, cf. 75.

612. μεταστήσω: 'I will exchange'.

613–19. = xv 113–19, where, however, it is almost certainly a post-Aristarchean interpolation, being omitted by some of the medieval MSS and by P. 28 (Pack² 1106, 3rd/4th cent.) and ignored in the *scholia minora* of *P.Amherst* 28 (Pack² 1211; 2nd cent. AD); see further Apthorp, *Evidence*, esp. 195 ff.

615. τετυγμένον: 'well made, well wrought'; see further Hoekstra on xiii 306.

616. Cf. 132 (of an Egyptian artefact).

617. ἔργον Ἡφαίστοιο: the phrase indicates superlative craftsmanship, not literally supernatural provenance; cf. *Il.* viii 195. **Φαίδιμος ἥρως**: plainly an *ad hoc* invention.

618. Σιδονίων: cf. 84; for Sidonian craftsmanship cf. *Il.* vi 289 ff. (textiles), xxiii 741 ff. (a similar metal bowl), cf. *Od.* xv 425 (Σιδῶνος πολυχάλκου). Phoenician pre-eminence in metal-working is also attested in the Old Testament narrative of the building of Solomon's temple (1 Kgs. 7: 13) in the tenth century; Solomon had to rely on a Phoenician artificer, Hiram of Tyre, who specialized in bronze-casting on a large scale. This passage should remind us that objects of Oriental provenance found in Greece may often represent the souvenirs of returned travellers. On Phoenician metal bowls see Glenn Markoe, *Phoenician Bronze and Silver Bowls from Cyprus and the Mediterranean* (Berkeley–Los Angeles, 1985).

Homer's references to Phoenicians have been the subject of much discussion: see further J. D. Muhly, 'Homer and the Phoenicians', *Berytus* xix (1970), 19–64 (esp. 41 ff.), who concludes that the Homeric picture of Phoenician activity corresponds to conditions in the poet's own day; see also Hoekstra on xiii 272, J. N. Coldstream, 'Greeks and Phoenicians in the Aegean', *Madrider Beiträge* viii (1982), 261 ff. Various late linguistic traits in passages referring to Phoenicians are noted by P. Wathelet, 'Les Phéniciens dans la composition formulaire de l'épopée grecque', *RBPh* lii (1974), 5–14. As was noted in antiquity (cf. Str. 756), Homer never mentions Tyre, although it was the chief city of the Phoenician homeland from the eleventh century until its power was destroyed by Nebuchadnezzar in 574; the supremacy of Sidon belonged to the Mycenaean age, but the rulers of Tyre took the title 'king of Sidon' (cf. 1 Kgs. 16: 31), and we should not see in Σιδονίων βασιλεύς a reflection of Bronze age tradition (*pace* Lorimer, *Monuments*, 67).[8]

619. κεῖσέ με νοστήσαντα: as I came there on my homeward journey'. **τεΐν**: on the form see Chantraine, *Grammaire*, i 265 § 124.

621–4. For our last glimpse of Sparta (until xv) we are offered a touch of local colour in the common meal to which all the diners contribute, regarded by other Greeks as characteristic of the Dorian way of life. This passage has often been suspected as an interpolation: there are some slight oddities of expression (see nn. on εὐήνορα (622) and καλλικρήδεμνοι (623)) and it is not clear how the preparations here described relate to the rest of the narrative—it might seem natural to take them as anticipating the feast

---

[8] Nor is it legitimate to argue that the Homeric identification of Sidonians with Phoenicians puts the composition of the *Od.* before the destruction of Sidon by Esarhaddon in 677 (so W. Helck, *Die Beziehungen Ägyptens u. Vorderasiens zur Ägäis bis ins 7. Jahrhundert v. Chr.* (Darmstadt, 1979), 158).

immediately preceding Telemachus' departure in xv, but there Menelaus quite plainly provides everything required (76 ff., 93 ff.), and it is not suggested that any other guests attend besides Telemachus and Pisistratus; see further Wilamowitz, *Untersuchungen*, 92 n. 5, Page, *Odyssey*, 69, 80. But without this passage the transition from Sparta to Ithaca would be extraordinarily abrupt, and the inconsistency with xv over the commissariat arrangements is less important than the effective contrast with the antisocial greed of the suitors, who feast continually at another's expense.

Eustathius supposed that the scene had already shifted to Ithaca, taking θείου βασιλῆος (621) to refer to Odysseus; θείου Ὀδυσῆος is actually given in a papyrus (*PSI* inv. CNR 66–7: see 556 n.). But this interpretation is impossible, as it requires us to take δαιτυμόνες (621) as servants who prepare the banquet, while the ἄλοχοι (623) must then be the maids who slept with the suitors.

621. θείου βασιλῆος: cf. θείων βασιλήων (691); the formula is probably a relatively late creation: see further Hoekstra, *Epic Verse before Homer* (Amsterdam, 1981), App. iii.

622. εὐήνορα οἶνον: εὐήνωρ is not elsewhere applied to οἶνος, and is otherwise found in Homer only at xiii 19 (εὐήνορα χαλκόν), though the personal name Εὐήνωρ is implied by Εὐηνορίδης (ii 242, xxii 294). It is best explained as a possessive cpd. (like πολυήνωρ), whose original meaning 'with good, i.e. brave, men' (cf. Pi. *O.* i 24) had faded by the time the *Odyssey* was composed; we may translate 'good for men'. See further Hoekstra on xiii 19, Leumann, *Wörter*, 110 n. 73.

623. καλλικρήδεμνοι: the epithet does not occur elsewhere in Homer; on the κρήδεμνον see i 334 n.

624–74. The suitors learn with astonishment of Telemachus' journey; Antinous proposes an ambush.

625–7. = xvii 167–9 (620 = xvii 166).

628–9. Cf. xxi 186–7. καθῆστο: sg., although there are really two subjects; the verb is evidently thought of as standing more closely with the former; cf. vi 171, *Il.* ii 858, xx 194. θεοειδής: 'handsome'; the epithet has no moral connotations. ἀρετῇ ... ἄριστοι: the clause explains why they were the leading suitors; we are reminded that Antinous and Eurymachus have already played a conspicuous part in i and ii.

630. On Noemon see ii 386 n.

632. ἴδμεν: polite use of the 1st pers. pl. where the 2nd would be more natural; cf. 138.

633. Noemon's question links this episode with the conversation in Sparta (594 ff.). νεῖτ': νέομαι is often used with future sense. ἠμαθόεντος: see i 93 n.

634. ἐμὲ δὲ χρεὼ γίγνεται: the phrase is not found elsewhere, but cf. *Il.* xxi 322–3 μιν χρεὼ | ἔσται and i 225 n.

635. Mules would be more useful than horses in country like Ithaca; Odysseus similarly has herds grazing on the mainland (xiv 100). εὐρύχορον: originally 'with broad dancing places', and perhaps always to be so understood in Homer, though the second element seems early to have been connected with χῶρος, not χόρος, so that the cpd. was taken in the less precise sense 'spacious'; see further Hainsworth on vi 4, Hoekstra on xiii 414.

636. = xxi 23. **θήλειαι:** θῆλυς/θήλεια is used in Homer of beasts and goddesses, but θηλύτεραι (pl. only) of humans. **ὑπό:** i.e. at the teat, unweaned.

638–40. The suitors' reaction shows how far they had underestimated Telemachus; having failed to take seriously his words at ii 318 ff., they had assumed that, like a child, he had gone off to seek sympathy for his discomfiture, and thus avoid having to face them.

638. ἔφαντο: 'thought, supposed', not 'said'.

639–40. Πύλον ... Νηλήϊον: cf. *Il.* xi 682; on the use of masc. forms of adjectives with fem. nouns see 442 n. **αὐτοῦ ἀγρῶν:** ἀγρῶν is best taken as epexegetic of αὐτοῦ, 'there (in Ithaca), on the estate'; cf. iii 251 οὐκ Ἄργεος ἦεν Ἀχαϊκοῦ, and see further Monro, *Homeric Dialect*, 143 § 149, Chantraine, *Grammaire*, ii 58–9 § 72. **συβώτη:** the casual reference to the swineherd is interesting; Eumaeus, who is to play a major role in the second half of the poem, has not yet been introduced, and it sounds as if he was a well-established character in the saga of Odysseus' homecoming.

642. ἔνισπε: as often, the use of the archaic ἐννέπω suggests that the matter is of importance or urgency to the speaker; on this form of the imperat. see Chantraine, *Grammaire*, i 467 § 222.

643. The punctuation is controversial, but most editors adopt that recommended in the scholia and put a question mark after ἕποντ' (so the OCT); the alternative punctuation, after ἐξαίρετοι, avoids an anomalous extension of κοῦροι, normally restricted to men of noble birth, to include θῆτες and δμῶες. **ἐξαίρετοι:** 'taken from', rather than 'chosen, picked'.

644. θῆτες: the noun is not found elsewhere in Homer, though θητεύω occurs at xi 489, xviii 357, *Il.* xxi 444. Homeric usage does not indicate a difference in status between θῆτες and δμῶες, and there is no reason to think that θῆτες are hired labourers, though they may be seen as essentially *outside* workers. See further G. Ramming, *Die Dienerschaft in der Odyssee* (Erlangen, 1973), 97–8. **δύναιτο ... τελέσσαι:** i.e. he had servants enough to man a ship with them; but elsewhere we get the impression that Telemachus cannot rely on the loyalty of most of his household.

646. Cf. *Il.* i 429–30 γυναικός | τήν ῥα βίη ἀέκοντος ἀπηύρων. The grammatical anomaly here is no doubt due to modification of this, or a similar, phrase; it is obviously tempting to see here an imitation of one of the most memorable passages of the *Iliad*. For other examples of a participle found in a different case from a preceding pronoun with which it might have been construed see Monro, *Homeric Dialect*, 211 § 243, 3 (d), Chantraine, *Grammaire*, ii 322–3 § 469; but the discrepancy here is unusually harsh.

649 ff. Noemon answers Antinous' questions in reverse order, a common feature of Homeric conversations; see further S. E. Bassett, '"Υστερον πρότερον Ὁμηρικῶς', *HSPh* xxxi (1920), 39–53. He evidently senses a

COMMENTARY

certain menace in Antinous' last question, in case it proves that he has sided with Telemachus.

650–1. ὁππότ' ... αἰτίζῃ: after ὅτε, ὅποτε the subj. is sometimes thus used without κεν or ἄν to indicate a case which may recur repeatedly, or at any time; see further Monro, *Homeric Dialect*, 263 § 289, 2 (a), Chantraine, *Grammaire*, ii 256 § 377.

652–3. That Telemachus could command so much popular support must come as a further unpleasant surprise to the suitors.

652. μεθ' ἡμέας: 'after us'; Noemon associates himself with the suitors (cf. ἴδμεν 632). (It has been suggested that it means 'among us' (i.e. the Ithacans in general), but with this sense the dat. is commoner, and we should lose the implication of solidarity with the suitors.)

653. οἵ: demonstrative, picking up κοῦροι.   ἐν: it is hard to say whether this should be taken with what precedes, 'among them', or with βαίνοντ', 'embarking', cf. ἔμβη (656).

654–6. Noemon seems surprisingly unimpressed by his own surmise that a god might have intervened to help Telemachus, and presumably the suggestion is not seriously intended; with the dramatic irony characteristic of the *Odyssey*, and particularly in connection with the suitors (see i 325–7, 384–5 nn.), Noemon is made to hit the truth in jest. Having assumed from Mentor's presence that he could expect to find his ship back, he is puzzled by what he interprets as evidence that Telemachus' party has split up. (It would be captious to wonder why he did not question Mentor himself.)

657. Noemon's part is now played, and he will not reappear.

658. ἀμφοτέροισιν: Antinous and Eurymachus.

659. μνηστῆρας: to be preferred to μνηστῆρες, the reading of most MSS; elsewhere in Homer καθίσαι is invariably trans., and παῦσαν similarly requires a direct obj.

661–2 = *Il.* i 103–4. The two lines were athetized here by Aristarchus as an interpolation from the *Iliad*, unsuitable in the present context; in support of his suspicions we may note that the relatively common formula τοῖς (τοῖσιν) ... μετέφη is elsewhere (except at *Il.* iv 153) immediately followed by the speech which it introduces. As often, it is hard to say whether φρένες are to be understood as a specific organ, most probably the lungs, regarded as the seat of consciousness and emotion, and the couplet interpreted in terms of a physiological process, or whether something more abstract is meant; on the problems of the Homeric use of φρένες see S. Ireland and F. L. D. Steel, *Glotta* liii (1975), 183–95.   **ἀμφιμέλαιναι**: in Homer always an epithet of φρένες: cf. *Il.* i 103, xvii 83, 499, 573; in antiquity it was sometimes treated as 2 words, ἀμφί being taken with the verb, but though it may have originated from a phrase in which ἀμφί was wrongly taken with μέλας and detached from the verb to which it belonged, the poet probably understood it here as a compound adjective, cf. ἀμφιδάσεια (*Il.* xv 309); see *LfgrE* s.v. ἀμφιμέλαινα, Leumann, *Wörter*, 73. Since the φρένες are not normally described as 'black' or 'dark', it seems clear that the epithet is used proleptically to express the effect of strong emotion, 'so as to become darkened on every side (with rage)'; cf. Thgn. 1199 κραδίην ἐπάταξε μέλαιναν, A. *Pers.* 115 ταῦτά μου μελαγχίτων φρὴν ἀμύσσεται φόβῳ, Ch. 413 σπλάγχνα δέ μοι κελαινοῦται.

663–4. Cf. xvi 346–7.

665. The asyndeton here and in 667 reflects Antinous' excitement. τοσσῶνδε should probably be taken ἀπὸ κοινοῦ with ἐκ and ἀέκητι, as the latter is not found elsewhere in Homer without a dependent genitive; Hartmann's conjecture εἰ for ἐκ (with only a comma after 666) avoids this slight oddity and produces a more smoothly running sentence.

667. ἄρξει ... ἔμμεναι: 'this beginning of his will mean further trouble': a curious phrase.

668. πρὶν ἥβης μέτρον ἱκέσθαι: the MSS are divided between this, the reading preferred by Aristarchus, and πρὶν ἡμῖν πῆμα γενέσθαι (φυτεῦσαι), cf. xvii 597, the reading of the κοινότεραι (ἐκδόσεις). Aristarchus' reading is very apt after νέος πάϊς (665); the variant looks as if it was intended to meet the objection that Telemachus cannot be under twenty.

669 ff. So Eurycleia predicted (ii 367–8); cf. also ii 332 ff.

669. A crew of twenty is modest: see i 280 n.

670. αὐτόν: this rather oddly suggests an emphatic contrast between Telemachus and someone else; we cannot take it as 'on his own', since Antinous does not plan to isolate Telemachus from the rest of his company. There is much to recommend Bentley's conjecture αὖτις, which supplies a very desirable indication that ἰόντα refers to Telemachus' return journey.
λοχήσομαι ἠδὲ φυλάξω: *hysteron proteron*; see iii 467 n.

671. Σάμοιο: Cephallenia; see i 246 n.; Σάμη is the usual form of the name.   παιπαλοέσσης: see iii 170 n.

672. ἐπισμυγερῶς: see iii 195 n.   ναυτίλλεται: this must be aor. med. subj.; many editors emend to ναυτίλεται which is found in one MS (see also Monro, *Homeric Dialect*, 69 § 82), but some defend the aor. in -λλ- as an Aeolic form like ὀφέλλειεν (ii 334, *Il.* xvi 651); see Chantraine, *Grammaire*, i 173 § 67.

We hear more of the suitors' plan to ambush Telemachus at xvi 364 ff., after he has eluded them, but the tactical details are left obscure. The suitors would have had the advantages of surprise, of the prevailing north wind, and, probably, of superior weapons (cf. xvi 473 ff.), but would not be numerically superior. No doubt in these circumstances an incident might easily be staged in which Telemachus drowned, but the suitors could not hope to avoid suspicion if any of his crew survived. An ambush on land would have stood a much better chance of success. However, the plan stands momentary inspection, and adds an element of suspense to Telemachus' journey; it also unambiguously reveals the suitors as something worse than thoughtless and rowdy free-loaders, and Athena sees that Odysseus is aware of it when he plans his vengeance (xiii 425 ff.). This development links Telemachus' journey more closely to events in Ithaca, and it has been argued by those who hold the Telemachy to have existed originally independently of the *Odyssey* (see above, pp. 17–8, 52 ff.) that the story of the ambush was invented, or at least drastically reworked, to connect Telemachus' journey with the rest of the poem. But though it seems quite probable that the suitors' counter-measures are a relatively late invention, I doubt if the inconcinnities of this incident throw much light on the relationship of the Telemachy to the epic as a whole. See further Page, *Odyssey*, 179 ff.

673. ἐπήνεον: 'approved, assented', not 'praised'; see Hoekstra on xiii 47.

675–767. Through the herald Medon Penelope learns of Telemachus' voyage and of the suitors' plot to kill him. She is at first overwhelmed by despair, but Eurycleia calms her by urging prayer. Penelope goes to her room and prays to Athena.

675. ἄπυστος: here active, as at v 127, 'unaware, ignorant'; passive at i 242.

676. βυσσοδόμευον: an Odyssean word, not found in the *Iliad*; it is always used metaphorically, of plotting mischief; see further Russo on xvii 66.

677. Medon is later described as the suitors' favourite attendant (xvii 172–3), no doubt to be taken as a tribute to his efficiency, rather than as an indication of disloyalty, since Telemachus testifies to Medon's concern for his interests (xxii 357–8)—well exemplified here, despite Penelope's reproaches.

678. Medon was eavesdropping while the suitors were plotting in the courtyard (cf. 625, 659); we may perhaps imagine him standing near the outer gates, concealed by the wall of the courtyard. (Some commentators take αὐλῆς ἐκτὸς ἐών as 'being outside in the courtyard', but this is most unnatural).

680 κατ' οὐδοῦ βάντα: the use of κατά in this phrase is exceptional; the idea is more commonly expressed with such phrases as ὑπὲρ οὐδοῦ βαίνειν, ὑπερβαίνειν οὐδόν, ἐπ' οὐδὸν ἰέναι, οὐδὸν ἱκέσθαι. κατά with the gen. in Homer normally means '*down*' either 'from' or 'over'; this suggests a raised threshold, which also seems to be indicated by 718 where Penelope sits ἐπ' οὐδοῦ: if she had simply wanted to sit on the floor, there is no reason why she should have chosen the threshold: cf. x 62–3, xvii 339. The high thresholds of the Geometric house models from Perachora and the Argive Heraeum (see Lorimer, *Monuments*, pl. xxxii, H. Drerup, *Archaeologia* O, pls. ii, iii) show that this was a feature of contemporary doorways; it does not suit the massive stone threshold of the Mycenaean megaron, but it is open to those who wish to interpret Homeric architecture, so far as possible, in Mycenaean terms to argue that some rooms in Mycenaean buildings may well have had high wooden thresholds. See further D. H. Gray, 'Houses in the *Odyssey*', *CQ* xlix (1955), 1 ff., M. O. Knox, 'Megarons and *ΜΕΓΑΡΑ*', *CQ* NS xxiii (1973), 1 ff.

682. ἢ εἰπέμεναι: ἢ εἰπ- must be scanned as a monosyllable by synizesis (despite the initial ϝ); cf. *Il.* v 466 ἢ εἰς ὅ κεν.

684. The syntax of the line is obviously irregular. The use of μή to negate the participles is influenced by the opt. in 685: Penelope begins as if she meant to continue with μηκέτι, or a similar word: 'Would that this might be the end of their wooing and their meeting together'. Some commentators take the participles as expressing a wish for the past—'Would that they had never wooed me nor met together on any other occasion'—but this seems less natural. There is a partial parallel at xi 613 μὴ τεχνησάμενος μηδ' ἄλλο τι τεχνήσαιτο, 'May he who fashioned it never fashion anything else like it' (where the context implies 'Would that he had never made it'), but there the main wish is a negative one, naturally introduced by μή. Cf. Monro, *Homeric Dialect*, 327 § 361, Chantraine, *Grammaire*, ii 336 § 491. **ἄλλοθ':** probably to be understood as ἄλλοτε, though the ι of ἄλλοθι is often elided. For the breach of Hermann's Bridge (caesura after the trochee of the fourth foot) cf. i 241.

685. For the wish cf. xx 116 ff.

686. κατακείρετε: Penelope now explicitly includes Medon with the suitors.

687–8. οὐδέ τι ... ἀκούετε: a question. **πατρῶν:** the form is also found at viii 245, likewise at the end of a line; despite its rarity it may be an archaism; see Ruijgh, *Elément*, 22. **τὸ πρόσθεν:** explained by παῖδες ἐόντες. **ἀκούετε:** best translated with a past tense: cf. iii 87 n.

689–93. Cf. ii 47, 71–2, 230 ff.

691. ἥ: the relative is attracted to the gender of the predicate. **δίκη:** 'custom', cf. xi 218, xiv 59, xviii 275, xix 43, 168, xxiv 255; not an Iliadic meaning.

692. ἐχθαίρῃσι ... φιλοίη: the subjunctive is used with future force, the optative implies a more remote possibility: 'he is sure to hate one, he may favour another'; for this use of different moods to express alternatives, the subjunctive giving that on which stress is laid, cf. *Il.* xviii 308 στήσομαι, ἤ κε φέρῃσι μέγα κράτος, ἦ κε φεροίμην: cf. Monro, *Homeric Dialect*, 253 § 275, Chantraine, *Grammaire*, ii 211 § 312. For the combination of ἐχθαίρω and φιλέω in gnomic expressions cf. xv 70 ff., Hes. *Op.* 300. **φιλοίη:** there is only one other example in Homer of the relatively late optative in -οίη, ix 320 φοροίη: cf. Chantraine, *Grammaire*, i 464 § 220, Wackernagel, *Untersuchungen*, 14.

693. The line picks up 690, ἀτάσθαλον corresponding to ἐξαίσιόν τι and ἄνδρα to τινά. **ἐώργει:** ἐόργει or ἐέοργει would be more correct: cf. Monro, *Homeric Dialect*, 61 § 67 (2), Chantraine, *Grammaire*, i 480 § 230.

695. εὐεργέων: gen. pl. neut., 'for benefits, acts of kindness'.

696. πεπνυμένα εἰδώς: see ii 38 n.

701. νισόμενον: on derivation and spelling see Hainsworth on v 19, Heubeck on ix 58.

703 ff. It is obviously unrealistic that Penelope should have remained so long unaware of her son's absence; the poet does not attempt an explanation, which would only have drawn attention to the improbability. She appears too shocked by Telemachus' clandestine departure to react immediately to Medon's far more alarming report of the suitors' plot.

704–5. = *Il.* xvii 695–6. ἀμφασίη is the spelling given by the majority of MSS in both places, but the μ merely serves to mark the first syllable as long, and has no etymological significance. **ἐπέων:** redundant; cf. iii 422 βοῶν ἐπιβουκόλος, and n. **ἔσχετο:** two readings were current in anti-

COMMENTARY

quity, but the schol. which gives this information is manifestly corrupt: ἔσχετο· αἱ Ἀριστάρχου ἔσκετο, ἀντὶ τοῦ ἐγένετο· γελοῖοι γὰρ εἰσιν οἱ γράφοντες ἔσχετο. It is clearly unreasonable to dismiss ἔσχετο as 'absurd', while ἔσκετο is nowhere attested, and does not make sense if it is taken as equivalent to ἐγένετο. Lehrs' transposition of ἔσκετο, ἀντὶ τοῦ ἐγένετο and ἔσχετο (see Ludwich, *AHT* i 548, 12), though drastic, is very attractive: ἔσκετο may simply be a copying error; certainly this unintelligible form cannot be due to conjecture. But it is conceivable that it represents the genuine form of the text here, implying an earlier *σέ-σκ-ετο, to be connected with Sanskrit *sa-sc-at*, 'hindrance, obstacle'; in that case, ἔσχετο should be interpreted as a conjecture, intended to remove a form no longer intelligible. See further W. Schulze, *Kleine Schriften*² (Göttingen, 1966), 368–9. But the meaning is unaffected.

707. οὐδέ ... χρεώ: see i 225 n.

708. ἁλὸς ἵπποι: here ἵπποι is almost equivalent to 'chariots' (Homeric heroes do not ride). For the comparison of ship to chariot cf. xiii 81 ff., A. *Supp.* 32, *Pr.* 468, Catul. lxiv 9. In Old English and Old Norse poetry ships are often called 'sea-' or 'wave-horses'. See further I. Waern, ΓΗΣ ΟΣΤΕΑ, *The Kenning in Pre-Christian Greek Poetry* (Uppsala, 1951), esp. 47 ff.

709. πουλὺν ἐφ' ὑγρήν: for the masc. form of adj. with fem. noun cf. 406, 442, and nn. ad loc. For πουλύν as fem. cf. *Il.* v 776, viii 50, x 27, always in the fifth foot; Witte (*Glotta* iii (1910), 106 ff.) suggests that the analogy of θῆλυς influenced the use of πουλύς and ἡδύς as feminines.   **ὑγρήν:** see i 97 n.

712. For the alternative explanations cf. vii 263, ix 339, xiv 178–9, xvi 356: all from speeches. This distinction in motivation is not found in the *Iliad*. See further A. Lesky, *Göttliche u. menschliche Motivation im homerischen Epos*, SHAW 1961, 4, 35 ff., H. Fränkel, *Dichtung u. Philosophie des frühen Griechentums* (New York, 1951), 127–8 (= *Early Greek Poetry and Philosophy* (Oxford, 1975), 90).

717. πολλῶν ... ἐόντων: 'although there were many chairs in the room' (not 'although a large company was present').   **οἶκον:** used rather loosely of one room (cf. i 356), not the whole house.

722 ff. Compare the opening of Thetis' speech at *Il.* xviii 429 ff.

723. τράφεν ἠδ' ἐγένοντο: on prothysteron as a characteristic feature of Homeric style see iii 467 n.   **τράφεν:** = ἐτράφησαν; also found at x 417, xiv 201, *Il.* i 251, 266, xxiii 348, in most places without variant, though here and at x 417 a few MSS have τράφον, which is preferred by those who hold ἐτράφην to be a post-Homeric form; see also Hoekstra on xiv 201.

724–6. = 814–6.   **θυμολέοντα:** on lions in Homer see 335 n.

726. = i 344; see n.

727. ἀνηρείψαντο θύελλαι: so most MSS; it better suits what follows than the variant ἀποκτεῖναι μεμάασιν (= v 18), and the wild exaggeration fits Penelope's mood. On ἀνηρείψαντο see i 241 n.

728. ἀκλέα: ἀκλεέ(α) would be more correct, and avoid hiatus; the epithet is explained by what follows, 'unbeknownst, without report'.

729. σχέτλιαι: implies tenacity of purpose, often with regard to an object which the speaker regards as unreasonable (cf. Hainsworth on v 118, Hoekstra on xiii 293); here we may detect an undertone of admiration for the women's solidarity with Telemachus.   **οὐδ' ὑμεῖς περ:** very emphatic, 'not even you (from whom I might have expected some loyalty)'.

733. τῷ κε μάλ' ἤ κεν μεῖνε: a unique use of double κε; for ἄν ... κε see v 361.

735 ff. Penelope's abortive proposal prepares us for xxiv 220 ff., where Odysseus finds Laertes in the κῆπος πολυδένδρεος while Dolius and his sons work elsewhere on the estate (222 ff., 386 ff.).[9] Dolius is also said to be the father of the unfaithful Melantheus and Melantho (xvii 212, xviii 322, xxii 159) and some have thought that two or even three homonymous slaves must be distinguished: so Page, *Odyssey*, 109, Erbse, *Beiträge*, 238 ff.; against, Heubeck on xxiv 222. On Laertes' curious situation see i 188–93 n.

735. καλέσειε: the opt. has the force of an imperat.

738. παρεζόμενος suggests the need for a long, undisturbed talk in order to explain the situation to the old man.

739. εἰ δή που: 'in the hope that'.

740. ὀδύρεται: aor. subj.   **οἵ:** virtually unintelligible: if Penelope supposed that the people as a whole were implicated in the suitors' plot to murder Telemachus (which goes far beyond what Medon has said), it is hard to see what good Laertes' complaint could do. We should expect Penelope to speak of the public exposure of the group's wicked scheme, and various conjectures produce the required sense quite simply: ὅ Nauck, εἰ Schwartz, ὡς Düntzer. But the poet may have been careless in expressing a proposal which is to be immediately rejected.

742 ff. Eurycleia replies with a frank confidence appropriate to her position as senior house-servant.

743–4. νύμφα: for this archaic short voc. of νύμφη cf. *Il.* iii 130; see further Chantraine, *Grammaire*, i 200 § 83. This may seem a surprising way to address a woman who has been married for over twenty years, but it reminds us that Eurycleia has been a member of Odysseus' household for longer than Penelope   **σὺ μὲν ... μεγάρῳ:** i.e. whether you slay me or spare me, I will not hide what I have to say. Eurycleia expresses herself somewhat similarly at xxiii 78–9.   **νηλέϊ:** on the hyphaeresis of ε (< νηλέει) see Chantraine, *Grammaire*, i 73–4 § 30; on the connotations of νηλέης see Hainsworth on viii 525.

745 ff. Cf. ii 349 ff.

746. μέθυ: in Homer only the nom. and acc. of this old word appear; its

[9] This should not be regarded as arguing the authenticity of xxiv; those who hold that what follows xxiii 296 is a later addition may maintain that these lines, together with 754–7, were inserted at the same time, to anchor the continuation more firmly to the rest of the poem.

cognates in many IE languages, including Sanskrit and Old Irish, meaning 'honey, mead' indicate that wine supplanted a more primitive intoxicant; see further Frisk, *GEW*.

747–9. Cf. ii 374–6.

750. ὑδρηναμένη: before prayer or sacrifice the hands must be washed: cf. iii 445 and n.

754 ff. The idea of reporting developments to Laertes is dismissed in a similarly unconvincing way at xvi 146 ff.

754. κάκου: = κάκοε, imperat. of κακόω.

755. Ἀρκεισιάδαο: Arkeisios was Laertes' father (xvi 118); Homer tells us nothing more about him, though the honorific way in which he is mentioned here and at xiv 182 (see Hoekstra's n.) should be noted. The name is perhaps a short form of Ἀρκεσίλαος (so Risch), the name which Eugammon of Cyrene gave to Telemachus' younger brother in the *Telegony* (fr. 1). A derivation from ἄρκτος was popular in antiquity; according to Aristotle's lost Ἰθακησίων πολιτεία (fr. 504 Rose) Arkeisios' mother was a bear, with whom his father Cephalus had mated on the instructions of the Delphic Oracle; for far-reaching speculations about the relevance of bears to the *Odyssey* see Rhys Carpenter, *Folk Tale, Fiction and Saga in the Homeric Epics* (Berkeley–Los Angeles, 1946), chs. vi, vii. Other versions of Arkeisios' parentage make him the son of Zeus and Euryodeia, or of Cephalus and Procris, or a grandson of Cephalus.

758. The repetition γόον ... γόοιο seems clumsy; Bentley conjectured χόλον for γόον, Schwartz ῥόοιο for γόοιο.

759–60. Cf. 750–1.

761 Contrast the use of barley (οὐλοχύτας) at iii 445. We are not told what Penelope does with it; commentators generally assume that the barley was poured from the basket like wine from a cup (presumably at 767), but there is no parallel for such a rite and no basis for this assumption. The barley is placed in the basket and thus dedicated to Athena; but it is not clear what was supposed to happen to it eventually. Conceivably the poet has simply invented a rite suitable for the rather restricted circumstances of a group of women engaged in surreptitious supplication in an upstairs room; though women may promise animal victims (xvii 50–1, *Il.* vi 302 ff.), blood sacrifice is reserved for men.

762 ff. The structure and phraseology of Penelope's prayer is strongly reminiscent of two prayers in the *Iliad*, that of Chryses (i 37 ff.) and that of Nestor (xv 373 ff.).

762. κλῦθί μευ: see 262 n.; μοι, the majority reading, would be preferable. **αἰγιόχοιο:** see iii 42 n. **Ἀτρυτώνη:** the title is exclusively Athena's; its derivation and meaning are obscure, and it is not attested in cult. It is conventionally translated 'unwearied', as if from ἄτρυτος, an interpretation which Aeschylus probably had in mind when he made Athena refer to her ἄτρυτον πόδα (*Eu.* 403). But the normal sense of ἄτρυτος is rather 'incessant, continual, unabating', and it is not used of persons until the Hellenistic age. Other attempts to find a Greek etymology are even more far-fetched, and most probably Ἀτρυτώνη is pre-Greek in origin. See further Hainsworth on vi 324, *LfgrE*.

764. On the burning of the thigh-bones see iii 9 n.

767. ὀλόλυξε: 'raised the ritual cry'; cf. iii 450 and n.   **οἱ:** 'for her'; the difference between gen. and dat. is here very slight.

767–86. The suitors prepare for their murder attempt.

768. = i 365; see n. Here ὁμάδησαν expresses the suitors' reaction as they misinterpret Penelope's ritual cry.

770–1. Page (*Odyssey*, 80 n. 15) finds this 'a silly inference from her ὀλολυγή'; but the combination of self-confidence, silliness, and ruthlessness is typical of the suitors, as is the poet's use of dramatic irony (on which see nn. on i 325–7, 384–5).

772. ἴσαν = ᾔδεσαν (ᾖσαν).

774–5. Antinous is aghast at the suitors' indiscretion.   **δαιμόνιοι:** as often in Homer, δαιμόνιος introduces a rebuke. The original meaning, 'acting under the monition of a daemon', was evidently no longer felt very precisely (Zeus can call Hera δαιμονίη (*Il.* iv 31)), and in translating it we need to concentrate on the speaker's surprise at what he regards (or affects to regard) as mental aberration, rather than seek an equivalent term. **ἐπαγγείλῃσι:** the ending in -σι in the 3rd pers. sg. of the thematic aor. subj. is a late development: see Chantraine, *Grammaire*, i 162–3 § 219, Wackernagel, *Untersuchungen*, 144–5.   **καὶ εἴσω:** in the women's quarters, i.e. to Penelope; the suitors themselves are already inside the palace (674).

776. ἀλλ' ἄγε σιγῇ τοῖον: cf. vii 30; τοῖον reinforces σιγῇ.

777. ἤραρεν: this should be 2nd aor. of ἀραρίσκω, which is normally transitive, though ἄραρον at *Il.* xvi 214 is intrans. But the sense required here 'pleased us, was agreeable to us' suggests that the poet may have intended a past tense of ἀρέσκω.

779 ff. Compare the description of Telemachus' preparations for his voyage at ii 414 ff., and nn. ad loc.

780–5. Cf. viii 51–5.

782. τροποῖς: leather loops passed round the oars and over the thole-pins (on which see ii 419 n.).

783. = viii 54, cf. x 506, *Il.* i 480; it is omitted by many of the medieval MSS and is surely a late interpolation.

784. τεύχεα: there is no reason why we should not take this in its normal sense, 'weapons', which the suitors would need for their assassination attempt, though τεύχεα is certainly used in a different sense at xv 218: see Hoekstra's n. and Kurt, *Fachausdrücke*, 158 ff.

785. ἐν νοτίῳ: only here and at viii 55; it apparently means 'the water near the shore', though its exact interpretation was disputed in antiquity. It should be noted that neither gangway nor dinghy is mentioned; we should imagine the ship with its prow well afloat (ὑψοῦ) and its stern on the beach or in shallow water: cf. D. H. F. Gray, *Archaeologia* G, 104. Aristophanes read εἰνοδίῳ (or perhaps ἐννοδίῳ or ἐννόδιον), but this is surely a conjecture. **ἐκ δ' ἔβαν:** the actual departure is described at 842.

787–841. Penelope finally falls asleep; Athena sends her a comforting dream.

788. For fasting as a reaction to grief cf. *Il.* xix 205 ff., 305 ff., *h.Cer* 47 (with Richardson's n.), S. *Aj.* 324 (perhaps a reminiscence of this line), E. *Med.* 24, *Hipp.* 135 ff., 274 ff., *Supp.* 1105–6, *Or.* 39–41, 189; see also Griffin, *Homer on Life and Death*, 15–17. A pointed contrast to the banqueting suitors. ἄσιτος, ἄπαστος: see i 242 n.

791 ff. On lion similes in Homer see 335–40 n. They are normally reserved for men, and this comparison of the drowsy Penelope to a lion at bay (cf. *Il.* xii 41 ff.) has struck many critics as inept. Thus Fränkel comments (*Gleichnisse*, 70): 'Alles in uns sträubt sich, mit dem Bilde der Frau die einschlummert, das eines Löwen in Verbindung zu bringen, der in seinen letzten Kampf geht'. We may suspect that the poet took over ready-made a simile originally devised for a warrior weighing various courses of action, not simply beset by anxieties; but its affinity with the simile earlier used for Odysseus (335 ff.) has a certain effectiveness which many will judge to outweigh its incongruity. περί: with ἄγωσι.

793–4. Rather typical of Penelope; cf. i 360–4, xvi 450–1, xviii 187 ff., xix 603–4, xxi 357–8, xxiii 16 ff. νήδυμος: in Homer applied only to ὕπνος. The original form was ἥδυμος, in some places given as a variant; νήδυμος developed when a preceding *nu ephelkystikon*, introduced to avoid hiatus, was wrongly attached to the following word; see Frisk, *GEW*, Leumann, *Wörter*, 44–5. (An analogous development took place in Middle English with *n*: *n* of the indefinite article *an* was frequently transferred to a following word beginning with a vowel, and a similar transference occurred with the *n* of *myn*, *thyn* (mine, thine): in a few cases the forms thus produced established themselves permanently, e.g. *nickname*, *newt*; a converse process has given such forms as *adder*, *apron*, *auger*.)

795 ff. Penelope's dream is of a type common in Homer, in which the sleeper is visited by a dream-figure; this is clearly regarded as an external, independently existing entity, not a creation of the sleeper's mind; compare Agamemnon's dream (*Il.* ii 16 ff.), Achilles' dream (xxiii 62 ff.), Nausicaa's dream (*Od.* vi 13 ff.); the dreams of Xerxes and Artabanus in Herodotus (vii 12 ff.) follow a very similar pattern. There is a tacit assumption that the sleeper's senses are awake and active, but the dreamer is usually more passive than Penelope is here, though there is some conversation in Achilles' dream; significantly, Achilles, like Penelope, is in a highly disturbed state when sleep overtakes him. This type of dream is certainly not common in our own dream-experience, but Homeric dreams (apart from the anxiety-dream of *Il.* xxii 199 ff.) are 'literary dreams' with a compositional function. Characters are made to have dreams appropriate to the story, but in no way indicative of their mental states; here it would obviously have been more realistic if Penelope had had an anxiety-dream. Dreams serve to motivate new developments in the action and provide a simple means for divine intervention in human affairs. Here Penelope has to be saved from total surrender to despair in a situation where no human friend could help her. She is at present more concerned about Telemachus than about Odysseus, and the thoughts which occupied her as she fell asleep come into the foreground in her dream; its reassurance rounds off this part of the story very satisfactorily, freeing Penelope (and us) from any anxiety about Telemachus' return. Despite Achilles' assumption that dreams come from Zeus (*Il.* i 63), as Agamemnon's deceptive dream in fact does (*Il.* ii 5 ff.), they are not regarded in Homer as the province of a single divinity; Athena is responsible not only for this dream and that of Nausicaa, but also for Rhesus' dream (*Il.* x 497), while Patroclus' ghost comes to Achilles in a dream without any divine prompting being mentioned (*Il.* xxiii 65 ff.). See further Arend, *Scenen*, 61 ff., E. R. Dodds, *The Greeks and the Irrational* (Berkeley–Los Angeles, 1951), 102 ff., A. H. M. Kessels, *Studies in the Dream in Greek Literature* (Utrecht, 1973), esp. 56–60, 73–4.

796. Athena creates the dream-figure *ex nihilo*, and when it has served its purpose it dissolves again into thin air (839). We may wonder why she does not herself visit Penelope, as she does Nausicaa (vi 13 ff.)—perhaps because it would have been difficult for her to refuse to satisfy Penelope's longing for news of Odysseus without appearing hard-hearted. **δέμας ... γυναικί:** on this formula see Hoekstra on xiii 288.

797. Penelope's sister is not mentioned elsewhere.

798. Eumelus, of Pherae in Thessaly, son of Admetus and Alcestis, is mentioned in the Catalogue of Ships (*Il.* ii 711 ff.) and is quite conspicuous in the funeral games of *Il.* xxiii.

800. ἧος: here used to introduce a purpose clause, though its function is primarily temporal: cf. v 386, vi 80, xix 367; this use is not found in the *Iliad*; ὄφρα similarly has both temporal and final senses: cf. Monro, *Homeric Dialect*, 281 § 307, Chantraine, *Grammaire*, ii 261 § 386. On the orthography of ἧος see iii 126 n., iv 90–1 n. The εἴδωλον is not given explicit instructions, which would have precluded the ensuing conversation with Penelope; contrast the precise briefing which Zeus gives Agamemnon's dream (*Il.* ii 8 ff.).

802. κληῖδος ἱμάντα: see i 442 n. Homeric bedrooms have neither window nor chimney; baby Hermes re-enters his bedroom in the same way (*h.Merc.* 145 ff.).

803. A conventional feature of such dreams: cf. vi 21, *Il.* ii 20, xxiii 68, Hdt. vii 12. 1, 14. 1, 17. 1.

804. Cf. *Il.* ii 23, xxiii 69; the dream visitant implies that the sleeper might be expected to be awake (cf. *Il.* xxiv 683).

805–8. Penelope's reaction shows that this does not carry enough weight to impress her.

805. οὐ μὲν ... οὐδέ: emphatic negative. **οὐδὲ ἔωσι:** this abnormal hiatus after the second trochee could be avoided by restoring the uncontracted form ἐάουσι.

807. θεοῖς: ethic dat., 'in the sight of the gods': cf. *Il.* xxiii 595 δαίμοσιν εἶναι ἀλιτρός. **ἀλιτήμενος:** on the accentuation, which is that preferred by Aristarchus, see Chantraine, *Grammaire*, i 190 § 78.

809. ἐν ὀνειρείῃσι πύλῃσιν: cf. xix 562 ff. The phrase seems to presuppose a belief that the dreamer's soul wanders to a distant land of dreams, though such a notion is not found in Homer and would here be strictly inconsistent with the details which firmly locate Penelope's dream-experience in her own bedroom. We cannot tell whether the location of the δῆμος ὀνείρων (and therefore presumably of the gates of dreams) at the entrance to Hades at xxiv 12 represents a widely held belief or an idiosyncratic fantasy.

810 ff. Penelope does not at first realize that she is not talking to a real woman.

810–11. πάρος ... πωλέαι: the present is regularly thus used with πάρος, cf. v 88, *Il.* xviii 386 πάρος γε μὲν οὔ τι θαμίζεις; see further Chantraine, *Grammaire*, ii 191 § 282, Wackernagel, *Vorlesungen²*, i 158. **πωλέαι:** cf. μυθέαι ii 202 and n.; the synizesis πωλέαι ἐπεί is very harsh.

814–16. = 724–6: see nn. ad loc.

818. Cf. Phoenix's description of the young Achilles, *Il.* ix 440–1 νήπιον, οὔ πω εἰδόθ' ὁμοιίου πολέμοιο | οὐδ' ἀγορέων, ἵνα τ' ἄνδρες ἀριπρεπέες τελέθουσι.

819. τοῦ δή: Telemachus (= τοῦ δ' 820 = ὅ γε 821).

821. ἵν': here more naturally taken as 'whither' (cf. vi 55) than in its normal sense 'where, in which place'.

824. = 835. ἀμαυρός is not found elsewhere in Homer.

829. Agamemnon's dream similarly identifies itself (*Il.* ii 26).

830 ff. Penelope now seizes the conversational initiative, a development for which Athena did not prepare the *eidolon*; the following dialogue presents several oddities, and we may wonder why the episode was not allowed to end at 829, which would have provided a more satisfactory, and cheering, conclusion than 836–7.

831. A very strange line. **εἰ μὲν δή** should mean 'if, in truth, as you say': cf. Denniston, *Particles*, 392; contrast the use of almost the same formula in Odysseus' speech to Nausicaa, vi 150, εἰ μέν τις θεός ἐσσι. But the εἴδωλον is not a god in any normal sense, and the second half of the line (cf. ii 297, xiv 89) is anticlimactic; it is no help to adopt ἔκλυον, the variant found in one MS, which makes it merely tautological. We should expect alternative hypotheses: 'If you are yourself a god, or have come on the instructions of a god'.

832. εἰ δ' ἄγε: see i 271 n. **κεῖνον ... κατάλεξον:** 'tell me about that man': an unusual construction, cf. 836 κεῖνον ... ἀγορεύσω.

836. διηνεκέως: the normal meaning is 'continuously, from beginning to end', but here it must be something like 'positively, explicitly'; a familiar formula (cf. vii 241, xii 56) has been carelessly used.

837. = xi 464. It is absurd that the dream-figure should thus allege lack of reliable information as grounds for its refusal.

838. σταθμοῖο: 'doorpost'.

839. ἀνόρουσε: a regular reaction to strong emotion, e.g. *Il.* i 248, ix 193, Hdt. vii 18. 1 καὶ ὃς ἀμβώσας μέγα ἀναθρώσκει.

841. νυκτὸς ἀμολγῷ: an Iliadic formula (xi 173, xv 324, xxii 28, 317), not elsewhere in the *Odyssey*. ἀμολγός must be related to ἀμέλγω, but a connection between milking and night is not obvious; the phrase was found puzzling in antiquity, and ἀμολγός had surely passed out of common use before the *Odyssey* was composed. It is generally understood to have a temporal reference, but, if so, it is used inconsistently: at *Il.* xxii 28 the reference to Sirius in late summer points to the time just before dawn, at xxii 317 the evening twilight is indicated, while elsewhere the sense seems to be 'at dead of night'. See further Chantraine, *Dictionnaire* s.v. ἀμέλγω, Frisk, *GEW*, *LfgrE*.

842-7. The suitors station their ambush.

844 ff. The only island in the channel between Ithaca and Cephallenia is Daskalio, a limestone reef about 200 m. long by 30 wide, lying west of Polis Bay and close to the shore of Cephallenia. Strabo (59) discusses the problem of its identification with Asteris, and notes the obvious difficulty that it scarcely offers a single safe anchorage; he explains the discrepancy from the twin harbours of the Odyssean Asteris by hypothesizing a change in the physical geography of the area, but this theory has not been supported by soundings in the Ithaca channel. Moreover, the subsequent account of the ambush (xvi 365 ff.) describes the suitors keeping watch from windy heights (ἄκριας ἠνεμοέσσας), which can certainly not be found on Daskalio, which hardly rises 4 m. above sea-level. Those who follow Dörpfeld's view that Homer's Ithaca is in fact Leucas have no difficulty here; the description of Asteris suits Arkhoudi, which is situated midway between Thiaki and Leucas in an excellent position for intercepting anyone making for Leucas from the south; it has twin bays and rises to a peak which affords an excellent view southwards. But geographical accuracy was not of first importance to the poet (see above, pp. 62 ff.), and (as with Pharos, 354 ff.) having set the story in an area unfamiliar to his audience he has created the sort of island required by his narrative. ἔστι δέ τις: see iii 293 n.

847. τόν γε: Telemachus, of whom we shall hear no more till xv.

BOOKS V–VIII

J. B. Hainsworth

BOOK V: INTRODUCTION

In v the poet must at last introduce his hero, Odysseus. Traditionally his personality was defined by a variety of epithets: διογενής, δῖος, πολύμητις, πολύτλας, πτολίπορθος, κτλ. Most of these are generic, applied to several and perhaps applicable to all heroes, but two are special to Odysseus: πολύτλας (= ταλασίφρονος in gen.), and πολύμητις (= πολυμήχανε in voc., and πολύφρονα, ποικιλομήτην in acc.). They describe a complex character, for the Homeric Odysseus is a figure of folk-tale as well as of heroic saga. Πολύτλας, for Homer, refers to the fortitude of Odysseus (see vii 1 n.). He therefore introduces Odysseus at a low ebb in his fortunes (151–9), a virtual prisoner, impotent and despondent. He reduces him even lower, to the condition of a friendless and naked castaway, for his evident intention is that the restoration of Odysseus to family and kingdom should begin from the lowest possible point. Even the hero's name seems to remind the poet of woe (ὀδύρομαι, cf. iv 110) and divine anger (ὀδύσσομαι, cf. i 62, v 340, xix 407, and see Risch in *Eumusia* (*Festgabe für E. Howald* (Zürich 1947), 82 ff.)—the real etymology is obscure cf. Frisk, *GEW* s.v. In this way the poet emphasizes by contrast the other aspect of Odysseus, the wily cunning, versatility, and opportunism by which he overcomes his difficulties. On this he touches, so as to complete the outline of the hero's personality on his first introduction, in the scene between Odysseus and Calypso (171–223).

Calypso herself is a creature of mystery. She contributes more to the structure than to the substance of *Odyssey*. The story requires Telemachus to be grown up and Odysseus to be presumed dead by all but his family and closest friends, so that he must be detained, hidden from the sight of men, till the twentieth year from his departure to Troy. Calypso is his 'concealer'—there is little doubt that for Homer this is what the name signified. (The form appears to be that of a hypocoristic, perhaps for *Καλυψάνειρα, cf. Heubeck, *Kadmos* iv (1965), 143.) In this sense Calypso was the invention of the singers of the story of Odysseus. Those who believe that behind the *Odyssey* as we have it it is possible to discern the outline of a simpler story easily remove her and take Odysseus directly from Thrinakia to Scheria (e.g. Schwartz, *Odyssee*, 5, fol-

249

lowing Wilamowitz, *Untersuchungen*, 134). However, it is the cus
tom of traditional poetry to borrow and adapt, not to creat
from nothing. Whence comes then such substance as Calypso pos
sesses? Some, notably Güntert, have speculated that she was a figur
of popular belief, a goddess of death, the *concealer of men*; her island
sort of Elysium. From our point of view the connection would be onl
at the deepest level. However, this view rests on the interpretation c
the goddess's name, for Calypso has no myth and no cult. Wilamow
itz derived her directly from Circe (*Untersuchungen*, 115 ff.). Th
parallel is suggestive, but not exact. Comparison with the Egyptia
tale of Sinuhe or Siduri of the Gilgamesh epic supports the view tha
her conception owed something to folk-tale: she is the enchantin
goddess of an enchanted isle. As such she has sometimes, though no
in this book, a slightly sinister aspect, cf. the epithet δολόεσσ
(vii 245).

The thematic structure of the book is simple. The poet mus
compose two episodes: the departure of Odysseus from Ogygia, an
his shipwreck upon Scheria.

The first is composed from the following themes: a council of th
gods (1–42), the departure and journey of Hermes (43–54), hi
arrival and welcome in Ogygia (55–94), his exchange with Calyps
(95–147), Calypso's report to Odysseus (148–227), and the boat
building (228–61). The second is composed from the voyag
(262–81), the storm (282–332), the intervention of Leucothe
(333–64), the shipwreck (365–87), Odysseus' perils (388–435), an
his landing on Scheria (436–93).

(In the most favourable circumstances, when a scene is of a ver
frequent kind, e.g. a council, or when the device of ring-compositio
marks off a scene, it is possible to discern the poet's units o
composition. Closer analysis, however, is apt to lose its objectiv
character. For the poet a given motif has no fixed status: he ma
elaborate it into a whole scene—or set of scenes—or make it a detai
in another; or he may change the character of a scene as he proceeds
Calypso's report of the gods' commands becomes, for Odysseus, a
πεῖρα: the landing on Scheria incorporates a supplication. Analysi
into themes, therefore, may legitimately vary from one critic t
another, and should always be understood to be 'for the sake o
argument'.)

The internal structure of the first episode offers no difficulty. Th
narrative proceeds in straightforward linear fashion, the themes ar
among the most frequent in Homer, and their sequence (council–
journey–report–reaction) is substantially identical with *Il*. ix 89 ff

The second episode is in fact equally straightforward, but in order to understand it it is necessary to recognize the methods by which the epic poet seeks to compose a grand and impressive scene. He seeks quality through quantity, and doubles and trebles the hero's woes. (This is one of the poetical 'laws' promulgated by F. Stürmer, *Die Rhapsodien der Odyssee* (Würzburg, 1921)). Unfortunately this was not understood by the earlier analytical critics. Schwartz, for example, having commended the first half of the book, sees the narrative begin to falter ('schaukeln') from 291: why does Odysseus have *both* the keel of his boat *and* the talisman of Leucothea to preserve him? His conclusion is to dissect out a Calypso-poem, in which Odysseus swam ashore, from a primitive Odyssey in which the storm was that which wrecked *his last ship* (cf. xii 403 ff.). This analysis was firmly rejected by von der Mühll (*RE* s.v. Odyssee, 713), and he has been followed by most recent analysts, e.g. Focke, *Odyssee*, 78–99, and Merkelbach, *Untersuchungen*, 210.

The fundamental integrity of this book is thus no longer an issue. However it must be connected with what precedes and what follows, and here the critic meets a problem of quite a different order. In each case, between iv and v and between v and vi, the poet must change the scene of his narrative and set in motion a new sequence of themes. Both times the text presents us with a well-tried and efficacious device: it is the gods who move the drama forward. On a strict view, however, the council of the gods which stands at the beginning of v is a superfluous repetition of that which stands at the beginning of i: in both the question was raised of Odysseus' release from Ogygia. Since Kirchhoff's discussion of the matter (*Odyssee*, 196), it has been recognized that with a little rewriting it is possible to make the dispatch of Hermes (v 28 ff.) follow Athena's suggestion to that effect (i 84 ff.), and to eliminate all the intervening material. Accordingly all critics who see in the Telemachy the hand of a second poet reject the repetition of the council theme. But even for unitarian critics who discount, as they must, the force of superfluity as an argument, the difficulties are still severe: in style the speech of Athena is uniquely unoriginal (see 7–20 n.), and the presence of a second council scene may conflict with a fundamental habit of epic narration.

The first council of the gods heard proposals for two courses of action: the dispatch of Hermes to Ogygia, and the visit of Athena to Ithaca. Like Alcinous (viii 46), Athena took assent to both projects for granted—as will the reader—and left at once. Two resolutions passed at a single meeting is nothing out of the ordinary. If a parallel is needed, *Il.* xv 154 ff. is a good example both for the taking of two decisions at a single time and for the mode of telling their execution. According to a celebrated 'law' given canonical form by Zieliński in 1897, both actions should be related in sequence, as if the second were suspended while the first was in progress. In fact the *Odyssey* does proceed in this way: Hermes does nothing while Athena is in Ithaca and Telemachus in Pylos and Sparta; Telemachus does nothing until Odysseus has landed on Ithaca, and only then begins his own return. Were the scale of these events as small as that in *Il.* xv, the second council of the gods would be unexpected and redundant, and Hermes would be properly sent on his way without further preparation. But the scale in fact is very large: nowhere else in archaic literature was such an interaction of parallel plots attempted. We are thus denied the most important of our critical resources, which is to appeal to the poet's normal and regular practices. K. Reinhardt (*Von Werken und Formen* (Godesberg, 1948), 38) tried to defend Athena's speech as being a deliberate allusion to the preceding books, such as would ease the transition. But the very perfunctory composition is against the assumption of so serious a purpose: it resembles that of other themes (e.g. banquets and sacrifices) whose presence and elaboration owes more to convention than to the strict requirements of context. D. L. Page (*Odyssey*, 70), a scholar familiar with the liberties of producers and actors in the theatre, suspected in the second council the work of some rhapsode who preferred to take the first four books of the *Odyssey* as read and begin his recital with Odysseus' departure from Ogygia: such a performance would require a short introduction to set the plot in motion. But in fact it is impossible to conceive of an *Odyssey* in which the Telemachy is integral and at the same time to merge the first and second divine councils, except at the cost of a signal implausibility: the critic would have to tolerate a council, albeit a council of gods, that remained in session for seven days, or postponed for that period the execution of its decision. Yet Page has pointed to a useful approach: the *Odyssey* proper calls for some sort of introduction, and an audience (or a poet for that matter, if we think of him as an oral composer) needs it after having been compelled to divert attention for so long to a sub-plot. The second council provides that introduction in an appropriate way, and reminds the audience again that the destiny of everyone in the poem is guided by Olympus.

Brief Bibliography

The characterization of Odysseus is the subject of a brief investigation by Paula Philippson, 'Die vorhomerische und die homerische Gestalt des Odysseus', *MH* iv (1947), 8–22, and of a study in detail by

G. Hunger, *Die Odysseus-Gestalt in Odyssee und Ilias* (Diss. Kiel, 1962). Hunger's standpoint is analytical, distinguishing an earlier conception of a daring Odysseus and a later one of the hero as the man of endurance. For the subsequent development of this ambiguous character, whose guile is not easily distinguished from deceit, see W. B. Stanford, *The Ulysses Theme* (Oxford, 1968).

On Calypso, H. Güntert, *Kalypso* (Halle, 1921), founded his interpretation on a comparison with Germanic and Scandinavian mythology and on the symbolism of the cave to identify the goddess as a death-daemon. This approach was at once rejected by K. Meuli, *Odyssee und Argonautika* (Berlin, 1921). However, the search for analogues has continued: F. Dirlmeier, 'Die "schreckliche" Kalypso', *Ausgewählte Schriften* (Heidelberg, 1970), 79–84, compares her with Siduri in the epic of Gilgamesh, and L. A. Stella, *Il Poema di Ulisse* (Firenze, 1955), and Germain, *Genèse*, adduce the influence of Near Eastern literature in more general terms. According to L. Radermacher, *SAWW* clxxviii (1915), Calypso is an *Elbin*, according to W. Kranz, *Hermes* i (1915), 93–112, a *Verbergerin*, a figure of folk-tale given artistic development. The skilful drawing of the Calypso scenes is emphasized by K. Reinhardt, *Tradition und Geist*, hg. v. C. Becker (Göttingen, 1960), 77–97, and by R. Harder, 'Odysseus und Kalypso', *Kleine Schriften* (München, 1960), 148–63. For an original view of Odysseus' detention on Calypso's island see Clay, *Wrath*.

In addition to Page most recent analysts have rejected the second divine assembly: von der Mühll, *Odyssey*, coll. 711 ff.; Focke, *Odyssee*, 74 ff.; Merkelbach, *Untersuchungen*, 155 ff.; Schadewaldt, *HSPh* lxiii (1958), 15–32. The best treatments of the function of the scene as it now stands are by Hölscher, *Untersuchungen*, 30 ff.; A. Heubeck, *Der Odyssee-Dichter und die Ilias* (Erlangen, 1954), 52 ff.; and T. Krischer, *Formale Konventionen der homerischen Epik* (Zetemata lvi, Munich, 1971), 95 ff. M. J. Apthorp, *CQ* xxvii (1977), 1–9, examines the language of the scene, on which Erbse, *Beiträge*, 127 ff. should also be consulted.

BOOK V: COMMENTARY

1–42. The second council of the gods. For the formal theme cf. i 26 ff., *Il.* viii 1 ff., xxiv 31 ff. In the human sphere also there are councils of chiefs, *Il.* ii 404 ff., ix 89 ff., where the theme incorporates the motif of the sacrificial meal, and public assemblies (ἀγοραί or ἀγῶνες) attended by the army, *Il.* i 54 ff., xix 40 ff., or the people, *Od.* ii 6 ff., viii 4 ff.: there is an ἀγορή of the gods (only at *Il.* xx 4 ff.) attended by the Rivers and Nymphs. In the economy of the epic the purpose of these scenes is to introduce an important narrative sequence, as is the case at this point. For the critical problems raised by the calling of a *second* council, after that in i, see introduction to v. Schol. try to distinguish the point of the first council, which had anticipated the decision to dispatch Hermes to Calypso's island, from that of the present (περὶ τοῦ σώζεσθαι Ὀδυσσέα against περὶ τοῦ πῶς), but the second council is merely resumptive after the retardation effected by the relation of Telemachus' journey. Accordingly, though the effect is brisk, the poet's invention is at a low ebb (see 7–20 n.).

1. **Ἠώς**: the new day, as usual, marks a new narrative step. The elaborated diction befits the importance of the following scenes (1–2 = *Il.* xi 1–2, cf. *Il.* xix 1–2 without the explicit personification). We are entering upon the *Odyssey* proper, just as *Il.* xi marks Agamemnon's supreme effort. Dawn-formulae are often highly ornamented and show many variants, see Kirk, *Commentary*, on *Il.* ii 48–9. **ἀγαυοῦ**: a complimentary epithet of wide application to persons and peoples. The sense of such epithets is likely to have been more precise, at least originally, then the vague equivalents favoured by translators (here 'illustrious', 'noble'), cf. Parry, *Blameless Aegisthus*. What aroused admiration (ἀγαυός < ἄγαμαι) in the Homeric world was especially personal beauty, cf. the formula εἶδος ἀγητός, and Tithonus is cited as a type of beauty by Tyrtaeus, fr. 12. 5 West. The -υ- is probably an Aeolism, despite the doubts of Wathelet, *Traits*, 150–1. All 12 instances of the gen. sg. occur in mid-verse, as here: a very ossified use probably fixed when the gen. sg. was still disyllabic (*-όο). **Τιθωνοῖο**: son of Laomedon, see the genealogy at *Il.* xx 230 ff. His unfortunate immortality (he was ἀθάνατος but not ἀγήραος) is first noted at *h.Ven.* 218–38 and Mimnermus fr. 4 West. Like others of his dynasty he may bear a genuinely Asiatic name, cf. von Kamptz, *Personennamen*, 363–4, and the Hesychian gloss τιτώ· ἠὼς ἢ αὔριον.

2. **φόως**: in the paradosis φάος is the normal spelling when the word is scanned ∪∪, φόως (by diectasis) when ∪–.

3. **θῶκόνδε**: cf. θοάζω, 'sit'. The sense is 'council', distinguished from the public ἀγορή, cf. ii 26. It is convened in Zeus' palace (as at i 26) in private, like Agamemnon's βουλαί in the *Iliad*. **καθίζανον** = κάθιζον: one of a series of poetical doublets in -άνω, cf. ἀλυσκάνω, ἰσχάνω, ἐρυκάνω, κευθάνω. The point of such alternants is to furnish a dactylic form before the bucolic diaeresis.

4. **οὗ τε κράτος ἐστὶ μέγιστον**: the prototype of this expression is ὅου (i.e. *ὅο) κ. ἐ. μ., attested at i 70, from which are derived also ὅ τε κ. ἐ. μ. (*Il.* ix 39, xiii 484), καί εὖ κ. ἐ μ. (*Il.* xxiv 293, 311), and τοῦ γὰρ κ. ἐ. μ. (*Il.* ii 118, ix 25), in accordance with the needs of metre and syntax. The τε is that which expresses a permanent fact or relation, see Chantraine, *Grammaire*, ii 240.

5. **λέγε**: 'related'. The verb is not yet used merely to supplement εἰπεῖν.

6. **δώμασι**: actually a cave (57), from a prototype such as δώματα Κίρκης or δώματα πατρός. **νύμφης**: Calypso, mentioned at i 14. This scene

presupposes i–iv also at 18, where παῖδ' would otherwise be unspecific
(= Telemachus) and the subject of μεμάασιν (the suitors) vague.

7–20. 7 = viii 306 etc., 8–12 = ii 230–4, 13 = *Il.* ii 721 (cf. *Od.* v 395, a
curious aural echo of this line with νούσῳ for νήσῳ), 14–17 = iv 557–60,
18ᵃ = iv 727ᵃ, 19–20 = iv 701–2. Page, *Odyssey*, 70, finds this 'an
abnormally artificial patchwork'. The uninventive composition would be
less conspicuous in an Iliadic battle book, where the recurrence of blocks of
lines is frequent. From contexts less dominated by formulaic diction the
best parallel is perhaps the wreck scene, xiv 301–9 = xii 403–6+415–19.
Other remarkable centos occur at *Il.* viii 28–72 and *Od.* xix 570–604, in
which every verse is found elsewhere. M. J. Apthorp, 'The Language of
Odyssey 5. 7–20', *CQ* xxvii (1977), 1–9, offers a good account of the
formular character or these lines. Athena is again taking advantage of the
prolonged absence of Poseidon, still feasting among the Ethiopians.

8. καὶ ἤπιος: μήδ', read by the 'wild' papyrus, P. 30, and also conjectured by
Nauck, is an unnecessary *facilior lectio* made to avoid the hiatus: the
pleonasm ἀγανὸς καὶ ἤπιος forms a unit of sense. **ἔστω:** εἴη P. 30, by
assimilation to the optatives of 10.

9. σκηπτοῦχος (*σκηπτροῦχος): the σκῆπτρον is a significant object, a symbol
of authority, especially regal authority, with overtones of divine right or at
least favour, cf. *Il.* i 279, ii 100 ff., 206 ff., ix 96 ff. and Griffin, *Homer on Life
and Death*, 9–12. **εἰδώς**, expressing a disposition, 34 times in the *Odyssey*.

11. θείοιο: the sense is 'godlike', in respect of appearance, endowments, or
exploits, like δῖος. The formation is *θεσ-ιος rather than *θεσ-γος, since 61
of the 75 occurrences imply an original -ει̃-, by locating the first syllable *in
thesi*, and 13 of the remainder are supplied by the one formula θεῖος ἀοιδός.
Hence the distribution in old formulae: nom. δῖος Ὀδυσσεύς, where θεῖος
was impossible, but gen. Ὀδυσσῆος θείοιο, where *διϝοιο was inelegant.
θεῖος, when it became available, was used for the ἀοιδός, to compliment his
genius and skill, because Homeric δῖος is appropriated to heroes.

12. πατὴρ δ' ὧς emphasizes the emotional link between Odysseus and his
home, but it was also prudent, in an ideal world, for a king to be just. For
the perils of a lawless community—storms and tempests—see *Il.* xvi
384–92 (simile) and, for more detail, Hes. *Op.* 225–47. The prototype,
both of the postponed ὧς and of the location of the phrase before the
bucolic diaeresis, is θεὸς (ϝ)ὧς (*Il.* xi 58, *Od.* xiv 205). The poet avails
himself of the Ionian vernacular loss of ϝ to introduce the connective
particle and use the formula in a new combination. The willingness of the
Ionian singers to mingle archaism and neologism, as explained by
Hoekstra, *Modifications*, 131 ff., brought the epic diction to a remarkable
degree of suppleness and ease.

13. The scholiasts, with typical over-precision, object to the physical over-
tones of κρατέρ' ἄλγεα πάσχων, when Odysseus' miseries are currently
spiritual (82 ff.), and would prefer τετιημένος ἦτορ. For ἄλγεα cf. xvii 142
φῆ μιν ὅ γ' ἐν νήσῳ ἰδέειν κρατέρ' ἄλγε' ἔχοντα (κατὰ δάκρυ χέοντα v.l. ap.
Eust.).

18. The ambush has been described in the three passages iv 660–74, 768–86, and 842–7.

19. νισόμενον: the conventional derivation from *ni-ns-omai*, a reduplicated present of the root *nes-, is morphologically impeccable but phonologically impossible (the result would be *νίνομαι) unless Schwyzer's 'retained or restored -σ-' is found credible: bibliography in Frisk, *GEW* s.v. νέομαι. Szemerényi, *Colloquium Mycenaeum* vi (Geneva, 1979) 338 n. 89, suggests *nes-ti > *nes-ty- > niss- by assimilation. The distinction between a present νίσσ- and future νίσ-, reported by Eustathius, is a figment.

20. ἠγαθέην = 'very holy': a generic epithet of places (Lesbos, Lemnos, Nysa, Pylos, Pytho), which need not, in a particular case, imply any superior sanctity. ἠμαθίην was read by Rhianus (an expert on Messenia), cf. ἠμαθόεις 9 times of Pylos, but is over-exact.   **δῖαν** is applied to the three localities, Arisbe, Elis, and Lacedaemon. LSJ do not notice this use, nor does Chantraine, *Dictionnaire* s.v. The precise (or original) sense of *epitheta ornantia* is not easily determined, since their use by definition is independent of context, but we may observe (1) an etymological sense 'of the god Zeus' (δῖος < *Διϝyος) found at *Il.* ix 538 and in Mycenaean (*di-u-ja, di-wi-ja*), the sole dialect to have the word in vernacular use, (2) a very common poetical use in the sense 'Zeus-like, sc. in appearance or ancestry', commonly rendered 'illustrious' or 'noble', and (3) a sense 'bright' in the formulae αἰθέρα/ἅλα δῖαν, preserving, even if indirectly, the force of the root *dei- (see Frisk, *GEW* s.v. Ζεύς). Since Homeric epithets for places generally allude to their physical, climatic, and agricultural amenities (πετρήεις, ἠνεμόεις, πολυστάφυλος, etc.) and not to their religious affiliations, sense (3) is here preferable. Lacedaemon in Homer usually denotes the district, but the regular epithet κοίλη is unavailable at the verse-end, being always placed as if trisyllabic.

21. νεφεληγερέτα: the nom. masc. sg. in -α of α-stems is confined to formulae (except for Θυέστ' at *Il.* ii 107), especially those for divinities. Metrical necessity or desirability (as here, where -της Ζεύς would be a harsh surallongement) is usually evident. The type is best derived from an original vocative (so Schwyzer, Chantraine, Palmer, Frisk). Masc. nominatives in -α in various dialects, sometimes adduced in this connection, appear to be secondary.

22–7. Zeus makes a brief but significant response to Athena's complaint. In the first council, at i 64–79, his reply to Athena had looked backward at the causes of Poseidon's anger toward Odysseus, now he adumbrates the climax of the *Odyssey* and, at 27, a major step towards it. Such foreshadowing is normal epic practice, for in relating a traditional story the poet eschews crude suspense, as explained by E. Auerbach, *Mimesis* (Bern, 1946), 1 ff. Suspense is a device less appropriate to the expansive epic manner than to the tension of the tragic stage.

22. ποῖον ... ὀδόντων: This whole-line formula is common to both epics (*Il.* twice, *Od.* 6 times), but *Il.* prefers the shorter expression ποῖον τὸν μῦθον ἔειπες (7 times).   **ἕρκος ὀδόντων** is a sort of 'kenning' or colourful paraphrase, not however noted as such by Ingrid Waern, *ΓΗΣ 'ΟΣΤΕΑ*: *The Kenning in Pre-Christian Greek Poetry* (Diss. Uppsala, 1951). The kenning, by meeting the need for alliteration, has a technical role in Germanic narrative poetry (see W. Whallon, *Formula, Character and Context* (Cambridge, Mass., 1969), 71–116); in Greek verse it is rare and is employed as an ornament of style. See also 43 and i 38 nn.

27. ἀπονέωνται: the lengthening of the initial syllable of this verb is habitual (20 times), but its origin is difficult to divine, except as an arbitrary licence, see A. Hoekstra, 'Metrical Lengthening and Epic Diction', *Mnemosyne* xxxi (1978) 1–26, and xv 308 n.

28–54. Departure of Hermes: see Arend, *Scenen*, 54. The most exact parallel is *Il.* xxiv 331 ff., cf. v 711 ff., with greater elaboration.

28. 'Ερμείας, cf. Mycenaean *e-ma-a*₂ PY Tn 316 etc. The Homeric spelling, according to C. J. Ruijgh, *Études du grec mycénien* (Amsterdam, 1967), 266, is a compromise between Ionic *Ἑρμέης* (< -ηής < -άας), and original -άας. Hermes is dispatched (rather than Iris, as usually in the *Iliad*) ὡς συγγενῆ ὄντα τῆς Ἀτλαντίδος Καλυψοῦς (schol.), or rather because he is persuasive (cf. *h.Cer.* 336, *h.Merc.* 317 ff.). Hermes as θεῶν κῆρυξ (Hesiod *Op.* 80, *Th.* 939, fr. 170) is not an explicit concept in Homer. **υἱὸν φίλον:** a few MSS read the unmetrical φίλον υἱόν, the most frequent realization of this formula, whence Nauck's φίλον υἱέα: an unnecessary conjecture, since the inversion of words in a formula is a well-established technique: see Hainsworth, *Flexibility*, 68. **φίλον:** the primary sense of φίλος has been much debated, most recently and effectively by A. W. H. Adkins, '"Friendship" and "Self-sufficiency" in Homer and Aristotle', *CQ* xiii (1963), 30–45, M. Landfester, *Das griechische Nomen φίλος und seine Ableitungen* (Hildesheim, 1966), and E. Benveniste, *Le Vocabulaire des institutions indo-européennes*, i (Paris, 1969), 335–53. The terminology which the modern reader naturally takes to be descriptive of inward states of mind in Homer describes the relations of the individual and the members of his group. φίλος thus opposes the 'insiders' of a community to the 'outsiders' (ξεῖνοι), cf. 135.

33. Classically σχεδία means 'raft', see Th. vi 2, X. *An.* ii 4, 28, though this is not what Odysseus constructs at 243–61 below. Germain's derivation from Egypt. *sḳdì* 'travel by water' (*Genèse*, 410) would be more convincing if there were more evidence of Egyptian loan-words in Greek, but finds favour with Szemerényi, *Festschrift für E. Risch*, Berlin 1986, 444–50. Ugaritic *ṯkt* may represent the term on passage to the Aegean. (On the meagre Egyptian contribution to the Greek lexicon see the sceptical paper of R. H. Pierce, 'Egyptian Loanwords in Ancient Greek?', *Symbolae Osloenses* xlvi (1971), 96–107.) A derivation from σχεδόν has only the difficulty that the sense 'improvised' is not actually attested in the root before ἐξ αὐτοσχεδίης h. *Merc.* 55. **πολυδέσμου:** 'πολλοὺς σχοίνους ἐχούσης' (schol. B) is certainly right: to equate with πολύγομφος, 'having many nails or pegs', epithet of the *ship* at Hes. *Op.* 660, as do scholl. EQ, is to relate the epithet to a peripheral (if not imaginary, see 243 n.) feature of rafts and, since the two epithets are metrically identical, violates the principle of a formular economy.

34. Von der Mühll's ἤματ' ἐικοστῷ (ἐεικοστῷ in the normal orthography, cf. ii 175 etc.) is correct as the original form of this expression, if formulaic, cf. ἐεικοστῷ ... ἤματι vi 170. Since, however, the κε is Homeric, cf. ἤματί κε τριτάτῳ *Il.* ix 363, with optative, the transmitted form could be accepted as a Homeric modification of the prototype, were it not for the fact that the tradition is in some disorder. The insertion of κ' by which the construction is made to correspond to classical Attic, is clearly the ultimate result of corruption, see van der Valk, *Textual Criticism*, 161. Mere ejection of the κ' or γ', with Bentley, is insufficient, since the ordinal is ἐ(ϝ)ικοστός with prothetic ἐ-.   **Σχερίην:** see vi 4 n.

35. ἀγχίθεοι refers to the Phaeacians' special relationship with the gods, rather than to their kinship. (The mythographers invented Phaeax, son of Poseidon and the nymph Asopis.) See vi 201–6.

36. περὶ κῆρι: formulaic (*Il.* 8 times, *Od.* 6 times), though that in itself proves nothing about the syntactical relation of the two words. Chantraine, *Grammaire*, ii 126, takes περί as adverbial and κῆρι as locative (as it must be at *Il.* ix 177, the only place where κῆρι is without περί). This suits the present line; sense, however, at vi 158 favours a prepositional περί. Formulaic usage allows variable syntax, see 162 n.   **τιμήσουσι,** according to the orthography of the vulgate, is fut. indic., not aor. subj. The construction is Homeric (Chantraine, *Grammaire*, ii 225), but here at least probably archaistic: the line is adapted from the prototype seen at xix 280 = xxiii 339, οἳ δή μιν περὶ κῆρι θεὸν ὣς τιμήσαντο.

38–40. The gifts are specified at viii 387 ff. and xiii 10 ff., thirteen changes of raiment and as many talents of gold. Yet this vast treasure (as the poet conceives it) could be stowed in a single chest, viii 438.

43–8. The epic invariably notes that on setting out a personage puts on appropriate gear, cf. i 96 ff., ii 1 ff., etc. The use of the long formula (44–8 = *Il.* xxiv 340–5; 44–6 = *Od.* i 96–8) suits the slow pace of the narrative.

43. διάκτορος ἀργειφόντης: a substantivized description or title, cf. περικλυτὸς ἀμφιγυήεις, γαιήοχος ἐννοσίγαιος, such as is commonly used for gods whose names are metrically difficult. The device is literary, since there is no correlation with the titles used in cult.   **διάκτορος,** conventionally rendered 'guide', whether of wayfarers generally or of the soul on its journey to Hades, cf. xxiv 1 ff. The attribute is suitable for the god, see E. T. Vermeule, *Archaeologia* V, 79, 90, with bibliography, but the word is not a normally formed agent noun of διάγω. For various speculations see Frisk, *GEW* s.v.   **ἀργειφόντης** 'Slayer of Argus': the story of Io and her guardian does not come within the purview of the Homeric poems, but is said to have been found in the Hesiodic corpus (schol. *Il.* xxiv 24). The sense 'Slayer of Argus' is implied by the form ἀνδρειφόντης, *Il.* ii 651 etc., whenever that epithet came into existence. But the formation Ἀργεϊ- is philologically impossible, unless -εϊ- (for -o-) is accepted as a metrical adaptation (so Kretschmer, *Glotta* x (1919), 45 and subsequent papers), cf.

χαλκεο-, πηγεσι- for χαλκο-, πηγο- —but there is no real parallel. See also i 38 n. and M. L. West's excursus, *Hesiod: Works and Days* (Oxford, 1978), 368-9.

It is remarkable that so many epithets of Hermes (cf. also ἀκάκητα, ἐριούνιος) should be of obscure meaning. The god seems to antedate the coming of the Greeks (cf. J. Chittenden, 'The Master of Animals', *Hesperia* xvi (1947), 89-114) and in all likelihood his name also, since the derivation from ἕρμα (in the sense 'cairn'), cf. Burkert, *Religion*, 156, is not free from philological difficulty.

45. **ἀμβρόσιος,** strictly 'undying' (< *ἀ-μρότ-ιος) is epithet of anything connected with the gods. **χρύσεια** because divine, and therefore magnificent: the *winged* sandals of iconography are a post-Homeric improvement.

47. The ῥάβδος (described at *h.Merc.* 528-32), like Athena's spear (i 99-101) and Poseidon's trident, is a permanent piece of the god's equipment. He will not use it on this expedition.

48. **ἐθέλει:** the subjunctive (ἐθέλῃ) is the better mood to express the sense 'of *all* those he wishes', see Chantraine, *Grammaire*, ii 245 and Ruijgh, τε *épique*, 378. **ὑπνώοντας,** a difficult form following, according to Meister, *Kunstsprache*, 91, the analogy of ἱδρώω. Schulze's idea, *Quaestiones*, 370-3, that the form conceals some sort of desiderative depends upon his over-precise assumption that the context requires the sense 'those who are weary'.

50. **Πιερίην:** the mountain range north of Olympus, the first point also at which Hera alighted on her way to Ida, *Il.* xiv 226. The goddess proceeded by Athos and Lemnos, but it is impossible to follow Hermes' journey or to identify the πόντος. The explicit association of Pieria with the Muses first appears in Hesiod, *Op.* 1 and *Th.* 53. Bérard's Πηρείην, a township in Thessaly according to the ancient lexica, is inspired by the confused MS tradition at *Il.* ii 766 (Πιερίη, Πηρείη, Πηρίη, Φηρίη).

51. **λάρῳ:** according to Thompson, *Glossary of Greek Birds* (Oxford, 1895), s.v., a gull or tern. It is distinguished from the αἴθυια, a diving bird, by Aristotle, *HA* v 9, 542 b. Hermes swoops down to the sea (ἔμπεσε πόντῳ) and skims across the surface. The comparison of a god to a bird is frequent (*Il.* v 778, vii 58, xiv 289, xv 237, xix 350, *Od.* i 320, iii 371, v 337, xxii 239) and natural, though, as Nilsson thought (*Minoan-Mycenaean Religion²*, (Lund, 1950), 491), it may ultimately derive from the cults of the second millennium BC to which the numerous bird figurines and bird motifs of the period are witness. The arrival or departure of a god is typically ornamented by a simile, see Moulton, *Similes* 138. It is unclear whether Hermes (and Leucothea at 337 and 353) acts in the *manner* of or in the *form* of a bird, on which see F. Dirlmeier, *Die Vogelgestalt homerischer Götter* (Heidelberg, 1967), and i 320 n.

52. **δεινούς** is metrically δϝεινούς, as in the formula μέγα τε δεινόν τε, iii 322, and often in the *Iliad*. Most Odyssean examples of the word occur initially.

54. The ancient critics desired concision and exactitude; hence the athetesis (προσέθηκέ τις οὐ δεόντως τὸν στίχον. καὶ μέντοι καὶ βραδύτερον πορεύεται μὴ χρώμενος τῷ ἰδίῳ τάχει). But the use of a resumptive line is normal epic

practice, called ring-composition. Ἑρμῆς, contracted, the usual form in
h.Merc., but 4 times only in Od., has also directed suspicion on the line.
55–147. Hermes and Calypso. The arrival and reception of a guest is one of
the most formalized contexts in the epic, see Arend, Scenen, 28–63, esp.
48–50. The following elements are usually present: (1) the scene is
described, (2) the stranger presents himself, (3) he is welcomed and offered
food, (4) lastly, he is invited to state his identity and business. See i 102 ff.
(a close parallel to the present scene), xiv 5 ff. Features of the supplication
scene are combined at vii 81 ff. Content and order may be disturbed if the
guest is well known to the host, as at Il. ix 182 ff. and xxiv 468 ff., or
unwelcome, as at Od. xvii 182 ff.
55. **νῆσον:** called Ὠγυγίη at i 85 and elsewhere: see vi 172 n.   **τηλόϑ'**
ἐοῦσαν: the consistent feature in the geography of Odysseus' wanderings is
extreme distance, as the poet conceived distance, cf. ἔσχατοι of the
Phaeacians, vi 205. Some Hellenistic scholars therefore, notably Eratos-
thenes, supposed that the poet actually represented the wanderings as
taking place in the outer ocean. For the ancient controversies see Strabo i
2, 9–15. Localizations of Calypso's isle in the real world are as numerous
as its investigators: (1) near Crete (Antimachus fr. 142 Wyss, reading
Ὠγυλίη for the name); (2) in or near Italy, (a) Gozo (Callimachus fr. 470
Pfeiffer—see Pfeiffer's n.), (b) Lacinium (Scylax 13), (c) Nymphaea (παρὰ
τῷ Ἀδρίᾳ, AR iv 574), (d) near Puteoli (DC xlviii 50), but when Propertius
(iii 12, 31) and Mela (ii 7, 18) call it Aeaea (Circe's island x 135 etc.) they
reveal nothing but their own confusion; (3) various places, ranging from
Malta and Gibraltar to Madeira and even the British Isles, according
to the reconstruction of the wanderings by modern scholars. (For the
history of modern speculation on this question see A. and H.-H. Wolf, Die
wirkliche Reise des Odysseus (Vienna, 1983) 143–206.) Even in antiquity
the radical view was not unknown, namely that the poet described
fictional places in fictional locations—whatever may have suggested
particular features of scenery and whatever may be the source of the
idea that distant lands existed beyond Cape Malea. Eratosthenes was its
best known protagonist. Such moral courage was rare and most saw the
issue as 'utrum ἐν τῇ ἔσω θαλάσσῃ Ulixes erraverit κατ' Ἀρίσταρχον an ἐν τῇ
ἔξω κατὰ Κράτητα' (Gellius xiv 6. 3). A technical term, ἐξωκεανισμός,
described the latter view. For an excellent discussion of the controversy see
F. W. Walbank, A Historical Commentary on Polybius, iii (Oxford, 1979),
577–87.
56. **ἤπειρον:** simply 'land', as at iii 90, x 56, etc.
57. **νύμφη:** in the Homeric version of Odysseus' return Calypso's role is
simply to detain the hero until Telemachus' maturity. It is likely therefore
that she is a poetical fiction created for that purpose, see Woodhouse,
Composition, 46–53, 215–16. She has no place in myth independent of the
Odyssey, unless we so count the appearance of a 'lovely Calypso' among the
daughters of Ocean at Hes. Th. 359. The poet of Hes. fr. 150 M–W 30–1,
who derived the Cephallenians from the union of Hermes and Calypso,

clearly used the present passage. There are parallels between Calypso and Circe, a figure of folk-tale, but they arise from the poet's conception of a pleasant isle inhabited by an amorous goddess. Wilamowitz's view, *Untersuchungen*, 115, that Calypso is actually modelled on Circe with some subsequent reaction of the conception of Calypso on that of Circe, is too narrowly that of an analytical critic. It is rejected e.g. by Lamer in *RE* s.v. Kalypso. Calypso is no witch, but a minor divinity of the Olympian religion. She appears not to exist strongly in the poet's mind, and consequently not in the reader's, so that Odysseus' departure does not arouse the ambiguous emotions excited, for example, by Aeneas' desertion of Dido. Nonetheless, for a thumbnail sketch her characterization is excellently done, cf. Austin, *Archery*, 149–52.

58. εὐπλόκαμος: πλόκαμος (< πλέκω) is properly a braided or plaited lock of hair, as explained at *Il.* xiv 175–7. The fashion is strikingly exemplified in Minoan-Mycenaean art, but is hardly ever unknown, cf. Marinatos, *Archaeologia* B, 1 ff. The poet uses a general word applicable to all females. The older goddesses wear a different style, denoted by ἐϋστέφανος (Artemis, *Il.* xxi 511; Aphrodite, *Od.* viii 267, *h.Ven.* 6 etc.; Demeter, *h.Cer.* 224 etc.).

59. ἐσχαρόφιν (< ἐσχάρη): a poetical form, like κοτυληδονόφιν (433), employing an ending -όφι extracted from *o*-stem nouns, where the -φι ending is probably itself a secondary development. In the Mycenaean dialect -φι is principally used to express the instrumental plural in consonantal and *a*-stems. The Homeric usage is very imprecise both as to number and case, since the disappearance of -φι from the vernaculars exempted the poets from the control of contemporary speech. See Chantraine, *Grammaire*, i 234–42, and Shipp, *Studies*, 1–16, *Essays in Mycenaean and Homeric Greek* (Melbourne 1961), 29–41. ἐσχαρόφι is certainly sg., but the case is doubtful: gen. and dat. are both possible.

60. κέδρου: not the cedar of Lebanon but the prickly cedar, *Juniperus oxycedrus*. θύου: probably the citronwood, *Callitris quadrivialis*. The classical θυία, *Juniperus foetidissima*, is certainly pungent but, at least according to Theophrastus, *HP* v 3. 7, principally a north African species.

61. ἀοιδιάουσ': a poetical formation, cf. ἀκροκελαινιόων, θαλπιόων, κελευτιόων, φαληριόωντα, φυσιόωντας, etc. It provides a nom. to ἀειδούσης ὀπὶ καλῇ (x 221) and a sg. to ἀμειβόμεναι ὀπὶ καλῇ (*Il.* i 604). Knight's ἀείδουσα (ϝ)οπί is metrically dubious: not only is the lengthening proper solely to words in *σϝ- (Chantraine, *Grammaire*, i, 146) but ϝ fell early before o-.

62. ἱστὸν ἐποιχομένη: the normal occupation of the Homeric woman, regardless of rank, cf. *Il.* xxii 440 (Andromache), *Od.* ii 94, xvii 97 (Penelope), iv 130 (Helen), vi 306 (Arete), x 222 (Circe). The loom is an upright structure from which the web hangs vertically, as represented in the Lin. B ideogram 159 ⌗ . The worker passes from one side to the other (ἐποίχεσθαι), as she threads the shuttle. The process is most fully described at *Il.* xxiii 760–3. It is natural that Calypso, like Circe (x 227), should sing while performing this repetitive task: it must be by chance that mortal women are not explicitly said to do so.

63–74. Calypso's island. The poet describes the Greek notion of an idyllic spot, cf. Pl. *Phdr.* 230 b–c—shade, water, and an exotic medley of luxuriant vegetation; only the view is missing, cf. the περίσκεπτος χῶρος of Circe's dwelling (x 211) and the sound of the cicadas (*Phdr.* 230 c). But the sociable Greek might discern a sinister overtone: there are no people in this paradise; Odysseus is both marooned and utterly alone. On the scenery see generally A. Parry, 'Landscape in Greek Poetry', *YClS* xv (1957), 3–29. It is doubtful if the poet wished to do more than describe an island fit for the habitation of a goddess: if it has something in common with Elysium (iv 565–8 q.v.) and the νῆσοι μακάρων (Hes. *Op.* 167–72: see West's n. ad loc.), that is because each is a paradise at the ends of the earth. The Garden of the Gods, where Zeus married Hera (Pherecydes, *FGrH* 3 F 16, Eur. *Hipp.* 742–51), has the same features. All lie in the far west, so as to be beyond the reach of human travel.

63–4. ὕλη: for Greek trees see R. Meiggs, *Trees and Timber in the Ancient Mediterranean World* (Oxford, 1982). The κλήθρη, 'alder', *Alnus glutinosa*, and αἴγειρος, 'black poplar', *Populus nigra*, are trees of wet ground, but the κυπάρισσος, *Cupressus sempervirens*, according to Theophrastus, *HP* ii 7. 1, prefers dry. The poet is above such botanical niceties, cf. 72.

65. τανυσίπτεροι: strictly 'with extended wings', the first element being derived from the verb τανύω, but the poets do not distinguish the form from τανύπτερος, 'with long wings'.

66. Calypso's birds: see D'Arcy Thompson, *A Glossary of Greek Birds* (Oxford, 1936), s.vv. **σκῶπες** are Little Horned Owls, *Otus scops*, if the word is used precisely, but these are shy, nocturnal birds resident in Greece only during the summer months: the Little Owl (γλαῦξ) is a much more visible bird. For the orthographic variants of the name (ἀείσκωψ, κῶπας, γῶπας, σκόπες) see Athen. ix 391 a–d. **ἵρηκες**: a generic term for the smaller hawks and falcons. Vergil's *sacer ales*, *A.* xi 721, implies a false etymology, for βείρακες· ἱέρακες Hesych. points to ϝ-, not present in ἱερός. **κορῶναι | εἰνάλιαι**: unhelpfully glossed by scholl. as αἴθυιαι, a term of even more uncertain meaning; presumably a cormorant, *Phalacrocorax carbo*, or shag, *Ph. aristotelis*, unless we have a poetical term for the ubiquitous gulls, *Larus* spp.

67. εἰνάλιαι: the lengthened first syllable is hardly etymological (as if from *ἐνσάλιος, or rather *ἐνhάλιος as Ruijgh argues, *Études du grec mycénien* (Amsterdam, 1967), 53, now that the loss of -σ- is shown to antedate the Mycenaean texts), for the provenance would be too remote, but rather from εἰν ἁλί where εἰν for ἐν arises from the analogy of εἰς/ἐς, see Wyatt, *Lengthening*, 90–2.

68. σπείους: The simplest explanation of this difficult form (6 times, cf. δείους twice < δέος) is that supported by Chantraine, *Grammaire*, i 7, according to which the original *σπέεος was in the archaic period spelled ΣΠΕΟΣ, a spelling subsequently interpreted as σπείους. But this is to ignore the tradition of the reciters. Moreover the acc. σπεῖος at 194 implies that the lengthened root syllable was already Homeric. Wyatt, *Lengthening*,

237, reasonably takes the lengthening to have arisen, in order to maintain the metrical shape of the word, by analogy with the many cases where epic -ειο- corresponded to vernacular -εο-. For the other case-forms see i 15 n.

70. πίσυρες: a curious epic form (6 times in nom. and acc.), much imitated by later epicists. The closest vernacular form is Lesbian πέσσυρες (and πέσυρα in Balbilla), with the characteristic Aeolic *k^we > πε-. πίσυρες might reflect *$k^{wo}tur$-, with reduced vowels in both root syllables, cf. M. Lejeune, *Phonétique historique du mycénien et du grec ancien* (Paris, 1972), 50, but the dialects, behind much analogical levelling, point to a normal IE declension: nom. *k^wetwor-es, acc. *k^wetur-ns, with gradation in the second syllable only, see O. Szemerényi, *Einführung in die vergleichende Sprachwissenschaft* (Darmstadt, 1970), 205: moreover the reflex of k^w before ι is regularly τ in all dialects. A development within the *Kunstsprache* must be assumed for πι, perhaps by assimilation to the fronted υ of Ionic.

The four springs presumably water every quarter of the island. Apollonius' baroque taste ran to different products, the four springs by Aeetes' palace (iii 222 ff.) supplying water (hot or cold according to season), wine, milk, and unguent.

72. σελίνου: 'celery', *Apium graveolens*, a plant of marshy places. Ptolemy Euergetes, in this an apt pupil of his grammarians, proposed σίου for ἴου. (σίον, a term for various umbelliferous marsh plants, perhaps the water parsnip, *Sium angustifolium*.) σία γὰρ μετὰ σελίνου φύεται, ἀλλὰ μὴ ἴα, Athen. ii 62 c.

74–6. The thrice repeated θηήσαιτο–θηεῖτο–θηήσατο is inelegant, an instance of Kirk's 'tired style' (*Songs*, 166–8).

79. It was difficult for *mortals* to recognize gods, cf. *Il.* v 127, and Odysseus' simulated uncertainty at *Od.* vi 149.

83–4. = 157–8. 157 is omitted by many MSS, and the scholl. to the present passage condemn 84 as superfluous (περιττός). The asyndeton is certainly harsh, but the Alexandrians were commonly offended at repeated groups of lines and dealt with them by omitting from one passage the lines they retained in the other: see van der Valk, *Textual Criticism*, 221.

85–96. The reception of Hermes. The literal interpretation of the text requires Hermes to be seated at 86 and at once made to stand up again at 91. Many codd. omit 91, the original text according to Apthorp, *Evidence*, 198–9, the intrusion of 91 being an example of 'concordance interpolation'. The natural sequence of events is illustrated at *Il.* xviii 381 ff.: Thetis comes to the house of Hephaestus. Charis welcomes her (385–6 = *Od.* v 87–8, with Thetis for Hermes) and leads her indoors (387 = 91), *then* seats her and calls her husband, whose privilege it is to enquire the visitor's business. Thus in the present scene 86 is the objectionable line: Hermes is seated *too soon*. D. M. Gunn, 'Narrative Inconsistency and the Oral Dictated Text in the Homeric Epic', *AJP* xci (1970) 192–203, esp. 198–9, defends the passage as if it were the verbatim record of an oral performance, 91 marking the point where the bard realized his error. Rather we have an unimportant passage constructed of conventional lines; it should not be scrutinized with more care than the poet used in its composition. M. W. Edwards, 'Type-scenes and Homeric Hospitality', *TAPhA* cv (1975), 61–7, diagnoses an overlap between 'messenger' and 'visit' scenes, together with a restarting of the scene at 85 after the notice of Odysseus' absence. The delay that intervenes between Calypso's question and Hermes' reply is not unusual: see Fenik, *Studies*, 80–2.

90. τετελεσμένον: a nuance of meaning must be added to the pf. ptcp. similar to that conveyed by the adjectival formant -τός: 'something that must come to pass'.

93. Ambrosia and nectar provide the sustenance of the gods. Beyond this it is uncertain that the epic had any clear conception of the nature of these substances. Ambrosia, for example, is a fluid at *Il.* xix 347, *Od.* ix 359; it is used as an unguent or embalming agent at *Il.* xvi 670, 680, xix 38, and xxiii 186, and as a cosmetic at *Il.* xiv 170 and *Od.* xviii 192. R. B. Onians, *Origins*, 292–5, divines that these substances are the Olympian equivalents of the ἄλειφαρ and wine offered by mortals to the gods. **κέρασσε ... ἐρυθρόν:** νέκταρ borrows the vocabulary appropriate to οἶνος. νέκταρ has no satisfactory Indo-European etymology (see Frisk, *GEW*, s.v.); it may conceivably be Semitic (< *nqtr* niph' al of *qtr*, 'to burn incense'), as argued by S. Levin, 'The Etymology of νέκταρ', *SMEA* xiii (1971), 31–50.

95. ἤραρε: 'suited, gratified'.

97–113. The decorated archaistic manner of the epic *Kunstsprache* has for the modern reader a certain uniformity. Sometimes the introductory line of a speech defines the tone: τὸν δ' ἐπικερτομέων (μέγ' ὀχθήσας, ὑπόδρα ἰδών, χολωσάμενος) προσέφη ... At other times emotion is concealed by a screen of formulaic diction. Scholl. discover a model of tact in Hermes' speech, because he stresses the distastefulness of his mission and makes no mention of Calypso's embarrassing love. It is hard to believe that this is correct. Hermes' distaste (101–2) is for the lack of the amenities to which he is accustomed. He is not to be blamed for the threatening manner he attributes, here and at 146–7, to Zeus, for that is traditional, cf. *Il.* xv 157–217, but the allusion to Odysseus, whom he cannot bring himself to name outright, is a contemptuous sneer. Calypso quite rightly replies, initially, with a tantrum.

97. θεὰ θεόν: polyptoton. The epic has no predilection for the rhetorical figures, but cf. 155 and the striking line ἀσπὶς ἄρ' ἀσπίδ' ἔρειδε, κόρυς κόρυν, ἀνέρα δ' ἀνήρ (*Il.* xiii 131 = xvi 215). The *o*-stem θεός is the normal feminine in Attic-Ionic, Arcado-Cypriot, and apparently also in Mycenaean; θεά must be an Aeolism in spite of the doubts of Wathelet (*Traits*, 354–5); it is strongly entrenched in certain formulae and fixed usages. In the *Odyssey* the frequency of the *o*-stem as feminine and *a*-stem forms is as follows (*a*-stem figures in parentheses): sg. nom. 15 (17 + 32 θεὰ γλαυκῶπις Ἀθήνη), voc. o (12), acc. 3 (0), gen. -οίο 6, -οῦ 3 (3), dat. 2 (0); pl. nom. o (2), gen. o (2 + 26 δῖα θεάων), dat. o (-ῆσι 1, -αῖς 1). In the nom. sg., where alone the two types are in serious competition, θεά may be (as here) a distinctive fem., but the decisive factor seems to be euphonic: see 194 and vii 41 nn.

101. ἄσπετον: the punctuation (;) is too heavy, for the co-ordinated clause οὐδέ τις ἄγχι ... is not functionally distinct, as an instance of cumulative sentence construction, from the relative clause that often follows the run-over epithet. (On the cumulative technique see now Kirk, *Commentary*, 30–5.) S. E. Bassett, 'The So-called Emphatic Position of the Run-over Word in the Homeric Hexameter', *TAPhA* lvii (1926), 116–48, denied that the run-over word had any especial stress, because it was a habitual feature of Homeric sentence structure. Few will be convinced.

105–11. Schol. dislike the repetition of 110–11 = 133–4, and find the lines 'superfluous' and 'at variance with the story'. Their content is indeed gratuitous, but only to Calypso not to us; and Hermes has to describe Odysseus somehow. They contradict the story because the lines seem to make the fate of Odysseus part of the same nexus of events, thematically and chronologically, as the νόστος Ἀχαιῶν of which Phemius sang (i 326)—and which could not, on that occasion, have included the sufferings of Odysseus.

105. ὀϊζυρώτατον ἄλλων: a frequent and convenient Homeric idiom, cf. *Il.* i 505, vi 295, x 434, *Od.* xv 108, and the common ἔξοχος ἄλλων 10 times. πάντων would be logical, but would not enter into this formular system.

106. τῶν ἀνδρῶν: for the structure of this sentence cf. *Il.* xix 103–5; the gen. is partitive and construes with ἄνδρα in 105.

108. Ἀθηναίην ἀλίτοντο: by the sacrilege of Ajax; for its consequences see iii 134 ff. Hermes speaks generally, not to say loosely: Poseidon wrecked Ajax, iv 500, and Zeus Odysseus, xii 405 and 132 below, on the complaint of Helios. Nor were Odysseus' travails, in our *Odyssey*, the result of Athena's displeasure, as the juxtaposition of 110–11 with 108–9 implies. (That Odysseus was in fact a victim of Athena's anger is, however, the thesis of Clay, *Wrath*.)

111. See the narrative, xii 420 ff.

113–14. In Homer αἶσα and μοῖρα form a synonymous pair beginning respectively with vowel and consonant, like ἄλγεα/κήδεα, ἐσθλός/δῖος, ἄλκιμος/φαίδιμος, etc. αἶσα is an 'Achaean' word regular outside the epic only in the Arcadian dialect (in the concrete sense 'part') with some attestation in Cypriot and Argolic: see Ruijgh, *Élément*, 118. For the Homeric idea of Fate see vii 196–8 n.

166. δῖα θεάων: a very common formula (33 times), mostly applied to minor goddesses (Calypso, Circe, Dione, Eidothea, Thetis) but also to Athena (5 times) and Hera (once). It is probably derivative from δῖα γυναικῶν, since (despite δι' Ἀφροδίτη and δῖα Καλυψώ) δῖος, 'god-like' *vel sim.*, is not appositely applied to divine persons.

118. An aural echo of *Il.* xxiv 33, with ζηλήμονες for δηλήμονες. **σχέτλιος:** a term of vague meaning, but applied especially to those who cannot be deterred from what the speaker regards as unreasonable behaviour.

119. θεαῖς: this dative, which is attested also at xxii 471 and twice in the *Iliad*, is of unexplained provenance: see Shipp, *Studies*, 57. Most dialects possessed the form from their earliest attestation, except Lesbian (-αισι in nouns), East Ionic (-ῃσι), Attic to mid-fifth century (-ασι/ῃσι), some forms of Cretan (-ασι), and early Argolic (-ασσι). It is found also in Hesiod and the *Hymns*, and to a greater extent than in Homer. -αισι (and therefore -αισ᾽) is unhomeric. Explanations of -αις as the consequence of interpolation or accident of transmission fail to account for the uniformity of the textual tradition, where -αις is attested, in face of the normal -ῃς/-ῃσι. For detailed discussion see G. M. Bolling, 'Dative Plural of the *O*- and *A*- Stems in Homer', *Language* xxii (1945), 261–4.

120. Some commentators have thought that this line implies a difference in attitude towards a mere amour and a more permanent liaison: but Olympus scarcely had a policy in the matter. Odysseus, who according to Calypso's logic would have been the victim of the gods' indignation, certainly felt no apprehension, whether with Circe or with Calypso: nor should he, for the crucial distinction, according to *h.Ven.* 281–8, was between a nymph, of whose favours a hero might boast with impunity, and a goddess whose μέγ᾽ ὄνειδος Zeus would infallibly avenge. See M. M. Willcock, 'Mythological Paradeigma in the *Iliad*', *CQ* xiv (1964), 141–54, for other instances of the free use of mythology to make a point in a special context.

121. Cursed, it was said, by Aphrodite in vengeance for an amour with Ares, Eos was especially susceptible to the charms of young mortals. The mighty hunter Orion was succeeded by Cephalus, Cleitus, Ganymede, and Tithonus (Athen. xiii 566 d). The erotic aspects of the Dawn-goddess seem to be part of IE mythology, see D. D. Boedeker, *Aphrodite's Entry into Greek Epic* (Leiden, 1974). The stories of Orion's death are various (see Roscher, *Lexicon* s.v.) but none attribute it directly to the consequences of his liaison with Eos. **'Ωρίων':** for the vocalism see 274 n.

122. ἠγάασθε follows the pattern of verbs in -άω (Meister, *Kunstsprache*, 87: the normal diectasis is seen in ἀγάασθε (119). **ῥεῖα ζώοντες:** a happy use of the formulaic epithet phrase (3 times). The latent contrast, of course, is normally between the μοῖραι of gods and men, not between the Olympians and the minor divinities.

123. ἕως < *ἦος. A trochaic form, ἦος or εἶος is restored by eds. in many formulae. There is slight evidence for εἶος but none at all for *ἦος (and none for *τῆος or *τεῖος) in the MS-tradition, which regularly has a monosyllabic ἕως or a disyllabic εἴως. The facts are well set out by M. L. West, 'Epica', *Glotta* xliv (1967), 135–9. The problem is to conjecture at what stage in the evolutio.. of the epic dialect (a continuous process, advanced not only by the ἀοιδοί but equally by rhapsodes and grammarians) *ἦος became ἕως + particle or pronoun. Hoekstra, *Modifications*, 35, infers that the process began in the aedic period, since the quantitative metathesis (ηο > εω) is already Homeric. **'Ορτυγίη:** 'Isle of Quails' (ὄρτυξ), mentioned also at xv 404 and *h.Ap.* 16 in the early literature: very variously identified, especially by the commentators on xv 404, but commonly supposed to be Delos (Strabo, x 5. 8, AR i 419, 537 with schol., Callimachus, *Ap.* 59) or an adjacent island (*h.Ap.* 16). **χρυσόθρονος:**

of Artemis also at *Il.* ix 533, but 3 times of Hera and 10 times of Eos, expands the verse-end formula *Ἀ. ἀγνή* 3 times. It is easy to see why Eos is golden, but the other goddesses are so called as part of the golden haze through which the poet contemplates all things divine. The Ionian *ἀοιδοί* doubtless connected the word with *θρόνος*, 'seat', as did the Hellenistic commentators, but there is a word *θρόνον*, 'sequin' or 'flower' (*Il.* xxii 441), with which the -*θρονος* may be ultimately associated: see G. M. Bolling, '*Ποικίλος* and *θρόνα*', *AJP* lxxix (1958), 275–85. The Mycenaean apparently had *θόρνος* (*to-no*), 'seat', not *θρόνος*. For full discussion see E. Risch, '*θρόνος/θρόνα* und die Komposita vom Typus *χρυσόθρονος*', *Studii Classice* xiv (1972), 17–25. A papyrus of the first century BC from Qaṣr Ibrîm (*JEA* lxii (1976), 118–19) reads *χρυσόρροος*, a simple mistake in an otherwise standard text. *χρυσόρροος* is not listed in LSJ and may be a reminiscence of *χρυσάορος*, an epithet of Apollo (2 times in *Il.*, 4 times in *Hymns*), but not attributed to Artemis before an oracle cited at Hdt. viii 77.

124. A formulaic line (*Il.* xxiv 759, and 5 times in *Od.*) used to attribute a quick and painless death to the action of Artemis or (with masc. *ἐποιχόμενος*) to Apollo, according to the sex of the victim. Its use here is therefore eccentric. The usual contrast is with a lingering death by illness (xi 172, xv 407–11), but see xi 324 for another instance of vindictive behaviour by Artemis. The vulgate reading, here and elsewhere, combines the short dative -*οις* with the long -*έεσσι*. A v. l. -*οισι* ... -*εσσι* is invariably found, but should not be preferred, since the *Kunstsprache* has an aversion for words of the rhythm ⌣εσσι and a liking for those ⌣⌣εσσι.

125–7. '*Ἰασίων*: a by-form *Ἰάσιος* also exists. The fruit of this union, said to have been consummated in Crete, was Plutus, hence the cynical popular etymology of *Ἰασίων*, *πάντα γὰρ ἰᾶται ὁ Πλοῦτος*. At Hes. fr. 177 (M–W) Eetion is named as the lover. Both are reported to be sons of Zeus.

127. *νειῷ ἔνι τριπόλῳ*: the allusion is to some primitive rite designed by sympathetic magic to improve the natural fertility of the ground: see Fraser, *Golden Bough*, ii, 97–104. Fallow was turned several times, but the idea that it was turned precisely three times arises from a misunderstanding of Hes. *Op.* 461–4: *τρίπολος* refers rather to the ploughing of three furrows as part of the ritual. *οὐδὲ δήν*, because < **δϝήν*.

128. *ἀργῆτι*, 'flashing'. The complementary formula with a consonantal initial sound has *ψολόεντι* 'murky', a curiously opposite meaning. There is, of course, no correlation between the epithets and their contexts. See 74–6 n. for the immediate re-use of the formula at 131.

132. (= vii 250); *ἐλάσας* is the paradosis. Aristarchus distinguished *βάλλειν* (of missiles) and *ἐλαύνειν* (of hand-held weapons), and so read *ἔλσας* in this line: see van der Valk, *Textual Criticism*, 100. But the distinction is not absolute, and the sense of *εἴλειν* in Homer is 'hold back', or 'confine', rather than the 'drive up and down' (as in Hippocrates *Morb.* iv 51) which is required. *οἴνοπι*: see i 183 n.

135. *φίλεον* 'welcome (as one of the household)': see 28 n.

136. *θήσειν ἀθάνατον*: either by feeding him nectar and ambrosia, Pi. *P.* ix

63 (Aristaeus), *h.Ven.* 232 (Tithonus), or by anointing him, Hes. fr. 23 (a) (M–W) 21 ff. (Iphigenia).   **ἀγήρων**: the vulgate here and elsewhere in early epic (vii 257, xxiii 336, *Il.* ii 447, etc., Hes. *Th.* 305, 955, fr. 23 (a) 24, *h.Cer.* 260) has the uncontracted ἀγήραος(-ον), which provides the expected dactylic rhythm. The contracted forms, however, occur both at the verse-end and medially (e.g. 218 below and vii 94) in variants of the formula ἀθάνατος καὶ ἀγήραος and were written everywhere by Aristarchus.

139. ἐρρέτω: with the usual imprecatory meaning, *abire in malam rem*, cf. *Il.* xx 349. Calypso maintains her petulant attitude here and in 140.

140. πέμψω implies the provision of means as well as permission for departure, cf. viii 30 ff.

141–2. Calypso uses a pair of formulaic lines (= iv 559–60, v 16–17). It would have been incongruous to suggest that she might have had ἑταῖροι on her island.

146. Διὸς δ᾽ ἐποπίζεο μῆνιν: the compound verb occurs only in the imperative and in this formula, cf. *h.Ven.* 290 and Thgn. 1297 (both with θεῶν for Διος): its modification, xiv 283, reverts to the normal simplex. Zeus' μῆνις would be specifically directed at Calypso's contumacy not at her original offence, which he had countenanced for seven years, just as in *h.Ven.* Anchises was threatened, not for sleeping with Aphrodite, but for boasting of it.

148–227. Odysseus and Calypso. We have waited almost 2,400 lines for this moment, our first meeting with Odysseus in person—and his introduction is singularly without fanfare. A modern writer, it may be supposed, would have sought at this point to impress upon us the morally important traits of the hero's character, his tenacity of purpose, ingenuity of mind, and fortitude in adversity, in short the moral courage that pervades the *Odyssey* as much as physical prowess does the *Iliad*. But for Homer this has already been done for him by the epic tradition that is shared by both poet and audience (cf. the muted introduction of man-slaying Hector at *Il.* iii 38). He therefore continues the κωμῳδία ἠθολογουμένη (Longinus *de Sublimitate* ix 4). The man for whom Calypso would have done so much has put the length of her island between them. In her motives he has no confidence. She herself, obliged to surrender her paramour, and that in favour of a mortal woman, is in a ridiculous position. Odysseus is made to handle her with superb discretion. The poet's ironical and playful mood in the description of personal relationships is a most successful part of his genius, and much in evidence from this point to the end of viii.

150. Ζηνὸς: the usage and distribution of the analogical oblique cases of Ζεύς is examined by P. Wathelet, 'Le Nom de Zeus', *Minos* xv (1974), 195–225. They occur sporadically in the Ionic dialects and elsewhere, but though rare in comparison with the regular forms are formulaic in Homer, e.g. Ζηνὸς Ὀλυμπίου 4 times. The notable archaism Ζῆν (acc. sg., *Il.* 3 times, Hes. *Th.* 885) is absent from the *Odyssey*.

152. δακρυόφιν: gen. pl., formed with -όφι from the regular nom. δάκρυ: for -όφι see 59 n.

The tears are not unheroic in themselves (cf. iv 113, viii 84 ff., 521-2), but Odysseus has, we may think, reason to weep: all that life means to a hero, activity, struggle, achievement, has been taken from him in exchange for eternal indolence and pleasure. We seem for a moment to confront the fallacy of Utopia, but neither here nor elsewhere does the poet ruminate on the profounder aspects of his story. Nor would he necessarily have seen Odysseus' predicament in this philosophical light: for those who toil the toil-free paradise of Ogygia (or Scheria, or Elysium, or Olympus) seems infinitely desirable.

155. σπέσσι: see i 15 n.

156-8. Odysseus is not 'looking out for a ship' (Stanford), an improbable sight in Ogygian waters, but expressing his despair and frustration, like Achilles at *Il.* xxiii 59.

157. Omitted by some MSS, see on 83-4 above. The text certainly reads better without the line at this point.

160. The fifth successive line ending in -ων: but all Greek poets are indifferent to such assonance.

When a character in the epic is ordered in plain language by a god to do something (as opposed to being prompted by a dream or omen), he makes no allusion to the visitation, cf. Achilles at *Il.* i 193 ff., Hector at *Il.* xi 195 ff., xv 236 ff. It is as if the theological explanation of behaviour were a poetical gloss upon action that could from another standpoint be described in more prosaic terms, see M. M. Willcock, 'Some Aspects of the Gods in the *Iliad*', *BICS* xvii (1970), 1-10. So here, as at 182 ff. and 203 ff., Calypso ignores the commands of Hermes and speaks as if she had finally acceded to Odysseus' implied entreaties (and takes credit for doing so at 190-1): 206 ff. amount to an invitation to remain, in defiance of Olympus. As they stand Calypso's three speeches provide excellent characterization: 'Very well, I shall let you go. I am not as heartless as you think. But you would stay if you knew what is in store for you. Besides I can offer you more than Penelope can': all the better for lacking the rhetoric in which Ovid's heroines clothe their analogous arguments.

161. πρόφρασσ(α): fem. of πρόφρων, < *προ-φρη̧-τια, after the analogy of -ντ- stems, type χαρίεντ- fem. χαρίεσσα (with -ε- after the masc. for the expected α < η̧).

162. δούρατα μακρά: 'timbers' here and 370, 'spears' at xxii 251 and *Il.* v 656: for the persistence of the formulaic word-group despite the change of sense cf. περικαλλέα δίφρον, 'chariot' (*Il.* iii 262 etc.), 'chair' (*Od.* xx 387); μάρμαρον ὀκριόεντα, 'piece of rock' (*Il.* xii 380), 'sparkling' (adj.) (*Il.* xvi 735); μενοεικέα πολλά, 'good things' (*Il.* ix 227), 'pleasing' (adj.) (*Od.* v 267).

163. ἴκρια: Herodotus (v 16), describing the lake-dwellings of the Paeonians, speaks of ἴκρια ἐπὶ σταυρῶν ὑψηλῶν ἐζευγμένα in a passage where ἴκρια clearly denotes a horizontal platform supported by vertical piles. None of the Homeric uses of ἴκρια is incompatible with this sense, 'deck' in a nautical context. ὑψοῦ (164), may imply something more than a flat surface built over the timbers of the raft, but the language here is too abbreviated to make plain the picture in the poet's mind. See further on 243–61.

Hermes, of course, did not mention the raft, but the epic convention permits the characters to know what the audience knows, if the narrative is thereby simplified.

165. ὕδωρ, because the Greek practice was to dilute the wine.

166. μενοεικέ(α): neut. pl., usually of food but here qualifying the three items mentioned in 165.

171. ῥίγησεν: the formula is used of a character's response to words or circumstances he sees as menacing, cf. 116, *Il.* iii 259, xv 34. Scholl., who are always on the look-out for climatic indications, comically refer the word to the winter season. (For the season, see 272 n.) **πολύτλας δῖος Ὀδυσσεύς:** the adjective δῖος (whose primary sense is 'like Zeus in appearance or attributes', cf. 20 n.) is the most frequent of generic epithets, being used of 32 different heroes, and therefore says little about any of them. Doubtless something less imprecise would be preferable for Odysseus, but metrics, i.e. the short space to be filled, rule out distinctive epithets at this point even for the foremost heroes (hence even δῖος Ἀχιλλεύς). **πολύτλας:** 'much enduring', cf. πολυτλήμων (xviii 319), is the distinctive epithet of Odysseus in the *Iliad* as well as in the *Odyssey*. It expresses in lapidary form the Homeric conception of his leading character, but in general terms: the same formula combines with opposed states of mind, with ῥίγησεν here but with γήθησεν at viii 199. What is uppermost at this point in the poet's mind, it soon appears, is not the hero's sufferings but the alertness of mind with which Odysseus deals with the resentful Calypso.

173–9. Calypso's reaction to this speech (182 ff.), like that of Athena in similar circumstances (xiii 287 ff.), is one of pleasure not resentment. Odysseus therefore displays, to excess, watchfulness and caution, but we should not, with the goddesses to guide us, stigmatize his attitude as mistrust or suspicion. κερδοσύνη is typical of Odysseus in all his encounters outside the earlier wanderings (with Calypso, Nausicaa, Athena on Ithaca, Eumaeus, the suitors, even Laertes) and forms part of the Odyssean concept of the heroic (crafty success rather than the Iliadic tragic honour).

174. λαῖτμα: possibly from the root otherwise attested only in λαι-μός, 'throat', but the Homeric usage, being mostly in complex formulae with parts of περάω, stresses the idea of extent.

176. ὠκύποροι: a formulaic epithet (gen. pl. 4 times, dat. pl. 5 times) shifted to the run-over position. It is doubtful if any contrast is intended with the sluggish σχεδίη.

177. ~ x 342, **178–9** = x 343–4, and so cut out by Hermann and others together with 184–7 (= *Il.* xv 36–8 + *Od.* x 300). Such treatment of repetitions no longer commends itself, cf. G. M. Calhoun, 'Homeric Repetitions', *Univ. Cal. Pub. in Class. Phil.* xii (1933), 1–25.

179. κακὸν ... ἄλλο: cf. 171, but Odysseus can be understood to mean a κακόν to crown all the κακά recounted in ix–xii.

181. ὀνόμαζεν: 'address' originally, doubtless, by name, but the weak sense is well established (6 times without voc., as here; 22 times with descriptive voc. only; 15 times with name), though not without dispute as to the exact nuance: see R. d'Avino, 'La funzionalità di ὀνομάζω', *Studia classica A. Pagliaro Oblata*, ii (Rome, 1969), 7–33.

182. ἀλιτρός: 'rogue', cf. ἀλιταίνω, used literally at *Il.* viii 361 but here in an ironical sense. **ἀποφώλια:** an Odyssean word (here and viii 177, xi 249, xiv 212) of uncertain sense, glossed by ἀπαίδευτος in scholl., and by ἀνεμώλιος, μάταιος in the Lexica. The etymologists fall back on the Hesychian gloss ἀποφεῖν [*sic*]· ἀπατᾶν, taking the -ο- as an Aeolism.

184. ἴστω: 'be witness', a common formula in oaths (*Il.* x 329 etc., 8 times). Mortals, of course, call gods to witness except on the most solemn occasions (as at *Il.* iii 276–9) when, like the gods themselves, they appeal to more fundamental cosmic principles. K. Reinhardt, *Von Werken und Formen* (Godesberg, 1948), 501, rightly points out that the majesty of Calypso's oath (contrast that of Circe, x 345) is commensurate with the moment: the wanderings are over, the return has begun. **γαῖα** etc. the oath appears to reflect the division of the cosmos into heavenly, terrestrial, and infernal regions, cf. *Il.* xv 187–9, *h.Ap.* 85–6. Yet in the epic imagination Styx is a river of that part of the underworld assigned to the human dead. Hesiod elaborates further: Styx is a goddess, daughter of Ocean, *Th.* 389. Schulze, however, pointed out (*Quaestiones*, 440) that Styx occurs in Homer only in the formula Στυγὸς ὕδωρ/ὕδατος, a unitary idea, whose original denotation remains unclear. See further J. Bollack, 'Styx et serments', *REG* lxxi (1958), 1–35, esp. 17–25, and cf. *Exod.* 20: 4 'in heaven above, or in the earth beneath, or in the water under the earth'.

185–6. μέγιστος | ὅρκος: The penalties of perjury are dwelt on by Hes. *Th.* 793–806, a year's deprivation of nectar and ambrosia followed by nine years of banishment from the society of the gods. For ordinary occasions the oath by Styx alone was sufficient, e.g. Hes. *Th.* 400 (where see West's n.) and *h.Cer.* 259.

188. φράσσομαι: 'will consider', not 'tell', a meaning that, according to Aristarchus, φράζειν never bears in Homer.

194. ἷξον: a 'mixed aorist', i.e. a first aor. with thematic conjugation. There is no normally conjugated first aor. ἷξα, indeed the only other active form known to the epic is the second aor. ἷκε restricted to the formula οὐρανὸν ἷκε and perhaps felt as an impf. C. Prince Roth, 'Thematic S-Aorists in Homer', *HSPh* lxxvii (1973), 181–6, plausibly suggests an analogy: ὦρτο: ὦρσε ~ ἷκτο (Hes. *Th.* 481): ἷξε. **σπείος:** see 68 n. **θεός:** the poet would have preferred the distinctive gender of θεά, cf. xx 393 θεὰ καὶ καρτερὸς ἀνήρ, but θεά is never scanned ◡◡ by correption: see also 97 n.

197. ἔσθειν: a poetical form, derived like the normal ἐσθίειν from the imperative ἔσθι (< *ἔδ-θι), perhaps attested at xvii 478, cf. Schwyzer, *Grammatik*, i 713.

201. Cf. *Il.* xi 780 (with τάρπημεν). Both halves of the line are formulaic, put together as an *ad hoc* replacement for the usual αὐτὰρ ἐπεὶ πόσιος καὶ ἐδητύος ἐξ ἔρον ἔντο (21 times).

202. The dat. pronoun in speech formulae supplies the indirect obj., so that τοῖς is anomalous where there is a single addressee: an inconsequence brought about by the use of a set formula.

203. W. B. Stanford, 'Homer's use of personal πολυ-compounds', *CPh* xlv (1950), 108–10, notes the clustering of such epithets about the name of Odysseus: πολύαινος, πολύμητις, πολυμήχανος, πολύτλας, πολύτροπος, πολύφρων. As in other cases, the formulaic system is extended from a traditional core, in this case by proliferating synonyms of the key epithet.

204. εἰ γοῦν τὸν σύνδεσμον [δή in this line] ἐξέλοις, συνεξαιρήσεις καὶ τὸ πάθος (Demetrius *de Elocutione* 57).

208. εὔχομαι: 'declare', 'claim', a very old use now attested in Mycenaean, on the Pylos tablets PY Eb 297 and Ep 704. For the semantic development see A. W. H. Adkins, 'Εὔχομαι, εὐχωλή and εὖχος in Homer', *CQ* xix (1969), 20–33, and J.-L. Perpillou, 'La Signification du verbe εὔχομαι dans l'épopée', *Mélanges Chantraine*, (Paris, 1972), 170–82.

212. οὐ δέμας οὐδὲ φυήν: Leaf (on *Il.* i 115) refers δέμας to outward appearance, φυήν to growth or stature: more precisely, as scholl. put it here, φυή is ἡ ἐκ πάντων μελῶν ἀναλογία: see also 217.

215–24. Odysseus takes up Calypso's points (her beauty, his longing for home, his future sufferings) *in reverse order*, according to the Homeric habit. The structure of Homeric discourse has been examined by D. Lohmann, *Die Komposition der Reden in der Ilias* (Berlin, 1970).

215. πότνα occurs in Homer only in this formula (3 times) and in the vocative case (cf. πότνα θεάων (*h.Cer.* 118), nom.): hence, according to Schulze, *Kleine Schriften*[2] (Göttingen, 1966), 325, < *πότνι cf. Sanskrit *patni*. Chantraine, *Grammaire*, i 170, takes the form as a spelling for πότνια with consonantalized iota, an orthography otherwise found only in δῆμον (δήμιον) at *Il.* xii 213. But the form is evidently artificial, after the many doublets in -ιος/-ος developed within the *Kunstsprache*.

217. ἀκιδνοτέρη: a pure gloss. Scholl. report two guesses, ἀσθενεστέρα and εὐτελεστέρα, neither evidently far from the mark. εἰσάντα: scholl. report Ἀρίσταρχος, εἰς ἄντα, αἱ κοινότεραι, εἰς σῶμα (εἰς ὦπα Porson). σῶμα is certainly wrong, but εἰς ὦπα, read here by Eustathius, could well be right, cf. xxii 405, xxiii 107 for the formula. Aristarchus would have been motivated by over-exactitude—ὦπα is strictly 'face', but Odysseus is speaking of μέγεθος 'height'; cf., however, ἐσάντα ἰδεῖν (*Il.* xvii 334, *Od.* xi 143). μέγεθος: regularly grouped with εἶδος, cf. vi 152, xi 337, xviii 249, xxiv 253. Height was an essential part of Greek beauty, cf. the superiority of Artemis to the nymphs, vi 107–8; in the classical period Aristotle, *EN* 1123 b 7, denied a short person could be handsome.

218. ἀγήρως: the medial formula is attested with the uncontracted -αος in the fourth foot, see 136 n., although Aristarchus preferred the contracted

-ως there also. The poet exploits the versatility provided by contraction to move the formula to the verse-end.

219–20. Dante, *Inferno* xxvi 90–142, imagines a heroic Odysseus who relentlessly seeks out danger and experience. There is some evidence of this concept of the heroic in the early episodes of the wanderings, e.g. ix 39 ff. (the Cicones) or ix 172 ff. (the Cyclopes), but generally the *Odyssey* shows a sense of moral achievement quite as important as physical courage. The marooned Odysseus is *doing* nothing, he is not even, like the defeated Satan in *Paradise Lost*, meditating escape and vengeance, but he is *being* supremely loyal to the things he values.

220. = iii 233 = viii 466, an unusual formula in that it presupposes the loss of digamma in (ϝ)ἰδέσθαι.

221–4. A fine expression of Odyssean heroism (which would have been out of place if Odysseus had known of the gods' decision to effect his return). The words are spoken with grim resolution, not swagger, although they have an ironic colour and anticipate the storm of 282 ff.

225. Ὣς ἔφατ': this speech is effectively Odysseus's farewell to Calypso, for the poet gives them no more direct speech. He does not in fact leave until four days later. The poet handles one topic only at a time, in accordance with the principle of archaic composition laid down by B. E. Perry, 'The Early Greek Capacity for Seeing Things Separately', *TAPhA* lxviii (1937), 403–27, and is now about to pass on to the boat-building.

225–7. For the casual attitude towards sexual relations cf. xx 6, *Il.* ix 663, and the revealing comment ἀγαθὸν δὲ γυναικί περ ἐν φιλότητι μίσγεσθαι (*Il.* xxiv 130).

227. τερπέσθην: dual, with plural participles. The hesitation is frequent, see Chantraine, *Grammaire*, ii 22 ff.

228–61. The boat-building. A good instance of 'ornamentation' (expansive and decorative treatment, see Lord, *Singer*, 86 ff.). In a technical matter such as this the poetical imagination, controlled as it is by the limits of the audience's credulity, is usually tempered by realism, see C. M. Bowra, *Heroic Poetry* (London, 1952), 147 ff. So here Odysseus' boat is a genuine vessel. Bérard, because he takes the boat for a mere raft, alleges 'un auditoire hellénique aurait souri d'un conte où un homme seul, fût-il l'ingénieux Ulysse, aurait sur une plage deserte fabriqué la coque, la membrure et toutes les parties d'un vaisseau creux'. But Gilgamesh, for example, was equally adroit (*Gilgamesh* x. iii 44–8). The point of the description is not the importance of the artefact (the boat is at once wrecked, nor does the shield of Achilles play a role commensurate with its divine workmanship), but to shed lustre on the hero by its magnificence or virtuosity.

230–2. = x 543–5. In the present passage Aristarchus altered ἐπέθηκε to ἐφύπερθε (the dative κεφαλῇ would then be construed with περὶ βάλετο), presumably because the veil is not put on top of the head, as if it were a helmet. But ἐπέθηκε in fact comes from the arming scene, e.g. *Il.* iii 334 ff., from which these lines are adapted.

273

234. ἄρμενον: athematic aor. med. ptcp.: Chantraine, *Grammaire*, i 383.

235. ἀμφοτέρωθεν ἀκαχμένον: used of the blade of a sword, xxii 80, where the natural interpretation is 'two-edged'. But a double axe, a votive rather than a practical implement, can hardly be meant here.

237. ἐΰξοον makes the same point as ἄρμενον ἐν παλάμῃσι (234): it is used of the job, i.e. in a passive sense 'smoothed', not of the action of the tool.

239. = 64 with the substitution of fir for cypress. Theophrastus *HP* v 7. 1 mentions ἐλάτη, πεύκη and κέδρος as ναυπηγήσιμα. But the ancient shipwright used what was available. Wrecks have revealed a great variety of woods, see L. Casson, *Ships and Seamanship in the Ancient World* (Princeton, 1971), 212–13, but not apparently alder or poplar, though the former is very frequently mentioned in the Latin poets.

240. αὖα πάλαι, περίκηλα: The phrase recurs at xviii 309 of firewood. The poet appears still to be thinking of a raft, for ship timber was not permitted to dry out, cf. Theophrastus *HP* v 7. 3 ναυπηγικὴ δὲ διὰ τὴν κάμψιν ἐνικμοτέρᾳ ἀναγκαῖον (ἐπεὶ πρός γε τὴν κόλλησιν ἡ ξηροτέρα συμφέρει). ἵσταται γὰρ καινὰ τὰ ναυπηγούμενα καὶ ὅταν συμπαγῇ καθελκυσθέντα συμμύει καὶ στέγει, πλὴν ἐὰν μὴ παντάπασι ἐξικμασθῇ, nor any timber destined for planing, sawing, or drilling, cf. id. *HP* v 6. 3. It would be wrong therefore to suppose that the timber was standing because it had been killed by girdling the bark, as described by Vitruvius (ii 9. 3) in order to season in the ground. No technical process is yet in question.

243–61. Odysseus' vessel. The literature on this passage is very extensive, see D. H. F. Gray, *Archaeologia* G, which has a full list to 1971. Casson, *Ships and Seamanship*, op. cit. (v 239 n.), 217–19, has the most recent discussion in detail. There is no doubt that whatever his primary intention what the poet describes is a boat not a raft: not only were the timbers shaped (245), but they were drilled (247), jointed, and pinned with treenails (248). The timbers of a raft are not treated in this way, but are lashed together with cables so as to permit the timbers some degree of movement in response to the waves. (The problems of building and sailing large sea-going rafts may be agreeably studied in Thor Heyerdahl, *The Kon-Tiki Expedition* (London, 1950), ch. v.) Depictions of the vessel on sixth-century and later vases (for which see Touchefeu-Meynier, *Thèmes*, nos. 343–51) have no independent value, and the remaining technical terms are unhelpful. τορνώσεται, 'strike a curve', is indecisive, since it occurs in a simile. The meaning of στάμινες and ἐπηνεγκίδες (252–3) is disputed: if 'ribs' and 'gunwales', the reference is again to the hull of a boat. The wicker bulwark (256) and dunnage (257) are of uncertain implication. Early representations of ships in art are published by Gray, op. cit., S. Marinatos, 'La Marine créto-mycénienne', *BCH* lvii (1933), 170–235, and G. S. Kirk, 'Ships on Geometric Vases', *ABSA* xliv (1949) 93–153: to these must be added the evidence of the Thera wall-paintings, see e.g. Casson, 'Bronze Age Ships', *IJNA* iv (1975), 3–10. Of known wrecks that at Cape Gelidonya, Lycia, has been published in detail by G. Bass and others, *Cape Gelidonya: A Bronze Age Shipwreck* (Philadelphia, 1967). The ancient shipwright laid a keel (τρόπις), to which stem (στείρη) and sternpost (ἄφλαστον) were attached. He then built up the shell with edge-joined planks, each one mortised at close intervals. When the joints were forced home (ἀράσσειν), the tenons were secured with treenails (γόμφοι). He then inserted ribs and deck-beams (ζυγά), see C. H. Ericsson, *Navis Oneraria* (Abo, 1984), 41–61. (The modern practice is to construct the skeleton of ribs first, and then to fit the planking of the hull.) Homer, it is clear, has omitted various parts and operations. The reason for his doing so is possibly the fact that, having no traditional formulae for the construction of a raft, he borrows from a description of shipbuilding such as would be required for the story of the Argo, cf. xii 70. Both the *Iliad* and the *Odyssey* seem able to draw on a greater body of diction concerning seafaring than they actually use, as noted by Kirk, *Commentary*, on *Il.* i 434 and 485–6.

The whole passage is a good instance of Homer's succinct descriptive style.

247. In practice the drilling of massive ship-timber called for a team of men, see ix 384–6. ἥρμοσεν: 'matched the joints' (Aristarchus).

252–3. σταμίνεσσι ... μακρῆσιν ἐπηγκενίδεσσι: I follow Casson, *Ships and Seamanship*, op. cit. (v 239 n.), 217–19 in taking these rare terms to refer to important members of the hull, i.e. the ribs and wales; but there can be no certainty. J. S. Morrison and R. T. Williams, *Greek Oared Ships* (Cambridge, 1968), 48, and S. Marinatos, *Excavations at Thera VI* (Paris 1974), refer to the superstructure of uprights and horizontal rails seen at the stern in early representations of ships, as if Odysseus were erecting a cabin. ποίει: probably intransitive, 'he worked away'.

257. ὕλην: as ballast according to scholl., as if there were no stones on Ogygia: the reference is rather to dunnage, on which to stow cargo clear of the bilge.

258. φᾶρε': φᾶρος is a sheet of material, more or less as it comes from the loom. It may serve, for example, as a winding-sheet (*Il.* xviii 353): for the shape cf. ideogram 159 of the Linear B script, ⊟.

261. Odysseus is in a hurry. Sound practice permitted the joints to settle for a while before launching, cf. Theophrastus *HP* v 7. 4, Plut. *Moralia* 321 d.

262–81. Odysseus' departure. The narrative is succinct and, though in the epic manner the poet omits no significant detail, it is clear he is interested in the wreck (282 ff.) and not in the voyage itself.

262–83. τέτρατον ... τετέλεστο ... πέμπτῳ πέμπ': a curious, but by no means unique assonance: see A. Shewan, 'Alliteration and Assonance in Homer', *CPh* xx (1929), 193–209, and cf. πῆλαι ... Πηλιάδα (*Il.* xvi 142–3), Δάμασον ... δάμασσε (*Il.* xii 183–6).

264. λούσασα: a good prothysteron. Like Circe (x 450), Calypso performs herself the chores usually left to menials (iv 49, vi 210, viii 449, xix 317) or to junior members of the household (iii 464), as if she were alone on her island with Odysseus. The δμῳαί of 199 are perhaps a mere slip.

266. τὸν ἕτερον: According to Wyatt, *Lengthening*, 217–18, this is one of the few genuinely acephalic lines. The rhythm arose easily in this case by the modification of a prototype in which the article (a frequent reinforcemen‹ of antithetical words) was naturally long or lengthened by connective δ'

267: μενοεικέα πολλά: formulaic, cf. *Il.* ix 227, with a curious echo at *Od.* xiv 232 τῶν ἐξαιρεύμην μενοεικέα, πολλὰ δ' ὀπίσσω.

272–7: *Il.* xviii 486–9 read Πληιάδας θ' Ὑάδας τε τό τε σθένος Ὠρίωνος and repeat 273–5. The two passages have an extensive literary progeny, cf. AR iii 745; Verg. *G.* i 138, 246; Propertius iii, v 35; Ovid *Met.* viii 206, xiii 725; *Ars Amat.* ii 53; Musaeus *Hero* 213. But neither the poets nor their commentators shed much light on the present passage.

For the *Astronomy* of Homer see D. R. Dicks, *Early Greek Astronomy to Aristotle* (London, 1970), 27–38. Beside the constellations named here and in *Il.* xviii Homer knew an 'autumn star' (*Il.* v 5 etc.), doubtless Sirius alias the 'Dog of Orion' (*Il.* xxii 29), and the 'morning' (*Od.* xiii 93, *Il.* xxiii 226) and 'evening' (*Il.* xxii 317) stars—the planet Venus, the identity of the 'stars' being unrecognized, or at least unstated. Hesiod adds some useful data together with the names Sirius and Arcturus. The configuratiun of the stars was not visibly different in antiquity from the present day, but their behaviour was altered by the changing position of the celestial pole about which the stars appear to turn. The Earth's axis performs a slow movement comparable to that of a slow-running top or gyroscope. Projected onto the celestial sphere this movement (called, from the effect noted below, *precession*) causes the poles to describe circles of *c*.47° angular diameter about the poles of the ecliptic, i.e. the axis of the Earth's orbit about the Sun projected onto the celestial sphere. The movement of the poles affects year by year the coordinates (Declination and Right Ascension) by which stars are located on the celestial sphere, and causes a displacement of the points (equinoxes) where the circles of the celestial equator and the ecliptic intersect. The equinoxes thus move westward at a rate of *c*.1° every 72 years. As a result the solar calendar dates of astral phenomena are up to 40 days earlier in antiquity than at the present day. From this it is possible to infer that the astronomical data in Hesiod (e.g. *Op.* 564–7), crude as they are, were formulated in or about the eighth century BC.

Homeric navigation, as befitted the inhabitants of the Aegean archipelago, normally relied on landfalls, cf. iii 159–83 and ix 39–81. The present passage contains the sole reference to stellar navigation. The technique depends on the observation that the rotation of the heavens pivots at a fixed point, the pole, by reference to which the ship was kept steady in a given direction. The mariner had to know, for he could not calculate, the relative positions of his starting point and destination. By an irony of fate, at the present day, when such aid is superfluous, the pole is marked within 1° by Polaris. Owing to precession, for Odysseus the situation was substantially as described by Aratus, δύω δέ μιν (the πόλος) ἀμφὶς ἔχουσαι Ἄρκτοι ἅμα τροχόωσι (*Phaen.* 26–7) or by Ovid, 'quaeque polo posita est glaciali proxima Serpens' (= the constellation Draco), (*Met.* ii 173). If he used the northerly stars of Ursa Major as a fixed beacon, a navigator would be off course to the maximum extent of *c*.13°, hardly a serious matter for a single night's voyage amid the vagaries of wind and current. Ursa Major therefore continued to be the Greek guide, cf. Aratus *Phaen.* 37. The Phoenicians had a less conspicuous but more accurate mark in Ursa Minor, then about 4° off the pole, cf. Aratus *Phaen.* 42, Strabo i 1. 6. The determination of the true pole awaited the science of Hipparchus.

The Pleiades (Right Ascension 3 hr. 45 min. at the present day) and Boötes (RA 14 hr 30 min.) lie at opposite sides of the celestial sphere. Both are unmistakable objects, the Pleiades being the closest and finest star cluster visible to the naked eye, and Arcturus (α Boötis) being at Magnitude 0.2 the brightest star in the northern celestial hemisphere. Yet both are usually adduced as indications of season, the heliacal rising of the Pleiades before sunrise (about mid-May in antiquity) marking the beginning of summer, that of Arcturus (mid-September) that of winter. The technique of their use in navigation can only be conjectured. For Homer both would rise and set in approximately ENE and WNW directions, and would culminate 70°–80° above the horizon, a track similar to that of the sun at midsummer. During the sailing season (50 days after the solstice according to Hesiod, *Op.* 663) one or both would be conveniently visible throughout the night. Errors would be large, but Homer divided the night into three watches (*Il.* x 253) and the navigator could use his sense of time to correct his course, just as he would in using the sun by day. However, the partial coincidence of these lines with *Il.* xviii 483 ff. raises the suspicion that they supply general astronomical, not specifically navigational or seasonal, data.

The course recommended to Odysseus was generally easterly, but the specification ('on his left') is vague and could mean SE or NE or any course in that quadrant.

J. A. Scott, *Unity of Homer* (Berkeley, 1921), 107–9, and Austin, *Archery*, 240–4, claim that the lines provide an indication of the *season* of the *Odyssey*'s action, namely between 1 September and 21 October. But they are obliged to make two assumptions, that Odysseus watched the Pleiades *all night*, and that ὀψὲ δύοντα is a *significant* epithet. Neither assumption is certainly required by the text. Astronomically this season was dominated by the heliacal *rising* of Arcturus, a traditional harbinger of stormy weather. Hesiod rightly advised the sailor μηδὲ μένειν οἶνόν τε νέον καὶ ὀπωρινὸν ὄμβρον (*Op.* 674).

272. ὀψὲ δύοντα: δύειν is used both of the annual and daily motion of stars, hence (1) 'setting late in the year', Dicks, op. cit. (272–7 n.), 30, because the heliacal setting occurred in early November—but we do not know at what point the Homeric year ended; (2) 'slow-setting', scholl., because the constellation sets along its long axis, cf. 'tardum occasum', Catullus lxvi 67—an unnatural sense of ὀψὲ; (3) 'late sinking', Stanford, ad loc., because the bright Arcturus is slow to fade in the dawn—an improbable sense of δύειν; (4) 'setting in the late evening': this is confirmed by δείελος ὀψὲ δύων

(*Il.* xxi 232), cf. *serus* in Latin (e.g. Propertius iii 5. 35). The epithet is decorative, as usual in such a list, and would be factually true only of late summer and early autumn, cf. Aratus, *Phaen.* 585.

273. ἄμαξαν: 'the Wagon' is the usual and sensible designation of the constellation except where the learned have imposed derivatives of Ἄρκτος, see A. Scherer, *Gestirnnamen bei den indogermanischen Völkern* (Heidelberg, 1953), 134. It is neatly argued by O. Szemerényi, *Innsbrucker Beiträge zur Kulturwissenschaft* xv (1962), 190–1, that Ἄρκτος itself is a popular etymology of a loanword derived from the Semitic root seen in Akkadian *ereqqu* 'wagon'.

274. Ὠρίωνα: an uncontracted form Ὠαρίων is attested in the lyric poets (Pi. *N.* ii 12 etc.) and in pretentious Hellenistic writers (Callimachus, *Dian.* 265, fr. 110, Nicander, *Ther.* 15). The epic tradition, however, confirmed by the practice of Aratus, has Ὠρίων everywhere. West, on Hes. *Op.* 657, compares epic ὠτώεις in contrast with Callimachus' οὐατόεις (*Aet.* fr. 1. 31): see also General Introduction, pp. 25–6. Orion is an important constellation in Hesiod (*Op.* 598–9, 615–16) where, however, it marks the turning-points of the farmer's year.   **δοκεύει**: 'keep a good lookout for', usually of an aggressor (*Il.* viii 340, xiii 545), but also (as here) of an intended victim (so *Il.* xvi 313). The mortal Orion was the Greek Nimrod, the mighty hunter of myth, cf. xi 572 ff.

275. οἴη: true of the stars *mentioned* in Homer and Hesiod, as was noted by the ancient commentary preserved in *P.Oxy.* 2888. Draco, Ursa Minor (allegedly introduced into Greece by Thales *c.*600 BC), and most of Cepheus were also circumpolar in antiquity to the puzzlement of the commentators. Aristotle (*Poet.* 1461 a 21) took the word κατὰ μεταφοράν, the best known being called the only one. Strabo (i 1. 6) supposed that the poet intended Ἄρκτος to signify ὁ ἀρκτικός (sc. κύκλος) which defined in Hellenistic astronomy the circumpolar zone on the celestial sphere. Crates, holding the same view, went on to change the gender of Ἄρκτος in accordance with it, and read οἶος. Owing to precession at the present day the courses of the most southerly stars of Ursa Major pass below the horizon for an observer stationed in Greek latitudes (35°–40° N.).   **λοετρῶν Ὠκεανοῖο**: the Homeric cosmology is far from explicit, but we shall not greatly err if we think of a flat disk-like earth surrounded by the river of Ocean. The firmament of heaven covers the whole like a dome, so that the stars, having traversed the sky, necessarily plunge into Ocean. Whether they then passed eastward under the earth or round the edge was a matter for speculation: see the discussion in Athen. 469 d ff.

277. ἐπ' ἀριστερὰ χειρός: an odd expression (3 times in *h.Merc.*). The gen. is partitive, construed with the substantivized epithet.

278–81. Homer relates what men said and did. If for a time they perform no deed worthy of record, there is nothing to tell: if it were not for his visitors we should be told nothing of Achilles' feelings between *Il.* i and xvi. Even so, eighteen days is a long time to be dismissed in a single line. Did

Odysseus not feel boredom or despair? Something seems to be lost if the promised landfall does not appear, as it were, as the light at the end of the tunnel. The poet has a simile for that circumstance, recovery after a long illness, but will use it at 394-7 below.

279. Periods of nine days are frequent in the Wanderings (ix 82, x 28, xii 447, xiv 314), cf. G. Germain, *Homère et la mystique des nombres* (Paris, 1954). If Odysseus went sleepless throughout this period (cf. 271), the feat is not, for an epic hero, incredible nor even without parallel, cf. J. Conrad, *The Shadow Line* ch. vi.

281. ὡς ὅτε ῥινόν: the initial consonant (< ϝρ-) would be expected to make position, hence the variant readings. The sense is evidently 'shield', not 'hide' (which gives an image no more intelligible than Aristarchus' ἐρινόν 'fig-tree'). The shield familiar to the poet was round and bossed (ὀμφα-λόεσσα), cf. Lorimer, *Monuments*, 153 ff., and lying on its inner side would make a satisfactory comparison with a mountain rising from the plain. But a shield could somehow also suggest a headland, cf. ἀκρωτήριον ὑψηλὸν καὶ περιφανές, οἷον ἀσπίς (Περίπλους τῆς μεγάλης θαλάσσης, 117 Müller).

282-493. Wreck of Odysseus and his landing on Scheria. The whole passage should be compared with the wreck of Odysseus' last ship (xii 403-50). The present episode has no greater number of essential elements, but the extensive elaboration, principally achieved by the introduction of divini-ties and the use of direct speech, makes it one of the most memorable in the *Odyssey*. Even so the colour was too rich for some: scholl. to 401 report that Homer was censured for ostentation (φιλοτιμία) in multiplying the woes of Odysseus. Modern critics have been especially suspicious of the Leucothea episode (333-67, with 459-63) and of the prompting of Athena (382-7), but it is in the nature of epic ornamentation that it is inorganic in character.

282. ἐξ Αἰθιόπων: Poseidon had gone there before the opening of the action of the *Odyssey*: see i 22-5 n.

283. τηλόθεν ἐκ Σολύμων: to be far-seeing is the especial faculty of Zeus (hence the epithet εὐρύοπα) and Helios (cf. viii 302), but it is credited to some extent to all the Olympians. Poseidon watched the battlefield at Troy from Samothrace (*Il.* xiii 11) as Zeus did from Ida. However, more than good sight is here in question. The Solymi (mentioned also at *Il.* vi 184, 204) are part of the pre-classical ethnography of Lycia–Pisidia, see Hdt. i 173. The name appears to have survived in Mt. Solyma, the eastern peaks of the Lycian massif and an excellent point from which to observe the nearby sea-routes; but the poet has hit on an odd location, even for a god, if Odysseus is sailing in western seas, so odd that Strabo (i 2. 10, i 2. 28) had recourse to an involved geometry to argue that the poet intended to refer to Ethiopia. (For traces of an alternative *nostos* of Odysseus see i 93 n.)

284. ἐχώσατο: in fulfilment of the Cyclops' curse (ix 526-35), cf. i 68-71. The trivial motivation is not untypical of primitive thought, but has been taken by some to represent a secondary feature in the growth of the

COMMENTARY

Odyssey story: see Marzullo, *Problema*, 103–8, and more generally J. Irm
scher, *Götterzorn bei Homer* (Leipzig, 1950).

285. The monologue is a device used six times in the elaboration of thi
episode, though occurring only four times in the rest of the *Odyssey*. Th
distribution in the *Iliad* is similarly unbalanced (once in xi, three times i
xvii, once in xviii, twice each in xx, xxi, and xxii).

288. αἶσα: see vii 197 n.

289. πεῖραρ ὀϊζύος: 'bondage of exile' (Fitzgerald), or 'trial of misery'
(Lattimore)? πεῖραρ is a traditional metaphor that has been so widely
extended in epic usage that the developments are not easily traced. Some
have supposed an interaction of distinct but homonymous words, se
Frisk, *GEW* s.v. The exhaustive discussion by Ann L. T. Bergren, *Th
Etymology and Usage of* ΠΕΙΡΑΡ *in Early Greek Poetry* (American Classica
Studies 2, New York, 1975), distinguishes a literal sense 'bounds'
(πείρατα γαίης) with abstract application (ὀλέθρου πείραθ' ἱκέσθαι), ἁ
development of this sense to 'that which binds' (literally at xii 51 o
Odysseus' bonds), with metaphors such as ὀλέθρου πείρατ' ἐφάπτεσθαι
She regards the present usage as one that 'activates all meanings and
associations of πεῖραρ: with his step upon Phaeacia, Odysseus will escape
the great "bond" and "boundary line" of his misery'. We should add the
influence of the semantically related τέλος, e.g. τέλος θανάτου ἀλεείνω
(326 below).

290. μιν ... ἄδην ἐλάαν κακότητος: for the construction cf. Τρῶας ἄδη
ἐλάσαι πολέμοιο (*Il.* xix 423) and μιν ἄδην ἐλόωσι ... πολέμοιο (*Il.* xiii 315
with Leaf's n. ad loc.). The gen. construes loosely with the adv. to give the
sense 'his fill of woe'.

291–6. The struggle of the winds. This fine image has inspired many poetical
storms, e.g. Verg. *A.* i 81–123; Ovid *Tristia* i 2, 27–32; Seneca *Agam.*
465–97; Lucan v 597–677. Note the enjambment and rapid movement o
the passage. The storms of the Mediterranean are often abrupt and
confused, especially near land (see R. Hampe, *Die Gleichnisse Homers und die
Bildkunst seiner Zeit* (Tübingen, 1952), 7–8 for a description), but it is
doubtful if any natural phenomenon is described: the lines (which greatly
elaborate the account of the wreck of Odysseus' last ship, xii 403 ff.)
combine the images of *two* winds in conflict which occur in Iliadic similes,
Il. ix 4–7 (Boreas and Zephyrus) and xvi 765–69 (Eurus and Notus).

The wreck was naturally a popular subject with the vase-painters: the
principal references are collected by Touchefeu-Meynier, *Thèmes*, nos.
355–60. There is a succinct account of the storm in literature in M. P. O.
Morford, *The Poet Lucan* (Oxford, 1967), 20–36.

296. αἰθρηγενέτης: a metrical variant of αἰθρηγενής (*Il.* xv 171, xix 358),
and so passive in sense, 'born of the aether'. **μέγα κῦμα κυλίνδων:**
echoed at xiv 315, μέγα κῦμα κύλινδον, where κῦμα is subj. of the ptcp.

297–387. The wrecking of Odysseus' raft is told through two parallel scenes,
297–353 and 354–87: see introduction to v. In each Odysseus delivers a
monologue, his raft (or its remnants) is shattered, he clings to the

timbers, and finally he is saved for the moment by divine intervention. The cumulative technique, once thought redolent of a redactor's methods, is characteristic of the epic. Fenik, *Studies*, 143-4, notes that the simple juxtaposition of the scenes is untypical, an Iliadic rather than an Odyssean practice.

297. γούνατα: 'limbs', used synonymously with γυῖα. Both words make many formulaic combinations with parts of λύειν.   **φίλον:** the so-called 'possessive' use of φίλος with parts of the body (ἦτορ, κῆρ, λαιμός, χεῖρες, γούνατα, γυῖα) is peculiar to epic diction. It is extended from the use of the word to express the relation between the community and its members: see 28 n.

304. Zeus and Poseidon are named as the bringers of storms at Hes. *Op.* 667-78. When ignorant of the truth, the mortals of Homer blame Zeus for their afflictions (cf. *Il.* xix 87), or whatever god seems specially appropriate (e.g. Paris blames Athena at *Il.* iii 439). Zeus in fact had brought about the wreck in xii. Odysseus' ignorance is a touch of verisimilitude, and sharpens the interest of the audience with the knowledge that they, through the poet, possess of the true nature of events.

305. σῶς: 'certain'. Uncontracted σάος could be substituted for the vulgate σῶς everywhere except *Il.* xxii 332, but the forms with diectasis (e.g. σόοι *Il.* i 344 etc.) imply σῶς: see M. Leumann, 'Griechisch σάος und σῶς', Μνήμης χάριν (*Gedenkschrift Kretschmer*), ii (Wiesbaden, 1957), 8-14.

309-10. The exploit is described in xxiv 36-42 in brief, and doubtless at greater length in the *Aethiopis*. The details would not have differed much from those of the fight over the body of Patroclus in *Il.* xvii: see B. Fenik, *Typical Battle Scenes* (Wiesbaden, 1968), 232-3.

311. To be unburied not only had disagreeable consequences in the afterlife (see *Il.* xxiii 69-74 and *Od.* xi 51-78), but was a humiliating disgrace fit to be inflicted on a hated foe, cf. *Il.* xxii 335-6 (Achilles to Hector). His funeral was a hero's crowning glory, and his tomb preserved his κλέος—καὶ ἐσσομένοισι πυθέσθαι, *Od.* xi 76, cf. xxiv 83-4.

312. Cf. *Il.* xxi 281, where Achilles fears that Scamander will overwhelm him. Scholl. accordingly decided that λευγάλεος was especially appropriate to drowning; the sense, however, must be general, as in the cognate form λυγρός.

313. κατ' ἄκρης: 'down from above'. The formulaic Iliadic usage (xiii 772 etc.) is restricted to the destruction of Troy, so that the feminine gender reflects an implied πόλιος, but the sense was first generalized, as here, and the phrase given the adverbial suffix -θεν. The result, κατ' ἄκρηθεν, is preserved as a variant at most points, but was early misunderstood as κατὰ κρῆθεν, as the derivative ἀπὸ κρῆθεν, [Hes.] *Sc.* 7, shows, and brought into association with κάρη (so Leumann, *Wörter*, 56-8). Hence the scholium here κατὰ παράλειψιν τῆς κεφάλης. 'Down on his head' would in fact be excluded only in the Iliadic passages.

314. ἐπεσσύμενον: Aristarchus took the form strictly as a pf. and emended, but his ἐπισσύμενον would be a *hapax legomenon*. The accentuation is supposed to be Aeolic but suggests that the perfective force of the form was not strongly felt by Ionian ἀοιδοί.

319. ὑπόβρυχα: the formation, whether an adv. or an acc. case, is the same as that of δίπτυχα beside adj. δίπτυχος.

328–9. The reference is apparently to the dried thistle plants themselves, not to the thistle-down (πάππος), cf. the parallel simile 368–70 (wind and chaff). Paired similes, such as 328–30 and 368–70, are discussed by Moulton, *Similes*, 19–27: the effect, of course, is to intensify the force of the image.

333–65. The intervention of Leucothea has been condemned, e.g. by Marzullo, *Problema*, 97–9, on the grounds that it is ignored in the sequel, and that the deification of a mortal is contrary to the doctrines of Homeric theology (unless we admit Heracles at xi 601–2). Moreover, Athena's intervention at 382–7 renders that of Leucothea superfluous. For the structure of the whole episode, however, see 297–387 n.: Leucothea corresponds to Athena in the first of two parallel scenes. Her function, like that of Calypso at 276, Nausicaa at vi 255, Athena at vii 28 and xiii 330, is to tell the hero what to do—or to foreshadow the course of the narrative: in both respects the closest parallel is the intervention of Eidothea to dispel Menelaus' perplexity at iv 363 ff.

333. τὸν δὲ ἴδεν: the transition is like the frequent τὸν δ᾽ ὡς οὖν ἐνόησε of the *Iliad*, and is equally without motivation in the immediate context. Later the Dioskouroi were believed to aid those in peril at sea, e.g. Alcaeus fr. 34 Page, Euripides, *El.* 1241.

333–4. Ἰνώ, Λευκοθέη: Ino, we learn from later sources (see Roscher, *Lexikon* s.v. Leukothea) leaped into the sea at Corinth with her son Melicertes (or Palaemon) to escape from her lunatic husband Athamas: see Burkert, *Homo Necans* (English transl., 1983) 178–9. She enjoyed cult in many places, sometimes in association with Leucothea, cf. Pausanias, i 42. 7 (Megara); iii 26. 1 (Thebes); iv 34. 4 (Corone). Blind to the obvious, scholl. derive the name Leucothea from the Λευκὸν Πεδίον of the Megarid, but the name was a generic appellation of sea-goddesses—Λευκοθέαι πᾶσαι αἱ πόντιοι (Hesychius). Although the wearing of talismans to protect from drowning is a well-known superstition (the initiates of the mysteries of Samothrace wore a band about the body, it is reported by schol. AR i 917), the introduction of Leucothea in this connection appears to be another example of the poet's free use of mythology: see 120 n. Her role, however, is a familiar one in folk literature. She is a 'donor' or 'divine helper' who encounters the hero at a moment of crisis to present him with a magic gift: see V. Y. Propp, *Morphology of the Folktale*[2] (Austin, 1970) 39–50, and Thompson, *Motif Index*, F 340–8 and N 810. **καλλίσφυρος,** i.e. *slim*-ankled, cf. Archil. fr. 206 West περὶ σφύρον παχεῖα, μισητὴ γυνή.

334. αὐδήεσσα: both here and in vi 125 the epithet seems to imply some distinctive quality of mortals as opposed to gods, yet the word is applied also to Circe and Calypso. J. Clay, 'Demas and Aude', *Hermes* cii (1974) 129–36, suggests that the Olympians had a special intonation, denoted by ὀμφή.

337. The line has been generally condemned. It may represent an early accretion to the text, inspired by 353, but the evidence against it was insufficient to satisfy Aristarchus: see G. M. Bolling, *External Evidence for Interpolation in Homer* (Oxford, 1925), 234, and van der Valk, *Textual Criticism*, 184. Some note, however, of Leucothea's point of departure is desirable, as in the epiphanies of Athena (*Il.* i 194) and Thetis (*Il.* i 357). The 'scientific' MSS that omitted the line conceivably misunderstood the comparison and took offence at a theriomorphic goddess. **αἰθυίη:** a generic and mostly poetical term for a sea-bird, a gull, *Larus* spp., according to Thompson, *Glossary of Greek Birds*, op. cit. (v 51 n.) s.v., but a diving bird seems here to be in question. **εἴκυῖα:** of manner, not appearance. **λίμνης:** 'sea', but not an obvious choice of word for stormy waters. λίμνη is equated with πόντος at *Il.* xxiv 79.

340. ὠδύσατ': Leucothea refers to Odysseus' present troubles, but uses a word in which, in the sigmatic aor., the poet seems to see a significant echo of his hero's name; see i 62 n., and for further discussion W. B. Stanford, *CP* xlvii (1952), 108–10; G. Dimock, *Hudson Review* ix (1956), 52–70 (= G. Steiner and R. Fagles (eds.), *Homer: A Collection of Critical Essays* (Englewood Cliffs, NJ, 1962), 106–9); and Clay, *Wrath*, 54–68. For the sense which this etymology may attribute to 'Odysseus' observe the apparent association of the name with ὀϊζύω at xxiii 307. **ἐκπάγλως <** **ἐκ-πλαγ-λως*, by dissimilation of λ–λ, used to protest at seemingly outrageous speech or behaviour.

342. ἀπινύσσειν: see vi 258 n.

344. νόστου: normally 'return home', but a generalized sense 'arrival at' is required here. This has seemed redolent of later usage, e.g. Euripides *IA* 966, 1261, to avoid which some critics expel 345.

346. τῇ: a demonstrative word (root **to-*) used imperatively, like δεῦρο. A pluralized form τῆτε is also found.

350. ἀπονόσφι τραπέσθαι: the injunction usually applies to dealings with chthonic or malevolent powers, cf. x 528, A. *Ch.* 98, Theoc. xxiv 96 with Gow's n. ad loc., etc., and for folkloric parallels Thompson, *Motif Index*, C 331–3.

354–64. A typical scene ('The hero ponders his course of action') of a class well represented in the *Iliad*: see Fenik, *Typical Battle Scenes* (Wiesbaden, 1968), 96–8. The hero exclaims in alarm (ὤμοι ἐγώ), considers one course of action, rejects it, and outlines the alternative.

357. ὅ τε or **ὅτε?** The nuance is in any case causal.

361. ὄφρ' ἂν μέν κεν: the formulaic use (cf. *Il.* xi 187, 202, *Od.* vi 259) as well as the occurrence of ἄν with κε elsewhere forbids correction.

365. The prototype of the initial formula is clearly **ἧος ὁ*. See 123 n. The MSS have ἕως or εἵως. 'Here, as elsewhere, the seeming vagaries of the manuscript tradition accord with the processes of oral poetry and thus bear witness to their faithfulness' (M. Parry, 'The Homeric Language as the Language of Oral Poetry', *HSPh* xliii (1932), 36–7, *Homeric Verse*, 353).

The process referred to is the continuous adjustment of the tradition to the vernacular dialect and the acceptance as 'correct' of whatever metrical rhythm results.

368. ἠΐων: 'chaff', hardly the same word as ᾗα (266 etc., = 'provisions'). For the function of the simile see 328–9 n.

371. κέληϑ': οἶδε μὲν ὁ ποιητὴς τὸν κέλητα, οὐκ εἰσάγει δὲ τοὺς ἥρωας αὐτῷ χρωμένους, scholl. Full discussion by J. Wiesner, *Archaeologia* F, 110–35.

377. ἀλόω: i.e. *ἀλάεο, 2nd sg. imperat. from ἀλάομαι. The transmitted form arises by diectasis of the Attic ἀλῶ (< ἀλάου), but is without precise parallel: see Cauer, *Homerkritik*, 93. The normal Ionic would be ἀλάευ.

378. διοτρεφέεσσι: a generic epithet (of kings and heroes); the special epithet is φιληρέτμοισι (386 etc.).

379. ὀνόσσεσϑαι: 'find fault with', i.e. 'think it insufficient', cf. 290.

381. Αἰγάς: Various places were so called. At *Il.* viii 203 Aegae is joined with Helice, a town in Achaea (*Il.* ii 575), as places were Poseidon was especially worshipped: but at *Il.* xiii 20–1 Aegae is four Olympian paces from Samothrace, in a passage reminiscent of the present. Poseidon was last located (283) on the mountains of the Solymi.

382–7. Athena's tutelage of the house of Odysseus has been much in evidence from the beginning of the poem. It is thus not at once apparent that the present intervention on behalf of Odysseus is the first that she has made since the hero departed from Troy. She was reluctant, she explains at xiii 341 (cf. vi 329) to offend Poseidon, whose wrath had been kindled by the blinding of Polyphemus. (A weak excuse, see vi 329 n.) It is reasonable, of course, that having set the return of Odysseus in motion she should help it along. Nevertheless many analysts have rejected the lines (details in Rüter, *Odysseeinterpretationen*, 230) as inessential.

386. ἧος ὁ: see 123 n. L. R. Palmer in *Companion*, 172, notes the final force of the conjunction, here and at iv 800, vi 80, ix 376, and xix 367.

391. = 168. Aristarchus read ἡ δὲ γαλήνη, but the contrast is rather between the weather and the sailor(s).

393. ἀρϑείς: probably an Attic form (Shipp, *Studies*, 50), though found also in the *Iliad* (xiii 63). For other linguistic and stylistic anomalies in 382–423 see Shipp, *Studies*, 326. **ὑπὸ κύματος:** Rhianus appears to have objected to the agent construction (ὑπό) for something as impersonal as a wave, and changed the preposition to ἐπί. κῦμα does not mean a breaker (the weather is now calm) but a broad heaving swell.

394–7. A remarkable and moving simile. Yet the association of rescue at sea with family reunion is probably traditional, for the two recur at xxiii 233–8, where, however, it is the rescue that illustrates the reunion.

395. κεῖται: probably a short vowel subj. (< *κεγεται).

396. δαίμων: ('he who deals out', cf. δαίω), an unspecific supernatural agency invoked as the cause of the inexplicable: cf. M. Untersteiner, 'Il concetto di δαίμων in Omero', *Atene e Roma* xli (1939), 95–134.

400. ὅσσον τε γέγωνε βοήσας: an Odyssean formula, cf. vi 294, ix 473, xii 181, but implied by *Il.* xii 337 βώσαντι γεγώνειν. The sense, concisely expressed, is obviously 'as far as he *could* make himself heard'. A straightforward use of ἐγέγωνε βοήσας occurs at Hes. fr. 75. 12.

402. The orator Demosthenes, it is said (Zosimus, *Vita Demosth.*), recited this onomatopoeic line to practise his elocution. **ξερόν**: only here in Homer; perhaps related to σχερός by metathesis: imitated by Homericizing poets, Nicander *Ther.* 704, AR iii 322, both with ποτί.

403. There are two verbs ἐρεύγομαι, (1) 'spew', of subjects with literal or metaphorical throats, and (2) 'roar'. The latter is preferable here, for what impressed Homer about the sea, after its colour, was its noise (cf. πολύφλοισβος).

405. σπιλάδες are half-submerged rocks, such as may wreck a ship (iii 298): the πάγοι, usually inland features, are part of the shoreline (cf. 411), running out seaward.

410. θύραζε: 'out', as at *Il.* xvi 408.

418. What Odysseus is looking for is a *shelving* beach, but this can hardly be expressed by παραπλῆγας ('struck aslant', with reference perhaps to the action of waves at the sides of a bay).

421. κῆτος: any sort of sea-monster, including, according to Aelian (*NA* ix 45) ζύγαινα, κριός, λέων, μάλθη, πρῆστις, ὕαινα, φύσαλος. This is the sole allusion in the *Odyssey* to such a danger, but impressively large sharks and whales are said to have entered the Mediterranean, at any rate until recently, in sufficient numbers to stimulate the imagination, if not to create a hazard.

422. Ἀμφιτρίτη: see iii 91 n. κλυτός: the use of the masc. form for the fem. occurs also at *Il.* ii 742 (κλυτὸς Ἱπποδάμεια), presumably for the sake of more elegant metre, cf. ἄγριον ἄτην (*Il.* xix 88), ἁλὸς πολιοῖο (*Il.* xx 229 etc.), πικρὸν ... ὀδμήν (*Od.* iv 406 (see n.)), ὀλοώτατος ὀδμή (iv 442). The practice is well established, under stronger metrical pressure, in the case of the -υς adjectives, e.g. θῆλυς ἐέρση (467 below).

The repetition of κλυτὸς in the next line, where κρείων Ἐνοσίχθων could have stood, is indicative of the general indifference of poet and audience to the decorative epithet, cf. vii 114–15.

426. ὀστέ': acc., like ῥινούς.

427. ἐπὶ φρεσὶ θῆκε: here absolutely, 'made a suggestion'; the formula is usually construed with the infin., e.g. xviii 158. γλαυκῶπις: it is uncertain how the poet understood this famous description, see i 44 n. and the long discussion in Leumann, *Wörter*, 148–54. Nothing in the Homeric text requires the first element to be associated with γλαύξ, 'owl', rather than γλαυκός, 'grey': the second element denotes either the eyes or the face. Hesiod seems to have taken the reference to be to the eyes, cf. κυανῶπις (fr. 23 (a) 27 etc.), and βοῶπις (fr. 23 (a) 5), both of mortal women.

432–5. Another striking simile. The point, however, is not that the octopus 'clings with its suckers as stubbornly as Odysseus clings to the rocks' (Stanford), but that the skin of his hands is left clinging to the rocks as the pebbles cling to the suckers of the octopus. The imagery in fact is slightly confused, since the octopus suffers no injury. The octopus, to take into account the wider implications of the simile, is the πολύτροπος and πολύμητις of the animal kingdom, cf. Thgn. 215–18.

433. -όφι is not original in consonant stems, see 59 n.

436 ὑπὲρ μόρον: Aristarchus took this phrase as a single word, inspired perhaps by such forms as the adjective ὑπέρμορα (*Il.* ii 155). For the thought see i 34–5 n.

438. κύματος is collective, hence the plural relative τά. ἐρεύγεται: see 403 n.

445. ὅτις ἐσσί: the preamble of a prayer would normally specify the god's titles or prerogatives, e.g. *Il* i 37, xvi 233, 514. Odysseus apologizes for his ignorance, as he does at much greater length before Nausicaa, vi 149 ff. πολύλλιστον: i.e. 'most welcome', cf. *Il.* viii 488 ἀσπασίη τρίλλιστος ... νύξ. ἱκάνω contains the nuance of supplication that is made explicit at 449 σά τε γούναθ' ἱκάνω.

447. αἰδοῖος: the claim of the suppliant, except in the heat of battle, was absolute against other men, and sanctioned by Ζεὺς ἱκετήσιος (xiii 213): a suppliant god (e.g. Thetis to Zeus, *Il.* i 500 ff.) would have an analogous claim against another god: but it expressed a hope rather than stated a fact to make the same claim when mortal confronted god.

458–90. the last scene of the book repeats the pattern of 400–57: a description of the hero's straits; a monologue (the choice of two evils); the prompting of the goddess; the hero's escape. Each sequence is ornamented by a simile (432–3, 488–90), but they are not 'associated' in Moulton's sense (*Similes*, 19). On the repetitions in the narrative of the wreck it should be observed that 'the repeated use of larger narrative units, like the smaller dictional formulae themselves, is part and parcel of the poet's technique. He repeats larger units just as he repeats the smaller phrase and sentence formulae. Moreover, when the repeated elements are arranged in studied sequences like the above, they lend a certain pleasing symmetry to the passage, and the repeated order is obviously a mechanical convenience as well. The storm and shipwreck scene is long; by proceeding along set, repetitive lines, the poet can easily maintain full control of the narrative.' (Fenik, *Studies*, 145.)

462. λιασθείς, 'having turned away from', a common Iliadic word. It leads on to the action σχοίνῳ ὑπεκλίνθη and cannot refer to Leucothea's injunction at 350, as Ameis–Hentze–Cauer suggest.

463. ζείδωρον: the first element (*ζεϝε-) of this word, like the second of φυσίζοος, is seen in the noun ζειαί 'kind of cereal'; but at least from the time of Aeschylus (*Supp.* 584) was associated with the root of ζῆν. If that etymology were as old as the *Odyssey* an interesting problem would arise here. The epithet is formulaic (12 times), and should therefore according to the normal use of decorative epithets be employed without reference to the immediate context: see M. Parry, *Epithète traditionnelle*, 147–81 (= *Homeric Verse*, 119–45). Yet no reader could fail to discern the pathetic force of the epithet in this context, however the poet had contrived to hit upon it: on this see further W. Whallon, 'The Homeric Epithets', *YClS* xvii (1961), 97–142, and Kirk, *Commentary*, on *Il.* iii 243–4.

467. θῆλυς: fem. A few other adjectives occasionally show -ύς/-ύν as a fem., but its frequency in this word (8 times) suggests that it is in some way prompted by the meaning. The sense here is disputed: τρόφιμος, schol., would be purely decorative, an awkward combination with στίβη κακή; 'gentle', *LSJ*⁹, is open to the same objection; hence the 'moist', 'soaking', 'chilly' of various commentators.

468. κεκαφηότα: only here and (in the same formula) at *Il.* v 698. Doubtless < *καπ-, cf. καπύω (*Il.* xxii 467). The -η- should mark an intrans. formation, so that the ptcp. may agree with μ', and θυμόν construe with it as an acc. of respect, cf. τετιημένος ἦτορ; but the formulaic combination suggests that κεκαφηότα and θυμόν go together, cf. τετιηότι θυμῷ. It is unlikely that κεκαφηότα is trans., as rendered in the paraphrase of Eustathius ἐκπεπνευκότα τὴν ψυχήν.

476. ἐν περιφαινομένῳ: it is hard to separate the sense of this phrase from that of the περίσκεπτοι χῶροι in which the house of Circe (x 211) and the piggery of Eumaeus (xiv 6) were built: hence 'beside a clearing' (where presently Nausicaa and her maids will play their game of ball, vi 99 ff.).

477. φυλίης: variously identified: a species of fig (Hesych.), a wild olive (schol.), or the evergreen thorn, *Rhamnus alaternus*, called φυλίκη in some modern Greek dialects.

478. Join ὑγρὸν ἀέντων (adverbial acc.).

478–80. These same lines are used at xix 440–2 to describe the lair of a wild boar. If they were traditionally used for such a purpose, their employment here like everything in this episode would emphasize the depths to which Odysseus has been reduced.

481. The 3rd pl. is properly ἔφῦν: see Schwyzer, *Grammatik*, i 664. But natural short syllables are tolerated before the caesura.

482. δύσετ': for this type of aor. see vi 321 n. **ἐπαμήσατο:** this middle verb, 'gather together', cf. ix 247, is usually separated from the active verb ἀμάω, 'mow', 'reap' (which has an unexplained long initial ἀ- in Homer), but these are technical words whose sense evolves with the skills they denote. The etymologies are disputed: see Chantraine, *Dictionnaire* s.v. ἀμάω.

488. δαλόν: < *δαϝελός, from the root *δαϝ-, cf. δαίω (< δαϝ-γω) 'burn'. It is not fanciful to think of Odysseus too as keeping alive the spark of life.

490. αὖοι (codd.) is a *hapax legomenon*, but the compound ἐναύειν, 'to give someone a light', is well attested. The etymology is uncertain. Allen's αὔῃ (the subjunctive is a grammarian's unnecessary correction to obtain a better sequence of tenses) is taken from Herodian and would be a derivative of αὖος, 'dry' (Attic αὖος).

492. The slightly awkward rhythm of the first hemistich arises from the adaptation of the verse-end formula ὕπνον ἐπὶ βλεφάροισιν ἔχευεν (-αν), xii 338, xx 54. **παύσειε:** the subject is ὕπνος, as shown by the masculine participle ἀμφικαλύψας (493).

493. δυσπονέος: apparently a blend of δυσπόνου and δυσπενέος, according to Schulze, *Quaestiones*, 244. The word fittingly sums up the bitter realism of this part of the *Odyssey*. This quality is a widespread feature of the poem (cf. H. Fränkel, *Dichtung und Philosophie des frühen Griechentums* (Munich, 1969), 96 ff.), but is especially effective at this point. It is the poet's wish that the recovery of Odysseus' fortunes shall begin from the lowest possible point.

As at the ends of i, ii, iii, and iv the narrative is broken off with nightfall or sleeping, so that a new episode may be begun with the following book.

BOOK VI: INTRODUCTION

Reduced, for its literary effect, to the lowest point of his fortunes, Odysseus has landed on Scheria, the land of the Phaeacians. Slowly he emerges from catastrophe to gain honour and recognition: this is the essence of vi–viii, the Phaiakis. Remote and isolated though they are (we are still in the land of myth, see 8 n.), the Phaeacians will be the first *men* whom Odysseus will have met since the loss of his companions eight years before. This fact may not be obvious, except to the alert reader, owing to the arrangement of the narrative in the *Odyssey*. The hero, therefore, is not made to cry with excitement, 'At last ἄνθρωποι!', as the Greeks cried 'Θάλαττα' on Mt. Theches. Instead, he apprehends yet another addition to his woes (119 ff.). This fact, taken together with the abrupt introduction of the world of fantasy when Odysseus passed from Cape Malea to the land of the Lotus-Eaters (ix 79 ff.), should prevent too ready an assumption that the Phaeacians are intended to be some sort of literary bridge between the world of folktale and the real world of Ithaca. But the Phaeacians are indeed unreal (cf. introduction to viii), and their unreality has provoked speculation about the origin of this episode. However, their fate (xiii 159 ff., see 8 n.) is sufficient warning that for the poet the Phaeacians, like Calypso, have only a literary existence, and that their ultimate provenance may have little bearing on their actual presentation. Welcker (see viii 557–63 n.) long ago compared them to the 'ferrymen of the dead' of northern folklore. This view still has its adherents, cf. Merkelbach, *Untersuchungen*, 173, 211), but it rests on little beyond a possible etymology (Φαίηκες < φαιός 'dark'): they performed a service for Rhadamanthys (vii 321–4), an inhabitant of Elysium at iv 564, but, it would seem, in this, not the other, life; a placename Βαιάκη in Epirus, a land of chthonic associations, may or may not recall their name. Even if valid, this comparison explains little, even at depth. On the surface of the narrative the poet seems to interweave three elements: (1) the Phaeacians as those who succour the shipwrecked, (2) Scheria as an earthly paradise, and (3) the princess Nausicaa as 'helper' for the hero. The first is the most obscure, for they were superseded in this role long before we have useful information about Greek popular belief. Reinhardt (*Vom Werken und Formen* (Godesberg, 1948), 155) compared this function to those of 'helpers', the semi-divine beings of folktale: it is impossible to be more precise. The second and third, like the stories of Calypso and Circe, seem to be variants of the tale of the 'Shipwrecked Sailor' known from Egyptian literature of the second millennium, except that the mistress of the isle is not predatory but perhaps herself the prize sought by rival suitors.

Such origins determine aspects of the background of the Phaiakis which are external to the οἰκονομία of the *Odyssey*. They do not determine the immediate structure of the narrative. This is very typical both in motifs—dream, journey, supplication, entertainment —and in the sequence of motifs. Although Schwartz (*Odyssee*, 9 ff.) discerned a discontinuity between the preface of the book (1–98)—which he attributed to the Calypso-poet—and the narrative proper—the work of the poet of the Wanderings—at the surface of vi is a simple linear structure, itself without obvious difficulty. 'The fine verses of Poet A have been preserved for us pretty well intact' (Merkelbach, *Untersuchungen*, 159), but for an episode whose essential purpose is to narrate the rescue of the hero the style is throughout slow and expansive. Many have thought that this betrayed a second hand. Von der Mühll (*RE* Suppl. vii 714) accepts the removal of 42–7, 120–1 (and 122?), 123–4 (and 125–6?), 181–5, 204–5, 209, 222, 244–5, 275–88, 306, 313–15, and 328–31, and is followed by Merkelbach: other suspected verses are 9^b–10^a, 31–5, 50–5, 77–80, 83–4, 103–4, 106, 108, 112–14, 129–30, 130–6, 144–6, 157, 161–74, 178–9, 193, 201–3, 207–8, 217–23, 236–47, 256–7, 259–90, 293, 300–15, and 318. Such wholesale excision cannot be right *in toto*. Indeed, no judgement can be passed on the pace of the narrative until its structure and purpose in the widest sense have been examined.

The pattern of the narrative bears an obvious resemblance to that of the landing of Odysseus on Ithaca and his meetings with Eumaeus and the suitors:

1. Dream: vi 13 ff. (Nausicaa) ~ xv 1 ff. (Telemachus). The motif begins a narrative bringing the hero and his helper together.
2. Awakening of the hero: vi 117 ff. ~ xiii 187 ff.
3. Supplication, welcome, and advice: vi 127 ff. ~ xiii 221 ff.

The Ithacan narrative is now duplicated, for Odysseus proceeds first to the homestead of Eumaeus (xiv ff.) and then to the town of Ithaca (xvii ff.).

4. Arrival at the palace/homestead, and description of the buildings: vii 14 ff. (with Athena introduced as 'helper', as at xiii 211) ~ xiv 5 ff. ~ xvii 204 ff.
5. Supplication and welcome: vii 133 ff. ~ xiv 29 ff. ~ xvii 328 ff.

6. The stranger's tale: vii 240 ff. ~ xiv 191 ff. ~ xvii 414 ff.
7. The testing of the stranger: viii 62 ff. ~ (xiv 459 ff., the stranger tests his host!) ~ xvii 445 ff. etc.
8. Relevation of his identity: ix 1 ff. ~ xvi 172 ff. (to Telemachus) ~ xxii 1 ff.

It is unnecessary and probably misleading to suggest that either of these episodes is modelled on the other. Both are instances of the same sequence of themes, and botɾ ɔw the minor incongruities inevitable when a general concept is applied to a particular instance. It is superfluous, or nearly so, that the Phaiakis should insist on the possibility of a hostile reception (vii 17, 30 ff., but cf. xvii 247 ff.), that Athena should meet Odysseus in the Phaeacian town (vii 18, but cf. xiii 221 ff.), that Odysseus should be concealed by mist (vii 14, 139, an obvious precaution on Ithaca, xiii 189), or that there should be a 'testing' of Eumaeus (xiv 459 ff.)

The themes themselves, however, call for a certain amount of description and discourse, inducing a leisurely style. In addition the poet has chosen to develop the character of Nausicaa, to the delight of every reader. The motif of her impending marriage probably has deep roots in folk-tale, as if the unknown stranger she assisted were to become her suitor. It supplies an amusing gloss to several passages here and in vii and viii, but it is potentially dangerous, as is apparent from the number of later authors and commentators who refused to limit the role of Nausicaa to this episode. Some married her to Telemachus, as Hellanicus *FGrH* 323 a F 156, and Aristotle, fr. 506 Rose, or even took seriously her dream of marriage to Odysseus (see 244 ff.), as Goethe in his unfinished tragedy. It is evident that the poet's intention lay elsewhere. In many respects Nausicaa is a feminine doublet of Telemachus, a model of decorum and courtesy. These are important matters in the Phaiakis (see 29–30 n.), and underscore its wider function, which is to contrast the peace of Scheria with the disorder of Ithaca during the absence of Odysseus. The Phaiakis thus complements the Telemachy (where the chief aim is to link the *Odyssey* with the greater heroic world). To accomplish this purpose a certain fullness of style is necessary, especially in discourse: in good manners small details are important.

Brief Bibliography

There are full accounts of the Phaeacians by Eitrem in *RE* xix 2, coll. 1518–33, and Jessen in Roscher, *Lexikon*, coll. 2203–19: modern contributions (to 1918) were listed with comments by A. Shewan in

CQ xiii (1919), 4–11 and 57–67 (= *Homeric Essays* (Oxford, 1935), 242–53, 253–68. Welcker's suggestions were first published in *RhM* i (1832) (= *Kl. Sch.* ii, 1 ff.), cf. Wilamowitz, *Ilias und Homer* (Berlin, 1916), 497–505. L. Radermacher, 'Die Erzahlungen der Odyssee', *SAWW* clxxvii (1916), 1–59, made the comparison with Egyptian popular literature: see also Germain, *Genèse*, 285, 299, and L. A. Stella, *Il Poema di Ulisse* (Firenze, 1955), 134–41 and 332–45. These tales are not specifically Egyptian, cf. D. L. Page, *Folktales in Homer's Odyssey* (Cambridge, Mass., 1973), 51–69. Van Leeuwen's idea of the suitor under test (*Mnemosyne* xxxix (1911), 25) was developed by Woodhouse, *Composition*, 54–65.

Marzullo, *Problema*, 173–408, has a close analysis of this book. The sequence of themes (on which see M. N. Nagler, *Spontaneity and Tradition* (Berkeley–Los Angeles, 1974), 112–30) is exploited by M. Lang, 'Homer and Oral Techniques', *Hesperia* xxxviii (1969), 159–68, as an adumbration of Odysseus' reception on Ithaca.

Nausicaa has attracted much affectionate criticism: see Woodhouse, *Composition* 54–65, and S. Besslich, 'Dichterische Funktion und Eigenwert der Person bei der Darstellung des jungen Menschen in der Odyssee', in *Gnomosyne*, Festschrift Walter Marg (Munich, 1981) 103–16. For the general purpose of the Phaiakis see F. Robert, *Homère* (Paris, 1950), 262, W. B. Stanford, *The Ulysses Theme* (Oxford, 1954), 51–5, Rüter, *Odysseeinterpretationen*, 219–24, 228–46, and Clay, *Wrath*, 125–32. For its possible function as a bridge between the worlds of myth and reality, see C. P. Segal, 'The Phaeacians and the Symbolism of Odysseus' Return', *Arion* i 4 (1962), 17–64.

BOOK VI: COMMENTARY

1–109. Nausicaa's washing. Like the *Iliad*, the epic of Odysseus proper has begun (v) with dramatic action and in brisk style. The poet now relaxes and the action proceeds slowly with full use of the epic apparatus and direct discourse. The change of pace invites appreciation of the poet's scene-painting and characterization. For the former it is enough to point to the idyllic pastoral scene beside the washing troughs (96 ff.), rudely shattered by the uncouth apparition of the naked castaway, and the ensuing panic of all but the intrepid princess: as for the latter, the whole book, but especially the treatment of Nausicaa, illustrates the κωμῳδία ἠϑολογουμένη that Longinus (*de Sublimitate* ix 4) discerned in the *Odyssey*.

1. Nightfall, implied at v 465 ff., marked as often the conclusion of a narrative episode. Exploiting the natural effect of contrast the poet turns from the δυσπονὴς κάματος (v 493) of the destitute Odysseus to the luxury of the Phaeacian court.   ἔνθα: in a thicket (v 476), beside a clearing near a river bank.

2. ἀρημένος, which is construed also with δύῃ (xviii 53, 81) and γήραϊ λυγρῷ (Il. xviii 434–5), is plausibly interpreted by schol. as βεβλαμμένος. No present (*ἄρημι?) or other parts are extant: see Bechtel, Lexilogus, 60, where it is noted that βεβλαμμένος is inappropriate with γήρᾳ λιπαρῷ at xi 136 = xxiii 283, and LfgrE s.v.   ᾿Αθήνη: she had returned to the aid of Odysseus at v 382 after neglecting him during the Wanderings proper out of deference, as was explained (vi 329, xiii 341), to the feelings of Poseidon.

3. δῆμον: cf. i 103: the sense of 'community' has been extended to the area chiefly occupied by it. Athena is already in the γαῖα Φαιήκων, if her presence is implied at v 491.

4–10. The migration of the Phaeacians. The element of fiction (magic ships, ever-fruiting gardens) in the Phaeacian episode is so strong that it would be unwise to see any shadow of historicity in these lines. The poet is explaining how it came about that the Phaeacians are ἔσχατοι (205 below), and uses a subject, colonization, that was topical from the mid-eighth century onwards. 9–10 give a minimal list of an oecist's duties in founding a new city, for apart from its regal palace the Phaeacian town appears to be conceived as a πόλις (cf. A. J. Graham, Colony and Mother City (Manchester, 1964), 29, Lorimer, Monuments, 506). The motivation of the colony, however, harassment at home, suits rather conditions at the end of the Mycenaean age than in the eighth century.

4. εὐρυχόρῳ: properly 'with broad dancing places', a common decorative epithet of cities and districts. In view of the importance of the χορός in the religious life of the Greeks this sense is perfectly acceptable, though some have supposed that the second element came to be associated with -χωρος, as if = εὐρυάγυια.   ῾Υπερείη = the 'land beyond the horizon'. Its location would depend on that of the Cyclopes (5 below), if the allusion did not read like free invention (cf. M. M. Willcock, 'Mythological Paradeigma in the Iliad', CQ xiv (1964), 141–54). The sense of the name (which is attested in the κρήνη ῾Υπέρεια (Il. ii 734, vi 457)) is in keeping with the Homeric idea of the extreme distance of the Phaeacians from the rest of mankind.

5. Κυκλώπων ἀνδρῶν: to judge by their lawless behaviour these are the same Cyclopes as those of ix (cf. ix 273 ff.) Hesiod (Th. 139) reports a different tradition, that of the Cyclopes as divine smiths (who, however, are also characterized by βίη, Hes. Th. 146). This is the only point where the Cyclopes are allowed to be human, but the poet appears to have adapted the formula-type Φαιήκων (Αἰγυπτίων, Θεσπρώτων, Κιμμερίων, Λωτοφά-γων, Φοινίκων) ἀνδρῶν. Unlike men the Cyclopes have no θέμιστες and stand in contrast to the super-civilized Phaeacians (cf. Eust. 1617. 59 on ix 106).

7. Ναυσίθοος: except in the regular case-forms of νηῦς itself, the epic retains the diphthong -αυ- (Chantraine, Grammaire, i 225). Apart from Arete,

Alcinous, Demodocus, and a few others, the Phaeacians have 'ship-names' in keeping with their principal preoccupation (they are ναυσικλυτοί). Most of them are transparent inventions: see the list, viii 111 ff.

8. ἐν Σχερίῃ is the paradosis: the epic uses both the prepositional construction (which is that of classical Attic) and the plain locatival dat. Aristarchus' reading (omitting ἐν) appears, however, to be conjectural. **Σχερίῃ**: cf. σχερός· ἀκτή, αἰγιαλός (Hesychius, perhaps in contrast to Ὑπέρεια), but the epic has at its disposal a number of ethnic and geographical terms (Τάφιοι, the Φαίηκες themselves, and most of those in the Wanderings) of uncertain provenance and very dubious etymology. For its location see the remarks on Ogygia (v 55). Modern identifications range from Istria to Cyrenaica but the favourite is Corfu. The last has the sanction of antiquity, being current in the fifth century BC (Hellanicus, FGrH 4 fr. 77, Thucydides i 25) and a commonplace later (e.g. Callimachus fr. 12 Pfeiffer, Apollonius iv 1209 ff., Tibullus i 3. 3). Yet for the poet the Phaeacians live beyond the limits of the known world (ἑκὰς ἀνδρῶν ἀλφηστάων here, ἔσχατοι 205 below). Erbse (Beiträge, 145) observes that the destruction of the Phaeacians (xiii 159–87), like the obliteration of the Achaean wall in the Iliad (xii 13–33), reads like a device to forestall the objections of the simple-minded whose conception of poetry had no place for fancy and invention: cf. schol. Il. xii 3 ff. ἐπεὶ δὲ αὐτὸς ἀνήγειρε τὸ τεῖχος, διὰ τοῦτο καὶ ἠφάνισεν αὐτό, τὸν ἔλεγχον συναφανίζων. **ἀλφηστάων**: cf. ἀλφηστῆσι· τοῖς εὑρετικοῖς καὶ συνετοῖς, Hesychios, as if from ἀλφάνω, but also ἀλφησταί· ἄνθρωποι, βασιλεῖς, ἔντιμοι: rather from ἄλφι- 'barley' + ἐδ- 'eat'. See also i 349 n.

10. νηούς: see Lorimer, Monuments, 433–45. An inadvertent anachronism, since monumental buildings are evidently intended. Homeric worship is normally performed at altars in the open air, e.g. iii 5 ff.

12. Ἀλκίνοος: a significant name would not be inappropriate. The obvious connection with νοέω gives a colourless sense if Ἀλκι- has its normal meaning 'valour'. Stanford suggests 'Minded to help', which invokes the secondary sense of ἀλκή. A connection with νέω, 'swim', to give a nautical name (cf. Ποντόνοος, vii 179 etc.) is whimsical, see von Kamptz, Personennamen, 75. Mühlestein's 'Mit Macht heimschaffende' (Živa Antika xxi (1971), 47), deriving the second element from the root of νέομαι, is worth consideration.

17. Ναυσικάα: -κάα perhaps for -κάστη (< καίνυμαι), 'Excelling in ships'.

19. ἐπέκειντο: -ντο for -ατο is an Atticism. Its use enables the poet to keep the rhythm of the active θύρας ἐπέθηκε φαεινάς.

21. The formula is used at xxiii 4 of the flesh-and-blood Eurycleia addressing the sleeping Penelope, but usually it is employed of more insubstantial beings: the goddess Athena in a penetrable disguise (xx 32), an εἴδωλον (iv 803), Baneful Dream (Il. ii 20), the ghost of Patroclus (Il. xxiii 68). Nausicaa is, of course, dreaming (see 49), her dream, like other activities of the mind in Homer, being externalized. The motif of the dream as a spur to action is discussed briefly by Arend, Scenen, 61–3. Its use is a well-elaborated instance of the principle that new steps in the narrative are introduced and so to speak motivated by some kind of divine intervention.

24. The line repeats the verb of speaking in the epic manner after the explanatory lines 22–3: *Il.* ii 790–5 is a precise parallel.

26. σιγαλόεντα: an epic word, derived by O. Szemerényi, *Studia Pagliaro*, iii (Rome, 1969), 245, from the Hittite and Luwian *šeḥeli-* 'clean' (ultimately from the Sumerian *sikil* 'pure'). Only the forms in -εντα and -εντι occur. Always, as here, a decorative epithet.

27. The matter of Nausicaa's marriage is raised also at 66, 180, 244, 277, and at vii 313. It adds a certain piquancy to the relations of Odysseus, Nausicaa, and Alcinous, but it is otherwise superfluous to this part of the *Odyssey*. There is no hint in the text of Odysseus' being detained, or desiring to remain, on Scheria with an amorous princess or her match-making parents, as he was detained by Calypso λιλαιομένη πόσιν εἶναι (i 15). It is likely that the marriage (and some other elements such as the games in viii) is mentioned because the poet is familiar with a folk-tale in which an unprepossessing suitor outwits glamorous but unworthy rivals, only to be revealed as a prince in disguise: see Woodhouse, *Composition*, 54–65.

29–30. There are many sententious passages in vi (182, 188, 275, cf. vii 159, 299, viii 167, 209) which point up the difference in behaviour between the person who is ἀτάσθαλος and that of the one who does and says ἄρτια. Such passages encouraged the classical and later view of Homer as the repository of all wisdom (Ὅμηρος ὁ σοφώτατος πεποίηκε σχεδὸν περὶ πάντων τῶν ἀνθρωπίνων. X. *Smp.* iv 6). Yet Homer is in no way a didactic poet (τέρπειν is his usual term for the effect of poetry). Nevertheless there is much worth consideration in Havelock's view (*Preface to Plato* (Oxford, 1963), 61–86) that in an age when the epic is the only developed form of art, then on the epic must devolve the duty of reinforcing and transmitting the ethos of its society.

30. χαίρουσιν δὲ = ὥστε χαίρειν: a good instance of epic paratactic construction, cf. the causal nuance of the δέ-clause at 6 above.

31–5. The structure of Athena's admonition follows that of the dreams in *Il.* ii 23 ff., xxiii 69 ff., and *Od.* xv 10 ff.: (1) you sleep and are negligent, (2) the circumstances are thus, (3) act as follows. In this case the exhortation is repeated (31 ἀλλ' ... and 36 ἀλλ' ...). In the sequel Dymas' daughter, whoever she may be, does not accompany Nausicaa. Düntzer and others, followed by Marzullo, *Problema*, 210–12, delete the lines, but they are in keeping with the principle of full narration by which the epic seems to answer the naïve questions of an unsophisticated audience: Nausicaa must meet Odysseus by the river; so she must have been washing clothes; so she must have been on the point of marriage; so she must have been courted by the ἀριστῆες. From this standpoint the lines are needed.

31. One does not imagine the royal ladies of the vast Mycenaean palaces washing their own linen, fetching their own water, or weaving their own cloth. Yet the *Odyssey* assumes without affectation that the womenfolk of the ἄριστοι do all these things (water carrying, x 105; weaving, xix 139), such is the distance to which the luxury of the Mycenaean age has receded: cf. Marzullo, *Problema*, 246–9, and for the Homeric woman's daily round Wickert-Micknat, *Archaeologia* R, 38–80.

35. ὅθι τοι ...: 'sine sensu' (Bérard). Schol. take the antecedent to be ἀριστῆες, but Φαιήκων is now generally preferred, as if the *native* suitors had some special advantage.

38. ζῶστρα: χιτῶνας καὶ τὰ τοιαῦτα (schol.). The πέπλοι are feminine garments.

40. πολλὸν: the distance, half a day's journey, is for the convenience of the story. The Trojan πλυνοί were more reasonably situated, adjacent to the city wall (*Il.* xxii 153).

42–7. This fine description (imitated by Lucretius iii 18–22, Lucan ii 271–3, Seneca *de Ira* iii 6) is very elaborate for a mere note of Athena's departure. It is reminiscent of the description of Elysium (iv 565–9) and inconsistent with the formulaic epithets of Olympus νιφόεις and ἀγάννιφος. Kirchhoff, accordingly, and many others have deleted it: most recently Marzullo, *Problema*, 212–21. But although it is true that the epithets of Olympus (μακρός, αἰπύς, μέγας, πολύπτυχος, πολυδειράς, αἰγλήεις, in addition to νιφόεις and ἀγάννιφος) describe a mountain, there is a tendency to equate it in some way with οὐρανός already in Homer: cf. *Il.* viii 18–27. R. Stieker, 'Die Beschreibung des Olympos', *Hermes* xcvii (1969), 136–61, strongly defends the lines.

45. ἀνέφελος: with long α as in ἀθάνατος etc. the spelling ἀνν- is unetymological, since νεφέλη, unlike (σ)νίφα, did not have initial *σν-: see Frisk, *GEW* s.v. νέφος.

47. γλαυκῶπις: for the meaning see v 427 n. Epithets of gods in the epic sometimes function as descriptive titles, and so may stand *tout court* in place of the divine name; Γαιήοχος, Ἐνοσίχθων, Ἐριούνιος are used in this way. The practice (doubtless an extension of the use of such periphrases as Ἀμφιγυήεις, Ἐννοσίγαιος, etc., which always replace the name and are never used as epithets with it) is more usual in the *Hymns*: it does not extend to the epithets of heroes.

48. ἐΰθρονος: adapted from χρυσόθρονος (10 times of Eos). For the sense of -θρονος see v 123 n.

49. ἀπεθαύμασ': Stanford takes the prefix as negative, with the sense 'ceased to wonder at'; but it is, rather, intensive, the prefix being a device to bring the verse-end formula back to the fourth foot caesura: see K. Witte's important paper, 'Homerische Sprach- und Versgeschichte', *Glotta* iv (1913), 1–22.

50. βῆ ἴμεναι: in this formula the MSS invariably fluctuate between the Ionic ἰέναι and the Aeolic ἴμεναι. The latter persists, though metrically equivalent to the Ionic infin., because it is supported by the briefer formula βῆ δ᾽ ἴμεν.

50–5. δώμαθ᾽ ... ἐσχάρη ... θύραζε ...: for the architecture see 303 n. The passage, however, illustrates the remark of Marzullo (*Problema*, 226), 'I poemi stessi descrivono, senza una topografia precisa, per particolari staccati e momentaneamente figurati, non convergenti. È lo stesso problema insomma, e non solubile, della piana di troia, e di ogni altra descrizione geografica, creata, ma per suo uso, dall'epica.' For the sociologist, could any lines define with more laconic exactitude than these the male and female roles as perceived in archaic Greece?

52. ἐπ' ἐσχάρῃ: her regular station, cf. 305 below and vii 141.

53. ἁλιπόρφυρα: a suitable tint for the product of the royal spindle according to schol., who compare ἰοδνεφές at iv 135 of Helen's wool: but Homer is innocent of such social niceties. It is not clear whether the sense was taken to be 'purple, the colour of the sea' or 'purple, the colour derived from the sea' (i.e. from the famous *murex*). But the epithet (only here = 306 and xiii 108) is evidently a hypostasis of the phrase ἅλα πορφυρέην (*Il.* xvi 391) *vel sim.* There, however, it is likely that πορφύρεος, at least originally, meant 'boiling' (< πορφύρω), so that ἁλιπόρφυρος would be 'gleaming/flashing like the sea', cf. the curious image of the gleaming textiles at vii 106. See further Marzullo, 'Afrodite Porporina', *Maia* iii (1950), 132–6. Alcman's ἁλιπόρφυρος ὄρνις (fr. 10 Page) presumably alludes to the bird's colour.

54. βασιλῆας: 'lords', evidently the same as the γέροντες of vii 189. They were twelve in number (viii 390).

57. πάππα: like τέττα (*Il.* iv 412), μαῖα (*Od.* ii 349), and ἄττα (xvi 31) a familiar term suitable for a wheedling child, cf. *Il.* v 408, Aristophanes *Pax* 120. Its use here defines the tone of Nausicaa's words, which would otherwise be concealed by the formulae of the epic diction.   ἀπήνην and ἄμαξαν (72) are synonyms. The vehicle is the same as that used by Priam in *Il.* xxiv. The decisive epithets describing the type are τετράκυκλος (*Il.* xxiv 324, *Od.* ix 242), ἡμιόνειος (*Il.* xxiv 189 etc., *Od.* vi 72), and ὑψηλός (58, 70 below). These distinguish the conveyance from the two-wheeled, horse-drawn ἅρμα of the military. Detailed discussion by J. Wiesner, *Archaeologia* F, 5 ff.

59. ῥερυπωμένα: the sole instance in Homer of this kind of reduplication (for ἐρρ-): ῥεραπισμένῳ (Anacr. fr. 112 (Page)) appears otherwise to be the earliest example. Yet the operation of analogy might give rise to such forms at any time.

61. βουλὰς βουλεύειν: the epic has a certain partiality for the σχῆμα ἐτυμολογικόν. Merry–Riddell list 18 examples.

62. πέντε ... υἷες: conversely, Dolon (*Il.* x 317) was an only son with five sisters. Three sons is the most popular number (*Il.* xi 59, xiv 115, xx 231), but a truly θαλερὸς γάμος (66 below) was much more productive, cf. Andromache's seven brothers (*Il.* vi 421), and Nestor's and Dolius' six (*Od.* iii 412, xxiv 497).

65. ἐμῇ φρενί: the sg., except in the formula κατὰ φρένα καὶ κατὰ θυμόν, is rare in Homer, and the dat. unique; but the usual formula, ἐνὶ φρεσὶ + personal verb, must be modified here to accommodate the impersonal μέμηλεν.

70. ὑπερτερίη: not a cover for the wagon, but the bodywork. This is evident from the list of parts given by Pl. *Tht.* 207 a (τροχοί, ἄξων, ὑπερτερία, ἄντυγες, ζυγόν). The Linear B ideograms for the chariot appear to envisage the body as separate from the chassis: see Ventris–Chadwick, *Documents*, 361.

71–84. Nausicaa's departure. The scene is very similar to that of Priam's departure in *Il.* xxiv 265–80, so that for the older critics the question of priority arose (cf. Marzullo, *Problema*, 236–46, where the Iliadic scene is pronounced secondary). But the staccato style and the occurrence of abbreviated versions (iii 477–86, xv 145–6 + 182–3) indicate that the poet is making use of a traditional typical scene: Arend, *Scenen*, 86–91.

73. Aristarchus, followed by Allen, favoured unaugmented verbal forms (i.e. ὅπλεον not ὥπλεον) in some places at least, cf. schol. *Il.* viii 55 Ἀρίσταρχος διὰ τοῦ ο ὁπλίζοντο. His reasons seem to have been euphonic: against him are codd., the Alexandrian epicists (e.g. ὡπλίζοντο (AR ii 995)), and the 'processes of oral poetry' (see v 365 n.), by which the *Kunstsprache* endeavoured to keep pace with the evolution of the vernaculars.

74. Aristophanes is reported to have read φέρον here and κατέθηκαν at 75, sc. the servants. Presumably he was offended that a person of Nausicaa's status should be represented as performing menial tasks, the Alexandrian critics being sensitive to ἀπρέπεια: but see 31 n. He must also have altered the subject κούρη (to κούρῃ Dindorf, κοῦραι Nauck, κοῦροι Allen).

76. κίστη: an Anatolian word, cf. Hittite *kistu-*. For this source of the Greek lexicon see now R. Gusmani, 'Isoglosse lessicali Greco-Ittite', *Studia Pisani* (Brescia, 1969), 501–14.

78. ἐπεβήσετ᾽: aor., see 321 n.

79. δῶκεν: sc. μήτηρ. The preceding clause is in parataxis ('as the girl mounted ...').

80. ἦος: see v 123 n. The final force of the conjunction (see Palmer in *Companion*, 172) is very clear. Schwyzer, *Grammatik*, ii 651, compares the converse development of ὄφρα. χυτλώσαιτο: 'anoint herself', but the thought is inseparable from bathing, in which sense the Hellenistic poets are accustomed to use the word, e.g. Callimachus, *Jov.* 17.

82. ἐλάαν: pres. infin. (< ἐλάω, by-form of ἐλαύνω). The object (sc. ἡμιόνους), as often, is suppressed.

84. οὐκ οἴην: cf. i 331, xviii 207, xix 601. Homeric ladies of good family did not appear in public unless escorted. The ἀμφίπολοι are a symbol of rank but also a guarantee of propriety, cf. xviii 182–4. (Europa's final wail as the bull plunged into the waves was πλάζομαι οἴη (Moschus ii 148).) A visit to the πλυνοί might give an alert seducer his opportunity, cf. xv 420.

87. ὑπεκπρορέει: the present tense, universally attested, is the same as those used in the description of Alcinous' palace (vii 104 ff.): see Chantraine, *Grammaire*, ii 191. The poet describes a permanent feature of the landscape; he might, however, equally have used a historic tense, as in the description of Calypso's cave, v 63–73.

91. ἐσφόρεον ... ὕδωρ: 'brought (the clothes) to the water'.

95. Take ποτὶ χέρσον with θάλασσα, 'the sea beating on the shore'. The reading ἀποπτύεσκε is an attempt to give the prepositional phrase an easier construction.

96. λίπ(α) is practically confined to the formula λίπ᾽ ἐλαίῳ (8 times), but occurs simply in the same context at 227 below. The formation (α < ṇ) is a remnant of the old Indo-European r/n flexion: E. Benveniste, *Origines de la formation des noms en indo-européen* (Paris, 1935), 92–4.

100. σφαίρῃ: Eustathius, anxious to defend the poet against any suspicion of levity, comments that πάλαι ποτε τὸ σφαιρίζειν διὰ σπουδῆς ἤγετο, and counted Alexander and Sophocles among its devotees! Such comments —and not all are as fatuous as this—were fostered by Hellenistic concepts of epic *gravitas* that would have seemed bizarre to the *Odyssey*-poet.　　ταὶ γ᾽: πᾶσαι (i.e. of Aristarchus' recension) διὰ τοῦ δ schol. δ᾽ would mark the apodosis of the sentence, but would be unusually delayed.　　ἀπὸ κρήδεμνα βαλοῦσαι: note the erotic overtone (the κρήδεμνον is a symbol of virtue and modesty). Such excursions as the present were a notorious hazard for young females (cf. *Il.* xvi 181–3, *h.Cer.* 2–5, Hesiod fr. 140 (M–W), Moschus ii 63–76), but by throwing off their veils in the presence (as the audience know) of a man, the girls are almost courting the fate that at 138 they clearly thought had overtaken them. The poet has already (3 ff.) hinted at the course of his narrative, according to his usual practice, but within the scene the element of suspense is skilfully retained.

101. λευκώλενος: the πέπλος does indeed leave the arm free for work or play, but λευκώλενος does not here draw attention to the fact (as Ameis–Henze– Cauer suppose): it is the regular epithet for women in the 3rd–4th feet, as δουρικλυτός for men. The pale colour was doubtless thought both beautiful and characteristically feminine. The epic, however, does not subscribe to the view of Greek painters that male flesh could be characterized as dark: there are no formulae for 'brown flesh', and even the uncompromisingly masculine Ajax had 'white flesh' (*Il.* xi 572).　　μολπῆς: Stanford's 'rhythmical ball-play controlled by a tune' tries to meet every difficulty. μέλπομαι certainly is used of song in some Homeric passages (*Il.* xviii 604, *Od.* iv 17, xiii 27) and probably in many, although Aristarchus (always reluctant to admit synonymy) appears to have wished to restrict the meaning to sports and dancing: see the discussion by K. Lehrs, *De Aristarchi studiis homericis* (Leipzig, 1865), 138–41, and for the self-sought difficulties of the modern critics Marzullo, *Problema*, 255–6. Athen. i 14 d, αἱ δὲ [ὀρχήσεις] διὰ τῆς σφαίρας, ἧς τὴν εὕρεσιν Ἀγαλλὶς ἡ Κερκυραία γραμματικὴ Ναυσικάᾳ ἀνατίθησιν ὡς πολίτιδι χαριζομένη, is one of scholarship's lighter moments.

102. οὔρεα gives a better sense than οὔρεος (a correction to obviate hiatus). The long initial vowel is probably extracted from compounds (Wyatt, *Lengthening*, 47–8).　　ἰοχέαιρα: if the second element is from χέω (which seems most likely, in spite of Heubeck's attempt to link it with χείρ, *Beiträge zur Namenforschung*, vii (1956), 275 = *Kleine Schriften* (Erlangen, 1984), 275–9), the formation is unusual, -αιρα being extracted from other feminines to make a word of convenient metrical shape.

103. Τηΰγετον: the range lying between Laconia and Messenia. Hesychius has a gloss ταΰς· μέγας. **Ἐρύμανθον**: the northern range of the Peloponnese. The Mycenaean *o-ru-ma-to* (PY Cn 3) may be the same word, but is hardly the same place. The names of these mountains do not occur elsewhere in Homeric epic, and the Telemachy (cf. iii 484 ff.) makes suspiciously light work of the passes of Taygetus. These are probably no more than evocative names to an Ionian poet, familiar from hero-tales, e.g. about Heracles.

104. τερπομένη κάπροισι: Artemis was πότνια θηρῶν, ἀγροτέρη (*Il.* xxi 470–1) in one of her most important aspects, a Greek version of the principal divinity of Minoan Crete and the pre-Hellenic Aegean. Erymanthus produced the celebrated boar, taken by Heracles as his fourth labour, and even in later times Taygetus was noted for its hunting (Pausanias, iii 20. 5).

106. In the second half of the verse Megaclides (a fourth-century peripatetic) read ἀνὰ δρία παιπαλόεντα, perhaps not understanding how Leto could observe her agile daughter. The correction is not Homeric (but cf. ἀνὰ δρία βησσήεντα, Hes. *Op.* 530).

107. In the Greek view height enhanced beauty: see v 217 n.

109. The point or *tertium comparationis* of this fine simile (which caught the attention of Verg. *A.* i 498–502) is the pre-eminence of Nausicaa, but it would be absurd to deny that the evocation of Artemis, most chaste of goddesses, was not intended to imply the purity of Nausicaa and the innocence of her sport. The goddess, racing across wild places with her nymphs and her bow, was (or became) the definitive picture of Artemis.

110–250. Odysseus' supplication. The theme of supplication is a common one (*c.*35 instances) in both epics: *Il.* i 493 ff., xxi 67 ff., and xxiv 468 ff. are the most explicit. Essentially, the suppliant should crouch and grasp (*Il.* i 500 etc.) or kiss (*Il.* viii 371, *Od.* xiv 279) the knees of his intended benefactor. Odysseus is afraid to do this literally (see 147)—the virtuous Nausicaa would surely recoil—just as he was unable literally to supplicate the river where he landed (v 445 ff.). The physical contact, however, had a potent ritual significance (as did contact with an altar, cf. xxii 332), and was always broken if the suppliant was rejected (e.g. *Il.* vi 62). The psychological point of the act, of course, is that by his abasement the suppliant shows that he constitutes no threat. In Homeric language he appeals to the αἰδώς of the stronger party: cf. the formulaic line γουνοῦμαι σ' Ἀχιλεῦ ('Οδυσεῦ), σὺ δέ μ' αἴδεο καί μ' ἐλέησον (*Il.* xxi 74, *Od.* xxii 312, 344). Moreover the suppliant was believed to enjoy powerful protection in the shape of Zeus ἱκέσιος, cf. vii 164 and see *RE* viii 1592–3 s.v. Hikesios. Notwithstanding, the suppliant usually mentioned such excuses, promises, or good wishes as expediency made desirable. If accepted (and in the Iliadic battle-scenes the plea is ruthlessly rejected), the suppliant is raised up and treated as a guest: he is invited to wash and to partake of food, i.e. made a φίλος: see further J. Kopperschmidt, *Die Hikesie als dramatische Form* (diss. Tübingen, 1967), and J. P. Gould, 'Hiketeia', *JHS* xciii (1973), 74–103.

111. ζεύξασ' must be taken closely with νέεσθαι, 'when she was about to yoke the mules and return home', for the ball game still continues at 115.

113. εὐώπιδα: only here and 142; perhaps adapted from ἑλικώπιδα (so Leumann, *Wörter*, 147). There is no other formulaic epithet of this shape with κούρην in the *Odyssey*.

119–21. Odysseus asked the same question on waking on Ithaca (119–21 = xiii 200–2, where the lines are widely condemned), and in a more confident mood on setting out to see the Cyclops (120–1 = ix 175–6). Strictly, Odysseus knew where he was, having been told by Leucothea (v 344).

119. τέων (= τίνων) is the usual Ionic form. The monosyllabic scansion is found only in this line.

121. The contrast of the ὑβρισταί and ἄγριοι with the δίκαιοι and θεουδεῖς is an important one for the *Odyssey*, an ethical concern that helps to make the poem and epic and not a romance: see H. D. F. Kitto, *Poiesis* (Berkeley, 1966), 116–52. **θεουδής** (< *θεο-δϝ-) is not found in the *Iliad* and might be thought to evoke the sort of picture drawn at xvii 485–7 and Hes. *Op.* 252–5 of gods alert to punish sinners, a picture in contrast to the comradely attitude of the Iliadic ἄριστοι towards their gods (but note the famous simile, *Il.* xvi 384–8, of the anger of Zeus against injustice). Yet in the closest Iliadic analogue to the present situation, the visit of Priam to Achilles, respect for the gods is urged by the suppliant (*Il.* xxiv 503). Even Achilles, when tempted to act like a ὑβριστής, admitted that it was better to respect the word of a god and obey (*Il.* i 216–18). **νόος**: 'disposition'; cf. G. Bona, *Il. νόος e i νόοι nell'Odissea* (Turin, 1959).

122. θῆλυς αὐτή: cf. ἡδὺς ἀὔτμή xii 369, an oft-noted aural echo. Such echoes pose special problems for the understanding of formular techniques: see M. N. Nagler, *Spontaneity and Tradition* (Berkeley, 1974), 1–5. The ear of the ἀοιδός was attuned to sound as well as to sense, and was doubtless pleased by the repeated sounds of -ήλυθε θῆλυς αὐτή: see W. B. Stanford, 'Euphonic Reasons for the Choice of Homeric Formulae?', *Hermathena* cviii (1969), 14–17, D. G. Miller, *Homer and the Ionian Epic Tradition* (Innsbruck, 1982), 57–69; the ancient authority is DH *Comp.* 14–16. But assonance is an art where hits are counted to the poet's credit and misses are ignored: for the general pattern of assonance in Homer see the comments and statistics in D. W. Packard, 'Sound-patterns in Homer', *TAPhA* civ (1974), 159–66, where the conclusion, cautiously expressed, is that the distribution of most sounds is close to random. See also 124 below.

123–4. Cf. *Il.* xx 8–9, *h.Ven.* 97–9. There were as many categories of nymphs as there were localities for them to inhabit. In Homer these minor divinities (often called daughters of Zeus, *Il.* vi 420, *Od.* ix 154, etc.) are chiefly water-goddesses (*Il.* vi 22, *Od.* xvii 240, etc.). Oreiads (called Ὀρεστιάδες) are mentioned at *Il.* vi 420 (cf. the nymphs at 105 above) where they plant *trees* about Eetion's tomb; but the dryads and hamadryads of later poets are not a distinguishable class in Homer: cf. Roscher, *Lexicon*, 502 s.v. Nymphen.

124. A striking, but rather pointless, alliteration on π. 'In Greek poetry, unlike Latin, this phenomenon [sc. alliteration] is sporadic and apparently accidental; some of the most marked instances in Homer occur in places where no particular effect can well be aimed at, e.g. *Il.* xviii 288–9, xx 217' (Leaf on *Il.* iii 50), perhaps as a result of an unconscious feeling for sound in the mind of an ἀοιδός: see also 122 n.

126. πειρήσομαι: in the same formula at xxi 159 the mood is certainly subjunctive. Here the imperatival nuance of the subjunctive is strongly suggested by the introductory formula ἀλλ' ἄγε.

127. ὑπεδύσετο: see 321 n., a so-called 'mixed' aor. **δῖος:** 'Zeus-like, scilicet in appearance, prowess or ancestry'. The poet makes no attempt, here or elsewhere, to change the formulaic epithets in keeping with the vicissitudes of the hero's fortunes.

128. χειρὶ παχείῃ: the relation of this formula to its metrical duplicate χ. βαρείῃ is unclear. A. C. Schlesinger, 'Penelope's Hand', *CPh* lxiv (1969), 236–7, makes χ. παχείῃ mean 'with the clenched fist'; but χ. παχείῃ (18 times) is fixed in shape, case, and position, whereas χ. βαρείῃ is used much more flexibly, being declined and inverted in word-order.

129. μήδεα: cf. μέζεα (Hes. *Op.* 512), μέδεα (Archilochus fr. 138 (Bergk) = 222 (West), q.v.). Both Frisk, *GEW* s.v., and Chantraine, *Dictionnaire* s.v., are sceptical of the proposed etymologies, but Wackernagel, *Untersuchungen*, 227, is surely right to see in μήδεα = αἰδοῖα a euphemistic adaptation of the other word. The epic has some areas of reticence, but is more inclined to avoid the vulgar word than the unseemly fact. F. Marx, *RhM* xlii (1887), 251–61, took offence at the unhomeric delicacy (as he saw it) of Odysseus' action, deleted 129, 136, and 221–2, read ἐπῆλθε for ἔμελλε at 135, and began a lively controversy: see Marzullo, *Problema*, 282–6. See further 217–22 n. In Marx's view Odysseus took the branch as a suppliant, cf. *Il.* i 14.

130–7. The point of the simile is seen principally in χρειώ (136) and secondly in σμερδαλέος (137). The facts of a simile not infrequently disagree with the narrative, but not the emotions: here, for example, we are not required to imagine Odysseus emerging from the thicket with eyes ablaze. Fränkel, *Gleichnisse*, 70, is critical of this unhappy lion, in which he sees a sad falling-off from the noble theme κέλεται δέ ἑ θυμὸς ἀγήνωρ of *Il.* xii 299–306 (another version of this comparison): but the present simile is in deliberate contrast with that at 102–9 above. The two similes are associated (see Moulton, *Similes*, 120) in order to define the relations of Nausicaa and Odysseus and, as an element of ornamentation, to emphasize the importance of the moment. For this function of the simile see W. C. Scott, *The Oral Nature of the Homeric Simile* (Leiden, 1974), 42–4. (Fränkel's general view of the simile, that it illustrates the whole picture of the action, has been criticized by G. Jachmann, *Die homerische Schiffskatalog und die Ilias* (Opladen, 1958), 267–338, with renewed emphasis on the *tertium comparationis*.)

131. εἶσ(ι): present tense.

139. Ἀθήνη: hardly more than a figure of speech, used because Nausicaa's bold behaviour calls for explanation. Athena was last seen departing for Olympus (47).

141. στῆ δ' ἄντα σχομένη: 'she stood still, holding her ground before him', but the interpretation is complicated by the formulaic line ἄντα παρειάων σχομένη λιπαρὰ κρήδεμνα (i 334 etc., 4 times) where σχομένη has an object. Schol. here suggest that τὰς χεῖρας or τὸ κρήδεμνον be understood.

This splendid moment inspired the artist of the Chest of Cypselus (Paus. v 19. 9) and Polygnotus himself (Paus. i 22. 6); for the vase-paintings see O. Touchefeu-Meynier, *Thèmes*, nos. 361–7.

142. γούνων λίσσοιτο λαβών adapts the formula λαβὼν (ἑλὼν) ἑλλίσσετο γούνων (*Il.* vi 45 etc., 3 times). γούνων construes both with the participle, cf. λάβε γούνων (*Il.* i 407 etc., 8 times) and with the verb, cf. ἦ γούνων λίσσοιτο παραΐξας Ὀδυσῆα xxii 337: a good instance of formulaic usage.

144. περιττός (schol.). The objection was that the verse introduced an extraneous thought, viz. the διάνοια of Nausicaa.

148. If we are intended to imagine Odysseus as shattered in spirit by his recent experiences (which is the thesis of Mattes's important monograph *Odysseus*), there is not much in the text at this crucial point to favour such a view. Odysseus is not so demoralized that he can utter no more than a piteous wail (like Lycaon at *Il.* xx 74–96): on the contrary he has his wits about him. At *Il.* xxiv 486–506 and 518–58, in a more doubtful situation, Priam and Achilles produce some serious arguments (see C. W. Macleod, *Iliad*, *Book xxiv* (Cambridge, 1982), 127, 131–2): fairyland demands a lighter touch, a κερδάλεος μῦθος. Schol. note the θεότητος ὑπόνοια, θωπεία, and εὐπορία ἐπαίνων of 149–63, the implicit claim to aristocratic status in 164, the claim to pity in 170, craftiness in 178 (μικρὰ μὲν ᾔτει, μεγάλα δὲ ἐδήλου), and mind-reading in 180: all suitable points for a μειλίχιον καὶ κερδάλεον μῦθον of highly diverting artfulness.

149. γουνοῦμαι: not 'kneel' but 'entreat you by your knees'. There is no reason to suppose that Odysseus does not remain standing throughout, as the vase-painters (see 141 n.) represent him. **ἄνασσα**: otherwise of goddesses, just as ἄναξ in classical times is restricted to gods.

151. σε ἐγώ: the hiatus is abnormal, but the emendations are all feeble *lectiones faciliores*.

153. τοὶ ἐπὶ χθονὶ ναιετάουσι: only here in Homer, surprisingly, the expression is easily generated from the formulaic usages of the prepositional phrase and the verb to give a contrast with the preceding τοὶ οὐρανὸν εὐρὺν ἔχουσι, but is itself probably formulaic; it occurs in Hesiod at *Th.* 564 (cf. 621 ὑπὸ χθονὶ ναιετάοντας).

157. θάλος ... εἰσοιχνεῦσαν: an easy *constructio ad sensum*. **θάλος**: literally 'shoot', a common metaphor, cf. ἔρνος, which Odysseus proceeds to develop, 162 ff.

158. περὶ is better than πέρι, since the superlative is expressed by μακάρτατος: but cf. v 36.

159. ἔεδνοισι βρίσας: both words are ambiguous. ἔεδνα (ἕδνα) appears to be 'brideprice' about 13 times (*Il.* xvi 178 etc.) but 'dowry' about 14 times (*Od.* i 277 (where see n.) etc.): see A. M. Snodgrass, 'An Historical Homeric Society?' *JHS* xciv (1974), 114–25. (Since the references are very laconic, it is unclear whether any of these refer to the custom of 'indirect dowry', by which the groom endows the bride with property for the new household.) βρίθειν is used transitively ('load') in the quasi-metaphorical sense required here at Pi. *N.* viii 18, but not elsewhere in Homer. The intrans. sense 'prevail' is clear at *Il*. xii 346 and xvii 512, and is generally preferred here; σ' is then obj. of ἀγάγηται.

160. τοιοῦτον ἐγὼ ἴδον: the reading of the MSS preferred by Allen appears to be an echo of iv 269. Many MSS have τοιοῦτον ἴδον βροτὸν ὀφθαλμοῖσιν, probably rightly, since ἐγώ in the first version of the line is pointlessly emphatic and the neglected ϝ of ἴδον in the second is no impediment in a modified formula: ἴδον (-εν) ὀφθαλμοῖσιν (11 times in *Od*.) would be split by the noun according to the usual pattern: see Hainsworth, *Flexibility*, 92. Schol. on i 1 quote the line with τοῖον εἶδον βροτον.

162. Δήλῳ: Odysseus appears to allude to his voyage to Troy (or Aulis), but a visit to Delos is otherwise quite unknown. The island and the cult of Apollo would have been familiar to the audience from the great Ionian πανήγυρις described at *h.Ap*. 146–64, which some doubtless had attended. (The hymn, however, is of disputed date. The archaeological material of the eighth century on Delos appears to be wholly Cycladic.)

163. φοίνικος νέον ἔρνος: the true palm, *Phoenix dactylifera*, is not indigenous to the northern shores of the Mediterranean and seldom fruits there: this is the sole Homeric mention. Fault has been found with the botany; for, in elaborating the simple comparison ἔρνεϊ ἶσος (xiv 175 etc.), the poet assumes that the young palm is tall and slender, like the mature specimen, whereas it is short and squat. There was a celebrated palm on Delos that was reputed to have supported Leto at the birth of Artemis and Apollo, although this can hardly have been thought (except by some confusion of mind) to have been a νέον ἔρνος at the putative date of Odysseus' visit. The literary fame of this tree naturally ensured its longevity: it was pointed out in Cicero's day (*Leg*. i 1), unless that was Leto's palm (cf. Pliny, *HN* xvi 99). The word was known in Greek in Mycenaean times (cf. *po-ni-ki-pi*, PY Ta 714).

164. The λαός was originally the people in their military capacity. A. Heubeck, 'Gedanken zu griechischem λαός', *Studi Pisani*, ii (Brescia, 1969), 535–44 = *Kleine Schriften* (Erlangen, 1984), 453–62, well discusses this word.

167. δόρυ: regularly of lengths of timber, but only here of the living tree-trunk.

168. δείδιά τ' αἰνῶς: the formula (cf. *Il*. xiii 481, xxiv 358) is strong language, more appropriate to a man in fear for his life. Like σέβας at 161 it keeps up the θεότητος ὑπόνοια of the discourse and reassures Nausicaa: if Odysseus is afraid of her, she need feel no alarm at him.

172. Ὠγυγίης: Calypso's island, so called at i 85, vii 244, 254. It was not identified by name in v. Ὠγυγίη always occurs with νῆσος, and has been taken as an adj. ('ancient' or 'of Ocean'): so Wilamowitz, *Untersuchungen*, 16–17. Later poets use the word with reference to Boeotia, Attica, and Cos. There is no satisfactory etymology, see Chantraine, *Dictionnaire* s.v., and i 85 n.. Ὤγυγος, a mythical ruler of Thebes (or Eleusis) is of no assistance.

175–85. Cf. *h.Cer*. 135–40 where the same points are made but in a different order: wish for prosperity, request for pity, request for aid and information.

177–8. πόλιν ... ἄστυ: the words are used as synonyms in Homer: cf. the formulae for Troy, Πριάμοιο πόλιν and ἄστυ μέγα Πριάμοιο.

178. The request is κερδάλεον according to schol., 'demander un oeuf', so to speak, 'pour avoir un boeuf'.

181–5. These moralistic lines, with their almost untranslatable conclusion, have been widely condemned (see Marzullo, *Problema*, 341–5) as a superfluous expansion, cumbrously expressed (κρεῖσσον neut., a novel usage; εὐμενέτῃσι, an unparalleled formation; ἔκλυον, an odd sense). At *Il.* xxiii 650, *Od.* ii 34, and xvii 355 the benediction (180) concludes the utterance: but those are laconic speeches, whereas the present is deliberately effusive. The sentiments are typical of the archaic period, cf. Thgn. 869, Sappho fr. 25 Diehl. With exquisite propriety, however, Odysseus forbears to mention to the maiden the offspring without which the happiness of this ideal household would have been incomplete.

183. ἤ is pleonastic after the gen. of comparison τοῦ, a common slip (cf. *Il.* xv 509) in all authors.

184–5. Odysseus, it is evident, cites three aspects of perfect contentment. The first two are commonplace; virtue was helping one's friends and harming one's enemies, e.g. Pl. *R.* 332 d. But what is the sense of the third colon μάλιστα δέ τ' ἔκλυον αὐτοί? Van Leeuwen, sensing an echo of μάλα τ' ἔκλυον αὐτοῦ (*Il.* i 218) understood from 180 θεοί as subject; but the general view is that the subject of ἔκλυον must be the husband and wife. Schol. gloss with αἰσθάνονται, as if the phrase were a pl. of μάλιστα δὲ καὐτὸς ἀνέγνω (*Il.* xiii 734): they record no variants, and apparently found no difficulty. They are followed generally by Merry–Riddell, Ameis–Hentze–Cauer, Stanford, *et al.* No similar equation of κλύειν with αἰσθάνεσθαι is quoted. However, the actions of the unvirtuous Paris are said to be πατρί τε σῷ μέγα πῆμα πόληΐ τε παντί τε δήμῳ, | δυσμενέσιν μὲν χάρμα, κατηφείην δὲ σοὶ αὐτῷ (*Il.* iii 50–1), the converse of the present couplet. Can then the third colon mean not 'they themselves perceive ⟨their happy situation⟩' but 'they themselves are in high repute'? The semantic development 'hear' → 'be reputed' → 'be well reputed' is widespread and well known in the adj. κλυτός but there is no parallel to κλύειν *tout court* in the sense required. See J. T. Hooker, *Zeitschrift für Vergleichende Sprachforschung* xciv (1980), 140–6 for a full discussion of the lines. Emendations (τε κλέος αὐτοῖς Schütz, δὲ κάλλιμον αὐοῖς Nestle) are as usual unconvincing.

186 ff. Tension, and with it the quality of the composition, relaxes till Odysseus enters the city: 'versi in verità poveri nella sostanza e nella forma, infarciti di luoghi comuni, di espressioni sfocate e non facilmente precisabili' (Marzullo, *Problema*, 347). The sententiousness is normal in formal situations, cf. iv 236, xviii 130, xx 195, *Il.* xxiv 518, *h.Cer.* 147.

187a. (= xxiv 402) οὐλέ τε καὶ μέγα χαῖρε θεοὶ δέ τοι ὄλβια δοῖεν, cited by Plu. *de profect. in virt.* 82 e, is an attempt to give a clearer construction to ἐπεί, but the rambling syntax of the causal sentence is not untypical, cf. iii 103, viii 236, xiv 149, xvii 185, etc. There is no reason to suppose, with Stanford, that Nausicaa is represented as confused. Indeed her self-possession (justified by 201 ff.) is amusingly evident throughout this book. The situation in which the poet has placed her is one in which he takes especial pleasure, that where one party to a confrontation is unknown to the other and anything but what he seems (see Fenik, *Studies*, 5–60). Social roles are inverted; the suitors insult a hero not a beggar and, with lighter effect, a virgin (254 ff.) delivers a lecture on behaviour to the Πολύμητις himself.

189. ὅπως ἐθέλησιν: the poet quotes a suitable *gnome*. The same sentiment appears at i 349, and iv 237. Elsewhere, of course, more confidence is shown in the justice of Zeus, e.g. i 32, xvii 483.

192–7. Nausicaa takes up Odysseus' questions in the usual inverted order.

199. φῶτα ἰδοῦσαι: the stress is not on Odysseus' masculinity. As the following lines show, the maids fled because they took Odysseus for the advance party of a gang of pirates, not out of outraged modesty.

201. Cf. xvi 437. The expression οὐκ ἔσθ᾽ οὗτος ἀνήρ is an Ionicism, cf. Hdt. iii 155, here expanded by the ornamental phrase διερὸς βροτός. The essential idea is 'There is no one who ...'. **διερός:** a notorious gloss. The poets, from Hes. *Op.* 460 αὔην καὶ διερήν, use the word in the sense 'moist', as if from διαίνω. Chantraine (*Dictionnaire* s.v.) sees no difficulty in this, nor in the semantic development towards 'vigorous' (ζῶν ἐρρωμένως schol.), for which see Onians, *Origins*, 254–6. The same sense is clear in διερῷ ποδί (ix 43), the only other Homeric occurrence.

204. πολυκλύστῳ ἐνὶ πόντῳ: those who take Σχερίη as meaning 'mainland' (e.g. Schwartz, *Odyssee*, 225) affirm that this phrase might equally mean 'by the sea' as 'in the midst of the sea'. But the natural sense of ἐνί, the usual nuance of πόντος 'high sea', and Homeric usage (cf. iv 354) suggest that Scheria is thought of as an island. The poet, however, is nowhere explicit.

205. ἔσχατοι: see Leumann, *Wörter*, 158. The word is not a superlative in origin. The sense is 'outside, sc. the known world', cf. i 23.

207–8. = xiv 57–8. Ameis–Henze–Cauer take φίλη as active ('mit Liebe'), rightly. The passive sense ('though small, is prized') is certain in the other independent occurrence of the phrase (*Il.* i 167), but would introduce an irrelevant point here. Nausicaa cares nothing at this moment for the attitude of Odysseus, whom she has decided is a harmless beggar. Her tone is one of amused disdain. 'Give the fellow a scrap', she observes, '*kindness costs nothing*'.

209. = 246. One MS (Ven. 456, 15th cent.) has an additional verse (ἀλλ᾽ ἄγε οἱ δότε φᾶρος εὔπλυνὲς ἠδὲ χιτῶνα), similar to viii 392. That Nausicaa should offer clothing now, which Odysseus asked for (178), and defer the matter of refreshment, which Odysseus did not mention, till 246, would be unexceptionable, and persuaded Kirchhoff and others that 209a is the genuine verse and 209 the interpolation. But 'the nature of these lines that crop out in single late MSS is too plain to allow us to take line 209a for anything but a late conjecture', Bolling, *Evidence*, 235.

210. λούσατε: for the root of this verb (disyllabic *λοϝε- and monosyllabic *λοϝ-) see Chantraine, *Grammaire*, i 34, Frisk, *GEW* s.v., and Shipp, *Studies*, 94. The easiest explanation, which is also in keeping with the evidence of the dialects for this verb, is to assume contraction, cf. λοῦσθαι (216) and ἀπολούσομαι (219). In formulaic uses the uncontracted λοε- is always possible, but this at most dates the origin of the formulae and does not justify the restoration of λοε- in the text.

215. χρυσέη: golden cups and ewers are standard epic equipment, but the poet may be thinking ahead to the luxury of Alcinous' palace, cf. vii 91, 100.

216. λοῦσθαι is middle ('wash himself'), but the assumption is that the maids will assist: cf. viii 449, where λούσασθαι ἀνώγει is followed by δμῳαὶ λοῦσαν (454).

217–22. Odysseus' modesty is odd, since Homeric etiquette required the man to be bathed by the woman, cf. iii 464, iv 48, v 264, viii 449, x 361, xvii 87, xix 317, xxiii 154, xxiv 366: hence some doubts as to the originality of the lines, cf. Marzullo, *Problema*, 364–9. Schol. offer two explanations of Odysseus' attitude: he was ξεῖνος, and the maids were πάρθενοι: but at iii 464 Telemachus and Pisistratus were unknown to their hosts, and at iv 48 we must assume the virginity of Polycaste, youngest daughter of Nestor. For Eustathius the problem is not the σωφροσύνη, as he calls it, of Odysseus but the normal custom, which (at iii 465) he puts down to the rough manners of an unrefined age. (In Nonnus' romantic epic Chalcomede could not bear to look upon λελουμένον ἄρσενα, *D.* xxxv 199 ff.). Stanford's suggestion, that Odysseus is ashamed of his filthy condition, is plausible: in his present state he does not wish to claim the privileges of an aristocrat, cf. his reluctance to take part in the games at viii 152 ff.

224–5. χρόα ... ἅλμην: the double acc. is regular, cf. *Il.* xviii 345 Πάτροκλον λούσειαν ἄπο βρότον.

227. λίπ': only here outside the formula λίπ' ἐλαίῳ, see 96 n. The line is a variant of the whole-line formula αὐτὰρ ἐπεὶ λοῦσέν τε καὶ ἔχρισεν λίπ' ἐλαίῳ (iii 466, x 364).

230. = xxiii 157. **κάρητος**: the formation is certainly secondary, cf. κατὰ κρατός, and does not occur in well established formulae: see Shipp, *Studies*, 69. The regular transformation scene (viii 17, xviii 192, xxiv 367) is more condensed in expression and does not mention the hair.

231. οὔλας (< *ϝόλνος or *ϝόλσος, but see Frisk, *GEW* s.v.): in spite of προσηνής, 'soft' (schol.), and 'crisp, close curling' (LSJ[9], after the use in Hdt. vii 70 of negroid hair), the predominant sense is rather 'thick'. Athena is rejuvenating Odysseus, so to speak; when she undoes this effect at xiii 431 she makes Odysseus bald. The primary sense is 'fleecy'. Archaic *kouroi* of the seventh century (there are none earlier) show a fashion for highly stylized spiral curls framing the brow and falling below the shoulder: an allusion to this fashion is not to be excluded. **ὑακινθίνῳ**: the point of the simile should be an amplification of οὔλας, a term of form and texture: hence some ancient commentators, followed by Ameis–Henze–Cauer and Stanford, took the point of comparison to be the curling of the petals. But it is hardly possible to ignore the colour of a flower. The ancient colour spectrum is notoriously perplexing, but it is certain that the ὑάκινθος, whether it be the modern wild hyacinth, *Scilla bifolia*, or an iris, *Iris germanica*, was perceived as dark. It was adduced by Theoc. (x 28) as something μέλας but handsome: cf. κυάνεος of Odysseus' natural beard at xvi 176. However, Odysseus' hair is ξανθός at xiii 399, 431 in accordance with the archaic taste. (Fashion changed, cf. Athen. xiii 604 b οὐδ' ὁ ποιητὴς [sc. ἀρέσκει] λέγων "χρυσοκόμαν Ἀπόλλωνα" [Pi. *O.* vi 41]· χρυσέας γὰρ εἰ ἐποίησεν ὁ ζωγράφος τὰς τοῦ θεοῦ κόμας καὶ μὴ μελαίνας, χεῖρον ἂν ἦν τὸ ζωγράφημα.) This is presumably a mere slip, though analysts, e.g. Schwarz, *Odyssee*, 83, naturally supposed that different poets had different conceptions of the hero: see further Marzullo, *Problema*, 366.

232. **περιχεύεται:** χεύειν expresses the act of pouring a material out of a vessel and its consequence: hence 'pile up' a heap or 'spread' one material over another. The word gives no clue to the technology—of which the poet was ill-informed if he supposed that anvils, hammers, and tongs were required (see iii 433–5): on the techniques (probably involving the use of gold leaf) see D. H. F. Gray, *JHS* lxxiv (1954), 4.

232–5. The crafts are not a common source for Homeric comparisons, but cf. ix 384 (shipbuilding), 391 (ironworking), and xxi 406 (minstrel). This simile, with the two preceding lines, is repeated *in toto* for the beautification of Odysseus before his reunion with Penelope, xxiii 159–62. The modern reader, who is trained in such matters, will probably recall the present use, with Nausicaa's reaction, on reading the second, and see in it a symbol of Odysseus as a bridegroom: it is possible that some such thinking unconsciously affected the poet's choice of imagery. However, the Homeric audience were too thoroughly accustomed to repetition for any particular instance to have been significant to them; the repetition therefore cannot have been conscious. (On repeated similes see W. C. Scott, *The Oral Nature of the Homeric Simile* (Leiden, 1974), 128–40.)

239. **κλῦτέ:** the imperat. of an athematic aor., see Chantraine, *Grammaire*, i 239. The -υ- is lengthened, as also in the singular κλῦθι, perhaps on the analogy of στῆθι, στῆτε, etc., cf. Wyatt, *Lengthening*, 211. The Iliadic formula is κέκλυτέ μευ (9 times). **μευ:** most MSS, both here and elsewhere, have the *facilior lectio* μευ: but κλῦτέ μοι is an old reading of the formula (P. 13 at xv 172).

242. **δέατ':** an old word, attested in classical times only in Arcadian inscriptions: cf. C. M. Bowra, 'Homeric Words in Arcadian Inscriptions', *CQ* xx (1926), 168–76.

244–5. The scholiast is worth quoting: δοκοῦσιν οἱ λόγοι ἀπρεπεῖς παρθένῳ εἶναι καὶ ἀκόλαστοι. λύουσι δὲ ἐκ τοῦ προσώπου. ὑπόκεινται γὰρ τρυφῶντες οἱ Φαίακες καὶ παντάπασιν ἁβροδίαιτοι. Ἔφορος μέντοι τοὔμπαλιν ἐπαινεῖ τὸν λόγον ὡς ἐξ εὐφυοῦς πρὸς ἀρετὴν ψυχῆς. Manners change. Most modern commentators find the verses naïvely charming. Nausicaa is, in effect, thinking aloud. She has been warned to expect marriage (27), but does not know to whom. On a less private occasion αἴδετο γάμον ἐξονομῆναι (66).

250. ἁρπαλέως: by popular etymology for *ἁρπαλέως. Hesychius has ἀλπά-
λεον· ἀγαπητόν, without the dissimilation. See Chantraine, *Dictionnaire* s.v.
ἄλπνιστος. But the sense is already passing from one of pleasure to that of
avidity.

251–331. Odysseus is taken to the city. ἀλλ' ἐνόησεν marks the beginning of a
new episode. The parallels indicate that the natural thing for the woman
to do would be to go and inform her father (*h.Cer.* 169 ff.) or husband (x
112 ff.) of the stranger's arrival. But this would destroy the fine scene at the
beginning of vii. The poet therefore, after adding more beguiling charac-
terization of Nausicaa and inventing the diverting picture of the stalwart
hero tramping behind the maiden's cart, is content to adumbrate what will
follow.

253. ἡμιόνους κρατερώνυχας: the simplex ὄνυξ normally denotes the claws of
an animal or bird (hence λύκοι κρατερώνυχες at x 218), but may distinguish
the hard from the soft parts of the hoof (ὁπλή) among those for whom the
distinction is important, e.g. X. *Eq.* i 3. The epithet is taken from the
formula-system for the horse where the two initial consonants κρ- are
metrically significant. From the metrical viewpoint the mules should
rather be καλλίτριχας, but mules are good on rough ground whereas
nothing about them is beautiful: the choice of epithet (also at *Il.* xxiv 277)
is not mechanical.

254. ἔπος τ' ἔφατ' ἔκ τ' ὀνόμαζεν: see v 181 n.

255–315. Nausicaa's discourse. Critical opinion has always found the speech
too long. 275–88 were athetized, and 313–15 are imperfectly attested.
O. Seeck, *Die Quellen der Odyssee* (Berlin, 1887), 147, discovered a combina-
tion of two speeches, 255–88 and 289–312. Schwartz, *Odyssee*, 205,
attributed much to the redactor, A. Fick, *Die Entstehung der Odyssee*
(Göttingen, 1910), 181 to the rhapsodes. See Marzullo, *Problema*, 379–404.
From the standpoint of οἰκονομία a fairly long scene is desirable to separate
the scene at the river from the scene in the town.

255. ὄρσεο: an artificial form designed to furnish the initial dactyl. ὄρσο (*Il.* iv
204 etc.) is the imperat. of the athematic aor. ὦρτο. Divided ὄρσ-ο it was
reinterpreted as a sigmatic aor. and given the thematic ending -εο: cf.
C. Prince Roth, 'Thematic S-aorists in Homer', *HSPh* lxxvii (1973), 181–6.

256. δαΐφρονος: 'warlike', the Iliadic sense, is never certainly required in the
Odyssey (cf. especially iv 687 of Telemachus, xv 356 of Penelope, and the
formula δαΐφρονα ποικιλομήτην iii 163 etc.). The derivation is felt to be
from δαῆναι, 'teach', not δαί, 'battle'. Translate 'wise'. Outside the
formulae Homer uses δαήμων in this sense.

258. ἀπινύσσειν: the primary sense 'be dazed' appears at *Il.* xv 10. The
formation must be by the analogy of other verbal derivatives of negative
adjectives, since ἀπίνυτος is not attested until post-classical times: see
O. Szemerényi, *Syncope in Greek and Indo-European* (Naples, 1964), 69.

259. ὄφρ' ἂν μέν κ': see v 361 n.   **ἔργ' ἀνθρώπων:** i.e. ploughed land. The
formula has the literal sense, with an epithet, at xiv 84: see v 162 n. for
other instances of variation in meaning of a formulaic word-group.

262–9. Alcinous' city. The poet describes a πόλις with town wall (not a fortified citadel), ἀγορή, and temple, in keeping with the ideas of the late eighth century (Lorimer, *Monuments*, 506). The site is a sea-girt peninsula, like those of Old Smyrna, Iasos, Melia, Miletus, Phocaea, Cyme, and others settled on the eastern shore of the Aegean after the Mycenaean age. The older mainland cities tended to form around defensible heights lying some distance inland (cf. Th. i 7, with Gomme's n.). Old Smyrna fits the Homeric picture well (cf. J. M. Cook, *ABSA* liii–liv (1953–4), 15), but so doubtless did many other places. It will be observed that the poet elaborates his picture of a well-defended settlement without regard for the point he had previously made (201–5) of the security of the Phaeacians.

262. ἐπιβήομεν: The orthography of the MSS has -ει- for -η- (both original and < ᾱ) before the back vowels where a form with -ε- continued in the vernacular, so στείομεν, cf. Ionic στέωμεν, *Il.* xv 297: see Werner, *H und ει vor Vokal*. The development (like that of ἕως, see v 123 n.) is progressive, and it is impossible to say what stage had been reached in the aedic period. The -η- of a few MSS is probably analogical (cf. ἔβη etc.).   πύργος: described in more detail at vii 44.

263–4. The description is generically conceived, cf. x 87–90, but adapts to a peninsula diction used elsewhere of an inlet. The double harbour was one of the amenities of Asteris (iv 846).

264. νῆες ... ἀμφιέλισσαι: an obscure part of the elaborate formula-system for the ship, on which see B. Alexanderson, 'Homeric Formulae for Ships', *Eranos* lx (1970), 1–46. For the sense see iii 162 n. S. Marinatos, *BCH* lvii (1933), 214 and *LfgrE* s.v. compares the lines of Minoan ships with tall curved stem and sternpost: traditionally the second element is referred to the verb ἑλίσσειν, hence ἀμφοτέρωθεν στρεφόμεναι ὑπὸ κωπῶν (schol.) and ἀμφοτέρωθεν ἐλαυνόμεναι (Hesych.). Further discussion in D. H. F. Gray, *Archaeologia* I G, 94.

265. εἰρύαται: doubtless from ἐρύω 'draw up', cf. *Il.* xiv 30, with ὁδόν as acc. of extent: but the sense 'protect' (< ῥύομαι) is in principle possible.   ἐπίστιον is evidently a slipway or ship-shed (ἐποίκιον, νεώριον (schol.)). Aristarchus (see schol. *Il.* ii 125) took the word as identical with the Ionic ἐπίστιον (< ἐφέστιον, 'household'), a derivation that was not recognized by the textual tradition, which elsewhere has ἐφέστιος. Modern etymologists prefer a connection with ἵστημι.

266. Ποσιδήϊον: an enclosure certainly (that is, a τέμενος in the classical sense), with an altar, cf. xiii 187, and perhaps including one of the νηοί mentioned at 10. Poseidon, the obvious patron of a seafaring people, was the progenitor of the Phaeacian royal house (vii 56).

267. Paved *roads* are not unknown even in the archaic period, e.g. at Karphi and Emporio, but a paved ἀγορή is a different matter. At viii 6, where the poet evidently has the same picture in mind, the stones (ξεστοῖσι λίθοισι) are used as seats. The ἀγορή therefore is defined by a wall.   ῥυτοῖσι (< ἐρύω): the Greek distinction appears to have been between blocks that

could be manhandled (cf. χερμάδια ἀνδραχθέα, x 121) and those that could
not (cf. λίθοι ἀμαξιαῖοι, Th. i 93): hence 'hauled', cf. W. Richter,
Archaeologia H, 27. The long -ῡ- is unexpected: C. J. Ruijgh, *Études sur la
grammaire du grec mycénien* (Amsterdam, 1967), suggests an analogy of the
type κερά-σαι: κρᾱτός ∼ ἐρύ-σαι: x. The Latin *rūta* (in the formula *ruta
caesa*, 'minerals and timber'), is a curious parallel, but embodies a different
idea, if the classical connection with *eruo* (*Dig.* xix 1. 17) is sound. **κα-
τωρυχέεσσ'**: a strange form, *metri gratia* (so Frisk, *GEW* s.v.) from a nom.
*κατῶρυξ.

268. ἀλέγουσι: always negated, except here and *Il.* ix 504, cf. the proper
name Οὐκαλέγων.

269. ἀποξύνουσιν: presumably in shaping the oar-blade so as to make it
προήκης (xii 205). Buttmann's ἀποξύουσιν, 'make smooth', accepted by
Ameis–Henze–Cauer and Bérard, has some support in the schol., τὸ δὲ
ἀποξύνουσι [leg. ἀποξύουσι?] ἤτοι τὸν φλοιὸν περιξέουσιν, but is hardly
necessary.

273–84. 'Nausicaa, malgrado tutti, è ragazza borghese, come tutta la società
dell'Odissea', Marzullo, *Problema*, 393. The effect is gently comic, like the
behaviour of Erysichthon's parents when their son is no longer presentable
in public (Callimachus *Cer.* 72–106).

273. ἀδευκέα: sense and derivation? Schol. are desperate (ἀπροσδόκητον,
πικράν, ἀφανῆ), nor are modern lexicographers any more confident.
'Malicious' would obviously be suitable, cf. the Hesychian gloss δεύκει·
φροντίζει, and the common Odyssean word ἐνδυκέως (vii 256 etc., 16
times) used of well-intended actions.

275–88. Aristarchus naturally found the lines unmaidenly, but they are the
best in a generally dull passage. Woodhouse, *Composition*, 58, commends
them as a κερδάλεος μῦθος whereby Nausicaa obliquely reveals her name,
status, and eligibility. It is no objection to this that subsequently (e.g. at vii
290 ff.) Odysseus is careful not to mention the princess by name.

278. κομίσσατο: cf. the sense of κομιδή, 'care', 'attention'.

284. πολέες τε καὶ ἐσθλοί: the acc. always has the *u*-stem form πολέας in this
formula, but the nom. fluctuates between πολέες and πολλοί (cf. viii 110).
The variation is unexplained.

287. The sense of the line ('against the wishes of her parents') is obvious, but
the construction, if precisely conceived, is unclear. The conventional view
(Ameis–Hentze–Cauer, Stanford) takes φίλων as a substantive dependent
on ἀέκητι and with πατρὸς καὶ μητρὸς in apposition to it, the participle
ἐόντων being supposed to mean 'while they are still alive', for which sense
an adverb (ἔτι) is sadly missed. Seelbach, *RhM* cv (1962), 288 takes the
genitives as absolute and construes ἀέκητι as an adv. with the ptcp.: but
epic usage assigns ἀέκητι (and ἕκητι) a prepositional construction. Schol.
have no comment. Eust. proposes ἐόντων = ζώντων.

288. μίσγηται: 'associate with'. In later usage the simple verb in such a
context is used as a euphemism for the sexual act. The line must have
sounded most odd to the classical age. Schol. have no comment, but Eust.

notes a gloss συνεῖναι beside παρεῖναι. vii 247 is an exact parallel to this sense of μίσγεσθαι.

289. ὦκ' ... ξυνίει: cf. ξύνες ὦκα (*Il.* ii 26), but ὦκ' is Aristarchus' correction, the paradosis being ὦδ'. Ar. (cf. Apollonius, *Lex. Hom.* 872 s.v. ὧδε) objected to weak and derivative uses of ὧδε, but it would be reasonable that Nausicaa should resume 'as I was saying' after her digression.

291. δήεις: a defective verb, synonymous with εὑρίσκειν but used in the epic as a future tense. The 2nd pers. sg. is the reading of the χαριέστεραι for which schol. (who read δήομεν like the medieval paradosis) offer no reason: perhaps an overcritical reading of the text, as if Nausicaa could not be said to 'find' the grove of Athena when she knew of its whereabouts, cf. van der Valk, *Textual Criticism*, 160.

293. τέμενος: cf. Apollonius, *Lex. Hom.* 240 s.v., πᾶς ἀποτετμημένος εἰς τιμὴν τόπος. The crucial passage is *Il.* xii 310–21, where it is explained that the βασιλῆες enjoy among other privileges the possession of a τέμενος and must therefore μετὰ πρώτοισιν ἐόντας ἑστάμεν ἠδὲ μάχης καυστείρης ἀντιβολῆσαι: see H. van Effenterre, 'Temenos', *REG* lxxx (1967), 17–26. The Homeric usage appears to describe a wholly secular institution, and it is possible to interpret the Mycenaean term (PY Er 312) in the same way, cf. Palmer, *Interpretation*[1], 83–5 (where, however, the sacral nature of the Pylian 'king' (*wanax*) is properly stressed). In later usage τέμενος denotes a precinct set aside for a god or hero, like the Ἀλκίνου τέμενος mentioned at Th. iii 70, but there are significant exceptions, e.g. Battus, king of Cyrene, held τεμένεα as well as ἱερωσύνας (Hdt. iv 161). Homer linked the term with τάμνω (cf. the etymologizing formula τέμενος τάμεν, *Il.* vi 194 and xx 184), but it is probably a loan-word, cf. Akkadian *temmenu*, Sumerian *TEMEN*, 'temple', as first pointed out by M. C. Astour, *Hellenosemitica* (Leiden, 1965), 338.   **ἀλωή** is properly a threshing-floor (cf. ἀλοιάω, 'beat'), as at *Il.* v 499 etc., but this and related words are widely used in the vernaculars for an enclosed garden; cf. Hesychius ἄλουα· κῆποι, Κύπριοι.

294. ὅσσον τε γέγωνε βοήσας: see v 400 n.

296. ἄστυδε ἔλθωμεν: emendations (ἄστυδ' ἀν-, ἄστυδ' ἐσ-, to which add P. 6 ἄστυ δι-) seek to obviate the hiatus which is not defended, as elsewhere in this position, by 'une coupe nette du sens' (Chantraine, *Grammaire*, i 89).

303. ἥρως: this is the spelling of the MS-tradition, with remarkable uniformity in view of the difficulty of the reading, and must represent the gen. case. As a contraction, however, or as the reflex of an orthographic representation of -ωος, the form is without parallel: hence ἥρω (a late form of the gen., by contamination with the 'Attic' declension) in a few MSS, and ἥρωος (Barnes); cf. βέβληαι (*Il.* xi 380) for the scansion. The nom. would be possible only with an epexegetic clause following, cf. *Il.* vi 396. Schol. moot the possibility of a voc., a desperate expedient.   **δόμοι:** the action of the *Odyssey*, both here and in the Ithacan scenes, presupposes the concept of a great house. The description is generic—it is applied in part to Eumaeus' pigsties (xiv 5 ff.)—and makes use of the central terms αὐλή, αἴθουσα, πρόδομος, μέγαρον, and θάλαμος. Just as the geographical descriptions fit many places, so the Homeric house can be drawn in accordance with many plans. The earliest modern view originated in the descriptions of classical houses in Plato, Xenophon, and Vitruvius. It identified the μέγαρον with the ἀνδρών, imagined a γυναικωνῖτις with θάλαμοι to its rear, and equated the αἴθουσα and πρόδομος. This picture could not survive the archaeological discoveries of the late nineteenth century. The μέγαρον became the square pillared hall of Tiryns or Mycenae, the πρόδομος the antechamber, the αἴθουσα the portico, and the θάλαμοι the detached suites entered from the πρόδομος. So certain did this seem that the Homeric terminology was adopted by the archaeologists. Yet we are left with 'the extreme difficulty of accounting for the knowledge which the poet apparently possessed of architecture of the LH III type', (Lorimer, *Monuments*, 407), when the palaces of the mainland had lain in ruins for four centuries. Old formulae might preserve a detail, but subject as they were to continuous replacement by new expressions they could not preserve the overall concept with its parts in their proper articulation. It is likely therefore that Drerup correctly describes the Homeric house as a heroically exaggerated form of the usual structures of the Geometric age (*Archaeologia* O, 128). It is necessary also to bear in mind that a palace, a city, or a battlefield is seen in Homer through the eyes of the heroes and not, so to speak, through the eye of Zeus. We do not watch Odysseus from afar threading his way through a precisely conceived labyrinth; we go with him through a succession of exotic and bewildering impressions. Most readers find this more satisfactory than exact description, because most people—and most poets—are unobservant of structure but receptive of impression. See the following n. When it is described below (vii 86–97) the palace is presented as one of unimaginable luxury.

304. μεγάροιο: the principal room of the Homeric house. The poet's usage and its correlation with the results of archaeology is examined by Drerup, *Archaeologia* O, 128–33, and in detail by M. O. Knox, 'Megarons and ΜΕΓΑΡΑ', *CQ* xxiii (1973), 1–21: she concludes, 'Most writers have expected to find Mycenaean elements playing an essential role in the story, with the Iron Age providing descriptive detail. As far as houses, at least, are concerned, the opposite seems now to be the case.' The Mycenaean halls are square, with central hearths between four pillars, a throne against a side-wall, and elegant decoration; those of the Geometric period are very variable, but are often rectangular with two or three pillars along the central axis: see Drerup, op. cit., 5–31. The Mycenaean room has a ceremonial air (note the painted floor and frescoes flanking the throne at Pylos): but in Homer the μέγαρον is used for all the ordinary purposes of life, except possibly cooking. It is dark (σκιόεις), but otherwise not strikingly characterized, and there is no objection to digging up the earth floor (xxi 120). It has pillars and a hearth, but the number and position of both are not specified.

For the scene drawn in 304–9 cf. A. Cambitoglou and J. J. Coulton, *Zagora I* (Sydney, 1971), 31, 'The long bench and large hearth in the centre suggest that H19 (the central room of a large house) was the main living room. The spindle whorls found on the floor near the bench show that it also served as an everyday room for women to sit and work.' (Zagora is a site of the Geometric period on Andros.)

305. μητέρ': Arete. For her status see on vii 66.

306. ἀλιπόρφυρα: see 53 n.

309. ἀθάνατος ὥς: The etymology *σƒως is reflected by the adverb's making metrical position in the two formular patterns $-\cup\cup- \ ὥς$ and $\cup- ὥς$.

313–15. = vii 75–7 with the trivial substitution of οἶκον ἐς ὑψόροφον at vii 77 for οἶκον ἐϋκτίμενον. They are omitted here by many codd. The lines give a reason of sorts why Arete and not her husband should be approached, but the connective τοι is that appropriate at vii 75. They are evidently plus-verses which have not yet spread throughout the MS-tradition. The scholia ignore them at this point. 312 (= vii 194) on the other hand, though not vital, is universally attested.

Nausicaa's speech has many linguistic infelicities (discussed at length by Marzullo, *Problema*, 388–404) and much loose and incomplete syntax. Stanford takes the latter as deliberate, expressing the maiden's agitation of mind (cf. ii 334, iii 103, 117, 187 above, vii 311, viii 236, ix 260, and xi 553)'. But there is no other indication of discomposure. Taken with the diction, the syntax shows that the poet's attention in this passage is generally at a low ebb.

316. φαεινῇ probably alludes to the finish or decoration of the leather (cf. ἥνια σιγαλόεντα), since it may be expanded by φοίνικι (*Il.* vi 219 etc.).

317. αἱ: mules are feminine in Homer, where the gender is clear, except at *Il.* xvii 742 (simile). The gender fluctuates in classical Greek.

318. πλίσσοντο: 'step out', 'trot'. The form is corrupted in the MSS (πλήσσοντο, ἐπλήσσοντο, or ὁπλίσσοντο), but is preserved in the scholia. The root appears to be πλιχ- (see Chantraine, *Dictionnaire* s.v. πλίσσομαι), but the etymology is obscure.

320. Nausicaa drives away and, but for a routine epilogue at the beginning of vii and a brief re-entry at viii 457–68, out of the story. This resolute dismissal by the poet of a sympathetic character cannot be other than an indication of his attitude towards her. The scene by the river is an episode, no more, a necessary and well-elaborated part of the οἰκονομία of the poem. The poet draws in outline an indulgent portrait of a well-bred girl: but there is no emotional involvement, least of all on the part of the hero. See introduction to vi.

321. δύσετο: a so-called 'mixed aorist', having the -σ- of the first aor. and the thematic conjugation of the second. Schol. *Il.* i 496 suggested that the type was an imperfect, but has not convinced either the MS-tradition (which has frequently introduced -σα- forms) or modern grammarians. The origins of the class are not uniform: see Chantraine, *Grammaire*, i 416–19 and *Od.* v 194 and vi 255 nn. The commonest group (βήσετο, δύσετο, etc.) appears to be the remnants of an abortive morphology which supplied past tenses to the future/desiderative formations: see

C. L. Prince, 'Some Mixed Aorists in Homer', *Glotta* xlviii (1970), 155–63 and lii (1974), 1–10.

324. μευ: cf. 239.

325. πάρος οὔ ποτ' ἄκουσας: Athena had aided the hero during his shipwreck (v 382), but her intervention on that occasion had not been evident to Odysseus.

326. ῥαιομένου, ὅτε μ' ἔρραιε ...: narrated at v 282–381. The words are an extreme example of the *schema etymologicum*: see the numerous examples collected by Fehling, *Wiederholungsfiguren*, 153–62.

328–31. The last four verses have been thought by some critics to have been added by rhapsodes to terminate a recitation; see Marzullo, *Problema*, 407–8. A resumptive verse (ὣς ὁ μὲν ἔνθ' ἠρᾶτο ...) also appears at vii 1. Unless the division into books is thought to be original (an unlikely contingency), some minor adjustment would be made as the separate ῥαψῳδίαι were established. The book division is discussed by S. West, *The Ptolemaic Papyri of Homer* (Cologne, 1967), 18–25: she concludes that it is earlier than Zenodotus but later than the fifth century.

328. Παλλάς: the old connections with παλλακή (= κόρη), accepted by Chantraine, *Dictionnaire* s.v. παλλακή, and παλλω are unconvincing. O. Carruba, 'Athena ed Ares preellenichi', *Atti del I Congresso di Micenologia* (Rome, 1968), 932–44, suggests that the word is an old title, a borrowing of the Semitic *ba'alat* (= πότνια, 'mistress'). Ancient speculations about the word may be read in *P.Oxy.* 2260. What sense, if any, the poet attributed to the term cannot be ascertained, since it is rigidly confined as the inessential element to the formula.

329. οὔ πω φαίνετ' ἐναντίη: she does not appear to him ἐναντίη in her own person until Odysseus has landed on Ithaca (xiii 287 ff.). Athena is the symbol of fortune and success, and from the moment of the shipwreck intervenes constantly (v 427, 437, vi 2, 112, vii 14, 19, viii 7, 193); see also v 382–7 n. The goddess's relationship with Odysseus is examined in detail by M. Müller, *Athene als göttliche Helferin in der Odyssee* (Heidelberg, 1968).

330. πατροκασίγνητον: Poseidon. **μενέαινεν:** because of the blinding of the god's offspring, Polyphemus (ix 526–36); see also v 284 and n. Athena's αἰδώς will not stand close examination as an excuse for her neglect. She had deserted Odysseus before the encounter with the Cyclops and gives no reason for her resumption of relations at this particular moment. No very convincing reasons have been adduced for her behaviour: Are the adventures of ix–xii better told for being without a divine mentor? Is the rational and enlightened Athena incompatible with the fictions and horrors of the adventures? Is Athena a symbol of the wisdom Odysseus has now acquired? Or of his imminent success? Is there a 'wrath' of Athena in the background? Was the poet constrained by a feature of some primitive *Abenteuergedicht*? (Some of these suggestions are discussed by Clay, *Wrath*, 43–4.)

BOOK VII: INTRODUCTION

Odysseus follows the advice given to him by Nausicaa at the end of vi. He enters the palace of Alcinous and appeals to Arete. The Phaeacian court welcomes him, and Alcinous promises aid and fitting entertainment the following day. Odysseus tells the royal pair the story of his last few days. For a book having so straightforward a content, vii is vexed by an exceptional number of critical problems. Analytical critics have unanimously divined deep inroads by the second poet or the redactor, to indulge his predilection for good manners and to prepare the way for viii (see Von der Mühll, *Odyssee*, coll. 718 ff.).

At the end of vi we are given to understand that an appeal to the Phaeacians is attended by some hazard. They are ὑπερφίαλοι (vi 274), and Odysseus is to address himself not to their king, but to their queen, on whose response all must depend (vi 310 ff.). The beginning of vii confirms our expectation. Athena shields Odysseus from κερτομία with a mist (14 ff., cf. 32 and 16–17 n.), and repeats the advice to approach the queen (53 ff., 75–7 = vi 314–16). All this seems very programmatic, yet it turns out to be without point. When Odysseus is revealed within the palace, he widens his appeal to include Alcinous and the other princes of the Phaeacians in addition to queen Arete (146 ff.); and *she* makes no response to his appeal, remaining silent in the background until 237. Alcinous on the other hand, after a moment of discomposure, is as gracious and generous as any suppliant could desire.

Thus far two problems arise: (1) why is Arete introduced as a person of importance, and (2) why is she not made to respond immediately? The issue, of course, in a work of fiction, is not the motivation of a real Arete or a real Odysseus, as if the narrative were of actual events, but the intention of the poet in describing his creations as he does, and his success in attaining his aim. The relation between literature and life is very complicated. On the one hand literature is more logical than life, because most of the events of life are accidental and irrelevant, and are eliminated from literature: on the other hand literature aims to move its audience and especially in the circumstances of oral ἀοιδή is beset by conventions of narration. In the one respect literature is more logical, in the other less logical, than life. It is characteristic of conventional analysm that it emphasizes the first aspect and neglects the second (see, on the present problem, Schwartz, *Odyssee*, 23, and Merkelbach, *Untersuchungen*, 161). The interlude following Odysseus' appeal, 153–233, is thus assigned to the second poet, as if a question logically entailed an immediate answer, or an adumbration a fulfilment. (The weakness of this approach is evident from the inferences drawn from the phrase αὔριον ἔς at 318 (see n.) 'Probably no other single phrase in the *Odyssey* has served as the basis for more elaborate or more confident analyst criticism and reconstruction'—Fenik, *Studies*, 108; yet its use in the circumstances is perfectly natural, and it is corrected at xi 350–1 when circumstances had changed.) The problem of Arete, however, is more than a matter of logical sequence. Fenik, *Studies*, 61 ff., following Hölscher, sees in the delayed response of Arete a convention of narration: the climax is deliberately retarded. Structurally the scene is indeed very like xxiii 85 ff., the notorious 'recognition scene' of Odysseus and Penelope. Where it is possible so to show how literature modifies life, a useful objectivity is brought into the discussion, and it is no longer necessary to rely on value-judgements concerning the 'harshness' or 'effectiveness' of Arete's abrupt question. But value-judgements are not wholly avoided. Fenik finds Arete's words 'full of menace', as they must be if her questions are so important as to be emphasized by retardation, but this cannot be independently demonstrated (see 230–9 n.). To see the structure of the scene in this way has another weakness: following those who excise 155–232, it accepts Arete's words (237 ff.) as the response to Odysseus' appeal at 146 ff. There is no need to take them in that way. The theme of ξείνια is well represented in both Homeric epics. If we compare the closely parallel sequence of themes through which the reception of Telemachus and Pisistratus at Sparta is narrated in iv 1 ff., it becomes evident that the root of the trouble lies in the ambiguity of the entertainment offered to Odysseus at 179 ff. The simple sequence of themes (as in iv) is Arrival–Being Noticed–Initial Minor Discourtesy–Welcome–Meal–Questions–Stranger's Story. For Alcinous the real ξείνια are yet to come: for Arete the stranger has been fed and wined, and may now be questioned. (The poet in any event wishes to divide the story of Odysseus into convenient parts: only the immediately relevant part of his story is rehearsed at 241 ff.)

That Odysseus should make his appeal to the Phaeacians through Arete is in itself not unreasonable: parallels are known to anthropology, cf. J. Pitt-Rivers, 'Women and Sanctuary in the Mediterranean', in J. Pouillon and P. Maranda (eds.), *Mélanges Levi-Strauss*, ii (The Hague, 1970), 862–75, and to Greek history, cf. J. N. Bremmer,

Mnemosyne xxxiii (1980), 366–8. However, for her status and alleged influence upon affairs there is no explanation within the text of our *Odyssey*: at xi 346 the poet himself seems to withdraw the point.

More problems follow. Arete asked the stranger's identity, and received no direct answer. The narrative is plausible enough: Odysseus began his story, but before completion it is overtaken by another topic—Alcinous' concern for proper courtesy (298 ff.). Why should the poet proceed in this way? There is general agreement that this is not the time and place for the castaway to say εἴμ' Ὀδυσεὺς Λαερτιάδης, ὃς πᾶσι δόλοισιν ἀνθρώποισι μέλω, καί μευ κλέος οὐρανὸν ἵκει (ix 19–20). To make such a statement credible we need the contents of viii (cf. Eust. 1586. 50). By postponing that revelation, moreover, the poet exploits the same effects he has already exploited in introducing a disguised Athena to Telemachus in i and an unrecognized Telemachus to Menelaus in iv, and which he is to exploit again on the grand scale when the beggar presents himself to the suitors. For Hölscher this sufficiently explains Odysseus' reticence: the requirements of literature have prevailed over the logic of life. Nor is the illogicality very great. The essence of the question τίς πόθεν ...; seems to be 'What brings you here?' Eumaeus (xiv 191 ff.) and Penelope (xix 221 ff.), having put the same question, had to be satisfied with no more than Arete receives here. Besslich (*Schweigen*) has made a perceptive analysis of Odysseus' story. It is a κερδάλεος μῦθος. Arete's maternal concern is for τίς τοι τάδε εἵματ' ἔδωκεν; The hero reassures her. His meeting with Nausicaa was wholly proper. All he desires is to return home. Alcinous takes up the implicit line of thought (311–15), 'Perhaps you would like to stay after all—and marry Nausicaa?'

If, however, the full force of τίς πόθεν ...; is insisted on, the critical dilemma is acute: either to admit a harsh discontinuity of thought (not, however, unique in the *Odyssey*), or to seek a motivation for Odysseus' reticence which the poet has failed to supply explicitly. The discontinuity can only be resolved by analysm—Kirchhoff, for example, thought that in the Ur-Odyssee the story of the wanderings immediately followed Arete's enquiry (on which see K. Reinhardt, *Tradition und Geist*, hg. v. C. Becker (Göttingen, 1960), 114). Schadewaldt and Mattes find a motivation in the hero's state of mind, as the poet must intend us to understand it. How must a hero feel, bereft of retinue, weapons, and even of clothes? In a world where showing respect means giving gifts can he recognize himself in such a condition? Is his identity not destroyed? The danger in such reasoning is the so-called 'documentary fallacy', to treat fiction as if it were the record of real events. Perhaps the only indication in the text of a psychological collapse is Odysseus' reluctance to accept service from Nausicaa's maids (vi 218 ff.): the stress is rather on his physical condition (vi 130 ff., vii 133 ff.). On the other hand the hero's κερδοσύνη is not diminished: it is explicit at vi 148, certain at vii 208 ff. and 303 ff., and probable (according to Besslich) at 241 ff.

Such cunning is balanced by the εὐήθεια of Alcinous, who stands to Odysseus rather as Croesus did to Alcmeon (see Hdt. vi 125). Humour is an elusive quality, but it is probably present in the portrayal of the Phaeacian king. He has some of the qualities of a περίεργος (cf. Theophrastus, *Char.* 13), displacing his eldest son to accommodate the unknown suppliant, wondering if his guest is a god, offering his daughter in marriage to an unknown stranger, issuing general invitations, boasting of the athleticism, luxury, and balletic accomplishments of his people, piling gift upon gift. The man of true experience caps his best efforts without difficulty.

Brief Bibliography

W. Nestle, 'Odyssee-Interpretationen I', *Hermes* lxxvii (1942), 46–77, and G. R. Rose, 'The Unfriendly Phaeacians', *TAPhA* c (1969), 387–406, discuss the characterization of Alcinous and his people: see also introduction to viii.

H. Kilb, *Strukturen epischen Gestaltens* (Munich, 1973), 26–107, Eisenberger, *Studien*, 107–29, and esp. Fenik, *Studies*, survey the critical literature on this book. Traditional analysm, which expunged 155–232 and (usually) viii and all that introduced it, goes back to Kirchhoff, *Odyssee*, and was consolidated by Schwartz, *Odyssee*, Von der Mühll, *Odyssee*, and Merkelbach, *Untersuchungen*. Focke, *Odyssee*, 129–39, reasserted the dramatic force of the retarded response. Reinhardt, *Tradition und Geist*, hg. v. C. Becker (Göttingen, 1960), 112–24, and Hölscher, *Untersuchungen*, 65–8, and 'Das Schweigen der Arete', *Hermes* lxxxviii (1960), 257–65, elucidated the underlying generic pattern of the narrative. Fenik develops this idea further. M. Lang, 'Homer and Oral Techniques', *Hesperia* xxxviii (1969), restricted the parallels to the scenes on Ithaca, but showed how the generic pattern and the particular instance may lead to illogicalities. For another view of the underlying structure see M. Müller, *Athene als göttliche Helferin in der Odysee* (Heidelberg, 1968).

W. Schadewaldt, 'Kleiderdinge: Zur Analyse der Odyssee', *Hermes* lxxxvii (1959), 13–26, and Mattes, *Odysseus*, seek the key to the action in the hero's psychology. Besslich, *Schweigen*, explains the oblique nature of Odysseus' discourse.

BOOK VII: COMMENTARY

1–13. Nausicaa returns home. This brief conventional scene is an appendage to the preceding book, put in to fulfil the epic desire for *complete* narrative. Without it the story of Nausicaa would have been broken off (vi 322) with the princess still far from home. She says nothing of her adventure, of course, as a maiden in such circumstances would normally do (cf. *h.Cer.* 171). We naturally may attribute her reticence to her αἰδώς, but the real reason is the poet's desire for an effective scene when Odysseus comes *unannounced* among the Phaeacian princes.

1. The line is functionally a duplicate of vi 328 ff.: see n. ad loc. ἔνθ': in the grove of Athena, just outside the city. πολύτλας δῖος Ὀδυσσεύς: This formula occurred also at vi 1 and at v 171 when Odysseus was first introduced in person. In later poets its use in such prominent places would doubtless give it a special significance, but in Homer the effect must be regarded as cumulative, for it is not obvious how a formula may be used casually in 40 places and significantly in a few others, unless there is something about the context of those few places that directs the audience's attention to the formula. πολύτλας is evidently interpreted by the poet as 'much-enduring' (cf. πολυτλήμων, xviii 319), but the original sense may have been 'much-daring': see G. Hunger, *Die Odysseusgestalt in Odyssee und Ilias* (Kiel, 1962), where an attempt is made to distinguish earlier and later poets by means of earlier and later conceptions of the hero. It is more likely that any change arose from the evolution of the formulaic diction.

7. πῦρ: the references to fires are persistently taken by schol. as an indication of the winter season. Some moderns have followed them (e.g. Wilamowitz, *Untersuchungen*, 87, *Heimkehr*, 149) at least in the Phaeacian and later Ithacan books, while maintaining that summer was the season of the Telemachy. But see J. A. Scott, 'Assumed Contradictions in the Seasons of the *Odyssey*', *CPh.* xi (1916), 148–55, and v 272–7 n. The correct clue is doubtless supplied by the expression used at xix 64 φόως ἔμεν ἠδὲ θέρεσθαι.

8. Ἀπειραίη: Ἀπείρη is doubtless < ἄπειρος, 'without bounds', a poetical fiction like Ὑπερείη (vi 4), the first home of the Phaeacians. The scholiasts' attempt to derive the name from Ἤπειρος is philologically impossible, and doubtless inspired by the equation of Scheria with Corcyra (see vi 8 n.). Germain, who believes that the story of the *Odyssey* is derived from an Egyptian tale, compares Egypt. '*pr*, 'prisoner' (*Genèse*, 305). Εὐρυμέδουσα: 'Wide-ruling', an odd name for a servant (for the masc. cf. 58 and *Il.* iv 228, viii 114, xi 620). The epic has a few names expressive of social standing or profession (Thersites, the spy Dolon, a singer Phemius, etc.), but there is no pool of names for the lower orders of society on which the poet can draw for incidental characters.

9–12. How Eurymedusa came to be in Scheria. The brief anecdote, common in the cataloguing style, is a way of introducing a minor character. The device is naturally much more common in the *Iliad*, where the cast must include many unimportant characters: for details see C. R. Beye, 'Homeric

Battle Narrative and Catalogues', *HSPh* lxviii (1964), 345–73. The poet presumably wishes to suggest that Eurymedusa was brought by slave-traders, like those who sold Eumaeus to Odysseus (xv 415 ff.), but the diction is that of a piratical raid. In either case the isolation of the Phaeacians (a special feature) is overlooked in favour of generic ideas about the provenance of slaves.

10. ἔξελον (3rd pl.): at xiv 232 Odysseus uses the 1st pers. in describing the allocation of booty, but nominally at least it is the λαός who assign prizes, cf. ix 550–1 and esp. *Il.* i 368–9.

11. θεοῦ δ' ὥς: a heavily modified form of the θεὸς (ϝ)ὥς prototype: see v 12 n.

13. εἴσω: of place, not motion, cf. *h.Merc.* 6 (ἔσω ναίουσα). This usage, and the fact that the line repeats the sense of 7ᵇ, caused Zenodotus at least to athetize it. But the line is a straightforward example of ring-composition, whereby the starting point of a passage is picked up by its conclusion. Nausicaa, in accordance with the universal Greek custom, did not banquet with the menfolk and their guests: cf. viii 458.

14–132. Arrival of Odysseus. Thematically the closest parallel is provided by the visit of Priam to Achilles in *Il.* xxiv. In both scenes the landmarks of the journey are noted, the traveller meets a divine guide in disguise, and the arrival is marked by an ekphrasis describing the scene. Both lead on to a scene of supplication. To the present passage further parallels may be found in the visit of Odysseus to Circe (x 274 ff.), in his journey to the town of Ithaca (xvii 204 ff.), in Hermes' visit to Calypso (v 43 ff.), and in Telemachus' wonderment at Menelaus' palace (iv 68 ff.): cf. Arend, *Scenen*, 42–4. Embellishment is lavish, for two reasons. First, to accommodate the length of the narrative to the length of the journey. Second, to postpone the crucial encounter of the hero with his patrons. This delay, together with the hints of Phaeacian xenophobia, creates a certain element of suspense within the scene, which is maintained in the first part of the following supplication.

14–15. ἀμφὶ ... ἠέρα χεῦε: αὐτάρ is read by a majority of codd., but the preposition appears elsewhere (*Il.* xvii 268–70 (ἀμφὶ), *Il.* viii 50, *Od.* vii 41–2 (κατά), *Il.* v 776, *Od.* vii 140, xiii 189 (περὶ)) in the expression of this idea, and should be retained here. The effect is to make Odysseus invisible, whereas in the *Iliad* ἀήρ denotes a palpable smokescreen (cf. ἠέρα τύψε, *Il.* xx 446). Perhaps for this reason Zenodotus thought the mist was shed over the Phaeacians: note his reading at 41 below. It is not recorded what he read here (αὐτάρ?), nor at 140 or 143.

The whole episode is closely imitated by Verg. *A.* i 411 ff.

16–17. Schol. (on 32) draw a distinction between the boorishness of a ναυτικὸς ὄχλος and the civilized manners of βασιλεῖς. Odysseus, of course, despite the princely tunic he has acquired from Nausicaa, is still a battered castaway without identity and without the retinue and accoutrements of an ἀριστεύς. His adventures in the palace of Ithaca demonstrate the sort of welcome that some considered suitable for the homeless, destitute, and unknown. By hinting at this, as schol. shrewdly note, the poet sets the scene for a prolonged episode in which Odysseus is gradually accepted for the king and hero that he is.

19 ff. Odysseus meets Athena disguised as a maiden. For the relations of Odysseus with his patroness see v 382–7 n. This scene, brief as it is, combines two themes: (1) a stranger meets a maiden at or near a well, cf. x 105, *h.Cer.* 98, and the Nausicaa episode itself (vi 110 ff.), and (2) the hero is met and aided by a god, cf. x 277, xiii 221, *Il.* xxiv 352. The closest analogue is that in xiii, where, however, Athena revealed her real identity (xiii 296 ff.).

24. ταλαπείριος: evidently ταλα-πείρ-ιος, 'who has undergone (many) trials'. The word puzzled the ancients, who sought to connect it with περάω (as if = πόρρωθεν πεπερακώς), or with ταλαίπωρος (Aristarchus). The epithet is formulaic with ξεῖνος (xvii 84, xix 379) and ἱκέτης (vi 193, xiv 511).

25. τηλόθεν ἐξ ἀπίης γαίης: ἀπίης is 'distant', at least in the poet's understanding, for τηλόθεν reads as a gloss on the word. It is confined to the formula with γαίης, and can hardly in view of such a restricted use be a genuine adjectival derivative of ἀπό. Carpenter, *AJA* lix (1950), 177, suspects a non-Greek provenance. Ἀπία, a poetical designation of the Peloponnese (A. *Supp.* 260 etc.), has long Ᾱ.

26. ἔργα νέμονται: cf. *Il.* ii 751. The alternative reading γαῖαν ἔχουσι appears to be intrusive from vi 177 and 195.

29. ναίει: we may understand either (δόμος Ἀλκινόου) ναίει (intrans., cf. *Il.* ii 626) ἐγγύθι (δόμου) πατρός, or (Ἀλκίνοος) ναίει ἐγγύθι πατρός. The latter is the more natural.

30–1. The text appears sound, though a lacuna may have been suspected in antiquity, for cod. Pal. has traces of a ligature for λείπει στίχος among the scholia. The difficulty would have arisen from a failure to recognize that ἐγὼ δ᾽ ὁδὸν ἡγεμονεύσω is parenthetic and ἴθι co-ordinate with προτιόσσεο.

32. See 16–17 n.

34. νηυσὶ θοῇσι ... ὠκείῃσι: Fick, *Die hom. Odyssee* (Göttingen, 1883), 94, maintained that θοός = 'sharp(-prowed)' not 'swift', and Ameis–Hentze–Cauer that νῆες θοαί = 'warships'. These are unnecessary expedients. The expression is a striking example of the inattention accorded to perpetual epithets, cf. τείχεα μακρὰ/ὑψηλά (44–5).

36. νόημα: the comparison was proverbial, cf. the saying of Thales, τάχιστος νοῦς· διὰ πάντος γὰρ τρέχει. An elaborated comparison is made at *Il.* xv 80–3 and at *h.Merc.* 43–4.

39–42. The lines were needlessly suspected by the older analysts. They constitute with 14–17 a good example of ring-composition.

41. For the reading of Zenodotus (ἤ σφισιν ἀχλὺν) see 14–15 n. **ἐϋπλόκαμος:** only here of Athena, see v 58 n. The word is derived from the formulaic sentence seen at 246 and 255 (cf. also v 58), which the poet here adapts. **δεινὴ θεός:** the o-stem form of the noun is invariable in this formula (7 times in *Od.*) and its derivatives (κυδρὴ θεός Hes. *Thg.* 442,

BOOK VII 17-54

h.Cer. 179, 292, and σεμνὴ θεός *h.Cer.* 1): θεά is never scanned ‿‿ by correction.

43. λιμένας: cf. vi 263. The site is conceived as a peninsula with harbours on either side of the isthmus.

44. τείχεα μακρά: it is natural to take the epithet to mean 'high', as in μακρὸς Ὄλυμπος etc., and this is not certainly excluded by ὑψηλά (45): cf. the duplication of ideas at 34.

45. σκολόπεσσιν ἀρηρότα: cf. the full description of the 'Achaean Wall' at *Il.* xii 54–7: κρημνοὶ γὰρ ἐπηρεφέες περὶ πᾶσαν | ἕστασαν ἀμφοτέρωθεν, ὕπερθεν δὲ σκολόπεσσιν | ὀξέσιν ἠρήρει, τοὺς ἵστασαν υἷες Ἀχαιῶν | πυκνοὺς καὶ μεγάλους, δηΐων ἀνδρῶν ἀλεωρήν. Drerup, *Archaeologia* O, 100, understands this to describe a stockaded earthwork (Pallisadenzaun): but the 'Achaean Wall', though a temporary and hasty construction, is represented at least at *Il.* xii 258–60 as a town wall with substantial foundations and substructure, above which timber towers or battlements were erected. See J. V. Nicholls, *ABSA* liii–liv (1958–9), 112–13, figs. 34, 35, for the timber fittings of the walls of Old Smyrna (8th and 7th cents.), in so far as these may be reconstructed.

47. τοῖσι: the usual formula (e.g. v 202), even though one person only is addressed.

49. βασιλῆας: called ἡγήτορας ἠδὲ μέδοντας at 136. They are twelve in number, cf. viii 390, and despite the use of the same term in the formula Ἀλκίνοον βασιλῆα (55 below etc.), are clearly outranked by Alcinous. The Homeric political vocabulary, however, is highly unspecific, and consistently distinguishes only the nobility (ἄνακτες, ἀριστῆες, ἄριστοι, ἄρχοι, βασιλῆες, ἡγέμονες, ἡγήτορες, κοίρανοι, μέδοντες) with their θεράποντες and ἑταῖροι, and the commons (λαός, δῆμος). Certain facts, e.g. the use of the term ἄναξ in old cults, and the failure in Homer to refer to the gods as βασιλῆες, suggest that βασιλεύς once denoted a humbler status than ἄναξ. Both terms occur in Mycenaean (Ventris–Chadwick, *Documents*, 121), but the βασιλεύς is there an officer of the provinces, not found at court. Neither word has any obvious etymology.

50–1: μηδέ τι ... τάρβει: the advice and the language in which it is expressed recall the aggressive tactics of Tydeus as a guest at Thebes, *Il.* iv 385 ff. Odyssean courtesy, cf. i 103, iv 20, demanded that the stranger wait ἐπὶ προθύροις until he was noticed.

52. ποθεν ἄλλοθεν: the reading μάλα τηλόθεν appears to be derived from vi 312 = vii 194. Bekker and others struck out the line to give a more sententious tone to 51, but there was no ancient athetesis.

53. πρῶτα κιχήσεαι: the natural rendering 'you will first encounter' abbreviates the language of vi 310–11, where Odysseus was recommended to go past Alcinous to reach Arete. Schol. circumvent this minor discrepancy by taking κιχήσεαι imperativally with a nuance of supplication 'you shall beseech', a sense of κιχάνω that seems to require explicit contextual indication, e.g. κιχανόμενοι τὰ σὰ γοῦνα (ix 266).

54–66. The Phaeacian royal house. If it is possible to take τοκῆες (54) in the sense of 'ancestors' and τέκον (55) in a corresponding sense, there is no difficulty. The genealogy, itself a regular motif for the introduction of a character, is clearly, however, an invention: at least twelve Periboeas and eight Eurymedons are known to the mythographers (see *RE* s.v.); Nausithous (also invented for an unhomeric son of Calypso and Odysseus at Hes. *Th.* 1017) is a typical Phaeacian 'ship-name', and Rhexenor a personification of a heroic epithet. A rival genealogy of Alcinous, making him son of Phaeax, son of Corcyra and Poseidon (Hellanicus fr. 77 Jacoby, DS iv 72. 4), is equally fanciful, and more tendentious. Arete is thus Alcinous' niece. Marriage of uncle and niece commended itself to classical Greek sentiment, from the time at least of the Hesiodic *Catalogue of Women*, cf. Cretheus and Tyro (fr. 30 M–W), but is not found among the traditional epic heroes. (The incestuous unions of divinities, of course, constitute a special case.) A loose use of τοκῆες is certainly found at iv 596, but there is nothing in the present context to prepare the audience for any but the etymological sense and the implication that Alcinous and Arete were siblings. The incestuous union was also affirmed by Hesiod (fr. 222 M–W) according to schol. on this passage. In that case the genealogy must be intrusive (Kirchhoff and others), or have been recast (Von der Mühll, *Odyssee*, 714), conceivably by the poet himself. The composition is elegant enough, and there is no ancient athetesis. The Argonautic legend furnishes no clue to the point of the brother–sister marriage.

54. Ἀρήτη: i.e. 'Prayed for (from the gods)', cf. Θεαίτητος. Stanford discerns a significant name, as if Ἀρήτη = 'Beseeched (by Odysseus)'. That would go neatly with Ἀλκίνοος if the second element of that name could mean 'sending home' (see vi 12 n.). Significant names, however, are usually given to minor characters of the poet's own invention (e.g. the Phaeacians at viii 111 ff.). The uncertain handling of Arete's role, however, (see introduction to vii) and the problem of her marriage (see preceding n.) suggest that the poet inherited her together with the story. She appears, together with Alcinous, in Apollonius' *Argonautica* (iv 993 ff.), but it hardly follows that Apollonius had any source but the *Odyssey* for his Phaeacians.

59. Γιγάντεσσιν: mentioned also at 206 and at x 120. The poet seems to regard them as the same sort of being as the Cyclopes, superhuman but subdivine. He betrays no acquaintance with the elaborate mythology of the Gigantomachia. The allusion to the Giants' defeat in 60, if not an *ad hoc* invention, is obscure.

60. ἀτάσθαλον: used of those who transgress the moral, ritual, and spiritual limits of their station, an important concept throughout the *Odyssey*, e.g. i 7, 34, xxii 317.

62. It is idle to enquire how a scion of the ἄγρια φῦλα Γιγάντων should become king of the gentle Phaeacians. Some mythographers discovered a connection: AR (iv 992) and his scholiast derive both Giants and Phaeacians from the blood of the mutilated Uranus, cf. Acusilaus, FGrH 2 F 4. This story was unknown to Hesiod, yet Phaeacians, Giants, and Cyclopes form some sort of nexus, cf. 206.

64. ἄκουρον: 'without a κοῦρος' (masc.). The point of παιδοποιία was to perpetuate a man's οἶκος: hence the issue that counted was *male* issue. The thought finds a precise parallel in Hdt. v 48 ἀπέθανε ἄπαις θυγατέρα μούνην λιπών. **βάλ' ... Ἀπόλλων:** of an untimely death, see v 124 n.

66 ff. Status of Arete. The explanation seems to lie ultimately outside the text. The exalted position of the queen provides a reason why Odysseus should be advised to direct his appeal to her. But since that appeal is without point in the ensuing narrative (see introduction to vii) her high station is without point also, except in the most general terms as a rehearsal of archaic courtesies. Arete has naturally appealed to those who are beguiled by the thought of a primitive matriarchal society (for details see K. Hirvonen, *Matriarchal Survivals* (Helsinki, 1968), 105–12), but there is no real clue to her provenance.

69. περὶ κῆρι: see v 36 n.   **τετίμηταί τε καὶ ἔστιν:** a parallel to this puzzling expression is Plato *Smp.* 195 b μετὰ δὲ νέων [ὁ Ἔρως] ἀεὶ ξύνεστί τε καὶ ἔστι [sc. νέος αὐτός], from which it appears that an adj. must be understood from the sense of the preceding words, viz. τιμητή or τιμήεσσα.

72. δειδέχαται: a present tense, expressing repeated actions, is required, rather than a stative perfect. The formation is therefore probably that of an athematic present, root *δεκ-, 'receive, welcome', with lengthened reduplication: cf. Chantraine, *Dictionnaire* s.v. δηδέχαται (δει- of the MSS would be a secondary orthography). A form in -σκ-, modified to δειδίσκομαι is also found (iii 41 etc.).

74. οἷσιν: the χαριέστεραι, recoiling from the thought of feminine arbitration, seek τὸ πρεπῶδες by reading ᾗσιν, as if Arete's jurisdiction were confined to matrimonial disputes; to which schol. P and T make the just and amusing reply, ὡς γελοίως, ὦ βέλτιστε. οὐ γὰρ τῷ δικαίῳ, ἀλλὰ τοῖς φίλοις φησὶν αὐτὴν βοηθεῖν.   **νείκεα λυει:** the long -ῡ- arises by conjugation of the formula, cf. νείκεα λύσω (*Il.* xiv 205) and Wyatt, *Lengthening*, 209.

79–80. See app. crit. to Allen's text. Aristarchus (who believed Homer to have been an Athenian) appears to have accepted the lines, but his pupil Chaeris suspected them. He has been followed by Bethe, Schwartz, Focke, and others who felt that the reference to Athens was too explicit, too knowledgeable, and too sycophantic for an Ionian poet. The parochial mythology of Attica, it should be noted, was not absorbed into the epic tradition. Most allusions to Athenian affairs have been suspected, see General Introduction, pp. 36–9 and the commentators on *Il.* i 265.

79. Σχερίην: the land of the Phaeacians: see vi 8 n.

81. δῦνε δ' Ἐρεχθῆος πυκινὸν δόμον: the words are odd, since we should expect Athena, having withdrawn to her favourite city, to take pleasure (like Aphrodite at viii 363) in the apparatus of cult (τέμενος βωμός τε θυήεις), and seem to express an old idea that gods dwelt in the palaces of kings, cf. xix 178 (Zeus and Minos) and see M. P. Nilsson, *Minoan–Mycenaean Religion*[2] (Lund, 1950), 488, and Burkert, *Religion*, 32. Throughout historical times Athena Polias and Erechtheus were worshipped together in a joint temple on the Athenian acropolis, cf. *Il.* ii 547–9.   **Ἐρεχθῆος:**

325

a legendary king of Athens, apparently a doublet conceived in more human terms of the half-serpentine Erichthonius. As a figure of cult he was *the* hero of Attica, the personification of the identity and autochthony of the people. **πυκινὸν δόμον**: doubtless on the acropolis, where Mycenaean palatial remains have been found around the periphery—the summit, of course, was cleared to the bedrock for the classical structures.

81–132. Alcinous' palace. The description falls into three sections: (1) the buildings and furnishings, 81–102; (2) the staff, 103–11; and (3) the gardens, 112–32. Throughout the poet's intention is to impress and astound, rather than to describe a precisely conceived structure (see vi 303 and 304 nn.): hence the lavish use of precious metal in the first section, for which it would be wrong to seek for exact analogues. In the second and third sections a utopian note enters: the Phaeacians have exceptional skills and dwell in a natural paradise of eternal plenty. (The emphasis of Hesiod (*Op.* 109–19, the Golden Age) is slightly different—the absence of toil. For other utopian notions, mostly jocular, see Athen. vi 267–70. See further M. I. Finley, 'Utopianism, Ancient and Modern', in K. H. Wolff and B. Moore (eds.), *The Critical Spirit: Essays in Honour of H. Marcuse* (Boston, 1967), 3–20 = *Use and Abuse of History* (London, 1975), 178–92.) The proper extent of an inorganic descriptive passage is difficult to determine, and various excisions have been proposed, ranging from the whole passage to single lines, especially the lines that occur elsewhere (84–5 = iv 45–6 with Menelaus for Alcinous, 94 cf. v 136, 99 = x 427, 111 = ii 117, 115–16 = xi 589–90): discussion in Marzullo, *Problema*, 386–7. Linguistic anomalies and secondary features are unusually frequent: see 86, 88, 94, 95, 107, 110, 114, 118, and 119 nn. Some description is appropriate at this point, cf. the descriptions that ornament the arrivals of Athena at Ithaca, i 106 ff., Telemachus at Sparta, iv 71 ff., Hermes at Ogygia, v 63 ff., Odysseus at Eumaeus' farmstead, xiv 5 ff., and at his palace, xvii 264 ff., but such descriptions may be very perfunctory and this elaborate passage invites the suspicion of rhapsodic reworking.

82. ἵε κλυτά: a neat modification of ἀγακλυτά, 4 times in this position with the noun δώματα in various parts of the verse.

83. χάλκεον οὐδόν: elsewhere specifically only of Tartarus, *Il.* viii 15, Hes. *Th.* 811. Odysseus' palace on Ithaca had only a stone threshhold (xvi 41 etc.).

86–7. The mention of the μυχός at 87 shows that these lines apply to the μέγαρον: they are, however, oddly reminiscent of the first stage (the αὐλή) of Odysseus' entry into his own palace, ἐπήσκηται δέ οἱ αὐλὴ | τοίχῳ καὶ θριγκοῖσι, θύραι δ' εὐερκέες εἰσὶ | δικλίδες, xvii 266–8.

86. χάλκεοι ... τοῖχοι: the brazen walls of the palace are symbolic of magnificence, just as the steel gates of Tartarus at *Il.* viii 15 are symbolic of incarceration. It is possible that, like the story of Danaë's brazen prison, the metallic walls reflect the Mycenaean use of bronze plaques to ornament, for example, the walls of the grander tholos tombs (see A. J. B. Wace, *Mycenae* (Princeton, 1949), 32). Mycenaean palace decoration was mostly fresco but of that Homer shows no knowledge. **ἐληλέατ':** 3rd pl.

plupf. pass. of ἐλαύνω. This is the reading of codd. of Allen's family b, a group that preserves a number of apparently old readings (see *PBSR* v (1910), 20–3). The stem is properly ἐληλά- as seen in the 3rd sg. form ἐλήλα-ται at 113. Codd. are much confused by this strange form: see app. crit. to OCT. The vulgate reading ἐληλέδατ' or ἐληλάδατ' is not necessarily wrong, although it may easily have been generated by contamination with ἐρηρέδατ' at 95, for analogies within the *Kunstsprache* can certainly produce a perfect in -δ-, cf. ἐρράδαται < ῥαίνω (xx 354 and *Il.* xii 431): see further Schwyzer, *Grammatik*, i 672, and Chantraine, *Grammaire*, i 435.

87. μυχόν is the rear part of the μέγαρον, a sleeping area at iii 402 and iv 304. In private buildings of the Mycenaean period it is sometimes screened off, but never in the palaces, where abundant θάλαμοι served its purposes more luxuriously. **θριγκὸς κυάνοιο:** cf. the inlay of blue paste in the frieze of the Great Megaron at Tiryns (Schliemann, *Tiryns* (London, 1886), 284–92). κύανος (cf. Hittite *kuwanna-*, 'precious stone', 'copper') denotes lapis lazuli (azurite), or more commonly a substitute, the σκευαστὸς κύανος of Theophrastus (*de Lapidibus* 55).

89. **ἀργύρεοι σταθμοὶ δ':** ἀργύρεοι δὲ σταθμοὶ is the barely metrical reading of the MSS (including P. 26), a striking testimony to the unity of the textual tradition. Correction weakens the rhetoric of this string of clauses by removing the adjective from its initial position (thus σταθμοὶ δ' ἀργύρεοι Barnes), or, like Bentley's emendation which Allen received into the OCT, postpones δέ in an unnatural way: postponed δέ is very rare in epic, and the *Odyssey* has no other instance of δέ placed after a noun–epithet group.

94. **ὄντας:** the Attic form (for Ionic ἐόντ-). Attic forms of εἰμί are certain also at xix 489, xxiv 491, *Il.* xiv 274, and xix 202. **ἀγήρως:** see v 136 n. The poet of this inorganic line has taken advantage of vowel contraction in the vernacular to decline the formula ἀγήραος (-ον) ἤματα πάντα into the acc. pl. The permutations of the expression 'immortal and unageing' are an instructive instance of the flexibility of formular composition.

95. **ἐρηρέδατ'** (< ἐρείδω), for *ἐρηρίδατο, possibly with Aeolic -ρε- for -ρι-, the reduced grade of the root, but more likely with -ρε- by analogy with the present, from which tense is derived the -ει- of ἠρήρειστο (*Il.* iii 358 etc.) and similar forms in later writers.

100. **χρύσειοι ... κοῦροι:** another note of luxury. The god Hephaestus had similar furniture, but his were additionally endowed with νόος, αὐδή, and σθένος (*Il.* xviii 417–20). In his description of Scheria the poet stops this side of unreality, as his age might be supposed to conceive it. Note that the palace of Odysseus on Ithaca was thought of in less utopian terms and made do with λαμπτῆρες, 'cressets', a sort of grating to hold blazing faggots, xviii 307 etc.

102. **φαίνοντες νύκτας:** not 'making the nights to shine', a use of φαίνω not recognized by LSJ⁹, but 'giving light by night' (φαίνω intrans. as at xix 25).

103. **δμῳαί:** the weight of philological opinion inclines to a derivation from δόμος, as οἰκέτης < οἶκος, see Chantraine, *Dictionnaire* s.v. δμώς, though δάμνημι provides an equally satisfactory provenance that seems to be

implied by the epic itself, cf. i 398 δμώων οὕς μοι ληίσσατο δῖος Ὀδυσσεύς,
and *Il.* xviii 28. If δμωαί are the product of pillage, how do the Phaeacians,
the most peaceable of men, come to possess them, and if they are foreigners
by what justice are their masters given the credit (110) for their skills?
Wickert-Micknat (*Archaeologia* R, 40) accordingly argues that these 'house-
hold women' (δμωή < δόμος) are free Phaeacian labourers. Others excise
108–11, but the contrasted skills of men and women look like a traditional
motif, cf. the embroidery of the women of Sidon, *Il.* vi 289, and the
metalwork of their menfolk, *Il.* xxiii 743. It is preferable to treat these
δμωαί, like the town walls of Scheria, as aspects of a normal epic
community that the poet has not troubled to adjust to the special
circumstances of the Phaeacians, cf. the δμωαί of Calypso, v
199.   **πεντήκοντα**, intended, as at xxii 421, to exemplify the magnifi-
cence of the heroic age, reflects only the meanness of contemporary times.
The kings of Mycenaean Cnossos and Pylos disposed of enormous staffs (cf.
Ventris–Chadwick, *Documents*, 155 ff., Palmer, *Interpretation*, 113 ff.): for a
truly imperial establishment cf. the booty taken by Alexander from Darius,
παλλακίδας μουσούργους τοῦ βασιλέως τριακοσίας εἴκοσι ἐννέα, ἄνδρας
στεφανηπλόκους ἑξ καὶ τεσσεράκοντα, ὀψοποιοὺς διακοσίους ἑβδομήκοντα
ἑπτά, χυτρεψοὺς εἴκοσι ἐννέα, γαλακτούργους τρισκαίδεκα, ποτηματοποιοὺς
ἑπτακαίδεκα, οἰνοηθητὰς ἑβδομήκοντα, μυροποιοὺς τεσσεράκοντα (Athen. xiii
608 a). Vergil too, imitating this passage (*A.* i 703 ff.) felt obliged to add
'centum aliae totidemque ministri'.   **οἱ** here and at 122 is Alcinous.
104. ἀλετρεύουσι: the present tenses of this and the following section are
descriptive, cf. Chantraine, *Grammaire*, ii 191. There is, of course, no
historic present in Homer.   **μύλης ἔπι μήλοπα καρπόν:** some ancient
commentators were induced by the Hellenistic preference for the masc.
μύλος, 'mill', to make the strange suggestion that μύλη is here the medical
term for the knee-joint. They then compounded this error by linking
μήλοπα ('having the appearance of a ripe apple, i.e. yellow', but found
only in this formula) with μῆλον, 'flock', and imagining some process of
wool-dressing. Aristarchus, citing xx 111 ἥ ῥα μύλην στήσασα, thought it
worth while to refute this nonsense. μήλοψ (only here and Hes. fr. 337) is
one of a series of old compounds, cf. αἴθοψ, ἤνοψ, νῶροψ, οἶνοψ, unproduc-
tive in later Greek (which prefers -ωψ, -ωπις, or -ωπος).
106. ἤμεναι applies to the spinning only, cf. xviii 315. It was necessary to
stand in order to weave (ἱστὸν ἐποίχεσθαι, v 62 etc.).   **οἶά τε φύλλα:** an
obscurely laconic comparison, whose point appears to be that the move-
ments of the spinsters' fingers are as rapid as the flickering leaves of the
aspen.
107. The obscurity of this line has been much reduced by Marinatos
(*Archaeologia* A, 4–5), who shows that in the preparation of woollen cloth a
bath of oil and other substances (called ἀμόργη) might be used as a bleach.
Oil, however, is also used in the preparation of linen (cf. Lorimer,
Monuments, 371), but if that sense of ὀθόναι is insisted upon, the context is
needlessly complicated.   **καιροσέων**, the reading of Aristarchus, is

philologically impossible. As schol. were aware, the underlying noun is καῖρος, a technical term for the fastenings of the loom by which the warp was attached. The form required is thus the gen. pl. fem. of the adj. καιρόεις, i.e. καιρουσσέων, of which the καιροσσέων of the MSS is an archaic orthography (cf. Chantraine, *Grammaire*, i 6). Despite the objections of Cauer (*Homerkritik*, 106), the word remains one of the clearest testimonies to a text in which secondary *OY* was represented by *O*.

110. ἱστῶν τεχνῆσσαι (contracted from τεχνήεσσαι, cf. τιμῆντα *Il.* xviii 475) is the *difficilior lectio* and rightly preferred by eds. since Bekker. With the vulgate ἱστὸν τεχνῆσαι (aor. infin.) understand ἴδριες from 108.

113. τετράγυος: usually derived from γύης, the stock of a plough, as if = 'of four days' ploughing'. The measure is quite uncertain: schol. say γύη denotes a square with sides of two stades (*c.*365 m.), an improbably large area; Hesychius more realistically equates with the πλέθρον (*c.*930 m²). At xviii 374 τετράγυος expresses the extent of a heroic day's ploughing with the best oxen. The τέμενος offered to Meleager (*Il.* ix 578), of which ἥμισυ οἰνοπέδοιο, was πεντηκοντόγυον, but that was meant to be an offer he could not refuse.

114. πεφύκει (3rd sg. plpf.) of the MSS (another striking instance of unanimity) could be accepted only as the result of careless formular composition, cf. δένδρεα μακρὰ πεφύκει (v 238, 241) and πεφύκει τηλεθόωσα (v 63). πεφύκᾱσι is therefore adopted by eds. from Herodian, but πεφύᾱσι (*Il.* iv 484 etc.), is the usual epic form, and there is but one other example of -ᾱσι as 3rd pl. pf. in Homer, viz. λελόγχᾱσι (*Od.* xi 304). It is possible that the poet of this passage intended πεφύκει as a pres., cf. ἐπέφυκον (Hes. *Th.* 152), and the common ἀνώγει: see Munro, *Homeric Dialect*, 30-1.   τηλεθόωντα: the orthography of this word (with or without diectasis) is very uncertain: P. 26, missing at 116, has τηλεθάοντα here.

115-16. (= xi 589-90, the punishment of Tantalus): the same trees, except for the pomegranate, were cultivated by Laertes, xxiv 340. Note the absence of the quince, μῆλον Κυδώνιον, known to Alcman (fr. 99 Page), and of the stone fruits, *Prunus* spp. (schol. assert that ὄγχνη includes the quince). W. Richter, *Archaeologia* H, 140-6, discusses the Homeric orchard.

116. The repetition of τηλεθόωσαι after τηλεθόωντα at 114 is awkward, but the formular style encourages indifference to such echoes, cf. v 422-3, viii 73-4. Some are even enshrined in formulaic runs of verses, e.g. χέρνιβα ... ἐπέχευε φέρουσα–σῖτον ... παρέθηκε φέρουσα i 136-40 = iv 52-6 = vii 172-6 = x 368-72 = xv 135-9 = xvii 91-5.

118. θέρευς: a rare contraction, cf. Shipp, *Studies*, 181.

119. Ζεφυρίη: the derivative form is found only here. The acephalous verse is unexplained, cf. Wyatt, *Lengthening*, 221.

121. Since ἐπὶ ῥοιῇ is good metre, it is unclear why for the pomegranates the poet substitutes grapes (σταφυλῇ), which belong in the next section. Aristotle (fr. 667) and derivative testimonia omit 120ᵇ-121ᵃ (μῆλον ... σταφυλή), but there is no Alexandrian athetesis.

122. ἀλωή implies, as a practical point, the facilities for wine-making, but there is no need to take ἐρρίζωται as a reference to the buildings, as if = 'be firmly fixed' (so Merry–Riddell, comparing xiii 163). The word is regularly used of plants, e.g. Xenophon *Oec.* xix 9, Theophrastus *HP* ii 5. 6.

123. θειλόπεδον: Bekker's ϑ' εἰλόπεδον is a ghost-word, known only to the scholiasts and glossographers, who were attracted by the etymology (< εἴλη, with the suffix of οἰνόπεδον etc.). Like the MSS, Homeric imitators in later times have only θειλόπεδον. (Bechtel, *Lexilogus*, 110, Leumann, *Wörter*, 44, Frisk, *GEW*, and Chantraine, *Dictionnaire*, however, all accept εἰλόπεδον.)

124. τέρσεται: as if θειλόπεδον denoted the crop as well the place where it was dried off; hence ἑτέρας (sc. σταφυλάς). The Phaeacians are not making currants or sultanas, but wine, cf. Hes. *Op.* 611 ff.τότε πάντας ἀποδρέπεν οἴκαδε βότρυς, | δεῖξαι δ' ἠελίῳ δέκα τ' ἤματα καὶ δέκα νύκτας, | πέντε δὲ συσκιάσαι, ἕκτῳ δ' εἰς ἄγγε' ἀφύσσαι | δῶρα Διωνύσου πολυγηθέος. **τρυγόωσιν:** see the fuller descriptions of this festive season at *Il.* xviii 561–72 and [Hes.] *Sc.* 292–301.

127. πρασιαί (< πράσον 'leek'): one of the very few references in the epic to green vegetables. (For discussion, see W. Richter, *Archaeologia* H, 123–7.) **νείατον**, 'at the bottom', 'last', is derived from νειός, 'deep ground', (see Chantraine's n., *Dictionnaire* s.v. νειός), not the adj. νέος (with which, however, it is undoubtedly sometimes associated).

133–52. Odysseus' appeal to Arete. The narration is rapid with many typical elements (e.g. 133–4, cf. v 75–6) and almost without decoration. The scene in the μέγαρον, of course, has already been described—twice in fact (vi 303–9, and 49–53 above). As for the appeal itself, Odysseus has already been given one κερδάλεος μῦθος (vi 149–85, to Nausicaa) and is about to be given a second (241–97 below, to Arete herself), and a third is hardly requisite. For supplication as a typical scene, see vi 110–250 n. Arete's response is delayed till 233 below, a postponement that has led to much Higher Criticism (see Fenik, *Studies*, 1–18, and more briefly introduction to vii, and 153–225 n.). Touchefeu-Meynier, *Thèmes*, nos. 369–70, lists the vase-paintings that seem to depict this supplication: none correspond closely to the Homeric narrative.

135. ἐβήσετο: a thematic *s*-aorist, see vi 321 n.

137. ἐΰσκόπῳ ἀργειφόντῃ: i.e. Hermes, see v 43 n. The words are used indifferently as epithets, with Ἑρμείας vel sim. elsewhere, or as epithet and noun, in order to circumvent the metrical problems of a divine name scanned – – –. On the supposed sense of ἀργείφόντης (Slayer of Argus) see i 38 and v 43 nn.

138. Hermes is honoured because he is the giver of sleep, cf. v 47, *Il.* xxiv 445. The line has a neat effect—Odysseus has come at the last moment!

143. θέσφατος: only here in Homer as an attributive epithet, but there is no reason to emend, cf. ἀχλὺν θεσπεσίην (41–2).

144. ἄνεῳ: -ῳ implies a nom. pl. of the 'Attic' declension. According to Apollonius Dyscolus (*Adv.* 554), Aristarchus (no doubt with a glance at the construction with a singular verb at xxiii 93) wrote the word as an adverb without iota. The etymology is unknown.

145. θαύμαζον: note that the motive of the Phaeacians' silence is defined as wonderment, not as hostility, cf. 16–17. Surprise is a standard reaction to the arrival of a visitor: cf. *Il.* ix 193, xxiv 480.

146. This verse must be recast by those who delete Arete's genealogy (56–74), e.g. Ἀρήτη, ἄλοχος μεγαλήτορος Ἀλκινόοιο (Kirchhoff).

150. γέρας: spelled out at *Il.* xii 310–13 τετιμήμεσθα μάλιστα | ἔδρῃ τε κρέασίν τε ἰδὲ πλείοις δεπάεσσιν | ἐν Λυκίῃ, πάντες δὲ θεοὺς ὣς εἰσορόωσι, | καὶ τέμενος νεμόμεσθα μέγα (Sarpedon to Glaucus).

153–225. Alcinous is prompted to welcome the stranger. Technically, as Besslich (*Schweigen*) and Fenik (*Studies*, 61–104) have argued, this passage is an 'interruption' by which the action is retarded, with suitable artistic effect. The delay is not extraneous to the action. In Homer the reception of a guest is represented as a matter controlled by the strictest etiquette, which provided those whose experience or presence of mind was deficient with ample opportunity for gaucherie: cf. the reception of Telemachus and Pisistratus by Eteoneus in the palace of Menelaus (iv 20–32). For the didactic and social significance of episodes such as this, see E. A. Havelock, *Preface to Plato* (Oxford, 1963), 61–86: it is the function of art to reaffirm the norms of society.

153. ἕζετ' ἐπ' ἐσχάρῃ: sitting on the ground is an expression of misery and despair, as at iv 716 ff., xxi 55. ἐσχάρη denotes any place for fire, whether for comfort (*Il.* x 418), or for ritual (xiv 420) or household use, and is not explicitly represented as a place of sanctity or asylum. A certain numinous quality, however, is implied in the formulaic lines ἴστω νῦν Ζεὺς πρῶτα θεῶν, ξενίη τε τράπεζα, | ἱστίη τε ... xiv 158–9 = xvii 155–6 = xx 230–1, cf. xix 303–4, where the more emotive word ἱστίη (= Attic ἑστία) is used.

154. ἀκήν: in Homer only in formulae and in this form. The sense is probably 'without movement' rather than 'without sound'. It is usually, and most probably, taken as an adverbial acc. of an *ἀκή (Pi. *P.* iv 156 has the dat. ἀκᾷ): see Chantraine, *Dictionnaire* s.v. and *LfgrE*.

155. Ἐχένηος is the 'Nestor' of the Phaeacians, privileged by his years to pontificate in moments of general perplexity: cf. ii 15 (Aegyptius), ii 157 (Halitherses). He reappears, in the same role, at xi 342.

156. Take Φαιήκων ἀνδρῶν as a partitive gen. with ὃς δὴ. **προγενέστερος** is without active comparative force.

161. ἰσχανόωνται: a common epic type of formation, providing useful metrical doublets in the fourth foot or, as here, at the verse-end, cf. καθίζανον (v 3).

163. εἷσον: aor. impf. of ἕζομαι/ἵζω (< *sed-, *sd-). The orthography (which is attested in similar forms also in Herodotus) is influenced by the indic. εἷσα. We should expect *ἔσσον (< *sed-s-) or (since ἐσσ- is the spelling for parts of ἕννυμι) *ἵσσον, cf. καθίσσας (*Il.* ix 488).

166. δόρπον: regularly of the evening meal in Homer.

COMMENTARY

167. ἱερὸν μένος Ἀλκινόοιο: a common type of periphrasis: *metri gratia* (ϝ)ίς alternates with μένος and κρατερόν with ἱερόν, or the epithet may be omitted. **ἱερόν:** the epic use of this word is very diverse, and has encouraged some to posit a conflation of different roots (e.g. Schulze, *Quaestiones*, 207: (1) (ϝ)ιερός, 'active', cf. (ϝ)ίεμαι; (2) ἱερός, cf. Skt. *iṣirá-*, 'strong'; and (3) ἱερός, cf. Italic *aisusis*, *aisis*, *erus*, 'sacred'). Recent authorities have preferred a single source, having the basic sense 'imbued with divine vigour'. See Frisk, *GEW*, and Chantraine, *Dictionnaire* s.v., and the literature there cited.

169. ἐσχαρόφιν: gen. sg., created *metri gratia*. -όφι, as to case (gen.), number (sg.), and form (extended from -φι and attached to an *a*-stem noun) belongs to the latest stage of the evolution of -φι within the *Kunstsprache*: cf. κοτυληδονόφι (v 433), and see Shipp, *Studies*[1] (Cambridge, 1953), 12–14.

170. ἀγαπήνορα has an active sense, 'welcoming heroes', see *LfgrE* s.v. It seems well chosen here, but alternates with μεγαλήτωρ in acc. and gen. sg. as a generic epithet of heroes.

171. μάλιστα δέ μιν φιλέεσκε: sc. Ἀλκίνοος as subject: a paratactic clause with causal nuance.

172–83. A routine and heavily formulaic passage (172–6 = i 136–40 = iv 52–6 = x 368–72 = xvii 91–5; 177 cf. v 94; 178–83 = xiii 49–54, with modification of the last verses). Nonetheless, two distinct scenes, the meal and the offering of libations, are brought together. The transitional line, 184, is repeated at 228, and thus marks the speech of Alcinous and Odysseus' reply, 186–225, as a digression within the libation scene. (The prayer of Achilles, *Il.* xvi 220–56, is inserted into the arming sequence in an analogous way.) The whole expanded 'libation' is inserted into the 'meal', whose final transitional element ('when he had finished eating ...') does not appear until 232. See also 215–21 n.

172–5. φέρουσα ... φέρουσα: for the repetition (which is here built into a fixed 'run' of verses) see 116 n.

183. ἐπαρξάμενος δεπάεσσιν, 'begin the ritual by pouring wine in the cups': a regular formula (7 times).

185. τοῖσιν δ(έ): the 'apodotic' δέ after ἐπεί (184) seems cumbrous, and in other occurrences of this common formula the δέ is connective. Nitsch therefore excised 184, but it is improbable that the full narrative style of the epic would have said that the ritual was begun, and have omitted to say that it was completed. Hoekstra (*Modifications*, 137) sees in the formula of which this line is an example one the late creations of the *Kunstsprache*, designed to accommodate names scanned –◡◡–.

186–206. Though Alcinous' remarks elicit a reply from Odysseus, they are explicitly directed to the Phaeacians. Etiquette forbade the interrogation of a stranger before he had finished eating, cf. iii 69–70.

188. In view of κείοντες etc. κατακείετε appears to be an imperative. It might syntactically be subjunctive (cf. σαώσετε, 'you are to save', *Il.* xiii 47, a rare idiom), and was so taken by the poet who conjugated it into the 1st person at xviii 419, ὄφρα ... κατακείομεν οἴκαδ' ἰόντες. The obvious

332

connection with κεῖμαι is hard to define, perhaps a short vowel subjunctive reinterpreted as a desiderative: discussion in Chantraine, *Grammaire*, i 453.

192. Observe the weak caesura in the fourth foot. Such a division of cola in Homer appears on average no more than once in a thousand lines.

195. μεσσηγύς: i.e. 'on his way', the word is used of space not time in Homer.

196–8. The Homeric concept of Fate has engendered much scholarship: useful are S. Eitrem, *RE* xv 2, 2449–60 s.v. Moira; W. Krause, 'Die Ausdrucke für das Schicksal bei Homer', *Glotta* xxv (1936), 143–52; U. Bianchi, Διὸς Αἶσα (Rome, 1953); B. C. Dietrich, *Death, Fate, and the Gods* (London, 1965).

The present passage is closely paralleled by *Il.* xx 127–8 (subject αἶσα) and *Il.* xxiv 209–11 (subject μοῖρα). αἶσα, unlike μοῖρα, is not elsewhere used in this half-personified sense, but is otherwise synonymous with μοῖρα (most clearly at v 113–14), for which it provides a useful metrical alternant. αἶσα is unknown in cult, and outside the epic is attested only in the conservative dialects (Arcadian, Cypriot, Argolic, Cretan): see Ruijgh, *Élément*, 118–19. The basic sense, like that of μοῖρα, is 'part', 'share', cf. Italic *aet-eis* (gen. sg.), 'partis'.

The function of μοῖρα in the epic is to mark at a man's birth the circumstances, and especially the moment, of his death. It is not thought to determine all the events of life, or their time and sequence, though in the *Odyssey* specific happenings are sometimes mentioned: cf. iii 269, v 206, ix 532, xiii 306. A μοῖρα may also be conditional: cf. *Il.* xviii 95–6 αὐτίκα γάρ τοι ἔπειτα μεθ' Ἕκτορα πότμος ἑτοῖμος, and *Od.* v 206–10 (Odysseus would stay with Calypso if he knew what he was fated to suffer). The Homeric age has no concept of natural law and its immutable chains of causation, and sees no contradiction in action ὑπὲρ αἶσαν, such action not being impossible so much as unthinkable. The best analogue to μοῖρα is therefore to be found in the Homeric sense of fitness and propriety, especially in the social order. In general, μοῖρα is mentioned as an explanation, more remote and general than the gods, for untimely or unwelcome events, but the decisions a man takes in response to those events remain his own: see A. W. H. Adkins, *Merit and Responsibility* (Oxford, 1960), 17–29. The effect of the belief in μοῖρα on heroic action is slight, except to encourage a certain bravado, e.g. *Il.* vi 487, xvi 860, unless a hero is privileged to know his μοῖρα, as Achilles knows that time is not on his side.

196. τόν is unnecessary, and in the wrong case, since the subjects of ἐπιβήμεναι and πάθῃσι are the same: but cf. i 210 πρίν γε τὸν ἐς Τροίην ἀναβήμεναι, where acc. τόν is correct.

197. Κλῶθες: a personification of κλώθειν, 'spin'. Κλωθώ, along with Ἄτροπος and Λάχεσις, first appears at Hes. *Th.* 218 and 905. Plural μοῖραι, common in cult and later literature, occur elsewhere in Homer, and questionably at that, only at *Il.* xxiv 49.

198. γεινομένῳ: for γεν-, aor. ptcp.; lengthened perhaps on the analogy of οὐλόμενος (so Wyatt, *Lengthening*, 119–20).   **νήσαντο**: On this metaphor see B. C. Dietrich, 'The Spinning of Fate in Homer', *Phoenix* xvi (1962), 86–101. The image is an old one and has a folkloric colour; cf. the 'Norns' of Old Norse, the 'Metten' of Anglo-Saxon, and the 'Gaschepfen' of Middle High German, who bestow skills *vel sim.* by their spinning at the moment of birth. But the Germanic analogues are not true figures of destiny, and the use of spinning as an image of the decrees of fate seems to be a product of the poetic tradition. The gods also issue their decrees by spinning: *Il.* xxiv 525, *Od.* i 17, iii 208, viii 579, xi 139, xx 196 (all ϑεοί), iv 208 (Zeus), xvi 64 (a δαίμων), though like μοῖρα they can work their will without recourse to the symbolic act. Since male gods are said to spin fate, the literal force of the image cannot be strongly felt, for spinning is a strictly feminine occupation in Homer.

199. Cf. Diomedes' dilemma at *Il.* vi 128. Alcinous is wary of the unpredictable behaviour of the Olympians and seeks reassurance before offence (or further offence, if the stranger has felt neglected) is given. Diomedes received a genealogy in reply to his query, but Odysseus (208–12) answers only the direct question 'Is he a god?' implied in Alcinous' remarks. That is proper; in the reception of a guest detailed explanations do not precede his entertainment.

200. ἄλλο: i.e. something other than they have done before; cf. v 179.

201. ϑεοὶ ... ἐναργεῖς: a utopian feature: cf. Catullus lxiv 384, Verg. *E.* iv 15. The Aethiopians, another people ἔσχατοι ἀνδρῶν (i 23) enjoyed the same privilege (*Il.* i 423).

205. ἐγγύϑεν, like ἀγχίϑεοι at v 35, expresses the special relationship of the Phaeacians with the gods, rather than geographical proximity (they are ἔσχατοι), or kinship (a distinction of the royal house).

207. Alcinous' remarks, though addressed to the Phaeacian princes, were an oblique question. Odysseus therefore is made to reply, and gently deprecates the king's impatience by self-mockery.

213. καὶ πλεῖον': καὶ μᾶλλον is the regular formula; cf. ii 334, iv 819, etc.

215–21. This amusing passage gave offence to schol., to Athenaeus (x 412 b), and to some of the moderns, either as bad manners (cf. ἐχρῆν γάρ, εἰ καὶ ἐλίμωττεν, διακαρτερεῖν ... ταῦτα γὰρ οὐδ' ἐκεῖνος ὁ Σαρδανάπαλλος εἰπεῖν ποτε ἂν ἐτόλμησεν, Athen. loc. cit.), or for incompatibility with epic dignity (cf. 'La fameuse tirade de Rabelais *Tout pour la tripe!* interpolée dans une tragedie de Racine ... ne détonnerait pas plus de cette tirade du ventre.' Bérard, *L'Odyssée* (Paris, 1947), n. ad loc.). Schol. T defends the lines as an attempt to disarm suspicion, as if Odysseus were representing himself as a πτωχός (cf. xvii 228, xviii 53, etc.), but this would clash with the evident intent of 224–5. The critic must not impose the taste of his own age on that of Homer. The imperative of hunger is mentioned in heroic contexts at iv 369 = xii 332, vi 133, and xv 344. Odysseus has in fact already eaten (cf. vi 249), though his words here seem to imply that nothing has passed his lips since his shipwreck.

216. κύντερον: a persistent image of shamelessness, cf. M. Faust, 'Die

künstliche Verwendung von κύων "Hund" in den homerischen Epos',
Glotta xlviii (1970), 8–31.

221. Aristarchus's ἐνιπλησθῆναι, 'to satisfy myself', softens the crude effect of
ἐνιπλήσασθαι, 'to stuff it'.

224. καί περ: always καί ... περ elsewhere in Homer.

225. κτῆσιν ἐμὴν δμῶάς τε: cf. schol. ἄμεινον ἂν ἔσχε, πατρίδ' ἐμὴν ἄλοχόν τε
(= *Il.* v 213), so as to avoid the unromantic emphasis upon property (for
which, however, cf. v 38 and the constant complaint that on top of their
other crimes Paris stole κτήματα and the suitors devoured the household of
Odysseus). But having mentioned πάτρη at 223, the poet uses a formulaic
line (= xix 526 [with δμῳάς fem.] = *Il.* xix 333). δμῶας and δῶμα are an
explication of κτῆσιν, not additions to it.

226–97. At the proper moment, when the meal is over, Arete asks Odysseus
to tell his story. He begins with his shipwreck on Calypso's isle (with which
he will break off his extended narrative, xii *ad fin.*) and concludes with his
meeting with Nausicaa. The style is succinct, and as is usually the case in
such recapitulatory passages there is much verbatim repetition of the
narrative.

229. κακκείοντες: see 188 n.

230–9. The brief and formulaic language of Arete's questions makes it
difficult to judge their tone. Fenik, who sees Arete as an 'unfriendly
Phaeacian', defines it as 'sharp' (*Studies*, 127), and finds an artistic effect in
the renewed perils of the hero. But Odysseus' reply is a straightforward
account such as would satisfy natural curiosity and excite pity. He does not
appear to be defending himself against an implied charge that, at the very
least, he had pillaged Nausicaa's laundry basket before (incongruously)
presenting himself to her parents. The questions, moreover, come at the
correct moment thematically (cf. xix 53–64 with 96–105) for this curiosity.

237. = xix 104, and cf. xix 509. 238ᵇ, the question about the clothes,
replaces the standard hemistich πόθι τοι πόλις ἠδὲ τοκῆες (i 170 etc., 6
times).

239. φῇς represents the present tense, φῆς the imperfect. Odysseus has not
said anything about his shipwreck, but neither has he deliberately
concealed it. The poet often proceeds as if immaterial details were as well
known to the characters as they are to the audience, or as if he supposed
the details had in fact been mentioned. (For instances of such unconscious
omissions in an actual oral tradition see A. B. Lord, *Serbo-Croatian Heroic
Songs* (Cambridge, Mass.–Belgrade, 1954), 342 n. 21, 343 n. 31, 351–2,
389 n. 14, 429 n. 14).

240. πολύμητις would be well chosen here, if the poet were exercising
choice; but the whole line is one of the most frequent formulae in Homer
(50 times).

241 ff. In the usual Homeric way Odysseus takes up Arete's questions in
reverse order: first how he had come ἐπὶ πόντον ἀλώμενος; second how he
had acquired his clothing. The convention helps to gloss over the fact that
Odysseus does not go on to answer her first question and reveal his

identity. The poet does not assign any motive to this reticence, but could, if pressed, have made the point he has Odysseus make at xix 115–18 τῷ ἐμὲ νῦν τὰ μὲν ἄλλα μετάλλα σῷ ἐνὶ οἴκῳ, | μηδ' ἐμὸν ἐξερέεινε γένος καὶ πατρίδα γαῖαν, | μή μοι μᾶλλον θυμὸν ἐνιπλήσῃς ὀδυνάων | μνησαμένῳ.

In Odysseus' narrative note that 242 = ix 15, 243 = xv 390, 249–51 = v 131–3 (Calypso to Hermes), 253–6 = xii 447–50, 256–7 = v 135–6 (Calypso to Hermes), 266 = v 268, 267–8 = v 278–9, 277 = iii 300 = xv 482, 281–2 = v 442–3 (with minor variations). Cf. the construction of Telemachus' report to Penelope at xvii 109 ff. (xvii 124–41 = iv 333–50, 142–6 = iv 556–60, 148–9 = iv 585–6 (Menelaus on his return).

242. οὐρανίωνες: strictly a patronymic 'children of Οὐρανός' (as at Il. v 898), but commonly used as equivalent of Ὀλύμπιοι.

244. Ὠγυγίη: see vi 172 n.

245 ff. The echo, 245–6 ~ 254–5, has prompted various excisions. 251–8 were athetized merely on the grounds of their repetition in xii. The thought and content of the passage, however, are unexceptionable.

245. Ἄτλαντος θυγάτηρ: as also at i 52. At Hes. Th. 359 and h.Cer. 422, she is an Oceanid (if that is the same Calypso).   **δολόεσσα:** Calypso has this ungenerous description only here, perhaps by contamination with expressions for her father (Ἄτλαντος ... ὀλοόφρονος i 52) or for Circe (Αἰαίη δολόεσσα x 32): cf. Κλυταιμνήστρη δολόμητις only at xi 422 after Αἴγισθος δολόμητις (5 times). Calypso has been uncooperative, in detaining Odysseus against his will, but is not guilty of malice or duplicity.

248. ἐφέστιον: the Attic form is universally read in Homer (for Ionic ἐπίστιος, Hdt. i 44 etc.).

249 ff. For ἀργῆτι (249), ἔλσας (250), ἐφίλει (256), and ἀγήρων (257), see v 128–36 n.

253. ἐννῆμαρ ... δεκάτη δέ: a common formular number, cf. ix 82, x 28, xii 447, xiv 314, and six occurrences in the Iliad, cf. ὀκτωκαιδεκάτη (268 below).

256. ἐνδυκέως: 'in a kindly manner' (ἐπιμελῶς schol.). This sense is suggested by the regular use with τρέφειν, φιλεῖν, κομίζειν, etc. A sense 'continuously' arose later (e.g. Bacchylides v 111), perhaps by misunderstanding of such passages as xv 490–1 or xxiv 211–12, cf. Leumann, Wörter, 311. The word is isolated, unless from the same root as ἀδευκής (vi 273).

259. ἑπτάετες: another formular number, cf. iii 304, xiv 285.

261–97 give an excellent outline of the entire action of v–vi: the only omission from the action as Odysseus knew it is the epiphany of Leucothea (v 333–53). The passage may be usefully regarded, not as a conscious shortening of v–vi, but as a list in sequence of the irreducible elements of the narrative which it was the business of the epic poet to fill out with description and discourse.

261. ὄγδοον: the harsh metre prompted Bentley's ὀγδόατον, an artificial form used elsewhere in the dat. and acc. fem. where the primary forms are intractable. Von der Mühll (in app. crit. ad loc.) suggests that a different numeral stood here in the Ur-Odyssee.   **ἐπιπλόμενον:** ἐπιπέλομαι, 'approach', is attested, e.g. xv 408, beside ἐπιτέλλομαι, but the aor. ptcp. (cf. Hes. *Th.* 493, *Sc.* 87) is used with ἔτος and ἐνιαυτός as an alternative to περιπλόμενος.

263. Calypso said nothing (v 160 ff.) of Hermes' visit, nor did Odysseus at that time ask the reason for her decision to release him.

271. Poseidon did in fact raise the storm (v 282 ff.), though Odysseus at the time attributed his danger to Zeus (v 304): see 286 n.

272. The pl. forms, κελεύθους (-α), read by some MSS, seem to be derived from the related formula ἀνέμων κατέδησε κελεύθους (-α). Both the acc. sg., 'prevented my journey', and the gen. (cf. iv 380 = 469), 'prevented me from journeying', give good sense.

273. ἀθέσφατον, 'that which god has not ordained', so 'extraordinary', 'huge': see *LfgrE*. Like many epithets of metrical shape ⏑–⏑⏑, it has no strong formular links with a single noun, but keeps a fixed position after the caesura (except *Il.* iii 4).

276. διέτμαγον: a ἅπαξ λεγόμενον (for -τμηξ-), formed after the aor. 2 pass. -ετμάγην.

283. θυμηγερέων: an artificial word, made from the formula θυμὸς ἀγέρθη (v 458 etc.). Leumann, *Wörter*, 116–17, notes ἀφραδέων, δυσμενέων, ὀλιγηπελέων, ὀλιγοδρανέων, ὑπερμενέων, ὑπερηφανέων, ὑπερηνορέων, and εὖ-, ἀλλο-, ὁμο-, δολο-, ἀ-, and χαλι-φρονέων. These are replacements for adjectival formations and not true verbal compounds.   ἀμβροσίη νύξ: a formula (iv 429 = 574, but cf. ix 404, xi 330, xv 8, *Il.* ii 57, etc.), but the sense of the epithet is unclear, see iv 429 n. There is no necessity, of course, for the sense to be appropriate in a particular instance. 283–4 modify the half-line expression ἐπὶ δ' ἤλυθεν ἀμβροσίη νύξ (iv 429 = 574).

284. διιπετέος: only in this formula in Homer. The sense, where contextually related, suggests that the first element was associated with Zeus (cf. διοπετής, Euripides, *IT* 977) and the second, if felt at all, with πίπτω: whence 'Iovis iussu et opera decurrens' (Schulze, *Quaestiones*, 238); even so, the dat. δι- (< δι(ϝ)ει-), is unexpected, and *h.Ven.* 4 οἰωνούς τε διιπετέας (the earliest non-formulaic example) seems to link the word with πέτομαι. M. Treu, 'Homerische Flusse fallen nicht vom Himmel', *Glotta* xxxvii (1958), 260–75, suggests an original διαι- (= δια-) as the first element: J. T. Hooker, *IF* lxxiv (1979), 115–17, reviews the theories, but shrinks from any firm conclusion.

288–9. δείλετο: δύσετο codd.: The language, if exact, should allude to the tripartite division of the Homeric day, cf. *Il.* xxi 111 ἢ ἠὼς ἢ δείλη ἢ μέσον ἦμαρ, and thus correspond to the narrative in vi, where at 96 ff. Nausicaa and her maids took their δεῖπνον (at midday) and then played ball; in the course of the game Odysseus was awakened. But δύσετο (an aor. tense, see vi 321 n.) refers to a moment of time, and is used, loc. cit., in the *same formula* as here to indicate a moment (sunset) substantially later than Odysseus' awakening. Aristarchus accordingly read δείλετο: for the formation cf. θέρμετο (viii 437 etc.); the impf. tense and the meaning (cf. δείλη, 'afternoon') are apposite. Unfortunately Aristarchus' authority is un-

337

known. If δείλετο is a conjecture inspired by over-exactitude (cf. van der Valk, *Textual Criticism*, 109), it must yield to the fact that the poet's evident desire in this passage is to exaggerate the length of Odysseus' exhausted sleep, even at the cost of inconsistency.

288. ἐπ' ἠῶ: an awkward rhythm and caesura. The last syllable of the old *s*-stems ἠώς and αἰδώς can always be resolved to *-όα (or *-ο') in Homer with some gain in elegance of metre. That is no reason to attribute the uncontracted form to the poet, for old habits in the placing of words died hard. The earliest irresoluble occurrences are *h.Merc.* 326 (ἠῶ) and Hes. *Op.* 324 and fr. 204. 82 (αἰδῶ).

291. ἐϊκυῖα θεῇσι: an echo of the simile οἵη δ' Ἄρτεμις εἶσι ... (vi 102–9). The distinctive feminine θεῇσι is normal in this formula (*Il.* twice, Hes. fr. 185. 23).

294. ἐρξέμεν (< ἔρδω) might be fut. or aor. infin. (with thematic vowel, like ἀξέμεν, see Chantraine, *Grammaire*, i 417). Schol. paraphrase with πρᾶξαι. Both constructions are Homeric.

295. αἴθοπα (< αἴθω 'blaze'): the sense 'bright', 'sparkling' seems obvious enough (it must be consonant with the common use for a quality of metal), but the Lexica (see *LfgrE* s.v.) suggest μέλας (as if 'burnt black in appearance', cf. the common etymology of Αἰθίοψ) ἢ θερμαντικός.

297. ἀχνύμενός περ: because to retell his woes is to relive their pain, cf. iv 183 ff., viii 83 ff., 521 ff., xix 115 ff.

298–347. Odysseus, having concluded his account with the gift of clothes, enables Alcinous to detect a discourtesy on Nausicaa's part. Odysseus adroitly excuses her, whereupon Alcinous offers her in marriage and (if that is unacceptable) renews his promise of a passage home. All then retire for the night.

Alcinous' generosity, though not out of character, has seemed excessive even to those willing to suspend their disbelief for the storyteller's benefit. It is a naïve variant of the more plausible designs of Circe and Calypso, who detain the hero λιλαιομένη πόσιν εἶναι (ix 30, 32): ultimately a motif of folk-tale, cf. D. L. Page, *Folktales in Homer's* Odyssey (Cambridge, Mass., 1973), 59–63.

301. ἡμέτερον: the gen. has MS-support in similar constructions at ii 55 and xvii 534, hence Aristarchus' reading here. Schol. call it an Ἀττικὸν σχῆμα. **πρώτην:** to accept a suppliant is to assume a lasting and full responsibility. Nausicaa ought not, Alcinous implies, to have passed the stranger on to others, cf. Arete's claim at xi 338 ξεῖνος δ' αὖτ' ἐμός ἐστιν.

303. ἀμύμονα: not a regular epithet of κούρη, and not usually taken here to be a decorative epithet, as if the sense were 'Do not reproach your daughter, for she is blameless'. But this kind of word-play is not in the Homeric manner. Odysseus is rather slipping in a decorative compliment: see further Parry, *Blameless Aegisthus*, 120–2.

304–6. Odysseus' statement, of course, contradicts the narrative at vi 251 ff. Kirchhoff, for whom the whole episode is secondary, takes this as evidence of careless redaction (*Odyssee*, 210), because there is no indication in the text that Odysseus is uttering a tactful falsehood. But indications of tone are very often lacking, cf. 230 ff. above and v 97 ff.

305. αἰσχυνόμενος: the middle (= αἰδέομαι) is rare in Homer (only here and xviii 12, xxi 323), but has become regular in classical prose.

311–16. There is no ancient athetesis, but τοὺς ἐξ Ἀρίσταρχος διστάζει Ὁμήρου εἶναι. εἰ δὲ καὶ Ὁμηρικοί, εἰκότως αὐτοὺς περιαιρεθῆναί φησι. πῶς γὰρ ἀγνοῶν τὸν ἄνδρα μνηστεύεται αὐτῷ τὴν θυγατέρα καὶ οὐ προτρεπόμενος, ἀλλὰ λιπαρῶν; schol. The defence was either that Alcinous was testing Odysseus (if he accepted, how could he claim to have refused Calypso?—but Alcinous is no πολύμητις), or that his conduct was scarcely more irresponsible than that of the fathers-in-law of Bellerophon, Tydeus, and Polyneices.

311–14. The construction is a blend of the wish (αἲ γάρ + optative) and the prayer (apostrophe of the god + infinitive): xxiv 376–81 is an exact parallel.

312. οἷος: ∪∪, as at xx 89 and *Il.* xviii 105.

318. αὔριον ἔς: since Alcinous is resolved to entertain in style (see 189 ff.), and since an overnight journey seems to be taken for granted, this is the only reasonable thing for Alcinous to say at this point. He was not to know that the stranger's story would take up half the following night and reveal an identity of such eminence that additional gifts and entertainment were called for (xiii 1 ff.), taking up a further day. The matter is thoroughly examined by W. Mattes, *Odysseus*. See introduction to vii.

321. ἑκαστέρω: comparative of ἑκάς 'far off'.   **Εὐβοίης:** it is conceivable the poet speaks momentarily from the standpoint of an Ionian Greek of unadventurous habits, or alludes to some proverbial comparison antedating the colonial era, otherwise it is hard to see why Euboea should be chosen as the type of distance. An ironical intent, to illustrate the blissful ignorance of the remote and happy Phaeacians, is unlikely, since they are assumed to know the saga of Troy and its background.

323. Rhadamanthys is an enigmatic figure: see iv 563–4 n. His name is clearly unhellenic (note the -νθ- element). Local Cretan mythology adduced a genealogy Cres–Talos–Hephaestus–Rhadamanthys, cited by Pausanias viii 53. 5, but this was too parochial for the epic tradition which makes R. a son of Zeus and Europa and brother of Minos (*Il.* xiv 321–2). He is one of the archetypal just men (Thgn. 701, Pi. *O.* ii 75, *P.* ii 74), now resident in Elysium (iv 564). He had, however, Boeotian connections, being married to Alcmene either in this life or the next. His tomb was shown at Haliartus (Plu. *De gen. Soc.* 577).   **ξανθός** appears to be the regular generic epithet at this point before names beginning with a consonant (κρείων for names with vocalic initial), but gives a pleasant jingle with Ῥαδάμανθυν.

324. Tityus was tormented in Hades as punishment for a criminal assault upon Leto (xi 576–81). He was a descendant, some said, of Minyas (or Orchomenus), and committed his crime in Phocis, so that Rhadamanthys is thought of as visiting Boeotia and being landed perhaps at Aulis opposite the Euboean town of Chalcis. The story appears to be an invention, for it is otherwise quite unknown to mythology. Schol. assume that Rhadamanthys is being conveyed from Elysium.   **Γαιήϊον:** 'son of Earth', either literally or, as some versions had it, because Zeus concealed his mother there to escape the indignation of Hera. -ιος is a patronymic formation, attested in the Mycenaean and Aeolic dialects, but archaic in the Ionian epic: no such form was created, for example, for Telemachus or for the suitors.

327–8. The naïve boast is in character, cf. viii 102, 252.

330. Note the threefold repetition of the idea of 'speaking': a good example of the 'tired style' (cf. Kirk, *Songs*, 167).   **ὀνόμαζε** (for the weak sense, see v 181 n.) is usually preceded by an indication of the person addressed. The MS variants, πρὸς ὃν μεγαλήτορα θυμόν and ἰδὼν εἰς οὐρανὸν εὐρύν, are no improvement, since Odysseus goes on to pray and not to speak to his θυμός, and is sitting in a smoky μέγαρον.

334–7. A conventional scene to complete the day's events. Note 334 = iv 620 etc.; 336–9 = iv 297–300; 340 = xxiii 291; 344 = vi 1; 345 = iii 399; 346–7 cf. iii 402–3. Cf. also *Il.* ix 658–7 and xxiv 643–8.

336. αἰθούσῃ: a porch or open-sided room in front of the μέγαρον, a permanent feature of Greek architecture (cf. Lorimer, *Monuments*, 414–17): despite the exposure it was the usual place for the accommodation of guests (cf. iii 399, iv 297, *Il.* xxiv 644).

337. τάπητας: seat or bed coverings (of wool, iv 124): never 'floor coverings' in Homer.

342. ὄρσο: i.e. ὀρ-σο, imperative of the athematic aor. ὦρτο.   **κέων:** the shortened root vowel (for κει-) occurs only here: see 188 n. and Wyatt, *Lengthening*, 132.

345. τρητοῖς: 'pierced', that is, in order to take the cords that served as mattress; see the illustrations in S. Laser, *Archaeologia* P, 15–34.

347. λέχος πόρσυνε: render 'shared his bed': strictly (especially in conjunction with εὐνήν) a euphemism for intercourse, cf. *Il.* iii 411; but here no more than a conventional phrase. -νν- is the form used by classical poets, AR has both -αιν- and -νν- (7 times each in Frankel's ed.), Aristarchus, it is noted at several places, preferred -αιν-.

BOOK VIII: INTRODUCTION

The critics of antiquity—always alert for useful moral exempla—sometimes praised the φιλανθρωπία of the Phaeacians. They might have gone further and commended the simple heroism with which Alcinous fulfils his promise to see Odysseus home in the face of the certainty of Poseidon's wrath. The conventional view, however, saw none of these things but only the elements of hedonism that seem to be inherent in a naïve notion of an ideal human existence: αἰεὶ δ' ἡμῖν δαίς τε φίλη κίθαρίς τε χοροί τε | εἵματά τ' ἐξημοιβὰ λοετρά τε θερμὰ καὶ εὐναί (248–9). The regular comments are:

τρυφεροί (τρυφή, τρυφᾶν) Heraclid. Pont. ap. schol. *Od*. xiii 119; schol. vi 53, 244, viii 248, 265; Athen. i 9 a, 14 c, v 192 d; Suda s.v. Ὅμηρος.

ἀβροδίαιτοι schol. vi 65, 244.

ἡδυπάθεια Theopompus, *FGrH* 115 F 114.

φιληδονία and ἀπολαυστικὸς βίος Heraclid. Pont. loc. cit.

ἑστίαι Suda loc. cit., cf. Sidon. Apol. xii 19.

Pingues Hor. *Epp*. i 15. 24, cf. i 2. 28, Auson. *Epp*. ix 15.

Worthy to be compared with Sardanapallus, Athen. viii 336.

A type to illustrate the lives of notorious voluptuaries, as Strato of Sidon, Theopompus loc. cit., or an unnamed Spaniard, Polyb. xxxiv 9. 15.

Modern commentators are accustomed to add a further gloss, e.g. 'Their life has no promise, no potentialities, no dynamism; to remain with them would drain Odysseus of his heroism by depriving him of any chance or need of action. It would be a living death.' (H. W. Clarke, *The Art of the* Odyssey (Englewood Cliffs, 1967), 54).

Such a viewpoint helped the scholiasts to explain the Phaeacians' uncivil desertion of Odysseus on the beach at Ithaca (xiii 116 ff.), or their enthusiastic reception of the Song of Ares and Aphrodite (viii 367 ff.)—which Odysseus also shared. But it cannot be accepted as an assessment of the poet's intention. Both the activities and the indulgences of the Phaeacians are paralleled elsewhere in the epics,

especially in the scenes of peace on the Shield of Achilles (*Il.* xviii
491 ff., 567 ff., 593 ff.), but also in the entertainments of Telema-
chus at Pylos and Sparta and in the less reprehensible relaxations of
Penelope's suitors (discus and javelin at iv 626 = xvii 168, ἀοιδή at i
325). The world of Scheria is thus a Homeric world from which war,
the curse as well as the glory of the heroic age, has been removed (vi
200). At the same time it is the sort of toilless world for which
Hesiod yearned (*Op.* 111 ff., 227 ff., *Ehoeae* fr. 1 Merkelbach–West
6 ff., cf. *Od.* vii 81–132 n.). There are some touches of additional
felicity, e.g. the presence of gods vii 201, and a striking difference,
the stress upon ships and seafaring, so often the symbols of man's
presumption.

The natural amenities of Scheria, peace, leisure, abundant crops,
are dreams special to no time and place: they were shared by Hebrew
prophets (Isaiah 2: 2–4, Micah 4: 1–5) and classical poets (A. *Suppl.*
625–709, *Eu.* 937–87) alike. In its social aspects Scheria was equally
blessed. Its site is perfect, at least for those who felt secure to seaward
but were nervous of the land. Its king is the ideal ruler, πρόφρων,
ἀγανός and ἤπιος (cf. ii 230 = v 8), he is θεῶν ἄπο μήδεα εἰδώς (vi 12),
concerned with αἴσιμα (vii 310), and generous to a fault. All men
hope for such rulers, but the poet has added such detail as might
suggest that he had something more specific in mind. The nature of
Homeric kingship, however, is nowhere precisely defined in the
poems, and has to be conjectured from two manifestly abnormal
situations, the position of Agamemnon as chief commander of a
confederate army in the field, and the position on Ithaca during the
absence of Odysseus. Kings always have a certain charisma, being
closer to the gods than other men, but their practical functions
include those of judge, lawgiver, war-leader, and priest. In Homer
leadership dominates, to the virtual exclusion of all else. Nilsson, who
saw in the citadels of Mycenae and Tiryns symbols of the sort of
leadership Homer described, argued that this aspect dated from the
Mycenaean age. It is doubtful if he would have done so, had the
documentary evidence for the character of Mycenaean society from
the archives of Pylos and Cnossos been available to him. It now
appears that the post-Mycenaean period was that which most
required its kings to be leaders. Alcinous enjoys the charisma of the
Homeric king—he is an ἄναξ of divine descent to whom men defer as
to a god (vii 10–11)—and his perquisites, including a fine τέμενος (vii
112 ff. cf. *Il.* xii 310 ff.); he is also leader (xi 346), insofar as there is a
leader among men who know not war. But he is attended, as is no
other Homeric king, by twelve βασιλῆες who are ἀρχοί (viii 390–1)

and who summon him to their council (vi 55). It is evident that these are not the *qa-si-re-we* of the Linear B tablets. The Mycenaean *qa-si-re-u* was a part, and only a part, of *provincial* administration: he did not live at court. Nor is βασιλεύς a precise word in Homer: it is used here as it is in i 394 for the ἄριστοι of the kingdom. Their status and precise number presumably reflect the evolution of government in the settled conditions of Ionia. If so, their presence is formally incompatible with the more archaic prerogatives of Alcinous. Attemps to see the 'constitution' of Scheria as a unity soon run into difficulties. Finsler, for example, was obliged to reduce Alcinous to president of a governing council, holding his τέμενος as an emolument of office, and took his epic epithets as his constitutional titles. As in other fields, however, so here the Homeric synthesis is only superficial. The poet uses what suits his story, or takes his fancy. His tradition supplies him with such detail as is inherent in the stories. Where he must amplify, he draws on the only other source available to him, his own experience. So the Phaeacian town is pictured as a foundation of the colonial age (see vi 262–9 n.), and certain aspects of its politics are drawn from the same source.

The content of viii is descriptive rather than narrative, and the story of the *Odyssey* makes little progress. The poet's problems in ordering his matter are consequently different from those of v–vii. He does not follow a sequence of themes whose course and direction ultimately rest on the nature of events, but seeks to give form to a paratactic assemblage of episodes. The poet disposes of a number of devices—adumbration, balance, repetition, contrast—but it is possible to overstate these. There is a constant problem of segmentation, since one critic will perceive a unit of composition where another will not. Where divisions are clear, often one episode dominates an indefinite list, as in the games of Patroclus (*Il.* xxiii) or the Nekyia (*Od.* xi). In *Od.* viii the assembly scene (1–61) is introductory to the entertainments. These are opened and closed by the two banquet scenes (62–103 and 469–586). As often in the *Odyssey* (cf. iv 97 ff., xiv 37 ff., xix 124 ff., 369 ff.) someone in the company raises, apparently spontaneously, a subject that interests the unknown hero. At once we wonder how he will respond. In the second banquet scene, whose scale (as usual when a motif is repeated) is more generous than that of the first, this effect is compounded by the natural but heedless action of the hero himself, who is made to set up the very situation that places him in peril (cf. xix 343 ff.). Between the two banquets there appear to be four principal episodes, as follows:

1. The games (104–30), narrated in very succinct fashion, as if no more than setting the scene for the next episode.
2. The quarrel (131–255), Euryalus offends Odysseus.
3. The Song of Ares and Aphrodite, bracketed by episodes of dance (256–65, 266–369, 370–85).
4. A complex scene of gift-giving, reconciliation, and further entertainment (386–468).

The artistic purpose of the book has been well defined by Mattes. It is to rehabilitate Odysseus, to infuse into him the heroic spirit: 'Just because he has eaten, bathed, and put on some borrowed clothes ... has he become once again the old brilliant Odysseus? No! Much has still to happen, precisely what is described in Book viii.' (*Odysseus*, 140.) The essential part of the book is thus the long quarrel scene. It is there, without any offence against verisimilitude, that Odysseus is converted from a ἱκέτης, a πτωχός without rank in society, into an ἄριστος, to be honoured with gifts and deference. Thus the scene is set for the narrative of the wanderings.

The book seems to be an integral whole, fulfilling a definite purpose and constructed in accordance with regular Homeric principles. It is easy, however, to excise inorganic episodes from a paratactically arranged string of scenes. Bérard and von der Mühll go further and cut out 93–531 (with 266–369 as an even later insertion) and 73–487 respectively. Suspicion has fallen heavily on two scenes: the first banquet, and the Song of Ares and Aphrodite. The objection to the first banquet is that it is a repetition, and a feeble copy, of the second. (Schwartz, *Odyssee*, 24, puts the argument in classic form.) It must now be recognized that this approach is misconceived: doublets are fundamental to the construction of epic narrative. The Song of Ares and Aphrodite offers a more intractable problem. The objections to it come down to matters of taste. Is it merely licentious and frivolous? If so, is this a comment on the Phaeacians (a view as old as schol. to 267), or a certificate of late degenerate taste? The view taken here (see 266–369 n.) is that the spirit of the episode does not differ materially from that of other Olympian scenes.

Brief Bibliography

On the characterization of the Phaeacians: A. Shewan, 'The Scheria of the *Odyssey*', *CQ* xiii (1919), 4–11 (= *Homeric Essays* (Oxford, 1935), 242–53) lists earlier work on the interpretation of the Phaeacians. The fullest recent statement of their hedonism is that of

F. R. Bliss, 'Homer and the Critics: The Structural Unity of *Od.* 8', *Bucknell Review* xvi (1968), 53–73: see also the observations of Eisenberger, *Studien*, 124. Much recent criticism seeks what sort of universal statement the poem makes in this episode: see Austin, *Archery*, 153–62, with bibliography pp. 171–4.

On Phaeacian politics: G. Finsler, *Homer* i 2 (Leipzig, 1924³), 132–5 and V. Bartoletti, 'Aristocrazia e monarchia nell'Odissea', *SIFC* xiii (1936), 213–65, address themselves directly to the Phaeacian question. The fullest statement is that of Sigrid Deger, *Herrschaftsformen bei Homer* (Wien, 1970), 157–78. Webster, *Mycenae*, 107–9, is confident the picture is Mycenaean, but cf. Ventris–Chadwick, *Documents*, 119–25, and the negative position of Palmer, *Interpretation*, 83–95. On Homeric kingship in general see also M. P. Nilsson, *Homer and Mycenae* (London, 1933), 215–26; Finley, *World*, 95–8, C. G. Thomas, 'The Roots of Homeric Kingship', *Historia* xv (1966), 387–407. No historical parallel was known to Aristotle, *Pol.* 1285 b —still a basic text. Homeric political terminology is imprecise: M. I. Finley, 'Homer and Mycenae: Property and Tenure', *Historia* vi (1957), 133–59 (= G. S. Kirk (ed.), *Language and Background of Homer* (Cambridge, 1964), 191–217), esp. 140–4. P. W. Rose, 'Class Ambivalence in the *Odyssey*', *Historia* xxiv (1975), 129–48, considers the poet's political standpoint.

On the structure of viii: F. R. Bliss, op. cit., proposes a loosely balancing arrangement, C. H. Whitman, *Homer and the Heroic Tradition* (Cambridge Mass., 1958), 288–90, a strict 'geometric' scheme. In 111–233 elements of the aristeia pattern appear, cf. R. Schröter, *Die Aristie als Grundform homerischer Dichtung* (Marburg, 1950), 162. At the deepest level Woodhouse, *Composition*, 59–71, perceived a complex of motifs associated with the rituals of wooing and marriage: the surface structure rests on the devices explored by J. A. Notopoulos, 'Continuity and Interconnection in Homeric Oral Composition', *TAPhA* lxxxii (1951), 81–101. For links with the rest of the *Odyssey*, see O. Andersen, 'Odysseus and the Wooden Horse', *SO* lii (1977), 7–18.

The analytical standpoint (Schwartz, *Odyssee*, 24, von der Mühll, *Odyssee*, col. 718, Focke, *Odyssee*, 139–55, Merkelbach, *Untersuchungen*, 168–75, W. Theiler, *MH* vii (1950), 102–4) is reviewed by Eisenberger, loc. cit. The epic use of doublets has been explored by F. Stürmer, *Die Rhapsoden der Odyssee* (Würzburg, 1921), 144–52, 562–9; Hölscher, *Untersuchungen*, 67–8; and especially by Fenik, *Studies*, 133–232. The comic presentation of the gods is an archaism: P. Friedländer, 'Lachende Götter', *Antike* x (1934), 209–26; K. Reinhardt, 'Das Parisurteil', *Tradition und Geist*, ed. C. Becker (Göttingen, 1960), 18–36; W. Burkert, 'Das Lied von Ares und Aphrodite', *RhM* ciii (1960), 130–44.

BOOK VIII: COMMENTARY

1–61. Alcinous convenes an assembly to grant Odysseus a ship to take him home and proclaims a day of feasting. For the theme cf. ii 1 ff., iii 137 ff., *Il.* i 53 ff., ii 48 ff., viii 489 ff., ix 9 ff., xviii 243 ff., xix 40 ff., and xx 3 ff. The common elements are: (1) heralds at the command of the king or other hero summon the δῆμος (or λαός if the context is military): attendance is not universal (at *Il.* xix 42 the exceptional attendance of κυβερνῆται and ταμίαι is noted); (2) the king proclaims his intentions; debate ensues only if there is perplexity or discord, and is confined (since Thersites (*Il.* ii 211 ff.) is clearly out of order) to the ἄριστοι; (3) the people signify their approval and disperse to execute their orders; they do not vote, nor, strictly speaking, decide anything, for the king may choose to disregard their clamours (cf. *Il.* i 22 ff.); (4) finally, the king invites the leaders to a formal feast. The Homeric assembly thus enjoys participation without power, a device well known to governments throughout the ages. The poet here takes the assent of the Phaeacians for granted.

On the assembly generally see R. Martin, *Reserches sur l'agora grecque* (Paris, 1952), and Finley, *World*, 86–90. G. M. Calhoun, 'Classes and Masses in Homer', *CPh* xxix (1934), 192–208, 301–16, collects the relevant passages.

The point of the scene is not clear, since nothing more than Alcinous' house-party was foreshadowed at vii 189 ff. But the poet wants us to imagine Odysseus on show before an impressive public audience. In style the scene is treated as a mere mechanism of plot. Thematically it is conventional and compressed, the sentences ramble, and the diction is verbose and careless.

1–61. This passage includes many whole-line and half-line formulae: 1–2 = ii 1–2; 4 = 421; 6 cf. 422; 9 = vi 14; 10 = ii 384; 15 = *Il.* v 792; 19 = vi 235; 20 = xviii 195; 24 = ii 9; 25–7 = vii 185–7; 34 = xvi 348; 36b = *Il.* xi 825; 38b = i 374; 40 = *Il.* ix 68; 46 = ii 413; 50 = ii 407; 51–5 = iv 780–3, 785; 61a = xix 421. The flat style is in large measure derived from this mode of composition.

1. Dawn is a suitable time at which to convene an assembly, cf. ii 1, but also, and more importantly, it is the proper moment with which to begin a major new episode of the poem. Dawn-formulae are consequently under frequent requisition: ἦμος δ᾽ ἠριγένεια ... occurs 22 times.

2. ἱερὸν μένος Ἀλκινόοιο: for this type of paraphrase see vii 167 n.

3. πτολιπόρθος: note the metrical effect of the initial πτ-. In the *Iliad* the epithet is generic (of Ares xx 152, Enyo v 333, Achilles xv 77, Odysseus ii 276, Oileus ii 728, and Otrynteus xx 384), but is restricted to Odysseus in the *Odyssey*, as if the sense were 'sacker of *the* city (i.e. Troy)', cf. i 2.

4. τοῖσιν: the plural is probably formulaic, cf. iii 386 and viii 421. Bérard missed a mention of the sons of Alcinous and wished to insert viii 118–19 (in an 'interpolated section') before this verse.

5. ἀγορήνδ': i.e. 'place of assembly'; the sense 'market place' (already in Hom. *Epigr.* 14. 5) is foreign to the epic. **παρὰ νηυσί:** as described at vi 264–9.

6. ξεστοῖσι: 'polished'; the epithet is glossed at iii 408 as λευκοὶ ἀποστίλβοντες ἀλείφατος.

7. Athena, among other things, is the symbol of achievement and success. Her introduction here is rather mechanical, for this is no real moment of crisis, but has the effect of stressing the size (16 ff.) and distinction of the assembly.

11. δεῦτ': a pluralized form of δεῦρο, an adv. used as an imperat., here oddly combined with the singular ἄγε. ἄγετε occurs, but in the weakened sense ('come now') ἄγε is virtually outside the sentence, cf. εἰπέ μοι, τί φειδόμεσθα τῶν λίθων (Ar. *Ach.* 319). **ἡγήτορες ἠδὲ μέδοντες:** a fairly wide group, but in any case that part of the assembly whose opinion was solicited, cf. 26 below and *Il.* ix 17.

15. Properly a formula of the battlefield (10 times in *Il.*).

18–20. Cf. vi 229–35. Since the epic has no diction with which to describe a person's mental state independent of his outer appearance, we should imagine Odysseus as proportionately gaining heroic confidence.

22–3. have been rejected by many critics (e.g. Schwartz, *Odyssee*, 312) on the grounds attributed by schol. to Zenodotus, that Odysseus was subjected to only one trial, the discus (186 ff. below). As in vii 318 (the notorious αὔριον) the language is perfectly natural in its place, and is mistakenly taken as programmatic. See the scornful remarks of Mattes, *Odysseus*, 63. Crates (of Mallos, *fl.* 168 BC) hoped to mend matters by taking ἀέθλους as πόνους generally, but this is controverted by xxi 180, where a similar formula is used of the bow-test.

22. δεινός τ' αἰδοῖός τε: the notions overlap in the epic, cf. *Cypria* fr. 23 (Allen) ἵνα γὰρ δέος, ἔνθα καὶ αἰδώς. δέος subsequently narrowed its meaning: see the discussion in Plato, *Euthphr.* 12 b.

28. οὐκ οἶδ' ὅς τις: Odysseus had carefully avoided Arete's direct question vii 237 (see introduction to vii), and does not reveal his identity till ix 19.

29. Alcinous quotes the cardinal points of the Homeric compass: cf. x 190 and *Il.* xii 239–40. 28–9 echo the formulaic direct question τίς πόθεν εἰς ἀνδρῶν; (i 170 etc.).

30. πομπὴν δ' ὀτρύνει: a loose echo of Odysseus' words (π. ὀτρύνετε) at vii 151. Properly it is the Phaeacians who are to 'hasten' his journey, as in 31.

35–6. Alcinous wanders from the first person (ἐρύσσομεν 34) to the third (κρινάσθων 36) and second (ἐκβῆτ' 38). **κρινάσθων** is in the middle voice with a vague unexpressed subject, hence κούρω is accusative dual. Schol. paraphrase as a passive (ἐπιλεχθήτωσαν), hence κοῦροι in some MSS. **κούρω** (cf. 48) is an irrational dual generated by the following δύω. The 52 κοῦροι appear to be the rowing complement of a pentekonter (cf. *Il.* ii 509, xvi 169), plus two supernumeraries, an ἀρχός (cf. *Il.* i 311, *Od.* iv 653) and κυβερνήτης, according to Gray, *Archaeologia* G, 108—or other 'officers' (πρωρεύς and κελευστής), since it is later (556) said that Phaeacian ships required no steering. On the manning of Greek ships see L. Casson, *Ships and Seamanship in the Ancient World* (Princeton, 1971), 300–2. Alcinous ordered out a first-rate to convey his guest: smaller vessels required only 20 rowers (*Il.* i 309, *Od.* ii 212, iv 669). 'Fifty', however, is a common round figure, cf. *Il.* iv 393 κούρους πεντήκοντα· δύω δ' ἡγήτορες ἦσαν ...

36. ὅσοι πάρος εἰσίν: the prototype of this expression (*Il.* xi 825, xvi 23) has ἦσαν, which has crept into some MSS here also. The nuance ('who have been hitherto') is not very felicitous, cf. ii 51.

38. θοήν: ἀντὶ τοῦ "θοῶς", ὡς "λῦσεν ἀγορὴν αἰψηρήν" (schol.), probably correctly, for Alcinous is anxious to proceed 'in haste', but not (cf. 59 ff.) to serve a 'hasty' meal.

41. σκηπτοῦχοι βασιλῆες: the σκῆπτρον is the symbol of royal power, cf. *Il.* ii 101 ff., and v 9 n. βασιλεύς means little more than 'lord', 'nobleman', as clearly at i 394 and as perhaps from Mycenaean times (cf. Lin. B *qa-si-re-u* and T. B. L. Webster in *Companion*, 457–8). In Scheria twelve were of especial distinction (390), but Alcinous' invitation is here taken very widely. Whatever picture the poet may have in mind, however, now or later, he seems to follow here the same thematic pattern as in *Il.* ii 404 ff. and ix 89 ff., where Agamemnon restricted his hospitality to the γέροντες.

44. Demodocus, like Phemius (i 337 etc.) has a suitable name (< δέκ-ομαι, Attic δέχομαι, 'welcome'), cf. λαοῖσι τετιμένος (viii 422). Such names are common (cf. viii 111 ff.): they are listed with comment by L. Ph. Rank, *Etymologiseering bij Homerus* (Assen, 1951), 130–5, see also H. Mühlestein, 'Redende Personennamen bei Homer', *SMEA* ix (1969), 67–94. The name Demodocus was borne, or usurped, by a poet of Leros (*RE* s.v. no. 7) in the sixth century, and was attributed by some to Agamemnon's ἀοιδός who was put in charge of Clytaemestra: see schol. *Od.* iii 267.

47. σκηπτοῦχοι is used substantivally, an unusual practice except in the case of the epithets of gods, as if it were a technical expression rather than *epitheton ornans*, cf. *Il.* xiv 93.

48–9. κούρω ... βήτην: irrational dual, cf. 35.

49. ἀτρυγέτοιο: a frequent but obscure epithet of the sea, very formulaic in use. The sense 'unharvested' (as if < ἀ-, τρυγάω) is traditional but philologically impossible: see Chantraine, *Dictionnaire* s.v. The expressions for the sea may be cited as a typical formular system (analysed by D. H. F. Gray, *CQ* xli (1947), 109–13), a *mélange* of archaism and innovation, comprehensive but not closed.

50–6. = iv 779–86 (with variations according to context). At iv 783 many MSS omit the line, but all MSS that have it read πέτασσαν: here all MSS have the line, but many read τάννσσαν. The half-line is formulaic (also at x 506, *Il.* i 480) and πέτασσαν is doubtless correct, whatever we think of the procedure of setting the sail and then leaving the vessel. The v.l. here and at iv 783 represent different attempts by Hellenistic critics to improve the sense (so van der Valk, *Textual Criticism*, 221).

55. Schol.'s note (cf. iv 785) points to a reading ἐννοδίῳ or εἰνοδίῳ (-διον Lehrs). Emendation by revised word-division was a favourite device of Alexandrian scholarship; νοτίῳ, like ὑγρήν (i 97 etc.), simply means the water as opposed to the shore.

57–8. Schol. joins δόμοι ἀνδρῶν and interprets as οἱ ἀνδρῶνες. This misconceives the nature of the Homeric house (see on vi 303, 304), but implies a text lacking 58, which is also missing from a large minority of the MSS. The line appears to be a 'plus verse', inspired by 17. There is no indication that the Alexandrians even read it (and therefore, of course, no note of athetesis).

59–61. A very truncated description of the sacrifice and feast (cf. *Il.* i 447–68, ii 402–31), one of the most regular 'typical scenes' of the epic: see Arend, *Scenen*, 64–78.

60. εἰλίποδας: a difficult gloss, conventionally explained as διὰ τὸ ἑλίσσειν τοὺς πόδας (Hesychius), as if < (ϝ)εἰλέω: but the ϝ is constantly neglected: see Frisk, *GEW* s.v. Hoekstra, *Modifications*, 67, defends the traditional derivation.

61. δέρον: strictly of the oxen. Porkers were prepared for the spit by singeing (*Il.* ix 468, xxiii 33).   ἕπον: distinguish this active verb (< *sep-) from the middle ἕπομαι (< *seqʷ-).

62–103. Demodocus entertains the company with an epic tale. This, together with the subsequent scenes (256 ff., 471 ff.) is an invaluable testimony to the nature and conditions of ἀοιδή as, ideally, the Homeric poet conceived them. See in general Schadewaldt, *Welt*, 54–86; for comparative material C. M. Bowra, *Heroic Poetry* (London, 1952), 404–42; and for particular points A. Pagliaro, 'Aedi e rapsodi', *Saggi di critica semantica* (Messina–Florence, 1953), 1–62, and R. di Donato, 'Problemi di tecnica formulare', *ASNP* xxxviii (1969), 243–94. The testimonia are well discussed by G. Lanata, *Poetica Preplatonica* (Firenze, 1963), 4–19. Note that the ἀοιδός is a professional but not necessarily retained by a permanent employer; he is both musician and poet; to perform poetry he sits and accompanies his chanting with the lyre; the performance is solo; the bard is open to suggestion, but may choose his own topic—in either case the matter is narrative, traditional, and concerned with the exploits of heroes or stories of gods; he pauses from time to time, and the audience respond with encouragement; if he does not please, he may be interrupted and silenced by his social superiors; the occasion of ἀοιδή is a banquet and its purpose is frankly entertainment; the nature of his skill is mysterious and attributable to divine aid and favour, but this does not set him apart from other craftsmen (diviners, doctors, and carpenters are mentioned at xvii 383–5) or give his art a value beyond that of acrobats and wrestlers. Since Scheria and Ithaca are opposed, order versus disorder, there is some contrast with the distasteful circumstances under which Phemius sang to the suitors (i 325–52). This has been stressed by W. Marg, *Homer über die*

Dichtung (Münster, 1957), 11, but the roles of both bards are conceived in closely similar terms. The picture is both traditional and contemporary (see M. Wegner, *Archaeologia* U, 1967), but the conditions described are not such as would naturally give rise to the art form of the monumental epic.

The scene is well conceived and vividly executed. The irony of Demodocus' choice of song and the consternation of Odysseus at once arrest attention, and at the same time the interest of the Phaeacians in Odysseus and his story is unobtrusively introduced.

62. ἐρίηρον: a gloss, cf. ἐρίηρες ἑταῖροι, interpreted as μεγάλως τιμώμενοι, ἀγαθοί, πρόθυμοι, εὐχάριστοι by Hesychius. There is a Mycenaean personal name *e-ri-we-ro* (PY Vn 130).

63. Μοῦσ': the canonical number, nine (though opinion varied), is first mentioned at xxiv 60 and Hes. *Th.* 60 (with list of names 77 ff.), but the vague singular is common. Homer mentions no personal names. They were daughters of Zeus (*Il.* ii 491 etc.) and Μνημοσύνη (first at Hes. *Th.* 54), a parentage usually considered significant for the nature of ἀοιδή. Their gift to the poet was not sublime inspiration, an idea not earlier than the fifth century (cf. Pl. *Phdr.* 245 a), but knowledge of the great storehouse of legend and saga: see E. R. Dodds, *The Greeks and the Irrational* (Berkeley, 1951), 80–2. The etymologies seek to connect the term with roots **men* cf. μέμονα, or **mont*, 'mountain', but founder on various difficulties. **ἀγα-θόν τε κακόν τε:** one must not expect the generosity of the gods to be unmixed, cf. the parable of Zeus' πίθοι (*Il.* xxiv 527).

64. For the blindness cf. Thamyris, according to some interpretations of the gloss πηρόν at *Il.* ii 599, the τυφλὸς ἀνήρ of *h.Ap.* 172, Daphnis, and Stesichorus: see R. G. A. Buxton, *JHS* c (1980), 27–30. Blind bards are attested in many epic traditions (cf. C. M. Bowra, *Heroic Poetry* (London, 1952), 420–2), though not as commonly as is sometimes thought. The tradition of Homer's own blindness (*Vita Herodotea* vii etc.) was doubtless promoted by the present passage.

65–6. Pontonous is one of Alcinous' κήρυκες, cf. vii 179 and xiii 50. He is evidently different from the κῆρυξ of 47, 62, 69, etc. Kirchhoff ejected the lines, to make the personnel consistent.

65. θρόνον ἀργυρόηλον: the θρόνος is a heavy piece of furniture, cf. S. Laser, *Archaeologia* P, 38–41 (it is only here said to be moved), not a ceremonial throne. For the decoration, cf. the epithets δαιδάλεος, περικαλλής, σιγαλόεις, and φαεινός.

66. μέσσῳ δαιτυμόνων: they sat around the walls, see vii 95.

67. πασσαλόφι: see v 59 n., gen. sg. **φόρμιγγα:** an accompanying instrument is regular in most oral epic traditions, except in their degenerate phases. Its use is closely related to the maintenance of correct metre, according to A. B. Lord, *Serbo-Croatian Heroic Songs*, i (Cambridge, Mass., 1954), 8. **λίγειαν:** used principally of winds (iv 567 etc.) and weeping (iv 259 etc.). The rendering 'sweet' (LSJ⁹) in bardic contexts is probably optimistic. Like the Hebrew prophet, the Homeric bard evidently 'lifted up' his voice to sing.

68. ἐπέφραδε: 'showed', not 'told'. Aristarchus maintained ὅτι τὸ φράσαι οὐδέποτε ἐπὶ τοῦ εἰπεῖν τάσσεται, according to Apollonius *Lex.* s.v. πεφράδοι.

73. κλέα ἀνδρῶν: cf. *Il.* ix 189 and *Od.* i 338 (ἔργ' ἀνδρῶν τε θεῶν τε, τά τε κλείουσιν ἀοιδοί). Owing to the following hiatus κλέα is often taken to represent *κλέε': so Chantraine, *Grammaire*, i 74. Apollonius Rhodius, writing κλέα φωτῶν (i 1), evidently took it as an instance of 'hyphaeresis' (i.e. a euphonic loss of one -ε-), as in θεουδέα (xix 364), νηλέι (iv 743), etc.

74. οἴμης: probably partitive genitive, not 'attractio inversa', since the Homeric poet thinks of the bard as taking up the narrative *from* a certain point in the tale, cf. viii 500 and the proems to both epics. The root is perhaps *sēi-, 'sing', though the association with οἶμος, 'path', was made early (e.g. οἶμος ἀοιδῆς, *h.Merc.* 451): see A. Pagliaro, 'Aedi e rapsodi', *Saggi di critica semantica* (Messina–Florence, 1953), 25–30. **κλέος** is (to the post-Homeric mind) awkwardly repeated after κλέα, but see vii 116 n.

75. The quarrel theme requires no illustration, but the dispute here mentioned is otherwise unknown. The *Cypria*, according to Proclus' summary, included a quarrel of Achilles and Agamemnon at Tenedos on the way to Troy, in which Sophocles (Σύνδειπνοι fr. 566 Pearson) appears to have made Odysseus a participant. Schol. refer to a symposium after the death of Hector, in which Achilles recommended ἀνδρεία, Odysseus σύνεσις, as a means of taking Troy. But the allusion seems to be an 'Augensblickerfindung' (so W. Marg, 'Das erste Lied des Demodokos', *Navicula Chiloniensis* (Festschrift Jacoby) (Leiden, 1956), 21), invented to meet the needs of the moment. Yet the exaltation of Odysseus into an opponent of Achilles (he has no such stature in the *Iliad*) is not without significance. Achilles was the last and greatest of those heroes who solved their problems by excess of violence: Odysseus represents a newer idea (though we might see the germ of it in Odysseus' rational admonition of the impatient Achilles in *Il.* xix 155–83), probably congenial to many in the Homeric audience, the cool opportunist, valiant but prudent, and not ashamed to stoop to conquer: cf. Rüter, *Odysseeinterpretationen*, 247–54; G. Nagy, *The Best of the Achaeans* (Baltimore, 1979), 42–58. The opposition of μῆτις and βίη, never remote from the action of the *Odyssey*, has generated much imaginative interpretation; see Nagy, and for supposed political overtones S. G. Farron, 'The *Odyssey* as an anti-aristocratic Statement', *Studies in Antiquity* i (1979–80), 59–101. Of older papers F. Jacoby, 'Die geistige Physiognomie der Odyssee', *Antike* 1933, 159–94, is obligatory.

79–82. Consultation of the Delphic oracle is mentioned only here in Homer, and the lines have been rejected, unnecessarily, for that reason: cf. Bolling, *Evidence*, 237–8. The original audience, no less than the interpolator, would expect some explanation for Agamemnon's unnatural pleasure. The athetesis, which is obscurely reported, concerns certainly only the gnomic lines 81–2. The sacred site of Delphi itself is at least as old as the mid-second millennium: cf. P. Amandry, *La Mantique apollinienne à Delphes* (Paris, 1950), 204. It is needless to doubt that its fame at an early period, like that of Dodona (*Il.* xvi 233, *Od.* xiv 327 = xix 296), justified a passing reference in Ionian epic. Later Delphi figured very prominently in classical and Hellenistic embroidery of the Trojan legend: see H. W. Parke and D. E. W. Wormell, *The Delphic Oracle*, i (Oxford, 1956), 309–19. The form of the oracle, an ambiguous promise of success misunderstood but ultimately fulfilled, is characteristic of many traditional stories of Delphi.

80. Πυθοῖ: the only name by which Homer, Hesiod, and the major Homeric Hymns refer to the site: *Δελφοί*, properly an ethnic term is first attested at *h.* xxvii 14.   **ἠγαθέῃ:** see v 20 n.   **ὅϑ' ὑπέρβη λάϊνον οὐδόν** is formulaic (4 times), and elsewhere merely amplifies *εἴσειμι*. Apollo's stone threshold, however, is mentioned also at *Il.* ix 404. It is perhaps implied that the oracle was delivered as soon as Agamemnon had entered the shrine, before the question was put, as in the case of the early oracles reputedly given to Lycurgus and Cypselus (Hdt. i 65, v 92 ε).

81. κυλίνδετο: a traditional metaphor (cf. *κακῶν τρικυμία* A. *Pr.* 1015): also at ii 163, *Il.* xi 347, xvii 688.

82. Διὸς … βουλάς: *βουλή* means strictly 'plan' not 'will' (W. Kullmann, 'Ein vorhomerisches motiv im Iliasproömium', *Philologus* xcix (1955), 173–92, *init.* discusses the epic passages), but the pl. is vague, and there is no need to see here an allusion to Zeus' plan (unknown to *Iliad* and *Odyssey*) to decimate the human race, as outlined in *Cypria* fr. 1. The Homeric view of divine causation permits any untoward event to be attributed to the designs of Zeus, cf. v 304.   **μεγάλου:** the regular epithet of Zeus in the genitive case. Oddly, since preternatural size is an attribute of deity, *μέγας* is used of no other god (save Cronus, *Il.* v 721 etc.), nor of Zeus in any other case.

83–95. Cf. 521 ff. below. The parallelism, both in word and thought, is normal in Homeric narrative, but has prompted various excisions from the present passage. Alcinous does not allude to Odysseus' distress, but that proves only that he is represented as a courteous and civilized host.

86. The idea of heroism calls on man to *suffer* for the sake of glory (cf. the summary of Demodocus's tale at 490, *ὅσσ' ἔρξαν τ' ἔπαθόν τε καὶ ὅσσ' ἐμόγησαν Ἀχαιοί*). The tears are not unmanly in themselves, but courtesy demanded their concealment unless the grief was shared, cf. iv 113 ff. and 183 ff.

88–9. ἔλεσκε … ἑλών: see vii 116 n.

89. δέπας ἀμφικύπελλον: The Mycenaean *di-pa*, to judge from the ideograms, was a large bowl, but except in the notorious passage *Il.* xi 632 ff. ('Nestor's Cup') the Homeric *δέπας* is a simple cup for drinking or pouring offerings (or ladling from a bowl—*Il.* xxiii 219). No context elucidates the sense attributed to *ἀμφικύπελλον* by the poet. *ἀμφι-* with reference to a cup is easily taken to allude to the rim (= 'all around') or handles (= 'on both sides') (cf. Hesych. *ἢ ἀπὸ τῆς τοῦ ὅλου περιφερείας ἢ ἀπὸ τῆς τῶν ὤτων* s.v. *ἀμφικύβωται*): hence 'two-handled' (Aristarchus, see Athen. 783 b for other ancient conjectures). What then of *-κύπελλον* (= 'cupped')? Aristotle used the term (*HA* 624 a) to illustrate the back-to-back structure of cells in a honeycomb. The primitive allusion may be to the Mycenaean

double cups joined at the rim: see G. Daux, *BCH* lxxxix (1965), 738 and
G. Bruns, *Archaeologia* Q, 25 and 42–4. The term δέπας itself is probably of
Anatolian provenance (Hitt. *tapisana-*), cf. E. Benveniste, *Hittite et indo-
européen* (Paris, 1962), 126.

92. κρᾶτα: acc., as if masc., of κάρη. Leumann, *Wörter*, 159, defines the
gradation as (1) *karasṇ > κάρη, and (2) *krāsn- > κράατος > κρατός.

98. Aristarchus' word-order, adopted by Allen, splits the formula δαιτὸς
ἐΐσης without any metrical convenience, and seems designed to bring the
more emphatic word to the head of the sentence.   **ἐΐσης**: only the fem.
has the prothetic vowel (except for the Hesychian gloss ἔισον· ἀγαθόν). The
sense ('equally shared') echoes the primitive meaning of δαίς (cf. δαίομαι,
'distribute'). Invitation to the feast, and the treatment received at it deeply
involve a man's honour, cf. xx 279–82, xiv 432–6; hence the epithet. The
sense is weakened in a few places (*Il.* iv 48 = xxiv 69, of offerings to Zeus),
and perhaps encouraged Zenodotus' conjecture (reported by Athen. 12 c)
that ἐΐση = ἀγαθή: see P. von der Mühll, 'Δαὶς ἐΐση', *WS* lxx (1966), 9–12.

100. ἀέθλων: masc. = 'contest': the neut. forms mean 'prize', according to
the grammarians, but see 108 below.

103. Cf. the classical pentathlon ἅλμα ποδωκείην δίσκον ἄκοντα πάλην. The
funeral games of Patroclus (*Il.* xxiii 262 ff.) omitted the jump, but added
the chariot, boxing, and discus, and the martial arts of spear-fighting and
archery. It is understandable that the peaceful Phaeacians did not attempt
the last: Alcinous withdrew their claims to eminence in the violent
exercises of boxing and wrestling as soon as Odysseus revealed his physical
strength (246).

104–255. The Phaeacian Games. Where the structure of the narrative has
set up a series of parallel scenes, it is regularly the case that one episode is
treated *in extenso*, e.g. the chariot race in Patroclus' games and the Cyclops
episode in the wanderings, and the rest in summary fashion. So here the
point of interest is not the games themselves (104–30), but the provocation
of Odysseus (131–233). The scene is one of excellent characterization and,
like the song of Demodocus, increases interest in the revelation of the
stranger's identity.

105. πασσαλόφι: see v 59 n.

107. αὐτήν: 'the same', as at x 263 etc.

109. πουλύς: the lengthened first syllable is usually assumed to have been
derived from *composita* such as πουλυβότειρα, see Wyatt, *Lengthening*, 195,
199: only here in the nom. case. The forms πολλός (-όν) are much the
commoner. The formula πουλὺς (-ὺν) ὅμιλος (-ον) perhaps follows πολὺν
καθ' ὅμιλον (3 times): note πολλὸς ... ὅμιλος (*Il.* xviii 603), when the word-
group is divided.

111–17. The choice, or invention, of names is a part of Homeric art: see
H. Mühlestein, 'Redende Personennamen bei Homer', *SMEA* ix (1969),
67–94. The poet's intention, as usual, is concealed by the consistent epic
style (see v 97–113 n.), but ranges from the grimly humorous (e.g. υἱὸς
Αὐτοφόνοιο μενεπτόλεμος Πολυφόντης (*Il.* iv 395), a murderer: see also

L. Deroy, 'Le Pays de Taphos et l'humour homérique', *AC* xv (1946), 227–39), to the romantic (e.g. the Nereids, *Il.* xviii 39–48), and whimsical (as here, cf. *Ἶρος*, the beggar, *οὔνεκ' ἀπαγγέλλεσκε κιών* xviii 7, like *Ἶρις*).

111. **Ἀκρόνεως** and 113 *Ἀναβησίνεως* show the quantitative metathesis (-νεως < -νηος < -να(ϝ)ος), a feature judged by Meister, *Kunstsprache*, 163, and Hoekstra, *Modifications*, 31, to be among the latest linguistic developments in Homer.

116. **Ναυβολίδης**: von Kamptz, *Personennamen*, 70, cites *Il.* xiii 628 *ἐν νηυσὶ ... πῦρ ὀλοὸν βαλέειν*, but the name is probably connected with *βόλις*, 'sounding-lead', rather than *βάλλω*. The *θ'* of many MSS should be deleted, since the patronymic is used as a substitute for the name only in the case of well-known heroes (*Πηλείδης, Τυδείδης*, etc.), and Euryalus, having a role in the sequel (158 ff.), deserves the full introduction.

117. **ἀμύμονα**: traditionally 'blameless', but a moral quality is not involved (cf. i 29). The epithet, where it is not mere ornament, seems to compliment personal appearance: see the exhaustive discussion by Parry, *Blameless Aesgisthus*.

121. **νύσσης**: usually *νύσσα* denotes the turning-post of a double course, but the sense ('a course was laid out for them (to and) from the turning-post') would be both difficult and dull. *νύσσα* is probably < *νυκ- (or νυχ-) -ya, cf. *νύσσω* (see, however, Frisk, *GEW* s.v.), meaning simply 'mark', here the starting line. **τέτατο δρόμος**: 'the running was strained', i.e. the speed was increased to the limit. The metaphor is common of anything requiring effort, especially battle. Note 121 = *Il.* xxiii 758, 122 = *Il.* xxiii 372, with slight variations. The use of stock lines shows that the focus of attention is elsewhere.

123. **ὄχ'**: used only as a reinforcement of *ἄριστος*. Formed, according to Leumann, *Wörter*, 133–6, by decomposition from *ἔξοχα*.

124–5. The same comparison is used at *Il.* x 351–2. *οὖρα* seem to be the 'limits' (cf. *ὅρ(ϝ)ος*), i.e. the side-limits, cf. *τέλσον*, 'end-limit', of a standard area of ploughland: hence 'distance', 'range'. See further W. Ridgeway, 'The Homeric Land System', *JHS* vi (1885), 319–39. The distance would be 20–30 m.

125. **λαούς**: the spectators. As with Patroclus' games, the events begin and end at the same point. **ἐλίποντο**: passive sense, cf. *Il.* xi 693 etc.

126. The noun–epithet formula is displaced from the verse-end (cf. *Il.* xxiii 701) by the heavy quadrisyllable *πειρήσαντο*.

127. **ἀπεκαίνυτο**: this present stem (pf. *κέκασμαι*) first appears in the *Odyssey*. It is clearly secondary, perhaps on the analogy of *δαίνυμαι: δέδασμαι*: so Schwyzer, *Grammatik*, i 698.

133. **Δεῦτε**: see 11 n.

134–6. Cf. the description of Odysseus at xviii 67–9 *φαῖνε δὲ μηροὺς | καλούς τε μεγάλους τε, φάνεν δέ οἱ εὐρέες ὦμοι | στήθεά τε στιβαροί τε βραχίονες*, the physique of a boxer or wrestler. The same picture is implied in the comparisons with Agamemnon and Menelaus, *Il.* iii 193–4, 210.

141. **Λαοδάμα**: the correct form of the vocative was disputed by the grammarians (see Bekker, *Anecdota*, 1183—long names should be without -ν). Zenodotus preferred -αν (schol. *Il.* xii 231), Aristarchus the analogical form (-δάμας, -δάμα after -ίδης, -ίδη).

142. πέφραδε: see 68 n. According to schol. none of the Alexandrian critics read this verse. The point of the omission is obscure, if the schol. is correctly referred to this verse (141 would be better, according to Schwartz, *Odyssee*, 312, or 146, according to Bérard, ad loc.).

145. ξεῖνε πάτερ should mark the following words as civil in tone, cf. vii 28, yet Odysseus (153) takes them to be κερτομία. The offence lies in the challenge to a guest, especially to a guest in Odysseus' condition. The insolent youths, Laodamas and, especially, Euryalus, lack the sense of proper conduct which the *Odyssey* is at pains to stress.

146. ἔοικε: 'it is fitting', as in the formula οὐδὲ ἔοικε (10 times), rather than 'it is likely'. Laodamas' argument is from the moral code (147–8), not from Odysseus' appearance. The line is not formulaic, though the first words echo 133–4, and the digamma is neglected twice (ϝέϝοικε, ϝίδμεν).

147–8. Laodamas speaks *ad hominem* and *ad tempus*. Homeric ἀρετή, the foundation of κλέος, embraces excellence in βουλή as well as πόλεμος (for which the sports are a peacetime substitute), though the martial arts are the more important. Laodamas himself was no stranger to μουσική (370 ff.).

153. κελεύετε: the plural includes Euryalus.

159. γάρ: i.e. 'I knew you would refuse, for ...'

160. ἄθλων: the contraction is found in various compounds and derivatives (ἀθλέω, ἀθλητήρ, ἀθλοφόρος), but only here in the simplex. The gender (see 100 n.) is obscure, for οἷά τε implies an unspecific antecedent, cf. κτῆσιν ... οἷά τε (xiv 63).

161–4. The object of aristocratic contempt is the itinerant trader, cf. xv 415 ff. (though the anti-Phoenician prejudice is there racial as well as social). Similar attitudes are widely quotable, both in fact and in literature (where the attitude is easily disguised as moral condemnation of avarice, cf. Horace, *Serm.* i 4. 29, *Ep.* i 1. 45; Tibullus i 3. 39; Propertius, iii 7; *Anth. Pal.* vii 586). The attitude softened in post-Homeric times, especially when confronted with high profits; see Hdt. iv 152 and Cic. *Off.* i 151 (an illuminating passage); and contempt shifted to κάπηλοι and artisans. In Homer the banausic arts (carpentry, medicine, metallurgy) are *infra dignitatem*, but not inherently illiberal.

161. νηὶ πολυκληῗδι: the formula (5 times and 6 times in dat. pl.) most naturally refers to a rowed warship (as certainly at xxiii 324, *Il.* viii 239); but even a φορτὶς εὐρεῖα (ix 323) could be ἐεικόσορος. There is no formulaic diction specifically for merchantmen.

162. πρηκτῆρες: 'traders', cf. πρῆξις (iii 72), 'business'. The usage is not classical.

163. Commentators have sought to distinguish φόρτος and ὁδαῖα (= ἐφόδια Eustath., ἐπιμήνια Apoll. Soph.) as 'outward and inward cargo'. The Homeric style does not demand a precise distinction.   **μνήμων** and ἐπίσκοπος ('having oversight') are probably both adjectival. As a noun μνήμων (= ἐπίπλους, γραμματεύς, ἐπιμελήτης schol.) is normally restricted to religious and political functionaries, chiefly in Dorian cities. Schol. note τοῦτο δέ τινες σημειοῦνται πρὸς τὸ ἀγνοεῖν γράμματα τοὺς ἥρωας.

166. ἀτασθάλῳ: the frequent association with ὑβρίζειν (e.g. iii 207), ὑβριστής (xxiv 282), and ὕβρις (e.g. xvi 86) is the best indication of the sense of this word, an arrogance of mind and deed strongly condemned throughout the *Odyssey*. There is no plausible etymology.

167. The thought is illogically expressed, since the sense required is 'the gods do not give all their gifts to anyone', not 'the gods do not give their gifts to everyone'; it is best understood as elliptical, sc. οὐ πάντεσσι θεοὶ ⟨πάντα⟩ χαρίεντα διδοῦσιν, cf. *Anth. Pal.* xii 96. 2 οὐ πάντα θεοὶ πᾶσιν ἔδωκαν ἔχειν: hence οὐχ ἅμα πάντα was read by Düntzer, for πάντεσσι.

169. ἀκιδνότερος: cf. vi 217.

170–3. The gift of speech: cf. Hes. *Th.* 83 ff. τῷ μὲν ἐπὶ γλώσσῃ γλυκερὴν χείουσιν ἐέρσην [sc. Μοῦσαι], | τοῦ δ' ἔπε' ἐκ στόματος ῥεῖ μείλιχα· οἱ δέ νυ λαοὶ | πάντες ἐς αὐτὸν ὁρῶσι διακρίνοντα θέμιστας | ἰθείῃσι δίκῃσιν· ὁ δ' ἀσφαλέως ἀγορεύων | … | ἐρχόμενον δ' ἀν' ἀγῶνα θεὸν ὧς ἱλάσκονται | αἰδοῖ μειλιχίῃ, μετὰ δὲ πρέπει ἀγρομένοισι. Parallel passages in Homer and Hesiod are discussed by I. Sellschopp, *Stilistische Untersuchungen zu Hesiod* (Hamburg, 1934) (assuming a direct relationship and Hesiodic priority), and F. Krafft, *Vergleichende Untersuchungen zu Homer und Hesiod* (Göttingen, 1963) (assuming Homeric priority). F. Solmsen, 'The "gift" of speech in Homer and Hesiod', *TAPhA* lxxxv (1954), 1–15, discusses the present passage at length, awarding priority to the *Odyssey*: further literature in West, *Theogony*, nn. to 84 ff., who reserves judgement. For oralists the problem does not present itself in these terms, since it is supposed that both poets, independently of each other, made use of a common tradition, cf. A. Hoekstra, 'Hésiode et la tradition orale,' *Mnemosyne* x (1957), 193–225. Hesiod's lines appear to expand the thought that is expressed in the *Odyssey* (cf. the way in which viii 362–6 are expanded at *h.Ven.* 58–65), but the *Odyssey* has certain awkwardnesses (see 172 n.) which suggest that its version is further removed from the original expression of these thoughts.

170. μορφὴν ἔπεσι στέφει: 'puts a crown of charm on'; μορφήν is an internal acc. and ἔπεσι a dat. of the remoter object. 175 has the same construction in the passive.

171. ἀσφαλέως: at *Il.* iii 213–15 the terms ἐπιτροχάδην and οὐδ' ἀφαμαρτοεπής are applied to the oratory of Menelaus. Xenophon's comment (*Mem.* iv 6. 15) on the ἀσφαλὴς ῥήτωρ—ὡς ἱκανὸν αὐτὸν ὄντα διὰ τῶν δοκούντων τοῖς ἀνθρώποις ἄγειν τοὺς λόγους—favours the latter, but what impressed the Homeric age about the orator was that he is articulate: cf. *Il.* i 249 ῥέεν αὐδή, *h.Ven.* 237 φωνὴ ῥεῖ ἄσπετος, and *Il.* iii 221–3.

172. αἰδοῖ μειλιχίῃ: see the discussion in Cauer, *Homerkritik*, 653–5. αἰδώς may denote a feeling inspired in others (e.g. *h.Cer.* 214), but is regularly used of one's own feeling. Hesiod construes the phrase with the equivalent of λεύσσουσιν (see *Th.* 91–2): αἰδώς is often indeed said to reside in the eyes, and the hyperbaton (making ὁ δ' ἀσφαλέως ἀγορεύει parenthetic), though extreme, is not impossible (cf. *Il.* xi 242–3, *Od.* xiv 62–5); but the sense would then clash with τερπόμενοι. The orator seems rather to be thought of as conciliatory, speaking μειλιχίοις or ἀγανοῖς ἐπέεσσι—a fitting contrast to the ἔπεα ἄκοσμα (*Il.* ii 213) of Euryalus.

173. θεὸν ὥς: the comparison in fact is usually presumptive of the physical beauty here disparaged. See Pi. *P.* iv 79–92 (Jason's appearance at Iolcus) for a vivid image in which the hero's θαητὰ γυῖα and πλόκαμοι ἀγλαοί put the onlookers in mind of Apollo or Ares.

175. ἀμφιπεριστέφεται: the archaic epic uses the doubled prefix only in the third to fourth feet of the hexameter, cf. xi 609, *Il.* viii 348, *h.Ven.* 271: later poets prefer the first to second feet. It is evident that the archaic poets perceived a caesura between ἀμφι- and -περι-, but to mark this (as do Ameis–Hentze–Cauer, Bérard, and others) by separating ἀμφὶ is to confer a false appearance of autonomy on the preposition.

177. ἀποφώλιος: see v 182 n.

179. νῆϊς: i.e. *νη-ϝιδ-. νη- is doubtless by analogy with νηλεής, νημερτής, etc., where it is the product of an early contraction.

180. μυθεῖαι: the sequence -ε-ε-αι has been contracted to -εῖ-αι not -έ-η (-ῇ), cf. νεῖαι xi 114, xii 141, and αἰδεῖο ix 269, *Il.* xxiv 503 (in the second example -ει- lies under the ictus and cannot be resolved).

182. ἔχομαι: 'in the grip of', as at xvii 318, xviii 123, xix 168, a metaphor from wrestling.

183. = xiii 91, 264, *Il.* xxiv 8.   πείρων, 'piercing' (frequent in culinary contexts), hence 'cleaving my way', cf. (νηῦς) πεῖρε κέλευθον (ii 434), must be taken also by zeugma with πτολέμους, almost as if it were associated with πειράω.

184–5. For the hero the challenge is virtually an absolute imperative, cf. *Il.* vii 92. To shirk it brings immediate reproach, e.g. *Il.* iii 30 ff. (Hector to Paris), *Il.* vii 120 ff. (Nestor to the Greeks).

186. αὐτῷ φάρει: 'cloak and all'. The dat. is sociative and in this idiom is not usually defined by a preposition (σύν xiii 118), as if the αὐτός (i.e. 'without change', 'as before') were sufficient. See Munro's note, *Homeric Dialect*, 138.

187. πάχετον: schol.'s suggestion that this form is a 'syncopated comparative' is, of course, impossible: the formation is that seen in περιμήκετος etc. The co-ordination with the two comparatives is awkward, but we may take μείζονα as 'rather big' and confine the comparative construction to στιβαρώτερον.   περ: intensive, as in 212: see Denniston, *Particles*, 482: an infrequent function in Homer.

188. Classical metal δίσκοι range from about 1.5 to 5.7 kg. Stone δίσκοι of the sixth century weigh as much as 7 kg., more than ample for a serious accident, cf. 190–1, and the death of Hyacinthus at the hands of Apollo. *Il.* xxiii 826 ff. has the term σόλος, a massive lump of unwrought iron 'enough to supply a farmer for five years'.   ἐδίσκεον ἀλλήλοισι: the dat. is transparent in sense 'with (i.e. against) each other', but is not easily defined syntactically: see Schwyzer, *Grammatik*, ii 161. An extension from

357

the dat. regular with verbs of competition to verbs used in a context of competition seems natural.

189. περιστρέψας: note the active voice (likewise at *Il.* xix 131), as if the missile was thrown solely with the arm, cf. δινήσας *Il.* xxiii 840. The classical action is described by Philostratus, *Imagines* i 24, and representations (including Myron's celebrated *Discobolus*) are frequent in the late archaic and classical periods: see E. N. Gardiner, *Athletics of the Ancient World* (Oxford, 1930), 154–68, and S. Laser, *Archaeologia* T, 58–62. The athlete raised the discus before him, turned his body as he swung it backward to shoulder height (sc. into the pose of the *Discobolus*), and with arm extended twisted the thighs and body to speed it forward. The modern action, in which the whole body is whirled around several times, was unknown in antiquity.

190. βόμβησεν: at *Il.* xiii 530, xvi 118, *Od.* xii 204, xviii 397 the context is that of a falling body, but the reference here is evidently to the flight of the discus.

191. Some commentators have detected irony in the honorific epithets used in unheroic circumstances; but the line is a formula (= 369, xiii 166), and therefore, other things being equal should be used without reference to its immediate context: see v 463 n.

192–3. From the following lines it appears that Odysseus threw from the correct line or box (called βαλβίς in the classical stadium), that the τέρματα (*plurale tantum*) denote the point that defined his throw, presumably the point where the discus first hit the ground, which the umpire was charged to observe, and that the σήματα (pegs are illustrated on the vases) mark the τέρματα. For Athena's role see 7 n.

194. ἔκ τ' ὀνόμαζε: see v 181 n.

198. A late epigram (*Anth. Pal.* Appendix 297) attributes a throw of 95 feet to the fifth-century pentathlete Phayllus. **τόδε γ'**: the MSS have τόν γ', sc. δίσκον or perhaps ἄεθλον. OCT's τόδε γ' is an emendation in favour of strict accuracy: see van der Valk, *Textual Criticism*, 126.

200. ἐνηέα: apparently = 'having goodwill', cf. Skt. *avas-*, 'aid', but a notorious gloss found only here in the *Odyssey*, once in Hesiod (*Th.* 651), and restricted in the *Iliad* to Patroclus. But it had meaning for the poet, for he formed the derivative ἐνηείη (*Il.* xvii 670).

201. κουφότερον: 'more light-heartedly', in contrast with his dejected appearance implied at 149. The pejorative sense 'frivolous' is also common, hence the gloss ἀλαζονώτερον in schol.

203. μᾶσσον: < *μάκ-γον (μακρός). The suffix is well represented in Homer, cf. βράσσων (βραχύς), πάσσων (παχύς), besides the forms retained in Attic: see also Schwyzer, *Grammatik*, i 538.

204. ὅτινα: Homer has (besides the ambiguous ὅτι) ὅτις, ὅτινα (also neut. pl.), and ὅτινας. The formation occurs alongside forms in -ττ- in Aeolic and Arcado-Cypriot, and sporadically elsewhere. These are dialects that use the article as a relative, but the nature of the first element is disputed: see Schwyzer, *Grammatik*, i 617.

208. Games, of course, led to argument, cf. *Il.* xxiii 539 ff.

209–11. A moralistic observation typical of the Phaeacian books, cf. vi 25, 66, 182, 187, 273, vii 159, 299, viii 166, 388. It is part of the function of the epic art in archaic society that 'relationships which are basic to the stability of the social structure are ... recapitulated' (E. A. Havelock, *Preface to Plato* (Oxford, 1963), 68).

210. ἔριδα προφέρηται: the phrase expresses challenge or emulation, as at vi 92; the literal use occurs at *Il.* iii 7.

212. οὐδ' ἀθερίζω: an epic verb, always negated in Homer. The Lexica interpret as 'flocci facere' (cf. ἀθέρες, 'chaff'), but schol. here have a different account ([οἱ ἀθέρες] ἐκτὸς ἐκφύονται καὶ προίασι πορρωτέρω): see *LfgrE* s.v. These look like learned conjectures. Risch compares Skt. *adhara-*, Lat. *inferus*: see *Wortbildung*, 92.

214–33. Odysseus for the second time lets slip a clue to his identity, cf. 83 ff. Various parts of the passage have been excised (esp. 218–28) to improve the relevance of his remarks and preserve his anonymity, but there was no ancient athetesis.

215–18. In the *Iliad* Teucer and Meriones are the contestants in archery (xxiii 859), and Odysseus appears throughout only as a spearman. Kirk (*Songs*, 290) finds this a 'radical difference' between the two epics, indicative of an independent development of the Odysseus-saga. Schol. suggest that the present passage προοικονομεῖ the massacre of the suitors, but that episode does not need the support of so distant and incidental a comment as this: see vi 232–5 n.

215. ἀμφαφάασθαι: i.e. 'handle', 'manage'. The hemistich (with ἀμφαφ-όωντας) recurs at xix 586 in the same sense. The action of Odysseus in examining his bow at xxi 393–400, which would have been literally ἀμφαφάασθαι, is peculiar to that context.

219. Φιλοκτήτης: *Il.* ii 716–28 and *Od.* iii 190 are the only other Homeric notices of this hero, but he must have figured largely in the *Il. Parva*, where he slew Paris with the bow inherited from Heracles.

221. ἐμέ φημι ... εἶναι: for the acc. and infin. construction where the subjects of the principal and subordinate verbs are the same cf. *Il.* vii 198, xiii 269: see Chantraine, *Grammaire*, ii 312.

222. ἐπὶ χθονὶ σῖτον ἔδοντες: the formula (also at ix 89 and x 101) is echoed by ἀρούρης καρπὸν ἔδοντες (*Il.* xxi 465 and (with ἔδουσι) *Il.* vi 142). The contrast is with the diet of the gods, cf. *Il.* xiii 322.

224. The bow, naturally a gift of Apollo (Apollodorus *Bibl.* ii 71), is the characteristic weapon of Heracles in Homer, cf. xi 606. His club is first reported in Stesichorus (fr. 229 Page). Eurytus according to legend advertised the hand of his daughter Iole as prize for anyone who could beat him in marksmanship. Heracles took up the challenge, defeated Eurytus and, being refused his reward, sacked Oechalia. The story (not directly attested in Homer) found literary form in the Οἰχαλίας ἅλωσις attributed to Creophylus and in the *Heracleias* of Panyassis, but the details remained fluid: see *RE* vi 1360. Theocritus (*Id.* xxiv 108) even has it that Eurytus was Heracles' instructor in archery. His bow (a gift of Apollo like that of Pandarus (*Il.* ii 827), as AR i 88 has it) descended through his son Iphitus to Odysseus: see the anecdote in xxi 11–41. **Οἰχαλιῆϊ**: towns named Oechalia are exceptionally numerous in myth, and those in Messenia, Thessaly, and Euboea are all associated with Eurytus by various sources. Homer, in *Il.* ii 595 ff. and *Od.* xxi 11 ff., seems to prefer the Messenian location.

225. ἐρίζεσκον: the point of the iterative imperfect ('un des traits nettement ioniens du dialecte épique', Chantraine, *Grammaire*, i 321) is obscure, especially since 226–8 imply the precise sense 'challenged to a contest'. Heracles drew his bow against Hera and Hades (*Il.* v 392, 395), but is not recorded as having issued any challenge to a trial of skill. Eurytus' challenge is echoed by AR i 89: other sources have him slain by Heracles at the sack of Oechalia.

226. αἶψ' ἔθανεν: cf. *Il.* vi 130, v 407–8 (οὐ δηναιὸς ὃς ἀθανάτοισι μάχηται | οὐδέ τί μιν παῖδες ποτὶ γούνασι παππάζουσιν).

229. ἀκοντίζω: The Homeric spear is a thrown javelin, except in a few instances (e.g. *Il.* xxiii 816), and the warrior carries two (i 256, xii 228, etc.): see Lorimer, *Monuments*, 258–61.

230. Odysseus' language at 206 (ἦ καὶ ποσί) suggested some doubt about his running. At the Games of Patroclus (*Il.* xxiii 740 ff.) he had gained the first prize (with some help from Athena).

232–3. κύμασιν ἐν πολλοῖς is easily taken as a reference to his two days and nights swimming in the sea (v 388); hence Bekker's excision of 232ᵇ and 233ᵃ. But the poet conceives Odysseus as having recovered from his δυσπονὴς κάματος (v 493), at least for feats of short exertion: it is the sustained effort of the footrace that he finds implausible for a man who has just spent three weeks on a raft. **κομιδή**: cf. xiv 124, xxiv 245, *Il.* viii 186, xxiii 411. The meaning is much wider than 'provisions', of which Odysseus had had a good supply (cf. v 265–7), and includes all that care for the body without which a man loses physical fitness.

234–55. The games, like the preceding banquet, end in a social contretemps. Alcinous dissipates his embarrassment in the same way, by ordering a change of scene.

234. ἀκήν: see vi 154 n. The silence expresses a range of emotion from enchantment (xi 333, xiii 1), to wonder (vii 154), and embarrassment (xvi 393, xx 320).

236. ἐπεί: no principal clause follows, cf. iii 103 ff., iv 204 ff. Like the common use of γάρ in classical Greek, the causal conjunction gives the speaker's reason for assenting to his interlocutor.

239. ὡς ἄν is a final construction (Chantraine, *Grammaire*, ii 270), and may easily be construed after ἀρετὴν σὴν φαινέμεν (so Stanford), but the additive Homeric style suggests that it is better taken in a modal sense explicative of νείκεσεν '... has insulted you in a way that no sensible man would' (so Bérard). Note that the negative is οὐ. The sense is then similar to *Il.* xiv 91–2 μῦθον, ὃν οὔ κεν ἀνήρ γε διὰ στόμα πάμπαν ἄγοιτο | ὅς τις ἐπίσταιτο κτλ. Merry–Riddell and Ameis–Hentze–Cauer seek to combine the modal sense with dependence on φαινέμεν, an unnecessary strain upon the thought.

240. ἐπίσταιτο ᾖσι: it is descriptively true that antispastic words (∪−−∪) lengthen the final syllable in the hexameter (see Schulze, *Quaestiones*, 8), but the licence is here assisted by the fact that the personal adjective is derived from *swos (strong grade *sewos), so that the reflex of initial σϝ- would, primitively, make position; but since the poet habitually sings e.g. φρεσὶ (φρεσὶν codd.) ᾖσι 18 times, he cannot be supposed to have distinguished the personal adjective from other words with initial ϝ-. For the metre then cf. Ὀδυσσῆα (ϝ)έπεα xxiv 494. A genuine reflex of original σϝ- is seen *within* certain formulae, e.g. θυγατέρα ἥν 4 times.

241–9. The rambling nature of Alcinous' discourse has suggested various excisions: see Ameis–Hentze–Cauer ad loc. The king makes allusion to Penelope, whom Odysseus has not mentioned, and, inaccurately, to his children; he superfluously confesses the luxurious and effete life-style of the Phaeacians; and then turning to his entourage he repeats himself (250–3). This is not epic discourse at its best, but the passage requires little attention from poet or audience, being no more than a transition to the dancing scene that follows.

243. δαινύῃ: it is impossible to reconcile the metrics with those of xix 328 (δαινύῃ + vowel). The common assumption is that both forms rest ultimately on *δαινύεαι, the short vowel subjunctive of an athematic verb. Schulze's δαίνῦαι represents another type of subjunctive formation: see Chantraine, *Grammaire*, i 458. **ἀλόχῳ:** Odysseus has just let slip that he was a member of the heroic class (cf. 221–2), but Alcinous in fact knows no more about his guest's family than he did at vii 311 ff., when he offered him Nausicaa in marriage. The principle operates that in minor matters the characters are permitted to assume what the poet and audience know.

245. ἐξέτι: 'ever since the time of', also at *Il.* ix 106.

247. νηυσὶν ἄριστοι: sc. εἶμεν, as at ii 60, vi 203, *Il.* viii 205, ix 225.

248–9. These lines naturally attracted the animadversions of the censorious, e.g. Heracleides Ponticus (ap. schol. *Od.* xiii 119) συνειδότας γὰρ ἑαυτοῖς φιληδονίαν καὶ ἀπολαυστικὸν τρόπον ..., Hor. *Epp.* i 2. 28–9 'sponsi Penelopae, nebulones, Alcinoique | in cute curanda *plus aequo* operata iuventus'. But the lines merely summarize the delights of a society at peace, cf. the contrasting line αἰεὶ γάρ τοι ἔρις τε φίλη πόλεμοί τε μάχαι τε (*Il.* i 177 = v 891), on which 248 is evidently modelled. Nor would any interpretation *in malam partem* be in keeping with the underlying contrast between the felicity of Scheria and the disorderly licence of the suitors' Ithaca.

249. Cf. the miseries of the campaign, εὐναὶ γὰρ ἦσαν δαίων πρὸς τείχεσιν, | ἐξ οὐρανοῦ δὲ κἀπὸ γῆς λειμώνιαι | δρόσοι κατεψάκαζον, ἔμπεδον σίνος, | ἐσθημάτων τιθέντες ἔνθηρον τρίχα (A. *A.* 559–62.) **εὐναὶ:** no more than 'bed' is required for the sense, cf. the passage just quoted and Hor. *Epp.* i 2. 30, 'in medios dormire dies', but the erotic nuance cannot be excluded. **ἐξημοιβά:** a pleasure not available (for instance) to Eumaeus and his men (xiv 513).

250. βητάρμονες: only here and 383 in Homer. Possibly a very old word, since both root elements are archaic in form: βη-τ(ι)- (< βαίνω) shows the compounding suffix as -τι- without assibilization, not as -σι-, as do some other epic compounds of archaic appearance, e.g. βωτιάνειρα, and the second element -αρ- does not show the aspiration acquired by classical ἁρμόζω: see Bechtel, *Lexilogus*, 81. The sense 'dancers' (ὀρχησταί Hsch) is not in doubt.

251. παίσατε: < παίζω not παίω. Hence the v.l. παίξατε, the regular Hellenistic form. Zenodotus' παίσατον, which avoids the hiatus, may look forward to 370 ff., a dance of two performers, but Zen. often abusively introduced the dual (cf. *Il.* iii 459, vi 112, xiii 627, etc., see N. Wecklein, 'Über Zenodot und Aristarch', *SBAW* 1919, Abh. 7, 36–9).

254–5. Observe the casual attitude taken towards the bard: cf. i 340 ff., viii 97 ff., 536 ff.

254. φόρμιγγα: the same instrument (for which κίθαρις (248) is a synonym) serves to accompany the dance as well as the solo singer. This is confirmed by early monuments which show the solo singer seated and the accompanist standing 'in the midst' (262) of the chorus, both bearing the same four-stringed lyre: see M. Wegner, *Archaeologia* U, and for further illustration and comment Renate Tölle, *Frühgriechische Reigentanz* (Hamburg, 1964). The seven-stringed instrument was said to have been invented by Terpander (Strabo xiii 2. 4). The monuments also show the dance accompanied by the flute (cf. *Il.* xviii 494–5), but the *Odyssey* has no interest in the wind instruments.

256–384. The section consists of three episodes, the Song of Ares and Aphrodite (266–369) bracketed by two exhibitions of dancing (256–65 and 370–84). The description of the first dance, however, is very laconic, and this, together with the way in which the bard Demodocus is introduced before the dance, has suggested the idea that the first dance and the Song are represented as simultaneous, the dance being a mime of the Song (e.g. Woodhouse, *Composition*, 62). Dance and song are indeed often linked (i 152, xxiii 144, *Il.* xviii 491, 569, 590, *h.Ap.* 149, *h.Merc.* 451), but the suggested scene would be reminiscent of a ritual (cf. *Il.* xviii 569—the Linus-song—and Webster, *Mycenae*, 62, 129, 286. Focke, *Odyssee*, 146 ff., rightly noted that Odysseus admires and compliments the dancers after their performance, and the singer after his, without the mention of any other party.

As a whole the episode completes the presentation of the arts of peace, γυμναστική and μουσική, in the enjoyment of which the Phaeacians spend their lives.

258. αἰσυμνῆται: 'umpires', a much debated word, see *LfgrE* s.v. At *Il.* xxiv 347 it (with suffix -τήρ, v.l. αἰσυητήρ) means 'prince', and is common in the Ionian world in the sense 'magistrate' (with which meaning, and in the form αἰσιμνάτάς it appears also in Megarian Doric). -υμν- suggests an Anatolian loan-word: see Chantraine, *Dictionnaire* s.v.

260. εὔρυναν ἀγῶνα: i.e. made the spectators step back. The setting seems

casual, just a convenient piece of ground; but a χορός could be specially
built, cf. that of Cnossos (*Il.* xviii 592).

262–3. A similar scene, reputedly Demodocus and the Phaeacians, was
represented on the throne of the Amyclaean Apollo (Pausanias iii 18).

262. κοῦροι: The monuments show choruses of men, women, and occasion-
ally of mixed sex, usually ἀλλήλων ἐπὶ καρπῷ χεῖρας ἔχοντες (*Il.* xviii 594):
cf. T. B. L. Webster, *The Greek Chorus* (London, 1970), 1 ff. The postures
depicted on Corinthian pottery have been classified by A. Seeberg,
'Astrabica', *SO* xli (1966), 48–74 (see 72), but do not permit the
identification of the present dance. The commoner dances are listed by
Pollux iv 99–105.

264. χορὸν: the dance (internal acc.) not the dance-floor as in 260. θεῖον
is a unique epithet, cf. καλὸν χορόν (*h.Ven.* 261, *h.* xxvii 15). Bérard's λεῖον,
with χορὸν = 'dancing place', would give a contextually related use of the
epithet out of keeping with the Homeric style.

266–369. The Song of Ares and Aphrodite. The literature upon this famous
episode is summarized by W. Burkert, 'Das Lied von Ares und Aphrodite',
RhM ciii (1960), 130–44. The scene offers a glimpse, unique in the *Odyssey*,
of the daily life of Olympus. Being a 'poem within the poem', however, the
scene is set at a certain distance (like the narratives of Nestor in the *Iliad* or
the lying tales of Odysseus), and the possibility that the sentiments
expressed are adapted to the character and his circumstances cannot be
entirely removed: cf. Athen. 14 c εἰδὼς ἐν τρυφερῷ τινι βίῳ τεθραμμένους
κἀντεῦθεν ὁμοιότατα τοῖς τρόποις αὐτῶν τὰ πρὸς ἀνάπαυσιν προφέρων. But
the scene, like the Διὸς ἀπάτη (*Il.* xiv 153–351), differs from the Θεομαχία
(*Il.* xxi 383–513) and the other Olympian scenes of the *Iliad* only in that
the subject matter is sexual, and so in the eyes of some moralists especially
sensitive. Even in the *Odyssey* it is unnecessary to look for an example of
moral anthropomorphism further than the political lack of scruple with
which Athena takes advantage of the absence of Poseidon from the
assembly of the gods in i and v. Artistically, such scenes have all the appeal
for common men inherent in the private lives of the great and powerful.
They do not imply disbelief or even disrespect, and so are not properly
called blasphemous: they occur in most anthropomorphic mythologies
(e.g. the Egyptian Re and Isis, J. B. Pritchard, *Ancient Near Eastern Texts*[2]
(Princeton, 1955), no. 12). For all Greeks, however, adultery was a serious
matter, not lightly to be treated in literature (cf. Ar. *Ra.* 1043–56). The
philosophers therefore reacted violently against the present episode (cf.
Xenophanes fr. 11, Pl. *R.* 390 c). Schol. (on 267) report the defence: the
tale is moral, since the guilty pair are caught; it is a traditional story, not
Homer's invention (for Homer represents a Charis as Hephaestus' con-
sort); moreover, Homer did not approve of such things, cf. i 47 ὡς ἀπόλοιτο
καὶ ἄλλος ὅτις τοιαῦτά τε ῥέζοι, and has Odysseus say μετάβηθι (492), as if
objecting to the subject matter. Straightforward excision (as lately by
Schadewaldt, *Homer, Die Odyssee* (Hamburg, 1958), 330) would be un-
usually easy, but the episode was read by all ancient critics of consequence.

Passages which are unusual in content commonly exhibit a certain number of forms and usages that call for comment, more so than passages of a more conventional nature. The present episode is no exception: note 267 ἀμφὶ + gen., 271 Ἥλιος, μιγαζομένους, 273 χαλκεῶνα, 276 Ἄρει, 278 χέε, 279 μελαθρόφιν, 284 ἀπασέων, 288 Κυθερείης, 292 τραπείομεν, 299 φυκτά, 312 τοκῆε, 315 κειέμεν, 325, 335 ἐάων, 332 τό, 334 Ἑρμῆν, 351 sense? 365 ἐπενήνοθεν. The formular diction of the episode has been examined by R. di Donato, 'Problemi di tecnica formulare e poesia orale nell'epica greca arcaica', *ASNP* xxxviii (1969), 243–94 (see 277 ff.): its intimate connection with the normal diction is evident, despite a number of quasi-formulaic expressions which for philological reasons cannot be traditional formulae in the strict sense; e.g. 287 περικλυτοῦ Ἡφαίστοιο, 288 ἐϋστεφάνου Κυθερείης, 360 κρατεροῦ περ ἐόντος. It is difficult to evaluate such data without recourse to some general theory about the evolution of the epic, beyond the observation that they show the traditional style in a highly evolved form.

266. = i 155 (where see n.).

267. Ares and Aphrodite are associated not only in archaic literature (cf. *Il.* v 357 ff., xxi 416 ff., Hes. *Th.* 933) but also in cult (see L. W. Farnell, *The Cults of the Greek States*, ii (Oxford, 1896), 745, n. 96), for example at Athens (Pausanias i 8. 4), between Argos and Mantinea (Pausanias ii 25. 1), in Crete (*Inscr. Cret.* iii 3B 14, and iii 4. 14—from Hierapytna), and subsequently at Rome in the Pantheon and the Augustan temple of Mars Ultor (Ovid *Trist.* ii 295). The connection gradually hardened into a presumption of matrimony, probably in Hes. *Th.* 933, and in the decoration of the Chest of Cypselus (Pausanias v 18. 5) and the François Vase in Florence, certainly in Pi. *P.* 4. 87, and A. *Supp.* 665. Hes. *Th.* 195, 197, provides the pair with offspring, Phobos, Deimos, and Harmonia. However, the divine cast of this little drama are thoroughly humanized: they are made to behave, and also to think, like the bourgeoisie of any place and age, and their roles as *gods* (on which see Burkert, *Greek Religion*, 152–6, 169–70, 220) is at best implied.   ἐϋστεφάνου: see v 58 n.

268. The marriage of Hephaestus and Aphrodite is scarcely attested outside the present passage, cf. AR i 859, and its source is very uncertain: see U. von Wilamowitz-Moellendorff, 'Hephaistos', *Kleine Schriften* v 2 (Berlin, 1937), 5–30, Dümmler, *RE* i 2747–8 s.v. Aphrodite, and the comments by Burkert, op. cit. (n. to 266–369), 132.

271. Ἥλιος: elsewhere always the uncontracted Ἠέλιος.   μιγαζομένους: only here, a denominative of μιγάδ-. The sun, in folktale and myth, is the all-seeing witness: see Roscher, *Lexikon*, i 2019–20. He is accordingly the guardian of truth and justice, cf. *Il.* iii 277, xix 259.

274. The δεσμοί are evidently chains. For another device of Hephaestus, a throne that imprisoned Hera when she sat on it, see Alcaeus, fr. 349 Page.

275. μένοιεν: sc. the lovers, though the thought would be obscure to an audience unfamiliar with the story. The *schema etymologicum*, with δεσμοί understood as subject, would require the relative οἵ.

276. Ἄρει: only here with the spondaic scansion, but the long Ᾱ (of doubtful provenance, cf. Wyatt, *Lengthening*, 88) is common enough.

277. φίλα: cf. φίλα εἵματα, and see v 28 n. This use of φίλος is almost untranslatable. Though not demonstrably formulaic, φίλα δέμνια should not be taken as an attempt at pathos (but cf. v 463 and n.)

278. The mechanics of Hephaestus' trap would be more intelligible if his bed were a four-poster, with curtains and canopy; but such a bed is unknown to the monuments (see S. Laser, *Archaeologia* P, 15-34), whose beds are surprisingly modern in appearance. The ἑρμῖνες are therefore 'legs' rather than 'posts'. In width all examples appear to be 'singles' rather than 'doubles'. χέε: this form is attested four times, against the regular χεῦε.

279. μελαθρόφιν: for -όφι see v 59 n.

283. Λῆμνον: the association of the island with Hephaestus is clear in Homer (*Il.* i 593—but the location of Hephaestus' forge, *Il.* xviii 368 ff., is not specified). A cult existed on Lemnos, whose chief town was named Hephaestia, and the association is intermittently acknowledged in literature: see L. W. Farnell, *The Cults of the Great States*, v (Oxford, 1896), 374-95. The island was the scene of metal-working, and for the poetical tradition of a volcanic Mt. Mosychlus (S. *Ph.* 800, Antimachus fr. 46 Wyss, etc.) see P. Y. Forsyth, 'Lemnos Reconsidered', *Echos du Monde Classique* xxviii (1974), 3-14. ἐϋκτίμενον: the verbal element is the pres. ptcp. of an athematic verb *κτειμι (cf. Myc. *ki-ti-je-si* 3rd pl.) displaced by κτίζω. The primary sense is 'inhabit', as in Skt. *kṣeti*, but the Myc. verb is already a technical term within the general field of 'settle', 'bring into cultivation', cf. Ventris–Chadwick, *Documents*, 232. It is used in Homer of islands (ix 130) and gardens (xxiv 226), as well as of towns. πτολίεθρον: the poet equates the city with the island, as at *Il.* xiv 230.

285. ἀλαοσκοπιήν: the compound, which occurs only in the present formula (cf. *Il.* x 515, xiii 10, xiv 135), is of a rare type (cf. ἀκρόπολις), but gives an effective oxymoron. χρυσήνιος: only here and (of Artemis) *Il.* vi 205. The equipment is golden because it is divine, cf. χρυσάμπυκες of Ares' horses (*Il.* v 358).

286. κλυτοτέχνην: a regular epithet of Hephaestus (4 times). The author of *h. xx* appears to understand it as summarizing his concept of Hephaestus as a culture god.

287. περικλυτοῦ: so also at xxiv 75, doubtless by declension from the prototype περικλυτὸς Ἀμφιγυήεις (9 times): the primary formula in the gen. would be πολύφρονος Ἡφαίστοιο (297, 327).

288. ἰσχανόων: an artificial formation, *metri gratia*, cf. Schwyzer, *Grammatik*, i 700. Κυθερείης: for the epithets of Aphrodite see D. D. Boedeker, *Aphrodite's Entry into Greek Epic* (Leiden, 1974), 18-42. Κυθέρεια appears to be a late addition to the resources of the *Kunstsprache*, occurring in Homer only here and at xviii 193 (but 5 times in *Hymns*), in spite of the metrical utility of the initial consonant. The goddess was so called, according to an etymology as old as Hesiod (*Th.* 198), because she emerged from the sea-foam on the shores of Cythera. Appropriately, there was a famous shrine of

Aphrodite on the island (cf. Hdt. i 105). But the normal ethnicon of
Κύθηρα is Κυθήριος (Il. x 268, xv 431), and the short -ε- is unexplained.
G. Morgan, TAPhA cviii (1978), 115–20, sees a reflex in the title of the IE
root *gᵂhedh- (whence πόθος, θέσσασθαι), as if = 'goddess of desire'. The
epithet ἐυ-στέφανος does not exclude a comparison with the Semitic ktr
'diadem'.

291. ἔκ τ' ὀνόμαζε: see v 181 n. The present instance bears out M. W.
Edwards's observation that the formula is predominantly used between
intimates, but 'is clearly fossilized to some extent, as ὀνόμαζε is sometimes
quite illogical in the context' (HSPh lxxviii (1968), 10 n. 18).

292. Eds. (including Ameis–Hentze–Cauer and Bérard) place a stop after
λέκτρονδε and assign a quasi-verbal sense ('come hither') to δεῦρο, cf. the
pluralized form δεῦτε at ii 410 etc. (7 times); but δεῦρο may be taken with
the hortatory subj. τραπείομεν as with the imperatives at 145 and
205. **τραπείομεν:** aor. pass. subj. (for -ει- see on vi 262) < τέρπω; for
τραπ- cf. δερκ- > δρακ-, but the metathesis is found only in this
formula. λέκτρονδε (which should be taken with εὐνηθέντες) might suggest
a derivation from τρέπω, but that would be incompatible with the tense of
the ptcp. In Il. iii 441 and xiv 314 the formula is expanded by (ἐν) φιλότητι,
and all connection with τρέπω is excluded. The Ionic aor. of τρέπω is
normally ἐτράφθην, e.g. xv 80, Hdt. ix 56, etc.

294. Σίντιας ἀγριοφώνους: the S. (only here, Il. i 594, and derivative
passages) were reputedly Thracian (so schol. = Hellanicus fr. 71 Jacoby),
though the name was derived from σίντης (see Eustath. on Il. i 594), not
the Σιντοί of the mainland. The island passed through many hands, see
Hdt. vi 137–40. ἀγριόφωνοι = βαρβαρόφωνοι (of the Carians, Il. ii 867).
Naïvely, the world of the narrative is monoglot.

298. A remarkable vase fragment from Lemnos c.550 BC (i.e. from the pre-
Hellenic period), discussed by Ch. Picard, RdA xx (1942–3), 97–124, shows
two crouching figures, a nude goddess and an armed warrior, *apparently in
fetters*. As it stands this does not illustrate the *Odyssey*'s telling of the story,
but suggests that the tale is not just an Ionian *jeu d'esprit*.

299. ὅ τ': the sentiment is the same as that at Hes. Op. 218 παθὼν δέ τε νήπιος
ἔγνω, so that the temporal construction, reading ὅτ(ε), would be preferable
to that of a noun clause with the reading ὅ τ'. **φυκτά:** schol., glossing
with φεύξιμα or λυτά, appear to understand δέσματα, but the word is easily
taken in a nominal sense, 'escape': cf. ἴσα, 'equality' (ii 203), ἄριστα,
'success' (iii 129). **πέλοντο:** the pl. concord with a neut. subject is
common in Homer, especially in the case of πέλονται, -ντο, cf. 160.

300. ἀμφιγυήεις: the sense of this famous epithet is still disputed, see e.g.
H. Humbach, 'Ἀμφίγυος und Ἀμφιγυήεις', Studi linguistici in onore di
V. Pisani, ii (Brescia, 1969), 569–78, suggesting 'user of the double axe'.
Bechtel, Lexilogus, 40, divorced the second element from γυῖον (an ancient
etymology responsible for the rendering 'skilled in both arms' found in
some modern commentators) and associated it with γύης 'curved stock',
thus restoring the ancient interpretation 'lame in both feet'. In form the

epithet is a metrical variant of ἀμφίγυος, see *LfgrE* s.v., and Chantraine, *Dictionnaire* s.v. γύη. Hephaestus, like the smiths Weyland in Germanic and Agni in Vedic mythology, was certainly conceived as lame, but ἀμφιγυήεις does not occur in any context that determines what sense it held for the poet.

303. = ii 298. The line is harmless enough as a resumption of the narrative after 302, and van der Valk, *Textual Criticism*, 270, finds τετιημένος psychologically effective. But it is evidently a plus-verse, unknown to schol. and omitted by the greater part of the medieval MS-tradition.

304. προθύροισι: cf. 325. In spite of θάλαμον (277), the poet now seems to visualize a modest house with the adulterers couched μυχῷ δόμου ὑψηλοῖο, i.e. in the 'megaron', and visible to spectators in the anteroom.

307. δεῦθ': see 11 n.   **γελαστά** has the unanimous support of the MSS, but apart from a conjectural reading at Babrius 45. 12 is ἅπαξ λεγόμενον. The sense is attractively ironical (so Stanford), but we should expect the connection with οὐκ ἐπιεικτά to be adversative (ἀλλά) not copulative (καί). ἀγέλαστα (also at *h.Cer.* 200 in an active sense) is reported by the Lexica and accepted by Wolf, Kirchhoff, Ameis–Hentze–Cauer, and others. The verbal adj. in -τος is regularly negative, see Schwyzer, i 502. Schol. (οὐκ εὐτελῆ) comment on the negative form. As usual, the tradition of the learned is less sensitive to artistic than to moral considerations.

308. Διὸς θυγάτηρ (9 times of Aphrodite) is metrically equivalent to φιλομμειδής (6 times). It might be a very old formula (cf. R. Schmitt, *Dichtung und Dichtersprache in indo-germanischer Zeit* (Wiesbaden, 1967), 173) with cognates in Vedic. In that case, however, the persistence of the breach of economy would be difficult to explain. D. D. Boedeker, *Aphrodite's entry into Greek epic* (Leiden, 1974), 32–42, argues that the distribution is related to context, φιλομμειδής being erotic. It seems more likely, on general principles, that Διὸς θυγάτηρ, a generic expression in Homer used also of Athena, Persephone and Ate, encroached on the domain of φιλομμειδής.

309. ἀΐδηλον, a poetical word (see *LfgrE* s.v.) meaning either 'making unseen', i.e. 'destructive', or 'unbearable to the sight', i.e. 'hateful'. The structure is evidently ἀ-ϝιδ-ηλος, but it is hard to separate original sense from popular etymology (with Ἀΐδης).

310. ἀρτίπος (for -πους): Ares is regularly θοός (8 times) in the *Iliad*, presupposing the opening fighting of the pre-hoplite age.

311. ἠπεδανὸς 'weakling': for the suffix cf. πευκεδανός, ῥιγεδανός; the origin of the stem is quite uncertain.

312. τοκῆε: Wackernagel, *Untersuchungen*, 55, observes that this dual, oddly enough, is very rare; cf. the plurals οἱ γονῆς, οἱ τεκόντες, οἱ γεινάμενοι, οἱ φύσαντες. Hesiod (*Th.* 927) preferred the story that Hephaestus was the progeny of Hera alone.

313. ὄψεσθ(ε): an imperat. rather than a simple fut. seems to be intended, as at *Il.* xxiv 709⁴. Similar forms are ἄξετε (xiv 414 etc.) and οἴσετε (xx 154 etc.), on which see C. L. Prince, 'Some Mixed Aorists in Homer', *Glotta* xlviii (1970), 155–63.

315. κειέμεν: an obscure formation, see vii 188 n. The desiderative force is here clear.

318. πατήρ: '*her* father'. The anthropomorphic language must ignore the fact that Zeus is here the father of both parties. **ἀποδῶσιν:** the subjunctive is usual in Homer after εἰς ὅ κε, but the short vowel aor. subjunctives (e.g. ποιήσεται, *Il.* iii 409) are readily misunderstood as futures, hence the future ἀποδώσει, the reading of most MSS, may well be correct here. **ἔεδνα:** the ambiguity of this word, 'brideprice' or 'dowry' (including 'indirect dowry' by which property is vested in the bride by the bridegroom), is notorious: see the excellent discussion by A. M. Snodgrass, 'An Historical Homeric Society?' *JHS* xcv (1974), 114–25. ἔεδνα (or ἔδνα) means 'brideprice' *c*.13 times, 'dowry' *c*.14 times. It is doubtful if these practices could coexist, except in some transitional phase between two norms, in the same social class (all Homeric marriages are between ἄριστοι), in a single society. They might be reconciled in terms of gift and counter-gift (so M. I. Finley, 'Marriage, Sale and Gift in the Homeric World', *Revue internationale des droits de l'antiquité* ii (1955), 167–94), but such a transaction is never recorded in the same passage of the same marriage, and is out of court here. The cultural world of Homer, like his material world, reflects a diversity of historical sources. See also i 277–8 n.

320. ἐχέθυμος: i.e. 'restraining θυμός', not 'possessing θυμός'. In Homer θυμός is the seat of passion, φρήν (cf. ἐχέφρων) the seat of sense and reason. For a discussion of these terms, with bibliography, see J. Bremmer, *The Early Greek Concept of the Soul* (Princeton, 1983), 54–6 (θυμός) and 61–2 (φρήν).

321. χαλκοβατὲς suits Hephaestus' arts and describes the palace he built for Zeus (*Il.* i 426 etc.); used exceptionally of Alcinous' house at xiii 4. The practice of armouring a floor or threshold (cf. the formula χάλκεος οὐδός, vii 83 etc.), though natural enough, is not certainly attested archaeologically, and probably reflects a poetical idea of divine luxury: cf. the very metallic character of Alcinous' palace at vii 81 ff.

322–3. Only three gods are named as responding to Hephaestus' summons. The lesser gods, who play a negligible role in Homer, are not thought of as resident on Olympus, and Dionysus, apart from four passing allusions, is ignored by Homer. Zeus as usual remains aloof from the antics of the other gods. There thus remain only Poseidon, Apollo, and Hermes of Hephaestus' neighbours, though the language at 326 ff. seems to imply more of a crowd. **Ποσειδάων γαιήοχος:** the form and etymology of the divine name are discussed by C. J. Ruijgh, 'Sur le nom de Poséidon et sur les noms en -α-ϝων, -ι-ϝων', *REG* lxxx (1967), 6–16. It is probable that the name consists of Ποσει- (an ossified vocative, cf. *Iuppiter*) + δα- 'earth', a calque of various oriental divine titles derived ultimately from the Sumerian EN.KI, 'Lord of the Earth': see Palmer, *Interpretation*, 255–6. The epithet γαιήοχος (< *wegh-, not *segh-, cf. Γαιάϝοχō *IG* v i 213), 'earth-bearing', is perhaps another version of the same title, with the nuance that the god is 'Lord of the Earth' because he is, or personifies, the 'water under the earth' on which the terrestrial disc, in Near Eastern cosmology, was conceived to float. Further literature in Burkert, *Greek Religion*, 402. **ἐριούνης** (cf. ἐριούνιος in mid-verse): the Lexica connect with ὀνίνημι and render 'gracious', but this leaves -ου- unaccounted for. The second element recalls glosses (e.g. οὔνει· δράμε, Ἀρκάδες) attributed to the Arcado-Cypriot dialects with the sense 'run' (so K. Latte, 'Zur griechischen Wortforschung II', *Glotta* xxxiv (1955), 190-202). 322 offers a curious echo of *Il.* xx 34 with ἦλθε ... ἦλθ' ... for ἠδὲ ... ἠδ' ... **Ἑρμεί-ας**: see v 28 n. **ἑκάεργος**: evidently < ἑκα- (cf. ἑκών) and ἔργον. The Lexica explain as ἕκαθεν εἴργων or ἕκαθεν ἐργαζόμενος, and the poets seem thus to have understood the word. **Ἀπόλλων**: no probable etymology has been proposed (see Chantraine, *Dictionnaire* s.v.). A Hieroglyphic Hittite *Apulunas*, which seemed to guarantee an Anatolian provenance, has proved illusory. W. Burkert, 'Apellai und Apollon', *RhM* cxviii (1975), 1-21, seeks to reaffirm a connection with the Doric term for an assembly.

325. ἐάων: only here, 335, and *Il.* xxiv 528 in Homer, but found also in Hesiod (4 times in *Th.*) and the *Hymns*. The sense ('good') and the gender (neut.) are fixed by the Iliadic passage. O. Szemerényi, 'Greek nouns in -εύς', *Μνήμης Χάριν* (Gedenkschrift Kretschmer), ii (Vienna, 1957), 159-81, assumes an inflexion *esus* *eswos* giving Greek ἐύς *ἧρος with the gen. refashioned into ἐῆος: similarly in the gen. pl. original *ἥρων was remade into *ἐήων and then into ἐάων. The older view (see Chantraine, *Dictionnaire* s.v. ἐύς) postulated a radical archaization of gen. *ἐέων (cf. ἡδύς ἡδέων) after the pattern of Ionic -έων: archaic -άων in nouns of the first declension. The spiritus asper appears to be by contamination with forms of the possessive ἑός, a frequent v.l. in the gen. sg. δωτῆρες ἑάων may be an extremely old formula; M. Durante, 'Ricerche sulla preistoria della lingua poetica greca', *Rendiconti Lincei* xvii (1962), 25-43 (= R. Schmitt (ed.), *Indogermanische Dichtersprache* (Darmstadt, 1968), 291-323) compares *dātā vásūnām*, an epithet of Indra in the Rig-Veda.

328. A whole-line formula: *Il.* ii 271 etc., 9 times (20 times if variants are included).

332. μοιχάγρι': only here, formed after ζωάγρια (462) etc.

333-42. This splendid joke (the subject, with pornographic elaborations, of Lucian, *Dialogues of the Gods* xxi) was inevitably censured: ἐν ἐνίοις οὐ φέρονται διὰ τὸ ἀπρέπειαν ἐμφαίνειν schol. Bolling, *Evidence*, 237, is inclined to accept the excision of 334-43, remarking 'we have no right to assume that interpolators were always clean-minded people'. But the idea that ἀπρέπεια was incompatible with epic dignity manifests itself early: *h.Cer.* 202 ff. omits any description of the vulgarities of Iambe by which Demeter was induced to smile. It is hard therefore to see how an indecent interpolation could have made headway. Moreover the focus of interest in Demodocus' song is not the paradox κιχάνει βραδὺς ὠκύν, but the personalities of those involved: the indignation of the cuckold, the embarrassed flight of the adulterers, the diplomacy of the old god Poseidon, to which the salacious flippancy of the younger gods makes a very suitable foil: see A. Lesky, 'Griechen lachen über ihre Götter', *Wiener humanistische Blätter* iv (1961), 30–40, and W. M. Hart, 'High comedy in the *Odyssey*', *Univ. California Publ. in Class. Phil.* xii (1943), 263–78. There is detailed criticism of Bolling's arguments, based chiefly on the disruption of thought that any excisions hereabouts entail, in Apthorp, *Evidence*, 87–91.

333. = *Il.* v 274 etc., 25 times, the regular formula corresponding to 328.

334. Ἑρμῆν: the contracted form occurs 4 times in the *Odyssey*. The *Iliad* prefers synezesis, Ἑρμέᾳ (v 390). None of these forms is integrated into the epic's system of formulae for the god.

335. διάκτορε: conventionally rendered 'Guide'; see v 43 n. δῶτορ: a poetical formation (δοτήρ is the form of the vernaculars) but correctly made: cf. βώτωρ: βοτήρ. The -ω- was extended to δώτηρ (325) to furnish a lengthened formula. ἐάων: see 325 n.

339. ἑκατηβόλ': the sense of the second element seems to imply the association of the first with ἑκάς (see 323 n.), but the formation defies exact analysis: see Chantraine, *Dictionnaire* s.v. for various conjectures. Perhaps a metrically conditioned reformation of ἑκηβόλος, cf. -γενέτης beside -γενής.

341. The full formula is πάντες τε θεοὶ πᾶσαί τε θέαιναι (3 times in *Il.*). θέαινα is confined to this formula and to some later derivative expressions. In later Greek -αινα, common as a fem. of nasal stems, is chiefly productive in the creation of terms for female *animals*, e.g. λύκαινα, ὕαινα.

342. Hermes had his wish! In its attested form the story of Hermaphroditus, the fruit of his union with Aphrodite, is a Hellenistic fantasy, however, cf. Ovid, *Met.* iv 347 ff., nor is his cult attested before the fourth century.

343. Uproarious laughter (γέλως) in Homer regularly contains an element of derision or 'Schadenfreude', cf. 326, xviii 100, 350, and *Il.* i 599.

344. The solemn note balances the humour of the earlier lines. For Homer, of course, the gods control the world and his attitude towards them cannot be wholly frivolous. He laughs *with* the gods, not *at* them.

346. ἔπεα πτερόεντα προσηύδα: this formula gave rise to an important controversy between G. M. Calhoun ('The Art of the Formula in Homer', *CPh* xxx (1935), 215–27) and M. Parry ('About Winged Words', *CPh* xxxii (1937), 59–63). Calhoun argued that the words, and especially the epithet πτερόεντα, signalled the emotional excitement of the speaker. Parry, for whom the formular epithet constituted a convenience of composition wholly independent of its context, insisted that the formula was used when the character who is about to speak has been named as the subject of the preceding sentence. The merits of the dispute would be easier to decide if the precise sense of πτερόεντα were clear. Many authorities compare the formula πτερόεντες ὀιστοί, where the epithet may mean literally 'feathered', not metaphorically 'winged', as if the words were implied to be like arrows in their emotional effect or intention. But 'winged' is an obvious and easy metaphor. See Chantraine, *Dictionnaire* s.v. πτέρον.

348. The penalties prescribed by the code of Gortyn (ii 20 ff.) provided for the detention of the adulterer as security for the payment of compensation; failure to pay put the adulterer at the mercy of his captor: αἰ κα τὰν ἐλευθέραν μοικίόν αἰλεθεῖ ... ἐν τõ ἀνδρός, ἑκατὸν στατῆρανς καταστασεῖ ... προΓειπάτō δὲ ἀντὶ μαιτύρōν τριõν τοῖς καδεσταῖς τõ ἐναιλεθέντος ἀλλύεθθαι ἐν ταῖς πέντ' ἀμέραις ... αἰ δέ κα μὲ ἀλλύσεται, ἐπὶ τοῖς ἐλόνσι ἔμεν κρέθθαι ὅπαι κα λείόντι. Attic law took a similar view, except that an apprehended adulterer might be lawfully killed on the spot, cf. Lysias i 25–7.   **μετ' ἀθανάτοισι θεοῖσι:** construe with τίσειν. Justice must be seen to be done, cf. Il. xix 172–4 (τὰ δὲ δῶρα ... οἰσέτω ἐς μέσσην ἀγορήν), xx 313–14.

350–3. Hephaestus' point is that Ares is certain to default and that then it would be embarrassing for him to take action against Poseidon. The proverb δειλαί τοι δειλῶν γε ... complements that reported to have been inscribed on the temple of Apollo at Delphi, ἐγγύη· πάρα δ' ἄτη. It is as imprudent to accept pledges as to give them. But the expression, as befits a proverb, is enigmatic. Schol. are perplexed whether to refer δειλῶν to Ares ('pledges given on behalf of a worthless fellow') or to Hephaestus ('pledges given to one of low status'). The second seems preferable, since Hephaestus is thinking chiefly of his own position in these lines. (The third possibility, that the proverb refers to pledges given *by* worthless men, is inapplicable here.) See further E. Cantarella, 'La ἐγγύη nell'Odissea', SIFC xxxvi (1964), 199–214.

352. δέοιμι: the literal sense ('bind'), which is probably correct, strained the credulity of the Hellenistic commentators: hence the interpretation of Aristarchus εὐθύνοιμι ('keep you to your undertaking'), and the anonymous emendation δήοιμι ('meet with') implied by the gloss εὑρίσκοιμι in schol. E.

355. χρεῖος: < *χρη-ος. For the phonology see v 365 n.

361–6. The lovers flee to their natural destinations. The association of Ares with Thrace (Il. xiii 301, cf. RE s.v.) is as regular as that of Aphrodite with Cyprus. 363–5 appear to be a traditional description; they are repeated, with the usual variations, at h.Ven. 59–63.

363. Πάφον: in SW Cyprus. Mentioned only here in Homer, but the site of a famous cult; cf. Hdt. i 105.   **ἔνθα τέ οἱ τέμενος ...** = Il. viii 48 and (with ὅθι τοι) xxiii 148. Except for this formula and an isolated use at Il. ii 696 the Homeric τέμενος is represented as the property of a king or hero: see vi 293 n.

364. = iv 49 = xvii 88, with the substitution of Χάριτες for δμωαί.   **Χάριτες:** the canonical number in art is three, after Hes. Th. 907; two are attested in some local myths, see the account in Pausanias ix 35. They are introduced here simply as suitable ladies-in-waiting for Aphrodite (as at Il. v 338 they weave her πέπλος). They have no known association with Cyprus, and have an independent cult.

365. οἷα: apparently adverbial ('how', 'as'), cf. ix 128, xi 364, with ἔλαιον understood as subject.   **ἐπενήνοθεν:** a popular (5 times) epic verb, used also of hair sprouting (Il. ii 219, x 134), blood flowing (Il. xi 266), and odour rising (Od. xvii 270). Both examples in the Odyssey are perfect in tense, those in the Iliad are preterite. Derivation and formation are alike unclear, see Chantraine, Dictionnaire s.v. ἀνήνοθε and Grammaire, i 423. ἀνήνοθε (Il. xi 266) implies that ἐπ-εν- (also κατ-εν- h.Cer. 279, Hes. Sc. 269, and παρ-εν- AR i 664, besides simple ἐν- at xvii 270) is a compound prefix, and permits a connection with ἄνθος (so J. M. Aitchison, 'Homeric ἄνθος', *Glotta* xli (1963), 271–8). There is no root *ἐνεθ-/ἐνθ- (ἐνθεῖν, though favoured by Frisk, *GEW* s.v., is a West Greek variant of ἐλθεῖν), but the forms appear to have been regarded as reduplicated perfects of such a root.

370–80. Homeric dances are vigorous (δινεῖν, ποσὶ σκαίρειν *Il.* xviii 494, 572) and accompanied by virtuoso performers called κυβιστητῆρες ('leapers' rather than 'tumblers' *Il.* xviii 605, *Od.* iv 18.). For representations in archaic art see M. Wegner, *Archaeologia* U, 65–8. Nothing quite matches the audacity of the performance here described. Eustathius, on 376, mentions an exercise called ἡ οὐρανία.

373. A rudimentary anecdote. The point of such comments (cf. the accounts of Pandarus' bow, *Il.* iv 105–11, or Andromache's veil, *Il.* xxii 470–2) is to enhance the value of the object described. Most can be regarded as the *ad hoc* inventions of the poet, cf. M. M. Willcock, 'Mythological Paradeigma in the *Iliad*', *CQ* xiv (1964), 141–54.   **Πόλυβος:** a common name, used in the *Odyssey* also of the father of the suitor Eurymachus (i 399 etc.), the king of Egyptian Thebes (iv 126), and one of the suitors (xxii 284).   **δαΐ-φρων:** see vi 256 n. The sense here is clearly 'skilful'.

374. ῥίπτασκε: an artificial iterative formation, echoing the -α- of ῥιπτάζω, cf. ἰσάσκετο (*Il.* xxiv 607) < ἰσάζω.

377. ἀν᾽ ἰθὺν: a difficult phrase. The sense required is 'up aloft', in contrast with ποτὶ χθονὶ (378). The epic noun ἰθύς, however, is a synonym of ὁρμή, 'impulse' (e.g. iv 434, xvi 304); hence ἀν᾽ ἰθύν, 'upstream' (*Il.* xxi 303). Some confusion with the adjective ἰθύς, 'straight', may be suspected in this passage.

379. ἐπελήκεον: impf. formed from the pf. ἐπι-λέληκα after some such analogy as γηθέω: γέγηθα (so Leumann, *Wörter*, 218).

382. ἀριδείκετε: the epithet occurs only in this and similar formulae (except at xi 540) where no meaning more precise than 'distinguished' is required —hence 'clear' at Empedocles fr. 20. 1 Diels. Schulze therefore (*Quaestiones*, 282) separated the root from δείκ-νυμι and assigned it to *dek- (cf. Lat. *decus*) with metrical lengthening. From the Greek viewpoint the prefix, like its doublet ἐρι-, is an intensifier. The one free use, however, at xi 540 commends courage *in war*: P. Thieme (in R. Schmitt (ed.), *Indogermanische Dichtersprache* (Darmstadt, 1968), 55) connects the prefix with Vedic *ari-* 'enemy'.

385–468. Two short scenes, smoothly run together, conclude the games and introduce the resumed banquet in the palace. The prize-giving (385–420) is an essential part of the sports, nor does Homer see any objection to the award of prizes to distinguished non-competitors, cf. *Il.* xxiii 884–97. But the gifts are also guest-gifts, since Odysseus is (as all believe) on the point of departure. The themes of gifts, banquet, and πομπή are repeated, after Odysseus' long story, at xiii 1–92. The bath, whose account is interwoven with that of the reception of the gifts, is the correct preparation for the banquet, cf. iii 464, xvii 84.

388. πεπνυμένος denotes one who observes the courtesies of life, especially in

372

speech (*Il.* ix 58, *Od.* iii 20 = 328, iv 204, xix 350, and perhaps xviii 125—all other occurrences are in formulae). It is seldom used of the great heroes (cf. iv 190 of Menelaus), but is a regular description of youthful or subordinate characters. There is a certain irony in calling the crafty warrior who had pillaged his way across the world a 'perfect gentlemen'.

The form πεπνυ- has given much trouble. Schulze (*Quaestiones*, 322) set up a special root *pnu-; Szemerényi (*Syncope in Greek and Indo-European* (Naples, 1964), 71–8) associates the form, by syncope, with πινυ-τός. A link with πνευ- poses semantic problems.

390. βασιλῆες: called γέροντες at vii 189. The word does not express a defined status but describes (from a political standpoint where the standpoint is clear, e.g. *Il.* iii 179) Agamemnon himself and Priam on the one hand and the suitors and nobility of Ithaca (i 394) on the other. See introduction to viii. In Linear B texts the *qa-si-re-u* is an officer attested only in provincial towns: see Ventris–Chadwick, *Documents*, 122. It is not clear why twelve princes was considered an appropriate number: the numeral is a common choice (36 times).

391. τρισκαιδέκατος δ' ἐγὼ αὐτός: cf. the appositional construction 'ordinal numeral + αὐτός' in classical Greek. It has been thought that the idiom expressed the pre-eminence that the subject often in fact possessed (as here), but such a nuance is unlikely: see K. J. Dover, '*ΔΕΚΑΤΟΣ ΑΥΤΟΣ*', *JHS* lxxx (1960), 61–77.

392–3. Other lists of gifts are given at *Il.* ix 122–8 (gold, vessels, tripods, horses, slaves), xxiv 229–34 (clothing, gold, vessels, tripods), *Od.* iv 128 (bathtubs, gold, tripods), iv 590–615 (gold, vessels, horses), and xxiv 274–7 (clothing, gold, vessels). Odysseus receives the tripods and vessels at xiii 13 ff. Between individuals the bestowal of gifts is not only an act of generosity but also a field in which ἀρετή may be displayed. The obligation upon the host to make gifts is clear, and so in the normal heroic world is the assumption that the generosity will, ultimately, be reciprocated (see xxiv 283–6, and Finley, *World*, 64–70). There is, however, no parallel in Homer to the collective generosity proposed by Alcinous. The individual tariff he suggests is modest, cf. the seven talents given by Maron to Odysseus (ix 202) and by the 'Stranger' to 'Odysseus' (xxiv 274), and the ten talents offered by Agamemnon to Achilles and given him by Priam (*Il.* ix 122, xxiv 230). Later Alcinous felt obliged to increase it (xiii 13).

393. τάλαντον: hardly a technical expression, whether we think of the Euboeic (25.86 kg.) or Aeginetan (37.80 kg.) standard; it would all go into a single box. Alcinous' cup (430) is implied to be of equal, or greater, value.

396. Odysseus is to be personally (αὐτόν) conciliated by Euryalus. The reflexive ἑαυτόν is unknown to Homer, but inevitably (and nonsensically) read by the MSS here. The other princes made the gifts through Alcinous, cf. 418.

398. ἐπήνεον ἠδ' ἐκέλευον: so always in the *Odyssey* (4 times): cf. ἐπήνεον ὡς ἐκέλευε (*Il.* iv 380, xxiii 539).

COMMENTARY

399. οἰσέμεναι: infin. of the 'mixed' aor.: see vi 321 n.   **κήρυκα:** the factotum of the Homeric world: note the equivalence with ὀτρηρὸς θεράπων (*Il.* i 321, *Od.* i 109).

403–5. Cf. *Il.* xxiii 560–2, describing the breastplate of Asteropaeus. The Iliadic passage has been thought more clear in its expression, and therefore the model for the present description. The model is more likely to lie in the whole class of technical descriptions in the epic tradition: cf. J. A. Davison, 'Quotations and Allusions in Early Greek Literature', *Eranos* liii (1955), 125–40.

Euryalus' sword is clearly a special article whose description owes less to reality than to epic ideas of heroic magnificence. The Bronze Age sword (see Lorimer, *Monuments*, 261–76) has a double-edged blade and a useful point. The hilt is made integral with the blade, and is designed to receive ornamental attachments. The decoration (of some perishable material) was secured by rivets plated with precious metal. Silver (cf. ἀργυρόηλον 406, 416) was used for this purpose during the earlier phases of the LH period, but not so commonly as gold (in Homer only at *Il.* xi 29–30), which was used throughout LH. Iron Age swords are forged with a separate hilt. The compound παγχάλκεον truthfully describes the Bronze Age sword, but as an epithet of the sword it is unique and is therefore unlikely to represent a genuine tradition. The silver hilt (attributed also to Achilles' sword, *Il.* i 219) is doubtless inspired by the ancient epithet ἀργυρόηλος with which it is equated by schol. *Il.* i 219. The ivory scabbard is without parallel in the monuments.

404. ἐλέφαντος: always the product 'ivory', never the beast 'elephant' before Hdt. iii 114, cf. M. Treu, 'Homer und das Elfenbein', *Philologus* xcix (1955), 149–58. The term, clearly a loan-word, is related in some way, though probably not by direct filiation, with the Hittite *laḫpas*: see E. Laroche, 'Sur le nom grec de l'ivoire', *RPh* xxxix (1965), 56–9.

405. ἀμφιδεδίνηται: the primary sense must be 'wind around', cf. Bacch. fr. 17. 105 (Snell) ἀμφὶ χαίταις ... δίνηντο ταινίαι, which in both Homeric passages is either much weakened (e.g. 'has been set to encircle', Stanford) or misconceived. At xix 56 δινωτὴν ἐλέφαντι describes the decoration of a throne in words almost identical with the formulae of the Pylian Ta Series, see Ventris–Chadwick, *Documents*, 332–46, where the rendering 'inlaid' of Myc. *qe-qi-no-* is suggested. See also D. M. Jones, 'Notes on Mycenaean Texts', *Glotta* xxxvii (1958), 112–18.

408–9. A conventional formula of conciliation, cf. *Il.* iv 362–3; likewise Odysseus' response at 413, cf. vii 148, xxiv 402.

410. ἄλοχον: see 243 n.

417. δύσετο: see vi 361 n.

421. τοῖσιν δ': i.e. the company, with imprecise reference. Some eds. see a contrast with the preceding παῖδες, but that would call for some amplification, as at iii 387.

422. ἐν ὑψηλοῖσι θρόνοισι: chairs with high backs (like the celebrated throne of Cnossos) are known at all periods: see S. Laser, *Archaeologia* P, 48–54:

but the dignity of the Homeric throne was also augmented by a footstool (i 131 etc.). The expression is unique, and formular economy is breached by the existence of ἐπὶ ξεστοῖσι θρόνοισι (xvi 408): traditional phrases for furniture are usually concerned with the decoration.

426. ἀμφὶ is construed with πυρί, cf. 434 and the epithet ἀμφίπυρος (S. *Aj.* 1405). Schol. (ἕνεκα δὲ αὐτοῦ) joins the preposition to οἱ.

429. ὕμνον: only here in Homer (4 times—and ὑμνεῖν 11 times—in the Homeric *Hymns*). In the strict sense ὕμνος celebrates a god, and though the longer examples of the genre regularly include a narrative element, it is not a proper term for heroic narrative poetry, such as is appropriate to the banquet (cf. i 325, viii 72, 492). ὕμνος in a generalized sense is found also at Hes. *Op.* 657, 662.

430–2. Cf. iv 591–2. A cup, for the reason given in the text, is a frequent gift, cf. also xv 85, *Il.* xxiv 429. Gold cups (which here illustrate the luxury of Scheria) are real enough, but are typical of the earlier rather than later Mycenaean period. Metal vessels of any kind are rare after the time of the Dendra tombs (LH III A 1).

433 ff. The following bathing scene (see vi 217–22 n.) is the fullest in Homer, probably because it is interrupted by the packaging of Odysseus' gifts. The diction is very formulaic: 434–7 = *Il.* xviii 344, 346–8, etc.; 450ᵃ = iv 48ᵃ, etc.; 454–5 = iv 49–50 etc.; 456ᵃ = iii 468ᵃ, etc. Cf. Arend, *Scenen*, 124–6.

434. εἰπεῖν is not elsewhere in Homer construed with oratio obliqua. The line could in principle be taken as oratio recta, with infin. for imperat., but Homer (unlike Hesiod) avoids speeches of such brevity.   **τρίποδα:** i.e. a three-footed cauldron.

435. πυρὶ κηλέῳ: a rather common formula (8 times), though in view of the contraction (κήλεος < κηϝάλεος), not an old one. Shipp, *Studies*, 21, suggests *κηϝάλεον πῦρ as the prototype.

443. δεσμὸν: i.e. a knot; the same term is used of the Gordian knot, cut by Alexander the Great (Plu. *Alex.* 18). The use of signet rings and sealings, so common in the Mycenaean period, is quite unknown to Homer.

444. αὖτε: a strong force 'once again' has been attributed to the adv. (e.g. in Ebeling, *Lexicon* s.v.), as if allusion were made to the escape of the winds (x 31 ff.) and the passage wrongly incorporated at this point. A weakened force 'next', 'by and by' is more likely.

448. δέδαε: causative aor. of *δάω, 'learn': φρεσὶν, 'in his heart' is carried over from the simple tenses.

Both Circe's instruction and the special knot itself seem to be passing inventions of the poet: neither is referred to again.

449. αὐτόδιον: only here. Presumably αὐτ-όδ-ιον, though the compounds of ὁδός normally show the aspirate. -όδ- need not be taken literally (as do schol.) but serves rather as *nomen actionis* of εἶμι ibo.

450–3. Since the theme of the bath is linked with that of the banquet, it is doubtful if the poet were concerned that Odysseus had bathed (actually a quick scrub in the river—vi 224–7) only the previous day. Nevertheless,

COMMENTARY

some commentators have detected a contradiction with vi: see the discussion in Marzullo, *Problema*, 369–70.

450. ἀσάμινθον: the sense (a cultural term), the phonology (intervocalic -σ-), and the morphology (suffix -νθ-) indicate a foreign word: see *LfgrE* s.v. (The 'Greek' word for 'tub' is πύελος (xix 553).) Seven of the eleven occurrences are preceded by ῥ': hence some suspicion that the oral tradition corrupted the form: see M. L. West, 'Epica', *Glotta* xliv (1967), 144–5: but this is now confirmed by Myc. *a-sa-mi-to* KN Ws 8497. Menelaus (iv 128) had silver tubs, but the specimens known to archaeology are all ceramic. They are rather short, to economize the water, and have a raised back, for the comfort of the bather. The Mycenaean palaces naturally had bathrooms, but no term for 'bathroom' is found in Homer: nothing explicitly indicates that the poet did not think of the bath being taken in the μέγαρον.

452. ἐπεὶ δή: the lengthened ε̄ is a well-established licence in this phrase (6 times). According to Leaf (on *Il.* xxii 379) and Wyatt, *Lengthening*, 219–20, the lengthening follows the analogy of the conjunctions ὅπη: ὅππη, ὅπως: ὅππως, etc. (themselves after ὅτι: ὅττι). The original realization of the lengthening would thus be *ἐππεί.

Odysseus had left Calypso's island three weeks previously, according to the reckoning of the fifth book.

453. θεῷ ὥς: see v 36. At v 151 it had suited the poet to picture Odysseus as wasting away from despair and misery.

454. δμῳαί: For the etiquette of the situation see vi 217–22 n.

455. Cf. x 365, xxiv 367. The regular epithet of χλαῖνα is οὔλη, as in the plural of this verse, iv 50, x 451, xvii 89.

456–68. The bath-scene is regularly followed by a note of admiration for the bather, now clean and refreshed: cf. iii 468, vi 229, xxiii 163, xxiv 367. The routine remark is adroitly combined with the farewell to Nausicaa to make a brief scene of memorable beauty. Since Odysseus (as all suppose) is to depart as soon as the banquet is over, this is the last moment at which Nausicaa could with propriety address him in the megaron: see also v 225 n.

458. A formulaic line (6 times), usually used of Penelope's appearances in the hall of Odysseus' palace. The σταθμός is apparently the furthest point a lady might go in approaching ἄνδρας οἰνοποτῆρας. In analogous scenes (e.g. i 330 ff.) the poet says, in effect, 'The lady entered (not alone, but accompanied by two maidservants) and stood by the pillar ...' Since Nausicaa is not entering the megaron but waiting there, the formulaic language compels the poet to omit the reference to the maids (cf. vi 18, 84), for there is no verb of motion with which the line may construe, and to use an awkward tense (στῆ, aor. for impf.).

462. ζώαγρι': cf. *Il.* xviii 407. The primary sense must be that of the ransom tendered by a defeated warrior to his captor, cf. the verb ζωγρέω 'take alive'.

465. ἐρίγδουπος πόσις Ἥρης: not a free alternant to πατὴρ ἀνδρῶν τε θεῶν τε

376

(except at *Il.* xiii 154), but a phrase, usually used in apposition, appropriate to the solemn language of prayer.

467. Ͽεῷ ὣς εὐχετοώμην: a traditional hyperbole, cf. *Il.* xxii 394 (Hector). No living mortal, present or absent, is represented in Homer as receiving divine cultus. It is sad to find, after this protestation, that in his account of his wanderings at xxiii 310 ff. Odysseus forgot Nausicaa but remembered Circe and Calypso.

469–586. The sequence of themes—the banquet, the minstrel's song, the distress of the guest, the courtesy of the host—repeats in a more elaborate form that found at 62–103 (q.v.). The earlier analysts responded to the close repetition by the excision of complementary passages, e.g. 93 ff. and 469–531. F. Sturmer's view (*Die Rhapsodien der Odyssee* (Würzburg, 1921), 182–192), that the repetition obeys certain 'poetical laws' of parallelism, contrast, and climax, has more to commend it. Oral composition tends to elaborate by the cumulation of traditional topics or, if the material is specific to some incident, by its repetition with progressively greater ornamentation (cf. B. Fenik, *Typical Battle Scenes* (Wiesbaden, 1968), 86, and *Studies*, 103). See also introduction to viii, and for the history of the problem W. Nestle, 'Odyssee-Interpretationen I', *Hermes* lxxvii (1942), 47–60.

471. ἐρίηρον: see 62 n.

472. Δημόδοκον: for the 'sense' of the name, paraphrased as λαοῖσι τετιμένον, see 44 n. Though Demodocus is part of the poet's ornamentation of the Phaeacian court, and therefore not a traditional figure *per se*, in our *Odyssey* his description has acquired a quasi-formulaic status and is repeated at xiii 28.

473 (= 66). **ἐρείσας:** a sitting posture is implied, cf. vi 307.

474–6 and 477–8. Both sentences consist of two clauses whose phrases are interlaced, a not infrequent accident in the cumulative style (cf. xiv 62–5 and 172 above). **Ͽαλερή ... ἀλοιφή** therefore is to be taken with πλεῖον ἐλέλειπτο and commends the magnificence of the portion remaining even after Odysseus' generosity: in 478 **προσπτύξομαι** (aor. subj., not fut. indic. in an independent sentence) is co-ordinated with ὄφρα φάγῃσι (477).

477. τῆ: see v 346 n.

478. προσπτύξομαι: literally 'embrace', as at xi 451, but here it is the appropriate sentiment, not the action, that is expressed, cf. γουνάζομαι (vi 149). **ἀχνύμενος:** a general application is best. Since their first mention at i 49 the poet's stress has been on Odysseus' πήματα and on his anxiety to return to Ithaca, cf. v 151–8, xiii 28–35, which are here in contrast with the delights of the feast. A precise allusion to the effect of Demodocus' first song (noticed only by Alcinous, 94) would not only be ungracious but goes badly with Odysseus' wish at 492 to hear more.

479–81. There is something inexplicable, and therefore numinous, in the ability of the singer: god must be his teacher, cf. 64, xxii 347, Hes. *Th.* 22, Archilochus fr. 1 West. The αἰδώς this ability commands is noted at xvii 518–20, cf. viii 170–3: τίμη means the giving of presents on an adequate

COMMENTARY

scale; as Stanford suggests, the lines express a hope rather than state a fact. The νῶτον, which Demodocus shared, was the prime cut, cf. *Il.* vii 321, given to Odysseus as the guest of honour.

481. οἴμας: see 74 n.

483. ἥρῳ Δημοδόκῳ: The scholar Istros (a 'pupil' of Callimachus) alleged that ἥρως was a qualification reserved for Homeric kings—and incurred the censure of Aristarchus (see schol. *Il.* ii 110, xii 165, xiii 629, xv 230). But Istros was nearly right: apart from the formulae ἥρωες Ἀχαιοί, ἥρωες Δαναοί, only the charioteers Cebriones and Automedon, other than fighting warriors, have the epithet in the *Iliad*. The *Odyssey* admits also Μούλιος, a κῆρυξ and θεράπων (xviii 423), and here Demodocus. The epic generally ignores the lower ranks of society as individuals and has no system of epithets for them. The type ἥρως –⏑⏑– is regular (8 names besides Demodocus). There is no sign in Homer of the semi-divine connotation of ἥρως first seen at Hes. *Op.* 159.

484–5. A stock pair of verses, 3 times in *Il.*, 8 times in *Od.* There is a set scene describing the preparation of meat, otherwise Homeric epic is interested in ἀναθήματα δαιτός not in the δαίς itself.

487. αἰνίζομ' (= αἰνέω): only in this half-line, here and *Il.* xiii 374.

488. Apollo is only here explicitly mentioned as a patron of ἀοιδοί in Homer, but although Apollo, like the Muses, knows all things that were, and are, and are to come, there is no need to see here an invocation of the god of prophecy, cf. Hes. *Th.* 94–5 (= *h.Hom.* xxv 2–3) ἐκ γάρ τοι Μουσέων καὶ ἑκηβόλου Ἀπόλλωνος | ἄνδρες ἀοιδοὶ ἔασιν ἐπὶ χθόνα καὶ κιθαρισταί.

489–91. Odysseus ignores the Song of Ares and Aphrodite, as if the present scene should stand immediately after the first song (72 ff.) or something similar (so Merkelbach, *Untersuchungen*, 170). But heroic song is the sort of song that is appropriate to the feast and, now that the banquet has been resumed, it is neither improbable nor illogical that Odysseus is made to recur to the point where the feast had been broken off.

489. κατὰ κόσμον: same point at *h.Merc.* 433, cf. κατὰ μοῖραν (496 below). In an oral tradition the sequence of themes that identifies a song is easily disordered, not merely by the incompetence of poor performers but also by the ambition of good singers to expand and ornament their work, an ambition which is potentially in conflict with the feeling that heroic poetry enshrines true history: for an expression of this fear by a modern ἀοιδός, see A. B. Lord, *Serbo-Croatian Heroic Songs*, i (Cambridge, Mass., 1954), 239–43.

492–3. Odysseus sets the story of the Wooden Horse, the final victory of the Achaeans at Troy, in contrast with their toils and miseries, the subject of Demodocus' first song; but it is a pleasing irony that Odysseus is himself the hero of the song and that it finally extorts from him a confession of his identity. Mattes (*Odysseus*, 112) sees in Odysseus' choice of song evidence of his awakening heroic confidence. He desires to hear of his greatest exploit. However, the text, as usual, is silent as to a character's inner feelings. **κόσμον:** i.e. κατασκευήν, οἰκονομίαν ἢ ὑπόθεσιν scholl. **ἵππου …**

378

δουρατέου: the allusion is obviously to a well-known story. The classical age knew the tale in the Cyclic epics *Ilias Parva* and *Iliou Persis*, and in the *Iliou Persis* of Stesichorus (cf. Verg. *A.* ii 13–267), and took the 'horse' in a literal sense. Famous representations existed on the Athenian acropolis and at Delphi (Paus. i 23. 8, x 9. 12, x 26. 2); cf. the Mykonos relief pithos, *Deltion* x viii (1963), 37–5, and the vases *CVA* 18, fr. 302 (Korinthian aryballos), and J. D. Beazley, *Attic Black Figure Vase Painters* (Oxford, 1956), 314. Its capacity was variously estimated, from a reasonable handful (9 in Verg. *A.* ii 261, 12 in Eustathius 1698, 23 in Lycophron 930) through 50 (Tryphiodorus 150) and 100 (Stesichorus ap. Eust. 1698) to a ludicrous 3000 (Apollodorus *Epit.* 5). The *Odyssey* scholia have no comment. Rationalism set in later, cf. Servius ad *Aen.* ii 15, 'ut enim Hyginus et Tubero dicunt, machinamentum bellicum fuit quod equus appellatur, sicut aries, sicut testudo, quibus muri vel discuti vel subrui solent'. Since Bethe (*Homer*, iii 190) it has been usual to see in the horse the elaboration of a motif of myth or folk-tale, cf. the Egyptian capture of Joppa by concealing men in *pithoi* (J. B. Pritchard, *Ancient Near-Eastern Texts*[2] (Princeton, 1955), 22–3). F. Schachermeyr surveys the whole question (*Poseidon und die Entstehung des griechischen Götterglaubens* (Bern, 1950), 189–203), and concludes that ῖππος ultimately conceals a theriomorphic conception of Poseidon, god of the earthquake, that shattered Troy VI. (A god 'Hippos' is indeed read by Palmer, *Interpretation*, 227–8, on the Pylos tablets Fa 16 and Eq 59). W. Burkert, *Homo Necans* (Berlin, 1972), 178–80, opines that the wooden (δουράτεος) horse is really a 'spear' (δούριος) horse, a sacred animal bringing doom to the enemy that receives it.

493. Ἐπειός appears elsewhere in Homer only as a boxer and weight thrower in the Games of Patroclus (*Il.* xxiii 664 and 838). Stesichorus (fr. 200 Page) made him ὑδροφόρος to the Atridae.   **σὺν Ἀθήνῃ**: because the horse was an ingenious creation, cf. στάθμη δόρυ νήϊον ἐξιθύνει | τέκτονος ἐν παλάμῃσι δαήμονος, ὅς ῥά τε πάσης | εὖ εἰδῇ σοφίης ὑποθημοσύνῃσιν Ἀθήνης (*Il.* xv 410–12).

494. ἀκρόπολιν: only here and 504, otherwise Homer uses the phrase πόλις ἄκρη (6 times).

499. ὁρμηθεὶς θεοῦ ἄρχετο: the grammarians (Schwyzer, *Grammatik*, ii 119, Chantraine, *Grammaire*, ii 61, 65) construe θεοῦ as *genitivus auctoris* with ὁρμηθείς and render 'inspired by the god he began'; but this use of the gen. case, though common in fifth-century writers, is otherwise alien to Homer; the sense would produce an awkward clash between syntax and metrical colon and leave ἄρχετο very weak, and ὁρμηθείς is normally used absolutely. Schol. T construes in this way but takes ὁρμηθεὶς θεοῦ to mean 'setting out from the god' (or 'goddess'), ἔθος γὰρ ἦν αὐτοῖς ἀπὸ θεοῦ προοιμιάζεσθαι. G. M. Calhoun (*CPh.* xxxiii (1938), 205–6) applies this sense to θεοῦ ἄρχετο. The allusion would be to preludes like the shorter Homeric *Hymns*. Like ἀναβάλλομαι (266) the expression would be a technical term of the art of ἀοιδή.

500–20. A remarkably concise and clear summary, except for the concluding lines 517–20 (q.v.). We are probably right to think of such a précis as the essence of an epic tale which it is the business of ἀοιδή to fill with interest and colour: cf. Lord, *Singer*, 95, 'I believe that it is accurate to say that the poet thinks of his song in terms of its broader themes ... the singer must "think how it goes, and then little by little it comes to him"'. Literary narratives of these events, probably dependent on the Cyclic Epics (see 492 n.), may be read in Verg. *A.* ii 13–267, and Quintus Smyrnaeus xii–xiii.

500. ἔνθεν ἑλών: cf. the prologues to both epics. The tale of Troy (like the tale of Thebes, the other cycle of heroic saga, cf. Hes. *Op.* 161–5) was a continuum from which the singer made an appropriate selection. Demodocus chooses his own starting-point within the prescribed episode.

501. ἀπέπλειον: the lengthening (-ει- for -ε-) is parallel to that seen in forms of θείω, 'run', the frequent πνείω, and (in Hesiod) χείω and ῥείω. All these are from roots ending in -ϝ, but there is no process in phonology by which the semivowel could affect vowel quantity. The forms are probably based on the analogy of verbs in -εσγω in which a vernacular -έω contrasted with an archaic and poetical -είω: see Wyatt, *Lengthening*, 126–34.

505. ἄκριτα is 'not able to be determined', hence 'confused', 'contradictory' (as here), 'confusing' (xix 560), 'indiscriminate' (*Il.* ii 246), or 'without end' (*Il.* iii 412 etc.).

508. 'drag it to the brink (ἐπ' ἄκρης) and pitch it down the cliffs (πετράων)'. What cliffs are these? They are unknown to the *Iliad*, and a precipice would be a doubtful description even of the steep northern slope of Hissarlik, the site of the later Ilium. Hence attempts to understand the sense as 'pitch it off the *walls*', cf. schol. ἐπὶ κρημνῶν ἢ ἐπὶ τῆς ἀκροπόλεως and ἐπί τινος ἄκρου τοῦ τείχους (Eust. ad loc.). Rather, the poet's thought is controlled by the context (βαλέειν suggests πέτραι), and not by a precise and permanent visual image.

510. τῇ is adverbial 'in that way', cf. ᾗ τελέει περ (*Il.* viii 415). **τελευτήσεσθαι ἔμελλεν:** the construction is impersonal, cf. the formula ὡς τετελεσμένον ἐστι (ἔσται) (*Il.* viii 286 etc.), of which the present phrase is a variant.

511. αἶσα ... ἐπὴν ... : a 'conditional' destiny, just as Odysseus was destined to be safe once he had landed on Scheria (v 288).

514–20. The narrative structure here envisaged is that of the major battle sequences in the *Iliad*, e.g. iv 422 ff., xvi 278 ff.: a general picture of the fighting, followed by the exploits of individual heroes and the *aristeia* of a single hero culminated by a duel with an opponent of the first rank.

514. υἷες Ἀχαιῶν: the ethnic use of υἷες is strange for Greek and is restricted to this common formula (61 times in nom. and acc.). The parallel κοῦροι Ἀχαιῶν (9 times) is giving way to δῖοι Ἀχαιοί (8 times): see D. L. Page, *History and the Homeric* Iliad (Berkeley–Los Angeles, 1959), 280.

515. Schol. are impressed by the ἐνάργεια of ἱππόθεν ἐκχύμενοι.

516. αἰπήν: a common epithet of towns (especially Troy, as here) with reference to the site (cf. the places Αἶπυ (*Il.* ii 592) and Αἴπεια (*Il.* ix 152, 294)) or rather to the fortifications (cf. the formula πτόλιν αἰπύ τε τεῖχος 3 times). Schol., e.g. on *Il.* ix 668, and the ancient Lexica give ὑψηλός as the primary sense. The thematic declension in -ός, -ή, found also in the neut. pl. αἰπά, is a poeticism, *metri gratia* and without exact parallel, although the poets may have felt the analogy of πουλύς: πολλή ~ αἰπύς: αἰπή. As feminines -ύς, -ύν are found only medially where short -ῠς, -ῠν are essential.

517. **Δηϊφόβοιο**: a son of Priam and Hecuba, unmentioned in the first half of the *Iliad* but prominent in the assault on the Achaean Wall (*Il.* xii 94 ff.) and afterwards. Schol. insist that his marriage to Helen after the death of Paris is the invention of οἱ μεταγενέστεροι, i.e. the poets of the Epic Cycle. The marriage is explicitly mentioned neither here nor in iv 271 ff., but seems to be assumed in both places.

520. **διὰ μεγάθυμον Ἀθήνην**: the positional lengthening before μεγα- is by analogy with words having original σμ-. The acc. of the frequent γλαυκῶπις Ἀθήνη (76 times) would meet the metrical requirement and is attested (*Od.* i 156, *H.Ap.* 314, *H.Ven.* 8, and in Hesiod), but with striking rarity. For the use of a common generic epithet in place of an archaic gloss in untypical circumstances, cf. χερσὶ ... κρατερῇσι (iv 287–8) for χερσὶ στιβαρῇσι (7 times).

522. Cf. 86. Weeping in Homer is the expression of a very wide range of emotion (fear, relief, vexation, pity, sense of loss, failure, or helplessness), but none exactly fit the case of a man who weeps at the recollection of victory. Mattes, *Odysseus*, 115–22, perceives in the simile, 523–30, a contrast applicable to Odysseus' present state between happiness (past for the woman, future for Odysseus) and humiliation; but it is doubtful if a simile can be interpreted with such exactitude. Heroic exploit is for Homer always an ἄεθλος leading to no permanent happiness, cf. in this regard the tears of Menelaus and others at iv 183, of Odysseus and the ghost of Agamemnon at xi 466, and of Achilles at *Il.* xxiv 511.

523–30. A remarkable and compelling simile. Pathos was recognized by ancient criticism as a special quality of Homer (cf. J. Griffin, 'Homeric Pathos and Objectivity', *CQ* xxvi (1976), 161–87), but most pathetic moments arise from the play of conventional motifs and are made inconspicuous by the speed of the narrative. A simile, however, by its nature amplifies the detail (αὔξει τοῖς οἰκείοις τὸ πένθος, ἀνὴρ καὶ φιλόπολις καὶ πεσὼν ἐν τῷ ἀμύνειν τοῖς ἑαυτοῦ Eust. ad loc.) and invites the audience to savour the scene. It is not easy for the modern reader to separate the anonymous woman from the Trojan captives implicit in 516. There would be a bitter irony in the equation of the πτολίπορθος himself and his victim; but we should expect the poet to mark a connection which he wished to be significant.

The subject-matter of these lines appears explicitly at ix 41, *Il.* vi 464–5, ix 593–4, xvi 833–4, xix 291 ff., and xxii 59 ff. Philosophers deprecated the enslavement of Greeks by Greeks (e.g. Pl. *R.* 469 b), yet it remained axiomatic, as long as slavery persisted, that the population of a defeated city was the victor's legitimate prize of war.

524–6. The lines recall the sentiments of Tyrtaeus (fr. 10 τεθνάμεναι γὰρ

COMMENTARY

καλὸν ...), and reflect a view of men's foremost duty in the age of the πόλις: P. A. L. Greenhalgh, 'Patriotism in the Homeric World', *Historia* xxi (1972), 528–37. ἀμυνέμεναι περὶ πάτρης is of course a heroic duty, but it is not so heroic as a successful offensive.

525. νηλεές: the second element is certainly ἔλεος, 'pity' (or was so understood) when applied to persons, in the formula νηλεὲς ἦτορ and in later usage, and was universally so taken until W. Schulze (*Kleine Schriften*[2] (Göttingen, 1966), 375), who derived the second element from ἀλέομαι, 'avoid', when the reference was to weapons, fate, or death: see Chantraine *Dictionnaire* s.v. Whether the day of doom is 'without pity' or 'unavoidable' is nuance indeterminable from the formulaic style.

529. εἴρερον: a ἅπαξ λεγόμενον = αἰχμαλωσία, δουλεία (schol.). The sense is clear but the etymology (see Chantraine, *Dictionnaire* s.v.) is desperate. The acc. construes with the εἰσ- of εἰσανάγουσι, cf. ἐσφόρεον ⟨εἵματα⟩ μέλαν ὕδωρ (vi 91).

531. δάκρυον εἶβεν is always accompanied (except at xxiv 234, 280) by an adj. (ἐλεεινόν, θαλερόν, πικρόν, τέρεν) whose sg. number is required by metre. The formula is thus a special kind of alternant to δάκρυα λείβειν. The etymology or provenance of εἴβειν is obscure, a creation of the epic *Kunstsprache* itself according to R. Stromberg, 'ΕΙΒΩ und ΛΕΙΒΩ bei Homer', *C&M.* xxi (1960), 15–17.

532. (= 93) **ἐλάνθανε:** with his cloak, cf. 83–5. Homeric λανθάνω (for λήθω) occurs only in this line and at *Il.* xiii 721.

539. ὦρορε: The archaic reduplicated aorists are normally causative in the active (not intransitive, as here), cf. Chantraine, *Grammaire*, i 397. ὦρορε cannot be pf. (ὄρωρε), and the coordinate δορπέομεν is impf. (inceptive, 'from the moment we began to eat').

544. τάδ': 'these honours': πομπή (545), like the English idiom 'send off', comprehends any accompanying celebrations. **τέτυκται ... τέτυκται (546):** for the repetition see v 422 n.

547. ἐπιψαύῃ πραπίδεσσι: a difficult expression. Homer knows a literal use of πράπιδες, 'midriff' (*Il.* xi 579 etc.), and a quasi-metaphorical use in the formula ἰδυίῃσι πραπίδεσσι (5 times, always of Hephaestus). Hes. *Th.* 656 etc. and *Hymns, h.Merc.* 49, have a less restricted use of the metaphor. The sense 'have some little grasp of wisdom' (for the dat. cf. *Il.* xiii 132) is better than that obtained by forcing an intrans. use on ἐπιψαύῃ in order to preserve the instrumental force of πραπίδεσσι.

548. νοήμασι κερδαλέοισι means a lie, cf. *h.Merc.* 162, 260, such as Odysseus told Eumaeus (xiv 192 ff.) and Penelope (xix 165 ff.). Alcinous makes the same point implicitly that Eumaeus made openly (xiv 361 ff.), that beggars are apt to speak to please, but there is irony in his making the remark to the Master of Lies himself.

550, 555, 572: Alcinous asks, in hugely expanded form, the questions usually condensed into the formula τίς πόθεν εἶς ἀνδρῶν, πόθι τοι πόλις ἠδὲ τοκῆες; and adds (572 ff.), in equally expanded form, the common supplementary question, 'How did he come to be here?'

382

552. ἀνώνυμος: only here in Homer. In this, the classical form of the word, the negative prefix (originally *n*- followed by a lengthened vowel, see Schwyzer, *Grammatik*, i 431) has been normalized to ἀν-. Elsewhere Homer has νώνυμος, νώνυμνος.

556. τιτυσκόμεναι φρεσί: 'intelligently aiming at their goal' cf. τυγχάνω. The expression is without exact parallel (τιτύσκομαι normally has an object expressed or implied), but is easily understood in its context.

557–63. The οἰκονομία of the *Odyssey* makes it convenient to pass from the Phaeacians, ἔσχατοι of men (vi 205), to the real world of Ithaca in a single night. The magic ships may therefore be no more than a happy invention to accomplish that end, in keeping with a land that knows no toil. Since the paper of F. G. Welcker, however ('Die homerischen Phäaken und die Inseln der Seligen', *Rh.M.* i (1832), 219–83 = *Kl. Schr.* ii 1 ff.) many commentators, including Wilamowitz and Bethe, have admitted a comparison with the north European belief that the souls of the dead were ferried to their abode in preternaturally swift ships: see Procopius *Bell. Goth.* iv 20. 48–58. But if such a conception underlies the Phaeacians, it must be understood to underlie the Homeric presentation at the deepest level. Objects which guide themselves, or move of their own accord, are very common in the folk-tales of all peoples and places: cf. Thompson, *Motif Index*, D 1520–1609.

557. Cf. 35, where (apparently) a κυβερνητήρ is included in the crew: cf. vi 201–5 with vi 9 and 262 (the walls of the town and the immunity of Scheria from invasion) for a similar conflict between specific statements made about the Phaeacians and the general narrative. The latter is controlled by its typology, the former by the imagination of the poet.

559–60. ἴσασι: i.e. *ἴσσασι < *(ϝ)ἴδ-σασι. This is the predominant (12 times) Homeric scansion.   πόλγας (likewise at 574, where the v.l. πόλεις is an Atticism): cf. gen. sg. πόλγος (*Il.* ii 811, xxi 567). The scansion is a well-established but infrequent licence.

562. ἠέρι καὶ νεφέλῃ κεκαλυμμέναι: i.e. 'invisible', cf. vii 14–15. As in 564–9 the poet seems to anticipate a naïve objection that, although he brings the Phaeacians momentarily into the real world, no one in fact had ever been known to have set eyes on them.

564–71. were athetized by the Alexandrians (see app. crit.). 565–9 = xiii 173–7 with unexplained variations in some MSS between the two passages. Schol. object that Odysseus would not have admitted he was a victim of the wrath of Poseidon (cf. ix 526–36) if he had been aware of this prophecy, but the epic does not aim at that degree of consistency. Alcinous' sequence of thought is unclear, but it is possible that the prophecy of disaster is prompted by the statement (562–3) that Phaeacian ships are immune from ordinary perils. However, it may be noted that when Alcinous recurs to this prophecy at xiii 172 ff. he presents it as if it were a new thought.

569. 'Throw a great mountain about our city', i.e., according to most commentators, blockade it and separate it from the sea, so as to put a stop to Phaeacian seafaring rather than to crush Scheria out of existence. In any event, the point of the prophecy is to explain why Scheria was unknown to the poet's audience: see vi 8 n.

570–1. The prophecy was fulfilled, at least in part (xiii 159–87). Poseidon turned the ship into a reef, and the narrative abandons the Phaeacians making sacrifice to avert the second part of their doom.

575–6. = vi 120–1 (see n.) = ix 175–6 = xiii 201–2.

578. Ἀργείων Δαναῶν: a unique expression. The formulaic diction for the Greeks and Trojans, as may be expected, is refined to a very high degree of economy, and no regular expression of this shape exists in the genitive case (cf. nom. ἥρωες Δαναοί). In the *Iliad* the combination would probably be impossible, since the three terms Ἀργεῖοι, Ἀχαιοί, Δαναοί are treated as nouns. The apparent refinement of a formulaic system is relative to the intensity of its use, and the poet of the *Odyssey* does not have Iliadic diction at the surface of his mind: if he had, he would not need to create an anomalous phrase.

579. ἐπεκλώσαντο: for the metaphor of spinning fate see vii 198 n.

580. ἧσι as it stands is an Atticism. ἔησι would be a trivial correction, restoring both dialect and smooth metre.

By the purpose clause Alcinous does not attribute an intention to the gods (which would give a satirical effect, like 'i demens ... ut pueris placeas et declamatio fias', Juvenal x 166–7) but expresses the inevitable connection between heroic exploits and their celebration in song. The singer, it is implied, is not to blame for what god has done: cf. i 346–55 where the same thought is expressed at length.

581–2. πηός, γαμβρός, πενθερός: all three terms are used in specific and generic senses, but it is clear that here πηός is the generic term ('relative by marriage', cf. xxiii 120, *Il.* iii 163, Hes. *Op.* 345), and γαμβρός ('son-in-law', but 'brother-in-law' at *Il.* v 474, xiii 464) and πενθερός ('father-in-law', i.e. 'wife's father', as opposed to ἑκυρός, 'husband's father') are specific terms: for the Homeric terminology of kinship see M. Miller, 'Greek Kinship Terminology', *JHS* lxxiii (1953), 46–52.

581. Ἰλιόθι πρό: one of a small group of phrases, cf. ἠῶθι πρό, οὐρανόθι πρό. The adverbial formation replaces an intractable gen. in -ου. Ἰλίου προπάροιθε (*Il.* xv 66 etc.) represents an alternative way of resolving the problem, but probably continues an inherited *Ἰλίοο.

583. κήδιστος is superlative of κήδειος, 'cared for'. It is not a kinship term in Homer: cf. x 225, *Il.* ix 642.

585–6. κασίγνητος at least sometimes (e.g. *Il.* xv 545) includes cousins as well as brothers. A wider term, denoting the full extent of a man's kin, is ἔτης. G. Glotz, *La Solidarité de la famille et le droit criminel en Grèce* (Paris, 1904), 85, made a famous, but unacceptable, attempt to equate ἔτης with ἑταῖρος. In the broadest sense ἔταρος, ἑταῖρος expresses the relation between a hero and his λαός, as in the common formula ἂψ δ' ἑτάρων εἰς ἔθνος ἐχάζετο (7 times): his ἑταῖροι rally round their chief (e.g. *Il.* xvii 117), and their chief defends his ἑταῖροι (e.g. *Il.* xvi 363); chief and ἑταῖροι fall together (cf. the formula πολέες δ' ἀμφ' αὐτὸν ἑταῖροι (3 times). But a narrower relationship between heroes themselves may also be indicated, such as that between Achilles and Patroclus or Antilochus, between heroes and their ξεῖνοι (*Il.* xvii 150), or between heroes accustomed to share the δαίς (*Il.* xvii 577): see the discussion by H. Jeanmaire, *Couroi et Courètes* (Lille, 1939), 97–111. We should think of one of the latter relationships in this passage.

INDEX

Greek words

387

INDEX

μέγαρον, 266
μέθυ, 239–40
μήδεα, 302
μολπή, 95–6, 299
μόρος, 78
μῶμος, 136

ναιετάω, 124
νέμεσις, 134
νήδυμος, 242
νηλεής, 382
νηνέω, 95
νηπιέη, 113
νίσσομαι, 256

Ὀδυσσεύς, 83
οἴμη, 351
οἶνοψ, 100
ὀλοόφρων, 82
ὁμοῖϊος, 174
ὀνήμενος, 131
-οο gen. sing., 26, 84, 254
ὁπλότατος, 189
ὄρομαι, 190
ὄρσεο, 309
Ὀρτίλοχος, 191
ὄρχαμος, 185
ὅς (reflexive possessive), 123–4
οὖλος, 307
-όφι, 261, 332

Παλλάς, 315
πάρδαλις, 221–2
πατροφονεύς, 113
πεπνυμένος, 102, 372
περίσκεπτος, 125–6
πίσυρες, 263
πολύτροπος, 69

πολύχαλκος, 158
Ποσειδάων, 368
πότνα, 272
πτερόεις, 92
πτολίεθρον, 70

ῥερυπωμένα, 297
ῥοδοδάκτυλος, 129
ῥυτός, 310

σιγαλόεις, 295
σπέος, 74, 262
σχεδίη, 257
σῶς, 281

ταλαπείριος, 322
τανηλεγής, 138
τετράγυος, 329, 354
τηλύγετος, 194
τῆος, see ἧος
τίνω, 80
τριτογένεια, 184

ὕμνος, 375
Ὑπερείη, 293
ὑπερτερίη, 298
ὑπερφίαλος, 93–4
ὑπονήϊος, 165

φίλος, 82, 257, 281
φρένες, 234

χρεῖος, 124, 183
χρυσηλάκατος, 201

Ὠγυγίη, -ος, 85–6, 304
ὠμοθετέω, 188–9

General

accentuation, 39, 71, 101, 124, 154,
    184, 217, 243
adultery, 370
Aegisthus, 57, 77, 78; see also Atreidae-
    Paradigm
Aeolic dialect, 24–5, 171, 296, 327, 340,
    358
Aeschylus, 99, 113, 216, 225, 240, 361
Aethiopis, see Cyclic epics
Africa, 198
Agamemnon, see Atreidae-Paradigm
Ajax, s. of Oileus, 116, 170, 223–4
Alcaeus, 116
Alcinous, 294, 319
Alexandrian scholarship, 41–8; see also
    Aristarchus, Aristophanes of
    Byzantium, Zenodotus
alliteration, 80, 133, 148, 301
Alpamysh, 56 n. 14
alphabet, 34, 39
amber, 197
ambrosia, 221, 264, 267–8
Amphitrite, 166
anachronism, 294
anaphora, 70
animals: bears, 240; birds, 262; boars,
    300; cattle (as standard of value),
    126–7; deer, 213–14; dogs, 129, 176,
    204; horses, 130, see also chariots;
    leopards, 221–2; lions, 213, 242, 302;
    mules, 232, 309; octopus, 285–6;
    panthers, 221–2; sea monsters, 285;
    seabirds, 259; seals, 219; sheep, 198
anointing of stones, 185
Antilochus, 167
Antimachus, 41, 86
Antinous, 121–2, 136, 149–50
ἀοιδή, 349, 379, 380; see also bards
aorist, gnomic, 103, 216; 'mixed' 76,
    117, 271, 314–15, 367, 374
Aphrodite, 363–71
Apollo, 177, 208, 267, 369, 378
Apollonius Rhodius, 44, 263
ἀπρέπεια, τὸ πρεπῶδες, 298, 308, 311,
    325, 369

Arcadian dialect, 308, 358, 369
archery, 91, 92, 107–8, 359–60
architecture, 88, 116, 117, 125, 151,
    312–13, 326; αἴθουσα, 185, 212, 340,
    367, 368; μέγαρον, 313; μυχός, 327;
    οὐδός, 236, 352, 368
Ares, 363–71
Arete, 316–18, 324, 325, 335
Argonauts, 20
Argos, see Ἄργος
Aristarchus, 39 n. 18, 40 n. 19, 41–2,
    45–7, 76, 80, 87, 96, 98, 117, 119,
    120, 124, 163, 164, 169, 199, 211,
    212, 271, 272, 273, 281, 284, 286,
    298, 299, 310, 311, 325, 330, 337–8,
    340, 351, 353, 355, 378; see also
    athetesis
Aristophanes (of Byzantium), 40 n. 19,
    45, 76, 164, 298; see also athetesis
Aristotle, 40, 41, 84, 163, 228
Arkeisios, 240
arms, 88, 107, 374
Artemis, 177, 201, 267, 300
assembly, see typical scenes
assonance, 80, 103, 107, 125, 164, 184,
    269, 275, 301
Assurbanipal, 202
Asteris, 245, 310
astronomy 276–7, 278
Athena, angry with Gk army, 116–17,
    168, 265; associated with seamanship,
    148; with weaving, 120; Ἀτρυτώνη,
    240–1; γλαυκῶπις, 80, 285; enhances
    protégé's appearance, 129, 307; sends
    dreams, 243, 294–5; special
    relationship with Od., 60–1, 173, 212,
    284; symbol of success 315, 347;
    transformed into bird 115–16, 183–4;
    Τριτογένεια, 184, 284; see also Mentes,
    Mentor
Athens, 36–9, 177, 180, 325–6; see also
    Panathenaea, Pisistratus
athetesis, 42, 46–7; by Aristarchus, 87,
    94, 98, 100, 119, 120, 130(?), 140,
    150, 164–5, 172, 175, 196, 204, 205,

390

INDEX

Sappho, 141, 170
sceptre, *see* staff
schema etymologicum, 112, 297, 315, 364; *see also* word-play
Scheria, as a colonial city, 293; etymology, 294; location, 294
season, 277, 320
sententiousness, 295, 310
Serbo-Croatian heroic songs, 8–9, 35, 378
shape-shifting, 217, 220
ships, 111, 153–4; compared to chariots, 238; construction, 274–5; crew, 347–8; epithets, 108, 169–70, 177, 179, 310; magic, 383; parts of, 156–7, 183, 241, 274–5; preparation for voyage, 153–4, 241
Sidon, *see* Phoenicians
similes, 213, 216, 242, 279, 284, 285, 300, 302, 307, 308, 322, 328, 338, 381
Simonides, 230
singers, *see* bards
slaves, slavery, 123, 194, 327–8
Smyrna, Old, 310, 323
Solon, 36, 77
Sparta, 193; local colour, 231–2
sports, 299, 342, 353, 358, 372
staff, 259; symbol of authority (sceptre), 131–2, 255
story-telling, 229
Strabo, 63, 64, 88, 99, 100, 106, 108, 159, 178, 183, 193, 198, 215, 231
Suitors, 53, 55–60, 76–7, 86, 89, 104, 106, 116, 118, 121, 125, 128, 133–40, 142–7, 151, 157, 158, 172, 213, 232, 233, 234, 235–6, 241, 245; *see also* Antinous, Eurymachus, Leocritus
supplication, *see* typical scenes
sword, 374

talent, 203
Tamassos, *see* Temesa
Taphians, 88
Telegony, *see* Cyclic epics
Telemachus, 51–5, 91–2, 106–214 *passim*, 229–30, 233, 234; πεπνυμένος, 102; piety, 157; resemblance to Od., 102, 167, 203
Telemachy, 17–18, 27 n. 10, 52–5, 109, 235, 251, 291, 300
temenos, 312, 329, 371

Temesa (Tempsa, Tamassos), 100
textiles: finishing, 328; loom, 261; Penelope's web, 137; spinning, 120, 201; (metaphorically) 74, 105, 108, 334; weaving, 120, 138, 328–9
Thebes, see Egypt
themes, 250; conflation, 263–4, 332; sequence of themes/motifs, 29, 289, 290–1, 317, 336, 375–6, 377, 379, 380
Themis, 135
Thrace, 371
Thrinacia, 71–2
Thucydides, 119, 165
Tithonus, 254
traders, 99–100, 355
Troy, 70, 130, 208–12, 380
typical scenes, 29; arrival, 321; assembly, 129–31, 253, 346; bath, 375; council, 253; deliberation between alternatives, 200, 283; departure, 257, 298; dream, 242–4, 290, 294, 317; journey, 87, 153, 290; landing, 161; libation, 157, 162, 182; meal, 76, 90, 94–5, 189, 332, 349; oath, 152–3; πεῖρα, 291; quarrel, 351; reception of visitor, 90–1, 159, 162, 195, 260, 263, 331; sacrifice, 160, 161, 182, 185–9, 215, 240, 349; supplication, 166, 290, 300, 330

utopian ideas, 326, 342

Vergil, 95, 158, 218, 280, 300, 321, 380

weeping, 118, 136, 199, 200, 205, 269, 352, 381
'wild' texts, *see* papyri
women: attended by maids, 117–18, 298; bathe men, 189, 210, 307; duties, 261, 295–6, 296–7; join men after supper, 117, 120; medical knowledge, 207; proper place, 120; *see also* textiles
Wooden Horse, 70, 210–12, 378–9
word-play, 80, 83, 103, 164, 178, 221, 275; *see also* schema etymologicum
writing, 12, 33–5

Yugoslav heroic poetry, *see* Serbo-Croatian

Zenodotus, 38 n. 15, 41–4, 70–1, 86–7,

395